THE GREAT DOMAINES OF

BURGUNDY

REMINGTON NORMAN

THE GREAT

DOMAINES

of

BURGUNDY

A Guide to the Finest Wine Producers of the Côte d'Or

SECOND EDITION

REMINGTON NORMAN

with a foreword by
MICHAEL BROADBENT

photographs by Janet Price and Geraldine Norman

HENRY HOLT AND COMPANY

NEW YORK

For Geraldine

Henry Holt and Company, Inc.
Publishers since 1866
115 West 18th Street
New York, New York 10011

Henry Holt ® is a registered trademark
of Henry Holt and Company, Inc.

First published in the United States in 1993 by
Henry Holt and Company, Inc.
Originally published in Great Britain in 1992 by
Kyle Cathie Ltd.

Library of Congress Cataloging-in-Publication Data
Norman, Remington.
     The great domaines of Burgundy: a guide to the finest wine
   producers of the Côte d'Or/Remington Norman; with a foreword by
   Michael Broadbent; photographs by Janet Price and Geraldine
   Norman—2nd American ed.
         p.   cm.
     Includes bibliographical references (p.   –   ) and index.
     1. Wine and wine making—France—Burgundy. I. Title.
   TP553.N67 1996   96-25441
   641.2'2'09444–dc20   CIP

ISBN 0-8050-4680-1

Henry Holt books are available for special promotions and premiums.
For details contact: Director, Special Markets.

First American Edition—1993
Second American Edition—1996

Designed by Geoff Hayes

Printed in Great Britain by
Jarrold Book Printing Ltd. Norfolk

All first editions are printed on acid-free paper. ∞
10 9 8 7 6 5 4 3 2 1

Abbreviations

Throughout the text and, in particular, in the tables, the following
abbreviations have been used:
BGO. *Bourgogne Grande Ordinaire.*
Bourg. *Bourgogne.* C. *Centigrade.* GC *Grand Cru.*
Ha *Hectare.* hl *Hectolitre.* hl/ha *Hectolitres per hectare.*
M. *Metayeur.* P. *Proprietaire.* PC *Premier Cru.*
PTG. *Passe-Tout-Grains.* R. *Regional Appellation.*
V. *Village Appellation.*

Explanation of Tables

1. *Grands Crus*: at the foot of the relevant commune chapter, for each
commune which has one or more Grand Crus, a table is given, giving the
name, area, number of proprietors and approximate annual yield in cases
of each Grand Cru.

2. *Domaines*: the vineyard holdings of almost all profiled Domaines
are tabulated at the end of the profile. These tables are taken from
information supplied by the Domaine and include the commune, name
and status—Grand Cru, Premier Cru etc.—of each vineyard, the
Domaine's holding, expressed in hectares and 100ths of a hectare, the
average vine age(s) or date of planting, and the status under which the
Domaine expoits the vines—proprietor, *Metayeur* or *Fermier*.

In reading these it should be remembered that a Domaine which exists as
a company may farm or share-crop vines belonging to its individual
owners—so F. or M. beside an entry does not necessarily mean that those
vines are owned by some third party. Equally, where a Domaine is a
Metayeur, the land holding shown may in some cases represent the total
area worked by the Domaine; if it has to cede half the crop to the landlord,
then the figure will not truly reflect its own production. Domaines were
asked to list vineyard areas which correspond to their own production.

This information was collected between October 1990 and February 1991
and between March and October 1995.

CONTENTS

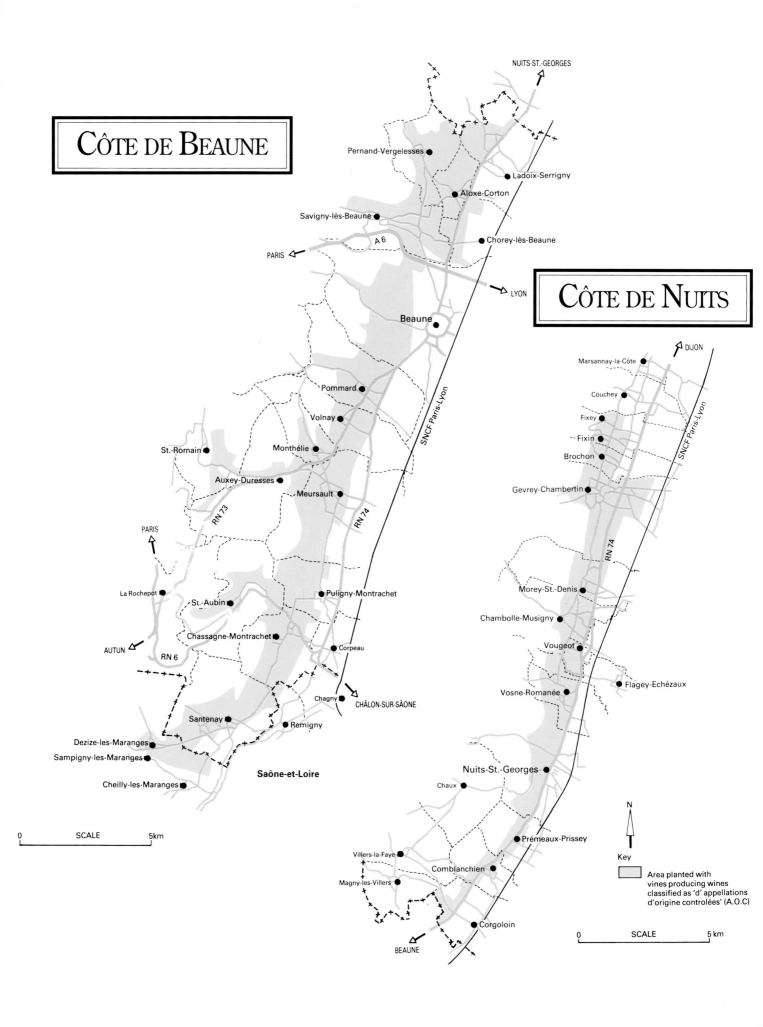

CÔTE DE BEAUNE

CÔTE DE NUITS

NUITS-ST.-GEORGES

Pernand-Vergelesses

Ladoix-Serrigny

Aloxe-Corton

Savigny-lès-Beaune

Chorey-lès-Beaune

PARIS

A 6

LYON

Beaune

Marsannay-la-Côte

Couchey

Fixey

Fixin

Brochon

Gevrey-Chambertin

Pommard

Volnay

St.-Romain

Monthélie

Auxey-Duresses

Meursault

RN 73

RN 74

SNCF Paris-Lyon

SNCF Paris-Lyon

DIJON

RN 74

PARIS

Morey-St.-Denis

Chambolle-Musigny

La Rochepot

St.-Aubin

Puligny-Montrachet

Vougeot

Flagey-Echézaux

AUTUN

RN 6

Chassagne-Montrachet

Corpeau

Vosne-Romanée

Chagny

CHÂLON-SUR-SÂONE

Santenay

Remigny

Nuits-St.-Georges

Dezize-les-Maranges

Chaux

Sampigny-les-Maranges

Saône-et-Loire

Cheilly-les-Maranges

Prémeaux-Prissey

N

Villers-la-Faye

Comblanchien

Magny-les-Villers

Key

SCALE   5km

Area planted with
vines producing wines
classified as 'd' appellations
d'origine controlées' (A.O.C)

Corgoloin

BEAUNE

SCALE   5 km

FOREWORD

There is no more heart-warming sight than the almost unbroken vista of vines carpeting the lower slopes of the Côte de Beaune. One drives, in a leisurely but careful way (the RN74 is notoriously dangerous), from Dijon to Beaune, a route punctuated by the most evocative signs to villages, the names of which sound like a roll call of the most voluptuous red wines of the world: Chambolle-Musigny, Vougeot, Vosne-Romanée . . . The vineyards themselves form a rhythmic pattern of parallel lines changing from the brown of winter, the light, bright green of the spring and early summer, the lush green of September and autumn russet after the harvest: one huge park more akin to a series of expensive individually-owned allotments.

Beyond the ancient walled town of Beaune, the expanse of vineyards continues, the view to the right being broader, the slopes further from the main road. But the rows of vines are endless, and the list of famous village names goes on: Volnay, Pommard, Meursault, Puligny, Chassagne . . .

It is within these villages that the growers live and maintain their cellars. Their way is quite different from Bordeaux. The countryside is different. The vineyards of Bordeaux, particularly in the Médoc, are smugly self-contained; each has its own château and chai within the confines of the property; each property has one resident or absentee proprietor. In Burgundy there is no equivalent to the 'château' of Bordeaux. The word 'Domaine' is proprietorial yet more nebulous – a personal or *société anonyme* estate made up of small vineyard parcels, often mere strips of vines, individually tended, the wines very individually made.

The man who introduced me to fine wine almost half a century ago, when asked what was the difference between Bordeaux and Burgundy, answered 'about 400 miles': the differences were too vast to explain. They are different worlds: different climate – one maritime, the other continental; different soils, different vine varieties but, above all, different people. I have always felt that Burgundians are closer to the soil. The vineyards are but a step outside each village boundary, some only a few minutes walk from the centre of that lovely, old – and very rich – town of Beaune.

The people and their 'domaines'; these are the keys to Burgundy and the subjects of this book.

In Burgundy, the name of the grower is as significant as that of the parcel of vines he tends, no matter how grand the *grand cru*. To get to know the maker and his domaine is to know the wine.

Not everyone, even nowadays, realises that there can be an immense difference in style and quality between one Nuits-St.-Georges – or Pommard or Meursault – and another; those more knowledgeable do know that wines made from vines grown in an individual but sub-divided, named vineyard can vary markedly. This book explains how and why.

There is no wine on earth as elevating as a great Burgundy: richness of 'robe', intensity of bouquet, a velvety liquid that expands in the mouth, reaching – flooding – the head and heart. This sort of wine does not make itself. It is made by individuals, by stalwart characters dedicated to making the best wine their well-tended vines can produce following an invariably unpredictable growing season. Burgundy is easy to drink, speciously easy to criticise, fiendishly difficult to make.

And what about the author? Remington Norman is not a writer new to wine. He is a fellow Master of Wine, with a lifetime in the wine trade. Based in London, principally as a retailer, he gained long experience buying and selling the wines of Burgundy, as well as those of Alsace and the Rhône valley, selecting the real thing for his most discerning clientèle from a mass of familiar and not so familiar names being touted by importers and *négociants*. He has been driven, inexorably, to explore the villages of Burgundy, to talk at length to the wine-makers and investigate their methods, discovering for himself first hand who, at the foot of those 'golden slopes', is making the best and the true.

Remington combines the soul of an artist, the level head of a businessman and an enquiring mind. No other book on Burgundy deals so thoroughly and approachably with the philosophy and techniques of individual growers and wine-makers. He writes lucidly, unpretentiously and with authority. What he has discerned and written about will add greatly to our understanding as well as our knowledge of one of the most complex and, at best, unsurpassed wines of the world.

FOREWORD TO SECOND EDITION

It does not surprise me in the least that the first edition of Remington's book has received critical acclaim and, with good reason, won prizes. One of the side effects to benefit readers of the second edition is that the success of the work has induced one or two previously reluctant wine producers to succumb, to open up, to co-operate, which together with some useful updates and including 37 totally new domaines will make this new edition doubly interesting and valuable.

Burgundy, the region and the wine, is complex but Remington has proved his mastery of the subject. All of us, from producer to consumer, benefit from his unique perspective. He enables us to see Burgundy with new eyes and to drink it with greater understanding and renewed pleasure.

Michael Broadbent
Christie's, London

Introduction

Of all the world's great wine regions, Burgundy is widely seen as one of the most difficult to understand. This reputation reflects both the impression that it is unpredictable – there seems to be no certainty that one bottle of a given appellation will taste anything like another – and the feeling that, all too frequently, price seems to bear no discernible relationship to quality. If to these inconsistencies one adds the difficulty of getting to grips with a seemingly structureless plethora of appellations, vineyards and growers, it is hardly surprising that amateurs and professionals alike are chary of further exploration. For too many, the effort to understand Burgundy is frustrated by its apparent complexity. Even seasoned wine-lovers, faced with a range of Burgundies on a shop shelf or restaurant wine-list, may turn towards the more predictable attractions of Bordeaux or elsewhere, rather than risk an expensive disappointment, whilst many wine professionals who would like to discover more, find it hard to know where to start.

This state of affairs is unfortunate, but understandable. Burgundy has unquestionably suffered from comparison with Bordeaux whose uncluttered structure of a few, clearly defined, appellations and a relatively small number of large estates, has undeniable appeal. There, knowing the appellation or property gives a measure of security and predictability which Burgundy manifestly lacks.

The region has also suffered needless, self-inflicted harm from giving its name to too much mediocre wine. Poor quality blurs differences between appellations, making wine from one commune taste much like that from another, and when expensive Grand Cru turns out dilute and meagre compared with Village wine at one-fifth of the price, the credibility of the grading system crumbles and the image of the region is inevitably tarnished. It only takes a handful of indifferent wines to goad a confused buyer into enquiring whether Vosne-Romanée really differs from Vougeot or Volnay, and whether producers' names have anything more than tangential bearing on the contents of the bottle. He might even be tempted to conclude that appellations are distinctions without differences and the Burgundy is nothing more than a disorderly patchwork of variegated brands.

This irritating unpredictability leaves many struggling to make sense of the appellation system whilst wondering what it is about Burgundy that seems to generate such excitement. Do the opulent, sensuous wines they have read about really exist, or are these simply the figments of wine-writers' over-stimulated imaginations?

Faced with such an unrewarding lottery, some abandon the quest for this elusive Grail; others soldier on, often limiting their researches to a favourite appellation or producer because of a bottle once enjoyed. In both cases, the best of Burgundy passes them by.

Fortunately, as this book demonstrates, great Burgundy still exists – and not just within the confines of a few famously expensive Domaines. Furthermore, despite its apparent complexity, the region is not particularly complicated. However, to understand the region properly it is essential to know how it is structured and to appreciate its rather unusual and fragmented system of production.

The primary purpose of this book is to demystify Burgundy and to enable those who have either lost heart, or else found the entire subject too intimidating, to navigate the minefield with confidence. By presenting this greatest of wine regions through the perspective of the entities which really determine quality – the Domaines – one can separate the real magic of the wines from the rather interwoven structures defining them.

The rest of this Introduction provides background to what follows; it summarises the scope and aims of the book, describes the structure of the Côte d'Or and explains the basis upon which the 131 great Domaines herein were selected. It concludes by outlining important recent trends, setting Burgundy into its modern context.

Scope :

Viticultural Burgundy extends over a large area of eastern France – comprising, from north to south: Chablis, the Côte d'Or, the Côte Chalonnaise, the Maconnais and the Beaujolais. Since covering all this thoroughly would far outcompass a single volume, the present scope is limited to the heart of Burgundy, the Côte d'Or – a narrow 55 km strip of land, extending south from the outskirts of Dijon to just beyond Santenay. Here are to be found the world-famous villages and vineyards, from which most of the region's finest wines are produced.

In this book, the Côte d'Or is viewed from three different perspectives. First, the finest Domaines and the people who run them are profiled in detail, together with an account of how they work, in order to discover how great wine is made and why some estates consistently out-perform others. Second, a short account is given of each of the Côte's principal communes – its history, wine and most important vineyards. These, accompanied by specially commissioned, detailed maps, are designed to show how each commune fits into the overall context of the Côte. Third, a section of background chapters draws together several important threads influencing viticulture and winemaking, and reflects on matters related to buying, tasting and enjoying Burgundy. An assessment of vintages from 1971–1995 is also included. These chapters show that tasting – important as it undoubtedly is – is only one element in true wine appreciation; one also needs to understand how wine is put together and the many factors which contribute to quality. A glossary of technical terms defines words italicised in the text. Some French terms translate poorly, but every effort has been made to render them intelligible.

In writing this book, I have tried to keep in view the 'typical reader' – someone, whether amateur or professional, who is interested in broadening their knowledge and appreciation of Burgundy. If the book is to have any permanent value for them beyond mere anecdote, some technical explanation is inevitable; this I have made as assimilable as possible without sacrificing important detail. There is nothing here which should baffle an intelligent reader, even someone with a non-technical background.

The structure of the Côte d'Or :

Geographically, the Côte is subdivided into some 28 different villages or communes – in effect, small parishes. Those comprising the northerly sector, from Marsannay to Corgoloin, are collectively known as the Côte de Nuits – based on the town of Nuits-St.-Georges; those adjoining them to the south, from Ladoix-Serrigny to Santenay, as the Côte de Beaune – based on the rather larger town of Beaune.

Surrounding each village is an area of vineyard which, as the maps show, is relatively small and heavily subdivided into individually named sites. Although to the passing visitor there is little to distinguish one patch of vines from another, all have been meticulously measured and mapped, and their borders

precisely delineated. With very few exceptions, ownership of each vineyard is divided among several different growers, each the proprietor of designated vines, from which he makes his own wine. For example, the Bâtard-Montrachet vineyard has some 49 individual owners and the Clos de Vougeot no fewer than 82. So, it would be possible, in theory at least, to line up 49 bottles of the one and 82 of the other in any given vintage, each bearing the name of a different producer. Although there might be broad similarities in taste between such bottles of the 'same' wine, these would be eclipsed by the differences in quality, reflecting the varying competences of individual vignerons. Such fragmentation vitiates parallels with Bordeaux – there is only one Château Latour 1995, whilst there are at least as many 1995 Bâtards or Clos de Vougeots as there are owners of these vineyards. It is this diversity which makes Burgundy so frustrating and yet such a fascinating challenge.

The skill of the grower is not the only determinant of quality. The vineyards themselves also differ significantly in quality potential – a fact reflected in the Appellation Contrôlée system which grades each vineyard into one of four categories: in ascending order, Régionale, Village, Premier Cru and Grand Cru. (See Appellations and Quality Control, p.246 for a more detailed explanation of the system.)

Superimposed on the differences between vineyard and growers are important differences in style (largely due to soils) between the wines of the communes themselves. So, whilst for example a Volnay Premier Cru may be expected to outclass a Volnay Village wine, both should differ in character from the wines of neighbouring Pommard. The pattern is thus complex – but logical.

Individual land-holdings are small – often no more than a fraction of a hectare in any one vineyard. So, to establish a viable business, a grower (or Domaine) will generally own a portfolio of vines spread across several sites and quality levels: a few rows here, half a hectare there etc. – not only within his home commune, but often further afield. These are likely to be spread over several quality levels. From each individual appellation, a different wine will be made and bottled separately. This again contrasts with Bordeaux, where Châteaux have a few large chunks of vines in a single appellation, all contributing to one or two wines at most. By comparison, the Côte d'Or is highly fragmented in its pattern of ownership and production.

The prospective buyer is therefore theoretically faced with a vast array of wine from which to choose: 28 communes, 4 separate quality levels, innumerable individual vineyard sites, and several thousand growers. Fortunately, it is neither necessary, nor realistic, to master even a fraction of these first hand. Anyone looking for reliable Burgundy of better than average quality needs only to concentrate on the relatively small number of estates for whom quality is top priority. Domaines differ considerably: some consistently produce magnificent wine, some manage excellence occasionally, and for others, one keeps the proverbial barge-pole permanently to hand.

The Côte must therefore be seen as a fragmented patchwork of small, independent estates, each producing a range of wines from basic Régionale to Premier or Grand Cru. Within this framework, the name of the producer is the single most reliable indicator of quality, transcending even the grading of the vineyard or the vintage. The grower/Domaine is therefore the key to unlocking Burgundy.

Selection :
Selecting the top 131 Domaines from the Côte's rich array was no easy task. The basis upon which it was done needs some explanation and, since no selection will please everyone, some justification.

The final choice reflects merit rather than either land-holdings or reputation – a lavish marketing budget and the consequent high profile are not always matched by wine quality. In deciding who to include, I have been influenced by two over-riding considerations: first, absolute quality – the ability to produce something especially fine, in its class; and second, consistency – that dimension of year-on-year excellence which gives one the impression that a bottle from this Domaine, whatever its appellation or vintage, would rarely disappoint. The Domaines profiled here fulfil both these criteria.

Although this book is devoted to the best, it is not entirely a paean of praise. There are several Domaines, often internationally known, which regularly turn out disgracefully poor wine. Some recognise their shortcomings, and are striving to put things right; others shrug off their mediocrity, seemingly content to enjoy the lavish profits which even poor Grands and Premiers Crus are still capable of generating. Within the bounds of fair comment, these Domaines are identified. Their continuing prosperity is, however, in doubt, as ever more value-conscious markets baulk at exorbitant asking-prices for indifferent quality.

Whilst it is relatively easy to produce a respectable wine given fine land and a good, ripe, growing season (although some even manage to fail this test), it is the skill at dealing with the lesser vintages which sorts out the great from the good. This observation must be tempered with the realisation that even the finest winemaker is not immune from mistakes – sometimes even disasters. These growers would be the first to admit to imperfection – and would probably ascribe to their failures some of the motivation which keeps them striving for excellence.

For this new edition, visits were made to all the original 111 Domaines and a further 40 rising stars. New visits comprised an in-depth interview covering history, viticultural and vinification practices and as extensive a tasting as possible – recent vintages on the spot, with samples of 1991s being taken back to London for further comparative assessment. From this, the list was whittled down to the 131 Domaines included here. Limitations of space unfortunately meant that vineyard holdings for some of the new entries had to be left out.

Unfortunately, there was a handful of owners who proved uncooperative: Engel, Pernin-Rossin and Jean Mongeard in Vosne and Ramonet in Chassagne. I have taken a view on these, based on tastings of recent vintages. Also, Dominique Laurent failed to keep an appointment, apparently in bed, as on two further attempts to visit him.

The Hospices de Beaune is deliberately omitted, since all its wine is dispersed in barrel at the famous auction each November, making their final quality dependent upon the skill in *élévage* of each purchaser. The estate therefore has no real identity beyond its vineyards. The talented André Porcheret is back at the helm here and there are rumours of Domaine bottling, so perhaps an important change is on the way. Also excluded are estates whose wines are normally made by others, such as Baron Thenard and the Duc de Magenta.

Although the aim was to cover the Côte d'Or, this was done with no prima facie idea of how the final selection would be distributed between the communes. No attempt was made to massage standards so that equal numbers of Domaines appeared in each commune. As they fell out, so they appear.

There are a few other factors affecting the final selection, which merit specific comment. It is generally recognised that some communes are inherently capable of producing better wine than others – Volnay than Monthélie or Puligny than St.-Aubin, for example – a matter of *terroir*. Even a moderately good Puligny Premier Cru will probably outclass a St.-Aubin Premier Cru. I have therefore allowed for such relative strengths and weaknesses, in assessing the Domaines.

No attempt has been made to rank the Domaines into any order of merit – since I believe these serve no useful purpose, especially in a region where a single estate may produce a score, or more, of wines in a single vintage. Neither should the profile lengths be taken as an indication of status – some vignerons are distinctly more innovative or loquacious than others. Conversely, the fact that a Domaine is omitted altogether doesn't mean that it produces poor wine. Quite simply, this selection creams off the finest; there are many other meritorious Domaines, producing excellent wines, if not at the topmost level.

In the end, whether a Domaine or an individual wine is considered great, rather than just good, is a matter of personal opinion. Nevertheless, any such selection is bound to have omissions and injustices. I trust that these are few, and that those who feel hard done by will appreciate the difficulties.

Recent trends (welcome) :
The Côte d'Or is a collection of strong-minded individuals who have their own perceptions of what constitutes fine wine and their own methods of realising them. From these deep-rooted convictions they are not easily shaken. However, recent years have

seen important developments in the broader context of Burgundy and its wines – not specific events, but welcome evolutions which are precursors of better all-round quality.

The most significant changes are those in the collective mentality of growers – in particular, the novel discovery that greater openness, instead of making one vulnerable, can be of mutual benefit. An older guard is now ceding responsibility to a younger, formally trained, generation, who discuss wine-making problems openly, with friends, and taste each others' wines together, critically. This is a far cry from the not so distant time when winemakers worked behind closed doors and coped alone to cover up any mistakes, preferably without anyone finding out about them.

This trend has come in the wake of another: much greater detailed knowledge and control of winemaking. So now, even modest-sized Domaines have both the knowledge and the technical means at their disposal to implement their ideas. Technically incompetent wines are fewer and growers have no credible excuse for sloppy wine-making. Older hands still talk much of 'tradition' although, more often than not, this means no more than slavish adherence to antiquated practices, both because they work with acceptable frequency and also because there was no alternative. Now that research has enabled growers who want to, to understand how means relate to ends, tradition is being replaced by flexibility – a willingness to adapt vinification to the character of the vintage – and the accumulated dogmatic baggage of generations is, albeit with some nostalgic reluctance, being slowly discarded.

Growers are also recognising that quality pays. They are aware of an enticingly vast, international market, but realise that, with substantial quantities of excellent, attractively-priced wines available from outside France, the competition for the consumer is severe.

Enlightened growers are adapting to this trend. They are prepared to make short-term sacrifices by declassifying substandard wine or by selling it in bulk, to harvest late and restrict yields, and to adopt vinification practices designed to produce wines of concentration and quality. They realise that the long-term advantages of such a policy far outweigh any immediate pecuniary gains. If you are recognised as a 'no compromise on quality' Domaine, then you can charge high prices and still have no difficulty in selling your wine.

As more and more Domaines produce better quality, they have also come to appreciate the financial advantages of marketing their own wines, rather than of selling them in bulk. In consequence, the great négociant

houses of Beaune and Nuits, which dominated the market in Burgundy until the 1970s, are finding their regular sources of supply drying up. Those dedicated to quality have secured their future by buying vineyards and will continue to produce excellent, reliable wines. Others, however, drift steadily downwards in quality, supplying that sector of the market which is only concerned with label and price. As a result, the market is becoming polarised, with the serious sector concentrating on the finest Domaines, for which buyers are prepared to pay top prices.

This trend has led to great prosperity, with Domaines becoming sufficiently profitable to attract the younger generation back to the Côte, either to take over family estates or to establish their own. Recent years have seen the emergence of many excellent enterprises from the embers of family bulk-selling operation; several are profiled here. Furthermore, the 'patron to the end' mentality is definitely in decline, with parents and grandparents increasingly prepared to hand over responsibility well before reaching retiring age.

Recent trends (unwelcome) :
Not all recent trends are beneficial. Many a vigneron trying to run his small estate, helped by his wife and a worker or two, finds himself beset by an ever increasing administrative workload. Selling in bulk was easy – one invoice, a few appellation certificates and that was it. Now, every bottle sale has to be accounted for, and many more individual customers and visitors dealt with, leading some growers to lament that they are being turned into glorified bureaucrats.

By far the worst recent trend to have hit the Côte's vignerons is the phenomenal increase in land values, brought about by heavy demand for the little good vineyard land offered for sale. Insurance companies, pension funds and banks in particular, seem willing to pay exorbitant prices, especially for Premiers and Grands Crus which, at current levels (estimated at 1–2% of notional capital value) show no realistic prospect of an economic return. For the small grower who may, on paper, be worth several million francs, this is of little benefit since it has no direct impact on his income.

What these exaggerated values do influence are inheritance and capital taxes. The former, levied on death, presents heart-rending difficulties, since, although notionally of high net worth, the inheritor(s) will rarely have enough disposable cash to meet their tax liabilities, and there is then no alternative to selling part of the family patrimony to pay the bill.

High vineyard values also affect the wealth tax levied annually on capital assets which, in France, is charged on both vineyards and stock. This militates against quality in two ways: the less cash a vigneron has, the more he is tempted to cut corners; also, obliged to pay tax on any stock in the cellars, many growers will succumb to the attractions of producing early-maturing wines to minimise their inventory.

On top of everything, the Code Napoléon, which governs inheritance in France, requires that assets, including land, be split equally between surviving children. This further subdivides estates, unless the legatees can be persuaded to keep their vines within a single exploiting company.

The more enlightened growers now operate under a corporate structure which provides a limited buffer against eventual taxation and subdivision, since it is only the shares which ultimately change hands. However, this is no more than a short-term palliative and there is a strong case for the French government acting to make a special case of viticulture, both to allow vignerons to keep their Domaines intact, and also to prevent this unique vineyard land from falling into the hands of remote banks and insurance companies, who may not always have quality as their top priority.

For the consumer, the most significant recent trend has been the encouragement of growers toward production of overblown, over-oaked, over-extracted reds – the antithesis of true Pinot Noir. This, driven chiefly by US critics, whose palates seem tuned towards 'drag 'em out and knock 'em down' instant impact styles, has led far too many gullible vignerons, seduced by the lure of lucrative foreign sales, to abandon their instinctive feel for Pinot and fashion wines to consumers' preferences. The volatility of the American market has fortunately brought most back to their senses, whilst many laudably refused to change in the first place.

Based on the distinctly contentious, and almost certainly, false premise that 'the more you extract, the better', this view of things crystalises the worst of Western materialism. It is simply not the case that a person with two cars/microwaves or whatever, or a wine with twice the amount of new wood, is *ipso facto* better than their apparently disadvantaged neighbours with only one. What many seem incapable of appreciating is that too much extraction is as much a flaw as too little. This 'philosophy of monsters' may be fine for producing sledge hammer Californian Cabernet, but has no place in Burgundy, where both grape and *terroir* scream out for finesse, and subtlety. It is to be hoped that, as with nouvelle cuisine, this exaggerated and distorting trend is given a quiet but speedy burial. Fortunately the signs are encouraging.

The outlook of the winemaker :
How a winemaker, wherever he happens to be, sets about making his wine, depends to a great extent on his philosophy – how he sees his role. For most, if not all, of these Great Domaines, the primary concern is to preserve, in each wine, the typicity of the vineyard which produced the grapes. This is indissolubly linked to the concept of *terroir* – to the idea that soil and micro-climate contribute significantly to the individual taste qualities of a wine, and thus to its quality-level. This is the anchor premise on which the entire appellation system is founded.

Although the notion of *terroir* is controversial and has yet to gain wide acceptance in the New World, where grape variety and fruit ripeness often take precedence over origin, there are few honest tasters who would deny its importance in the Côte d'Or, where consistent differences exist between the wine of one commune or vineyard and that of its neighbours.

This contrast points up two entirely different winemaking perspectives, both found in Burgundy. Some see themselves as mere intermediaries between *terroir* and wine – vinous midwives, whose role is to assist the grapes they have harvested to deliver their maximum potential for expressing their origins. In this, they are essentially passive players, only intervening when absolutely necessary.

Others take the view that, like chefs, their job is to create – to use the means at their disposal to transform the grapes into a wine style of their own choosing. They do not deny the importance of *terroir*, but argue that fine wine is perfectly compatible with several different expressions of the same origin. Theirs is an active, interventionist role. Although each would probably hotly contest the argument, neither approach is obviously wrong, and both are capable of producing top-class wine.

Shortcomings of the system :
Whilst the Domaines profiled here, and others, will continue as producers of excellence, there is much that the regulatory authorities could do to rid the market of the persistent tide of untypical, mediocre Burgundy, and to prevent some of the blatant abuses of the system they are supposed to control. Some of these measures are discussed in the text, but in the (probably vain) hope that this might provoke some action, it is worth restating the most urgently needed reforms.

Firstly, there should be an AC-specific register of permitted clones and rootstocks for use in Côte d'Or vineyards – this would prevent the planting of maladapted or inferior material responsible for much indifferent wine. Secondly, greater effort should be made to police the existing crop restrictions and to limit permitted yields to healthy vineyards; allowing a grower to harvest the maximum from a diseased vineyard, where many of the vines are dead or missing, is a manifest absurdity. Thirdly, fractional *chaptalisation* should be legalised forthwith – at present it is only tolerated; growers and independent experts alike recognise it as indispensable to quality. Finally, and most importantly, the existing controls should be rigorously enforced to ensure that mediocre wine submitted for tasting, for appellation approval, is declassified or rejected altogether. This means setting clear standards and having tasting juries who are independent of the local market and its vested interests. Collectively, these measures would go far to improving the quality to which everyone involved never ceases to tell you they are eternally dedicated.

For all its fragmentation and idiosyncrasy, or perhaps because of it, the Côte d'Or is a magical place; small, intimate and doggedly individual. At its best it produces sensational, sensuous wines, which leave one marvelling, almost in disbelief, that the contents of a glass are no more than the transformation of bunches of grapes.

The growers are as interesting a range of personalities as can be found anywhere – warm, friendly, abundantly welcoming and hard-working, for whom the bonhomie and joie de vivre which invariably accompany good wine, conceal a profound dedication to the unique land with which they have been entrusted. This book brings some of these vignerons and their Domaines into more public relief. I hope that they, and the Côte d'Or, will benefit from that process.

MARSANNAY-LA-CÔTE

Leaving the traffic clot which is central Dijon, the visitor, if he manages to fathom the eccentricities of French sign-posting and locates the correct artery will soon find himself on Napoleon III's RN 74 – la Voie Royale – travelling down the Côte de Nuits towards Nuits St.-Georges and Beaune.

Although most of the vineyards on the outskirts of Dijon – La Côte Dijonnaise – have long been swallowed up by urban sprawl, a few remain, notably the 'Montre-Cul', so named because women working there involuntarily showed off their ample bottoms, so steep is the incline.

The first wine commune of any significance one encounters is Marsannay, a rather pedestrian village of some 6000 souls which keeps alive on a modest tourist trade, encouraged by a developing wine industry. In 1783, probably fearful of being gobbled up by its larger neighbour, it tacked 'La Côte' on to its designation, to remind predatory officials in Dijon of where its real allegiance lay.

Marsannay has a long connection with viticulture: wine was being produced here under religious aegis in the middle of the 7th century, and Charlemagne is said to have rested under a tree next to a fountain in La Charme. Despite this recommendation, the advent of the railway in the middle of the nineteenth century engineered the replacement of the Gamays of Marsannay with the

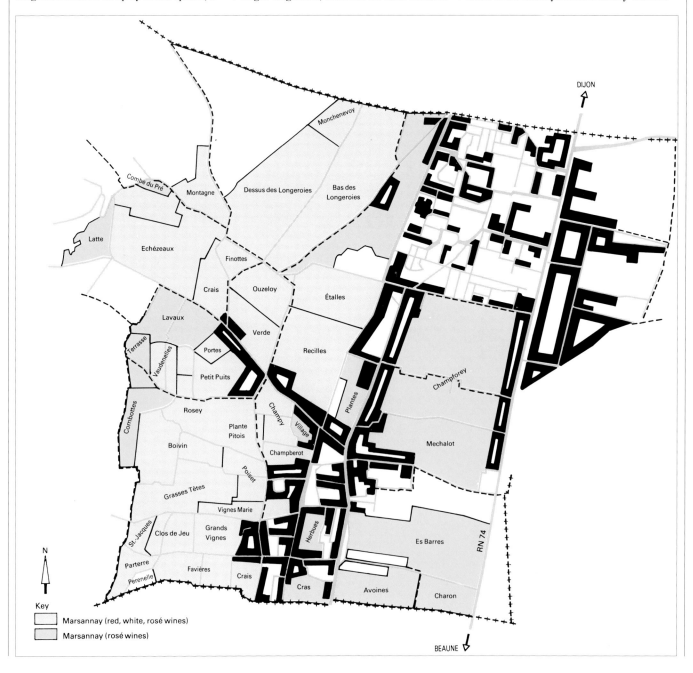

Key
Marsannay (red, white, rosé wines)
Marsannay (rosé wines)

The Mairie

more robust, alcoholic beverages of the Midi.

The commune saw its fortunes steadily decline until, by the beginning of this century, matters had become so serious that the village was reduced to within a hair's breadth of financial ruin. Then, in what amounted to a stroke of marketing genius, a local grower, Joseph Clair, decided that the impetus of a new product was needed. Accordingly, 'on 22nd September 1919' to quote Anthony Hanson, he invented Marsannay Rosé. This wine, made by light pressing of Pinot Noir and vinification 'à gris', rapidly became the fashionable drink of Dijon café society of the day and its popularity restored the fortunes of the growers and put the village back on the wine map.

However, things got worse when the appellations were delimited in the 1930s, because the commune was given neither its own AC nor the right to the catch-all designation of Côte de Nuits-Villages. It seemed to have been forgotten in the rush, ending up with mere Bourgogne, or Côte Dijonnaise, which no-one wanted anyway. Decline again set in: by 1962 the area of land under vine amounted to 29 ha and during the 20 years which followed it sank to virtual extinction at a mere 19 ha.

The vignerons decided that they were entitled to their own AC and set about a legal battle to convince the INAO of their case. Some twenty years later, in 1987, Marsannay, together with northerly neighbour Chenove and southerly Couchey, were granted the appellation Marsannay for red, white and rosé wines.

Fortunes restored, growers set about capitalising on their hard-won appellation which presently covers some 512 ha of land. Much of the 300 ha currently in production had to be reclaimed from scrub before it could be

replanted. Whilst most of the lower lying land bordering the RN 74 is designated for rosé alone, the more steeply sloping vineyards behind the village are considered finer and zoned for red, white or rosé.

Since the grant of AC status, there has been a strong revival of interest in Marsannay. Land continues to be reclaimed and replanted at a fierce rate, and anything available is easily sold, for high prices.

The heart of the appellation is some 65 *climats* stretching from Chenove to just south of Couchey. These vineyards, exposed marginally south of east, exhibit a mixture of soils, of which the principal constituent is limestone. Patches of richer clay soil are restricted to regional appellations, such as Bourgogne Grande Ordinaire. Some, on higher, better drained ground, are prone to suffer from drought in particularly hot and dry years, such as 1990 and 1993.

There has been much debate over the question of whether some favoured sites merit Premier Cru status. Although some 20 individual vineyards are considered to produce finer wine than the rest, there seem to be no imminent moves towards reclassification.

Marsannay has some 40 growers producing some 22,000 cases of white, 120,000 cases of red and between 13,000 and 33,000 cases of rosé annually. In particularly abundant years, the proportion of rosé increases as vignerons *saigner* their red *cuves*.

The white, made principally from Chardonnay, although there is still some Pinot Beurot and Aligoté in the vineyards, can be good, somewhat rustic, sappy stuff. It will age, but is best drunk young.

The rosé, though no longer fashionable, has a small faithful following. It is a sound, firm, dry wine which can stand up to a variety of food, especially the rather rich reconstituted offerings which pass for the gastronomic end of charcuterie in the area, although it is much better as an aperitif or with a piece of cold fish. Bruno Clair, grandson of the inventor, makes by far the best version.

The future will undoubtedly bring more recognition to Marsannay; the acquisition in 1985 by Louis Jadot of the village's greatest Domaine, Clair Däu, has already raised its profile significantly and the collective efforts of the commune to establish an identity for themselves seem to be bearing fruit.

Behind the church

Domaine Bruno Clair

MARSANNAY

Bruno Clair's Domaine has evolved from some Burgundian misfortune. His grandfather, Joseph Clair married a Mlle Däu in 1910, a union which gave birth to three children, Marsannay Rosé and the Domaine Clair-Däu, formed in 1950 and generally regarded as one of the finest in the Côte.

Things worked smoothly until family dissension erupted in the late 1970s. One of the children wanted to take out as much as possible, the others to plough the profits back. Matters came to a head in 1980, when Bruno's father Bernard Clair, exasperated by increasingly bitter family warfare, left to start up on his own. In 1985, his sister Noëlle, having failed to quell the dissension, sold her vines to Louis Jadot in Beaune. A great Domaine was split up.

Bruno, left without the Estate which he might otherwise have expected to run, had started up his own enterprise in 1978, replanting some Marsannay, renting some Fixin and buying some unplanted scrub in Morey. During 1985–86 his mother and father, together with four brothers and a sister, formed a company with Bruno to farm their own vineyards, now marketed under the label 'Domaine Bruno Clair'. Plots of Corton-Charlemagne – bordering Pernand – and Aloxe Village were added in 1993 along with replantings of Marsannay Blanc and 1.6 ha of Chambolle Village.

Shortly after all this upheaval, Bruno Clair recruited the winemaking talents of Philippe Brun. Philippe is engagingly enthusiastic about his wines – relishing his rare fortune at working with wines from throughout Burgundy. 'Let's make a little tour round the Côte,' he invites, waving his pipette at a bank of barrels.

The fast-talking Bruno Clair has a deep knowledge of the Côte in general and of Marsannay in particular with expertise – and experience – extending beyond the mere theoretical to vineyard and cellar work.

For him, sound viticulture comes from knowing the personality and characteristics of each plot of vines and from minimum interference with their environment. His vineyards are treated as organically as possible, using only humus and organic fertilisers and adjusting soils for potassium, nitrogen and phosphorus deficiencies. Magnesium is also carefully monitored, both to counteract the excess of potassium put on the soil after the last war and also because

'it is essential, for plants as well as humans'.

Whilst clones, properly mastered, are beneficial, most replanting is by individual replacement from a *sélection massale*, except for larger parcels where a clonal mix is used. Older vines, such as the 90-year-old *massale* Pinot plot in Savigny La Dominode, need a special feel rather than strict rules.

From an extensive range, Bruno and Philippe's 'signature' is indubitably their Marsannay Rosé – a wine deliberately designed to show true Pinot Noir character rather than just using Pinot to make a tinted white wine.

This result is achieved by an *assemblage* of ¼–⅓ 'vin gris' from direct pressing of the black grapes and juice from a 2–4 day cold *macération pélliculaire*, followed by *écoulage* and then pressing. Both elements contribute to the final wine: 'press direct' gives a subtle aromatic aspect, whilst *macération* contributes the pure Pinot flavours, which are its hallmark. The juice is vinified in bulk, without new wood, by slow fermentation at low temperature, ensuring even development. The result is fresh, not lively, with marked variety.

Then come Bruno's trio of distinctly individual white wines: a Marsannay – about 2,500 bottles annually – made from equal proportions of Chardonnay for finesse and

Pinot Gris for richness, a combination which results in a gorgeous ripe mouthful, especially in vintages with a touch of botrytis, such as 1994. Next, a Morey St-Denis – from 100% Chardonnay – of which he is one of only a handful of producers. The Morey vines are a series of 15 scattered plots in the *climat* 'En la Rue de Vergy', just above the Clos de Tart, which Bruno reclaimed from scrub in the late 1970s. Third, a Corton-Charlemagne, vinified, as the others, in cask, (mainly second and third year oak) for a long, slow fermentation, which, being less tumultuous, Bruno considers better for extraction of glycerols and finesse.

For his red wines, Bruno also seeks a slow fermentation and a long *cuvaison*. The bunches are 40–100% destalked (completely in 1994), vatted and given regular *pigéage* – 'about 5–6 times a day if we can do it' – to maximise extraction.

Macerating wine and skins after fermentation is not eschewed, even though this extracts tannins which make the wines 'a little hard to start with. In 1990 and 1993, *cuvaisons* lasted a total of 17–22 days, which is nothing exceptional chez Bruno.

With press-wine incorporated, part of each *cuve* is decanted into large 13-14 hectolitre oak vats and the rest – about 33%

VINEYARD HOLDINGS

Commune	Level	Lieu-dit/Climat	Area	Vine Age	Status
Marsannay	V	(Blanc – Various)	2.09	15	F
Marsannay	V	(Rosé – Various)	2.92	25	F
Marsannay	V	(Rouge – Various)	1.12	35	F
Marsannay	V	Les Vaudenelles (R)	1.99	25	F
Marsannay	V	Les Longeroies (R)	1.55	40	F
Marsannay	V	Les Grasses Têtes(R)	1.33	25	F
Savigny	PC	La Dominode	1.12	90	F
Savigny	PC	La Dominode	0.59	10	F
Morey	V	En la Rue de Vergy	0.65(R)	15	F
Morey	V	En la Rue de Vergy	0.51(W)	15	F
Gevrey	PC	Bel Air	0.43	20	F
Gevrey	PC	Les Cazetiers	0.67	40	F
Gevrey	PC	Clos du Fonteny	0.68	20	F
Gevrey	PC	Clos St Jacques	1.00	35	F
Gevrey	GC	Clos de Bèze	0.98	2/3 1/3 25	F
Vosne	V	Les Champs Perdrix	0.93	2/3 801/3 25	F
Chambolle	V	Les Veroilles	1.04	6	F
Aloxe	V	Les Valozières / Les Bruyères / Les Cras	0.34	4–33	F
Aloxe	GC	Le Charlemagne (W)	0.34	20	F
Regionales		(R & W)	1.78		F
		Total:	**21.06 ha**		

– into new wood. Each appellation has the quaint luxury of its own particular *foudre*, to make it feel more at home. The wines in small oak are racked cask-to-cask – the more important appellations being rotated from new to old wood. The Marsannay Rouge matures in second and third year casks with only a touch of new wood. The period Clair reds spend in cask, is a function of each wine's inherent structure – 6-12 months being the average.

Bruno sees wine as 'l'expression d'un terroir et d'un homme'. Tasting wines from different Marsannay vineyards, one is left in no doubt of his commitment to this philosophy. His intimate knowledge of his vineyards and their wine characteristics allows a healthy scepticism on technical correctness, preferring instinct to constant adjustments for imbalance. He cites the still magnificent 1959s, whose analytically hopeless acid deficiency made them 'almost dead' – no technologists then to cow growers into acidification.

The Domaine's reds have high tannins and marked acidity, but age well – 'tannin is good for you,' according to Bruno. The Marsannays are excellent with plenty of depth and finesse. Bruno's red 'signature' is his splendid Savigny La Dominode, from 90-year-old vines (younger fruit appears as generic Savigny-les-Beaune). In 1993, these near-antiques yielded 28 hl/ha and produced a firm, deliciously coarse-grained wine of marked austerity, needing a decade at least to mature.

From a more complex, richer and more elegant trio of Premier Cru Gevreys, the palm falls between Cazetiers and Clos St-Jacques – entirely different wines from adjacent vines of broadly similar age. The greater finesse of the Clos St-Jacques contrasts with the distinctly more rugged structure of Cazetiers with its note of attractive rusticity. Cazetiers is perhaps the more typically Gevrey of the pair.

Their sole red Grand Cru comes from nearly a hectare of Clos de Bèze – top class wine in vintages such as 1993 with the structure and complexity derived from fine land and mature vines.

Bruno Clair contrasts the Côte with Bordeaux, where 'when you choose the wine, you also choose the vigneron', an equation manifestly false in Burgundy. Although he may lament the demise of Clair-Däu, something of its fine old tradition seems, fortunately, to have rubbed off. Bruno and Philippe make a fine team and a range of wines which are unlikely to disappoint.

Domaine Philippe Naddef

COUCHEY

Two-and-a-half hectares of splendidly old Gevrey vines owned by his mother form the nucleus of this fine Domaine, built up since 1983, by the slim, earnest Philippe Naddef. Rented vines in Marsannay and Fixin have doubled this and, for the present, expansion has ceased.

The Domaine is based in Couchey, just north of Fixin, whose vines come under the Marsannay Appellation. Here, in a skilfully restored set of buildings behind the church, Philippe works with his attractive wife, Anne-Marie – a native of the Midi-Pyrénées, whose acquaintance with fine wine dates from her meeting her future husband.

The Gevrey vines are usefully mature and, with care but not undue interference, yield quality fruit; replacements, where necessary, are made individually and the general regime tends towards the least toxic treatments. Harvest is deliberately late, with the white (Chardonnay) Marsannay grapes being picked ideally *surmature*, generally 15 days after the reds – a policy which, in a wet vintage such as 1994, coupled with rigorous discarding of unripe fruit produced a good quiver of reds and a gorgeous white, enriched by 50% botrytis.

Vinification, in stainless steel, takes place in a *cuverie* custom-built into the upper storey of an ex-hayloft. Red fermentations are characterised by a finishing burst at 40–45^{0}C to ensure conversion of the last gram of sugar and maximum extraction – especially of tannins – and the vats are *saignéed* 0-40%, depending on the wine. Maturation lasts 12-18 months in wood – with 50-100% new wood for the Mazis and old-vine bottlings (Cazetiers, Champeaux and Gevrey Village *cuvée*).

The Naddefs have 11 different Appellations, starting with an attractive, light, Bourgogne Rouge and include red, white and Rosé Marsannays. The Mazis-Chambertin and three Gevreys 'Vieilles Vignes' bottlings form the pick of this quality cellar. The Gevrey village *cuvée* is deep, classy with a delicious silky elegance, ripe grape tannins (1993) balanced by just enough supporting oak. To these estimable qualities, the Champeaux and Cazetiers add power and succulence; the former, from especially well-drained hillside ground shows a characteristic dry tannic aspect, well covered with plush, ripe fruit, whilst the Cazetiers seems livelier and indeed a shade finer. This is an excellent source – no formulae, just care and sensitivity.

VINEYARD HOLDINGS

Commune	Level	Lieu-dit/Climat	Area	Vine Age	Status
Gevrey	GC	Mazis-Chambertin	0.42	60+	F
Gevrey	PC	Les Cazetiers	0.32	45	F
Gevrey	PC	Les Champeau	0.44	45	F
Gevrey	V	——	0.60	40	F
Gevrey	V	——	0.60	15	F
Fixin	V	——	0.21	10+	F
Marsannay (Rouge)	V	——	1.00	35	F
Marsannay (Blanc)	V	——	0.30	45	F
Couchey	V	Bourgogne Rouge	0.32	20	F
Couchey	V	Bourgogne Blanc	0.21	20	F
Marsannay / Fixin	V	——	0.20	1994/5	F
Total:			**4.64 ha**		

FIXIN

Fixin is an attractive little village of some 1,000 inhabitants, sitting on a slight incline to the immediate south of Couchey. A much underrated commune, suffering perhaps in the shadow of its illustrious neighbour Gevrey, it is pleasantly encircled by its vineyards with an enchanting 14th century lizard-roofed church which stares out over the vines as if somehow personally responsible for them.

Fixin is in fact the fusion of two ancient hamlets – Fixin and Fixey – each of which used to boast its own silk-worm industry. However, this is now long gone and wine and its attendant tourism have taken over. The village is well worth a detour for its fine old buildings, in particular the splendid 19th century wash-house which still functions, although the red soils colour the water, casting some doubt on its cleansing properties.

The main attraction is the 15 ha Parc Noisot at the top of the village, surrounding a house built by Claude Noisot, one of

Napoleon Bonaparte's Imperial Guard commanders, as a replica of that on St Helena where Napoleon died. This now houses a small museum of Napoleonic memorabilia whilst an over-fed bronze statue of the Emperor, sculpted by François Rude, looks down on the scene.

Also of interest is La Résidence de la Perrière, named after the nearby quarry from which stone was extracted to build the church. Originally the summer retreat of the Dukes of Burgundy it became a rest-house for monks when it was ceded to the Abbey of Cîteaux in 1192. It offers a fine panorama of the surrounding countryside and, on a clear day, of the Jura and distant Alps. Meanwhile, Fixey's church is a mélange of romanesque and renaissance with incongruous later additions and a varnish-tiled roof.

When you have finally exhausted the history and yourself, 'Chez Jeanette' and 'Au Clos Napoléon' keep travellers well victualled with simple local fare, washed down with a

Autumn vine colours mirrored in Fixin's church roof

decent bottle of Fixin.

The vines are on mainly gentle slopes rising from 270 to 360 m and exposed due east. Although they cover some 326 ha in total, only 107 have the appellation Fixin and 22 Fixin Premier Cru, the remaining 197 ha being Côte de Nuits-Villages.

Due to an administrative anomaly, 1.62 ha of Fixin Premier Cru extends into next door Brochon which has a fine Château – now part of the local Lycée Viticole – but no appellation of its own and is thus forced to borrow from its neighbours – Gevrey and Fixin.

Fixin's 6 Premiers Crus all lie at the top of the village. The largest, the 5.36 ha Clos de la Perrière, is on a 12–14 % slope, surrounding La Résidence with the 4.78 ha Clos du Chapître just below.

Les Hervelets (3.83 ha) and Les Arvelets (3.36 ha) to the north, are separated by the smallest Premier Cru, Le Meix Bas (1.38 ha). The Clos Napoléon, opposite the Clos du Chapître, was originally 'Aux Cheusots' before Claude Noisot married its owner and changed both their names. Overlooking the village, this makes a splendid spot for a glass.

Until the end of the 17th century Fixins were of greater repute than Gevreys, whose character they often resemble; masculine wines, with plenty of robust, muscular fruit.The best need keeping, and although never exceptional, bottles can be delicious after a decade or so.

Apart from Pierre Gelin, Philippe Joliet's Clos de la Perrière is worth seeking out and there are worthy Fixins from Clair, Charlopin, Jadot and Faiveley. Fixin, like Marsannay, deserves a better press. The best wines are excellent, especially if given time to develop, and also notable value!

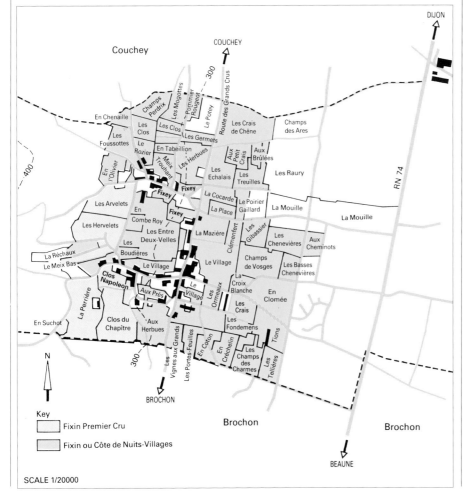

Couchey

COUCHEY

DIJON

Champs Perdrix
Les Mogottes
Pommier Rougeot
Le Potey
Route des Grands Crus

En Chenaille
Les Clos
Les Clos
Les Germets
Les Crais de Chêne
Champs des Ares

Les Foussottes
Le Rozier
En Tabeillion
Meix Trouhant
Les Herbues
Aux Petit Crais
Aux Brûlées

Les Echalais
Les Treuilles
Les Raury

Fixey
La Cocarde
Le Poirier Gaillard
La Mouille
La Mouille

Les Arvelets
En Combe Roy
Fixey
La Place

Les Hervelets
Les Entre Deux-Velles
La Mazière
Clémenfert
Les Gibassier
Les Chenevières
Aux Cheminots

La Réchaux
Le Meix Bas
Les Boudières
Le Village
Champs de Vosges
Les Basses Chenevières

Clos Napoléon
Le Village
Aux Prés
Les Ormeaux
La Croix Blanche
En Clomée

En Suchot
La Perrière
Clos du Chapître
Aux Herbues
Les Crais
Les Fondemens

Les Vignes aux Grands
Les Portes-Feuilles
En Coton
En Créchelin
Les Champs des Charmes
Les Tellières
Les Tions

N

BROCHON

RN 74

La Mouille

Brochon

Brochon

BEAUNE

Key

Fixin Premier Cru

Fixin ou Côte de Nuits-Villages

SCALE 1/20000

16

Domaine Pierre Gelin

FIXIN

Here is a splendid smallish Domaine, making wines which, with the welcome renaissance of Fixin and Marsannay, are destined to become more widely known and appreciated.

The history of the Domaine is briefly told: Pierre Gelin, a native of Fixin, bought some vines in the commune between 1925–1930. His son Stephen, who came to work with him in 1959, at the age of 21, took over the running of the Domaine in 1978 on the death of his father, at the same time giving it its present name. His original partner, André Molin, a long-time employee of Pierre's, retired in 1995, leaving the quiet, self-effacing Stephen in charge, helped by his wife, Marie-Odile.

The vineyards comprise the best of Fixin, together with some Village, Premier Cru and Grand Cru Gevreys. The Domaine has the 'Monopole' of the Clos de Meixvelles – a Gevrey village vineyard – and of Fixin's Clos Napoléon. It also boasts a pair of Grands Crus: 37 ares of Mazis-Chambertin and 60 ares of Chambertin Clos de Bèze. Until 1995, when it was sold by the owners, Stephen Gelin had the sole rights to Fixin's 4.78 ha Clos du Chapître. This loss – with others to follow – will make an unwelcome hole in his Domaine. None the less the quality remains uniformly fine.

The majority of the vines are 25–40 years old, except for the Clos de Bèze which has seen some 65 vintages and low yields are a priority. Stephen Gelin prefers to spring prune, when the sap has started to rise, and prunes very short, if he can without breaking the fragile fruiting cane. Once the shoots appear, there is a severe *ébrossage* to remove excess buds. What counts is not the average yield, but the yield per vine: 'A vine which has too many bunches is like a woman who has too many children – she has difficulty feeding them.' It is essential to realise that, although quantitatively identical, the produce of 1,000 vines yielding 10 bunches apiece and 500 vines producing 20 bunches apiece, are far from qualitatively identical.

A further problem for the Fixin grape-grower is that this part of the Côte is the 'secteur tardif'. Being more northerly, with much of its vineyards area exposed north or north-east, ripening is late and fruit prone to the risks of autumn wind and rains. Gelin tries to counteract this by planting his vines on early-ripening SO4 roots; whilst this can help, the increased risk of *coulure* (loss of flowers) can result in significantly reduced crops. However, he refuses to green-prune:

'from principle, I never go against nature' – believing perhaps that one fine day, nature might turn round and take some unspecified revenge.

The vinification is what might best be described as 'modified traditional' – 100% destalking, and long, slow fermentation in open wooden *cuves*, without any pre-fermentive maceration, at up to 36°C with 7–8 *pigéages* interspersed with *remontage*.

The modification, introduced with the 1988 vintage, comes at the end of the 15–20 day *cuvaison*; when all the sugar has been fermented out, the vats are heated to 35–45°C and left overnight before being decanted at about 20 degrees. This brief heating helps extract colour and flavour components from the grapes, but requires that the last milligram of sugar has been fermented first.

The wines then pass into cask. Fixins are matured partly in *foudre* and partly in older casks – depending on space available and on the characteristics of the wine. Stephen Gelin finds that they evolve more gently in large cooperage, giving a touch of softness to the final blend. Their high natural tannins would certainly not benefit further from new oak. However the Grands Crus are permitted the luxury of some 70% new wood before fining and passing into the hands of a contract bottler some 16–18 months later.

Stephen Gelin is not a grower who is prepared to adapt his style to the whims of his customers. The *terroir* at Fixin, in particular, gives naturally tannic, long-lived wines, which he happens to prefer. 'The customers adapt to us, not we to the customers,' he explains, so if the style is not to your taste, then you go elsewhere.

Whilst the Gevreys are generally well-made, interesting wines – the 1993 Grand Crus are lush and fine, especially the Mazis – it is the Fixins which make this Domaine's reputation. Of the Premiers Crus, Les

Hervelets generally shows more expressive fruit aromas than the Clos Napoléon, which has more natural power and evinces the more animal, musky, spicy, peppery side of the Pinot Noir.

The 1993 Hervelets was mid-purple in hue with a soft, smoky, plummy nose; on the palate quite lean, with bright acidity and firm structure supporting a good layer of ripe fruit. In character, it showed greater finesse than the Clos Napoléon and promised interesting development. The Hervelets vineyard has significantly stonier topsoil and a higher iron content than the Clos, which contains more pink clay. This latter tends to impart a broader, more muscular structure which is noticeably more *sauvage* on both nose and palate. Stephen's policy of very late harvesting explains the great richness one finds in these wines.

For many years the wines of Fixin have been unfairly regarded as the 'little' wines of the Côte. Consequently neither merchants nor collectors will give them cellar space. This is a pity – and an injustice, as Fixins will make fine old bottles, given half the chance. A 1961 Clos du Chapître was still magnificent 30 years on – a fine, deep colour, with richness and complexity both on nose and palate, and a very long, warm finish. Not a Gevrey Grand Cru certainly, but infinitely preferable to many wines of greater pretension at several times the price.

It is about time that people took the wine of this part of the Côte more seriously – Stephen Gelin has more than enough ammunition to make them sit up and think.

VINEYARD HOLDINGS

Commune	Level	Lieu-dit/Climat	Area	Vine Age	Status
Fixin	PC	Clos Napoléon	1.80	40	P/M
Fixin	PC	Les Hervelets	0.57	25	F
Fixin	V	————	2.50	20/30	P
Gevrey	V	Clos de Meixvelles	1.80	30	P/M
Gevrey	PC	Clos Prieur	0.23	28	P
Gevrey	GC	Mazis-Chambertin	0.37	40	P
Gevrey	GC	Clos de Bèze	0.60	65	P
Total:			**12.65 ha**		

GEVREY-CHAMBERTIN

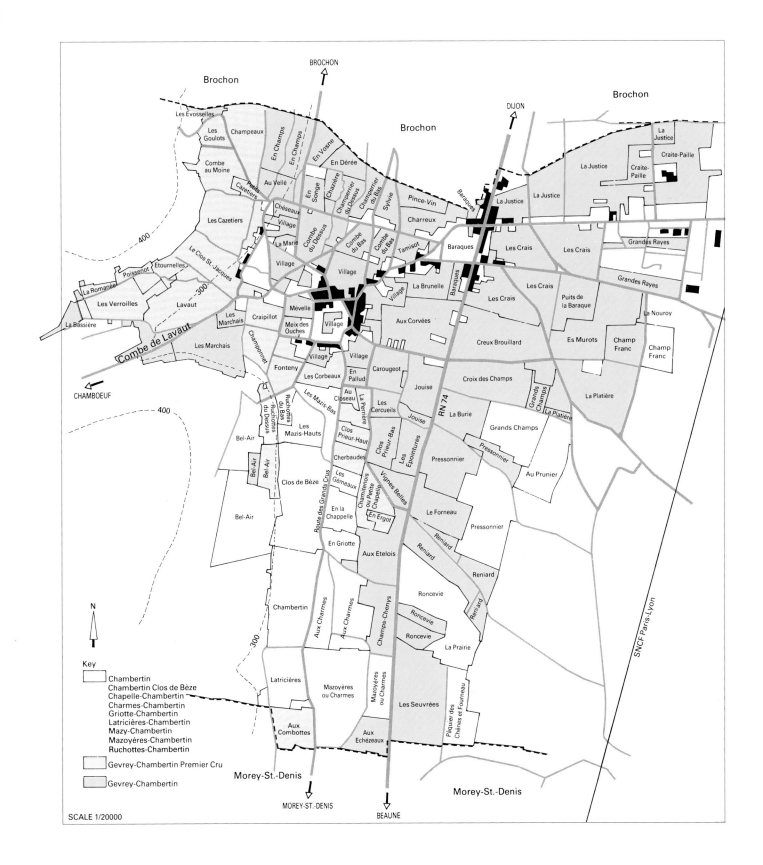

BROCHON

Brochon

Brochon

Brochon

DIJON

Les Evosselles

Champeaux

Les Goulots

En Champs

En Champs

En Vosne

La Justice

Craite-Paille

Combe au Moine

En Dérée

Craite-Paille

Petits Cazetiers

Au Vellé

En Songe

Chazière

Champerrier du Dessus

Champerrier du Bas

Sylvie

Pince-Vin

Baraques

La Justice

La Justice

Les Cazetiers

Chéseaux

Village

Combe du Dessus

Charreux

Grandes Rayes

Le Clos St.-Jacques

La Marie

Combe du Bas

Combe du Bas

Tamisot

Baraques

Les Crais

Les Crais

Poissenot

Etournelles

Village

Village

La Brunelle

Baraques

Les Crais

Grandes Rayes

La Romanée

Lavaut

Village

Les Crais

Puits de la Baraque

La Nouroy

Les Verroilles

Mévelle

Village

Aux Corvées

Les Crais

La Bassière

Les Marchais

Craipillot

Meix des Ouches

Village

Creux Brouillard

Es Murots

Champ Franc

Champ Franc

Combe de Lavaut

Les Marchais

Championnet

Village

Village

Carougeot

Croix des Champs

La Platiére

CHAMBOEUF

Fonteny

Les Corbeaux

En Pallud

Jouise

Grands Champs

La Platiére

Au Closeau

Les Cercueils

Jouise

La Burie

Les Mazis-Bas

La Perrière

Ruchottes du Bas

Ruchottes du Dessus

Les Mazis-Hauts

Clos Prieur-Haut

Clos Prieur-Bas

Les Epointures

Pressonnier

Grands Champs

Pressonnier

Bel-Air

Cherbaudes

Vignes Belles

Au Prunier

Bel-Air

Bel-Air

Clos de Bèze

Les Gémeaux

Chamitenois ou Petite Chapelle

Le Forneau

Pressonnier

Bel-Air

Route des Grands Crus

En la Chapelle

En Ergot

Reniard

En Griotte

Aux Etelois

Reniard

Reniard

Chambertin

Aux Charmes

Aux Charmes

Champs-Chenys

Roncevie

Roncevie

Reniard

Roncevie

La Prairie

SNCF Paris-Lyon

Key

Latricières

Mazoyères ou Charmes

Mazoyères ou Charmes

Les Seuvrées

Pâquier des Chênes et Fourneau

Chambertin
Chambertin Clos de Bèze
Chapelle-Chambertin
Charmes-Chambertin
Griotte-Chambertin
Latricières-Chambertin
Mazy-Chambertin
Mazoyères-Chambertin
Ruchottes-Chambertin

Aux Combottes

Aux Echézeaux

Gevrey-Chambertin Premier Cru

Gevrey-Chambertin

Morey-St.-Denis

Morey-St.-Denis

SCALE 1/20000

MOREY-ST.-DENIS

BEAUNE

N

400

300

400

300

For many, Gevrey-Chambertin marks the true northern limit of the Côte d'Or. With its 9 Grands Crus, it is by far the largest commune in the Côte de Nuits and very much its flagship.

The village, recorded as Gabriacus in 640, belonged to the Abbots of Bèze whose monks were largely responsible for clearing the ground and pioneering the original vine plantations. In 1257, the Abbot of Cluny decided that fortifications were desirable and started the construction of a Château, the remains of which can still be seen at the top of the village.

Nothing momentous happened thereafter until 1553–58 when the plague struck with devastating effect and massive infestations of insects laid waste the vines for over a century. In 1847 a Royal decree granted the commune the right to add the name of its most renowned Grand Cru to its designation; thus was Gevrey-Chambertin born.

Gevrey is really a small town. Its 2,600 inhabitants benefit from shops, a wine-bar, a bistro, a hotel and a couple of prestigious restaurants, reflecting expansion, especially on the eastern side of the RN 74.

The vineyards extend to 532 ha; 9 Grands Crus account for 87, 26 Premiers Crus for 86, leaving 359 ha of Village appellation, including 11 *climats* from Brochon which are entitled to call their wine Gevrey-Chambertin.

The Village vines extend on both sides of the Dijon Beaune road, mainly to the east and north of the village centre. The Premiers Crus lie in two bands, one to the south and the other, larger, section to the west towards the Combe de Lavaux. This latter, generally regarded as the first division of Premiers Crus, includes Les Cazetiers, La Combe aux Moines, Le Clos S.-Jacques, Lavaux St.-Jacques and Etournelles St.-Jacques.

The Grands Crus are sited south of the village on a magnificent swathe of east-facing, gently sloping hillside at a height of 260–320m, protected from wind-chill by the forest above. The commune has taken the unusually extrovert step – for Burgundy – of identifying each Grand Cru with a prominent sign for the benefit of its numerous visitors.

Micro-climates are particularly important here, since the Combe de Lavaux, a steep-sided valley behind the village, acts as a funnel for bad weather, especially for hail. Fortunately the higher ground is inimical to frost, which, like water runs off to the flatter land near the main road. In 1985, whilst more than 80 ha of village vineyards were destroyed by frost, the Premiers and Grands Crus escaped virtually unscathed. The relative coolness of the upper slopes slows down the ripening process, making these vineyards less successful in marginal vintages or when bad weather necessitates an early harvest.

For centuries, Chambertin's combination of 'grace and vigour, firmness and strength, finesse and delicacy . . . the summit of Burgundy's potential' has inspired writers to exotic prose. Together with its neighbour Clos de Bèze, Chambertin is widely considered as *primus inter pares* among the Grand Crus. Administrative idiosyncrasy permits wine from Clos de Bèze to be labelled Chambertin, but not vice versa.

Gevrey's soils exhibit wide diversity. The Grands Crus are planted on a base of compacted limestone – its substratum is clearly visible from an incision marking the site of a disused quarry on the left of the Route des Grands Crus entering Gevrey from Morey-St.-Denis. Topsoils are more or less rich in clay particles – less in Griotte-Chambertin and Chapelle-Chambertin more in Mazoyères, which is altogether more fecund arable soil, with a 30–35 cm outcrop of well-drained gravel. Another administrative oddity permits wine from the Mazoyères-Chambertin *climat* to be called Charmes-Chambertin, but not vice versa.

Latricières- and Ruchottes-Chambertin are on higher ground, with a topsoil of white marl; a highish limestone content tends to give the wines a more marked dimension of hardness and tannin than the other Grand Crus.

Griotte-Chambertin, the smallest of the Grand Crus, takes its name not from any cherry-tree planted there, nor from the supposed whiff of cherry in its wine, but rather from its shape, a concave bowl which trapped the sun so much in summer that it was like a little grill or 'grillotte'.

Elsewhere in the commune, soil depths vary; topsoils are frequently thin with clearly visible rock outcrops. The flat land on either side of the road, where Village and Regional appellations are concentrated, have more clay in their composition, giving breadth and body, but less finesse.

Such a large commune – some 110 growers in Gevrey itself – is inevitably home to a wide variety of quality and styles. A Chambertin from Jean Trapet, emphasising delicacy and finesse, will have little in common with Charles Rousseau's denser, more structured version. Whilst Gevreys are broadly characterised by power and muscle, tending to start compact and needing time

A vigneron's house in Gevrey-Chambertin; grand houses are the exception in the Côte d'Or

to unpack, the best do not lack finesse. Premiers and Grands Crus from top vintages can develop well over 30 years or more.

Recent years have seen the emergence of a number of excellent 'new' Domaines – some of which are profiled here. Many are long-established family enterprises which are now – usually under the aegis of a new generation – Domaine bottling, rather than selling everything in bulk, whilst others have emerged from divisions of vineyards between different members of the family. Elsewhere, poorly-performing Domaines have been transformed with the arrival of a new hand on the tiller.

Apart from the obvious stars, there are a number of estates which have all the ingredients for stardom but lack the consistency of the best. Lamentably, there are also too many Domaines which continue to underperform. Common faults are excessive yields, sloppy vinification, keeping wine too long in cask and evisceratingly harsh filtration – often incompetence masquerading as 'tradition'. This is doubly inexcusable, as it both damages the reputation of the appellations produced and denies abler winemakers, who could do a much better job, access to scarce land. The shortage might just tempt someone to a charitable experiment!

THE GRAND CRUS OF GEVREY-CHAMBERTIN

Lieu-dit	Area	Props.	Av. Prod.
Chambertin	12.90.31	25	4000 C/S
Chambertin Clos de Bèze	15.38.87	18	5200 C/S
Chapelle-Chambertin	5.48.53	9	2000 C/S
Charmes-Chambertin +			
Mazoyères-Chambertin	30.83.24	67	10500 C/S
Griotte-Chambertin	2.69.18	9	800 C/S
Latricières-Chambertin	7.35.44	12	2500 C/S
Mazis-Chambertin	9.10.34	28	3000 C/S
Ruchottes-Chambertin	3.30.37	8	1000 C/S
Totals:	**87.06.28 ha**		**29000 C/S**

Domaine Bachelet

GEVREY-CHAMBERTIN

Denis Bachelet is a thirty-something modern young man with a centuries-old traditional Domaine with which, despite the serious disparity in their ages, he gets on remarkably well. Perched on a couple of plastic wine boxes in the *cuverie*, he self-confidently discusses his charge, his slim figure, outsize brown eyes and large ears giving him the appearance of an animated gallic version of E.T..

The family house was originally the post-house for Gevrey in the reign of the Sun King. The original Bachelet, Victor, was a tonnelier in the area, but Denis was uncertain precisely where – 'perhaps Grandmother . . .' He has a clearer memory of his grandparents who 'bought vineyards right and left' – an expression meant to convey quantity rather than orientation. Included in these whirling purchases was a parcel of Grand Cru Charmes-Chambertin, which remains the pride of the Domaine.

On his demise in 1984, Grandfather bequeathed 5 ha of vines which were divided between Denis' father, Bernard and his aunt, Michelle who cared for the estate until Denis completed his studies in 1983.

At present the vineyards are owned by his father, who went to Belgium in the 1960s to pursue his career as an electromecanicien. Although Denis' wife is now involved, he admits that the full 'Equipe technique' at present consists of himself, his father and 'Grandmother'.

Denis' Domaine may be short on hectares, but on neither quality nor commitment. His concern is to maintain, and where necessary improve, the traditions he has inherited. In the vineyards this means a high average vine age and only organic fertilisers which, with low herbicide doses and hand working of the soil, help retain these ancient plants – some in Charmes-Chambertin having already seen their century.

Each year some 200 vines per hectare need replacing – victims of disease, natural decrepitude or tractor accidents. This entails digging a hole, disinfecting the soil and then covering it up for the winter. In the spring the new vine is planted – one of 3 or 4 chosen clones – and carefully nurtured until it is 4 years old. Young vines planted between two old vines often give particularly good fruit – the old plants take much of the light and spread their foliage, obliging the impoverished newcomer to struggle for nourishment. Further, after its initial 'clean soil' period and once roots are established, it becomes

infected with nematodes from its neighbours; these restrict youthful vigour and give the fruit a depth and concentration compatible with *Grand Vin*.

Low yields seem to just happen. Denis has never had to green-prune to remove excess bunches and dislikes the practice. The 1988 and 1990 figures indicate the small rendements achieved: Charmes-Chambertin 25–30 and 37+ hl/ha respectively; in corresponding Gevrey yields were 35 and 45 hl/ha – about 17% higher. In 1993, Charmes yielded just 28 hl/ha – 5 casks of wine.

To eliminate rot, pickers are trained to make two separate cuts on each bunch – first to remove rot, then to cut the bunch itself. In particularly difficult vintages – 1983 for example – a further *trie* is made at the *cuverie*. *Pourriture sec* is the least welcome form of rot, imparting an ineradicable flavour to the wine. *Pourriture humide* taints less, if present only in small quantities.

About all this Denis is philosophical: 'costly, but the price to pay for *Grand Vin* . . . we can't afford to get it wrong; every drop of wine counts.' He is acutely aware of the financial consequences of even minor spoilage, and equally mindful of the vulnerability of a fragile reputation: 'when you're at the top, it's so easy to slip' – a reflection more perhaps on the volatility of critical acclaim than on his own ability as a winemaker.

What happens in the cellar is often constrained by money. 'I can't afford to cool or heat the *must* – I haven't got the equipment.' All he can do is to extract 300 litres from one overheating *cuve* at a time, cool and return it, hoping that this will moderate the temperature. Sulphur, which knocks out the feebler yeasts producing least alcohol, is affordable and so systematically used.

Denis' and grandmother's philosophy is that the grapes contain everything needful for making good wine. Thus, the 7–11 days of fermentation are preceded by 3–4 days of maceration to maximise extraction. Every drop of press-wine is added to the free-run

wine – 'we can't afford to leave any aside' – before transfer to casks – 100% new oak for the Grand Cru and 50% for the Premier Cru. These remain in a specially cold part of the cellar for the entire winter, to ensure the slowest possible start to malolactic fermentation. 'My grandfather had no means of heating to start his *malos*, but made good wine all the same. After *malo* the lees are dead, so it is better to keep the wine on lees as long as possible before.' In early summer the wines are racked off their lees and returned to cask, thence to a deeper, cooler cellar before the onset of high summer temperatures.

Each cask is fined with fresh egg white, rested for one month, then hand-bottled without filtration. If Denis manages 4 casks in a day, his supper is well earned.

Bachelet wines are expressly *vins de garde*; they are also supple and attractively *tendre* in their youth. Denis prefers these qualities and is not interested in extracting concentrations of raw tannins which render wines unapproachable for years. The determination of how long a *cuvaison* is appropriate for each wine and when to bottle is the province of the omnipotent triumvirate of Denis, Bernard and grandmother.

To date, Denis considers the 1988 Charmes-Chambertin as his single greatest achievement. The 1989 is no slouch – with an aristocratic, highly seductive perfume and combining a soft, ripe structure with rounded and harmonious tannins – strongly redolent of a Musigny. Denis professes a love of Chambolles and looks for their elegance and finesse in his own *cuvées*. Meanwhile the 1993s show considerable promise – including a remarkable Côte de Nuits-Villages from vines at nearby Brochon – and the 1994s have delicacy and interest, for earlier drinking. A curiosity – from 1989 – is an Aligoté from Gevrey vines, vinified and matured for 18 months in cask – 'à la Meursault'.

Denis' wines are conscientiously thought out and expertly crafted. The amalgam of youth and tradition is a resounding success.

VINEYARD HOLDINGS

Commune	Level	Lieu-dit/Climat	Area	Vine Age	Status
Gevrey	GC	Charmes-Chambertin	0.44	80/100	P
Gevrey	PC	Les Corbeaux	0.42	75	P
Gevrey	V	(Several parcels)	0.91	60	P
Brochon	R	Côtes de Nuits-Villages	0.38	35	P
Gevrey	R	Bourgogne Rouge	0.60	18	P
Gevrey	R	Bourgogne Aligoté	0.19	9	P
Total:			**2.94 ha**		

Domaine Alain Burguet

GEVREY-CHAMBERTIN

This small Domaine has made a disproportionate impact in Gevrey in recent years. Alain Burguet, its founder and proprietor, is a solid, sometimes rather abrasive individual, a man of determination with a clear, though inflexible, idea of how things should be done. Success seems to have softened him somewhat and lessened his distrust of critics.

After working with his father from 1964 to 1972, he spent two years with Domaine Tortochot in Gevrey before leaving to create his own estate. In 1974 he acquired 2.1 hectares of Gevrey on a share-cropping basis from an elderly farmer, the contract requiring him to deliver ⅓ of the crop, as grapes, to his landlord and to pay all the costs of exploitation. In 1976 he bought the house at 18 Rue de l'Eglise in Gevrey, vinified his 1977 and then set about constructing a *cuverie* next door. He has recently bought a fine old cellar at the top of the village, used for cask-ageing and bottle storage.

From the beginning, Burguet was interested in nothing less than top quality. A sojourn in Oregon gave him a fascination for America and a profound respect for *terroir*. His first vintages brought little profit, as he stood by and watched his neighbours making fortunes from excessive yields and indifferent wine. However, he was encouraged to continue his policy of quality by friends who tried his 1978s and were impressed.

Of the Domaine's le 5.53 ha, 1.5 are owned outright, the rest being share-cropped Gevrey Village vineyards, much over 50 years old. There is a miniscule patch of young-vine Gevrey-Chambertin Premier Cru Les Champeaux first released in 1993.

Old vines and rigorous pruning keep yields low and concentration high. Burguet takes considerable care with the health of his vines, with up to 3 separate annual treatments for grape-worm and 2 for red spider. Bordeaux mixture is also used, with 6 treatments for mildew and 5 for *oïdium*.

No herbicides are used, Burguet preferring to hoe the land several times a year. In the winter, soil is ploughed up round the vine roots both as direct frost-protection and to aerate the earth because 'the softer the earth, the less the frost penetrates', he claims.

He regards his task as 'not trying to make the best Gevrey, but to make 'true' wine'. This means not relying on technical wizardry, if this threatens the typicity of either vintage or *terroir*.

The grapes are lightly crushed and destemmed: 'nearly 100% – it depends on the vintage'; in riper years including a few stalks helps maintain an acceptable level of acidity.

Only indigenous yeasts are used, although there may be a *pied de cuve* should things appear sluggish, as Burguet prefers fermentation to start as soon as possible. No sulphur is added to the crushed grapes to delay fermentation artificially, but no-one minds if a natural delay means that skins and juice macerate together for a few extra days.

The policy is to ferment at the riskier high end of the temperature scale – about 35°C. 'This,' Alain explains, 'is like washing clothes, the higher the temperature the more you extract.' The risks of stuck fermentations or jammy flavours don't appear to concern him.

After 15–20 days in the sultry habitat of a Burguet cement fermenting vat, only disturbed by the occasional *pigéage* (no pumping over here), the wine is decanted and amalgamated with its pressings. Burguet used not to believe in post-fermentive maceration, but now a few days are allowed to extract tannins and stabilise colour. The new wine is then removed, with or without lees (depending on their quality) to mature in oak casks.

About 5% of the casks are new Allier oak. Having tried Limousin – 'too strong' – Vosges and Charente, Alain decided that Allier gave the best structure and finest tannins. The Bourgogne Rouge has 2–3% of new oak, the Gevrey 'traditionel' 10%, the Vieilles Vignes 25% and the Champeaux 60%.

A rapid *malo* is followed by a full year's maturation on fine lees, provided these are healthy. If not, the wine is racked earlier. At racking, the various casks are equalised, and the wine subjected to a single Kieselguhr filtration; a further polishing plate filtration has been discarded.

Burguet does not fine his wines because they contain dissolved CO_2; if you want to fine them you have to degassify them first and this perforce removes some freshness;

QED no fining. As he points out, 'Degassifying a wine may add suppleness but I am not looking for suppleness. I want wine which will keep for 15 years, so I am not looking for it to be flattering at the start.'

His Gevrey Village can still be remarkably approachable young, with a deepish colour, black fruit aromas, an almost sweet undertone and a dimension of concentration derived from low yielding old vines.

In comparison, the Gevrey Vieilles Vignes is generally tighter on the nose and palate – with fine concentration corseted by a layer of harmonious ripe tannins and a distinctly spicy flavour. With singular modesty, Burguet attributes the quality of this wine to 'old vines . . . and me', the inflexion implying more than just the fact that he made it. In top-class vintages (esp. 1990 and 1993) the concentration of tannins and obvious acidity means 5 years, or more, in bottle before it is remotely ready to drink. Burguet's uncompromising high tannin style makes naturally leaner vintages less successful; a meaty and four-square 1992, for example, with an excess of dry tannin – not bad, but lacking in flesh and charm.

As one expects from a Premier Cru, Les Champeaux is a dimension more complex and profound. Its 60% new oak dominates initially, but the wine's natural concentration and power is capable of absorbing it in time. The fine 1993, with an exuberant nose, masses of ripe, fleshy fruit, all encased in the usual Burguet envelope of tannins is a wine for a decade of maturation.

This Domaine gets better and better, in particular with handling of lesser vintages. The 1991s and 1994s here are excellent wines which the general misinformed clamour about 'poor vintages' should not deter anyone from buying. Alain Burguet is shedding his bulldog image and a correspondingly softer persona is showing in his wines. Both are welcome changes.

VINEYARD HOLDINGS

Commune	Level	Lieu-dit/Climat	Area	Vine Age	Status
Gevrey	PC	Les Champeaux	0.18	9	P
Gevrey	V	Pince-Vin	1.20	50	P/F
Gevrey	V	Aux Corvées	0.50	40	P/F
Gevrey	V	Jouise	0.42	50	P/F
Gevrey	V	Creux Brouillard	0.90	50	P/F
Gevrey	V	La Justice	0.30	60	P/F
Gevrey	V	Reniard	1.26	35	P/F
Gevrey	R	Pince-Vin/Genevrière (Bourgogne R)	0.77	35	P/F
		Total:	**5.53 ha**		

Domaine Philippe Leclerc

GEVREY-CHAMBERTIN

This is an unusual Domaine in that it has tradition, but no past. When Philippe Leclerc received 4.3 ha as his share of the family vines in 1974, at the age of 23, he was already steeped in wine, having worked with his father since leaving school at 13. Time spent talking to older vignerons in Gevrey taught him to appreciate traditional practice with, no doubt, some traditional tasting into the bargain.

Nonetheless, in his desire to make big, uncompromisingly tannic wines, which take years to evolve, Philippe is something of an iconoclast. The results are often stunning – wines of great depth and hefty structure, but not without matching finesse.

Low-yielding old vines provide his raw material, improved by as late a harvest as practicable – usually a week after everyone else. In 1994 he didn't finish picking until 3rd October, giving 8 days of sunshine after the heavy rain to dry and ripen the grapes. He likes the crop as cool as possible – so doesn't pick when it is very hot, if he can avoid it – but with the added ripeness of a late harvest.

He used to leave 50% of stalks in his vats but has reduced this to 20%, having discovered that stalk tannins virtually never harmonise, whilst oak tannins usually do. The crushed grapes are encouraged by cooling and sulphur, to macerate for as long as possible before natural yeasts start fermenting the sugars. Over eight days or so, tannins and colour are extracted, which also gives Philippe time to finish the harvest: 'You can't concentrate on picking and deal with a problem *cuve* at the same time.'

Once fermentation has started, it is persuaded to proceed as slowly as possible – a long, gentle extraction. As temperatures rarely exceed 30°C, *cuvaison* can last for up to a month. As soon as all the sugar has been transformed the wine is run off and the *marc* lightly pressed. Philippe admits that for him an excess of tannin does not exist, since his aim is true, old-fashioned *vins de garde*.

What happens next is less than traditional: having cooled the *cuverie* and sulphured his wines, Philippe then blankets them with liquid paraffin. This effectively blocks the *malo* until the last but one vintage has been bottled in January/February, when space is freed to transfer the new wine to casks. Philippe insists that having the *malo* in cask extracts noticeably rounder and more harmonious tannins.

The two Premiers Crus find their way into 100% new Nevers oak, the Village Gevrey has 50% and the Bourgogne Rouge 15%. Here the *malo* passes off, unhurried, at its own pace, since the wine will not be racked until the following November. The period under paraffin helps rid the wine of all but its fine lees, reducing the need for racking and helping clarification. Philippe considers that having *malos* on lees, provided that they are healthy, adds a further dimension of richness.

The wines spend two years or more in cask before bottling: 'two summers for the *malos* and three winters for clarification,' is how he sees it. This extended *élévage* enables him to bottle with neither fining nor filtration and thereby to retain the maximum of each wine's natural stuffing.

This is a highly individual and unusual vinification – yet entirely logical. 'I don't pretend to always be right,' admits Philippe, in a burst of modesty; 'I like to try this and that, then analyse the results and adjust here and there. One must always question things, that is the only way to the summit of quality.'

Philippe's wines are intense and fine, although difficult to evaluate whilst still in cask. The Bourgogne Rouge – his largest appellation – is a big, sappy wine, with dryish tannins and plenty of sound, firm fruit. Not a wine for early drinking, but lovely after half a decade in bottle.

There are two Gevrey Village wines: one from Les Platières – a vineyard no more than 150 metres from the main railway line on the opposite side of the RN74 – whose richish soil and 40-year-old vines give a characteristically broad, meaty structure – evident in both 1990 and 1993. The En Champs *cuvée*, from 50-year-old vines, is altogether richer, tighter and more powerful and integrates its new oak more fully. 1993 saw the addition of an excellent Village Chambolle-Musigny – characteristically elegant and less aggressively muscular than the Gevreys.

The pair of Gevrey Premiers Crus, Les Cazetiers and La Combe Aux Moines, are next door to each other in the north-west corner of the commune, in that superb band which also includes Lavaux St.-Jacques and Clos St.-Jacques. The *terroir's* natural power and a preference for heavily charred casks impart a structure which makes cellaring essential, especially in vintages such as 1990 and 1993. The Combe Aux Moines is the denser and more complex of the two, but both are sizeable, muscular wines, of high quality – even in vintages such as 1994.

It is often the lesser vintages which put the winemakers to the severest test. In 1987 and 1986 Philippe passed with flying colours. The 1987 Premier Crus were deeply coloured wines, with the Cazetiers developing attractive aromas of *fruits noirs* and the Combe Aux Moines those of a more 'sauvage', tarry style. Both had sound, firm, ripe fruit, a good balance and plenty of depth. Not as complex or profound as the 1988s, but notwithstanding, fine wines to enjoy during the mid 1990s. The 1986 Combe Aux Moines is a triumph. A gorgeous, complex, nose of ripe strawberries, with a finely judged layer of tannins supporting ripe, stylish, almost sweet fruit. Not a wine of hallmark Leclerc density, but one of seductive opulence, and a great success for the vintage. The generally unsung 1991s are also good here – no shortage of flesh or character, with underlying complexity for those prepared to wait.

Philippe Leclerc will tell you that he has difficulty in finding inner serenity. He is a restless man who appears to be ceaselessly questing for something perpetually elusive – a loner. It is not unknown for him to disappear for a few days, when he feels he needs to escape. He shares his brother René's passion for cars – and is the proud possessor of an American 'Excalibur'. His wines obviously give him both pleasure and pain – never entirely right, always something that might have been done differently. However, the results are usually excellent, and for most growers that would be adequate compensation for the occasional imperfection!

VINEYARD HOLDINGS

Commune	Level	Lieu-dit/Climat	Area	Vine Age	Status
Gevrey	V	Les Platières	1.00	40	P
Gevrey	V	En Champs	0.75	50	P
Gevrey	PC	Champonnets	0.25	40	P
Gevrey	PC	Les Champeaux	0.50	40	P
Gevrey	PC	Les Cazetiers	0.50	55	P
Gevrey	PC	La Combe Aux Moines	0.67	50	P
Chambolle	V	Les Babillaires	0.50	40	P
Chambolle	R	(Bourgogne Rouge)	4.00	40	P
		Total:	**8.17 ha**		

Domaine Charles Mortet

GEVREY-CHAMBERTIN

Denis Mortet is a talented young vigneron, custodian of more than 30 different plots, developed from an original ha entailed by his grandfather to his father, Charles, in the 1950s. These include 2.3 ha of white varieties planted on reclaimed fruit orchards near the family home in Dijon. His brother, Thierry, who worked with him, left to establish his own Domaine in 1991, when Charles retired.

The quality here is remarkable. From the first skirmish with the Bourgogne Rouge, it is clear that Denis has the art of winemaking at his fingertips. His guiding principle is to work as naturally as possible.

He admits to attaching far greater importance now to his vineyards. Soils are hoed to deepen root-systems and weeds controlled organically, whilst pests are dealt with by standard sprays applied early to avoid traces finding their way into the wine. Denis admits to particular difficulty with the proliferous red spider where effective control is only possible if everyone treats conscientiously. If not: 'well I see them enough in the vineyards', and if that doesn't work, then 'you can always spray their vines to protect your own'.

Experiments with green pruning young Chambolle and Gevrey vines produced 'superb results'. Excising the largest, most shaded, bunches aerates the entire vine and increases overall ripeness; so, when necessary, the practice continues. With tighter pruning, yields are now notably lower than before – around 30–35 hl/ha in Premier Cru in 1993 – and it shows in the wines.

The Mortet harvest is unusually early – there is no point delaying when grapes are fully ripe – although in less favourable seasons, Denis is happy to wait for autumn sunshine to add ripeness and a touch more concentration.

Picking is scrupulously careful. The pickers, 'gens très sérieux', are drilled to excise anything that appears substandard. Not content with their efforts, Denis purchased a *table de trie* in 1993. One is left with the impression that a rotten Mortet grape would be pretty well friendless.

Vinification is fairly orthodox and stalks are completely taboo – 'never, never, never – there are other ways of having good structure in the wine'. To wit: a long fermentation at 29–32°C and 2–3 firm *pigéages* each day. Yeasting is beyond the pale: when the fermentation won't start, a *pied de cuve* is used to get things going. The 13–15 days of vatting now include 4–5 of prefermentive maceration.

Once the press-wine has been added, the Village Gevreys and the Bourgogne Rouge *cuvées* are assembled, weeding out those destined for the négoce – a pity some of the grander Domaines don't follow this example – before transferring the wines to cask.

Experiment has evolved a preferred mixture of Allier, Nevers and Vosges oak for the Gevreys (33% new), whereas Premiers and Grands Crus, and wine from old vines, fare best in Vosges which, though slower to marry, eventually gives something finer.

At first racking, where possible, new wood is exchanged for old. For the Villages this means that some wine remains in older wood, whereas for the Premiers Crus (50–60% new wood) there is a simple exchange of new casks with old. The Grands Crus, being in 75% or more new wood, remain where they are.

After 17 months maturation, without fining to avoid a further racking which tires the wine, the various *cuvées* are unified, lightly Kieselguhr filtered, then bottled by a visiting bottler whose competence Denis trusts. The small lots of Clos Vougeot and Chambertin are hand-bottled, by Denis himself.

Although he started working with his father in 1976 it was not until 1984 that they first exported. Now much of the 3,000–4,000 case production finds its way out of France.

The wines are characterised by suppleness and succulent fruit complex. The Bourgognes Rouge and Blanc, from family vineyards at Daix, are specially precious. The red is tender and quite fat, with attractive ripe fruit, a firm backbone and distinct earthiness. Both are exceptionally good for their Appellation, as is the red Marsannay and Les Longeroies, which arrived in 1993.

The Gevreys differ markedly: the Village tends to length and roundness, quite tightly structured, with aromatic and flavour com-plexity needing 5 years plus in good vintages to fully open out. The En Motrot, a Village *lieu-dit*, has greater angularity and acidity but ultimately, greater elegance. The 1993 was very fine – notes of *mures* and cassis – not vastly robust, more in finesse.

Au Velle, in contrast, is characterised by its *charpente* and underlying power – a true *vin de garde*, more typically Gevrey than En Motrot. En Champs – 70+–year-old vines, 200 m from Velle – exudes depth starting as a tight-budded wine but which in good vintages repays a decade of cellaring.

The Premier Cru Champeaux – situated high up beyond Cazetiers – has a stronger character yet with greater delicacy and finesse and significantly more acidity. The vineyard is a mixture of flat and sloping ground, with much iron and rock in its soil.

The Chambolle Les Beaux-Bruns, matured in 50% new Vosges oak, has all the quality of this fine Premier Cru and typifies its origin: a very good 1993 showed abundant silky fruit, excellent length – a delicate, complete wine with exemplary balance. By contrast, the Clos Vougeot, from vines situated near Ch. de la Tour, is a heady cocktail of tannin, acidity and fruit. The firmly-structured 1993, matured in 80% new wood, was intense, deeply coloured, with aromas of *fruits noirs* overlaying a layer of powerful, fat fruit.

These were eclipsed by the Chambertin's sheer class, from a tiny parcel of 35-year-old vines. Here, a fine deep colour, a remarkably complex fruit-based nose with a residuum of its 100% new oak to absorb, bags of very concentrated, multi-dimensional flavour and an extraordinarily long, peacock's tail of a finish (only 25 hl/ha in 1993). This has it all!

Denis Mortet's wines are among Gevrey's best and more than merit a place in any cellar of fine red Burgundy.

VINEYARD HOLDINGS

Commune	Level	Lieu-dit/Climat	Area	Vine Age	Status
Gevrey	GC	Chambertin	0.15	39	F
Vougeot	GC	Clos Vougeot	0.32	18	F
Gevrey	PC	Les Champeaux	0.29	65	F
Chambolle	PC	Les Beaux-Bruns	0.23	11	F
Gevrey	V	En Champs	0.86	70	F
Gevrey	V	Au Velle	1.16	45	F
Gevrey	V	En Motrot	0.49	35	F
Gevrey	V	(30 different plots)	2.69	40	P/F
Marsannay	V	Les Longeroies	0.48	36	F
Daix	R	(Bourgogne Rouge)	0.94	18	P
Daix	R	(Bourgogne Chardonnay)	0.60	10	P
Daix	R	(Bourgogne Aligoté)	0.30	12	P
Total:			**8.51 ha**		

Domaine Maume

GEVREY-CHAMBERTIN

Whilst the 1970s and 1980s have brought considerable prosperity to the Côte, evident to anyone driving through its attractive, scrupulously kept villages, a few Domaines appear to have got stuck in a previous age and have no obvious intention of being brought up to date.

Bernard Maume and his son Bertrand run one such. The visitor stepping off the easterly pavement at number 56, Route de Beaune, leaves the present decade for an epoch which has more to do with the 1920s than with the turn of the 21st century. A double-glazing of evergreen trees hides a house of 1850s construction from passing traffic and the gaze of curious passers-by. There is nothing to indicate the Domaine nor any clue of the riches of the various cellars which underpin – and undermine – the house.

Bernard Maume, a charming, courteous man strikes a scholarly attitude which conceals a quick passion for his work. The Domaine was started by his great-uncle – Louis Mariller – whose father had vineyards at Gevrey during the 19th century. Bernard was brought up in Dijon, but spent his holidays with Louis at Gevrey, playing around the casks and *cuverie*, and helping during the harvest. At Dijon University he distinguished himself as a biochemist, met his future wife and, fortuitously, added Diplomas in Oenology and Viticulture to his qualifications.

In 1956, while Bernard was still a student, great-uncle Louis died, childless, prematurely pitching him into running the estate. He vinified his first wine in 1957, and thereafter managed to continue both his work at the Domaine and at the University. A research post in Texas and other important work, led to his being offered Dijon's Chair of Oenology. He declined, and returned with his wife, to run his Domaine.

His academic interests remain, with some lecturing and supervision of students, his own research into yeasts and sterols, collaborating with Michel Feuillat, the current holder of the Chair at Dijon which he turned down. His various absorptions are evident from his study – a friendly clutter of academia interspersed with piles of 'in' and 'out' and a general air of 'work in progress'.

The Domaine has grown piecemeal to its present size. To the original holding, Louis added the Mazis-Chambertin, from the estate of Thomas Collignon – of which one-third went to the Hospices de Beaune, for the Cuvée bearing his wife's name. Although Bernard did not acquire the Charmes until

shortly after taking over, he says many of Burgundy's significant changes in land ownership came in the wake of the 1929 crash.

Bernard's intellectual background exacts a thorough and reflective approach to everything. The core of his philosophy lies in his belief that 'much of what is considered innovative today in fact derives from old and traditional practices'. 'Intellectually,' he maintains, 'there is little new to discover' (about winemaking). There is no point in tinkering with a tradition which already produces excellent wine without convincing justification.

In the vineyards, average vine age is kept high by individual *répiquage* with plant material selected by Bernard from his own land. Until 1988 he grafted the wood himself, but now it goes to a nursery he trusts, to be grafted on to rootstocks 161/49 and 3309 (a low-yielding Riparia-Rupestris cross).

During the harvest three separate *tries* ensure that any rotten fruit is removed before it reaches the vats. This, and the high proportion of old vines, mean yields which must be among the lowest in Gevrey. In Mazis, for example, yields recorded were (in hl/ha): 1984 – 13.5; 1985 – 23.0; 1986 – 32.0; 1987 – 23.0; 1988 – 36.0; 1989 -33.0; 1993 – 13.0. In Charmes, the average figure is hardly more generous – between 13 and 30 hl/ha. Set against an authorised yield of 37 hl/ha these seem positively niggardly. Would that others followed suit!

Once past the selection process, a bunch of Maume grapes may expect to be 100% destemmed and lightly crushed. 3 or 4 days pre-fermentive maceration at ambient cellar temperature precede a long, slow alcoholic

Bernard Maume

fermentation in large old oak *foudres* which line the wall of the ground floor *cuverie*.

A pecularity of Louis Mariller's vinification was the use of a liquid, cultured yeast which he bought annually from a specialist in Dijon. Bernard continues the practice, convinced that these produce a better result than natural yeasts, which mix more and less desirable strains.

Cuvaison lasts up to 4 weeks, including a short period of post-fermentive maceration after which the new wine is run off into one of a remarkable battery of underground glass-tiled *cuves,* built by great-uncle Louis. The remaining pulp is removed by hand and fed into a horizontal plate press. This article – a museum piece constructed in 1929 – although 'un peu particulier', was still working well in 1995, giving a gentle, slow extraction of good quality press-wine. This contraption also rotates, driven by an interesting assemblage of a lorry engine mounted on a wooden table, complete with 5-speed gear-box harnessed to a do-it-yourself system of belts and wheels. If, for any reason, reverse gear is required, this is achieved by the simple expedient of changing round the polarity on the lorry-motor contacts.

On the rare occasions it breaks down, a back-up is dusted off and, so to speak, pressed into service. This, even more antiquated, is a monstrous wooden 19th century square screw-press, mounted on thick legs. Given that it takes 3 strong men considerable time to remove the large blocks of wood which weight down the wooden pressure plate, Bertrand expends much effort to keep the 1929 running sweetly.

By whatever means it is extracted, the press-wine is added to the free-run wine. For the Grands Crus, only the first pressing is added, whilst for Premier Cru and Village wines both first and second pressings are used. Each *cuve* is allowed a few days to homogenise in great-uncle Louis' underground vats, before transfer to cask.

The Grands Crus see about 40% new wood whilst for the other wines the proportion is 20–25%. The Mazis and Gevrey En Pallud are kept in Nevers oak, whilst the other Gevrey Villages and Charmes are put into Vosges. For the Lavaux St.-Jacques the new wood is 50:50 Vosges : Nevers. Vosges imparts a softer tannin, with hints of vanillin, whilst the Nevers gives the wine a stronger foundation of tannin and considerable body.

The casks are then put into a small cobwebby cellar underneath the house, which is

Late autumn landscape in the Côte d'Or

heated to about 17°C to start the *malolactic* fermentation. The Village Gevreys invariably go first, followed closely by the Lavaux St.-Jacques and the Charmes. The Village En Pallud and the Mazis are the last to start.

The bare minimum of racking often means casks remain untouched until bottling. Should racking be needed after *malo* then the wine is returned to its original cask; this enables the Maumes to follow each wine's evolution and to assess the impact of different types of wood.

After about 20 months in wood, wines are fined with fresh egg-whites. Larger lots are then assembled by amalgamating 4 barrels – 3 old to 1 new and each 4-barrel lot bottled separately. The smaller lots – for example the two casks of Charmes – are simply bottled barrel by barrel. All Maume wines are un-filtered – 'filtration – that strips the wine'.

Tasting chez Maume is an unforgettable experience. Expansion of the Domaine has meant that casks are scattered in all sorts of obscure corners to make room for others; so, one trots from one *cuve* to another, from one cellar to the next looking for whatever is sought. In 1995 they constructed a new cask and vinification cellar to reduce handling and pumping, and finished tunnelling to link up the other small chambers.

The young wines, reposing in great-uncle Louis' glass-lined apartments are got at by lifting a species of iron-grid drain cover interposed with a sheet of thick plastic. An elegant 19th century silver Tastevin – won by Louis at skittles – is then dipped into the liquid and carefully extracted, along with any resident flies, for considered appraisal.

The cellar is a delightfully eccentric muddle – rather like Bernard's cosy study one gets the impression that things are generally 'in progress', but sometimes, with the pressures of work, never quite getting anywhere.

Despite appearances however, the Maumes' wines are superbly crafted and unquestionably among the best in Gevrey. Their style is dominated by a concentration derived from a deliberately late harvest, low yields and old vines. The care with which the wood is chosen and used results in a sensible balance of wood and grape tannins – enough to bolster the natural structure without dominating it.

There are broadly three types of wine in this cellar – reflecting the differences between one sector of Gevrey and another: the southerly *côteaux* – En Pallud, Mazis and the Premier Cru *cuvée* – give relatively substantial, powerful wines, with plenty of *charpente*. The Lavaux St.-Jacques and Champeaux tend to be more *tendre,* emphasising fruit rather than structure. The Charmes-Chambertin has a more floral, slightly mint-leaf aromatic dimension.

The Gevrey En Pallud, from 40–year-old vines just below the Route des Grands Crus, is characterised by attractive succulence and power with an overlying finesse and cask aromas of red fruits and blackcurrant, whilst the Gevrey Village is rather softer and rounder with noticeably ripe, well-integrated tannins and aromas of vanilla and cocoa beans.

By contrast, the Lavaux St.-Jacques has more finesse, with a foundation of restrained power and very ripe tannins. The primary aromas – griotte cherry and fleshy ripe fruit on the 1993 in cask – characteristically transform into the secondary and tertiary derivatives of *sous-bois* and mushroom combined with a noticeably floral element. The Lavaux tends to retain the structure of its youth whilst developing these mature aromas.

The Gevrey-Chambertin Premier Cru – a blend of wines from 30–year-old vines in Perrières and 70+ in Cherbaudes vineyards – has greater acidity than the Lavaux but noticeably less class and finesse – though not without interest and ageing potential. In the 1993 this hallmark acidity was somewhat masked by a fine concentration of fruit – a wine of good length and richness. Of the two Grands Crus, the Charmes has greater finesse, often with hints of cassis, and liquorice on the nose and plenty of power. The contents of the

single cask of 1993 added a dimension of concentration to all these qualities. A fine, complex wine – but something of a gypsy.

The Mazis is undoubtedly Maume's best wine. Tasting from one of only 3 casks of 1993 showed the concentration of old vine fruit and unquestionable Grand Cru complexity. Tightish at the outset, with a note of violets on the nose and some spiciness on the palate, this will be very good indeed.

These fine 1993s and very promising, if less opulent, 1994s are a tribute to Bertrand, who took over vinification in 1991. On the 'if it ain't busted, don't fix it' principle, he continues his father's tradition; the only change – a bit more *pigéage*. Bernard clearly enjoys working with his son and is proud of what he is achieving.

Underneath the house a small part of the cellar is allocated to a few stone bins of older vintages – plus a little old Vin Jaune from Château Chalon in the Jura and a bottle or two of Californian Pinot Noir brought by a friend. Bernard consulted some mouldy cards on top of several of these bins, before removing a bottle and extending an invitation upstairs to share its contents.

Installed underneath the remarkable staircase leading to the first floor from the hall – a spiral of flag-stone steps only supported by the weight of one upon the other – he uncorked the bottle and poured the contents into outsized Burgundian ballons. The wine – chosen to show what a Maume wine becomes after suitable ageing – had a really lovely limpid, deep cherry-red colour and an extraordinarily complex aroma of *sous-bois* and forest fruits. In the mouth it was a magnificent, complete envelope of ripe, almost sweet fruit, with a well-nigh impeccable balance and great finesse and length. It was a pleasure to share this 1978 Gevrey-Chambertin Lavaux St.-Jacques with its kind and thoughtful progenitor.

Although relatively small, Domaine Maume is one of the finest in Gevrey. You may just as soon find Bernard up an Alp cross-country skiing or climbing, as in his cellars, but seek out his wines and you are unlikely to be disappointed.

VINEYARD HOLDINGS

Commune	Level	Lieu-dit/Climat	Area	Vine Age	Status
Gevrey	GC	Mazis-Chambertin	0.67	65	P
Gevrey	GC	Charmes-Chambertin	0.17	41	P
Gevrey	PC	Lavaux St.-Jacques	0.29	45	P
Gevrey	PC	Champeaux	0.28	12	P
Gevrey	PC	Cherbaudes/Perrières	0.18	70/30	P
Gevrey	V	En Pallud	0.66	40	F
Gevrey	V	La Justice+Etelois+ Combes du Dessus + Les Fourneaux + Clos Prieur Bas	1.47	30	P
Gevrey	R	Vigne Blanche	0.52	15	P
		Total:	**4.24 ha**		

Domaine Joseph Roty

GEVREY-CHAMBERTIN

Among Burgundian viticulteurs – a decidedly heterogeneous collection of individualists – Joseph Roty stands out. If his weathered complexion, copious whiskers and quotidien overalls, all vigorously animated by a wicked grin, did not set him apart, his decision of purpose and sometimes iconoclastic ideas would do the trick in their stead. Here is an obstinate character whose distaste for pomposity combines with a mischievous sense of humour.

Roty's philosophy rests on foundations as solid as his shoes: wine, he believes, is the product of *terroir*, climate and vigneron, in equal contributions; and – his grandfather's maxim: 'The job of the vigneron is observation.' When you buy land, don't just look at a plan, prostrate yourself in the vineyard, touch the soil, look at exposition, slope and surroundings, then decide. One vineyard Roty was offered was within a few metres of the water-table – he spied the well, and declined the offer. Equally, when the grapes arrive at the *cuverie*, look at them, taste them, try and find out how best to treat them.

He spends a lot of his time observing. When he married, his son was conceived in the first week : 'I wanted to find out what it was all about – how it all worked,' he exclaims with a broad grin.

Rotys have been winemaking in Gevrey since 1710. Joseph is the 10th generation and his Domaine owes much to his thriftiness and skill. When his father died, it took 7 years to pay the death duties, and thereafter, the maximum has been reinvested in land.

As to his acreage, Jo Roty is close: 'No one but me knows the age of my wife or the extent of my vineyards . . . my importers will think I'm a millionaire and will want to know why there isn't more wine,' he muses, so one is left to guess.

He started in 1968 with a legacy from his grandfather, Joseph Antoine, which, the maxim apart, included Charmes-, Mazis-, Griotte-Chambertin, Gevrey Premier Cru and Village land. Jo learned his trade by working vineyards for others; fair prices and careful work made him much in demand.

Now he seeks to pass on his fine land, and his stamp collection ('nearly as big as the Queen's') to his children. His father died aged 35, when Jo was 7, so he is determined to give his children the best possible start. The Rotys appear to live modestly – a pleasant house on the northern side of the village, with cellars everywhere: 'I can never be found that way,' explains Jo.

His way of working is ruthlessly logical, and highly individual. He is scathing of those who work by formulae and who fail to think through what they are doing. Roty vines are treated with exemplary care. Trained to 'the true taille of Dr Guyot' – that is to say a maximum of 6 eyes on the *baguette* and 2 on the *courson*, fertilisers are limited to an occasional dose of 'guano', and frequent workings of the soil made to cut any surface lateral roots. 'Those who use chemical fertilisers and don't work the soil are not vignerons – they are jokers,' laughs Jo. To ensure that laterals have a short life, he hoes round the root of each vine – no inconsiderable labour, with some 10–12,000 vines per ha.

'Vineyards are like horses, one must be in tune with them and drive them' – a question of coaxing the best by good husbandry and empathy rather than letting fertiliser and treatment salesman loose. Jo's dealings with pests illustrate this: no insecticides are permitted – even the rapacious, rot-inducing, grape-worm is allowed to munch away to its heart's content. 'In the middle ages they would have simply excommunicated them,' reflects Jo. Now, he considers, with an air of mock gravity, that by far the best treatment is . . . a hammer; just squash them.

An average vine age of 60+, with 60–80% on original roots and deliberately late picking reduces yields and increases concentration.

Each batch of grapes is examined and tasted by Jo – a grand-paternal practice which indicates pip-ripeness, skin-thickness, tannin-quality and sugar and acidity levels. Destemming, which depends on the vintage (1990, 100%), is followed by a week's cold maceration at 15°C, to maximise colour extraction. Sulphur is rarely added to the pulp: 'Why take aspirin if you are perfectly well.'

The wines are fermented at below 30°C in open wooden *cuves*, giving a slow, gentle maceration 'like tea', declares Jo (he obviously doesn't drink French tea very often).

Cuvaison lasts up to 3 weeks, then Roty decants the wine off its solids with around 1.5 grams/litre of sugar remaining. Provided it is neither too harsh or unbalanced, the press-wine is added to the free-run wine.

After *assemblage*, the various *cuves* of wine are left for 7–15 days to settle (compared with 12–48 hours elsewhere). During this *débourbage*, the remaining sugar ferments, releasing CO_2 gas which sits on top of the wine protecting it from oxidation.

As one might expect, cask-maker and wood are both chosen with the usual Roty thoroughness. The wood is air-dried for 3 years and the only heat it sees is when the staves are fired to bend them. The tonnelier is instructed to char each cask well. This high-toast Burgundy and Chatillonais oak gives a slow release of tannins into the wine. The Cîteaux monks air-dried their wood for 6–8 years but this, Roty ruefully admits, is no longer a commercial proposition.

Until 1968 Jo Roty made all his own casks, making him a fine judge of the finished article and only too ready to reject anything substandard. Each year's intake is subjected to a meticulous scrutiny, by inserting an inspection-lamp through the bung-hole of a randomly selected cask. If its quality is doubtful, it is dismembered for further inspection. 'Given the size of the cheque I pay my tonnelier each year, he will only cheat me once I am not buying a piece of furniture.'

The proportion of new wood depends on both vintage and the *cuvée*. 'It can be 0 – 100%; there are no rules.'

Racking is not part of Roty's vinification. Jo is clear that the purpose of racking is not to get it off its lees but to aerate it. So, his wines generally remain on their fine lees as long as possible – even until bottling.

During their *élevage*, the wines are periodically roused to distribute the lees evenly through the mass – a common Burgundian practice to add richness to whites, but not for reds. However, Jo Roty believes that with fine lees – both in size and quality – there is no risk of the yeasty, cardboardy *goût de lie* which easily renders a wine flat and disgreeable. He is not alone in this view – André Porcheret, winemaker at the Hospices de Beaune, also *batonés* his reds.

After such consummate care, Jo has no intention of compromising by fining or filtration. So, the various casks of each wine are assembled in bulk fifteen minutes before bottling. The humblest Roty red, the Passetoutgrains, generally spends some 12–14 months in cask, the grander *cuvées* up to 30 months.

Jo Roty makes exceptional Burgundies. With a high proportion of very old vines, even in Village and Regional appellations, low yields and long maceration produce atypically black wines with remarkable depth of fruit and immense potential longevity.

Base level is a pair of Bourgogne Grand Ordinaires – one from Gamay grapes from Marsannay, the other from Pinot Noir from Brochon/Gevrey, both deeply coloured with warm, long flavours. The Pinot is generally tighter, with plenty of stuffing. Their vinification is not skimped – *élevage* in cask with all the care of Grands Crus.

The Bourgogne Pressonniers comes from both AC Bourgogne and AC Gevrey sections of this vineyard, and is sold with the lower appellation. It is usually deep black-cherry in hue and with a structure and depth well above its official classification; a wine to cellar for at least 5 years in good vintages.

Jo's Marsannay Rouge – from a parcel of well-sited 60-year-old vines is deeply coloured and harmoniously structured, with plenty of old-vine concentration and some attractive complexity; another 5 year wait!

The Gevreys Champs-Chenys comes from a vineyard bordered by Grands Crus – Charmes- and Mazoyères-Chambertin. The soil is a mixture of pebbles, flat rocks and limestone, with a significant proportion of iron-pyrites in the subsoil, which together with 25% of pre-1914 vines, contributes to the wine's density and style. Although dubbed by Jo his 'petit Charmes', there is nothing little about it – dense black-cherry hue, with excellent concentration, but more delicacy and complexity than the Pressoniers. With age it takes on an attractive caramellised, vanilla and liquorice aspect. A Village wine, this, of exceptional quality.

The Gevrey Brunelle comes from the Brunelle and the Clos de la Brunelle vineyards, vinified as a single *cuvée*. Not as dark or dense as Champs-Chenys the wine is often marginally more forward. Given that Roty's wines start life at double the density of everyone else's, this Brunelle is still a big item.

The third Village is Clos Prieur – the superior part being Premier Cru and the lower section AC Gevrey. The soils are richer here – no stones but 'têtes de loup' and a clay

bed, giving sturdy wine which ages well.

Jo's sole Premier Cru is Les Fontenys, a corruption of old French for 'little fountains' – a reference to wells some 30 m below the vineyards. At its top, layers of clay and sandy marls reflect Ruchottes-Chambertin, which borders it here; lower down, the ground resembles Mazis. This amalgam, together with vines so old that no-one has a record of their planting, gives a massively dense, firmly-structured wine needing years to evolve. A wine of power and finesse, with aromas of *fruits sauvages* and a spicy, tarry character results; in good vintages, unquestionably Grand Cru quality.

The Grands Crus, all from old vines, are remarkable. They start out deep, impenetrable black-cherry in colour, with a vast structure of tannins and acidity supporting an equally massive concentration of fruit; in vintages of the calibre of 1988, 1989, 1990 and 1993 they will take decades to soften out and unpack.

Despite their daunting structures, these wines by no means lack charm. On the contrary, delving, as it were, below the corsets, one finds sweet ripe flesh, considerable finesse and magnificent complexity.

The Mazis- and Griottes-Chambertin are mouthfillers – vinified for longevity and seeming fit to last a century. In the Charmes-Chambertin – from 1881 vines, one finds a virtually black wine with colours more redolent of young Syrah than of Pinot Noir, suffusing the palate with a staggering concentration of pure fruit and massive extract.

It matters little to Jo Roty that his wines differ in style from those of others. In a way, they mirror him – his intractability, stubbornness and bulldog tenacity. His fellow vignerons regard him with bemused respect, as 'un type' and something of an unknown quantity. Visitors are subjected to a similar degree of scrutiny as the casks (but not dismembered) and are unceremoniously thrown out if they presume to disagree or try to accelerate the painfully slow tasting progress, which includes looking at harvest photographs and hearing about the stamp collection. The idiosyncrasies may irritate, but this is winemaking of exceptional quality at every level.

VINEYARD HOLDINGS

Commune	Level	Lieu-dit/Climat	Area	Vine Age	Status
Gevrey	GC	Griottes-Chambertin	N/A	N/A	N/A
Gevrey	GC	Mazis-Chambertin	N/A	N/A	N/A
Gevrey	GC	Charmes-Chambertin	N/A	N/A	N/A
Gevrey	PC	Fontenys	N/A	N/A	N/A
Gevrey	V	Champs-Chenys	N/A	N/A	N/A
Gevrey	V	La Brunelle	N/A	N/A	N/A
Gevrey	V	Clos Prieur	N/A	N/A	N/A
Gevrey	V	Les Crais/Charreux	N/A	N/A	N/A
Gevrey	R	(Bourgogne Blanc)	N/A	N/A	N/A
Gevrey	R	Les Pressoniers	N/A	N/A	N/A
Gevrey	R	BGO – Les Marcellys	N/A	N/A	N/A
Marsannay	R	(R/V/Rose)	N/A	N/A	N/A

Cleared for take-off; an early dose of fertiliser

Domaine Philippe Charlopin-Parizot

GEVREY-CHAMBERTIN

Philippe Charlopin, who looks rather like a stocky French version of the English King Charles II, with a mass of frizzy dark hair and a friendly chubby face, is a rising star. Having started in 1976 with 1.8 ha from his father, he has gradually increased his Domaine to its present 13 ha. In 1987 the *cuverie* and cellars moved from Gevrey to Marsannay; in 1993 they moved back again to Gevrey, into the ex-Quillardet buildings on the RN 74.

The wines are carefully thought out, on the principle that the precise qualities of the grapes determine the precise details of vinification. Old vines play a particularly important part in Philippe's thinking, a fact reflected in the vineyard management. This is designed to interfere as little as possible with nature, while yet encouraging the vine to produce small yields of highly concentrated fruit. Vines are left until they cease producing altogether – only then are they grubbed up.

Maximum life expectancy is achieved by only working the soil – except for spot weed-killing to get rid of deep-rooted Iseron grass – using sulphur and copper-based products as much as possible. He uses a yellow-oil treatment before budburst, when the temperature has risen above $15°C$, to protect the vines from infestation and to 'clean them'.

Philippe puts particular stress on *évasivage* to remove any double or excess shoots, but will not countenance green-pruning. In his view, this is a waste of time, since it has apparently been proved to his satisfaction that if you eliminate 50% of the bunches, the others yield more in compensation, so you are effectively back where you started. In addition, bunches remaining afterwards tend to have thinner skins than normal and 'you can't make *Grand Vin* with thin skins'.

Since 1990 the crop has been totally destalked. In earlier years most of the stalks were left in the vats, but consultation with Henri Jayer reluctantly persuaded Philippe that they only brought astringency and no benefits. So, the policy was changed. There is also a heavy elimination of unripe or rotten grapes, and a *saignée de cuve* in years such as 1994 which threaten to be unusually dilute.

There is no Charlopin vinification recipe; everything depends on the particular qualities of the fruit being handled. Philippe generally prefers as long a pre-fermentive maceration as possible to extract colour, fat and the aromas of ripe fruit. It can last 4–5 days or up to twice as long. 'This,' Philippe adds, 'requires really ripe and healthy grapes'

– hence the severe *tri*. This is performed on a custom-built moving belt, white to highlight skin colour – a Charlopin innovation apparently copied by Romanée-Conti.

During fermentation, there is, unusually, no pumping-over because the oxygenation involved dissipates aromas which cannot be recaptured. Rather there is frequent and lengthy *pigéage*, up to ten times per day, to extract maximum colour and matter.

Vatting time depends on the state of the grapes: in 1990, for example, the skins were quite thick and the volume of juice quite small, therefore *cuvaison* was reduced to 10–12 days to avoid excessive tannin extraction; by contrast, in 1989 maceration was continued for 25 days in view of the relatively fine skins and the dilution of the juice – although Philippe admits he might have overdone it somewhat.

Another point of quality is that only press-wine extracted from the lightest of pressings by the new Bucher press – 200 grams – is added; 'almost free-run wine,' claims Philippe. There is no *débourbage*, because after such long *cuvaison*, the amount of fine lees left is small and the chances of the *malo* starting spontaneously would be much diminished by removing yet more.

From there 30% of the wines pass into new casks (25% for the red Marsannay), very heavily charred to avoid the extraction of harsh tannins and to maximise the aromas of coffee and vanilla. The remainder is kept in large stainless-steel tanks. In 1990 the new casks were a mixture of Chatillon and Jura wood – 'That's all my cask-maker could give me – the Bordelais had taken all the Tronçais and Allier,' confessed Philippe, ruefully.

To minimise loss of fugitive fruit aromas, the wines remain on their lees for just under a year without racking before a light Kieselguhr filtration and bottling.

Aroma and freshness are also conserved by retaining natural carbon-dioxide gas (a normal by-product of fermentation) dissolved in the wine. Philippe has worked out that, at bottling, the CO_2 should titrate at 4–500 mg/litre and since the wine in tank has double the concentration of gas of the wine in cask, there is some juggling to be done to arrive at the desired level. If necessary, Philippe will either pump in CO_2 to top up or else use a sparge of nitrogen to reduce the level. At these low concentrations, it is undetectable on the palate.

As one might predict, the wines are distinctly on the meaty side. They are also well made and invariably need keeping, even in lesser vintages. There is an attractive Marsannay Blanc, made from Chardonnay vines planted in patches of limestone soils and excellent Village Vosne, Morey and Chambolle – all from respectably old vines.

The cream of the cellar are the Gevrey-Chambertin, Clos St.-Denis and Charmes-Chambertin. The produce of less than 40-year-old Gevrey vines are vinified and sold to local négociants, leaving that of the 40–70-year-old plants for the Domaine. This is good wine – with a fine concentration of old-vine fruit and real depth. Something to keep for 5–10 years, or longer in better vintages.

Of the Grands Crus, the Charmes-Chambertin, from 40-year-old vines, is on the meaty side of normal, but has finesse and underlying richness which keep it from becoming lumpen. The Clos St.-Denis is also big – but with a touch more suppleness than the Charmes. Both are fine Grands Crus and are worth looking out for. Chambertin joined the team in 1995.

Philippe Charlopin has made great strides both in quality and reputation in recent years. If some attractive, seductively concentrated 1993s are anything to judge by, things seem to have settled down now. A reliable and interesting source.

VINEYARD HOLDINGS

Commune	Level	Lieu-dit/Climat	Area	Vine Age	Status
Gevrey	GC	Mazoyères-Chambertin	0.20	40	P
Gevrey	GC	Chambertin	0.21	40	F
Morey	GC	Clos St.-Denis	0.20	40	P
Gevrey	V	(Various *climats*)	5.00	7/70	P/F
Morey	V	Clos Solon/Les Crais	1.00	50	P
Chambolle	V	Les Herbues	0.60	–	P
Vosne	V	Les Ormes	0.40	30	P
Fixin	V	Les Germets	0.30	7/40	M
Marsannay	V	(Red / White / Rosé)	4.00	20	P/F
Bourgogne	R	(Red)	1.00	15	P
		Total:	**12.91 ha**		

Domaine Serafin Père et Fils

GEVREY-CHAMBERTIN

Domaine Serafin is a young establishment, having been founded by Serafin Père in 1947, with the acquisition of a patch of Gevrey-Chambertin. Further additions brought the estate up to 4.32 ha at his death in 1988. His son, Christian, took over in the early 1960s and, in 1993, bought another 18 ares of Grand Cru Charmes-Chambertin.

Overseeing all this is Mme Serafin Mère, a quiet, speckled old lady, who lives in the family residence above the cellars, just below the Cazetiers vineyard next to the commune's crumbling Château. Built in the early 1960s 'stone by stone' by Christian and his father, this incorporates a multitude of little neo-gothic windows and a splendid small tower which is an almost exact replica of that atop the Château opposite. So, rather like Wemmick's 'Aged P', Mme Serafin reigns over her modern castle, no doubt considerably cosier than the ancient monument itself.

Christian is quiet and dedicated to quality. His viticulture is as organic as possible with the aim of low yields and old vines. Shortish pruning, rigorous *évasivage* and, in abundant vintages, a green-pruning reduce yields whilst scrupulous removal of *verjus* which saps strength from the vine into useless fruit, bolsters concentration.

Vinification is still evolving. After a 70% destalking the pulp is macerated for 3–5 days. Once fermentation has started, *remontage* stops and twice daily hand-*pigéage* takes over to break up the cap. Artificial yeasts are not favoured, rather a *pied de cuve* is used should fermentation fail to start naturally, in the particularly cold cellar.

Christian is dubious about his tradition of leaving 30% of the stalks with the pulp. 'The oenologue tells me to do it,' he moans, 'but I don't like it.' Although stalks add tannin and acidity, make the pulp easier to work with and extract more colour, 'they absorb as much as they put in, so where are you?' His Bourgogne Rouge is, however, 100% destalked, for suppleness and early drinking.

Fermentation, at up to 35°C, is followed by a long period of post-fermentive maceration. In 1990 Christian experimented with a *cuvaison* of three weeks, though, as he hastens to point out, it is normally 15–18 days. He considers he loses a touch of colour by long *cuvaison*, but since his aim is to make *vins de garde*, he believes he has no alternative.

2–3 days *débourbage* precede the passage of the wine into casks. There is noticeable hesitancy here: 'I was rather against new

Christian Serafin – skilled hands

wood, but my American importer pushed me into trying some new oak for the first time in 1987. I think it gives something to the wine, especially in years like 1984 when the new wood hides some of the acidity.'

He obviously finds some benefit, as the proportion has increased to 80%. In general, the Gevrey Village sees 50% new oak, whilst the Vieilles Vignes, Premiers Crus and Charmes have 100%. Even the Bourgogne Rouge had 100% in 1993, but only 20% in 1992. Christian will tell you he is convinced by the results – but his look says otherwise.

In 1990, following Romanée-Conti, he delayed first racking until after the next harvest. The wines thus spent 15 months in cask before racking and fining around November, left *sur colle* for 2–3 months and then bottled. He seems uncertain what this achieves but is content to follow the practice of such an illustrious Domaine.

Christian regards filtration as an unacceptable interference, and considers a little deposit essential to a wine's longevity. He has kept samples of Gevrey Fonteny neither fined nor filtered and seems wedded to eliminating both processes if he can. His excellent 1993s were bottled unmanipulated.

Two *cuvées* of Gevrey form the major part of the annual 2,500 case production; one from 15-year-old vines and a Vieilles Vignes from several plots of 45-year-old vines, many

planted in 1920. A recently acquired plot in Les Corbeaux, reclaimed from parkland, has recently reverted to its original status of Premier Cru, to join Les Cazetiers and Fonteny.

Christian's wines have style and finesse, together with the weight derived from long *cuvaison*. The basic Gevrey reflects Chambolle in its delicacy and finesse, without lacking in fruit or underlying power. The Vieilles Vignes, assembled early from the various lots, is altogether more concentrated and firmer, old vine fruit imparting attractive depth and complexity. In good vintages these come well up to Premier Cru level.

The Premier Cru Cazetiers comes from a vineyard with poor soil, with visible 'cats heads' of limestone outcrops. These differ in structure from the Gevreys – more *charpente*, more obvious acidity and a touch of bitter cherry flavour. Underneath, there is ample fruit destined to open out and give the wine character and breed. Christian reckons, with a twinkle in his eye that 'Cazetiers is for men, Charmes for the ladies'.

The Premier Cru Fonteny is different again from Cazetiers. The vineyard, at Gevrey's southern end, has a more southeasterly exposition and relatively richer, rocky soils. The wine has a greater immediate appeal – with soft, red fruit flavours.

The recent addition of 18 ares in the *secteur Mazoyères* means a little more Grand Cru Charmes-Chambertin – the Domaine's top wine. Christian manages to extract something special from his 0.3 ha. A soft redpurple matures to a limpid red-velvet and the nose opens to reveal complex of aromas dominated by griotte cherry, raspberry with overtones of violets. Further ageing brings a spicier, vegetation side to the nose, whilst succulent, elegant flavours evolve on the palate. The wine bears the indelible marks of Grand Cru – that paradoxical combination of power and finesse; a fine summit to a thoroughly conscientious and attractive range.

VINEYARD HOLDINGS

Commune	Level	Lieu-dit/Climat	Area	Vine Age	Status
Gevrey	GC	Charmes-Chambertin	0.31	55	P
Gevrey	PC	Les Cazetiers	0.23	39	P
Gevrey	PC	Le Fonteny	0.33	35	P
Gevrey	PC	Les Corbeaux	0.45	27	P
Gevrey	V	(Vieilles Vignes)	1.09	45	P
Gevrey	V	(Basic cuvée)	1.58	15	P
Gevrey	R	(Bourgogne Pinot & Chard.)	0.51	27	P
		Total:	**4.50 ha**		

Domaine Armand Rousseau

GEVREY-CHAMBERTIN

There are two distinct types of Great Domaine in the Côte d'Or. The one evinces constant experimentation and innovation; the other gives a feeling of tradition honed down to a fine art. Domaine Rousseau is definitely of the latter style.

Charles Rousseau, who has run this superb estate since the premature death of his father in a car accident in 1959, is one of the kindliest and most genuine people one might wish to meet. Eager to expound his own philosophy, he is quietly confident of the quality of his wines, which are unquestionably among the finest in the Côte.

Rousseau's land-holdings are mouthwatering: nearly 8 ha of Grands Crus, 3.5 of Premiers Crus and 2.25 of Gevrey Village land. Since 1959 he has added several vineyards to his 7 ha inheritance: Clos St.-Jacques, Clos des Ruchottes, Clos de Bèze and Chambertin – a bit more of the latter pair in 1993. Altogether one of the most impressive portfolios in the Côtes de Nuits.

However, whilst quality land may be a desirable prerequisite, it does not, by itself, guarantee fine wine. Charles Rousseau's criteria are clear: fine land plus old vines plus low yields. So, he keeps his vines as long as they are remotely productive and is certain that this high average vine age contributes significantly to the quality of his wines.

This is not a Domaine to be described in terms of techniques, but better thought of as an estate where the wines are made by care and by feeling for their soul. That is not to say that technique is lacking, rather that Charles and his son Eric prefer to trust their instincts than to have their labour driven by laboratories and oenologists.

Meticulous care is taken to harvest only the best fruit. Minimum fertilisation is used, never chemical but all organic, horse and sheep droppings and some humus. Every 20–25 years each plot is treated in this way; the vines on the poorer soils of the Côteaux are treated slightly more often – every 15–20 years – with a dose of compost superadded.

Rousseau has reason to be particularly careful about soil management. After the last war, his father was persuaded, along with other growers, that the soil needed massive enriching doses of potassium after years of wartime neglect, promoting extra vine-vigour and thereby increasing sugar levels. Charles vividly remembers lorry-loads of potassium turning up at the *cuverie*. This turned out to be a signal error: the potassium infiltrated the soil at the rate of 1 cm per year and the

vine roots were effectively saturated. Being chemically 'basic' rather than 'acidic', it tended to lower the natural acidity of the grapes and thus of the wine.

The first serious indication of problems were wines found to be apparently re-fermenting in bottle. At first it was thought that bacteria from imperfectly washed bottles was to blame, but when this didn't solve the problem they sought elsewhere for a solution. Whilst bacterial activity was clearly responsible no one could understand, with Rousseau's scrupulous hygiene, where it was coming from.

Charles tried everything from heating the bottles to 30°C to cooling them to −15°C , before the answer was found. It appeared that bacteria normally dormant were being activated by the reduced acidity levels caused by the increased potassium.

Further investigation revealed that the re-activated bacteria were in fact breaking down the tartaric acid usually found to some degree in both red and white wines. The problem for Rousseau became, therefore, one of how to reduce the pH in his wines. Removing the potassium already in the soil was impossible, so the only remaining solution was to acidify the wines, which satisfactorily solved the problem.

Harvesting is scrupulously careful: Charles Rousseau reckons that if he watches over his pickers like a hawk on the first day then things go smoothly thereafter, averring that, 'unlike most vignerons, my place is in the vineyards, not in the *cuverie*'. At harvest, 'I let any visitors look around but they have none of my time.' So strict is he about excising rotten fruit that, in 1986 there was a carpet of grapes in the vineyards. For as long as he can remember the small hods of grapes were required to be emptied slowly into the crusher, to avoid unnecessary crushing and enabling pickers to make a final check for rotten fruit which could, even at this late stage, be kept out of the *cuves*.

A stemmer-crusher removes 80–90% of the stalks and the lightly sulphured crush passes to a battery of stainless-steel tanks for fermentation. Rousseau prefers to keep some stalks with the pulp to give a better distribution of heat through each *cuve*. Fermentation is never induced with cultured yeasts, but starts normally; 'once the first *cuve* goes then the others all go . . . woooof' – with a grin and a broad wave of his hand. So, a few days' delay amounts to a pre-fermentive maceration (now used deliberately by many).

Charles Rousseau in his cellar – nothing great was ever achieved without enthusiasm!

However, he is not much in favour of the deliberate heavy sulphuring of the pulp, *à l'Accad*, to extend pre-fermentive maceration.

Rousseau has never seen the need to *saigner* his *cuves* – a normal practice among conscientious growers in relatively dilute years; 'With old vines and low yields, there is never a problem of poor concentration.' Alcoholic fermentation proceeds at 31–33°C ('I am not in the business of making jam') and lasts about 15 days. An old balloon-shaped contrivance with a sealed refrigerant in tubes inside serves to cool the *must* if things look as though they will get out of hand.

The free-run wine is settled for 24 hours before being run into casks. A Vaslin press extracts the same yield from the press, with significantly lower pressure, thus avoiding harsh stalk and pip tannins. The press-wine is then added to the free-run wine.

The Chambertin and Clos de Bèze enjoy 100% new Allier oak; the Clos St.-Jacques sees 70%; the Ruchottes Chambertin, Clos des Ruchottes have 20–30% and the Charmes-Chambertin, Mazis-Chambertin, Clos de la Roche, Premiers Crus and the Village Gevrey have 100% of second year casks employed for the previous year's Grands Crus. Rousseau believes that the essential elegance and femininity of the Charmes-, Mazis-Chambertin etc. would be destroyed by any contact with new oak. In this he is clearly in a minority – but the sublime elegance of these wines makes argument difficult. On new wood he holds strong convictions: 'You can't put a little wine into new wood and expect to have *Grand Vin*.'

A Rousseau wine spends 18–24 months in cask with 2 rackings – the second of which is preceded by an egg-white fining. Equalising the various casks of the same wine follows an unusual procedure: 'I unify the wine and I don't unify the wine' is Charles Rousseau's cryptic description: the casks are lined up on a pair of wooden railway tracks, 4–6 at a time, then connected up to a system of pipes ending in a common feeder pipe. Turning the taps simultaneously runs the wines together into the feeder which delivers them to the most delicate of filtration plates and thence to the bottling machine.

A tradition of excellence, backed by sound intuition, pervades the Rousseaus, who are masters of everything from the first vine shoot to bottling.

Descending into the cellars beneath the *cuverie* through several galleries of different ages, brings forth an assessment of vintages at the Domaine since 1970. Apart from excellent, and generally underrated, 1972s, that decade was not remarkable. The 1970s themselves are holding up, but the 1971s 'had too much overripeness'. 1973s were good but not great, and the 1974s rather light. 1975 was for most in the Côtes de Nuits 'an unmitigated disaster' as a result of extensive hailstorms which had their epicentre round Vosne and Chambolle. However, Rousseau's stringent harvesting methods yielded a small but sound crop and much praise for his 1975s. The 1976s, particularly in the Grands Crus, are rated a great success – just coming to drinkability for those with the patience to wait. The 1977s have turned out worthy wines despite being badly affected by the bacterial problem. 1978 was a good, but not great vintage for Rousseau; whilst not obviously faulty, they seem to lack precision and depth.

1979 produced special problems. Charles Rousseau took his laboratory's advice and called in a contract bottler to flash pasteurise half of the crop; this worthy correctly passed the wine over a flame to deactivate all known microbes, but omitted to cool it afterwards. The bottles were so hot that Rousseau could hardly hold them. The 'unactinised' wines are probably sound, but dull, the rest distinctly problematical.

The 1980s however, has been an excellent decade: 1980 was 'one of the best vintages I have ever made'. Having tasted most of the Grands Crus it is easy to see why. Although generally decried as a mediocre vintage, these wines whilst quite light in colour have a superb silky elegance and lack nothing in attractive, complex Pinot flavours. 1981 and 1982 are good sound vintages whilst 1983 is excellent, without any traces of the rot which tainted so many otherwise fine *cuvées*. 1984 is light, but elegant, 1985 a very fine, ripe succulent success and 1986 of good, but not spectacular quality. Rousseau rates the 1987s highly; the 1988s are for long keeping – austere but with remarkable depth and

balance, needing years to unpack; the 1989s full and fleshy, and the 1990s (Chambertin and Clos de Bèze in particular) classics, for long maturation.

The 1991s, from a harvest reduced by two hailstorms, are concentrated and well-balanced – wines which will drink well from the late 1990s onwards. Of the 1992s Charles merely says: 'pfof – beaucoup de fruits'. He judges his 1993s, which have full firm structures, to be somewhere between 1988 and 1990; fortunately, at 30–35 hl/ha yields were normal. The 1994s were as challenging for the Rousseaus as for everyone else.

Tasting the range is a striking proof of the superb quality of the Rousseaus' wines, but also an opportunity to compare the characteristics of the different *climats*. Charles lays no claim to any particular style, his intention being to preserve as much of the delicacy and elegance of the Pinot Noir produced as he can.

His Gevrey shows well what great wine-making and old vines can do with a simple Village appellation: soft, succulent fruit, attractively *framboisé*, supported by a firm structure, balanced acidity, ripe tannins and good length. Quite meaty, all in all.

Of the Premiers Crus, the Cazetiers is the most closed and the Clos St.-Jacques the most muscular and rustic – although still very fine. The Charmes- and Mazis-Chambertin are characterised by the length one would expect of Grands Crus, with considerable finesse and elegance. Even in their first year in cask, the 1993s left no doubt of their intrinsic qualities. Of the pair, the Charmes shows more delicacy – greater elegance than the Cazetiers for example – but with time, both will be rich, long, seductive thoroughbreds.

In Morey-St.-Denis, Rousseau's Clos de la Roche seems to take on something of the Gevrey tone of its stable-mates, with mineral flavours and muscularity which mark out its youth – 'Kräftige!', expostulates Charles. With age it develops the majestically complex *sous-bois*, vegetal, secondary aromas of old Pinot and, in good vintages has great longevity. The 1957 Clos de la Roche was still

going strong in 1990 – a sublime glassful, of great concentration and complexity with no signs of imminent decline.

In contrast, the Ruchottes Chambertin, Clos des Ruchottes, a Rousseau 'Monopole', is much softer and more tender in its youth. The 1993 had less intensity of both colour and flavour than the Clos de la Roche, and more obvious finesse and open aromas. This, most of all Rousseau's wines, tends to retain its youthful characteristics into old age.

In Charles and Eric Rousseau's hands, the Clos St.-Jacques verges on Grand Cru quality – especially in vintages of the natural concentration of 1990 and 1993. It combines, effortlessly, power and finesse, with naturally highish acidity and balanced tannins.

The 1993 Chambertin Clos de Bèze showed, as expected, strongish oak influence from the 100% new wood. Although Clos de Bèze tends to support rather less oak than Chambertin, the dominance of wood-derived aromas and flavours will disappear with maturity. A further difference is that Clos de Bèze has less soil depth than Chambertin, endowing it with more obvious power. In 1993 (and 1990) these two wines were magisterial – with enormous depth, remarkable concentration and complexity. The 1993 Chambertin, in particular, will be truly sensational when it finally unpacks. These two are the product of old vines, which have less foliage, exposing more of the bunches to direct sunlight, which further concentrates the fruit and ripens the skins.

Charles Rousseau is a modest, kindly man; one of those rare people who exudes quality in everything he touches. A youthful late 70s – though you'd never guess it – the joy and depth he manages to extract from a life he so obviously enjoys, is amply reflected in his wines. The struggle he had with the bacteria demonstrates his determination to succeed. Fortunately that problem is behind him; no doubt there will be others – nothing is stable or certain in a vigneron's life. He and Eric seem intellectually more than adequately equipped to face whatever the future may bring. It is to be hoped that it will include an abundance of Rousseau wines.

VINEYARD HOLDINGS

Commune	Level	Lieu-dit/Climat	Area	Vine Age	Status
Gevrey	V	(Various climats)	2.20	35	P
Gevrey	PC	Estournelles St.-Jacques	0.20	25	P
Gevrey	PC	Lavaux St.-Jacques	0.50	55	P
Gevrey	PC	Les Cazetiers	0.60	50	P
Gevrey	PC	Clos St.-Jacques	2.20	45	P
Gevrey	GC	Mazis-Chambertin	0.50	35	P
Gevrey	GC	Charmes/Mazoyères	1.50	35	P
Gevrey	GC	Clos de Bèze	1.40	40	P
Gevrey	GC	Chambertin	2.20	50	P
Gevrey	GC	Ruchottes Chambertin, Clos des Ruchottes	1.10	45	P
Morey	GC	Clos de la Roche	1.50	40	P
		Total:	**13.90 ha**		

Domaine Louis Trapet

GEVREY-CHAMBERTIN

Domaine Trapet is one of those engaging establishments where it is difficult to decide whether you are in the last century or the next. There is a strong feeling of 'esprit familiale' which, together with the accumulated baggage of six generations, respectfully referred to as 'Tradition', remains quietly in the background as the ultimate justification either for doing something or not doing it, as the case may be.

To visit the cellars and offices is to be transported back to the earlier 1900s. One can imagine ancient frock-coated, top-hatted Trapets holding their counsels and their celebrations in these small, formal rooms – deciding whether to buy this or that parcel of land, or welcoming a younger member of the family into the deliberations of the house.

Celebrations there must have been, for it is almost a Trapet tradition for each generation to add its 'stone to the edifice', in the form of a parcel of vines. The original Louis Trapet, from distant Chambolle-Musigny, started it all by marrying an orphan from Gevrey and moving there.

Around 1870, Louis' son Arthur – great-grandfather of the present head of the house, Jean Trapet – realising that it was possible to rehabilitate phylloxera-infested vineyards by grafting on to resistant rootstocks, began to acquire Village land in Gevrey – Grands Crus Chambertin and Latricières-Chambertin were added around 1904. He was in fact among the earlier converts to this way of working and his success gave a strong impetus to the Domaine to produce better wine than their competitors.

In common with many Domaines, the Trapets suffered during the 1920s and 1930s from insufficient labour and a weak market and up to the end of the 1940s Louis Trapet (II) sold most of his production in barrel to local négociants. The early 1950s saw the gradual introduction of Domaine bottling which by 1975 had spread to the entire annual production of some 4,000 cases – about half of which is exported.

Tradition imbues the Trapet spirit. Louis (II), who died in 1991, added his wisdom to Trapet deliberations which helped preserve the sense of oral tradition which so clearly matters to the family. After 25 years at the helm, Jean Trapet – a short, kindly man, with an air of honest and old-fashioned courtesy, now in his late fifties – is slowly handing over the reins, and probably some of the 'accumulated', to his own son, Jean-Louis, who joined the firm in 1987 and has been in sole charge

of vinification since 1990.

One suspects that the traditional methods have been entrenched here longer than might have been entirely desirable. The wines have been generally upper-middle in quality with the occasional remarkably fine bottles and some occasional lapses. Criticism has focused on high yields and the emphasis of finesse at the expense of real depth.

Jean-Louis is an earnest, self-confident and deliberate man with his father's courteous disposition. Exposure to other growers' wine, as a member of the 'Groupe des Jeunes' – a dynamic forum for young vignerons – has imbued a determination to make the best in Gevrey, not just in one but in every vintage. His father is proud to have him in the firm, and admits that changes are overdue.

The first task was a thorough review of all the Domaine's practices, starting in the vineyards: here, the aim is to preserve the maximum natural humus and fauna in Gevrey's clay-limestone soils. Now, minimum fertiliser and much hoeing have replaced the more usual herbicides, and strong chemicals, which are slow to degrade, and denature the soil destroying its fragile balance, are avoided. These also kill useful predators on pests such as grape-worm and red spider, so a more ecologically friendly regime of precisely targeted insecticides has been introduced, and herbicides restricted to spot eradication of stubborn grasses.

The Domaine suffered – as did many in the Côte de Nuits – from excessive potassium enrichment of the soil after the last war. This is gradually working its way out of the land; but meanwhile, small deficiencies in other minerals such as magnesium are corrected only after extensive expert soil analyses.

Although the Trapets were among the earlier users of clones in the 1950s, Jean-Louis is considering reintroducing the traditional *sélection massale* for some of his plant material. He still believes it essential to have several different clones in a single vineyard, both to guard against a clone-specific malady, and to add complexity. He is cultivating both his own vineyard policies and his nurseryman to find out which rootstocks are best adapted to the calcareous Gevrey soils.

The problem of rot is part of life in the Côte de Nuits, where the autumns can be wet, where summer hail can split the grapes and where the destructive grape caterpillar is endemic. Jean-Louis is concerned that too rich a soil, especially in nitrogen and sodium,

Jean Trapet – with his hand firmly on technology – at the service of the vigneron but never dictating to him

encourages *botrytis*. To combat rot, he is investigating clones of Pinot Noir which have phenotypically thicker skins and give less compact, more regular bunches.

Yields per vine have been deliberately reduced to add concentration to the wines. Low fertilisation, the use of low-vigour rootstocks and a very severe *ébourgonnage*, to cut off excess buds early in the growing season all help. De-budding has the additional benefit of spreading out the vine's vegetation and thus encouraging more efficient photosynthesis. Vine vigour is further restrained by planting vines at relatively high density – 12,000 vines per hectare, compared with the more usual 9 or 10,000. Appellation rules limit the number of buds per hectare to 80,000, so one is at liberty to achieve this by longer pruning on a lower density, or by short pruning on a high density, which is Trapet's preferred solution.

In 1990, a trial green-pruning was performed, to excise some 30% of the bunches. Jean-Louis believes that this is an optimum, because above this level the vines compensate, leaving the same quantity, but with thinner skins and more dilute juice.

A diminishing, but still prevalent, malady is *court-noué* or 'fan-leaf' virus which systematically destroys a vine's leaves, diminishing its photosynthetic efficiency and therefore its production of sugar. Trials with selected resistant rootstocks are in progress, but meanwhile, the only solution is to grub up affected vines, disinfect the soil and replant.

As one might expect, harvesting is entirely manual. Jean and Jean-Louis recoil in horror from the thought of harvesting machines in the Côte. They aim to pick at maximum maturity, and are encouraged by their recent experiments with a form of high wire culture to expand the height of the Pinot foliage; this increases both grape sugar content and the concentration of polyphenols – which help to fix colour in young wine and add structure.

The grapes are hand-sorted both in the vineyards and at the *cuverie* – costly, but important details which help make the difference between good and really fine wine. Once any substandard grapes have been eliminated, the crop is destemmed – up to 95% depending on the vintage – and lightly crushed. The policy is to extract tannins from the skins with a longish *cuvaison* rather than adding stems which also impart tannins, but of a harsher character. Since the 1990 vintage there has been a deliberate pre-fermentive maceration: the grapes are sulphured at the rate of 1 litre per tonne (=1000 kilos = 3 barrels) and then cooled to 16–18°C and then left to macerate for 5 days. This extracts both glycerols, which give wines a certain fleshiness and fatness, and anthocyanins which are valuable colour compounds.

Jean-Louis is also interested by the work of Guy Accad, whom he met in 1990. He has already made some experiments with different levels of pre-fermentive sulphuring, to see how the wines react and, whilst it is too early to evaluate the results, seems inclined to pursue this line of thought further.

The first *cuves* are yeasted to get fermentation going – 'we have good yeasts at Gevrey' – and the rest soon follow naturally. Alcoholic fermentation and maceration, in open, temperature controlled, cement vats lasts for up to 19 days. Pumping over the juice at strategic moments to ensure temperature equilibrium is interspersed with the use of an overhead piston device to break up the cap.

Tasting rather than analysis is used to determine when tannin extraction is at its optimum; the new wine is then decanted off its lees, given 12 hours *débourbage*, and run into casks. The lees are gently pressed and the resulting wine added only if it is needed. Jean-Louis believes that tasting is of primary importance in every choice he and his father make. Technical analyses are secondary – background information to be used in conjunction with whatever the palate reports.

The Trapets make sure that all their wood is air-dried, and not force-dried in kilns. They regard new oak not as a source of additional structure, but rather as a means of providing young wines with an environment of controlled oxidation. At present, their Grands Crus see 30–40% of new wood and the

Short pruning on a high density of vines

Premiers Crus about 20%. Vosges, Allier and Tronçais oak are all employed – a proportion of each for each *cuvée*.

The following February, after the *malo*, each lot is tasted, racked and unified before being returned to barrels. Altogether, the wines spend 11–18 months in cask – least for Village Gevreys and most for the Grands Crus. In June or July of the second year, wines still in cask are racked and assembled in tank before being albumen-fined and, only if necessary, lightly plate-filtered.

The aim of all this is to produce wines which respect to the maximum the characteristics of *terroir* and vintage: 'le plus naturel que possible'. The Trapets seek to work with nature and not try to force it to produce a certain style of wine every year.

Do not expect massive, blockbusting wines. The Trapet style tends towards elegance and finesse, with a hallmark backbone of succulent old vine fruit and a gentle lace-like delicacy. Despite this apparent lack of overt muscle, the wines age extremely well. They have structure, no doubt derived from the high proportion of old vines, which seem to sustain and nurture, without making them in any way burly or clumsy.

Whilst the Gevrey Premier Cru tends to an attractive nose of redcurrants and raspberries, more pronounced in riper years, it is the Trapet's Grands Crus Chapelle-Chambertin, Latricières-Chambertin and Chambertin itself which have established their reputation for superb winemaking.

Part of the uniqueness of the Grands Cru is attributable to the way they react to rainfall: the vine needs a short period of dryness at *veraison* – the moment when the grapes change green to black – so that they can derive maximum benefit from soil nutrients. Being on slopes, the Grands Crus tend to drain off water better than the flatter Village vineyards lower down.

Trapet's Grands Crus have uniformly deeper colours and noticeably greater concentration and complexity than the rest. This is, of course, as it should be. Chez Trapet, as elsewhere, they are not to be hurried: closed up and difficult to taste for a time, then slowly opening out, almost imperceptibly, like the moving hands of a clock. They tend to be complete, but without any of the lumpiness that one so often finds in this commune.

In 1993, against the instincts of Jean Trapet, Jean-Louis finished the fermentations of all his Grands Crus in cask. This gave the wines an extra touch of 'berryishness' and opulence without compromising on tannin extraction or on overall balance. As always, the Chapelle-Chambertin is the more obviously elegant of the trio, but is by no means outclassed by a very fine Latricières-Chambertin, although the magisterial Chambertin 'tout court' has a notch more of everything than either.

There used to be a much sought-after Chambertin Vieilles Vignes. In 1990, following an exchange of Chambertin vines with Domaine Jacques Prieur (qv), this was discontinued. In Jean-Louis' view: 'Chambertin should be unique – not several *cuvées.*' So now there is just one, from 40–80-year-old vines. In fine vintages this is a voluptuous, aristocratic creation, deep-coloured, with complex flavours, splendid length and all the class one expects from this King of Grands Crus.

Jean and Jean-Louis Trapet have made great strides since 1990, particularly in improving the quality of their raw material. Both quality and overall consistency have improved and criticisms in the late1970s and early 1980s for lack of concentration are no longer justified. They seem to be a family dedicated to quality and to the maxim that, as for the winemaker so for the drinker, 'a pleasure implies an effort'.

VINEYARD HOLDINGS

Commune	Level	Lieu-dit/Climat	Area	Vine Age	Status
Gevrey	GC	Chambertin	1.80	40 / 80	P
Gevrey	GC	Chapelle-Chambertin	0.60	45	P
Gevrey	GC	Latricières-Chambertin	0.80	45	P
Gevrey	PC	Petite-Chapelle + Clos Prieur	1.50	20 / 40	P
Gevrey	V	Derée + Petite Jouise + Champerrier + Vigne Belle	5.00	15–60	P
Marsannay	V	Le Poirier + Grasses Têtes	1.50	25	
———	R	(Bourgogne R/W; Passe-Tout-Grains)	1.00	15–20	P
		Total:	**12.20 ha**		

Domaine Pierre Damoy

As so often in family-run businesses, a change of management portends a change of fortune. With 8 hectares of Grand Cru – including an enviable 5.36 hectare slab of Clos de Bèze, mostly planted in 1920, Pierre Damoy should have been making top-class wine. Instead, there was unremitting mediocrity. In 1992, after the death of his wife and son within two months of each other, he retired, broken, and handed over the Domaine to his nephew, also Pierre Damoy. In the space of a few years, this energetic, talkative, young man has transformed it into one of Gevrey's more promising sources.

His work, developing agricultural treatment products in northern France, and time spent with winemakers in Gevrey 'tasting a lot', were seminal in forming his ideas on how things should progress. He believes that 'you must have a feeling for the vine and for wine' (which his uncle did not) and rejects the unspoken perception of many 'traditional' Gevrey proprietors that because 'we've been there for five generations, we must be making fine wine'. Pierre saw the failings and changed virtually everything – personnel, *cuves*, casks, even the bottle.

In the vineyards, modernisation has been dramatic: Cordon training, no fertilisers, just humus to keep a balanced level of organic matter and small adjustments in soil trace-elements, the minimum of spray treatments, no weed-killers, rather ploughing the soil, and most important, a significant reduction in yields.

Small *cuves* enable Pierre to vinify his Clos de Bèze in small lots, according to age and location of the vines (even within a single vineyard, there are genuine differences between one plot and another). He then separates out the 40-50% to be sold *en négoce* which is kept in stainless-steel, in contrast to the Domaine wine which has 60-100% new wood. A touch of stems (20% is average) help drain the juice through the solids and facilitate the three daily double-*pigéages*; 'we are champions at this' Pierre boasts.

The wines reflect these improvements. Apart from a rather angular Pinot Noir white from juice *saignéed* from Clos de Bèze and Chapelle-Chambertin vats and a fresh, uncomplicated rosé, the range comprises a generic Bourgogne Rouge, two Village Gevreys – the better from 62 year-old vines in Clos Tamisot, behind the Domaine's grand house of the same name, and three Grands Crus: Chapelle-Chambertin, Chambertin and Chambertin Clos de Bèze.

The Damoy style emphasises elegance and is generally on the softer, more *tendre* side of Gevrey – which shouldn't be taken as implying any lack of structure, rather an attractive suppleness in wines designed for medium-term cellaring, rather than the more monstrously tannic *cuvées* found elsewhere in the village. A carefully judged seasoning of moderately charred new wood – Allier for the Chapelle, Allier and Nevers for the Clos de Bèze – and 15-20 months of *élévage* – impart an attractive hint of torrefaction – not oakiness, but char-grill (people who talk of over-oaking often confuse them), which shows, particularly in the Grands Crus.

The 1994s are well made and generally well-balanced, especially the Chapelle-Chambertin and Clos de Bèze, both of which have real depth and finesse, the latter being much the firmer and tighter of the pair. The 1993s provided a stern test of willingness to sacrifice yield to quality. Pierre was rigorous in discarding mildewed and rotten fruit and the quality shows. The Gevrey Clos Tamisot has plenty of quality, although starting out somewhat *brut* in structure. The Chapelle and Clos de Bèze (only 12 and 17 hl/ha respectively in this vintage) are very different. The former – Pierre's avowed favourite because it manages to combine quintessentially the opposite qualities of power and finesse – has a very opulent, super-concentrated nose, which leads to an equally rich and potentially complex palate; altogether a wine of real depth and class which will take a decade to harmonise and evolve. The latter shows the same opulence and complexity, with perhaps a shade less intensity, but on a firmer, more austere canvas. Both will undoubtedly be splendid, given time.

Among Gevrey's new generation, Pierre Damoy has to be one of most fortunate. The inestimable advantage of first-class vineyards, gives him the potential to become a Burgundy super-star with one of the finest estates in the entire Côte. However, there is still concern over yields, which need to be strictly controlled and selection for the Grands Crus which must be rigorously based on quality. Nonetheless, the signs are promising.

Domaine Vachet-Rousseau

The swarthy, bearded Gérard Vachet is a careful winemaker, working 6.22 ha. of Gevrey vineyards, encompassing all four levels of quality. The fourth generation of Vachets here – his late mother was a Rousseau – he took over 5 ha from his father in 1978, having learned in the field and part-time in an Ecole Familiale Viticole in Beaune.

Gérard's wines are somewhat unusual, in that he vinifies much of his crop, including the Lavaux St-Jacques and Mazis-Chambertin in roto-tanks acquired in 1981. This saves space in his small cellar, preserves aromas, and extracts 'gras et onctuosité'. The results are wines with considerable depth and richness, but without the aggressively tannic structure one often finds in Gevrey. In vintages such as 1993, there is an abundance of ripe, concentrated fruit underpinned by very soft, fine, tannins. Wines more for the medium term but none the worse for that.

New wood is used, but skilfully judged so as not to stifle the fruit. The Gevrey Village *cuvée*, Premier Cru Lavaux St-Jacques and Mazis-Chambertin have around one-third of new oak, rather less for the Bourgogne Rouge – there is also a Passe-tout-Grains and a Rosé de *saignée*.

Gérard likes nature – now that he is no longer President of the growers' Syndicat he has more time for walking in the mountains with his wife – and lets it do most of the work in the cellar. There are just two rackings – one, after *malo*, with vigorous pumping to aerate the wine, the other, under an anaerobic cover of nitrogen, to assemble each *cuvée*. The wines are Kieselguhr filtered but generally not fined, before being consigned to the well-known Maurice Ninot, for bottling. One disadvantage of this is that all the wines are bottled at the same time, which is rarely desirable.

Apart from the Bourgognes, there are three wines: a Village Gevrey, from 17 different parcels, a fine, tight and fleshy Lavaux St-Jacques (6 different plots here) and a notably more intense, powerful and complex Mazis-Chambertin from 3 separate plots of 30 year-old vines. These are all excellent, with a characeristically gentle elegance more evocative of Chambolle-Musigny than of Gevrey. Altogether this is an excellent, well-run, small Domaine.

Domaine Dugat-Py

In contrast to his more reserved brother Claude, Bernard Dugat is an extrovert, lively man. His Domaine started with a patch of village Gevrey bought in 1973 when he was 15 and he made his first wine 2 years later. The Domaine has grown gradually to its present 5 ha – all owned – in particular with gifts from his father of some old Gevrey vines and Charmes-Chambertin in 1987. Some Petite Chapelle was acquired in 1993 and Lavaux St.-Jacques in 1994.

The Domaine operates from a heavily restored house on the Combe de Lavaut road at the top of the village. Bernard's wife, Jocelyne (née Py), who used to run a haberdashery shop near Dijon, works with him in the vineyards and cellar, and tends their lovely wild cottage garden which gives onto the Le Marchais vineyard behind the house. The three cellars range from 1980 to a magnificent vaulted chamber with a small leaded window, dating from the 12th century when it was used to house lepers.

Until 1989, everything, save a few bottles for the family, was sold to the négoce – including Leroy who bought Gevrey and Charmes. The produce of younger and less well-sited plots still goes that way (30–35% of production) but the major part, including Premiers and Grand Crus, is now matured in wood for Domaine bottling.

The vines are tended with as much skill as the garden – short Guyot pruning and ploughing up the soil to cut laterals and protect the main roots in winter (*buttage*) – a traditional practice which lost favour but is now creeping back into the Côte. Bernard harvests early in the morning cool – though the *négoce* Gevrey and Bourgogne Rouge have to wait until the afternoon. Great care is taken in weeding out poor grapes – he resorted to tweezers in 1991 to discard individual hail-damaged berries from Charmes.

Vinification is relatively straightforward: 'I let nature work for me,' Bernard explains. However, it won't *piger*, which is done manually, or add the several small doses of sugar which help prolong fermentation to give more glycerol and fat in the wines. Unlike many of his colleagues, he does not *saigner* his *cuves* – 'this is the escape route for vignerons' – believing that if you work properly in the vineyards and at harvest, this should be unnecessary.

Elévage is complicated by the fact that the leper cellar is not entirely underground; its temperature rises to 17°C in summer, speeding up maturation, and falls to 5°C in winter which makes for painfully slow *malos* – 18 months for some 1993s. Bernard is philosophical: 'We don't use chemicals and work the soil, so acidities are higher and *malos* slower; in any case, rapid *malos* produce harsh tannins.' Since 1991, the wines are neither fined nor filtered.

The results are a very fine range of wines: two *cuvées* of Gevrey – a Vieilles Vignes from 40-year-old vines in Les Epointures and a 'Coeur du Roy' from vines averaging 65 in Le Marchais and Combe du Dessus vineyards. This latter a classy offering, the 1993 showing plenty of depth, ripe tannins, good acidity and excellent aromatic potential from yields of around 35 hl/ha. These have 30-50% of new oak. A further village Gevrey, Les Evocelles, arrived in 1995.

The top of the range consists of Premiers Crus Lavaux St.-Jacques (first vintage 1994) and Petite Chapelle (one cask only here – new oak, topped up with precious Charmes), Charmes-Chambertin and, since 1995, Grands Crus Mazoyères and Mazis-Chambertin. These see 50–100% new wood – half Vosges, a quarter each Allier and Nevers. After 14–18 months in oak, Bernard bottles these and the Coeur du Roy himself, the rest being entrusted to the ubiquitous Maurice Ninot's travelling bottling plant.

Bernard is frank in admitting shortcomings. 'My 1990s needed more concentration – we would do better now.' In fact the Charmes was rather good, long and elegant, just starting to open out; perhaps a bit weak in the middle, but the vines were then only 9 years old. The 1993 Charmes (29 hl/ha) showed much greater depth, good length, well-integrated oak and underlying finesse – real Grand Cru quality and a fine result. Care and a severe *trie* produced a notably successful raft of 1994s, the Char-mes in particular. This is a fine, reliable Domaine which is gaining rapidly in confidence.

Domaine Esmonin, M

Sylvie Esmonin holds the respected title of *ingénieur agronome* from Montpellier where she specialised in viticulture. When, in 1986, her father Michel asked if she would return to the family Domaine, 'I laid down conditions, because I have character.' He agreed, and in a few years, this vibrant 30-year-old has tranformed a sleepy estate, selling entirely to *négociants* into an excellent source of wine.

Her training as a consultant oenologist in the Maconnais and Beaujolais gave her a deep insight into winemakers' problems. However, she felt unable to take the risks she feels necessary to make fine wine – consultants are expected to be cautious. 'Growers,' she laments, 'only tell you half the story' – either because they have something to hide, or else because they have simply forgotten what they did.

The first Esmonin bottling came in 1989. Now there are 6 wines – a Bourgogne Rouge, a Côtes de Nuits Villages from Brochon, 2 Village Gevreys (the Vieilles Vignes from 60 year-old vines) a Premier Cru, and, most recently, a Bourgogne Blanc and Volnay Santenots, both from vines in Meursault, owned by friends. The pick of the bunch is the Gevrey Clos St-Jacques, a deep, silky wine from vines behind the family home near the Combe de Lavaut.

Sylvie's wines exude classiness and, in fine vintages such as 1993, good extract and ripeness. Even the Bourgogne Rouge – an excellent test of any Domaine – has interest and complexity, without that raw, rustic, rough edge which often accompanies lesser Appellations. The Côtes de Nuits Villages is a shade fuller and richer – delicious drinking after a few years.

Vinification is designed to avoid bitter tannins. The crop is invariably destemmed – 'we don't even ask the question' – and vatted for 3 weeks, with plenty of *pigéage*. Then into cask – only Burgundian Chatillon oak is used, an Esmonin tradition: 'It's written in our genes,' muses Sylvie, 'I've been brought up on its taste; in any case, that's what Burgundian winemakers used 40 years ago. She considers it a fine oak, imparting a hint of liquorice. It needs careful use; the Clos St.-Jacques gets no more than 50% and the Vieilles Vignes Gevrey 20%, which is increasing as finances permit. There is neither filtration nor fining – 'we touch the wines as little as possible'.

The Vieilles Vignes and Clos St.-Jacques are fine expressions of Gevrey. The former is the attractive and old-viney fruit, with more succulence and better structure than the 'standard' Gevrey, good as that is. The Clos produces a wine of real class. The 1993 and 1991 both showed a seductive soft fleshiness, the former with an extra dimension of concentration. The 1990 and 1989 were good, but less successful, the one a bit rustic and the other with a strong alcohol imbalance.

Her father bottled little, so there are few back vintages to compare the vinification of father and daughter. When Sylvie reproached him thus, he replied: 'you can't have lots of friends and old wine; I have lots of friends.' There seem little doubt that the future will bring them more.

Domaine Geantet-Pansiot

The Geantets are a delightful, friendly family who, since 1954, have built up a fine 9 ha Domaine from Madame Pansiot's original 3. Vincent Geantet, in his mid-30s, is now in charge, having taken over progressively from his father, since 1982. Fortunately his parents are still there to help, as he is presently head of Gevrey's fire brigade and has to rush off whenever the siren goes – which it does all too often.

The whole family inhabit a large establishment on the main road – Vincent and his wife have one wing whilst 'les parents' live over the tasting room. Madame G., a lively, white-haired lady, bursts with pride at her son's achievements – though whether as a winemaker, fireman or pilot is not immediately clear.

Vincent's philosophy is to continue the tradition, although what this comprises is a matter of friendly, but animated, dispute between father and son. He is prepared to accept clones – 'we'll get good results with these'; father disagrees, preferring his *sélection massale* which has worked well since 1960. 'The old 115 (clone) is too productive,' argues Vincent; 'It's simple,' retorts father, 'just prune it shorter.' Then they're disagreeing about *vendange verte*: 'We've never green-pruned Champs Perdrix,' expostulates M Geantet senior . . . 'Yes we have, don't you remember'. These minor discords hide a fine working relationship.

The range comprises 5 Bourgognes – two reds, Passetoutgrain, Grand Ordinaire (Gamay) and Rosé – a Marsannay Rouge (Champs Perdrix), two Chambolles (Vieilles Vignes and a Premier Cru assembled from 3 vineyards), younger and older vine Gevreys, and Gevrey Premier Cru and a Charmes-Chambertin.

Since 1987, up to 6 days of cool maceration precede fermentation. The crop is destemmed but, unusually, not crushed to retain the maximum of berries intact which conserves fruitiness. The grapes are yeasted and enzymed (to help clarification) – then fermented at up to 36°C – a total *cuvaison* of around 18 days. Apart from the Bourgogne Rouge which has 4–5%, one-third new wood is the rule – spread evenly across the range. The Grand Cru Charmes gets no favours here!

Vincent sees fine wine as 'well coloured, fruity and rich, tannic – but not aggressively; and with a good balance'. His wines well reflect this conception – in particular the Chambolles and the Gevreys. The Gevrey 'Les Jeunes Rois', from 40-year-old vines is a substantial wine, with round tannins, ripe, silky fruit, and a touch of spiciness. The Vieilles Vignes Gevrey comes from 17 different parcels of 50–90+ year-old vines co-fermented in two separate lots. These endow the wine, which tends to start rather more closed-in and burlier than its younger brother, with an added dollop of concentration. Both these *cuvées* are very fine indeed for Village quality.

The Premier Cru Les Poissenots is altogether more feminine (for a Gevrey) and elegant, with more obvious aromatic potential – a wine of greater intrinsic class than the Villages.

Domaine Rossignol-Trapet

This, another of Gevrey's newer Domaines, came to life in 1990, when Jacques Rossignol and his sons, Nicolas and David, took back their family vines and set up on their own account. The vines came from Jacques' wife, Mado, daughter of Louis Trapet who died in 1991, whose brother Jean had been responsible for tending them and making the wine from 1961 to 1989.

There is no shortage of expertise in the Domaine's new cellars in Gevrey's Rue de la Petite Issue. Jacques comes from a dynasty of vignerons in Volnay – his brothers Yves, Régis and Michel all make wine – and both Nicolas and David have appropriate qualifications. Mado's family, originally from Chambolle, are no parvenus, having made wine in Gevrey for over a century.

The estate covers nearly 13 ha, all in Gevrey save a patch of Morey-St-Denis and some Beaune and Savigny which latter pair come from Nicolas' wife – née Perrot-Minot, from nearby Morey. The vines are respectably old, especially in the three Grands Crus, Chapelle- , Latricières- and Chambertin itself where many pre-date the first world war.

Great care is taken not to destroy soil micro-flora and fauna which play an important part in the long-term health of the vine and in the short-term typicity of the wine from each *terroir*. Yields are low – with an ideal of 35–37 hl/ha. Winemaking is broadly classical, although in weaker vintages (eg 1992) marginally more stems (30% as against 20% in 1990) are retained to add structure. The overriding principle is to control vinification within sensible parameters, but not to seek to direct it in any predetermined path.

After 12-18 days' *cuvaison*, the wines are transferred to cask for their *malos* – something to which the Rossignols attach importance, especially for wine in new oak, as promoting better tannin integration. After two rackings – one a month after *malo*, the other just before the following harvest – the wines are fined, possibly plate filtered, and bottled in November or December – a total *élévage* of 14 months.

The house style combines *rondeur* and *gras* with a finely-tuned balance and the structure to age over the medium term. The maximum of Pinot Noir character is sought, together with the ripest possible tannins. These are not wines for great ageing, but rather more accessible and supple in style. This desire for elegance is reflected in the use of new wood – just 20% for the Villages, 30% for the Premiers Crus and 40-50% for the Grands Crus – oak from Nevers, the Vosges and the Jura. Here, the fruit comes first, at all costs.

The results are fine winemaking by any standards. From a well-balanced, succulent, Bourgogne Rouge, from vines in Marsannay, the range progresses by way of Beaune – a lovely, smoky, accessible Teurons (1993) – to Gevrey and the Grands Crus. Five scattered hectares of Gevrey Village vines give the opportunity to separate several different *cuvées* and watch their evolution, before finally selecting those to be assembled for Domaine bottling. The 1993 Village was open, ripe and stylish, with a silky mouth-feel and well-integrated tannins – only marred by the merest note of stalkiness.

The Rossignol Gevrey Clos Prieur is in the Premier Cru section of that vineyard – unlike those of Denis Mortet and Harmand Geoffroy which are in the Village—designated section. The wine is deeper, more powerful and complex than the straight Gevrey Villages with (1993) a touch of greenness at the edge. A wine to keep for 5-10 years or so.

The Grands Crus start with an elegant, quite firm, Chapelle-Chambertin – more restrained and discreet than either Village or Premiers Crus; new oak is evident but carefully titrated to ensure that the fruit remains the dominant partner in the blend. This, from shallow soils has finesse rather than muscle, in contrast to the Latricières or Chambertin itself, both of which have greater weight and firmness. The Rossignol-Trapet Chambertin, in particular, is a very fine wine – real old vine concentration, supported by softish, ripe, nicely charry oak tannins, with a long, seductive finish. Evidence, indeed, for the quality and standards which this excellent Domaine has set itself.

Domaine Harmand-Geoffroy

The lean, *sympa* Gérard Harmand is one of those vignerons who married the job. An ex-fighter-pilot, he met his future wife, Martine Geoffroy, and took over the Domaine in 1980. From having his head mainly in the air, he now works with his feet firmly planted in the soil.

Gérard is one of Gevrey's emerging stars, producing a splendid octet of wines from 6 well-sited hectares. He is driven by hard work – 'only this makes quality'. Unusually, the Domaine's vines are 90% Pinot Droit – an upright variant of Pinot Noir, which overcrops unless you restrict it severely. However, properly handled, it produces greater fruitiness and is less prone to rot and disease. A *sélection massale* is used for replanting – e.g. the hectare of Gevrey

lost in the frosts of 1985 – as Gérard dislikes clones, and ploughing-up each winter cuts unwanted superficial roots: '*terroir* is deep down, not on the surface'.

Since 1982, vinification is entirely in roto-tank. This detaches more colour and fruit, finer tannins and produces greater aromatic complexity. A few days pre-fermentive soaking makes for *cuvaisons* of around 15 days. Some 14 months of cask maturation with 25% new oak (Vosges, Allier and Nevers, depending on the wine) follow, then bottling with a 'symbolic' – i.e. minimal – polishing filtration. Gérard considers an early *mise* helps retain freshness, fruit and richness.

The wines are consistently good, often very good, benefitting from a high average vine age, especially Clos Prieur. Part of this vineyard is classified Village and part Premier Cru. As Gérard's land straddles both, he uses the lesser designation. This has both finesse and *puissance* and plenty of Gevrey muscle, but markedly less than the tiny Monopole Premier Cru, La Bossière,

despite its relatively young vines.

The La Perrière and Champeaux are very different. The one from predominantly stony soil is more floral in character, with lively acidity and notable finesse. The other, from very poor, rocky, limestone soils at the Brochon end of a fine band of Premiers Crus, has greater aromatic intensity and depth of flavour (a very fine 1993 in particular), and rather more length.

The sole Harmand Grand Cru –17 ares of Mazis-Chambertin (Mazis-Bas) – adds a further level of complexity and power. Whilst the 1994 lacked the power or depth for true Grand Cru, the 1993 showed a fine balance of components, gorgeously concentrated silky fruit and real class.

Gérard clearly has a masterly touch. His wines are all too attractive young, but age well, if a 1985 Gevrey Premier Cru (when he blended all three rather than releasing them separately) and a 1976 Clos Prieur were representative examples. This is a fine, confident Domaine.

Domaine Claude Dugat

This is a small Domaine turning out stylish wines from 3 ha (2 owned, 1 rented). In charge, the quietly-spoken, reserved, Claude Dugat, the fifth generation of Dugats at Gevrey. Its headquarters are a splendid mainly 13th century Abbatial 'dependence' opposite the Church at the top of the village, sympathetically restored by Claude, who works skilfully with wood and stone. A splendid underground cask cellar was hewn out by him and his father in 1976.

Claude delights in being out of doors – whether walking with his family or tending his vines. For these latter – but presumably not the former – his motto is 'make them suffer', adding 'not to the point of malady'. A high average vine age, mini-

mum interference and long pruning 'to stretch out the vegetation' is sufficient to produce low yields and well-constituted fruit. His view is that severe pruning reduces not only the crop but also the area of foliage and thus sugar production. Green-pruning where necessary ensures small, concentrated bunches which are harvested relatively early to retain acidity.

This is a fine source of Gevreys – from a good, firm Villages *cuvée* matured in 50% new oak through a Premier Cru from Crapillot and La Perrière, an excellent Lavaux St.-Jacques to a pair of Grands Crus: an elegant, yet tight, Charmes-Chambertin from 35-year-old vines and a paltry two *piéces* of Griotte-Chambertin from a patch of 40- year-old vines.

Vinification is broadly classical – open cement *cuves*, plenty of *pigéage* and temperatures peaking at around 30–32⁰C, press-wine (from a 30-year-old Vaslin press)

added back and then 12–16 months in cask before bottling without either fining or filtration. The Premiers and Grands Crus enjoy 100% new Allier oak and longer in it, the Village and Bourgogne Rouge, 50% new wood for shorter duration.

Sulphur is kept to a minimum throughout – apart from 1.5 litres per tonne at crush, the only further additions come indirectly from sulphur candles burnt to disinfect the casks.

This is a good source, bordering on excellent. One may perhaps question the use of 100% new wood for the Premier Cru, which dominated the fruit in the 1993 – a policy perhaps influenced by a strong US market. Even in this concentrated vintage, the wine would have been better balanced with a fraction less oak. Otherwise, the plums in this cellar are the splendid Lavaux St.-Jacques and the rare and delicious Griottes (if you can find it!).

Domaine Frédéric Esmonin

Young Frédéric Esmonin came to work with his father – the somewhat phlegmatic André – in 1988, after learning his trade in Beaune. He is a cousin of Sylvie (qv) whose father, Michel, is André's brother. Together, André and Frédéric have propelled their Domaine into the upper échelons of Gevrey quality. André founded the Domaine in the 1970s with purchases, *metayages* and *fermages* making wine which,

until 1988, was entirely sold to the négoce. Although some Premier Cru and Village Gevrey still goes out in bulk, the cream is now Domaine bottled.

Although small – only 3.9 ha – the Esmonin vineyards are of high quality: three Gevrey Grands Crus (Mazis, Ruchottes, and Griotte-Chambertin), a pair of Premiers Crus (Lavaux- and Estournelles St-Jacques) and two Villages, including the fine Clos Prieur.

There is little unusual or controversial here, except perhaps for their use, in part, of Limousin oak, which tends to impart rather coarse-grained tannins. Fortunately, they have the sense to balance it with a ma-

jority of Allier, so the effects are not destructive. New wood averages 20% across the Domaine, with the Ruchottes-Chambertin getting around one-third, the Premiers and other Grand Crus more.

The standard is uniformly high – the 1994's particularly successful, although not up to the fine 1993s. The Ruchottes and Mazis vie for top place – both are long and complex, with Grand Cru power and concentration. The former has a notch more substance and 'tendresse', the latter perhaps a shade greater complexity, although it is the more reserved of the pair.

This is another of Gevrey's quality new recruits. A Domaine to watch.

MOREY-ST.-DENIS

Morey-St.-Denis is the rather somnolent filling in the sandwich of which the outsides are Gevrey-Chambertin and Chambolle-Musigny. A compact little village of some 800 inhabitants, it has long suffered from lack of exposure and from the renown of its more illustrious neighbours with the result that its wines are among the least well-known in the Côte de Nuits.

There is no obvious reason for this. Although small – some 150 ha compared with 180 in Chambolle and a massive 532 in Gevrey – Morey has its fair share of excellent growers, and 4 potentially fine Grand Crus, plus a patch of Bonnes-Mares curiously left over from Chambolle-Musigny when they drew up the appellation maps in 1936.

Even now, many of Morey's 20 Premiers Crus are relatively unknown, being frequently sold as a blend of several under the designation Morey-St.-Denis Premier Cru without the name of the individual *climat* which cannot but compound the problem.

However with the efforts of the commune's 65 growers, Morey is gradually establishing its own identity. Fine wines from Domaines Dujac, Clos de Tart, Groffier, Clos de Lambrays, Hubert and Georges Lignier, Ponsot and others in the village, together with those from Roumier, Pernin-Rossin, Rousseau and others outside it, are giving Morey the recognition it has long merited.

This pleasant little commune has had a mixed history. Known as Moriacum, or Muriacum, its origins have been incontrovertibly established by archaeologists as Gallo-Roman. First mentioned in 1120, it has been something of a shuttlecock, belonging variously to the Abbeys of Cîteaux, La Bussières-sur-Ouche and St.Germain-des-Prés, near Paris. In 1636, during the 30 years war, it was completely destroyed by fire. Perhaps all this has led to parochial introversion and an ineradicable sense of collective insecurity.

Like so many others along the Côte, the village itself seems to be permanently asleep. Apart from the occasional passage of a straddle-tractor along the Route des Grands Crus, which bisects it, nothing much stirs. The road in from the RN74 leads to the church and a small 'rond-point' illuminated by a painted scroll announcing that you have arrived at the 'Centre des Grands Crus' and a signpost telling you to turn left for Chambolle and right for Gevrey.

Obeying the first injunction will take you smartly out of the commune passing below Les Bonnes-Mares, whilst a right turn leads upwards to the top of the village. There you will find a large municipal concrete space with a bench, another roundabout and a cluttered, one-eyed shop, selling everything from batteries to beetroot, presided over by a lady who gives the distinct impression that customers are an inconvenience she could well do without.

Here the road forks – right for Gevrey and left, up the hill to the newer part of Morey – a festival of modern brick and dubious architectural taste. Planning regulations seem non-existent in this corner of France.

The vineyards cluster tightly round the village. The Grands Crus continue Gevrey's band of hard Bathonian limestone, although with markedly more gradient. A vein of marlstone traverses Bonnes-Mares and the Clos de Tart, both of which have a topsoil of thickish scree. This peters out in the upper sections of the Clos des Lambrays which has more sand-sized particles in its topsoil. The Clos St.-Denis and the Clos de la Roche, to the north of the village, both predominantly at the base of the hillside, have soils richer in brown limestone and also benefit from a particularly sheltered micro-climate.

At Morey's northernmost edge, just under the wood, is the Monts Luisants vineyard. This is something of a double curiosity: firstly, it is the principal source of the minuscule production of Morey-St.-Denis Blanc and secondly, it is zoned into across all three quality designations: the topmost section (2.19 ha) is AC Morey-St.-Denis, the strip below (5.39 ha) is Premier Cru Monts Luisants and the lowest section contributes 3.74 ha to the Grand Cru Clos de la Roche.

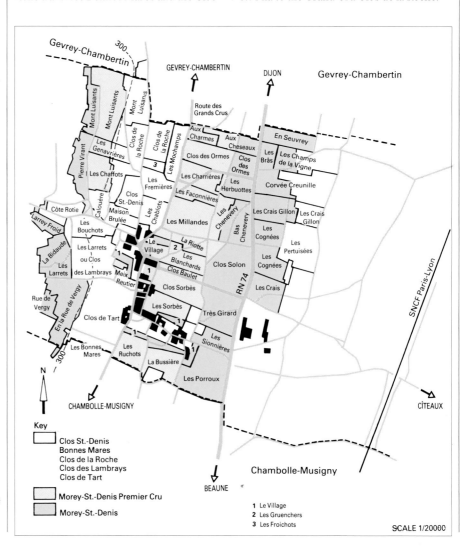

Key

Clos St.-Denis
Bonnes Mares
Clos de la Roche
Clos des Lambrays
Clos de Tart

Morey-St.-Denis Premier Cru

Morey-St.-Denis

1 Le Village
2 Les Gruenchers
3 Les Froichots

SCALE 1/20000

Morey-St.-Denis from the La Bussière vineyard

Morey Blanc is unusual and rare – only a few hundred cases are made annually. Although the appellation rules allow any Village or Premier Cru Morey to produce white wine, its production is in fact confined to the Monts Luisants and the En la Rue de Vergy vineyards, because their relatively poor soil, high in gravel and iron, with virtually no clay, is considered ideal for Chardonnay. The exception is Jacques Seysses' plot of Chardonnay between his house and the main road, which is on richer, more fertile soil.

Seysses apart, there are two other principal producers of white wine – Bruno Clair from Marsannay, who reclaimed much of his land from scrub and the Ponsot family (qv). Clair uses 100% Chardonnay for his wine, but Ponsot, who has some 1.5 ha of Monts Luisants, vinifies a mixture of old Aligoté, Chardonnay and 'le vrai Pinot Blanc'.

Morey Blanc is a gustatory oddity – broad in flavour, with plenty of guts but rarely much delicacy. It can support quite highly sauced dishes, and ages moderately well. In common with Musigny blanc, it has little to do with mainstream white Burgundy.

Moreys reds are usually characterised as combining the firmness and muscle of Gevrey with the finesse and elegance of Chambolle. However, the wide stylistic differences between growers far outweigh any common factors, vitiating generalisations. The pure fruit elegance of Jacques Seysses' wines, or the velvet silkiness of the Clos de Tart, when it is on form, share little with the more masculine style of the Ligniers, Robert Groffier or the Ponsots.

There are fewer thoroughly disappointing Domaines here than in Gevrey. Some, such as Pierre Amiot, Clos de Tart and the Clos des Lambrays lack consistency, producing some excellent wines and then for no obvious reason lapsing into mediocrity.

Nonetheless, Morey's wines are well worth searching out and the village worth a visit – if not to wander in the Grands Crus, then to dine by the fire at the Castel Très Girard where, if your pocket was deep enough, you used to be able to enjoy a bottle of 1945 Clos de Lambrays whilst contemplating, in all wisdom, the prospect of the Clos Solon beyond.

THE GRAND CRUS OF MOREY-ST.-DENIS

Lieu-dit	Area	Props.	Av. Prod.
Clos St.-Denis	6.62.60	20	1900 C/S
Clos de la Roche	16.90.27	40	4850 C/S
Clos des Lambrays	8.83.94	4	2300 C/S
Clos de Tart	7.53.28	1	2100 C/S
Bonnes Mares	1.51.55	2 or 3	500 C/S
Totals:	**41.41.64 ha**		**11650 C/S**

Domaine Dujac

MOREY-ST.-DENIS

Jacques Seysses is a rare species – a cross between the young, knowledgeable and passionate for quality and those great winemakers of the old tradition whose influence still suffuses the Côte. In his 30 years in Burgundy he has built up not only a fine Domaine but a reputation for winemaking which has helped many of those who have passed through his hands, on their own way to success.

Arriving in Burgundy in 1966 with the inestimable benefits of maturity and money and the doubtful benefit of inexperience, Jacques spent two vintages at the Domaine Pousse d'Or in Volnay before buying the 4.5 ha Domaine Graillet in Morey-St.-Denis in May 1968. He continued working with the family biscuit business in Paris for five years until he felt that the wine sales might reasonably support him and his American wife, Rosalind, whom he met in 1971 when she came to help with the vintage.

Meanwhile, the original 4.5 Graillet ha were growing – with the addition in 1969 of 69 ares of Echezeaux. Since then land has been added piece by piece to bring the Domaine up to its present size of 11.21 ha. Jacques calculated that, when he finally moved to Burgundy in the mid 1970s, the price of his Paris flat would have bought enough good vineyard land to support a small family. Unfortunately, this is no longer the case since the price of his Echézeaux has risen by a multiple in excess of sixty.

Jacques' father's love of good food and fine wine enabled him to taste old vintages and thus to experience what great wine was all about. The awareness that marvellous wines were produced before the last war, with minimal technological support – and a passing Diploma in Oenology from Dijon – laid the foundation of his winemaking philosophy which remains steadfast: 'Use knowledge and technology to counter accidents – for example, bad weather – but if all is going well, don't interfere.' This principle – although not entirely as 'laisser faire' as it might sound – governs much of what goes on in the vineyards and cellars.

Care of the vineyards is confided to Christophe Morin, a native of the Loire, who arrived via California, Chagny and Bordeaux; he is also consultant to one of Jacques' erstwhile apprentices, Jean-Pierre de Smet, at the Domaine de l'Arlot.

Christophe is charged with producing the healthiest and ripest possible fruit for Jacques to vinify. Much work has been devoted to finding clones which improve consistency of yields and give smaller berries and bunches. The ideal is six bunches per vine which is equivalent to 35 hl/ha given normal bunch weight of 80 grams. Fickle weather can reduce this to 70 or increase it to 100 – in which latter case you have dilution and corrective measures, e.g. *saignée* or artificial concentration are necessary to maintain balance. As their 60-year-old pre-clone vines in Les Gruenchers give very small, healthy berries and bunches, these are used as a mother vineyard for a regular *sélection massale*. Since 1977 they have also used clone 123 – not recommended because of its endemic leaf-roll virus. For some unaccountable reason, it has shown no disease and consistently produced fine quality fruit.

Rootstocks are also important. Earlier plantings on the precocious SO4 – ill-adapted to the limestone hillside soils of the Côte – had to be replaced. Jacques also tested the hypothesis that the more clones in a vineyard, the greater complexity of the resulting wine – a theory still widely held in Burgundy. Tasting 'clone' wine versus that from old *massale* vines clearly demonstrated the

Jacques Seysses in his cellar

theory to be false. Neither within a single vineyard nor between different vineyards is complexity dependent on the number of contributing clones. Since other variables were equated, it must come from *terroir*. This conclusion, entrenched in the collective psyche of generations of Burgundians, has yet to be accepted by those who spray vines indiscriminately around the New World.

The relative value of 'working' or 'hoeing' the vineyards to deal with grasses and weeds, and using defoliants or herbicides (one burns, the other destroys the roots) was also studied. Hoeing breaks up the soil which is good for aeration and for retaining a balanced population of micro-flora, including yeasts. However, the more friable the soil the more prone it is to erosion, especially on the hillsides of Burgundy; carrying it back up again is both time-consuming and expensive.

Herbicides, through helping to keep surface stones in place to store up heat for the vines during the summer, being chemical products can alter the ecology of the soil. Containing water, they tend to encourage the proliferation of less desirable surface lateral roots which discourage the main tap root from seeking nourishment deeper down in the ground. Jacques' regime is a compromise: 1–2 years herbicide followed by a similar period of working the soil. This was not easy for the field-workers to accept, since it tended to leave the vineyards generally less neat than they otherwise might have been. However, the manicured 'English garden' look is not what Christophe Morin is after.

Producing top-quality fruit entails hard work during the 6–7 months growing season. Achieving suitably low yields requires short pruning – a maximum of six eyes on each cane, not what is generally stated to be six eyes, which on scrutiny turns out to be 7 or 8 – a strict spring *évasivage* followed by green-pruning just before *veraison*, usually in mid-July. Jacques Seysses disagrees with those who contend that the need to remove bunches is an indication of overproduction, arguing that the natural vigour, especially of young vines, cannot be adequately controlled by short pruning alone. It is these vines which tend to be most severely green-pruned.

Timing is critical: if you prune too early the vines will compensate, producing larger berries – the reverse of what you want; if you wait until *veraison* this doesn't happen and yields reduce. As an illustration Jacques cites 1988, 1989 and 1990: most growers produced more in 1989 than in 1988 and again more in

1990. Dujac yields diminished by 10% between 1988 and 1989 and the 1990 yield remained at the 1988 level.

The Domaine encourages higher vine foliage – both at base and apex – to increase the area for sugar production. Experiments have shown that this augments potential alcohol by up to 2 degrees. Useful by-products are an improvement in the micro-climate within the vine – more air circulation which reduces the likelihood of rot – and better penetration of sprays, which means less frequency and concentration of treatments.

Dujac now limits sprays to periods of risk, using less toxic products and encouraging natural predators on pests. Jacques is firmly not organic and dislikes the cult image which such labels seem to entrain.

The Domaine's greatest recent investment has been in the unlikely sphere of harvest; between 1985 and 1990 the cost doubled and increased again by 35% between 1990 and 1995. Jacques considers it as nonsensical to ask a winemaker to turn rotten fruit into fine wine as to expect a starred chef to transform a battery-reared chicken into a decent Coq au Vin. So there are now more pickers taking longer over each bunch, carefully weeding out green, pink and red berries, leaving only those which are black and thus fully ripe. It is such attention to detail which marks out Great Domaines from the merely good.

By what alchemy does Jacques Seysses transform this cosseted ripe fruit into such fine wine? He will tell you, with a mischievous, yet genuinely surprised look, that there are no tricks. His own skill has been gleaned not from theory, but from observing what goes on here and there, and chatting to old winemakers steeped in local tradition.

In retrospect his two Volnay vintages appear to have been a seminal influence. Whilst he learned the ways of tradition from older folk, it was Pousse d'Or's modern equipment and hygiene which left an indelible impression: 'Potel used three times more water than wine, so I started like that.'

Bits of 'tradition' have also stuck: in particular, the absence of cooling the *must* (none, except for 1985), and an unwillingness to destalk. Jacques does not destalk, not because he wants the stalks, but because removing them would split and crush the berries, liberating juice for hungry yeasts to work on, thus advancing the start of fermentation. 'If I could find a way of destemming, without crushing, I would do so,' he confesses. It is perhaps superfluous to add that if there were any conceivable way, Jacques would certainly by now have discovered it.

This no-destemming is not just a bow to tradition, but a conviction buttressed by experiments with grapes from the same vineyard either left whole or destemmed. Whilst stalks absorb colour – Dujac wines are char-

acteristically lighter than darker – an enforced 3–5 days of intra-cellular fermentation of whole bunches adds an element of finesse which destemming would sacrifice.

As well as slowing down fermentation, stalks help maintain an even exchange of heat throughout the vat. For the remainder of the 16–21 days of *cuvaison*, Jacques' policy is to interfere as little as possible. In the natural course of events, temperatures rarely rise above 31–32°C, so cooling is only necessary in extreme circumstances. Plenty of *pigéage* helps to increase extraction and enzymes are added to facilitate clarification and thus minimise the need for filtration.

According to Jacques Seysses, the balance of great wine requires 11.5–12 degrees of alcohol. As in Burgundy's marginal climate it is rare to harvest a Grand Cru at above 12 degrees potential alcohol, *chaptalisation* is a concomitant of almost every vintage. Even with a natural 12 degrees, some alcohol is inevitably lost during vinification. Given Jacques' belief that the best extraction occurs later, he adds sugar in several small doses during the final phase of fermentation. This also prolongs the process, which would otherwise only last for 10–12 days.

Once the free-run wine has been decanted, the pulp is pressed very lightly in a pneumatic press. Normal practice is to add the press-wine immediately; Seysses prefers to vinify it separately, deferring its suitability for incorporation into the final wine until later: 'Work at it first, then see.'

The wine then goes into cask. Wood is a subject on which Jacques is especially knowledgeable, having served in 1976 on a commission researching into *élévage* in wood. Finding that he invariably preferred wines matured in new oak, he didn't wait for the results but started to put all his Grands and Premier Crus into 100% new casks, irrespective of the vintage. This practice remains – the Crus have new oak, the Village wines only second year or older wood.

Certainty about the quantity of oak was matched by doubt about the quality. So Jacques, and a group of like-minded friends, now buy their own Allier oak and have it air-dried for three years before use.

It must be emphasised that new oak is not used for its taste, but for its ability to impart a long, slow oxygenation to young wine. This not only reduces the need for sulphur, but most importantly leaches out tannins which bring stability, in particular to colour pigments. Strong firing of cask staves burns tannins which then don't work properly – and moreover give a hard, charry flavour which tends to dominate. So Seysses casks have the lightest toast possible.

The wines spend up to 16 months in cask and are racked just once, after the *malo* (which tends to happen sooner in new casks

than in old). They remain in cask until bottling, when they are racked and unified in 8 cask lots. Since it is physically impossible to equalise, for example, 40–50 casks of Morey-St.-Denis, the lots are chosen by tasting to ensure maximum uniformity.

The care taken over fruit enables Dujac reds to be bottled unfined in most years and unfiltered in all. Jacques argues that using enzymes and pressing gently for a clearer juice, the wine will fall bright naturally, so filtration is unnecessary.

This obsession with detail results in a remarkable galaxy of wines. It also makes vintages matter less than they otherwise might. If Jaques bottles a wine, one can be sure that it will be not just acceptable, but complex and interesting. In fact, some so-called 'lesser' vintages have been among Jacques' notable successes – e.g. 1980, 1982, 1987 and 1992. Nowhere is the absurdity of an inflexible belief in vintages more apparent than at Domaines such as this.

Dujac wines have an individual style which spans the range, tending to be lightish in colour – rather a limpid sort of crushed strawberry hue of varying depth – with a fine, almost succulent nose of ripe Pinot; in great vintages such as 1985, 1989, 1990 and 1993 they comes as close to being quintessential Pinot as that grape is likely to get. The flavours are equally seductive – sometimes lighter, sometimes richer, yet always complex, fine and often marvellously silky.

As Jacques himself is constructively critical of his own wines, it is perhaps worth contrasting the 1993s and 1994s. The former show a well-nigh perfect balance throughout the range, with matching concentration and length. There was no mildew in the crop, thanks to Christophe Morin's spending most of the time – including weekends – from flowering to harvest on his tractor nipping any outbreak in the bud. 'He saved the crop.' In contrast, 1994 produced attractive wines with plenty of fruit for relatively early drinking. Despite their best efforts, the crop size was huge, demanding the biggest green harvest ever and 15% *saignée*. *Saignée* included, yields touched 45 hl/ha in Morey Village.

The 1989s, 1990s and 1993s are classic Dujacs. In 1989 low yields gave an extraordinary concentration and finesse which started to unpack relatively early. Jacques recalls the mocking laughter of his neighbours when they saw him green-pruning that July. Almost open disbelief greeted his announcement that he had not sent any wine to distillation that year – some even accused him of hiding wine and falsifying his declarations to cover up overproduction. The wines are delicious, with fine balance and depth of extract; the Clos la Roche is magnificent – extraordinary silky elegance, mouthfilling fruit and an indescribable dimension of pure Pinot class.

A corner of Jacques' private cellar

The 1990s are equally fine, if different combining 1988's structure with 1989's gorgeously decadant fruit – atypical perhaps, but magnificent none the less. The 1993s are as good, but with greater typicity and a longer prospective evolution.

The situation of the vineyards often contributes to their quality; for example, the Gevrey-Chambertin, Aux Combottes, a Premier Cru, is entirely surrounded by Grands Crus and, in good vintages could convincingly pass as one. In most vintages there is little to choose between the Clos la Roche and the Clos St.-Denis; perhaps the latter is a shade more masculine and firmer but that is all. The Charmes-Chambertin is generally a wine of great delicacy and class – packed with almost creamy soft fruit and underpinned with harmonious tannins.

The Echézeaux and Bonnes-Mares complete the Grands Crus. The Echézeaux, from the Champs Traversins *climat*, tends to start with a lively acidity, which helps its long-term balance. The quality of the wine vindicates the decision to plant with selected clones; even though the vines are still young, the concentration they give is remarkable.

The Bonnes-Mares comes from the Morey end of this extended vineyard. It tends to have more obvious power than the Echézeaux, with the Seysses hallmark of almost creamy, old-vine fruit and considerable length. Jacques reckons that at least part of the complexity of his wines derives from the short period of whole-bunch quasi-carbonic maceration, which delivers extract into the juice without adding tannin.

There is also a little white wine: a few barrels of Meursault, from grapes from his parents-in-law, which is not sold in Europe,

and an equally small quantity (10–15 barrels) of a delicious Morey Blanc, made from Chardonnay vines planted after the frosts of 1985 on a patch of moderately rich soil between the Seysses' house and the RN 74.

Dujac claims to be the first Domaine in Burgundy to use *maceration pélliculaire* for its whites. This process consists of a few hours skin-contact – too much and you risk a dominance of exotic-fruit flavours – which adds *gras* and structure. The juice is fermented in cask – 75% new wood – with plenty of *batonnage*. After 8–9 months, the wine is racked, keeping some of the fine lees to further enhance complexity. Bottling is deliberately early – after 10–11 months – to retain maximum freshness and fruitiness. 'I make white wine the way I like it,' explains Jacques, adding 'when they are young you should feel that you are cracking berries.'

The results are triumphant: a wine with an open mineral/acacia nose, moderately powerful and concentrated with excellent length and attractive complexity – in style, a Corton-Charlemagne rather than a Puligny –

but, in reality, neither – just *sui generis*.

Jacques Seysses lives far from the parochial lifestyle of many vignerons on the Côte. Apart from spending as much time as he can with his three sons – one now at Oxford – he manages to cycle some 3–4,000 miles each year. These jamborees, in the company of friends, are not rudderless pedallings, but carefully planned circuits, usually studded with gastronomic overnight stops at the restaurants of chefs whom he admires, and who are often friends as well.

The most notable excursion Jacques recalls, was in 1989 from Venice to the restaurant of Frédy Girardet, at Crissier in Switzerland. Girardet also happens to be potty on cycling.

Manifestly unable to sit still, the Seysses's have acquired, with Aubert de Villaine and another friend, the 46 ha Domaine de Triennes, in the Var. After much T-budding of the existing roots on to Syrah and Cabernet, the first harvest was picked in 1990. Sitting in a corner of the *cuverie*, exhausted, Jacques remembers reflecting: 'You are very stupid to come 'ere.' However, as the wine and vineyards mature, he is clearly relishing this new challenge.

Domaine Dujac is a remarkable synthesis of talent and opportunity. Jacques' private cellar is a testimony to his father's early influence. A litany of France's greatest non-Burgundian wine-producing Domaines, each represented by a small or not-so-small pile of mycelium-covered bottles annotated in chalk on a piece of slate, attests to the breadth of his taste, and no doubt, to the eagerness of Domaine owners elsewhere, to exchange their precious wine for some of his.

Although thankful for the past, Jacques Seysses is not a nostalgic man. His confidence in Burgundy's new generation is boundless – 'The young have patience,' he says, 'whereas the older generation had to make a living; kids can study now, which gives them the chance to meet and talk to each other.' If his faith is justified, the future of Burgundy is indeed in good hands.

VINEYARD HOLDINGS

Commune	Level	Lieu-dit/Climat	Area	Vine Age	Status
Morey	GC	Clos de la Roche	1.95	Old+Young	P
Morey	GC	Clos-St.-Denis	1.43	8–35–50	P
Morey	PC	(Various climats)	0.54	½ Repl'nt.	P
Morey	V	(Various climats)	2.50	15–20	P
Morey	V	(Chardonnay)	0.70	11	P
Chambolle	GC	Bonnes Mares	0.44	18	P
Chambolle	PC	Les Gruenchers	0.33	60+ (most)	P
Chambolle	V	Les Drazeys	0.53	15–65	P
Gevrey	GC	Charmes-Chambertin	0.70	20	P
Gevrey	PC	Aux Combottes	1.15	18	P
Flagey	GC	Echézeaux	0.69	18	P
Vosne	PC	Les Beaumonts	0.25	10	F
Morey	R	(Bourgogne Blanc)	0.12	20	P
Total:			**11.33 ha**		

Domaine Hubert Lignier

MOREY-ST.-DENIS

Hubert Lignier, like his cousin Georges who lives next door, is not a self-publicist. However, in their own understated ways, they both make excellent wine – not perhaps as consistent as the superstars, but definitely at the top end of the scale.

Hubert is a jovial, self-effacing person – modestly content to do the best he can and make a living from it, without the need for ego-boosting headlines. Until recently he was content to sell more than half his total production to the négociant market; now his son Roman has joined him, most of the output is Domaine bottled.

The wines are made and the vineyards tended with care. Hubert and Roman go for sensible yields from old vines, with as much *répiquage* and as little chemicals as they can manage. One idiosyncrasy of Lignier viticulture is a machine, designed to cut any small roots which appear above the level of the graft – known as *racines à collé* – in the varietal part of the plant, which, should they get as far as the soil, would effectively by-pass the rootstock and become easy prey for soil infections in general, and *phylloxera* in particular.

Once he has overseen the harvest, Hubert returns to his *cuverie*, 'has a good shower', and gets into the *cuves* himself, with four friends to ensure adequate *pigéage*; 'un travail amicale', as he calls it! Vinification is classical, with no frills: 100% destalking, and fermentation in cement *cuves* – 'better for temperature insulation' – and a minimum of 15 days *cuvaison*, with the temperature peaking at 33–34°C.

Only natural yeasts are used – if the fermentation won't start itself within a few days of vatting, they simply warm the *cuverie* and pump over again to help the yeasts to work. Hubert is certain that the best extraction occurs during the principal phase of fermentation, rather than with *maceration* before or afterwards.

Most, but not invariably all, of the press-wine is added to the free-run wine before being left to its *malo*. Hubert admits that there are no rules, just a matter of expediency. If he has the time and space the wine goes into cask, if not, it stays in bulk, either under a floating platform seal, or else under a protective blanket of liquid paraffin.

Considerations of expediency also govern the cooperage: the Grands and Premier Crus normally have up to 50% new oak; the Morey, Gevrey and Chambolle being treated to an

Morey-St.-Denis from the Clos de Tart

amount which seems to depend on how many sound casks are left over from the previous vintage.

When it comes to a preference for the provenance of his wood, Hubert evinces a weary scepticism: 'There is no appellation controlée for wood,' he remarks quizzically; 'perhaps an 'Allier' cask may 10% of Allier and the rest from elsewhere'. He does however believe that the quality of the wood is of greater importance than its precise provenance – making a virtue out of necessity perhaps?

Since 1992 fining and filtration are not part of the Lignier procedure. So after some 18–24 months in cask, the wines are bottled *puris naturalibus* – 80% at the Domaine, the rest sold off in bulk.

Hubert's and Roman's style looks distinctly more towards the finesse and elegance of Chambolle rather than to the more muscular renditions of Gevrey. The style generally exudes *tendresse*, even in firmly stubborn vintages such as 1987 and 1991. There is a fine spread to choose from: Village *cuvées* of Gevrey, Morey and Chambolle-Musigny, two Morey Premiers Crus – one

from old vines, the other (Les Chaffots) a recent release; Chambolle-Musigny Les Baudes and Gevrey-Chambertin Les Combottes in Premier Cru plus Grands Crus Clos de la Roche and Charmes-Chambertin.

Of the Premiers Crus, the Chambolle Les Baudes, from 36-year-old vines next to Bonnes-Mares, is probably the most elegant. The pair of Moreys are excellent, especially the Vieilles Vignes which comes from vineyards straddling two Premiers Crus, adjacent to Clos de la Roche. This has a fine kernel of old-viney fruit, a subtle, but unobtrusive oak support from 50% of new wood and the Lignier caresse of ripe, plump fruit – broad in flavour but most attractive. In vintages of the quality of 1993, a wine to buy and keep for 5–10 years. The Gevrey Combottes is a stop more elegant, but equally cellar-worthy.

There is not a great deal to choose between the two Lignier Grands Crus. The Clos de la Roche is usually the more closed and structured of the two, the Charmes-Chambertin showing more finesse in youth with perhaps a shade less concentration and complexity. There is no significant difference in vine age to account for this, just the natural tendency of Charmes to elegance and Clos de la Roche to meaty firmness. Both wines more than live up to their classification, and are worthy summits of the Lignier vinous pyramid. Try the splendid 1991 if you want to see what skill can achieve in a difficult year.

Despite an air of laid-back indifference – a clock with the spring truly unwound – this is a fine, reliable, Domaine and one to trust even in second-division vintages.

VINEYARD HOLDINGS

Commune	Level	Lieu-dit/Climat	Area	Vine Age	Status
Morey	GC	Clos de la Roche	0.79	30–40	M/P
Morey	PC	(Several climats)	1.29	27–55	P
Morey	PC	Les Chaffots	——	——	P
Morey	V	(Several climats)	2.06	10–45	M/P
Gevrey	GC	Charmes-Chambertin	0.09	36	P
Gevrey	PC	Les Combottes	0.14	34	M
Gevrey	V	——	1.03	30–40	P
Chambolle	PC	Les Baudes	0.17	36	P
Chambolle	V	——	0.50	40	P
——	R	(Bourg./BGO/Aligoté)	1.74	15–40	P
		Total :	**7.81 ha**		

Domaine Robert Groffier

MOREY-ST.-DENIS

Robert Groffier is, like his wines, a man of considerable depth and charm. A kindly reflective, Pickwickian person, he lives in a substantial post-war house in the Route des Grands Crus on the Chambolle-Musigny side of Morey-St.-Denis, at the southern extremity of the village.

His establishment frames 3 sides of a large courtyard, the other 2 being the *cuverie* and cellars. This is a family business, with his son, Serge, now 37, working with him and a small grandson dashing everywhere and contriving to fall over everything.

In contrast to her relaxed husband, Mme Groffier, whose role seems to be to manage the office and who is most likely to answer the telephone if you ring, appears to be in a permanent state of the utmost confusion. This renders even the slightest request 'impossible'. Despite a long-standing appointment, carefully re-confirmed the day before, one was met with 'impossible, Monsieur, my husband is far too busy bottling to receive you'. Fortunately, at that moment Robert turned up and the crisis was resolved; but the Groffiers' customers must find this 'front of house' technique bizarre, to say the least.

Despite the antics of his P.R. department Robert Groffier is one of the best winemakers in the Côte. His efforts are helped by 7 ha of fine vineyards, including nearly 1 ha of Bonnes-Mares, some Chambertin Clos de Bèze and 1.5 ha of 15–30-year-old vines situated 'just below the Clos de Vougeot', which supplies his excellent Bourgogne Rouge.

Robert's father, Jules, put the Domaine together in the 1950s having inherited some vineyards from his father. In 1960, he split the land between Robert, his brother and sister, upon which his brother 'went into fruit and vegetables' enabling Robert to buy him out. This added Amoureuses, Gevrey and the Chambolle Premier Cru Les Hauts Doix to the Bonnes-Mares and Bourgogne he had already.

Having worked with his father since leaving school at 14, Robert had a good basic understanding of how things were done, but no formal training. In time, his son, Serge, joined him straight from school in the late 1960s, presumably undergoing a similarly osmotic apprenticeship.

The Groffier vines are conscientiously tended. Young plants – up to 18 years – are ploughed up round the roots each winter and unploughed in the spring. A light herbicide is applied to treat weeds and grasses and from May onwards the soil is hoed. New vines are given large doses of humus for 4 years after planting, otherwise a small amount of organic fertiliser is used as needed.

Following the frosts of 1985, new plant material is a *sélection clonale* rather than the more traditional *sélection massale*, always planted on to 161/49 rootstock: 'more finesse, less yield, better quality,' reckons Robert. Treatment for *cryptogamic* diseases – *oïdium*, mildew, *botrytis* etc. – is with Bordeaux mixture, and pests are dealt with by modern insecticide sprays.

Although they prune quite long – 7 eyes on each fruiting cane – Robert is very severe in removing any excess vegetation and wood to reduce yields and increase concentration. Robert is clear about the importance of these measures: 'It's not the pruning which counts, it's the debudding.'

As at any top-class Domaine, there is nothing inflexible about the vinification. Whether to leave stalks in the fermenting vats, and if so, what proportion is an annual decision. In 1990, none were left 'because of the volume of pulp'; in 1984 all the stalks remained; in 1987 and 1988 50% were removed – and so on. Stalks give tannins, which can often be green and aggressive if the wood isn't fully ripe, and also add a certain substance to the wine. However, they physically absorb colour, which is undesirable.

In common with most other growers, Robert *chaptalises* his wines in less sugar-rich vintages. He would infinitely prefer to do so in several stages 'if it were permitted'. In this way he would get a long, slow fermentation – 'It is necessary to feed the *cuve* from time to time,' he says , adding ruefully, 'but it is not permitted.' The authorities who man their regulatory desks in Beaune and Dijon, would do well to take note of what Robert and other vignerons are telling them. It may help to control over-*chaptalisation* to permit only one dosing, but no-one interested in top quality is in doubt that the process gives far better results when performed in stages. Although still technically illegal, fractional *chaptalisation* is now 'tolerated', official-speak for turning a couple of blind eyes – but nothing is certain . . .

Once vatted, the pulp is sulphured and left to macerate for 5–6 days 'à froid', that is to say 20–25°C. During the first stages of fermentation, the cap is broken up at least 3 or 4 times a day. Even the nights are not sacrosanct: Robert and Serge may have to get out of bed a 3 a.m. to do this if necessary as in 1988 and 1989. Mme G. must be severely discomposed when this is in progress!

An inoculation of good dried yeasts is then used to get fermentation going; according to Robert, they give an additional aromatic dimension to the wines. There is a little pumping-over at the start of fermentation, but the Groffiers prefer *pigéage* to ensure that there is as much fine tannin and colour extraction from the skins as possible, even if it means sleepless nights.

Yet greater vigilance is demanded during the active phase of fermentation, since Robert and Serge prefer their *cuves* to rise to the risky temperature of 35°C. Robert believes vehemently, that 'you need a good heat to dislodge flesh and matter', adding dismissively, 'those who *cuve* at 30°C have no colour'. In other words, the higher the temperature of the pot, the more you extract.

After reaching the giddy heights of 35°C the *cuves* are allowed to cool to about 30°C for the remainder of their fermentation which is then followed by some 5 days of further maceration. Robert insists that all through this period one must 'crush, crush, crush' to macerate the juice properly with the solids.

When the temperature finally arrives at 20–25°C, they start to decant the wine off the skins. The pulp which remains is then pressed more or less (which means nudged rather than squeezed dry), and the wine extracted amalgamated with the free-run wine. This press-wine is of course harsher and more tannic, but 'one must, it's necessary' says Robert cheerfully.

The knotty problem of new oak gives Robert headaches. He likes it: 'It gives us more tannin, more colour and roundness. We make superb things in these new barrels – but my wife doesn't approve of them very much.' He's clearly up against it: 'We tried some new casks in 1978, but the clients didn't care for it; you see, my wife listens to the 'reflections', she knows; you mustn't overdo things.' At present there seems to be an uneasy truce: for the Clos de Bèze, the Bonnes-Mares and the Amoureuses (which Robert considers, with justification, merits Grand Cru treatment), there is 70% (1993) – 100% (1990) of new Vosges oak, every year; the other wines mature in one-year-old casks. For the small, hail-damaged harvest of 1991 no new wood was used – 'it might accentuate any *goût de grèle*'. Some of the new casks come from Drouhin, in Beaune, to whom the Groffiers sell 20% of each year's crop – 'a few barrels of each *cuvée*'. The Drouhin barrels are distinctively varnished, Robert's are not. 'They look nicer,' says Robert, 'but I don't know why else they do it.' On the origin of the oak, Robert is openly sceptical: 'My tonnelier tells me that it's Vosges, and the bill says it's Vosges, but . . .'

After their *malos* the wines are racked cask-to-cask, although not completely off their fine lees. Then, at any time between the following October and the second year spring – a moment determined by tasting – the wines are again racked, this time clear. They are returned to casks and generally fined with albumin or egg white.

In the month or two following, the wines are racked off their fining, assembled in *cuves*, then bottled. Kieselguhr filtration sometimes replaces fining, if tests show that a wine is unlikely to clarify properly without it. The sumptuous 1993s were neither fined nor filtered. Bottling thus takes place 12–18 months after the harvest – the wines in new wood, unusually, being bottled earliest as Robert and Serge believe that new casks, being more porous, contain significantly more oxygen which develops the wine faster.

The Groffiers have their own bottling machine. 'Assisted' by Robert's grandson, who sits contentedly with his feet in a pallet full of new bottles, enveloped in shrink-wrap, sticking four little fingers in the tops of four bottles before handing them over to be filled, the line whirrs into action. Occasionally it breaks down, issuing a small fountain of precious, elegant Amoureuses all over itself and the concrete floor. 'On a quelquefois des petits problèmes,' muses Robert, phlegmatically. Mercifully, Mme G. sees nothing, as she hurries off across the courtyard to dispense a bit more 'front-of-house'.

Robert is in no doubt of the style of wine he is aiming at: 'a good structure, powerful, with plenty of colour and tannin, for long keeping . . . real Burgundy'. Of these desirable qualities, he particularly stresses colour; looking at his wines in the glass, one is left in no doubt that they are meant to last – high colours, deep and vivid in youth, but holding their hue well in bottle.

The Amoureuses, direct from the flooded bottling line, is already delicious – full of supple, ripe, succulent fruit, with impressive finesse and well-rounded and harmonious tannins. It would be sheer infanticide, though, to broach it yet. This vineyard and Robert's skill produces wine with plenty of power, considerable length and a firm underlying structure to sustain it.

The Bonnes-Mares is generally deeper and richer still. The 1993 showed a fine nose of super-ripe fruit and a real *fond* of flavour sustained by a touch of oak and good acidity – more masculinity and burly muscle at the outset, but with an extraordinary depth of fruit and *charpente* to ensure years of life.

Robert Groffier preparing for an assault on Mme G's vinous bottom drawer

The Clos de Bèze is deeper still, richer and profound on the nose and palate. The 1993 is five-star quality – long, very fine and even more complex than the Bonnes-Mares.

A maze of cellars underneath the house leads eventually into a large open room, fitted out with leather-padded mushroom seats around a few small tables. The walls are covered in bins full of older vintages – some 1972 Bonnes-Mares here, a pile of 1978 Charmes there. 'My wife insists that I keep some bottles back every year,' explains Robert, gesticulating at the walls. 'I would have sold everything, but she makes me do it. I'm not meant to open them, they're hers.'

A bottle is fetched from somewhere else to assist in the contemplation of Mme Groffier's vinous bottom-drawer – a Bonnes-Mares 1986. The wine is just as Robert would have his Burgundy – deeply coloured, very little sign of any age, with a seductively complex mixture of *sous-bois*, game and cinnamon aromas beginning to poke their collective heads above their rather tannic parapet. On the palate: lovely old-style Burgundy, ripe, long and mouthfilling with a magnificent balance. A really excellent bottle, which gives the lie to much of the adverse publicity surrounding the vintage – as do so many of the wines from these great growers.

Robert Groffier's sole aim is to give pleasure through his wines: 'People must taste good wines.' He's doing his best to ensure that they do.

VINEYARD HOLDINGS

Commune	Level	Lieu-dit/Climat	Area	Vine Age	Status
Gevrey	GC	Chambertin Clos de Bèze	0.42	45	P
Gevrey	V	Les Seuvrées	0.95	10 and 55	P
Chambolle	GC	Bonnes-Mares	0.98	35	P
Chambolle	PC	Les Amoureuses	1.15	35	P
Chambolle	PC	Les Hauts Doix	1.00	30	P
Chambolle	PC	Les Sentiers	1.07	40	P
Chambolle	R	(Bourgogne Rouge)	1.50	20–35	P
		Total:	**7.07 ha**		

Domaine des Lambrays
(DOMAINE SAIER)

MOREY-ST.-DENIS

This estate's chequered recent history made its inclusion here marginal. The *terroir* of Clos des Lambrays has been proven exceptional, but for many years seems to have been jinxed into producing wine which, although often fine, lacked the frisson one expects from a Côte de Nuits Grand Cru. Having to search for the class, for the depth and breed, is the antithesis of the spirit of Grand Cru.

The Clos is documented as existing in 1365 and as belonging to the Abbé at Cîteaux, a substantial local landowner. Its recorded history thus post-dates that of its neighbour the Clos de Tart, by some two centuries. It passed the Middle Ages, the Renaissance and le Grand Siècle without major incident; it took the great Revolution of 1789 to shatter its calm. Its precious 8.84 hectares were subdivided among 74 different owners, an arrangement which continued until 1836 when they were all somehow bought out – a major achievement, given French peasant farmers' capacity for obstinacy – and the Clos reverted to a single piece, owned by a single family – the Jolys, négociants of Nuits-St.-Georges.

The modern chronicle of this Domaine follows the history of several notable families who followed Joly. In 1865 it was bought by M. Albert Rodier, a 'sub-inspector of Domaines' from Dijon. In 1938 the Clos des Lambrays again changed hands, coming into the possession of the Cosson family. M. Cosson was a Parisian banker, and his wife a sculptress who had managed both to win the Prix de Rome, and to have a lengthy affair with Camille Rodier – Albert's grandson.

Sadly, the Cossons did not look after their great Domaine; the latter part of their 42-year custodianship saw it crumble, bit by bit, into disrepair. The vines were neglected and vinification became haphazard and sloppy – at one time much of the wine spent 6 years in cask before they got round to bottling it.

In 1979 the wheel turned once again, with the acquisition of the Domaine by the wealthy Algerian Saier brothers – Fabien and Lucien, together with a M. Rolland Pelletier. In addition to the Clos, they have a large wine estate (Domaine des Quatre Vents) in Algeria, and important land holdings in Mercurey, as well as about 4 ha of vineyards in Aloxe, Puligny and Morey.

The Saiers expended considerable effort and resources in reconstructing the Domaine's buildings and installations, as well as putting the vineyard back into good order. Those who criticised the wines have all too often relied on a supposed complete replanting as a convenient scapegoat. This belief is mistaken. In fact, whilst the vineyards were generally tidied up and dead or hopelessly old vines individually replaced, replanting only accounted for 2.44 hectares – less than ⅓ of the total surface. The majority of the old vines were left intact, and it was only the northernmost part of the vineyard – that abutting the Clos St.-Denis – which, in 1981, was grubbed up and replaced.

Two further matters of fact are worth noting: firstly, the Clos is not a *Monopole* – there are 3 other owners of small parcels, 2 of whom have courtyards or gardens which are classified but not planted, whilst the other, Jean Taupenot, has only 430 sq m at the bottom of the slope next to his house.

Secondly, when the Saiers bought the Domaine, the Clos was only classified as Premier Cru. In 1981, it was upgraded to Grand Cru. It may seem extraordinary that after a period of appalling neglect, with the vineyard in a dishevelled state, the authorities should have agreed to an upward revision. However, it must be remembered that what is classified in Burgundy is neither the wine, nor the vines, but the quality potential of each plot of land. The fine bottles of the earlier Cosson period and the considerable reputation built up during the Rodier era was clearly enough to convince the inspectors. If the vineyard had been planted to carrots it probably would have received the same treatment – such is the way of appellations in the Côte d'Or! It might have been more prudent to have granted a 20-year probation – presenting the Saiers with a bill rather than a receipt.

Realising that vineyards are useless without skilled personnel, the Saier's engaged a distinguished young oenological graduate from Dijon, Thierry Brouin, to run the Domaine and its sister establishment in Mercurey. They were determined to use their substantial resources (gained largely from the grocery business) to restore the Clos, and its reputation, to its former level.

Thierry Brouin is something of a poacher turned gamekeeper, since he was for a time employed by the 'repression des fraudes', searching out those whose vinification practices were not always what they should be.

The Domaine from the Clos des Ormes

After 15 years at the Domaine, he has had ample opportunity to show what he, and his vineyard, are capable of. What are the results?

The practices which Brouin has introduced, both for vineyard management and in the cellars, include nothing that is not found in other top Domaines. He is aware of the risks of over-fertilising, and in the profligate use of chemicals on the vines. Treatments are kept to a safe minimum with an emphasis on organic products and on working the soil in preference to using herbicides. Yields are deliberately low – from 27 hl/ha in 1991 to a relatively abundant 39 hl/ha in 1992 – and maintained at these levels with the use of low-vigour clones and rootstock, strict *évasivage* and a green-pruning whenever necessary, especially in the younger vines. In addition, a sorting table enables the removal of any rotten or unripe grapes as the small harvesting boxes are emptied.

Once sorted, the grapes are partially destalked before being lightly crushed, sulphured and vatted. Thierry has definite ideas about grape stalks. They have, he says, many advantages: they help keep fermentation temperature down and aerate the *must*; they promote a gentle lowering of temperature at the end of fermentation, and a slow, even, rise in temperature during its active phase; they provide a natural juice duct so that the juice runs freely off the skins when the time comes and they help promote an even pressing of the pulp which remains. Moreover, wines from non-destalked grapes are less sensitive to oxidation. However, he admits that stalks have compensatory disadvantages: they provide generally poor quality tannins and moreover absorb colour which would otherwise find its way into the wine. All in all this seems a perfectly fair rationale for a policy of variable destemming – 20–100%.

There is nothing curious or iconoclastic about the vinification either: fermentation at 30–32°C in one of an impressive battery of stainless-steel *cuves*, about 21 days of *cuvaison*, 5 being spent in pre-fermentive *maceration,* 5 or more in fermentation itself and the rest in post-fermentive *maceration* with the *cuve* covered. A *saignée de cuve,* to increase juice:skins ratio is practised in dilute vintages, as it should be at all conscientious Domaines. The press wine is extracted gently with a Bucher press and added more or less, according to the vintage, at the moment the free-run wine is decanted. Only natural yeasts are used for fermentation and *chaptalisation* performed in several stages to prolong fermentation and to maximise extraction.

Maturation is entirely traditional: the Clos des Lambrays goes into 50% new Nevers oak plus about 5% Vosges – after trials with the 1986 and 1987 vintages proved the suitability of this wood. Thierry Brouin looks for an

early end to the malolactic fermentations 'so that I can bottle the previous year's crop'. Thus, in February or so, the young wine is racked off its fine lees into another cask and then left for a further year. It is never fined nor is it filtered, unless the lees are fat and unhealthy in which case Kieselguhr is used. This is helped by the use of pectolytic enzymes, added during fermentation to help remove excess proteins, which otherwise would need to be fined out.

This is then, careful, no-expense-spared, traditional winemaking – nothing fancy, except the plethora of stainless steel and perhaps the somewhat luxuriously spaced-out and back-lit casks. Trials with a rotating fermenting tank have not proved successful, so this will certainly not be used for the Grand Vin. Thierry Brouin may lament the lack of space for his machines and tanks but he is unquestionably better off than most vignerons who often have plenty of space but lack the machinery their dreams would buy to fill it.

The wines themselves are invariably correct – with the prominent exception of a disgraceful 1983 – with good colour and a firm structure of acidity and tannins; but is the Clos des Lambrays itself of sufficient depth and complexity to justify Grand Cru status?

Through the late 1980s the answer had to be in the balance. The problem seemed to lie in the depth of fruit; the concentration just wasn't there – the flavours simply tailed off leaving the impression that a pretty girl has undressed and then mysteriously vanished.

The 1987 was all in finesse – a gentle, soft wine from a small harvest of healthy grapes. However, an element of dilution beneath the ripe, succulent fruit, leaves a note of doubt about its future. The 1988 is altogether better: ripe, quite sweet fruit, good acidity and tannins and fair length. Whether, with evolution, the tannins will come to dominate the somewhat delicate and ephemeral fruit is a question only time can answer.

In 1989 perfectly ripened grapes produced a deep hued Clos des Lambrays with plenty of round tannins and adequate acidity. However underneath, the wine lacks concentration. There is enough fruit for balance, but not the depth and complexity for Grand Cru.

Thierry Brouin

Indicating the symptoms of the Domaine's problems does not suggest an obvious solution. Care, cash and expertise are not in question, nor is the will to produce top-class wine. There is equally little doubt that the Clos is capable of producing Grand Cru quality – although there are (unsubstantiated) suggestions that it comprises two distinct veins of soil: one, the strip adjoining the Clos de Tart, being superb and the other, northerly sector, less propitious. In addition, yields are entirely compatible with top quality. It may be that too rapid a replanting programme – even though it covered less than a third of the Clos, has also contributed to poor concentrations. All this would be easily resolved by separate vinification of different plots and a more rigorous cask selection for the Grand Vin. Although the 1990s appear to have brought improvement – the 1993 in particular has all the richness, depth and character expected of a Morey Grand Cru – the verdict remains open.

In 1994, circumstances gave a further twist to the story as difficulties with their grocery business forced the Saiers to put the estate up for sale. By late 1995, no serious suitors had materialised and a Dutch auction appeared to be in progress with the price in steady decline. Meanwhile Thierry Brouin soldiers manfully on. Let's hope that a White Knight appears before everyone loses enthusiasm for this potentially fine Domaine.

VINEYARD HOLDINGS					
Commune	*Level*	*Lieu-dit/Climat*	*Area*	*Vine Age*	*Status*
Morey	GC	Clos des Lambrays	8.70	45	P
Morey	PC	Le Village/La Riotte	0.34	50	P
Morey	V	La Bidaude	0.90	12	P
Aloxe	GC	Corton, Clos des Maréchaudes	0.50	50	P
Aloxe	PC	Corton, Clos des Maréchaudes	1.50	¾:55	
				¼ 1986	P
Aloxe	V	Les Citernes	0.50	40+	P
Puligny	PC	Les Caillerets	0.34	1947–8	P
Puligny	PC	Les Folatières	0.30	20	P
		Total:	**13.08 ha**		

Domaine Ponsot

MOREY-ST.-DENIS

This estate has shown itself capable of producing some of Burgundy's finest wine. After an uneven patch in the mid-1980s, for which it was justly criticised, it is now back on form, in the conscientious hands of Laurent Ponsot – an affable man in his forties. An outwardly serious mien hides a strong *joie de vivre*, reinforced by serious injuries from a car accident in 1986, from which he has almost fully recovered. He has since taken up flying as has his son, who obtained his pilot's licence on his fifteenth birthday. The titular head of the house, Laurent's father, Jean-Marie, from whom he took over in 1983, is a bluff, gruff man of didactic manner and rigid views. As long-time Mayor of Morey, he is also a minor politician, much 'pris à la Mairie', a dull yellow corner building opposite the village well.

The Domaine was established by William Ponsot in 1772 after the Prussian war. However, it was not until the late 19th century that it began to take its present shape with Jean-Marie's great uncle who had the indubitable blessing of 3 ha of vineyards but no children. When his nephew, Jean-Marie's father, took over in 1922, the inheritance had dwindled to a solitary hectare.

Land purchases meant that by the time Jean-Marie started working in 1949, there were 6 ha. Taking sole charge in 1957, he added a further 2.6 ha of share-cropped vineyards in Morey, Gevrey and Chambolle, mainly from the Domaine de Chezeaux owned by a banker, M. Mercier. The usual *metayage* arrangement for Grands Crus divides the fruit equally between proprietor and *metayeur*. The Ponsots negotiated one-third for the Merciers, which is paid in bottled wine (apart from the Griotte-Chambertin which is taken in cask).

The Domaine's vineyards include a fine selection of Grands Crus in Gevrey and Morey. Their most important parcel is 3.15 ha of 55-year-old vines in Morey's Clos de la Roche, from which a Cuvée Vieilles Vignes is produced. For two years – 1988 and 1989 only – there was a special Clos de la Roche Cuvée William, from a parcel of very old vines. Sadly, problems with high demand and insufficient supply put an end to that, so now there is just a standard Vieilles Vignes *cuvée*. Young vines (under 18) from this vineyard together with Pinot from adjoining Monts Luisants contribute to a Morey-St.-Denis Premier Cru, Cuvée des Alouettes. The Gevrey and Morey Village wines are sold as Cuvée l'Abeille and Cuvée des Grives respectively.

Jean-Marie Ponsot – preparing to inflate something

The Ponsots were among the first in Burgundy to recognise the value of, and to use, clones. In addition, their vineyards have provided the mother vines for most of today's finest Pinot Noir clones.

To develop a single clone takes years of propagating, selecting and virus-indexing each batch of plant material. The original Ponsot *sélection massale* aimed to have nothing more than clean, healthy plants, which is still the most important factor in the selection of plant material. Their part in the development of clones is something of which the Ponsot family can justifiably be proud.

Herbicides, and then only biodegradables, are used as little as possible to avoid infecting the soil and developing resistance. In general, they resist the blandishments of product salesmen, and continue to what has worked perfectly well for several decades. Jean-Marie Ponsot is distinctly cynical about the new breed of people who appear to have just discovered ecology: 'The true ecologists are people of the soil, like me, who have never abused the equilibriums of nature, not the people who ring me up at the Mairie and ask to plant trees in the commune.'

The Ponsot hand-picked, rot-excised grapes are passed through a Demoisy crusher-stemmer. This marvel of modernity also removes any berries affected by rot – but only dry rot. Jean-Marie Ponsot admits to trying what he colourfully describes as 'all sorts of fantasies', including everything from 0–100% destemming. He concluded that stems bring nothing to quality and that

'whole bunches will help bring down the temperature of fermentation and provide a reserve of yeasts which are liberated at a late stage in fermentation', thus prolonging it. So, Ponsot grapes are now destemmed 'for the most part', although a small proportion of stems may be left if deemed fit.

Fermentation is carried out in a battery of old wooden *foudres,* housed in a new *cuverie,* built next to Jean-Marie's residence overlooking the village, in 1989. Vatting lasts 8–20 days with three daily *pigéages à pied*. 'More than Papa,' Laurent admits, adding, 'I am more a purist than him.' So fermentation proceeds with natural yeasts and there is no interference to delay its onset and thus no deliberate pre-fermentive maceration. Temperatures are allowed to rise to 35–36°C and *chaptalisation*, when necessary – it wasn't apparently in 1988/89/90 or 91 – is performed, unusually, in the middle of fermentation, rather than towards the end.

The Ponsot press, used for both red and white grapes, is a marvellous 1945 model, of the vertical screw design. It sits, majestically, on a contemporary trolley, ready to be trundled round to where it is needed next. A system of cogs and wheels, powered by a small motor, turns the screw to drive the press and incorporates an early servo cut-off mechanism, triggered when the pressure becomes excessive. At the end of each vintage, this picturesque antique is left to dry naturally to prevent the wood splitting.

After a short period of *débourbage* to settle out the gross lees, the wines are put into old casks – 'up to 30 years old; if they're sound, we use them'. Laurent follows his father in evincing a strong dislike of new wood. 'It's fine at the start, for those who like their wine young, but why ****** yourself to get fine new oak, if in the end, the differences are obliterated anyway?' New wood also speeds up a wine's evolution by too strong an exchange of air (oxygen); in an old cask a wine develops more slowly and finely. 'It's like love,' Laurent philosophises, 'the most durable relationships are those slowest formed.' Indeed, but perhaps tempestuous, torrid affairs are sometimes more exciting.

New wood also distorts aromas and flavours and blurs differences in *terroir* to which true Burgundians, and certainly the Ponsots, attach prime importance. Laurent cites plots of Latricières and Chambertin, separated only by a narrow path. The Latricières went in 1994 (they could not afford to buy both this and the Clos de la

. . . perhaps Laurent's anti-hail rocket

Premier Cru, with pronounced silkiness, ripe, succulent fruit and splendid length.

The Chapelle-Chambertin – until 1989 this fruit was sold off through lack of cellar space to keep the wine – exudes essence of Pinot with its pronounced crushed summer-fruit nose and concentrated elegance. A fine balance of fruit, alcohol, acid and tannins give it a feel of real class. In contrast, this penultimate vintage of Latricières was relatively closed-in; the fruit and finesse are there, waiting only for time to unlock them.

The Griotte-Chambertin is distinctly more structured and powerful with yet more complexity and finesse than either Chapelle or Latricières. In this small, rare, Grand Cru, the *terroir* seems to amalgamate the contrasting qualities of suppleness and firmness; the 1993 is almost drinkable from the cask but, given time, will develop into something infinitely finer. As expected, the Chambertin has more power and underlying muscle than the other Gevrey Grands Crus – except the Griotte which goes a distinct step further.

The Clos de la Roche Vieilles Vignes is equally fine, with an opaque-centred limpid colour and a tight, but very promising, nose. The 1993 – the product of 18 hl/ha (against a permitted 35 hl/ha) – is deceptively easy to drink; the concentration is there, but so good is the balance that the acidity and tannins seem almost hidden by its rich, chocolatey silkiness. By no means an overpowering wine, its qualities are all in finesse with an underlying reserve of power and sinew which ensure it a relatively long life.

The Clos St.-Denis Vieilles Vignes shares many of the qualities of the Clos de la Roche – above all its finesse, concentration, structure and exemplary length. Laurent Ponsot's 1993s exude class and distinction – wines of marvellous depth and poise, with no hint of a shadow over their future.

In the ungenerous 1994 Laurent declassified his Grands Crus (all but the *Griotte*) to Premier Cru and some Premiers Crus to village "to respect the Appellations" – a courageous and laudable decision.

Things are well and truly back on track chez Ponsot. Once more a five-star Domaine.

Roche on offer), but Jean-Marie vinified both for years and they were consistently 'completely different. We have the most original subsoil in the world and must respect this.'

Laurent dislikes fining, filtration and sulphur with equal vehemence. Since 1985, his wines have generally been subject to none of them, and since 1988 sulphur has been limited to what is absorbed from burning sulphur candles in the casks to disinfect them.

The reds are racked twice: once, with aeration, up to 6 months after *malo,* and again when the different casks of each *cuvée* are blended together to harmonise the wine.

In addition to excellent reds, the Domaine also makes a rare and delicious Morey Blanc from the Monts-Luisants vineyard. Although widely believed to be Chardonnay, this in fact consists of 60% Aligoté – from vines planted in 1911 just below the miniature Château at the top of the vineyard – plus 25% Chardonnay and 15% of 'Pinot blanc vrai' sourced originally from Gouges in Nuits-St.-Georges. Ponsot's Monts-Luisants has a further peculiarity, being one of only two white Premiers Crus in the Côte de Nuits (the other is Clos l'Arlot) and the only Premier Cru of which Aligoté is a legal component.

The wine is made without *malo,* to retain acidity, and put into cask in the spring following the vintage, where it remains for 18 months before bottling unfined and lightly filtered. It is generally deep green-gold in colour, with characteristic aromas of quince and acacia, and a broad, almost mineral flavour; altogether opulent, powerful and unusual. By chance, Laurent recently found William's original 1772 purchase deed for the

'Clos Monts-Luisants' so, from the successful 1992 vintage, this wine is now so labelled.

Ponsot's reds are among the Côte's finest. Their style emphasises finesse with structures derived from old vine fruit and a dimension of opulence. The Clos de la Roche Vieilles Vignes is usually best of the bunch with a marvellous depth and Grand Cru length and persistence. In 1993 it was outshone by an extraordinary Clos St.-Denis Vieilles Vignes – little more than a single cask – from 75-year-old vines yielding just 8 hl/ha.

The 1993s showed a variety of profiles, all with ripe, round tannins, good acidity and seductive velvety fruit, well exemplifying the general characteristics of each *climat.* The two Village wines have good, limpid hues, the Gevrey being marginally firmer and more muscular than the Morey, and show the concentration of low yields and the purity of fruit from scrupulous grape sorting. The Morey Premier Cru Cuvée des Alouettes is altogether richer than its Village sibling, although this 1993 had a slight hollowness which time should fill. The Chambolle Charmes is a fine example of this top

VINEYARD HOLDINGS

Commune	Level	Lieu-dit/Climat	Area	Vine Age	Status
Gevrey	GC	Griotte-Chambertin	0.89	1947/1982	M
Gevrey	GC	Chambertin	0.14	1961	M
Gevrey	GC	Chapelle-Chambertin	0.47	1955/72/87	P
Gevrey	V	(Single plot of vines)	0.51	1960	P
Morey	GC	Clos de la Roche	3.15	55	P
Morey	GC	Clos St.-Denis	0.38	75	P
Morey	PC	Monts-Luisants	0.68	40	P
Morey	V	(Several plots)	0.62	1966/69	P
Morey	PC	Clos des Monts-Luisants (Blanc)	1.33	1911 -1980	P
Chambolle	PC	Les Charmes	0.58	35	M
Total:			**8.75 ha**		

Le Clos de Tart

MOREY-ST.-DENIS

This is a rare example of a Côte d'Or Grand Cru which has remained intact since its creation. In the mid 12th century the Benedictine monks of the Abbey of Tart-le-Haut bought the site which was then known as the Climat-des-Forges and in 1184 changed this to Clos de Tart. Since then it has remained undivided, under single ownership, and was classified Grand Cru in 1939. In 1932 it was acquired from descendants of the Marey family – of Marey-Monge lineage – by the Mommessins of Charnay-les-Macon and remains in their ownership.

In addition to the vineyard, the site comprises buildings from the 12th and 15th centuries, including one housing an old wheel-press from 1570, which processed 3 tonnes at a time and was still working in 1924. In 1850 a two-level cellar was constructed on the Domaine's eastern side, the lower of which is 9.5 metres below ground.

From 1969 until his retirement in 1996, charge of the Clos and vinification of its single wine was in the hands of Henri Perraud – a charming and informative man who has lost none of his enthusiasm for what he regards as his personal Grand Cru. Despite considerable changes, including a brief dalliance with Guy Accad for the 1992 and 1993 vintages (largely from marketing motives, it would seem), he still believes in what he terms 'méthodes traditionelles', although these include putting all the stalks into the vats – a thoroughly untraditional proceeding.

Henri is at one with his job. Following winemaking through from the young graft to mature bottle provides him with the utmost satisfaction imaginable and whatever modernists might say about 'tradition' he is content to abide by it and to enjoy its fruits.

His Clos is a superbly sited 7.53 ha plot just above the southern extremity of the village, sandwiched between Bonnes-Mares and the Clos des Lambrays. A peculiarity of the Clos is that it originally contained 27.80 ares of Bonnes-Mares and a 7-are parcel of Village Morey. However these were obligingly reclassified as part of the Clos in 1956.

The oldest part of the vineyard was planted in 1918. Now every 3 years ⅓ ha is grubbed up in a single piece and replanted. Otherwise, vines are replaced individually as they expire. The 'méthodes traditionelles' do not appear to care much for clones. Henri conducted some tests with them on 60 ares (the last two triennial replantings) but is privately content that it requires a decade to assess their effect on his wine – by which time he will have been long retired!

The soil is *argilo-calcaire,* with markedly more *argile* than *calcaire.* Interestingly, the vines are planted transversely, across the fall-line. This helps to contain soil erosion and, more importantly, to maximise insolation – the morning sun reaching one side of each row and the evening sun the other.

Most of the vineyard work is 'méthode ancienne', with no concessions to modern materials. There is preventive spraying, for *court noué, ver de la grappe,* etc., using the minimum practicable dosage. The soil is ploughed regularly, by hand, with a pick and rake, which Henri admitted is 'du travail'.

Each spring, the vines are pruned and trained *Guyot simple*. Even the oldest plants are somehow coaxed into this form, although it takes skill and care to bend the fruiting cane of a tall 60-year-old without damaging it. Henri did point to a vine or two which they had allowed to grow straight and then tied up with straw. The most determined traditionalist can't force a frail old lady to bend over backwards – even to please Mommessin! Severe selection at harvest ensures that only healthy bunches reach the *cuverie.*

Fermentation in ancient cement *cuves* lasts about 15 days, including 9 days of *maceration* after the active phase. The temperature is not allowed to exceed 33°C – 'The yeasts stop working at about 35 and then you have problems with *volatile* (acidity) and restarting it!' Henri puts some grapes from the 2 ha of younger vines into each *cuve* for balance – a sort of pre-*assemblage*. With its press-wine blended, the wine is put into 100% new oak – 80% Allier and 20% Tronçais – and taken down to the first level cellar.

All the subsequent cellar operations are carried out without pumping. This includes the first racking – after the *malo* – and the second in June/July following the vintage. The casks are fined with egg-white after a final assemblage then returned to the lower cellar for bottling – cask by cask.

Henri's wine – Mommessin would be deluding themselves if they regarded it as theirs – has received mixed reviews. It has been deemed pleasant and correct, but not the stuff of Grand Cru. Clos de Tart is certainly not a blockbuster; it is not designed to be. Neither the *terroir* of Morey nor Henri Perraud is capable of producing wines of this kind. Their style is demonstrably 'en finesse'.

The comment that the wines sometimes lack substance is justified. However, this fault is slight when set against their superb complexity and refined elegance. It is surely infinitely preferable to have of delicacy and finesse which could do with a touch more flesh than a clumsy, clod-hopping artisan.

Henri does not go for broke in his vineyard – yields of 30 hl/ha, with another 5 in abundant vintages make over-production not a credible criticism. Any dilution is easily corrected with a short prefermentive *maceration* and a more traditional level of *égrappage*.

Tasting recent vintages, it would seem that any deficiencies are quietly being corrected. The wines are powerful, but still supremely elegant, with no disequilibrium from 100% new wood, or from fermentation with 100% stalks. Aromas of black cherry, griottes, sometimes pepper and often *petits fruits rouges* suffuse the wine, which has characteristic length and an impeccable balance.

Tasting Accad and Perraud versions from 1992 and 1993, the former showed greater elegance, the latter a shade more depth. A 50:50 blend was superior to either.

Much criticism stems from the erroneous expectation that Grand Cru must be big, over-extracted wine. This has never been the style of the Clos de Tart, nor should it be. The wines are consistently fine, though sometimes lacking the substance ideal for balance. They also age well. A 1978 sipped on a warm October morning under the stone wall at the top of the Clos was as opulent and complete a wine as one could wish for: a magnificent spectrum of mature Pinot aromas – *sous-bois*, mushrooms, cinnamon, spice and more, with a mouthfilling presence of considerable complexity and distinction.

The critics, of course, might cavil that 1985–93 have seen some exceptional vintages, and that it needs another 1984 to put the question fully to the test. Henri Perraud can retire confident that in the 1978, 1985, 1988, 1990 and 1993 he has left Mommessin a fine legacy to prove them wrong.

VINEYARD HOLDINGS

Commune	Level	Lieu-dit/Climat	Area	Vine Age	Status
Morey	GC	Clos de Tart	7.53	40	P
		Total:	**7.53 ha**		

Domaine Perrot-Minot

MOREY-ST.-DENIS

In 1973, Armande Merme's Morey Domaine was split in two. Half went to Jean Taupenot's wife Denise (née Merme), half to her sister, the wife of Henri Perrot-Minot who operates from cellars opposite them, just above the Mairie in the Route des Grands Crus.

Henri's core activity was as a négociant and broker, so until his son Christophe joined him in 1990, 50% of his wine was sold in bulk. Now, everything except 15 casks of Passetoutgrain is Domaine bottled.

Christophe, young and articulate, has worked with his father and their oenologist to develop overall policy guidelines. For him, the natural noblesse of Pinot Noir demands strenuous efforts to harvest only healthy fruit and yields which do not exceed 33 hl/ha in Premier Cru and 40-43 hl/ha in Village.

He is clearly 'passioné' and 'sérieux' about his wine, and, if early results are any indication, is making a more than respectable shift of things. A tasting room wallpapered with gold medal certificates suggests that something is going right. As Christophe crystallises his approach: 'With all the competition, you must show the difference either with price or with quality; we go for quality.'

However, bold as may be the aim, achievement is another matter. The main problem seems to be mastering the equilibrium between structure and finesse. It's easy to have one or the other but retaining and balancing both with Pinot Noir is, as Christophe admits, an annual challenge.

His loquacious self-confidence barely conceals a strongly heuristic streak. He is still at the experimental stage – trying out different fermentation temperatures, more or less *maceration* and various sorts of casks and coopers. Security means using a selected Champagne yeast which gives consistently satisfactory results without compromising the typicity of each *terroir*.

With his oenologist, M. Lede, better known in Champagne and Chablis and also used by Olivier Leflaive in Puligny, he discusses the orientation of each vinification and *élévage,* and plans his viticultural regime. New oak is kept to 40% for the Charmes-Chambertin, the Domaine's sole Grand Cru, with less for the Premiers Crus and Village *cuvées.*

Elévage lasts 13–15 months. Christophe tried bottling unfiltered which increased ampleur, but at the expense of adding a touch of rusticity. Now the wines are Kieselguhr and cartridge filtered, but not fined before bottling by a local bottler. Natural clarification is greatly helped by throwing open the cellar doors when the temperature is 1–2°C – hardly 'high-tech', but highly effective.

The range extends across the adjacent communes of Gevrey, Morey and Chambolle. The style tends to emphasise finesse, possibly at the expense of structure. Bottling after only 13-15 months certainly gives an element of freshness and finesse, but sometimes leaves tannins which are rather dry and unrefined.

This is not to say that the wines are indifferent. Far from it, they generally have fine aromas, excellent concentration, good length and Christophe's feel for balance.

The pick of the cellar is the Charmes-Chambertin – a fullish, fat, long wine in good vintages, with a firm backbone often lacking in Charmes. It is run a close second by a very fine Chambolle-Musigny Premier Cru Combe d'Orveau, which exudes essence of pure Pinot in vintages of the quality of 1993. The Perrot-Minot's also have 60-year-old vines in the Village-designated section of this vineyard, from which they make a splendid, deep, old-viney Chambolle-Musigny.

The Gevrey *cuvée* presents Christophe with the constant challenge of extracting finesse into a naturally rather massive, burly wine. The tannins here are sometimes slightly aggressive, needing longer than the Chambolles to meld with the fruit.

Of the two Moreys, the En la Rue de Vergy, (in the split, the Taupenots got the Belair, the Perrot-Minots this) from the top of the vignoble is more in finesse than size – well-balanced, *framboisé* with a good base of succulent fruit in 1993. In contrast, the Premier Cru, La Riotte tends to be fuller and fleshier, with the greater depth and complexity one expects from the superior classification.

Christophe, in common with many other rejuvenated family estates in the Côte de Nuits, is making fine wine and shows every sign of turning a merely very good Domaine into a truly great one.

Christophe Perrot-Minot

VINEYARD HOLDINGS

Commune	Level	Lieu-dit/Climat	Area	Vine Age	Status
Gevrey	GC	Charmes-Chambertin	1.20	25	P
Gevrey	GC	Mazoyères-Chambertin	0.40	40	P
Gevrey	V	———	1.50	20	P
Morey	PC	La Riotte	0.58	30	P
Morey	V	En la Rue de Vergy	1.50	22	P
Chambolle	PC	La Combe d'Orvaux	0.60	80	P
Chambolle	V	———	0.60	50	P
———	R	(Bourgogne Rouge)	0.35	25	P
———	R	(Bourgogne Passetoutgrain)	2.00	35	P
———	R	(Bourgogne Aligoté)	0.40	11	P
Total:			**9.13 ha**		

CHAMBOLLE-MUSIGNY

Chambolle-Musigny is one of the most delightful and unspoilt villages of the entire Côte. Driving south along the RN74, just before the road bends east to by-pass Vougeot, a great sign proclaiming 'Chambolle-Musigny . . . Son site . . . Ses vins', attracts the visitor's eye to the right. There, in the mid distance, with its ecclesiastical head just above its parochial vines, is Chambolle-Musigny, a gently elevated village with its medieval bell tower clearly visible against the backdrop of the limestone escarpments of the Combe d'Ambin.

The settlement is of no great antiquity, compared with others along the Côte. It appears in records as Cambolla in 1110, when the monks of Cîteaux took up residence. By 1302 the name had changed to Chambolle – thought to be a corruption of 'champ boullant', meaning a 'boiling field', a reference to the frequent storms which caused the little river Grone to overflow into the fields (most recently in 1965).

Thereafter, until 1500 when permission was granted to build a Church, the hamlet was in the fief of nearby Gilly-les-Cîteaux. In 1878 it annexed the name of its most illustrious vineyard – Le Musigny – and became Chambolle-Musigny, and in 1960 decided to widen its horizons further by twinning itself with Sonoma, near San Francisco, USA.

It is often said that the wines of Chambolle epitomise the finesse of which Burgundy is capable. Gaston Roupnel wrote of 'silk and lace' and of 'supreme delicacy', and others have emphasised the stylistic differences between it and its neighbours – Vougeot to the south and Morey-St.-Denis to the north.

Although such generalisations inevitably mask a diversity of styles, there is geological support for the view that the wines of Chambolle emphasise finesse at the expense of weight or muscle. Erosion of the limestone escarpments of the Combe d'Ambin has deposited a layer of fine, gravelly scree on to the land, as far down as the régionale vineyard sites on the opposite side of the RN74. This, combined with substantial topsoil erosion in the more sloping Grands and Premiers Crus, has left a meagre base for viticulture. With the exception of the northerly section of Bonnes-Mares towards Morey, there is little clay to be found in these soils.

This limestone-dominated geology is completely different from that of Morey and Gevrey. This endows Chambolle's wines with high initial acidity and a dimension of elegance which particularly expresses itself in aromatic purity and finesse, without the breadth and power of its neighbours. Fine young Chambolle often smells of crushed strawberries – sometimes almost essential.

Chambolle has some 180 ha of vines of which Village land accounts for half. The 22 Premiers Crus cover 60.78.20 ha, and two Grands Crus, Bonnes-Mares, towards Morey, and Musigny, towards Vougeot, occupy a further 24.24.40 ha.

In quality potential, the Premiers Crus are a mixed bag. Les Amoureuses, which is very similar in soil to Musigny, is the finest and most prestigious and moreover, the most plausible candidate for elevation to Grand Cru, in the unlikely event of a reclassification. Les Charmes is also excellent, followed closely by Les Beaux-Bruns, Les Cras and Les Fuées. Whilst Les Charmes and Les Amoureuses are close in style to Musigny, Les Cras and Les Fuées more resemble Bonnes-Mares, of which they form an extension.

Many of the smaller, lesser known Premiers Crus are sold simply as Chambolle-Musigny Premier Cru, an *assemblage* of more than one named vineyard. These wines, whilst often fine, rarely reach the heights of an Amoureuses or a Charmes.

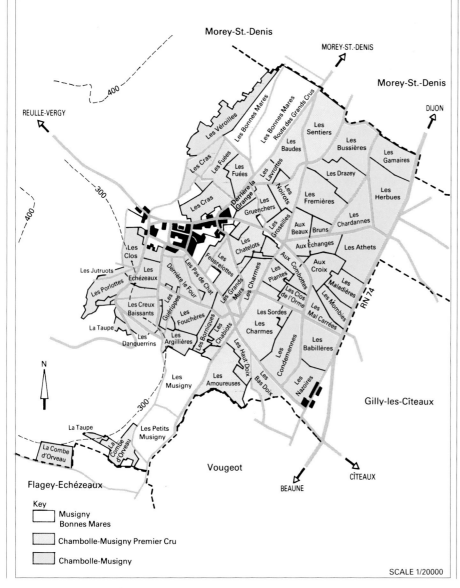

Key
Musigny
Bonnes Mares
Chambolle-Musigny Premier Cru
Chambolle-Musigny

SCALE 1/20000

The two Grands Crus mark the commune's northerly and southerly boundaries. Bonnes-Mares, which abuts Morey's Clos de Tart and which is putatively named after the sisters, Les Bonnes Mères, of the Abbey of Tart-le-Haut, is composed of a mixture of soils. There is a gradation from the relatively clay-limestone of Morey, with a deepish topsoil of marl, towards the redder clay and iron-bearing soils of Chambolle, which are generally thinner and finer in texture. So a Bonnes-Mares from the Clair-Däu (Jadot) section, in the commune of Morey, is likely to have more tannin and power, but less 'rondeur' and finesse, than the same wine from the Chambolle end of the vineyard.

Musigny, at the opposite end of the village and at a lower elevation than Bonnes-Mares, is divided into Les (Grands) Musigny and Les Petits Musigny. The first, oriented to the south-east with a 10–14 % slope, is predominantly limestone with a high proportion of pebbles and some ferruginous clay. The second, exposed almost due south, has deeper soil with a higher proportion of clay with surface rock outcrops. Since the Domaine Comte Georges de Vogüé owns 71% of the entire Musigny vineyard, the wine usually represents a blend of both parcels.

Petit Musigny also contains 0.5 ha of Chardonnay from which de Vogüé produce 1–2,000 bottles of Musigny Blanc. The wine is *sui generis*, quite heavy and rich, hideously expensive, and ages well.

A fine red Musigny is a magnificent wine, combining seductive power and unrepentant aristocracy with an extraordinary spectrum of aromas – crushed strawberries when young, *sous-bois* and liquorice later on. Fully mature after 10–20 years it is often the quintessence of finesse and from a great vintage, an unforgettable experience.

Apart from the five estates profiled here, a number of other outside growers produce noteworthy Chambolle Grands Crus: Drouhin, Dujac, Robert Groffier and Georges Lignier have Bonnes-Mares and Drouhin; Faiveley, Leroy and Jadot offer Musigny.

Nothing momentous seems to happen in Chambolle, although, in the early 1950s, there was a gripping dispute between the Mugniers and the Grivelets over the right to use the designation 'Château de Chambolle-Musigny' for their wines. Both families live in the village, the Mugniers in the Château, and the Grivelets in another substantial, 18th century building round the corner. It appears that, many years ago, the Mugniers ceded the 'brand' designation 'Château de Chambolle-Musigny' to the Grivelets. Latterly, the Grivelets became unhappy with the Mugniers' continued use of it on their labels, even as their address. The matter rumbled along in the courts, but, according to Henri Cannard, was never finally adjudi-

Jean Moisson's and Chambolle's restored church looking towards distant Morey-St.-Denis

cated having been amicably settled in favour of the Mugniers in 1956.

At any season the village is a place of quiet and serenity. There is no commerce here – apart from a solitary restaurant – and only 49 growers – making it an attractive alternative to the main tourist circuit.

Whether under snow in winter, in the fragrance of a still summer evening, or glowing in the warm russets of an autumn afternoon, it is a delight to wander through Chambolle's little streets redolent of the past, musing perhaps on some of the great wines which have

left here to give pleasure on many a less tranquil shore.

The 'vrai' Château is an attractive mid 19th century building with an imposing carriage-sweep, surrounded by a pleasant, wooded park. A circuit from the Church through the village will take you past its gates, perhaps on the way to lunch at the friendly little Le Chambolle-Musigny, where meat and fish are grilled on a large open fire, and the prices are remarkably reasonable.

GRAND CRUS OF CHAMBOLLE-MUSIGNY:

Lieu-dit	Area	Props.	Av. Prod.
Musigny	10.70.23	17	3000 C/S (red) 160 C/S (white)
Bonnes-Mares	13.54.17+ 1.51.55 (Morey)	35	4500 C/S
Totals:	**25.75.95**	**52**	**7660 c/s**

Domaine Barthod-Noëllat

CHAMBOLLE-MUSIGNY

Whilst a top Burgundy Domaine's popularity fluctuates publicly with the quality of its wines, it is a pleasure to highlight establishments whose steady, fine quality is bringing them into the limelight.

Ghislaine Barthod and her courteous father run one such small estate from a substantial turn of the century building on the edge of Chambolle-Musigny. Although the Domaine has existed from the late 1920s, they only recently acquired these premises, from the Savigny négociants Henri de Villamont, who in turn bought them from Bernard Grivelet's mother. Only in recent years have the Barthods' wines attracted any serious attention.

There are 5.86 hectares in all – worked by Ghislaine and one labourer, plus occasional help from her mother in the vineyards and her father in the cellars.

This is not a Domaine where one should expect to find pioneering theoretical advances – trials with clones, experiments with wood, deep pondering over vine maintenance regimes or biodynamics – but sound, careful winemaking from relatively old, well-tended vines; more perhaps excellent provincial fare rather than studied grande cuisine.

The Barthods tend to harvest early. The distillation of Ghislaine's father's 30 years' experience is that better wines are made from earlier picking, avoiding the considerable risks from waiting too long in Burgundy's capricious autumn. Moreover, they are not in favour of green pruning, preferring to remove any potential excess earlier on in the growing season.

A maximum of one-third of the stalks are left in the vats to help maintain the fermentation temperature at no higher than 32°C, and only natural yeasts are used. Whole bunches are deliberately put into the middle of the mass in each vat to encourage a long, slow extraction of colour, aromas and tannins. Alcoholic fermentation is preceded by 2–5 days of *maceration* – depending on the temperature at which the grapes reach the *cuverie*.

Except for the Bourgognes, the wines see about 25% new wood for about 20 months. Ghislaine complains gently, with a broad affectionate smile, that her father racks sooner than she does, but this apart, she and Monsieur Barthod seem in general agreement as to how their wines should be treated.

Until 1985 they bottled the wines them-

Chambolle's village pump – one way of watering the flowers

selves; now a contract bottler does the job for them. Curiously, some wines are just fined – if the customer wishes it this way; for those that do not, their wines are given a light 'white Kieselguhr' filtration.

Perhaps their past obscurity owes something to their strong home sales base. Of the 100–110 barrels production, the lesser appellations are virtually all sold in France, although there is a growing export following for their excellent Bourgogne Rouge. After 30 years' or more loyal custom, many private clients have become family friends, accounting for a significant proportion of annual sales. Most of the Premiers Crus and Village Chambolle find their way into foreign hands.

The Domaine is clearly in the international ascendant. Ghislaine, a charming girl in her 30s, with 2 years at Beaune's Lycée Viticole behind her, is working hard to consolidate and improve on what has already been established. Her partner, Louis Boillot from Gevrey, helps when he can spare the time

from his own *cuverie*, and will no doubt exercise an increasingly important influence over the Domaine's future since the birth of their son, Clément, in 1995.

The wines are already attracting considerable plaudits. They range from a beautifully balanced Aligoté – well above its class in quality – through a delicious, long, Chambolle Village to a septet of fine Premier Crus: Les Beaux Bruns, part Premier Cru and part Village, which has a base of ripe, concentrated fruit, and an underlying structure more reminiscent of masculine Morey than of feminine Chambolle; Les Cras – an extension of Grand Cru Bonnes Mares towards Chambolle which contrasts yet firmer depth of fruit with the Beaux Bruns; Les Veroilles, only a Premier Cru since 1987, which was largely replanted from scrub land; this has a markedly more *sauvage* character with a deep colour and relatively high tannin and acidity and an attractive amplitude on the palate. Les Fuées, which adjoins Bonnes-Mares at the northern end of the village, was first released in 1992. From 1991, Les Baudes and Les Châtelots were bottled separately, rather than being amalgamated with the Chambolle Village *cuvée*.

The pick of the Barthod cellar is undoubtedly the Premier Cru Les Charmes. Its hallmark is concentration and length, with an attractively promising youthful aromatic complexity which cries out to be kept for several years to show its paces.

This is a very fine stable of conscientious winemaking. One gets the impression of youth and age combining their experience wisely to great effect. This is not a Domaine of theory, but one of practical experience backed by a sound nose for quality. Ghislaine and her parents are people of immense quality and charm and their wines run them a close race in this regard.

VINEYARD HOLDINGS

Commune	Level	Lieu-dit/Climat	Area	Vine Age	Status
Chambolle	PC	Les Charmes	0.25	36	P/M
Chambolle	PC	Les Cras	0.86	34	P/M
Chambolle	PC	Les Beaux-Bruns	0.73	21	P/M
Chambolle	PC	Les Veroilles	0.37	28	P/M
Chambolle	PC	Les Baudes	0.19	24	P/M
Chambolle	PC	Les Châtelots	0.23	16	P/M
Chambolle	PC	Les Fuées	0.24	–	M
Chambolle	V	(Several climats)	1.24	31	P/M
Chambolle / Gilly les Cîteaux	R	(Bourg. Rouge / Aligoté)	1.75	24	P/M
Total:			**5.86 ha**		

Domaine Georges Roumier

CHAMBOLLE-MUSIGNY

The Domaine Georges Roumier is one of the many beneficiaries of a new perception that the reputation of an estate, especially such small enterprises as those of the Côte d'Or, rests largely on its winemaker. Until quite recently, people talked of Domaine X or Y as if they turned out bottles in some mysterious manner which did not involve human intervention. Now, a change of winemaker at an important estate triggers a reassessment of its standing.

This willingness to evaluate each vintage from each property afresh is beneficial for the Domaine as well as for the consumer. It diminishes the ability to rely on past reputation – and equally, gives a Domaine which has been through a rough period, the chance to wipe clean the slate.

Up to 1982 Jean-Marie Roumier had made good, but not headline-making wines. The arrival of his son Christophe, however, soon rocketed the Domaine into the cult league, as people began to realise that this articulate, intelligent young man had exceptional wine-making talent. Subsequent vintages have done nothing to diminish that impression.

Christophe's Domaine consists of 12 ha, the nucleus of which is a dowry of land in Chambolle brought by a local girl to her wedding to his grandfather, Georges, in 1924: Les Amoureuses, Les Fuées and some Bonnes-Mares. A further parcel of Bonnes-Mares – next to the Clair-Däu vines – was added in 1952, together with some Clos de Vougeot, when Georges bought a third share of the Domaine Belorger. In 1953 he acquired the whole of Morey's Clos de la Bussière – now the family home. The final additions were made by Christophe's parents: in 1969 his mother bought 0.2 ha of Corton-Charlemagne, and his father 0.09 ha of Musigny, already *en fermage*, in 1978.

On his retirement in 1961 Georges divided his vines between his 7 children and formed a company to keep the Domaine intact. After his death in 1965, this arrangement continued, with Christophe's father, Jean-Marie, running the Domaine and making the wine.

In the early 1980s Jean-Marie and two of his brothers – Alain (ex-manager of the de Vogüé estate) and Paul – formed a limited company for their own vineyard holdings, which, together with those of the rest of the family, remained rented to the Domaine. The last major change came in 1990, when Christophe bought out his two uncles. Thus he and his father now own the Domaine, although some of its vineyards belong to other members of the family.

Jean-Marie and his charming wife have more or less retired to their attractive house in the Clos de la Bussière, away from the bustle of day-to-day life in Chambolle. Part of the garden is devoted to Mme Roumier's vegetable patch, the source of splendidly flavourful tomatoes, potatoes, cabbages and other leguminous delights.

Christophe, now in his late thirties, is a man of quietly impressive confidence. Trained at Dijon University's Faculty of Oenology, he took full charge of technical matters in 1982. He thinks deeply about everything he does and has made a considerable impact, not only on the Domaine's affairs and standing, but also upon other young winemakers in the Côte, amongst whom he is much respected.

Nothing is systematic, that is to say determined in advance, as each growing season and thus each crop of grapes is different. This may appear trivial, but, in a region where growers are only too ready to tell you that they do X or Y 'tous les ans', it has greater portent than one might imagine.

Vineyard policy is directed to maintaining as diverse and healthy a population of natural yeasts as possible. This means using Bordeaux mixture to protect against *cryptogamic* diseases – *botrytis*, *oidium*, mildew, etc. – rather than strong, synthetic products which would effectively sterilise the soils, destroying valuable yeasts as well as the undesirable *cryptogams*. 'Yeasts are a mushroom – there are lots of different species ; we must respect this.'

'Culture biologique' was used on the entire Domaine in 1992 – and worked well. However, things changed sharply in 1993, with high levels of mildew (especially in Chambolle and Vosne) which forced Christophe to reconsider. His guiding principle, that the vine must be allowed to express itself through the soil, is coupled with a strong desire to 'respect the natural balances'

The family home in the Clos de la Bussière

between and within the plant and its environment. This brings a definite emphasis on organic treatments, with the overriding selection criteria being an amalgam of least residue and longest lasting effect.

Minimum herbicides and maximum hoeing aerates the soil, encouraging the development of micro-flora and cutting lateral roots. This forces the vine to establish a deep rooting system which maximises extraction of the elements which stamp the typicity of each vineyard – differences Christophe strives to protect.

When a patch of vines reaches the age of 50, individual replacement ceases in favour of larger replanting. Christophe aims to mimic the qualities of the traditional *sélection massale* by using the maximum diversity of clones in each vineyard. This is achieved by dividing each parcel to be replanted into seven sub-areas in each of which a clone is planted. Trials with selected clones have proved highly successful. Most of those used – 113/114/115/167/777 and 778 – come from mother vines on the Ponsot estate in Morey and are planted on to classic rootstocks: 161/49 with a touch of SO4 on hillsides with colder micro-climates or high limestone content.

Yields are deliberately small and controlled by a high average vine age, and also by careful *évasivage* and green-pruning. Christophe is contemptuous of those who regularly green prune it reveals that their vines are too productive in the first place. Chez Roumier they never get near to the maximum authorised yields whereas most vignerons complain that these aren't generous enough! The Domaine's 10–year average (1985–94), including *saignée de cuve* , was 29 hl/ha.

Vine foliage is tended with exemplary care. Experiments have convinced Christophe that fruit quality is improved by increasing foliage height and when summer pruning reduces foliage width at the top of the vine. Part of the benefit comes from a reduction in *verjus* – small, unripe bunches near the tip of the vine – which adds to the concentration of the important bunches lower down.

Christophe seeks to adapt the level of stalks to the vintage, the vines and the particular vineyard site. Whilst stalks impart undesirable astringency to a wine, they also play a useful physical role in inhibiting the speed of fermentation, draining the cap which forms at the top of the vat, and helping to protect the *must* against oxidation during the period of pre-fermentive *maceration.*

Destalking used to be a minimum of 20%; now this is a maximum, except for the Musigny and Chambolle Charmes where all the stalks remain (à la Dujac). Christophe's tendency in recent years has been to destem more, although there is no predetermined

level; in 1985 none of the stalks were removed, whilst in 1990 only 30% were left, since there was much *millerandange* at flowering and the stems were much larger. Where whole bunches remain – usually from old vines – they are put into the middle of the *cuve*, promoting a long, intra-cellular fermentation which releases an element of fruitiness and soft tannins into the mix.

This *maceration* lasts for between two and eight days, and extracts 'practically all the colour' into the juice; however this colouring matter consists of unstable anthocyanins which need to be 'fixed' by tannins which are progressively leached out by alcohol during the fermentation. The enzymatic process which mediates this important colour extraction also delivers much of the future aroma compounds into the juice.

During this time, the natural yeast population gradually multiplies generating a slow and spontaneous start to fermentation. Christophe is in no doubt that these days of pre-fermentive *maceration* add significantly to the structure, harmony, richness and aroma of his wines.

Whilst the chemical intricacies of fermentation are not yet fully understood, it is known that a diversity of yeast species seems to provoke a series of separate reactions which are generally believed to impart significantly more complexity to a wine than fermentation with a single species of cultured yeast. For this reason, Christophe never

resorts to cultured yeasts.

In the *cuverie*, his principal thought is to extract the maximum from the grapes: 'You must get everything out into the wine.' Fermentation is thus 'as long and as intense as possible; for me this is fundamental.'

Cuvaison lasts for 17–21 days at as near to 30°C as practicable. Christophe confesses that he would like to reduce fermentation temperatures a degree or two to maximise what he calls the 'discreet aromas' – the indiscreet ones are the more obvious fruit aromas such as those of crushed strawberries – and to keep the fermentation going as long and as slowly as possible. He also admits that 'it's an error on my part if it goes to 32°C; that means I haven't intervened quickly enough.'

Pigéage is also important, occurring twice a day during the active phase and once a day during pre-fermentive *maceration. Remontage* with aeration extracts glycerol and richness into the wine, although it is made without aeration after the active phase is on the wane. When *chaptalisation* is needed it is carried out in at least four stages to further prolong fermentation.

Christophe prefers to extract before and during fermentation for the greatest 'delicatesse et typicité' and believes, conversely, that extracts obtained after fermentation are not by and large of positive benefit to the wine. His aim is therefore to make the *cuvaison* coterminus with fermentation so there is consequently a strong emphasis on pre-

Christophe and Jean-Marie Roumier

fermentive maceration. In 1990 the charts showed one *cuve* which macerated for 8 days before fermentation started – which suggests heavier than normal doses of SO_2 – perhaps he is beginning to 'Accadise' just a little?

The press wine is vinified separately – a rare occurrence in Burgundy, though more common in Bordeaux – because the quality of extract obtained is inferior. Christophe uses it for topping up casks but only as a function of its taste qualities. 'After all,' as he points out, 'it only accounts for 5% of each *cuve,* so that is hardly a great sacrifice.'

Christophe is equally clear about his wood: 'The provenance of the wood is less important than having wood which is dried properly and naturally.' New casks bought by the Domaine each year thus come from a tonnelier who guarantees that his wood – usually Allier – is dried slowly rather than in a kiln. It is also essential that the amount of wood used enhances rather than destroys the typicity of each wine, so a maximum of 30% is new, 'according to the year; never more . . . whatever happens'.

How much new oak any given wine gets is estimated on the principle that the greater its natural grape tannin structure and concentration, the more it can support new wood. 'New wood is the best mask for wine faults; when I taste a wine in a new cask, I want to taste the wine before the cask.' With Chambolle-Musignys, whose hallmark is supreme delicacy, the overriding need is for a discreet touch of oak, rather than a massive wooden pie-crust. There has been reproach for not using more new wood. Christophe, whilst accepting that, for example, his 1991s might have been rounder with a touch more new oak, dismisses the overall thrust of this criticism. He dislikes new wood and is entirely content with results at the present levels.

Racking is left as long as possible after *malo* to extract the maximum from the lees. Tasting determines the precise moment of racking, when wine in a new cask is transferred to an old cask and vice versa by gravity, of course, without contact with the air. Provided they are healthy, some fine lees are left in each cask until the following September when the wine is racked clear.

In preparation for bottling, the wines are egg-white fined. This is intended to stabilise their colour by eliminating any unstable colours rather than fixing those which are already there. A careful fining also eliminates gross lees and 'refines' the wine's aromas.

Filtration is avoided, unless a wine has not clarified sufficiently in cask: none from 1991–3, save for a *cuvée* of Chambolle Villages in 1992. As to the bottling date: 'it's the wine which makes the rules'. The 1989s, for example, were bottled relatively early in 1991, to preserve their fresh, succulent fruit, whereas the 1988s were bottled between

April and June 1990 – nothing is immutable!

Christophe Roumier gives one the impression, with characteristic modesty, that he regards his role as that of an intermediary between *terroir*, nature, the grape and the wine. Along this chain of transformation he is required to intervene from time to time as a sort of vinous midwife, to help extract the pure expression of the soil through the medium of the grape. His philosophy is both articulate and persuasive: 'We don't make Pinot Noir, we make wines from *terroir* which expresses itself through Pinot Noir.'

His own wines are designed – or at least intended – to give prominence to the structure and typicity of each *terroir*, not to emphasise the fruit. Wines which are 'fruité' Christophe regards as 'simple and therefore, not Grand Vin'; the expression of fruit alone is fugitive, impermanent. Some vintages – for example 1987 – are characterised by a dominance of fruit, and are not, to Christophe's way of thinking really the expression of 'terroir véritable', but of the grape variety instead. His overriding aim therefore, is to ensure that his wines are dominated by the *terroir* and not by the grape.

He has travelled and tasted widely outside France and seems genuinely appalled by winemakers, especially in the New World, who seem to regard the vine as of secondary importance to the winemaking process – some sort of utility which is there to produce the grapes they vinify. To make great wine one must go beyond the simple expression of fruit, to the expression of *terroir*. Unfortunately, in the USA and elsewhere, people are not attached to *terroirs*, in the way in which Europeans are – indeed, on the whole, they have yet to find them.

His own wines express his philosophy admirably. Whilst their balance and harmony are impeccably tuned, they differ markedly one from another in underlying character. The Chambolle-Musigny (which contains some Premier Cru fruit) has a gentle softness underneath a plump, yet tight, envelope, attractive young fruit aromas, and a good length. The Clos de la Bussière, however,

shows its predominantly clay soil in a much tighter, firmer profile, with more *charpente* and a notch more vinosity. Both Chambolle Premiers Crus are finely-crafted and elegant wines. Les Cras, definitely the less refined of the pair, although still long, deeply flavoured and gorgeously elegant; whilst Les Amoureuses combines this elegance with a more complex and powerful base. In vintages of the quality of 1990 and 1993 it has a remarkable floral nose, smelling decidedly of violets, sumptuous concentration and the class and power of a Grand Cru (which it would be, were it not for the reluctance of 'les officiels' to embark upon a reclassification). A Roumier Amoureuses is a complete wine, well-nigh impeccably balanced and structured to develop interest in bottle for a considerable number of years.

The Bonnes-Mares comes from two separate plots – half on *terre rouge*, half on whiter soil. The fruit from each is vinified separately then blended later. This soil imparts a solid, firm and more muscular structure – the soil is also deeper here – than the Musigny. This (just two casks) combines great power and attractive old-vineyness, with the exceptional elegance which is the hallmark of this great vineyard. Though very different, both have the Roumier softness and length, and generally make fine bottles for the medium to long term. The Corton-Charlemagne, whilst invariably good, is rarely great, coming from the late-ripening, westerly, Pernand sector of the vineyard.

This then, is a Domaine of great quality, as reliable and authentic in lesser vintages as in greater. Because he is passionate about what he is doing, and firm in his belief that 'the essentials of a good wine are made in the vineyard', as well as being a fine winemaker, Christophe Roumier will continue to succeed. 'Winemaking is not an art, it is a craft – nature is like a dog on a lead, you have to be led around by it. You must let nature make the choices, and occasionally point it in the right direction.' Those high-tech winemakers elsewhere, who believe in total control, would do well to heed his advice.

VINEYARD HOLDINGS

Commune	Level	Lieu-dit/Climat	Area	Vine Age	Status
Chambolle	GC	Bonnes-Mares	1.46	32	F
Chambolle	GC	Musigny	0.10	65	F
Chambolle	PC	Les Amoureuses	0.40	33	F
Chambolle	PC	Les Cras	1.76	40	F
Chambolle	V	Les Veroilles+ Les Pas de Chat+ Les Combottes	3.98	25–30	F
Pernand	GC	Corton-Charlemagne	0.20	1971	F
Morey	PC	Clos de la Bussière	2.59	28	F
Chambolle	R	(Bourgogne Rouge/PTG)	1.27	17	F
Vougeot	GC	Clos Vougeot	0.32	42	F
		Total:	**12.08 ha**		

Domaine Amiot-Servelle

CHAMBOLLE-MUSIGNY

This is another of Burgundy's lack-lustre Domaines transformed by an energetic son-in-law. Christian Amiot, a stocky, bearded man – son of Pierre Amiot of Morey St. Denis – worked with M. Servelle from 1980 until he died in 1989. Since taking over he has added Premiers Crus Les Charmes and the lesser known Derrière la Grange and replanted some Village Chambolle. He is often to be found taking the air outside his Domaine in the Rue des Tilleuls.

A high proportion of old vines keeps yields low and a policy of minimum treatments keeps vine health high. Christian considers that 'le grand-pere's' perception of Chambolle wines as 'very light and elegant' was misconceived, and has instituted improvements to inject more depth and complexity. In particular, *cuvaison* has been lengthened from 8 days to 15 with plenty of *pigeage* and the crop totally destemmed. 'Le grand-père' did not renew his casks, so this had to be dealt with. Now the three Chambolle Premiers Crus and the Clos Vougeot have 30% of new wood, the Chambolle Village 10% until the first racking between April and June, when they return to second year casks. In Christian's view: 'that's enough new oak'.

When he took over, there was nothing in stock – 'mother-in-law had it all' – so he was forced to sell to the negoce to keep the Domaine going. Until 1992, bottling was carried out by a contractor; now it is done with their own, shared, equipment. The eventual aim is to Domaine bottle everything and sell none in bulk.

At present, exports account for most of the sales – the US in particular. French sales are limited to individual customers and a few grand restaurants.

Christian is rather reticent, but thoroughly likeable. He is by no means an iconoclast – athough he has saddled his daughters with the names Prune and Violet – but someone determined to do whatever is necessary to achieve quality. His apparent hesitancy about what he is doing contrasts with the confident quality of his wines.

As President of Chambolle's growers Syndicat, he needs sound diplomatic skills to keep different interests pulling in the same direction. In 1993, he refused the PLC (which increases yields by 10%) because, in his view (rightly) it wasn't merited. It's not easy: 'There's always someone who pleads for an extra ten litres to make up a *cuvée*'.

An attractive, if slightly rustic, Bourgogne Rouge and a sound, somewhat meaty and muscular, Clos Vougeot are the only non-Chambolle wines on offer. The pick of this cellar are undoubtedly the *cuvees* of Derriere la Grange, Charmes and Amoureuses.

The first is a tiny Premier Cru from a well-exposed enclave adjoining Les Fuees, of which this Domaine is one of only two proprietors (the other is Domaine Louis Remy). Its soil is shallow clay-limestone, giving wine which tends to be fuller and sturdier than the other two, with good acidity and plenty of class, but a shade less obvious elegance (very good 1990, 1993 especially, and an entirely respectable 1994).

The Charmes runs true to form – not vastly substantial but vastly elegant. Less intensely coloured than Derrière la Grange, very *flatteur* in character (particularly in 1990 and 1993), with flavours of griotte cherry and red fruits, fine length and good ageing potential.

The Amoureuses – generally reckoned to be the top Chambolle Premier Cru and of Grand Cru potential – combines Derrière la Grange's fat and concentration with Charmes' aromatic complexity and elegance, adding a dash of *puissance* along the way. Christian Amiot's version is excellent, with plenty of depth and succulence, good acidity and enough structure to keep it going until the various components open out. The 1993 will be sublime – the 1994 seems less harmonious.

Christian runs a good ship and knows what fine wine is about. Although not quite at the level of Frédy Mugnier, de Vogue or Christophe Roumier, this is a thoroughly dependable source.

VINEYARD HOLDINGS

Commune	Level	Lieu-dit/Climat	Area	Vine Age	Status
Chambolle	R	Bourgognes Rouge, Aligoté, PTG	1.22	20–40	P
Chambolle	V	(15 parcels)	3.14	25	P
Chambolle	PC	Les Charmes	1.21	30	P
Chambolle	PC	Derrière la Grange	0.35	8–60	P
Chambolle	PC	Les Amoureuses	0.45	55	P
Vougeot	GC	Clos Vougeot	0.41	55	P
Total:			**6.78 ha**		

Domaine Jacques-Frédéric Mugnier

CHAMBOLLE-MUSIGNY

Frédéric (Frédy) Mugnier came late to winemaking. When his father died in 1980 he was pursuing a successful career as an off-shore oil engineer, travelling the world from Africa to Aberdeen in what he confesses was by no means a culture-rich life.

His father, a Parisian banker, being no winemaker himself, left the management of his Domaine in the hands of Bernard Clair (Bruno Clair's father), co-owner and manager of the Domaine Clair-Däu in Marsannay. Between 1978 and 1985 Clair was responsible for the estate and its wines, most of which were sold in cask to négociants.

In 1985 Frédy decided to take a sabbatical from oil and to return to Chambolle-Musigny to see what the family Domaine was all about; he became so attached to the way of life, that 1985 was the last the oil industry saw of him. In order to gain expertise he enrolled at the Lycée Viticole for a 6-month crash course. This both enabled him to take over management of the Domaine and provided a source of many useful contacts throughout the Côte.

Not content to be in charge of one of Burgundy's finest estates, Frédy also wanted passionately to pursue his other interest, flying. Obtaining his commercial pilot's licence in 1988, he now flies Fokkers three days each week for the French airline TAT, spending the rest of his time at Chambolle.

His flying is not entirely self-indulgence; it gives him a measure of financial independence from the Domaine, owned jointly by him and his family, and allows him to take a slightly more risky line with his winemaking. For example, he prefers to harvest late, and to ferment at relatively high temperatures, both of which would entail an unacceptable level of risk for vignerons whose sole source of income was wine. Tangentially, having what he pleasantly refers to as 'pocket money' from the airline, gives him the chance to hold back some of his best bottles to mature at the Château.

This enviable position grew out of a prescient great-great-grandfather, also Frédéric Mugnier, who established himself in the last 30 years of the 19th century as a manufacturer of liqueurs and négociant in Cognac and wine in Dijon. This enterprise financed the purchase of some 9 ha in Chambolle, Clos Vougeot and Nuits St.-Georges, and the magnificent Château de Chambolle-Musigny, bought from the Marey-Monge family in 1889. In 1945 the vineyards were divided between different members of the family, and

rented on a long-term contract to the large house of Faiveley in Nuits.

In 1977 Frédy's father decided to take back the family vineyards into his own management. However, the French laws being designed to protect farmers, great or small, and Guy Faiveley being a skilled lawyer, this was not achieved without difficulty and compromise. The deal that was finally struck ceded the Clos Vougeot land absolutely to Faiveley and the Nuits Premier Cru Clos de la Maréchale to them on a long-term contract until 2003, when it will revert to the Mugnier family. Whether the principles of French law intended such consequences is not clear.

Frédy's own principles are both clear and direct: 'Everything is contained in the grape; what you include and what you exclude is a matter of your own choosing.'

In the years since he took charge, he has come to several important conclusions. Firstly, one must use fertilisers as sparingly as possible. Apart from a small plot of Amoureuses which, curiously for this part of Burgundy, lacked potassium, no fertilisers whatsoever have been used since 1987. Secondly, insecticides are employed to the minimum extent compatible with keeping infestations at bay. Frédy is content to tolerate a mild outbreak of yellow spider, for example, rather than to treat at maximum level to protect his vines from pests. Also, repeated, strong chemical treatments only eradicate pests at the expense of killing the insects which naturally predate on them.

The vines are deliberately pruned to a reasonable length because he believes that the conventional short pruning, to restrict yields is misguided: 'If you prune too short, you augment the vigour of what remains and therefore increase the area of foliage in a smaller space.' He prefers instead to leave a longish *baguette* on each vine and to excise unwanted growth and shoots during a rigorous *évasivage* each May.

He also dislikes green-pruning; this, like *saigner* is 'only a means of dealing with mistakes elsewhere'. Far better to use appropriate clones and well-adapted rootstocks, together with foliage control and severe *triage* to obtain a low yield of maximally concentrated fruit. Rootstocks, clones and no fertilisation are the best control mechanisms, which Frédy uses to the full.

His yields bear out his words, averaging 34 hl/ha over a decade – 1 hl/ha below the *rendement de base* for Grands Crus, and 6

hl/ha below that for Village wines. He believes that, to make real Grand Cru, yields should not exceed 30 hl/ha. There are few Domaines who content themselves with this level of production, even for their Grand Crus.

So severe is Frédy over *triage* that his mother complained that during the 1990 vintage he had as many members of the family as he could muster sitting up until midnight in the *cuverie* sorting grapes before these were allowed anywhere near the *cuves*. 'It took me three weeks to get my hands back to their proper colour,' groaned Mme Mugnier, waving the palms of her elegant hands in the air with a disarming smile.

In the cellar, matters proceed with much equal attention to detail. Stalks, being either good or bad according to their ripeness are added to the pulp, up to a maximum of 40%. 'People who talk about selection are usually concerned with the quality of the grapes and not with the quality of the stalks,' argues Frédy. 'The qualities they bring to the wine depend upon the type selected.' Selection of stalks requires equal care to the selection of

Frédy Mugnier – vigneron and commercial pilot

grapes; some parcels of vines yield riper and better constituted stalks than others.

Pre-fermentive *maceration* lasts for about 4 days: 'If you want to prolong this you have a problem without massive doses of sulphur.' So fermentation starts naturally, with no need of cultured yeasts. Frédy seeks to prolong fermentation but without closed vats – his are splendidly ancient open vats – and an inert gas blanket, there is not much he can do. When the temperature reaches 36–37°C, a system of heat-exchangers in each *cuve* lowers it.

Frequent *pigéage* – as much as 5 times per day – ensures the maximum contact between liquid and solids. *Cuvaison* lasts for 15–17 days before the wine is passed into cask for its *malo*.

The press-wine is vinified separately and blended, or not, with the free-run wine just before bottling. This gives yet another chance to add a further element to the composition of the final wine, which would have been denied to him, had Frédy followed the usual Burgundian policy of assembling both wines before transfer into cask.

One quarter of each harvest goes into new Allier oak, with the Grands Crus having 5% or so more than the rest. The tonnelier, known for a rather heavy toast on their casks, is instructed to give Mugnier's only a light charring. Frédy abhors excessively grilled aromas and rinses each cask with steam and hot water to leach out some of the more aggressive tannins before they impregnate his wine. Dissatisfied with the quality of some of his casks, in 1992 he bought some oak and dried it for 36 months at the Château. The casks were tried out on various *cuvées* of the 1995 vintage.

Casks bring to a wine both extracts from the particular character of the wood used, and also a more-or-less controlled oxidation through air retained in the interstices of the staves. New wood adds depth of colour and richness to wine, in addition to its own aromatic contribution but needs careful usage since it has a tendency to uniformity of flavour, and to dominate a wine. This is undesirable when the aim is to express the typicity of the individual *terroirs* which make Burgundy such an enigmatic place. Wood is a matter of particular concern in Chambolle-Musigny whose wines are, above all, of considerable delicacy, a character easily stifled with too much oak or too clumsy a structure.

Elévage follows no predetermined timetable. There will be a first racking, from cask to cask, in about May, but thereafter tasting determines what happens. If a wine is unduly 'reduced' in aroma and flavour, it is likely to be racked again any time between the following August and November. In general, the wines remain about 18 months in cask before fining with fresh egg-white a

month before bottling. Frédy dislikes filtration, but has found that recent vintages have been too turbid to avoid it, a circumstance he attributes to his deliberately not using pectolytic enzymes to aid clarification – something which he has come to regret. The various casks of each wine are finally unified in a splendid rank of 2,700-litre casks before Domaine bottling.

Frédy Mugnier's wines are characterised by both elegance and power, often represented as hallmarks of Chambolle, but so often lacking. These are not wines which can, despite their distinctive finesse, be hurried; they take time to undress and to show their hidden charms. The Village wine, and indeed the Premiers Crus can start life noticeably ungainly – difficult to taste and unforthcoming, particularly on the nose. However, left alone, they blossom into wines of great delicacy, underpinned by restrained but powerful structures.

The Chambolle Village in fact comes equally from the Premier Cru Les Plantes and from the Village Combe d'Orveau. In volume the younger vines of Les Plantes yield more, so the true mix is nearer 60:40. The result is a quite plush, rich wine, with good *puissance* and length. Not surprisingly, the Les Amoureuses is generally the better of the two Premiers Crus; here a relatively superficial, highish limestone soil gives a wine which starts out with marked acidity and a firm structure, but with ultimately more depth and complexity – more discreet perhaps, but greater length. In contrast, Les Fuées has a higher clay content in the soil, giving a broader more fleshy style of wine – definitely Mahler rather than Wagner. This is not to belittle one at the expense of the other – both are very fine.

Frédy Mugnier admits an admiration for the skills and wines of his neighbour, Christophe Roumier, and there is more than a passing resemblance in style between the two Domaines. Frédy's wines, however, tend to be less approachable to start with than Christophe's but share the same underlying balance, depth of fruit and delicacy. He tends to evaluate his own wines in terms of their structure rather than of their aromas, reasoning that in an infant Burgundy – as elsewhere

– this is the only immutable anchor. Week by week, racking by racking, the aromas change in type and intensity, whereas, by and large, the bricks and mortar of the building remain constant.

Of the two Grands Crus, the Bonnes-Mares, from a plot geographically midway between Chambolle and Morey, is usually the chunkier – the more overtly muscular and masculine. It has some similarities to Les Fuées, but is rather firmer and tighter, slightly squarer in profile, although decidedly more Chambolle than Morey in the Bonnes-Mares spectrum.

Frédy replanted half his Bonnes-Mares recently because the clones were proving erratic in both yield and quality. The 1988 was the first vintage which he considered truly regained typicity. The wine is sturdy and long, but the reduction in vine age shows in a more open-knit texture and lack of real Grand Cru concentration.

The Musigny however has no such problems. Until 1989 there were two *cuvées* – a 'standard' and a Vieilles Vignes. Now, there is just a single bottling, as Frédy considered the blend superior to either component. 'In any case, everyone wanted the Vieilles Vignes, no-one wanted 'second class' Musigny.' The rule was broken in 1992 when a single cask of Vieilles Vignes was made to celebrate the birth of Frédy and Josceline's daughter, following their marriage in 1989.

The Mugnier Musigny has all the power and concentration one expects from a Grand Cru, and all the finesse and silkiness one expects from a Musigny. Not an easy wine to taste young because of its tight, often lively tannins and obvious acidity, but one of great underlying depth, opulent, velvety and multifaceted. In fine vintages, something to keep for a decade or longer, but in all its plenitude, well worth the wait.

Frédy Mugnier is a very fine winemaker. The care and intelligence he brings to each vintage results in consistently excellent wines of supreme elegance and typicity. In his short tenure he has achieved, and obviously learned, a great deal; experience which will stand him in good stead in the years to come.

VINEYARD HOLDINGS

Commune	Level	Lieu-dit/Climat	Area	Vine Age	Status
Chambolle	V	Les Combottes + Les Plantes + La Combe d'Orveaux	1.30	35	P
Chambolle	PC	Les Fuées	0.71	35	P
Chambolle	PC	Les Amoureuses	0.53	40	P
Chambolle	GC	Bonnes-Mares	0.36	1/3:35 1/4:15 5/12:5	P
Chambolle	GC	Musigny	1.13	37	P
		Total:	**4.03 ha**		

Domaine Comte Georges de Vogüé

CHAMBOLLE-MUSIGNY

This Domaine is, as Charles Dickens put it, in quite another context, 'as old as the hills and infinitely more respectable'. The Musigny family, who gave their name to the famous vineyard in the 14th century before vanishing into obscurity, lived in the small hamlet which was later to become Chambolle. About 1450, a Jean Moisson constructed there a small chapel which later, under the protection of Cardinal Rollin, son of the Burgundian Chancellor Nicolas Rollin, became its parish church. In 1528, the grand-daughter of Jean Moisson married a Dijon négociant Michel Millières, bringing with her, as a dowry, the first vines of the future Domaine de Vogüé.

It was not, however, until 1766, that the name de Vogüé first appears in the records, when the Moissons' last direct female descendant, Catherine Bouhier, married Cerice François Melchior de Vogüé. Since then, five generations of de Vogüés have managed the Domaine, each adding, by acquisition or exchange, something to its vineyards.

Most, no doubt, chose to live in Jean Moisson's elegant 15th century house in the Rue de Barbe, with its tall, plain casement windows, which faces on to his attractive, though now enlarged, parish church.

In post-war years it was Comte Georges de Vogüé whose name was inextricably linked with the Domaine. By all accounts a lively old-fashioned aristocrat of great charm, he came often to Chambolle from his home in Paris, to discuss and oversee the work of a closely-knit team, led by the forthright and irrepressible Alain Roumier. Sadly, Comte Georges died in 1987, the same year that Roumier retired after 30 years' service.

Georges' wife took over, but left the Domaine's day-to-day management to her daughter, Elizabeth de Ladoucette. In spring 1986, a new team was installed, consisting of oenologue François Millet and Gerald Gaudeau who arrived as Chef de Culture. The aimiable and urbane Jean-Luc Pepin was appointed 'commercial attaché' in 1988, to superintend sales and marketing operations.

There was much to be done. Since the late 1970s there had been disquiet in expert circles about the Domaine's wines which were widely felt to be less concentrated and consistent than before; even in great vintages, such as 1978, there seemed scant sign of the extraordinary quality seen in legendary vintages such as 1945, 1947, 1959, 1969 and 1972. The potential was clearly there but the managers simply weren't realising it. Given the high price of its wines, the Domaine's reputation inevitably suffered.

It is difficult to discover whether there really was a problem. The Domaine itself kept virtually no stocks of older vintages, so there are none of impeccable provenance to taste. It may also be commented that Musigny – the core of the estate's production – is often misjudged, being a wine of naturally lightish colour and predominantly characterised by finesse and elegance. Those expecting the colour or style of neighbouring Morey-St.-Denis or of Vougeot, might wrongly conclude that the wine is unusually light in fruit. With Pinot Noir in general, and with Chambolle-Musigny and its wines in particular, colour is often a poor indicator of flavour. A wine of pale rose hue often turns out to be packed with fruit and to have considerable power and depth.

Even so, the critics are unlikely to have all been wide of the mark. What is far from clear is precisely what happened during the 1970s and early 1980s. Some talked of over-production, others of excessive filtration to please the US market (they liked it then!); the first is verifiable, and false, the second possible but implausible given Alain Roumier's experience and Georges de Vogüé's undoubted commitment to quality. It should be noted that between 1973, when the rot is generally supposed to have set in, and 1986 when the new regime took over, there was only one really outstanding vintage – 1978.

The new team is now firmly bedded in, and it is by their output that the Domaine must be judged. François Millet comes with excellent credentials: after extensive studies at Dijon University he spent 12 years as a consultant oenologist to various houses 'from Mâcon to Montelimar'. A somewhat deliberate, taciturn person, he distrusts rigid formulae of any sort and stresses the importance of approaching each vintage with an open mind. What may be good for one particular lot of grapes may not necessarily suit the next.

The result of this vintage-by-vintage, *cuvée*-by-*cuvée* policy is that it makes no sense to speak of a system of vinification. Moreover, François is adamant that it will take longer than the decade he has been at the Domaine to establish a real rapport between him and his wines and for him to grow into the de Vogüé mould. However, he takes great care to avoid isolation, in his nineteenth century cellars, from what is going on elsewhere;

François Millet and Jean-Luc Pepin – looking into the future

tasting other wines, not just Burgundies, and making regular visits to vineyards elsewhere, he regards as an integral part of his job. It is all too easy to become so closely involved that you can no longer see where you are going – so François Millet travels and tastes.

Even allowing for the 'no-formulae' approach, trying to discover how the Domaine sets about vinifying its impeccably nurtured fruit is met with singular reticence.

The stated aim is, as far as possible, to tailor vinification to the year and to the particular vineyard or lot of grapes concerned. Even given healthy grapes all round, there may be significant differences in the way each vineyard's produce is dealt with. Getting to know the pecularities and idiosyncrasies of each patch of vines, and each patch of *terroir* is, in François' view, a cornerstone of his work.

This willingness to remain flexible, to take decisions as individual circumstances dictate, does not exclude preferences. The grapes are usually destemmed – between 30 and 100% – how much varying with vintage, appellation and the individual parcel of vines. 'Stems,' according to François Millet, 'are difficult to evaluate; tannins vary in quality, and soil is an important factor.' Equally, some parts of a vineyard tend to give more natural grape tannin than others, lessening the need for the addition of stem tannin. Furthermore, tannin has several sources, and it may be possible to extract better tannins from a longer *cuvaison* than from a greater proportion of stems in the vats.

In all but the the worst of rot-infected years, a short period of *maceration* precedes fermentation in large open wooden vats. François Millet likes 'to work with nature – the sun and the earth' and is less than enthusiastic about those who dose their crushed grapes with massive amounts of sulphur to ensure a long cool pre-fermentive *maceration*. As he quaintly puts it: 'This is not natural – not a way to thank God for his work.'

Yeasting, with dried Burgundy yeasts, may be used on vats which are sluggish in starting to ferment. Thereafter, temperature is controlled at a maximum of 32–33°C with length of *cuvaison* adapted to the parcel being vinified. In general, the longer the *cuvaison* the better, although it has been noted that some vineyards produce better results with 15 days, others with a month.

François Millet believes that the length of *maceration* after fermentation is of greater importance than the length of fermentation itself. The pulp left after the wine has been run off is gently pressed and the wine extracted kept apart. Whilst the chances are that this will all be added to the free-run wine, this is only done after several tastings and when the time is deemed right. 'Chambolles,' François points out, 'are characteristically feminine so it is rare not to include 100% of the *vin de presse*, even in riper years, to add an element of backbone and structure.'

The Domaine's policy on casks appears to be still evolving. There is 40–70% of new wood, depending on vintage, parcel of vines etc. . . . and efforts are being made to determine which forest provides the most suitable oak for each particular wine. So far François has tentatively decided that Nevers adapts well to Bonnes-Mares – or is it the other way round? There are no firm conclusions, beyond the negative statement that they do not want to go the way of many growers and simply use new casks of several different provenances as a cautious averaging.

A further complication is that wood from the same forest can differ from year to year. So the Domaine is trying to educate its barrel-maker by inviting him to taste and to become more involved in their thinking.

Whether a wine is racked at all – except, of course, for bottling – and if it is, when and how often – is a matter for individual decision. What is certain is that if a cask is racked then gravity not pumping is used. There is a general tendency to rack shortly after *malo*, but this decision is tempered by the desire to keep enough lees in the cask.

The moment of *assemblage* is equally fluid. It may happen before fining or just after, or may be delayed until just before bottling. The later each blend is made the more precise it can be; 'It is like a painting, there are more colours to use.'

Fining is not an unvarying piece of the de Vogüé vinification jigsaw. 'Fining undresses a wine,' chorus both François and Jean-Luc. So a separate decision is taken on each cask. If fining is deemed necessary, samples are analysed to determine the optimum fining agent. Fresh egg whites are generally preferred, but gelatine may sometimes be more efficient. Neither is filtration a cornerstone: 'It is ridiculous to filter a wine if it is brilliant.'

When necessary, Kieselguhr or plate filters are used or, in extreme cases, both.

Perhaps the most exigent decision a winemaker faces is when to bottle. Here, at least, there seems to be a policy: 'We are looking for a wine that is beginning to open out. This is not easy to figure out, but we do not want a wine which is too open.' Cask maturation has both a good and a bad side – too much cask age can dry out a wine and destroy the delicate Pinot Noir fruit, whereas the right amount can greatly enhance a wine's quality and life expectancy. 'One is taking a wine out of his house and putting it into a bottle.'

It has taken almost a decade, but now the new team are producing wines of indisputably top-class ranking. Although these are still young, in terms of their long-term evolution – a fine Musigny needs 10–20 years in bottle – one can see both quality and consistency; not just the occasional flash in the pan, but year-on-year confidence. It would seem that the frisson, the indefinable thrill, of great Bonnes-Mares, great Amoureuses and, above all, of great silken, opulent Musigny, is steadily being recaptured.

The Domaine produces about 4,000 cases a year comprising five wines: Musigny Blanc: a minuscule output of some 160 cases of a most sought-after and unusual wine from Chardonnay grown on Grand Cru Côte de Nuits soil. This curious cross-fertilisation produces a wine of striking power and considerable presence, without the indelible finesse of a great Puligny; rather more like a Corton-Charlemagne with a hairy chest. For some it is the ultimate in dry white wine, for others just an interesting curiosity. Whichever camp you support, making up your mind is an expensive pastime.

Alain Roumier wanted the Domaine to have some plain Chambolle Village land, to have more stock to offer its loyal customers, but Comte Georges would not entertain the idea, feeling that nothing less than Premier Cru would do. Now, there is a straight Chambolle, from 1.8 ha of Village vineyards.

Otherwise, the red range begins with the Chambolle Premier Cru Les Amoureuses. The soil in this particular vineyard has a high limestone content which characteristically gives a wine of great finesse and delicacy, with a lightish colour and a soft, mouthfilling flavour. The wines of Chambolle-Musigny tend to have a good natural balance of tannin

and acidity and the Amoureuses beautifully exemplifies this. François will tell you – with a broad grin – that he never acidifies his wines – which leaves one marvelling even more at the quality of Chambolle's soils!

The Domaine's Bonnes-Mares vines are located nearer to Chambolle than to Morey. The wine is invariably both denser and darker in appearance than the Amoureuses, with more weight and structure. It tends to age into a fine spectrum of aromas, at first fruit based and then more vegetal; altogether, a much wilder wine than its brother Musigny, with a little less raw power, but with considerable finesse and concentration; a wine of more masculine tone, but with no less breed and length.

The Musigny, of which the Domaine de Vogüé is by far the largest owner, with some 80% of the entire vineyard, comes as a single *cuvée* labelled Vieilles Vignes. Capable of divine sublimity, it disarms the drinker with its limpid light colour and hue of red silk taffeta, which belie the purity and depth of fruit underneath. The nose develops into a harmonious amalgam of discrete, but seductive aromas of great class and finesse, each sniff offering a different facet and a new perspective. On the palate, a superb concentration of ripe fruit, with generally well rounded tannins, is offset by a fine balance of acidity. The most striking characteristic of this wine, as evident in lesser vintages as in great, is its length and persistence. The former shows as a 'peacock's tail' of flavours, whilst the latter allows those flavours to remain on the palate long after swallowing. In fine vintages the de Vogüé Musigny is a wine of great profundity and one of Burgundy's rare and remarkable treasures. The 1993, helped by a fair amount of *millerandage*, is a masterpiece.

This is one of the Côte d'Or's noblest estates, of whose potential for making some of the finest and most remarkable Burgundies no-one is in any serious doubt. Whilst the team continue to consolidate their feel for the great vineyards under their control, the confidence and quality of the wines they have so far produced has done much to revitalise the Domaine's fortunes. The restoration of this magnificent estate to its former pre-eminence will be heartily applauded by all Burgundy lovers. De Vogüé is now back on top form.

VINEYARD HOLDINGS

Commune	Level	Lieu-dit/Climat	Area	Vine Age	Status
Chambolle	GC	Musigny	6.70	N/A	P
Chambolle	GC	Bonnes-Mares	2.60	N/A	P
Chambolle	GC	Musigny (blanc)	0.50	N/A	P
Chambolle	PC	Les Amoureuses	0.60	N/A	P
Chambolle	V	———	1.80	N/A	P
		Total:	**12.20 ha**		

VOUGEOT

With only 67.08 ha of vines, Vougeot is the smallest commune in the Côte d'Or. Yet through the work of the Confrérie des Chevaliers du Tastevin, based at the Château du Clos de Vougeot, its name is known throughout the wine-loving world.

Outside the activities of the Confrérie, the village's reputation rests principally on the vines from the magnificent 50.59 ha of walled vineyard known as the Clos de Vougeot – the largest Clos in the Côte d'Or. The red and white wines from the remaining 16.59 ha, which are only entitled to the appellation Vougeot, or Vougeot Premier Cru, remain for most Burgundy lovers an obscure curiosity.

Vougeot is a small village of some 200 inhabitants, reached from a short spur off the RN74, which now by-passes it. In the spring, summer and autumn months a seemingly constant river of tourists are to be seen visiting the Château and buying wines from one or other of the large cellars which act as shrimping nets. There is a half-hearted general store, a few predictably expensive restaurants and, for the hot weather, an excellent municipal swimming-pool. If you feel like staying, Domaine Bertagna has an attractive small hotel in the vineyards or there is the luxuriously restored Château de Gilly, a blissfully peaceful Relais et Châteaux with a tennis court and an excellent restaurant, a kilometre away on the opposite side of the RN74.

The village takes its name from the little river Vouge which has its source near Chambolle-Musigny. In the 12th century it was in fact called Vooget, although its existence was already known three centuries earlier, thanks to a toll established at the river.

Before the monks of Cîteaux arrived at the beginning of the 12th century, the ground which is now the Clos was either forest or fallow. Gifts of land to the Abbey of Cîteaux encouraged the clearing of scrub and the plantation of vines. However, unable to complete the Clos from donations, the brothers were obliged to spend lavishly between 1227 and 1370 to buy up the remaining plots of land at elevated prices. By the 15th century a great wall had been constructed round some 50 ha forming the Clos as it is today.

According to Henri Cannard's excellent concise history, the Clos and the Château de Gilly were ransacked during the wars of religion. Although Gilly was rebuilt, the Clos was left with no more than a few utilitarian buildings for the making and storage of wine,

and remained so until 1551 when the present Château, designed as a fortress, was constructed. Cannard also notes that, apart from a small Oratory, the Château contains no Chapel, confirming its status as a dependency of the Abbey of Cîteaux.

Meanwhile illustrious visitors appeared: Louis XIV came to the Abbey in the course of a cure, consisting chiefly of Nuits wines, prescribed by his doctor, Fagon, and it is reported that numerous 'auberges reputées' sprang up in the village to cater for visitors who generally preferred to stay in Vougeot rather than in Nuits.

In 1860 a group of English businessmen tried to buy the Château, but the owners refused, selling instead to the Thenard family in 1869. Thereafter the estate remained in single ownership until 1889 when the vines were divided between some 15 different proprietors. Among those, Léonce Bocquet, who spent much effort and money on the buildings, is particularly remembered, being buried – presumably upright – in the entrance gate.

The buildings gradually fell into disrepair, until finally coming into the hands of Etienne Camuzet, whose legatees sold them to the

Chevaliers de Tastevin on 29th November 1944. The Château now belongs to a company called Les Amis du Château du Clos Vougeot and remains the headquarters of the Chevaliers du Tastevin.

This Confrérie, founded ten years earlier, in 1934, was designed as a promotional organisation, at a time when sales were particularly difficult. Today, lavish banquets, noted more for their length than anything else, are accompanied by 'Intronisations' at Vougeot and elsewhere, of luminaries who are esteemed valuable to Burgundy's reputation around the world.

Over the years, however, becoming a Chevalier du Tastevin has come to be regarded as evidence of expertise. As Anthony Hanson remarks: 'Certainly the idea is widely held that membership of the order is some sort of qualification.' If so, this is entirely without justification; but as a marketing gimmick it is masterly!

There are some 4.82 ha of appellation Vougeot land and three Premiers Crus which account for a further 11.68 ha. These latter – Les Cras, La Vigne Blanche and Les Petits Vougeot (part of which is Bertagna's Clos de la Perrière) – are not widely known, probably

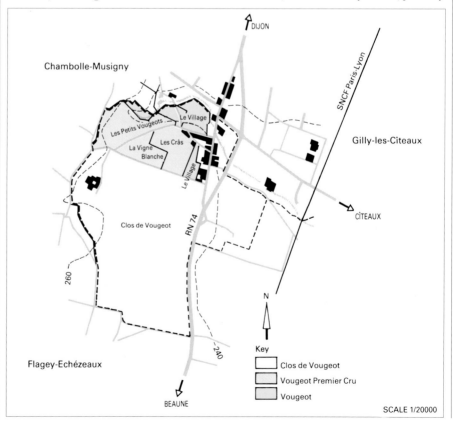

The Château and the upper part of the Clos de Vougeot – the most subdivided vineyard in the Côte d'Or, with 82 owners

by virtue of their size. The wines tend to solidity and tannicity, but can sometimes develop finesse with age. Some 5–600 cases of Vougeot Blanc are made annually; this can be delicious or dull, depending on the grower and the vintage.

The Clos' fifty hectares are now in the hands of some 82 different owners – companies, individuals, Domaines large and small, with a corner belonging to the French department of roads and bridges – so there is considerable variation in quality.

The Clos de Vougeot is one of the few Grands Crus where the location of vines within the vineyard really matters. The monks of Cîteaux, having accepted, gratefully, everything they were offered, found themselves with a great diversity of land. Mme Rolande Gadille (1957) has described no fewer than six different soil types within the Clos, and honest growers themselves recognise the better drained top section, nearest to the Château, as superior to that next to the RN74, which has a higher humidity and thus increased risk of mildew and frost. Moreover, since the turn of the century successive local authorities have contrived to raise the road level by about two metres, further increasing moisture

retention in the lower part of the Clos.

Although from the road it appears quite flat, the Clos is in fact on a gentle 3–4 degree slope, with a vertical displacement of some 30 metres towards the Château. Soils at the top are mainly limestone-based and of fossil origin, whereas those by the road are considerably deeper, with an increased pro- portion of clay, and closer to the water-table. The middle section has a significant clay content, with soils of some 40–50 cm in depth which are stony and well drained.

Jean Grivot claims that the best wines come from a mixture of grapes from both top and bottom sections – a generously frank sentiment given that much of his own large plot is right next to the road, marked by an ornate wrought-iron gate. In truth, the skill of the vigneron is probably more important than the location of the vines, although this may play a negative role in particularly wet or dry years. However, so ingrained is the primacy of position that one is at pains to find

a grower who admits to owning vines at the bottom of the Clos. Most tell you that their patch is 'at the top', usually adding 'up near the Château' for good measure.

Wines from the Clos too often disappoint, ranging from dreadfully thin and acidic to the few which genuinely merit Grand Cru status. The majority are usually lumpen and tannic without the promise of ever blossoming. Invariably expensive, Clos de Vougeot scores highly on the price/disappointment scale.

Among the best producers are: Hudelot-Noëllat, Jadot, Méo-Camuset, Chopin-Groffier, Jean Gros, Gros (Frère et Soeur), Dom. Georges Mugneret, Jean Grivot, Roumier, Drouhin and Jacky Confuron-Cotéditot.

There is a strong case for re-examining the Clos with a view to down-grading the less good land. This, together with a more stringent tasting assessment, would do much to restore the rather tarnished image of this noble Grand Cru.

GRAND CRU OF VOUGEOT

Lieu-dit	Area	Props.	Av. Prod.
Clos (de) Vougeot	50.59.10	82	16,500 C/S

Domaine Bertagna

VOUGEOT

Although originally created by Monsieur Bertagna, an Algerian businessman, in the late 1940s, Domaine Bertagna has recently passed into the young hands of 30-year-old Eva Reh and her English husband Mark Siddle. Eva's business and marketing training and Mark's work experience with Robert Mondavi in the Napa are bringing strenuous efforts to bear to re-establish the Domaine's reputation, which slipped badly during the 1970s.

The enterprise is part of an unusual family group of businesses, each of which is run by one of Karl Reh's five children. The system is simple: the managing family member holds the majority interest in his or her particular enterprise, the others owning the balance. Other group holdings include a large Sekt house, the Reichsrat von Kesselstadt estate in Trier and important hotel interests. The backing of substantial financial resources has permitted significant vineyard purchases and capital investment in recent years.

Since taking over in 1982, Eva and Mark have worked hard with their winemaker, Roland Masse, to bring the cellars up to date and to replant where it was considered necessary. Installations include an impressive battery of computer-controlled fermentation tanks, providing temperature control and automatic *pigéage*, an ingenious system for extracting the lees without decanting the wine, and state-of-the-art vacuum bottling.

The vineyards are harvested several times over to pick only the ripest fruit; green-pruning is preferred to a *saignée de cuve* – although there is not much to suggest that these are genuine alternatives. The number of different individual lots of grapes presents handling problems, providing an additional motive for restricting yields.

Vinification is designed to return to what Mark calls 'traditional Burgundy' – that is to say, the extraction of concentrated, obvious Pinot flavours and aromas. 'Burgundy is unique soil, so it is not just a question of making good wine, but of making good Burgundy.' The tanks are filled brim-full of completely destalked grapes so there is little need for sulphur; *cuvaison*, including 5–8 days pre-fermentive *maceration*, generally lasts 3 weeks, with temperatures kept below 30°C.

Concern about the wood used by barrel-makers has led to the Domaine buying its own trees in the Vosges, so that from 1991 it had complete control over cask quality. A major effort has gone into tailoring the amount and charring of new wood to each

wine and vintage. This and the ability to order the casks as near as possible to harvest-time has greatly improved the overall structural balance of the wines. The average is 30% new wood, with the range spanning 40–100%. The accent remains on Vosges, but Alliers, and to a lesser extent Nevers, are also used.

Bottling takes place about 18 months after the vintage, and is preceded by 3 rackings and an egg-white fining. Roland Masse is currently experimenting with different bottling intervals, and there have also been small trials with machine-harvesting of a plot of Nuits St.-Georges in 1985.

The unusual Vougeot Blanc is evidence that this is not just a red Domaine – a good omen for the newly-acquired Corton-Charlemagne. It comes from one hectare of Chardonnay in Les Cras, half planted after the frost damage of 1985 and half a decade later. The wine is quite broad in profile with a lively acidity and good length – in style, something between a Premier Cru Meursault and a more masculine Corton-Charlemagne. As the vines age, it is deepening in texture and richness; a delicious curiosity, which has the structure to age well over a few years.

Recent years have seen careful, judicious, additions to the portfolio. Corton (from above Ch. Corton André) and Corton-Charlemagne (from the Ladoix sector) came on stream in the 1994 vintage and there is also some Premier Cru Vosne-Romanée Les Beaumonts. Two ha of red Hautes Côtes de Nuits, in what ought to be AC Nuits St.-Georges, just below Château Gris, have also been added – a shrewd investment if they can engineer a reclassification.

As time passes, Bertagna's wines are becoming more confident and increasing in definition and typicity. The red Vougeots are on the masculine side of that Appellation, with a rather sturdy feel to them. Of the trio of Premiers Crus, Les Cras and Les Petits Vougeots are a shade lighter and more feminine than the *monopole* Clos de la Perrière – which generally sees around 60% of new wood compared with 40% for the other two. In 1993, two-thirds was heavy toast Allier, evident from a firm, charry nose, which threatens to dominate the wine, although its superior concentration and complexity should win through. There is obviously more fine-tuning to be done on the oak front before the balance is absolutely right.

The Grands Crus are good – especially the Clos St.-Denis and the Chambertin. They run almost neck and neck in quality, although the latter seems to have marginally greater style and complexity than the former. It will be interesting to see how the Corton turns out.

Things are moving in the right direction at Bertagna and the efforts are bearing fruit in wines of typicity and good concentrations from sensible yields. Some of the reds, especially the Vougeots, can show a rustic edge – less toast and more middle palate would put this right. Otherwise, a fine range. Mark and Eva have now bought the Moingeon Cremant business – the German operation has abundant technical expertise here – which will significantly increase volume. It is to be hoped that this, and their new daughter Nicole, will not prove too much of a distraction from continuing the excellent progress they have already made at Vougeot.

VINEYARD HOLDINGS

Commune	Level	Lieu-dit/Climat	Area	Vine Age	Status
Vougeot	GC	Clos de Vougeot	0.30	70%:50+	P
Vougeot	PC	Clos de la Perrière	2.20	70%:35	P
Vougeot	PC	Les Petits Vougeots	2.40	100%:40	P
Vougeot	PC	Les Cras (Chardonnay)	1.00	Pl.1985/95	P
Vougeot	PC	Les Cras (Pinot Noir)	0.40	30	P
Vougeot	V	————	0.80	100%:18	P
Chambolle	V	————	0.40	1950	
Chambolle	PC	Les Plantes	0.20	1988	P
Morey	GC	Clos St-Denis	0.50	1/31950/ 2/3 1975	P
Gevrey	GC	Chambertin	0.20	1965	P
Nuits	PC	Aux Meurgeys	1.00	45	P
Vosne	PC	Les Beaumonts	0.90	35	P
Ladoix	GC	Corton-Charlemagne	0.26	30	P
Aloxe	GC	Corton	0.25	35	P
Nuits	R	Htes. Ctes. de Nuit (R)	2.00	1974	P
Total:			**12.81 ha**		

Domaine Georges Clerget

VOUGEOT

From its unpretentious base in Vougeot's Grande Rue, Georges Clerget, now well into his sixties, presides over a 4.7 hectare Domaine spread across Morey-St.-Denis, Vougeot, Vosne-Romanée and Chambolle-Musigny. The Domaine was created by contributions of vines from Georges' maternal grandmother and grandfather, the one from Flagey and the other from Chambolle. What remained after the obligatory division between him and his brother, together with vineyards bought by his mother, provided Georges with the nucleus of what he has today.

Georges is a charming, friendly man, rooted firmly in the traditional mould of working, who, whilst he is quite prepared to follow the advice of his oenologist, has healthily sceptical views on modern technology. His father died when Georges was a boy of nine; his mother thereupon took up the reins of their six-hectare Domaine and roped in her two sons – Georges and his brother Michel – to help her with the work and to learn the trade at the same time. Georges remembers being given 'a vine or two to keep me interested' – which stratagem obviously worked well, since he has never left the job.

In 1978 the vineyards were divided, Georges and his brother each receiving about 3 ha. Now, his son, Christian, in his thirties, who works with him, has taken Michel's vines as well as 0.5 ha of Grand Cru Echézeaux, which Georges let him have on *en fermage*. Christian's studies at the Lycée Viticole in Beaune will hopefully keep both Domaines in tune with modern developments.

Whilst the vineyards are now tended by hand and by tractor, Georges remembers vividly the days of horsepower. Then, he will tell you, the vines were planted deeper than today, which meant that one had to be very careful, after ploughing down the soil which had been ploughed up to protect the roots for the winter, to ensure that any lateral roots put out by the French scion, were cut off, to avoid infection. With modern shallower planting, the risk is minimised, but the Clergets are no less careful in their spring *évasivage*.

This traditional ploughing up – *buttage* – continues. As well as covering the roots and thereby lowering the frost-risk, Georges argues that, when he ploughs back the soil level the following spring, he has the chance to mix in any small allowance of fertiliser he may have administered, so it is well integrated with the top-soil.

Yields are kept as low as economically sensible. George's team of regular pickers are trained to spot any unripe or rotten fruit, and are fully aware of what constitutes an acceptable 'Clerget' bunch of grapes.

The wines are vinified in cement, enamelled-steel or old wooden *foudres*, and kept in a plethora of ground-level garages and small underground cellars near his house just off the RN74 at the northern end of Vougeot. Whilst the intention is to destalk the bunches completely, such is the age of the Clerget destalking machine, that some 10–15% of stalks usually remain after it has done its work.

There is no equipment for cooling the pulp. In consequence, the important phase of pre-fermentive *maceration* is excluded if the grapes arrive at the *cuverie* warm, since the yeasts multiply rapidly and begin to ferment the sugars immediately.

The wine is decanted within a day or two of finishing fermentation and the *marc* given 'two gentle pressings', explains Georges, turning an imaginary knob in the air in front of him. The wine from both is then added to the free-run wine. *Elévage* lasts around 19–22 months, with some one-third of new oak for the Chambolle Charmes and Premier Cru Les Petits Vougeot and 50% for the Echézeaux. The wines are racked cask-to-cask – old wood to new and vice versa.

In general the Clergets turn out excellent wines. These have two broadly distinct styles: the Village appellations tend to an elegant, lighter frame, with the pure crushed strawberry aromas and red fruit flavours of young Pinot Noir. Usually quite succulent and slightly peppery, they have a delicate balance of tannin, but are not of massive structure; wines for the medium term.

In contrast, the wines which have the benefit of new wood are much richer, with a firmer backbone and naturally greater power.

Georges and a client

The new casks suit the Echézeaux, and would, in moderation, definitely benefit the Vougeot and Chambolle-Musigny Charmes.

Although claiming to be officially retired, Georges shows no signs of taking a back seat. He obviously values having Christian to help him with the work, but remains firmly in charge – no devolution of responsibility here! When Georges is next sitting on his customary Spanish beach, on his annual summer visit, he might give this some serious thought.

VINEYARD HOLDINGS

Commune	Level	Lieu-dit/Climat	Area	Vine Age	Status
Flagey	GC	Echézeaux (en Orveaux)	1.10	40 and 50	P
Chambolle	PC	Les Charmes	0.30	40 and 20	P
Chambolle	V	Les Babillières+			
		Les Condemennes	1.50	40 and 25	P
Vougeot	PC	Les Petits Vougeots	0.50	25 and 10	P
Morey	V	Les Crays	0.40	10 and 30	P
Vosne	V	Les Violettes	0.38	1946/49	P
Vosne/Flagey					
Gilly	R	(Bourgogne Rouge)	0.50	10/25/40	P
		Total:	**4.68 ha**		

Domaine Alain Hudelot-Noëllat

VOUGEOT

Alain Hudelot-Noëllat's wines have been among the best in the Côte for many years – full of charm and exuberance, but with considerable depths for those who care to look for them. Alain mirrors his wines: a solid, hard-working man, with short-cropped hair and a broad friendly face, exuding passion for his work and an abundant enjoyment of wine and the people that go with it. Talking to him, in front of a roaring November fire of vine prunings blazing away in a massive chimney-piece, one is aware of a mischievous grin which, when coupled with a brief, but totally deliberate wink of his left eye, rapidly divorces his real meaning from whatever he happens to be saying.

He receives his visitors in what appears to be a large converted garage with a set of curiously ornate, wood-framed doors squeezed into the front. One wall is binned with stock, whilst another is occupied with a variety of ancient viticultural tools – brightly polished copper hand-sprays, disinfecting syringes and so on. On top of the mantel a couple of boxes of cartridges, being gently warmed by the fire below, betray Alain's interest in hunting. Suspended above the fire is a double cattle-yolk, with the names 'Hudelot' and 'Noëllat' inscribed one on each side.

The history of the Domaine runs no deeper than the history of Alain and his wife. Leaving school young, he started working in the vineyards of Drouhin and Champy – négociant houses of Beaune. In 1960 – his twenty-first year – he was given two small plots of vines by his father Noël in Chambolle-Musigny Les Charmes and in Chambolle-Musigny itself.

At that time, much of the vineyard work was done by horsepower, so Alain saved up enough to buy a tractor and rented himself and his équipage out in the locality. With the money he earned, he bought more vineyard land to add to his Domaine. In 1977, the addition of 42 ares of Clos Vougeot *en fermage* from his father, brought the Domaine up to 5 ha.

In 1960 the young Alain Hudelot married the young grand-daughter of Charles Noëllat from Vosne-Romanée, bringing with her entitlement to several choice parcels of vineyards from that commune. Unfortunately, one of her relatives refused to release the vineyards to her and she and Alain were obliged to fight a legal battle to regain possession. This took 15 years and substantially drained their

resources; however they won and the land finally became theirs in 1977.

The Domaine now stands at nearly 10 ha – including over a hectare of Clos Vougeot and just under half a hectare of Romanée-St.-Vivant with a small parcel of Richebourg and a 3 ha chunk of Chambolle-Musigny.

Vine age is kept deliberately high by a systematic grubbing up and replanting schedule. The Romanée-St.-Vivant vines are so old that Alain prefers to replace them individually rather than to completely grub up such a small area. He has further difficulties, of a more emotional nature, with his plot of Vosne-Romanée Les Suchots; he wanted to grub it up and replant, but the ancient vines continued to produce such marvellous grapes that he couldn't bring himself to do it; thus, they remain in situ, getting gradually more venerable, and no doubt less productive, as the years go by.

Alain's way of working in his vineyards follows broadly traditional lines. One peculiarity is his choice of SO4, which is known for its precocious growth and abundant foliage, as one of his rootstocks. Alain is not unduly worried: 'The more the foliage, the better the grapes are nourished!' Treatments are rotated to avoid the build-up of resistance, and the soils ploughed up regularly.

Despite a relatively standard viticultural regime, Alain does have dislikes and

preferences. He abhors green-pruning to remove excess bunches of grapes, preferring to *saigner* his *cuves* in particularly abundant years. 'Never refuse what the good Lord gives you.' In any case 'green-pruning changes the balance of the vine,' he barks, adding, 'I don't like going against nature,' throwing up his hands in the air, and winking.

His scepticism was reinforced when he went into one famous vineyard nearby during the summer of 1990 and saw some much-photographed workers green-pruning the vines. 'C'était la folklore, c'était de la grande musique' (meaning roughly, 'all show and no real effect'). Apparently they were much more interested in being photographed than attending to the job they were supposed to be doing. Alain was horrified to see them cutting off heaven knows what, and worse still, handling the young bunches of grapes which affects their natural bloom.

He considers that many who chose to green-prune did not make a success of the 1990 vintage, since, when the much-needed rain came later in early September, the vines blotted up the water so rapidly that many of the berries on the less-charged vines swelled up and burst, giving rise to rot. 'Pure theatre, la musique, nothing to do with Grand Vin.'

Alain Hudelot proudly sporting his Irish cap

On yields, Alain is less than conventional, declaring that it is perfectly possible to make excellent Grand Cru with 'healthy yields'. This comes from the time, when the powerful Alexis Lichine awarded the unknown 26-year-old Alain Hudelot a silver cup for his 1964 Clos de Vougeot. 'The best wine of the Côte,' chuckles Alain, 'it beat all the Richebourgs and Romanée St.-Vivants – everyone else was furious, hopping mad. I made 1 barrel per *ouvrée* (= 55 hl/ha). There was lots of publicity; all these grand people came to wander through my vineyard to see how the vines were pruned, planted, trained,' adding, with a wink, 'truly, de la grande musique!'

In the cellar, fermentation proceeds with natural yeasts, and is allowed to reach 32°C before the *must* is cooled to 25°C. Alain dislikes stalks, but generally leaves up to 25% in the vats, for no particular reason – his father and grandfather worked like that, so why change; after all, it keeps the customers happy! In 1990 however, fearing a repetition of the excessively hard and unyielding tannins of 1976, he decided to remove all the stalks. Total *cuvaison* generally lasts 15–18 days, although Alain firmly believes that *maceration* before fermentation extracts more finesse and complexity into his wines than *maceration* after fermentation.

When it comes to the question of wood, Alain grows particularly animated. He seems to have tried every forest in France for his casks, and yet to have found nothing completely satisfactory. His usual tonnelier provides new barrels each year from Nevers, Allier, and even Limousin into which Alain puts 100% of his Grands Crus. He has recently started working with a small barrel-maker who supplies him with local wood – Cîteaux and Châtillon. Alain likes the results from Cîteaux and will probably increase the proportion of this in future.

In general he is thoroughly disbelieving of the nuances, or lack of them, from different types of wood: 'c'est de la musique, de la grande, grande, grande musique; moi, j'estime que c'est de la grande musique!' However, he took the matter seriously enough in 1990 to put some of his Vosne-Romanée Les Suchots into new wood – from where he couldn't quite remember.

The wines are racked cask-to-cask in March following the vintage – 'My grandfather did it this way, my father did it this way, so I do it this way.' A second racking around the following September precedes egg-white fining, plate filtration and bottling in May of the second year, or 'when I have the time'.

The Domaine used to bottle its own wines; then Alain felt that it might be better done by a contract bottler, and gave one a try. However, this worthy, being remunerated on a piece-work basis, bottled the wines so rapidly – which is not good for them – that Alain decided to take bottling back into his own hands. His three workers are at full stretch in the vineyards during the early summer so bottling has to be fitted in with whatever else is going on.

Alain Hudelot is at a loss to explain why his wines are so much finer and better constructed than those of many of his neighbours. Talking to him, it is clear that he finds it difficult to believe in the quality of what he is producing: 'I don't think I really have any good wines,' and, when pressed, 'There is nothing particularly special about my wines.' This crisis of confidence sits oddly on a man of such acclaim, but his doubt is genuine.

A group of French customers turn up at the door in search of some of his Richebourg – they had read about this wine in the respected *Guide Hachette des Vins*. 'I'm not really in there, am I?' asks Alain, grabbing the book. Then, finding the reference: 'That's very kind of them.' Sadly there is no Richebourg left; he has only two casks and it's all sold. In vain he suggests the Romanée-St.-Vivant as a suitable alternative – 'I have about twice as much,' he tells them. To no avail, they make some feeble enquiry about the next vintage of Richebourg, which they are informed is still in cask, and leave. Such is the power of the press!

Alain's style tends to supple, aromatic wines, of great elegance. They are not designed for early drinking but to be kept a long time to show their full potential. His avowed aim is to make wines which combine power and finesse and which typify their origins.

Although his Chambolle-Musigny and his Nuits Les Murgers are usually very successful, it is his Vosne-Romanées for which he is best known. The Vosne Village *cuvée* is invariably beautifully balanced and quite delicate. The 1993 was almost sweet in tone, with flavours of crushed strawberry and spice. Not a big wine, but one with plenty of *mache*, good length and supple fruit.

The Vosne-Romanée Les Suchots, from Alain's precious 75-year-old vines, has characteristic fat and depth. The 1993 showed a fine concentration of opulent, silky fruit, with overtones of cassis, with a well judged underpinning of oak, and excellent length – a really lovely wine, which shouldn't be touched for 7–10 years.

Alain's Clos Vougeot is one of the best from that frequently disappointing Grand Cru. The 1993 is a wine of class, rarely found in the Clos – plump, stylish ripe fruit, rich and concentrated, with none of the burly rusticity which so often appears in other growers' wines. It has real depth and length – a wine to start drinking a little after the Suchots.

The Richebourg and Romanée-St.-Vivant represent the summit of Alain's considerable achievements and follow, though in a more complex and powerful manner, the general Hudelot line. Although the 65-year-old vines in Romanée-St.-Vivant give it an extra dimension of depth, neither wine is overbalanced by clumsy fruit which might threaten the underlying finesse. The Richebourg is altogether bigger than the Romanée-St.-Vivant, with great power and majestic depth, a bass compared with a tenor. The Romanée, in contrast, has more obvious refinement and elegance – yet with fine, restrained power.

In common with several colleagues the difficult market conditions of recent years have led Alain to sell wine (including apparently Grands Crus) to the trade. This is surprising for such a talented winemaker.

Searching for a clue as to why his wines are so much finer than those of his neighbours with equally good vineyards, Alain suggests that too long a *cuvaison* is often a cause of loss of finesse. Delaying decanting the wines off their solids after fermentation can, he believes, lead to a certain dryness and 'coldness' which closes up the aromas and stunts their future development. Beyond that, he shrugs his shoulders and chucks another fifteen logs on to the blazing fire – presumably 'c'est la grande musique' as well.

VINEYARD HOLDINGS

Commune	Level	Lieu-dit/Climat	Area	Vine Age	Status
Chambolle	V	(Various climats)	3.00	5–25	P
Vougeot	PC	Les Petits Vougeots	0.50	35	F
Vougeot	GC	Clos de Vougeot	1.08	35	P/F
Vosne	V	————	0.68	17	P
Vosne	GC	Romanée-St-Vivant	0.48	65	P
Vosne	PC	Les Suchots	0.45	75	P
Vosne	GC	Richebourg	0.28	45	P
Vosne	PC	Les Malconsorts	0.20	40	P
Vosne	PC	Les Beaumonts	0.32	40	P
Nuits	PC	Les Murgers	0.80	40	P
Chambolle+ Gilly	R	(Bourgogne Rouge)	2.00	30	P
Total:			**9.79 ha**		

VOSNE-ROMANÉE AND FLAGEY-ECHÉZEAUX

There can be little doubt that, in the firmament of the Côte de Nuits, Vosne-Romanée is the brightest star. Turning off the RN74 into the village never fails to evoke a feeling of pilgrimage, a sense that this unpretentious little village and its backdrop of magnificent vineyards are something special and that those who own this precious land must be among the most fortunate souls on earth.

The pilgrim needs no other reason to visit Vosne than to wander through its streets up to the slopes behind, perhaps to taste at a grower's cellar, or just to picnic among the vines on a warm afternoon, inwardly marvelling that from this ordinary-looking land come some of the world's legendary, most sumptuous and extraordinary wines.

By comparison to the Côte's other communes, Vosne is not large – just 182 ha of vines, but vines of a quality that brings one to one's knees. To the east and south-east of the Post Office lies the lion's share of the Village appellation – 98.57 ha, mainly of thin but well-drained clay-limestone soils, topped with a pebbles and limestone scree. These produce wines which balance depth and richness with elegance and breed; often described as silky, they are usually marked by finesse and perfume which, together with their natural power, age beautifully.

Scattered round to both sides and to the west, are Vosne's 16 Premiers Crus. These occupy some 57.19 ha, often on slopes of up to 15%, and are mainly exposed to either the east or south-east. These soils tend to have less depth and to contain a higher proportion of limestone than those in Village vineyards and the topsoil is mainly scree, making for excellent drainage. Although there is no marked quality distinction between them, Les Suchots (13.07 ha), Les Beaux Monts (11.39 ha), Aux Malconsorts (5.86 ha) and Les Chaumes (6.46 ha) are the largest and therefore somewhat better known.

The associated commune of Flagey-Echézeaux – whose vineyards are generally considered as part of Vosne – is something of a curiosity. This perfunctory hamlet of some 450 souls lies not along the main flank of the Côte, but on the eastern side of the RN74 beyond the railway tracks. Tradition has it that the name 'Flagey' derives from the flagellative scything action used by the peasants to harvest corn in the 6th century. 'Echézeaux' was tacked on in 1886. With no appellation of their own for Village and Premiers Crus, the handful of vineyards falling into these categories are accorded the relevant Vosne-Romanée appellation. Were it not for its two Grands Crus – Echézeaux and Grands Echézeaux – Flagey would barely merit notice. However, the village now has an excellent small restaurant, owned and run by Robert Losset, an ex-chef from the liner *France,* which for some mysterious reason only opens at lunchtime and closes altogether on Wednesdays.

Vosne's Grands Crus are capable of producing quintessential Burgundy – wines of such opulence, depth and refinement that it is difficult to believe that they are solely the product of bunches of grapes.

Of these, Les Echézeaux is both the largest

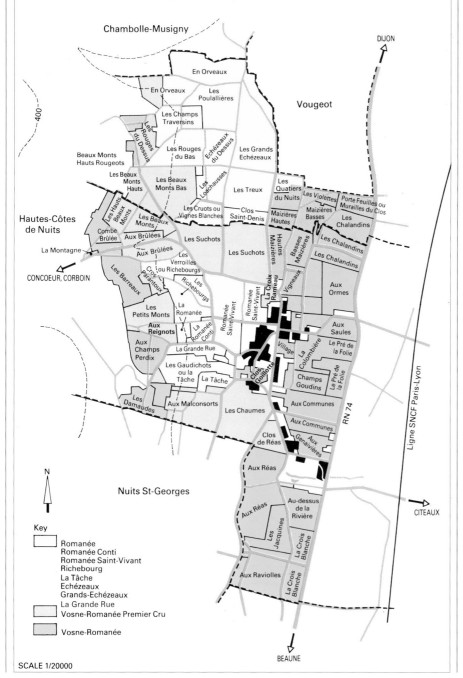

and the most variable in quality. Many believe that most of its 11 constituent *climats* deserve no more than Premier Cru status and should not have been included when the 1936 Grand Cru delimitation, which only extended to the 3.57 ha of Les Echézeaux Dessus, was subsequently revised.

The Echézeaux vines extend to the dizzy height of 360 m above sea level on slopes of up to 15%. The soils vary within the vineyard, but are relatively deep, even in the top sections, being composed chiefly of fine siltstone, clay and pebbles, over the hard limestone base on which most of Vosne-Romanée rests. It is this depth and richness which gives the potential for quality.

Indisputably Grand Cru, however, is Les Grands Echézeaux, a 9.14 ha slab of moderately flat land bordering the western edge of the Clos de Vougeot, with soils of similar content and structure to Les Echézeaux. Of the 8 Vosne Grands Crus these (and possibly Lamarche's Grande Rue) are the only ones which come anywhere near to a sensible quality:price ratio. In good vintages, Grands Echézeaux from Domaines such as Clos Frantin, Drouhin, Jean Mongeard, Engel and the Romanée-Conti, are excellent.

At 0.85 ha, La Romanée, on a 16% slope, sandwiched between La Romanée-Conti to the east and Premier Cru Aux Raignots to the west, with Les Richebourgs to the north and La Grande Rue to the south, is the smallest Grand Cru in the Côte d'Or. Originally joined to the Romanée-Conti vineyard, it was split in 1760 when the Prince de Conti bought the lower section. Owned since 1815 by the Liger-Belair family, its 300 case output is sold by the négociants Bouchard Père et Fils. The wine comes no where near equalling that of its illustrious neighbour.

In contrast, Romanée St.-Vivant is situated on virtually flat ground to the north and west of the village. The soil is unusually deep, dominated by limestone with a high clay content. More than half of its 9.43.74 ha are owned by the Domaine de la Romanée-Conti who acquired them from the Marey-Monge family in 1988. Its wine can be excellent, but is often overshadowed by the other Grands Crus. Domaine de l'Arlot and Alain Hudelot-Noëllat also make fine examples.

Les Richebourgs, which Camille Rodier described as 'one of the most sumptuous Crus of Burgundy', is an amalgam of 5.05 ha of genuine Richebourg and 2.98 ha of Vosne Premier Cru Les Verroilles which was tacked on later. Oriented eastwards, the vineyard is mainly on limestone with some clay, giving its wines characteristic meaty robustness and firm *charpente* ; whence its longevity. The finest examples come from Romanée-Conti, Méo-Camuset, Henri Jayer, Alain Hudelot-Noëllat, Jean Gros and Jean Grivot, in no particular order

Vosne's next generation of vignerons enjoying the hospitality of a rather famous wall

The 1.65 ha strip of La Grande Rue was, until 1991, one of those anomalies of classification one sometimes encounters in the Côte d'Or – a Premier Cru sandwiched between two Grands Crus – in this case La Tâche and Romanée-Conti. It has belonged to the Domaine Lamarche (qv) ever since Henri Lamarche was given it as a wedding present in 1933. The present generation, François and Marie-Blanche Lamarche, finally succeeded, after a long and persistent campaign, in persuading the authorities to reclassify it as Grand Cru, chiefly on the ground that it shares the same soil band as its neighbours. Twenty ares are in fact in Les Gaudichots.

The remaining pair of Grands Crus, La Tâche and Romanée-Conti – both *Monopoles* of the Domaine de la Romanée-Conti – represent the summit of what Burgundy and the Pinot Noir grape are capable. The one lies to the south-west of the Post Office, covering a broad strip reaching almost to the summit of the Côte, whilst the other sits majestically, compact, in the heart of the Grands Crus, marked by a simple stone cross.

Wine from these precious plots exudes breed and elegance. At once silky, opulent and fine, with mature aromas of spice and violets they offer multi-faceted flavours of glorious richness and length. Words – even if suitable ones could be found, which is doubtful – are woefully inadequate when faced with such superlative examples of the winemaker's art and attempts at description easily degenerate into senseless pretension. These are the wines of which vignerons throughout the Côte and well beyond, whether they admit it or not, stand in awe, hoarding a few treasured bottles in their own cellars to crown some special occasion. These are the apotheosis of Vosne-Romanée, and Vosne-Romanée is the apotheosis of Burgundy.

GRAND CRUS OF VOSNE-ROMANÉE

Lieu-dit	Area	Props.	Prod.
La Grande Rue	1.65.25	1	600 c/s
Echézeaux	37.69.22	84	10,500 c/s
Grands-Echézeaux	9.14.45	21	2,750 c/s
Romanée Saint-Vivant	9.43.74	6	2,600 c/s
Richebourg	8.03.45	10	2,500 c/s
La Tâche	6.06.20	1	1,870 c/s
La Romanée	0.84.52	1	300 c/s
Romanée-Conti	1.80.50	1	500 c/s
Totals:	**74.67.33**	**125**	**21,620 c/s**

Domaine Robert Arnoux

Robert Arnoux, who died in 1995, was a man of abundant vivacity, he wandered his cellar, pipette in hand, expounding his philosophy to visitors who turned up at his door on the main Nuits St-Georges road. Unfortunately, the quality of his wares declined during the 1980s, and it has taken considerable effort by his son-in-law, Pascal Lachaux to turn things round. He arrived in 1985, aged 23, at Robert's request, with only his qualification as a pharmacist and promptly went off to Dijon on a crash course to ingest the rudiments of oenology.

His influence has been radical. Robert's splendid guiding principle: 'we vinify what nature brings us' has been abandoned in favour of lower yields, with rigorous *évasivage* and crop-thinning if necessary. In 1994, Pascal even removed embryos at flowering, to encourage super-concentrated *millerands*, and has started trials to evaluate clones which give smaller bunches and berries. If he succeeds it could advance maturity by several days.

In the cellars, developments have been equally dramatic. Total destemming, cold *maceration*, enzymation, lower fermentation temperatures, more new oak, *saignées* if required and fractional *chaptalisation* have all impacted on the depth and balance of the Arnoux wines. Now they are left in cask after *malo* 'to fatten up' before racking. Pascal follows Robert in disliking filtration, but still plate-filters all his wines for security.

Old, well-placed vines help, especially in Nuits Les Poisets, Les Suchots, Romanée-St.-Vivant and curiously, their Nuits Bourgogne Rouge vineyards, all of which regularly, and inexplicably, produce a high proportion of super-concentrated *millerands,* whatever the vintage, adding substance to what are already low yields.

Pascal attributes the quality of his wines to a lowish fermentation temperature (peak 31–32⁰C) and to limiting *pigéage* and *remontage*. This, with shortish, gentle *cuvaisons* of 12–14 days – a simmer not a boil – puts nobler tannin, plusher fruit and more elegance into the wines. A few days of pre-fermentive *maceration* bring total vatting time to around 19 days and contribute further finesse, 'great concentration and substance'. The wines are matured for 15–16 months then bottled filtered but unfined.

Tasting Pascal's 1993s leaves one in no doubt of his quality. Even the Bourgogne Rouge exudes class, with only a hint of rusticity to betray its Appellation. Heavily *millerandées* 50-year-old vines, in the southerly, Prémeaux sector of Nuits, yielding 30–35 hl/ha and matured with 15% new oak all contribute to what could be one of the lushest, silkiest Bourgognes around.

The Nuits are particularly interesting in that the quality doesn't quite follow the classification. Les Procès, from a vineyard just below Château Gris, on the southern edge of the town, is a Premier Cru – only two owners and only Arnoux labels his wine Procès – is fine enough: Lachaux silkiness, perhaps mildly severe tannins to start with, but real fat underneath. However, the wine from the Village vineyard Les Poisets, is indubitably finer. Its situation plus 60+ year-old vines which regularly *millerand*, combine to give a wine of fine concentration and natural balance, with a hint of Nuits muscularity supporting Vosne power and class – a perfect ballet couple. Les Corvées Pagets, which abuts the Clos des Corvées in Prémeaux follows in the same line, with perhaps a hint more elegance and length.

The Vosnes – two Village *cuvées* and a trio of Premiers Crus – are equally exciting. The more interesting of the Villages is Les Hautes Maizières, formerly Robert's Vosne Premier Cru *cuvée*, until the entire vineyard, which straddles Premier Cru and Village, was declassified into Village in 1982. Of the Premiers Crus the Suchots is particularly good – the 1993 certainly of Grand Cru quality. Low yields, plenty of *millerands* and 70% new wood fuse into an opulent, silky, almost voluptuous whole, powerful yet beautifully balanced. This is more complex and complete than either the Echézeaux or Clos Vougeot.

The finest Arnoux Grand Cru, Romanée-St.-Vivant, comes from 0.35 hectares of 70-year-old vines and goes a dimension further in power and complexity. The 1993 had a fine, limpid, purplish black cherry colour, fruit-based aromas of great class and inherent complexity, a palate-suffusing richness of silky fruit and remarkable length – a real masterpiece with a fine future.

Pascal is an open, uncomplicated man, who thoroughly enjoys his life of wine. His wife helps with clients and the ever-increasing administrative workload, and looks after their two children, Charles and Antoine. Meanwhile, in 1995 he was elected to Vosne's local council – no great triumph, as he readily admits, eleven candidates and eleven places. Robert Arnoux would be proud of the new team.

Domaine A et F Gros

The boyish, elfin, Anne Gros took over her father, François' Domaine in 1988. Now wine formerly sold *en negoce* is Domaine bottled. François, one of four of Louis Gros' children, inherited vines, including 60 ares of Richebourg, the common denominator uniting this tentacular family.

Anne's studies in Beaune and Dijon, and six months at Rosemount in Australia, seem to have given her an appetite for experimentation. 'I'm always experimenting with something', she confesses, with an impish grin. Whether its 'culture biologique', developing her own living compost for the vines, different types, chars and suppliers of oak for maturation, or almost every conceivable combination of fining and different filtration mediums, she's tried it or intends to. 'Nothing systematic – nothing fixed', best describes her approach. With only a few vintages under her belt, she admits that her experience is limited, so is happy to explore different avenues to increase her feel for her wines.

These – just five in all, spanning the range from generic Bourgogne Rouge to Grand Cru – are excellent. In between there is a delicious, quite bright, Chambolle-Musigny from scree soil on the lower section of the Combe d'Orveau; this is humid land and rather a frost-pocket. The village Vosne-Romanee, from *lieu-dit* Les Barreaux, a well-sited, hillside vineyard above Cros Parantoux, Aux Brulées and Les Richebourgs – is much denser. Its weight, aromatic potential and concentration put the 1993 on the verge of Premier Cru quality.

The two Grands Crus are entirely different. Clos Vougeot – from the Le Grand Maupertuis part of the Clos, between Vosne and the Château, next door to Les Grands Echézeaux, has all the richness of the old vines from which it comes (many over 90), with the tannic structure derived from 15–18 months in 80–90% new oak. For such ancient vines, yields are generally good (35 hl/ha in 1994 but only 22 hl/ha in 1993 because of mildew): 'These vines are in super form', Anne laughs. So, in both vintages, is the wine – complex aromas and flavours of black fruits, rich, and satisfying with a very long follow-through on the 1993. The Richebourg has less obvious breadth, but greater finesse – a long, voluptuous, very sexy, silky 1993 – with more complexity and *puissance* than the Clos Vougeot.

Her Australian *stage* resulted in her meeting Jean-Paul Tollot, one of the Tollots-Beaut from Chorey (Rosemount's winemaker, Phillip Shaw was apparently the go-between). Now, they live together and have two small children. Fortunately, these don't seem to distract her unduly from her task of developing her fine Domaine.

Domaine Cathiard

Sylvain Cathiard trained at the Ecole Viticole in Beaune, then worked with his father André – who lives next door – for 15 years before starting out on his own in 1984. A decade later, his father ceded his vines to him *en metayage*, so there are now around 4 ha of good vineyards spread across Vosne, Chambolle and Nuits.

Sylvain is a careful winemaker with a feel for quality. His vinification is thoroughly traditional – 17–20 days *cuvaison* of destemmed fruit, with neither yeasting or enzyming, and a level of *pigéage* adapted to the vintage and the individual wine. The Bourgogne Rouge is kept in *cuve* and the rest of the range matured in cask, with a judicious larding of between 40 and 100% new oak to add structure and *rondeur*. Sylvain prefers Allier – 'finer than Vosges', which is also used, but believes that for proper balance you need both. After 18-20 months and a single racking, the wines are assembled, lightly plate-filtered and bottled.

The style here emphasises finesse and fruit, rather than being massively structured. Many of the vines are well into their 40s, which adds natural concentration and balance to the wines. The Vosnes are particularly good – the En Orveaux, from the Echézeaux sector of the vignoble, adjoining Chambolle-Musigny, is perhaps the sturdiest of the Premiers Crus, with almost Vougeot meatiness. The Reignots, particularly well-sited, above La Romanée and Romanée-Conti, exudes both *puissance* and depth, with plenty of finesse underneath. The Malconsorts, which borders Nuits, starts with an angular aspect to it – higher acidity and firmer tannins – which makes for a longer evolution. Premiers Crus Vosne Les Suchots and Nuits Les Murgers and Grand Cru Romanée-St.-Vivant, were added in 1996.

Sylvain Cathiard and his wife do all the work between them – vineyards, cellars, sales and accounting. In time, their son, now approaching his teens and distinctly more attracted by pistols than pipettes, will hopefully join them to share the burden. This is a fine source.

Domaine Clavelier-Brosson

This is one of a flush of emergent Burgundy Domaines, transformed from a family enterprise selling entirely *en négoce*. The widespread tradition of bulk sales reflected more a desire for security than any defect in the wines which, in many cases, including that of the Claveliers, came from fine land.

Bruno Clavelier – a slim, handsome man in his 30s – is the 7th generation at Vosne. In 1988, he returned from *stages* in Bordeaux and Meursault to take over 5.47 ha of vines from his maternal grandmother. Now everything is Domaine-bottled and the standard is uniformly high.

One can immediately sense quality from Bruno's articulateness – nothing glib, but a careful approach which is both flexible and self-critical, and confidence that the main direction is right.

The vines are relatively old, an immediate advantage which shows in the concentration and balance of the wines. 'Our vines control their own production,' Bruno comments, noting that he rarely needs to crop-thin to reduce yields, but adding: 'I bless grandfather for putting only manure on the vineyards, not potassium which reduces acidities; you see, he kept cows and horses, here in the stable.' Everything which comes from vines over 45 is automatically labelled 'Vieilles Vignes'.

The emphasis is on Vosne-Romanée – with two Premiers Crus and a quartet of vineyard-designated Villages. Otherwise, the range includes Nuits, Gevrey and Chambolle Premiers Crus, red and white Régionales and an interesting Chardonnay Vin de Pays de Côte d'Or from vines at nearby Boncourt.

Bruno's principal objective is quality, which he describes as a finely-judged balance of constituents, none of which should dominate. In particular, new wood needs careful thought and is presently limited to 25–30%: 'We're not craftsmen in oak.' He buys casks from several barrel-makers, pitting one against another, to keep them on their collective toes.

The house style puts *terroir* and fruit in the driving-seat, with around 10% of whole bunches left in the vats to increase glycerol production during the few days of cool *maceration* which precedes fermentation. Three weeks of *cuvaison*, scrupulously avoiding any sharp peak in temperature, helps add *gras* and, in Bruno's view, substitutes fine for coarse tannins. After 18–22 months, the wines are assembled, without pumping, and bottled unfined (excepting some 1992s) and unfiltered.

The Vosnes provide an unequivocal demonstration of the importance of *terroir*. The Hautes-Maizières, from a Village vineyard on eroded soil below Premier Cru Les Suchots, exudes elegance, with round tannins and Chambolle-like finesse. Despite being separated by just 50 metres, the Village Combe Brulées and Premier Cru Aux Brulees differ markedly in character: the former, from stony soils, has a firm structure, quite powerful with finesse underneath – a wine which evolves slowly. The latter, from deeper soil, has a meatier, spicy quality, highish acidity and more obvious tannins. The Vosne Les Beaumonts, 200 metres from Les Brulées, combines structure and elegance with more natural power than either of the other two.

In a few years, Bruno Clavelier has established a solid reputation – no publicity, just recommendation, among 'particuliers', especially from Switzerland, who constitute half his sales. He bemoans the American merchants who only appear when some guru or other tells them that a vintage is worth buying. In years such as 1994 – his are particularly good – it will be merchants and customers who lose out, not Bruno. Clavelier is definitely a name to watch.

Bruno Clavelier and his father

THE GREAT DOMAINES OF BURGUNDY

Domaine Forey Père et Fils

Régis Forey lives opposite the Domaine de la Romanée-Conti, which is entirely appropriate since he is responsible for both vines and wine of Grand Cru, La Romanée – at 0.85 ha the smallest Appellation in the world – adjoining the Romanée-Conti vineyard, and also has some Les Gaudichots, which abuts DRCs La Tâche.

Although his family have made wine since 1870, when his great-grandfather, François Forey, bought Les Gaudichots and Chalandins, it is only from 1983 that there has been any Domaine bottling. Then there were 2,000, now there are 20–25,000, 80% of which is sold to 'particuliers'.

In 1988, having worked with his father for several years, in the USA, and with the Peyrauds at Domaine Tempier in Bandol, Régis finally took control. He bought some Echézeaux and was approached by négociants Bouchard Père et Fils to share crop their La Romanée and Vosne Premier Cru Aux Reignots on behalf of the proprietors, the Liger-Belair family, an arrangement which expires shortly. Although Régis is entitled to half the crop from these two vineyards, all the wine is *élévé* and sold by Bouchard, in order to preserve La

Romanée's *Monopole* designation. The Liger-Belairs also own the Château de Vosne-Romanée, a fine, but sad and little-used building, in the splendid, film-set cellars of which Régis stores his casks and bottles. He is busy making plans for new cellars for the turn of the century.

A tall, hirsute swarthy man with a somewhat rectangular head, he builds his wines to last: plenty of new wood – 100% for Les Gaudichots and the Grands Crus, 50% for the Nuits Les St.-Georges and progressively less for the rest; 18–25 days *cuvaison* with plenty of *pigéage* to maximise extraction; then 15–24 months' maturation (1993 and 1990 respectively). So cold are the Château's cellars that finings won't settle out properly; so, since 1992, Régis has replaced fining with enzymes added at fermentation, to improve clarification and avoid filtration.

Given 50 pickers, he can harvest his 8 hectares in 5 days – an advantage in uncertain weather; this and a rigorous *trie* gives him good control over fruit quality. The results show in the wines. The three Nuits – all from the Prémeaux sector – have plenty of stuffing balanced by an attractive Vosne-ish elegance. The Village and Premier Cru

Les St.-Georges have firmer structures and greater power than Les Perrières which, in the 1994 vintage, was more voluminous, with 'sweeter' fruit, good grip and considerable style. Les St.-Georges has more clay and limestone than Perrières, which is poorer, stonier, ground.

The Gaudichots, a Vosne Premier Cru in which La Tâche was embedded, is a rarity – both in quantity (450–550 bottles) and in the sense of being little seen. This, and the Echézeaux – from the favourably-sited *lieus-dits* Les Treux and Clos St.-Denis, adjoining Clos Vougeot and Grands-Echézeaux – vie for top place in Régis' cellar. The Forey-Gaudichots is perhaps the silkier of the pair whilst the Echézeaux, which Régis describes as his 'most difficult *cuvée*' on account of its tendency to overproduce, is somewhat broader. Both are fine quality indeed – great successes in 1993 and 1994 – but you'll be lucky to get any Gaudichots.

The Forey family are long-established in Vosne – François and his son Henri were instrumental in founding the commune's co-operate which flourished before WW2. They are once again making an impact and seem set to continue doing so.

Domaine Emmanuel Rouget

Emmanuel Rouget, a solid, rather gruff 30-year-old, has the advantage, and inestimable privilege, of having worked alongside Henri Jayer, one of Burgundy's greatest winemakers since 1977. Needing extra help, Jayer, his uncle, offered Emmanuel, a tractor mechanic, a job.

In 1985, he took on some vines of his own – Echézeaux, Vosne and Nuits Villages – *en metayage* from Henri's brother Lucien Jayer. Two years later, another brother, Georges, offered more Echézeaux and Nuits on the same basis, and starred restaurateur, Jean Crottet, asked him to share-crop his Bourgogne Rouge vines. In 1989 came more vines, this time from Henri Jayer himself, in Nuits, Vosne Village and Premiers Crus Les Beaux-Monts and Cros Parantoux. Latest additions (1990/1) were Savigny, Vosne and Nuits – owned by Jean Crottet and friends.

All these vines are share-cropped on a 50:50 basis. This means that Emmanuel works the vines and vinifies the wine, giving half to the owner and keeping half for

himself – each selling under his own label.

This is straightforward enough, apart from the Echézeaux, which gives rise to splendidly convoluted Burgundian complications, since Henri's vines are in one *climat* (Cruots), Lucien's in another (Les Treux), whilst Georges has vines in both. The law demands a strict split – so three separate *cuvées* are produced – one for each brother. Once they have taken their share, what remains is blended together and bottled by Emmanuel under his own label.

The quality of his wines is uniformly high. Starting with a supple Bourgogne Rouge, the range progresses through a silky Savigny and very Vosne-ish Nuits Village, to a fine top trio. First, an attractive, mid-weight, Vosne Premier Cru Les Beaumonts, deftly balancing elegance and power from predominantly thin stony soils. Next, comes the 'cocktail' Echézeaux, a firm, deep, broad-framed wine with plenty of grip and power. The high clay soil of Les Treux imparts substance, whilst Cruots contributes suppleness and 'extraordinary' complexity.

The whole invariably transcends its components and, for once in this often disappointing *climat*, fully merits its Grand Cru status.

Finally, Cros Parantoux, a Vosne Premier Cru situated above Les Richebourgs to the north and east, with Petits Monts to the south and Vosne Village vines to the west. Here the poverty of the soil virtually precludes cultivation and vine roots show through to the surface. Such a struggle results in a wine of majestic subtlety – somehow fusing power, elegance, complexity and ampleur into an effortlessly harmonious whole, as only the greatest Burgundy is capable of. In vintages of the quality of 1993, it certainly outclasses the Echézeaux .

Emmanuel's ideas and general guidelines follow closely those of Henri Jayer (q.v.), under whose watchful eye and in whose *cuverie*, everything is vinified. Once shared out, his wines are taken to the cellar beneath his house in Flagey-Rouget Echézeaux for *élévage*. This is no young iconoclast, but a masterfully trained traditionalist and worthy successor to his mentor.

Domaine René Engel

VOSNE-ROMANÉE

René Engel was one of the great personalities of post-war Burgundy and of Vosne-Romanée in particular. A co-founder of the Confrérie des Chevaliers de Tastevin, for 35 years Professor of Oenology at Dijon University and a respected writer on Burgundy and its wines (a 'Vade Mecum pour Viticulteurs' and 'Vosne-Romanée, l'histoire du Village' are the best-known works), he was dedicated to the Côte d'Or and to improving quality.

He died aged 94, in 1986, five years after his son Pierre. When his grandson, Philippe, finally took over, in 1981, much needed to be done to remedy neglect evident in the vineyards where dead vines had not been replaced and the soil contained excess nitrogen and potassium. In the cellars, casks and *foudres* were in poor repair.

Gradually Philippe put things right and began to stamp his own personality upon the Domaine. Although it has taken time for him to shake off the legacy of illustrious ancestry, things have improved considerably, the wines becoming more consistent.

Philippe is clear about his preferred style of wine and the exponents of it he most admires. Philippe Charlopin and Alain Burguet are his friends, occasional dining companions and informal consultants. Not for him lacy finesse and feminine elegance, rather richly-structured wines with plenty of meaty fruit.

Nonetheless, much of family tradition is retained. Up to 21 days *cuvaison,* total destalking, no pumps and twice daily *pigéage* during fermentation. Surprisingly, cultured yeasts are sometimes used to start fermentation; perhaps more of a panic measure than a necessity. Hopefully this practice will be discontinued.

Philippe is not afraid to take risks. When, for example, a *cuvée* of 1985 Clos de Vougeot resisted all attempts at cooling and continued fermenting up to the dizzy heights of 36⁰C, he consulted René on what should be done. The advice: 'leave it alone'. Philippe did, the wine was superb. So now, he is happy to let his *cuves* rise to 35⁰C to render the wine 'bien gras'.

René Engel liked to add only the wine from the first, gentler pressing. Philippe, having experimented with a Premier Cru without press-wine, and with first press-wine, continues in this way. However, in years when the harvest is small, there is a second press-wine which is vinified apart and then either added or not at assemblage, just before bottling, or 'kept for a year which has less structure'.

Although the wines see 30% new wood, Philippe would prefer more. He cites the cost of new casks, the 'poor image' of new wood (hard to believe) as deterrents, but admits that those of his wines which see most new oak are universally preferred by his customers. He also cites the wines of Jean-Nicolas Méo, vinified in 100% new oak, as among his personal favourites.

The wines are generally racked 'a l'air', with a push of nitrogen to avoid pumping. This generally happened after *malo* in spring of the first year; however, having once left the wines on their lees for 18 months convinced him that 'vins solides' may safely be left unracked, which also helps retain their freshness. Equally, pumping adds a grassy dimension and detracts from a wine's freshness. So now, minimum racking and no pumping.

René Engel apparently studied the question of when to bottle in some detail and discovered that after a certain time in cask a wine does not further evolve – at least, not beneficially. Whilst some in Gevrey, for example, bottle their wines after only 9 months in cask, in a misguided attempt to mimic the freshness and delicacy of a Vosne-Romanée, Philippe Engel leaves his wines for 18 months before bottling, generally with an albumin fining in bulk and a Kieselguhr and/or plate filtration. In his view, fining rounds out a wine and endows it with a brilliance which filtered wine lacks. Filtration, however careful, tends to remove some of a wine's stuffing, and is increasingly avoided.

An interesting experiment tested the relative importance of vinification and vineyard on the character of a wine. Engel exchanged a tonne of Vosne grapes with Burguet and Charlopin and they delivered Gevrey grapes to him. Not surprisingly, he made rather Vosne-like wine with his Gevrey grapes whereas Burguet and Charlopin made heavier structured and Gevrey-ish Vosne-Romanées. There seems to be considerable scope for imaginative experimentation along these lines elsewhere to dissociate the relative contributions of yeasts and *terroir.* How about Leflaive grapes vinified at Bonneau de Martray or some Monthélie grapes vinified in Chambolle-Musigny?

Although large chunks of spare time are scarce, Philippe Engel is not completely tied to his cellars. He indulges his passion for motor-cycling round the locality and sails on nearby lakes. He follows in his father's and grandfather's footsteps at the Château de Clos Vougeot, where he takes his duties as a member of the 'Grand Conseil' seriously. This requires attendance at twenty Chapters a year, and his knowledge of the history of both Château and Confrérie lets him in for conducting visitors round the building.

Consonant with his preferred style, Engel wines are darkly-coloured and brooding in their youth, with a firm structure of tannins and acidity, beneath which lurks considerable substance. Their density is accentuated by a *saignée de cuve* when necessary; in 1990, for instance, against the advice of his oenologist, Philippe *saignéed* many of his *cuves.*

Of the range, the Clos Vougeot is the tightest at birth, with something of the structure of Burguet's Gevrey-Chambertin Vieilles Vignes. The Vosne-Romanée, Les Brulées is distinctly better than its Village sibling, with more breed and complexity. The Echézeaux with its deep, limpid black-cherry hue and nose of griottes, liquorice and *fruits noirs* , although sometimes excellent (1990), can be disappointing and clumsy (1989). The Grands-Echézeaux is a distinctly masculine interpretation of that Cru. If there is a general fault, it is that the fruit is too often supported by what some might regard as an overkill of tannin. Such judgements must be a matter of personal taste, but the wines would benefit enormously from slightly less scaffolding so that one can more easily appreciate the building underneath.

Commune	Level	Lieu-dit/Climat	Area	Vine Age	Status
Flagey	GC	Echézeaux	0.55	25 and 80	P
Flagey	GC	Grands Echézeaux	0.50	75	P
Vougeout	GC	Clos de Vougeot	1.37	55	P
Vosne	PC	Les Brulées	1.05	45	P
Vosne	V	————	2.54	50	P
		Total:	**6.01 ha**		

Domaine Confuron-Cotétidot

VOSNE-ROMANÉE

Jacky Confuron is an individual – a person who, once met, is difficult to forget. Physically striking with short hair, sometimes swept back, sometimes standing up on end, he is short and stocky with slightly bowed legs. His personality matches his mien – rather rugged, determined and not to be gainsaid or swayed – he is someone for whom the world is either black or white, with few shades in between.

He lives with his wife Bernadette in a large, pleasant house in one of the feeder roads into Vosne from the RN74. From here, they run their 7.14 ha Domaine with the help of their two sons – oenologist Jean-Pierre and, since 1995, his younger brother Yves – a distinctly gruff, rough-edged, individual.

The Confurons – of which those at Premeaux are another branch – have been in Vosne for a long time: 'My great, great grandfather, at least, started the Domaine.' Generations later, when 'Le Père', as Jacky refers to his father, decided to divide up his 18 ha in 1964, Jacky received 2.5 ha as his share – 'Le Père' having resolved to keep the largest slice for himself. Gradually more land was bought – Chambolle-Musigny, Gevrey-Chambertin, Nuits-St.-Georges and Bourgogne – to turn it into an enterprise which would comfortably support a wife and two children.

It takes only a few minutes' conversation to realise that Jacky Confuron is not someone who acts on impulse, but who weighs every decision with the utmost care and precision. For him there is no short cut to quality.

In 1977, he sought the advice of Guy Accad to help bring back an equilibrium to his soils, but Accad's influence soon extended into the cellars. However, it would be a mistake to think that Jacky abrogated his responsibilities there to Accad – as long as the advice is good he will take it, otherwise he is perfectly capable of making up his own mind. 'It takes 25 years to get a client and it is so easy to lose them,' Jacky adds reflectively. His wines are rapidly sold out, so for the moment the clientele seems totally faithful. Although Accad's services were dispensed with in 1990, the exchange has left indelible marks on the Confuron way of working.

Part of Jacky's philosophy is a hearty dislike of anything of which he is not completely sure. Clones fall into this category. He did try them but was dissatisfied with the quality: 'The vine perished in 15 years. No clones – I

make my own plant selection.' There is no compromise – the plant selection is grafted by Jacky himself on to riparia rootstock – a traditional root which is returning to favour in the Côte for its low yield and berry quality – 'good on to good'.

Generally the vines are pruned in the customary *Guyot simple* mode, limited further by Jacky to 5 or 6 eyes on each cane. If an individual plant is becoming feeble, then it is trained *en gobelet* to encourage it to produce. This is expert work for which he enlists the skills of his wife: 'It is like making love,' he explains, 'you must concentrate.'

As one might expect, Jacky Confuron prefers low yields and works hard to limit them. In this he is helped by the vines themselves, many of which are a venerable 60–75 years old. A young vine for Jacky would be an old one for most other growers. The figures speak for themselves – in 1988 and 1989 average Confuron yields were 30 hl/ha – against permitted base for Vosne Village and Premier Cru of 40 hl/ha and 35 hl/ha for Grand Cru. In 1990 they climbed to 40 hl/ha for Village and to 35 hl/ha for the Premiers and Grands Crus, with rather less in 1993.

All this is achieved by meticulous attention to detail – plenty of *repiquéage*, the barest minimum, if any, fertilisation, rigorous *évasivage*, the minimum of treatments and certainly no anti-rot sprays. In addition, the foliage is summer-pruned 'much higher than

Jacky Confuron stamping out his grafts – most vignerons buy them in

normal', to encourage photosynthesis and thus maximise sugar levels; any second generation bunches are scrupulously removed each August.

The right moment to harvest is one of the most important decisions a conscientious vigneron has to make. In Jacky's case there is no difficulty – 'We harvest late to have the maximum degrees,' he remarks, as if this were a self-evident truth, adding 'you must take risks'. He cites some tests carried out by a French wine-writer, in which samples of grapes were taken from a number of vineyards during harvest – many were found to be far short of proper maturity.

In the cellars beneath the house the work continues: 'I operate on the ancient method,' says Jacky, referring no doubt to his old wooden *cuves* and to the 150-year-old press, originally used by his great-grandfather.

The grapes are not destalked, but vatted whole, where they receive a 1–1.5 litre per tonne dose of SO_2 – 0.5 less than in Accad's vintages. Selection in the vineyard is so rigorous that 'there are never any rotten grapes here', so the sulphur simply serves to knock out the yeasts and, together with cooling to 8–10°C, to delay the onset of fermentation.

At the end of this cold *maceration*, yeasts are added to get fermentation started. The average length of *cuvaison* is 3 weeks, during which time the temperature is permitted to rise to no more than 28°C – 'Above that you get evaporation and the risk of *volatile acidity*.'

The 'méthode ancienne' extends to the '3 good *pigéages*' to which each *cuve* is subjected daily. This involves Jacky and his sons, completely naked, immersing all but their heads in the *cuve*. His wife is spared this ordeal – 'She is the head and I am the arms,' is how Jacky seems to view his conjugal corporate structure.

Chaptalisation is kept to the minimum and performed in one fell swoop. Once most of the sugar has been fermented out the free-run wine is drawn off and the remaining pulp forked into the 150-year-old press which is then galvanised into action with the aid of a hand pump. A single pressing is enough – for the pulp and, one suspects, for Jacky as well.

The press-wine is then tasted and, if up to scratch, added to the original wine which is allowed to settle further for 2–8 days, depending on the state of the lees, before transfer to casks to begin its *élevage*.

Because he considers that not destalking gives his wines enough tannin, Jacky sees no

The Confurons' house on the edge of Vosne

reason to add any more in the form of new oak. Therefore only 10% of his casks are renewed annually, and they last him for 5–10 years.

The *élevage* here is highly individual: the wines spend some 24–30 months in wood, a timescale more Bordelais than Burgundian. Each February/March and August the casks are racked, the final racking being into bulk to unify the different lots of each wine. The wine is then returned to cask, the sulphur adjusted, and then it is carefully bottled by hand, direct from cask.

Jacky's 'méthode ancienne' tolerates neither fining nor filtration. 'Wine,' he remarks dryly, 'is living, and should be treated like a person. Filtration takes the trousers off a wine – it removes everything.' In his view careful racking keeps the trousers intact without destroying the stuffing and balance of a wine.

Whatever his rationale, Jacky's wines are remarkably good. Some commentators heaped opprobrium on him for producing what they referred to as 'méthode Accad' wines. These criticisms were offensive and usually concealed a limited understanding of what Accad and his clients were trying to achieve.

What cannot be denied is that long, cold, *maceration* produces wines which start life with deep colours – this is not, let it be said, unique to this system of vinification. They also tend to have somewhat exuberant aromas – which are extracted, and fixed, by a relatively low fermentation temperature.

The wines remain excellent, and good examples of their appellations, even though Accad has departed. The Vosne Village *cuvée*

is generally quite a dense, meaty wine, well-concentrated, with plenty of depth and considerable length. The 1993 showed firm tannins and highish acidity, otherwise, it ran true to form. The Nuits-St.-Georges is entirely different – rather more breadth and earthiness – fatter and more structured. The 1993 had open aromas of *fruits noires* with good length and rather dry tannins. The vineyard is situated on the Vosne side of Nuits, which would tend to emphasise similarities rather than differences.

The Chambolle-Musigny is generally the least typical of its origins. Such a determined extraction imparts almost too much depth and structure for a really copybook Chambolle – this is not an argument about the quality of the wine, rather about its typicity. The 1993 lacked a bit of *puissance* and seemed altogether rather flat. Perhaps it will flesh out and regain its form with a few years in bottle.

The Confuron vinification particularly suits Nuits and Gevreys. The *cuvée* of 1993 Gevrey-Chambertin, from 80-year-old vines, has incredible depth, a dark, brooding nose with a substantial layer of ripe fruit underneath. The wine – still in cask in June 1995 – seemed rather blurred and diffuse and finished with a note of bitterness. Possibly a touch over-extracted. The Nuits Premier Cru – an assemblage of fruit from 70-year-old vines in Les Murgers and Les Vignesrondes – has similar depth, massive structure and plenty of very ripe fruit; something of a brick shed in character which will take some time to become user-friendly.

The 1993 Vosne-Romanée Les Suchots is constructed on a less grandiose scale – bright flavours, enough new oak and excellent length and persistence. This will be very good indeed – one can see a cleaner line on to its evolution.

The Echézeaux, from 42-year-old vines in Les Treux, is fairly broad in character, concentrated, long and satisfying, but without quite the power one expects from a Grand Cru. This may change after bottling, but, as seen, this is somewhat one-dimensional, and not up to the usual Confuron Echézeaux standard.

The Clos-Vougeot, from 65-year-old vines, is denser and noticeably earthier. Underneath, a splendid concentration of fruit and notable elegance, with a carefully-judged dose of new oak. This will be very good.

Now that the Accad furore has died down, critics will hopefully revert to tasting the wine rather than the vinification. Such debates should not blind people who seek only to enjoy their wines, from trying some of the very fine bottles to be had from such as Jacky Confuron and his sons – wines as carefully crafted as it is possible to make them – albeit in Jacky's individual mould. Jacky and Bernadette Confuron can sell every drop they produce – a position of which many lesser winemakers might be thoroughly envious. Those who denigrate should pause to reflect on this before rushing into print.

VINEYARD HOLDINGS

Commune	Level	Lieu-dit/Climat	Area	Vine Age	Status
Flagey	GC	Echézeaux (Les Treux)	0.46	42	P
Vougeot	GC	Clos de Vougeot	0.26	65	P
Vosne	PC	Les Suchots	1.34	–	P
Vosne	V	Porte Feuilles du Clos + Jacquines	1.45	10–40	M/P
Nuits	PC	Murgers + Vignesrondes	1.00	75	M
Nuits	V	Bas de Combes + Lavières	0.55	75	P
Gevrey	V	Les Champs Chenys	0.40	80	P
Chambolle	V	(Various *climats*)	0.71	50	P
———	R	(Bourg. R / Aligoté)	0.98	40	P
Total:			**7.14 ha**		

Domaine Jean Grivot

VOSNE-ROMANÉE

The Domaine Jean Grivot is generally regarded as one of the finest in the Côte d'Or. An old Domaine, its origins date back to the French Revolution at the end of the 18th century, when Grivots from the Jura first appeared in Vosne. Whilst the maternal branch came from Italy's Val d'Aosta, the paternal roots were local farmers, barrel-makers and blacksmiths. Gradually, viticulture superseded the agricultural and forging activities until, by the end of the 19th century, Gaston Grivot had built up a Domaine of considerable quality.

He had foresight – selling several disparate parcels of vines, including those in the Hautes Côtes at Chaux, and replacing them with 1.68 ha of Clos Vougeot, a single strip from the RN74 to abeam the Ch. de la Tour at the upper end of the Clos, which remains one of the Domaines most important holdings.

Gaston's planning extended to marriage – to Madeleine Grivot (no relation) who had some good vines in Nuits; so the Domaine grew yet again. He also earned a Diplome d'Oenologie from Dijon University, being one of the earliest students of that now famous faculty.

The sound understanding of the technical complexities of viticulture and vinification thus acquired led, in 1919–20, to him bottling his own wines and selling in bottle. Together with Henri Gouges and the Marquis d'Angerville, Gaston was among the first in the Côte to Domaine-bottle, both as a guarantee of authenticity and as a measure of protection against adulteration.

Jean Grivot took over on his father's death in 1955 with, as his son Etienne puts it, 'all the oenological baggage'. Since 1959 the Domaine's wines have all been sold in bottle, except in lesser vintages when it proved financially more interesting to sell in bulk. Now everything is sold in bottle.

Under Jean's hand the Domaine flourished and achieved a high reputation for the typicity and quality of its wines. Bottles from the Gaston and earlier Jean Grivot era are a remarkable tribute to the skill and quality of two great vignerons.

Recent years have seen significant changes which demand a reappraisal of this great estate. In 1982, Jean's son Etienne, fresh from the Lycée Viticole in Beaune with a Diploma in oenology and viticulture and solid work experience in France and California, joined his father.

Gradually Jean handed over responsibility

Etienne and Jean Grivot

for the technical aspects of the Domaine to Etienne, who is now in full charge of vineyards and winemaking. His father, meanwhile, looks after sales and sees most of the many admiring clients who visit the Domaine – self-imposed tasks which he clearly enjoys.

This change entrained controversy. To put this into proper perspective it is necessary to underline that Etienne is both intelligent and of the utmost integrity. The radical changes he made since 1987 are not the fruit of youthful rebellion, but rather the result of deep conviction and considerable heart-searching. Whatever may be thought of their effects, the sincerity of the motives behind them is beyond question.

Tasting his own and others' wines over many vintages, Etienne found himself dissatisfied with what the Domaine was producing;

in his opinion, the wines generally lacked colour, structure and longevity. He desperately wanted to improve on what he regarded as a disparity between actual and potential quality and believed that he had the ability to do so.

The core question was: why are the wines of recent years so elegant yet lacking in guts, whilst those of earlier times are so rich and such long keepers? Preliminary conclusions were that the relatively feeble fertilisation in previous decades gave a much higher level of grape maturity and further that if one did not crush the grapes deliberately, then the temperature of fermentation rarely exceeded 32°C, so it lasted longer and produced a greater extraction of colour and tannins.

These thoughts led further: Etienne considered that the most important factor in the production of fine wine is the health of the grapes and this could only be maximised by a soil which was in as near perfect equilibrium as possible. Furthermore, since the maximum quality potential is in the grapes, it can be destroyed or maintained, but never surpassed. These two propositions, together with that relating the uniqueness of each soil to each wine type, triggered a reappraisal of his viticulture in the quest for perfect soils and fruit.

Given that this happened at a time when Domaine Jean Grivot was regarded as one of the best in the Côte, to question the fundamentals of its quality was an act of great courage. It must also be realised that handing over the Domaine's magnificent vineyards to Etienne to pursue his goals was an act of equal courage and considerable faith on the part of Jean Grivot.

Since taking over, Etienne's priority has been to re-establish a true equilibrium of soil constituents. In this, he was influenced and helped by an oenologist, Guy Accad, whose views he shares. They set about adjusting the excesses of nitrogen, potassium and phosphorus which were seen as a serious threat to soil balance. The nitrogen was especially worrying since it blocked natural magnesium so essential for photosynthesis and thus for the production of chlorophyll. Chlorophyll is effectively the vine's factory, and so any lack will slow down production, affecting grape-sugar levels and maturity.

The legacy of years of over-fertilising was a severe soil disequilibrium which Etienne was not alone in seeking to rectify. The principles upon which he and Accad worked were that: i) any element is acceptable up to a certain level of concentration, above which it becomes toxic; ii) the soil mechanism should be regarded as an integrated whole – break one link in the chain and that integrity is destroyed and iii) that it is all too easy to add an element to the soil, but less simple to correct an excess.

Once soil balance was in hand, attention was turned to the plant material being used and, in particular, to clonal selection. Clones, Etienne judged, were generally good, but risked excessive production. It is essential to have the competence to adjust fertilisers and pruning to each clone and to its soil, rather than just planting them out and trusting to nature.

In 1985 the Domaine instituted trials using the maximum available number of quality clones and planting them in 2–3 row stands on different rootstocks. These will continue to be evaluated for several years.

The manner and length of the *taille* and density of planting are no less important. Etienne has concluded that for optimal fruit quality it is essential both to prune the vines *en cordon* and, against the current trend of

reducing density, to increase the number of vines per ha from the present 10–12,000 to 15,000.

These improvements have resulted in both higher and more consistent yields. Furthermore, the better condition of the soil and the nourishment of the vines have increased protection against infestation, reinforcing Etienne's policy of using as few treatments as possible, and then only in minimum dose. His guiding philosophy is that one should regard a vineyard as a complex, integrated biological mechanism and should avoid tinkering with individual bits without having careful regard to the effects upon the whole. All this holistic viticulture is designed to optimise the functioning of the vegetal machine – that is the production of sugar and the ripening of skins and wood, and the production of pips – the next generation.

It might be thought that such careful husbandry would only increase yields at the expense of a drop in quality – since there is generally thought to be an inverse relationship between the two. Etienne addresses this question by suggesting that the only sensible way of reducing yields is to harvest late, and further, that one can only hope to do this effectively if the vines are thoroughly healthy.

To those who claim that beyond a certain level of maturity there is no further beneficial development so there is no point in delaying harvest, Grivot counters that one only has to watch the *verjus* – the second crop of grapes – mature perfectly well, even when the vine has shed all its leaves, to explode that argument. Moreover, he argues, if customers are to be expected to pay high prices for fine Burgundy they have the right to expect vignerons to accept the risks of late harvesting to ensure that the wine is of the highest quality – which rather begs the question.

Grand Cru vegetables maturing in the Grivot cellar

In 1990, to test his theories, he left a plot of Vosne-Romanée until 16th October when it was harvested with a potential alcohol – that is to say, the alcohol level if all the natural sugar were fermented out – of 13.7 degrees; the resulting two *cuvées* were, in his view, far above Village quality.

Feeling increasingly in tune with what Guy Accad was trying to achieve, in 1987 Etienne persuaded his father to extend his consultancy to the Grivot vinification. This decision brought them both considerable criticism. It was said that Accad's methods had nothing to do with 'proper Burgundy' and that they effectively amounted to cheating by adding colour, acidity and tannins to the wines. Others who sought Accad's services came in for similar opprobrium.

The cornerstone of that philosophy is that much of what passes for 'traditional' vinification in the Côte d'Or is a crystallisation of bad habits resulting from starting off with poor quality raw material – hence the stress on viticulture and the best possible grapes. However, this by itself will not do: there are examples aplenty of superbly made Burgundies, young and old, vinified without recourse to Accad. One may, without inconsistency, agree with the viticultural principles but not accept the modifications in vinification. One does not follow from the other.

Although Accad's consultancy ended amicably, in February 1993, 'ma période', as Etienne refers to these years, has clearly left him defensive and wounded. 'I had to bear the brunt of everyone's criticism; people even asked me whether my wines were legal because of the sulphur.' Much was learned, on both sides, and Etienne is now striving to regain his self-confidence.

The keys to Etienne's vinification remain unaltered: i) one must have the maximum potential quality in the grapes one harvests; ii) they must be vinified in such a way as to extract the maximum of that potential. In order to achieve this, it is necessary to vinify to augment those elements – chiefly solidity and tannins – which protect the wine through a long, slow evolution in cask and in bottle and to minimise those unfavourable elements which gradually degrade a wine – namely, the oxidases – an excess of which induce browning and premature ageing. In his 'third period', he wants wines which have ageing potential but which are 'easier to understand young'. Just that elusive union of apparent opposites which many a quality-conscious vigneron strives to achieve.

Etienne asks himself why the 1964s, for example, are still delicious, but the 1980s have mostly fallen apart. The staying power of some of the older vintages caused him to reflect on their longevity – concluding that the natural accident of supremely healthy, ripe fruit in certain years, maximised the favourable elements for ageing at the expense of the unfavourable ones. So if one can remove the uncertainty – by producing healthy fruit and by controlled, properly directed vinification, it should be possible to replicate this phenomenon on a regular basis.

Added to these fundamentals is one which might, in some quarters, be considered heretical: namely, that the Pinot Noir, far from being the fragile grape it is generally considered, is robust and sturdy. Vinified properly it has both power and subtlety and considerable potential for long ageing.

The specific key to making long-lasting wine is, according to Etienne, its underlying structure. That means, in essence, its level of tannins and extract – the stuffing extracted from the skins of the grapes. Tannins – the most effective natural protection of the wine against oxidation – are extracted by long *maceration* before fermentation, which is achieved by cooling the pulp to around 5°C and dosing it with enough sulphur to kill any natural bacteria and to protect the juice from oxidation until the tannins take over. These, along with important colour, flavour and aroma compounds are thus slowly extracted before fermentation begins. It is important to understand that the Grivots, and Accad, consider that a much finer extraction occurs in aqueous solution – i.e. before fermentation – and that alcohol is regarded as far too powerful a solvent for the extraction of subtle aroma and flavour compounds. Hence the long pre-fermentive *maceration*.

After 4–5 days of *maceration*, enzymes are added to help clarification and cultured yeasts to kick-start fermentation. As this progresses further tannins are leached from the grapes, reducing the yeasts' natural exuberance and slowing down fermentation. This keeps temperatures within desired limits, allowing a long *cuvaison* of 15–21 days for further extraction of tannins, aroma and flavour. These tannins also act to stabilise colour extracted before fermentation. All this effort results in the cleanest possible wine being put into casks for maturation. Etienne believes that the wine's best protection against oxidation, is a healthy, tannic structure.

However, Etienne is broadly against new wood as a means of achieving this, believing that it accelerates ageing, producing earlier maturity and faster evolution in bottle. Most importantly, he feels that oak masks the individuality of a wine – something which goes completely against his most basic beliefs. Despite this there is a touch more new oak post-Accad – 25–30% for everything above Village for the first year – and he readily admits that there are other perfectly good methods of making fine wine, including those which use 100% new oak.

Before nearing a cask, Grivot's wines spend their first winter in tanks, under a blanket of liquid paraffin. The following February, even if *malos* have not finished, they are racked into cask. Rackings – of which there are three (one more than is normal in the Côte) – are performed with deliberate aeration. Etienne considers that his vinification augments the naturally reduced state of the wines and that they therefore need oxygen to re-establish their proper qualities.

The time each wine spends in cask is determined by the vintage – the better the wine the longer the *élevage* it needs. Grivot disagrees with those who believe that the Pinot Noir needs to be bottled early to retain its freshness and fruit. His wines are robust, not delicate, and need no such precaution. There are no formulae – just tasting; for example the 1984s were bottled after some 16 months, whilst others remain in cask for nearly two years.

Etienne's somewhat informal argument is that 'if a wine is going to keep for 20 years in bottle, it should be capable of holding out for two years in cask'. This is hardly the point. What matters is that the wine should be bottled when it has derived maximum benefit from staying in cask and not allowed to linger to the detriment of its balance and overall structure.

The results of this vinification tend to be deeply coloured wines, which are slow to evolve and retain their youthful tones for some considerable time. They start off noticeably reduced in aromas and flavours – that is to say, with an initially disagreeable side which takes some time to disappear. Their generally big structure tends initally to mask the taste and aroma qualities which define their typicities – so they are more difficult to taste young than the wines of other producers.

Etienne realises that, in some quarters, this gives them less market acceptability and has deliberately adapted his winemaking towards a more approachable style. The 1990s (Accad) and 1993s (post-Accad) are both excellent at all levels. The latter, from average yields of 30 hl/ha, have biggish frames, but not so austere as to mask their underlying elegance. The Nuits Boudots and Clos Vougeot, for example, will be eminently approachable within a decade – a normal span for such a concentrated vintage.

Only time will desensitise Etienne Grivot from what has been a traumatic experience. When he can distance himself from the past, he will realise that he still has a fine Domaine, with a first-class reputation, which, in the tradition of his father, grandfather and great-grandfather, and for the sake of his own two children, he must strive to maintain.

VINEYARD HOLDINGS

Commune	Level	Lieu-dit/Climat	Area	Vine Age	Status
Flagey	GC	Echézeaux	0.61	48	P
Vougeot	GC	Clos de Vougeot	1.86	43	P
Vosne	GC	Richebourg	0.31	60	P
Vosne	PC	Les Beaumonts	0.90	40	P
Vosne	PC	Les Brulées	0.25	38	P
Vosne	PC	Les Chaumes	0.15	42	P
Vosne	PC	Les Suchots	0.21	52	P
Vosne	PC	Les Reignots	0.08	60	P
Vosne	V	Bossières	0.66	50	P
Vosne	V	(Various *climats*)	2.37	38	P
Chambolle	V	La Combe d'Orvaux	0.62	35	P
Nuits	PC	Les Boudots	0.85	75	P
Nuits	PC	Les Pruliers	0.76	30	P
Nuits	PC	Les Roncières	0.50	42	P
Nuits	V	Les Lavières	0.65	35	P
Nuits	V	Les Charmois	0.52	30	P
————	R	(Bourg/PTG/BGO/Chard.)	2.72	8–55	P
		Total:	**14.12 ha**		

Domaine Jean Tardy

VOSNE-ROMANÉE

A short, slim man, with close-cropped grey hair, Jean Tardy exudes assiduity and passion for his job and discusses this or that point with gallic animation. When something of particular importance arises his voice jumps a couple of octaves and repeats the phrase for further emphasis.

Jean Tardy's father, from whom he took over in 1970, did not own a single vine, but share-cropped on a 'half-fruit' rental, much from Méo-Camuzet (q.v.). In 1972, Jean bought 2.5 ha mainly in *Régionales* and some Nuits Village. He would like to add further to his Domaine, since he now has more customers than wine to sell, but current prices make buying or renting uneconomic.

At present, the Domaine – 5 ha, spread over Vosne, Nuits and Chambolle – comprises two parcels of good Premiers Crus – Nuits Les Boudots (a steep vineyard with a very thin topsoil on rock) and Vosne, Les Chaumes, with a little Clos Vougeot and some Chambolle and Nuits Village. The remainder is Passe-tout-grains, BGO and Aligoté.

Jean is meticulous about everything he does and scathing of those who have fine land and yet produce sloppy, indifferent wine. He enjoys being out-of-doors and relishes hard work; whether putting back earth washed down Les Boudots, or dealing 'very severely' with an outbreak of grape-worm or red spider.

Careful *repiquéage* to ensure that no vines are missing is coupled with a complete replanting programme, at the stately rate of 10 rows per year. So, at its present size, the entire Domaine will be replaced every 28 years – otherwise, a fairly orthodox viticultural cycle. 'The vine is like wine, it must be cared for,' comes with the added warning: 'They can be too well looked-after and this makes them lazy!'

The oldest vines are picked first, since their smaller crop tends to ripen sooner; chez Tardy this generally means the 45-year-old Nuits Boudots and Clos Vougeot.

Thereafter, what is sought is the longest, slowest possible fermentation. Though each year is different, Jean normally achieves a *cuvaison* of 15–20 days; in 1982 the average was 23 days, but that was exceptional.

One practice, however, is invariant: every year the *cuves* are *saignéed*, to concentrate the wine further. Surprisingly, even the old vines of Les Boudots, which naturally produce very little, were *saignéed* in 1990. Such sacrifices show in the depth of Tardy's wines.

Another peculiarity concerns his use of new oak. Up to 1985 the proportion was 50% but, convinced that the extra expense and trouble were justified, he used 100% for all the Villages, Premiers and Grand Cru. The mere thought of colleagues who 'use 25 year-old casks, badly filled' brings him out in a muck sweat. His own new casks are never prepared or treated in any way – 'no rinsing, never a drop, never a drop,' he trills, an octave up.

The idea of 100% new oak, which must seem to some as heresy, is no whim, but a considered policy. 'The *élevage* of a wine is very important; one must be obsessive,' he argues, adding that with low yields, long *cuvaison* and 'grosses *saignées*', even a vintage like 1984 can support 100% new wood.

The wines spend 16–18 months in cask. Jean vehemently opposes any kind of fining and of most types of filtration. He reckons that fining takes too much out of a wine and has no time whatever for the Kieselguhr filtration used by many of his colleagues: 'C'est lamentable,' he shrieks, 'there is nothing left in the wine.'

If making the wine to his satisfaction is difficult enough, the business of dealing with his customers is even more problematical. His 2,000 cases a year simply won't go round. Having to deny a constant stream of hopeful suitors leaves him in near desperation: 'I have refused the Japanese three times; a German who wanted 1,200 bottles was allocated 300 – that was really very generous, very generous.' Fortunately, he can see the mild humour in his situation: 'Oh, là là, oh, là là,' he shrills, 'the clients want the wine and I haven't got it!' He was found packing up 600 bottles of 1987 in mid 1995, so things can't be all that desperate. His simple maxim: 'If you sell everything the cellar's empty, and you pay too much tax; that's no good.'

Despite this minor trial, Jean Tardy clearly enjoys his celebrity and derives obvious pleasure from a dozen top Swiss restaurateurs and their sommeliers tasting in his cellar.

There is no doubt that his manic obsession with detail pays off; although by no means all the wines are great, the overall standard is high with some spectacular successes. However, even with the oldest vines, Jean's Nuits Boudots is sometimes rather dull; not badly made, just lacking in nuance.

This cannot be said of the Chambolle Villages, Vosne, Les Chaumes or of the Clos Vougeot. Jean admits that long *cuvaison* may unbalance the delicacy of Chambolle, but seems determined to stick to his methods. The Chambolle is very fine – the 1993 had aromas of ripe burlat cherries and *fruits noirs sauvages* with plenty of depth of flavour. The extra *maceration* shows in a heavier structure – more Morey than Chambolle.

The 1993 Chaumes from poor, predominantly limestone soil, has sound, fleshy fruit and a nice touch of new oak, plenty of aromatic potential and underlying finesse.

The Clos Vougeot is even richer and more complex, with added power and vinosity. Jean's vines, located in the part known as 'Aux Grands Maupertuis', adjacent to Grands Echézeaux, has the depth and power of a Grand Cru, without the rustic earthiness which so often characterises wines from the Clos. The 1992 is only marginally less deep than the 1993, its aromas in transition to a more mature secondary character; real depth here, good power and length, a touch hollow, but very satisfying for the vintage.

Jean's voice leaps involuntarily as he bemoans those who have criticised his 1993s. 'They say that they lack colour, but look . . .' Indeed they are dark, although marginally less intense than others. What matters is that their flavour and balance are correct, and of that there is no room for doubt.

Jean Tardy's style is for well-structured, long-lived wines. If you can lay your hands on a case or two, they are well worth having. Let's hope that somehow he manages to find some more vineyards before his *metayage* agreement expires in 2007, otherwise the Swiss restaurateurs will collar the lot!

VINEYARD HOLDINGS

Commune	Level	Lieu-dit/Climat	Area	Vine Age	Status
Vosne	PC	Les Chaumes	1.55	20	M
Nuits	V	Les Bas de Combes	0.45	40	P
Nuits	PC	Les Boudots	1.04	45/65	M
Vougeot	GC	Clos de Vougeot	0.23	45	M
Chambolle	V	Les Athets	0.32	17	P
———	R	(BGO/PTG/Bourg.)	1.20	25–45	P
		Total:	**4.79 ha**		

Domaine Jean Gros

VOSNE-ROMANÉE

There are a score or so of Domaines along the length of the Côte which simply sing quality. There is no doubt about their ability to make wine at the finest level, almost irrespective of the vintage. When you encounter them, it is merely a matter of the first whiff or two – even the young wines, chilled as they are in their winter casks, reek of quality. No need to delve beneath a searingly brutal or miserably dilute exterior in the vain prospect of finding something unbelievably fine which one has somehow overlooked. You know you can relax and enjoy the fruits of a master's art.

Madame Jean Gros personifies the elegance of her Domaine. A dignified and charming lady, she was Vosne's Mayoress for 24 years until relinquishing the office in 1995. Her class pervades the family house, in a quiet backstreet, near enough to the Mairie, from which she administers the affairs of nine fine hectares. This attractive pre-Revolution residence – divided between the Domaines Gros and neighbouring Mugneret-Gibourg – is full of elegant period furniture and combines grace with cosy family comfort.

The fragmentation of the original Louis Gros Domaine between each of his four children spawned at least three separate 'Gros' enterprises. Jean's vineyards are now run by Mme Gros and the wine made by her son, Michel – who has also created his own Domaine principally from purchases in the Hautes Côtes and Vosne. The vines of two other of Louis' children – Gustave, now dead, and Colette, a somewhat feeble old person, still living – were amalgamated and are vinified by Michel's brother Bernard under the Domaine 'Gros, Frère et Soeur'. The fourth of Louis' children, François, exploits his share of the vines with his daughter Anne, under the Domaine 'Anne et François Gros' whilst Mme Gros' daughter, Anne-Françoise, runs Domaine A-F Gros with her husband, François Parent, from Pommard.

Jean Gros seems to take little interest in his Domaine – preferring to shoot game. His brother, François also takes life easily adding 'resting' to hunting as his preferred recreations. The senior members of the Gros family are gradually divesting themselves of their vineyards in favour of their children. Anne-Françoise, for example, has taken her 20 ares of Richebourg out of the Jean Gros ambit – the remaining 40 will in time be divided between her two brothers, Michel and Bernard. With such a plethora of lega-

tees, this important Domaine is constantly in flux.

Michel Gros – an amiable, short-cropped man in his forties – is the Domaine's wine-maker and technician. Able and conscientious, he clearly enjoys his job and thinks carefully about his responsibilities. A traditionalist by conviction, he is happy to experiment with anything in the vineyard or in the cellar which might lead to an improvement.

However, it is in the vineyard that Michel is found at his most interesting and articulate. He has evidently thought deeply about the ways of the vine and takes pride in the nurture of those entrusted to his care.

The aim of the viticultural year is to produce both optimum quality and a yield which makes commercial sense, without forcing the vines. Michel has observed that up to a certain level, increased yield is not detrimental to quality, merely the point on an imaginary curve at which quality starts to decline varies from year to year. Thus in one vintage he could harvest 50 hl/ha from one plot of vines and make top quality wine whereas the following year quality in the same vines may start to fall off at two thirds of that figure. The conclusion is that one must adjust one's expectations year by year and not aspire to some preconceived fixed annual yield.

To achieve the optimum, Michel believes that one must replace individual vines, wherever possible. Once a Gros vine fails to produce half the permitted maximum yield, its days are numbered. He admits, however, that he is sometimes forced to replant whole parcels when successive interbreeding results in virus infection and degeneration. Fortunately this is not a frequent occurrence, as most of his vines are young – replanted in the 1960s and 1970s, presumably because of the progressive degeneration of post-war plants and rootstocks.

Vignerons, such as Michel, combine technical expertise with an artist's feel for their vines. This empathy enables each plot to be treated as an individual, adapting pruning, spraying, planting and harvesting to its idiosyncrasies, rather than coaxing them all into one common viticultural mould.

Experiments with bilateral *cordon* training and wide spacing in the Hautes Côtes and Bourgogne Rouge parcels in Vosne, have given Michel further insight into the way vines behave and provided valuable economies in labour and materials.

In his quest for the mastery of yields, Michel considers it preferable to remove any

potential excess of buds or of shoots as early as possible in the growing season. Realising that an advance knowledge of the likely fecundity of the vines would be a distinct advantage, he has developed a technique for early estimation of a vine's future output. This relies on the fact that a vine will form the bud material for one year during the previous June. By soaking a cutting in hot water he can count the number of embryo buds and extrapolate. So far this information has enabled him to avoid removing fully developed bunches in August – a practice he abhors. One must realise, he will tell you, that the vine is an irregular producer. One year you may get fifteen bunches, the next year only five.

Michel's intimate knowledge of his vines also helps him plan his harvest. In general, the Domaine has two separate pickings: the first, at the normal time takes place in the vineyards on the Côte; the second, a late harvest in the Hautes Côtes, starts once the crush from the Côtes has finished fermenting and there is space in the *cuves*. The order of harvesting in each area tends to be the same from year to year – some plots of vines just happen to ripen earlier or later, and Michel knows which they are.

As for vinification, nothing is systematic. Grapes arriving at the *cuverie* will generally be 66–75% destemmed, even totally, in years where there is much *millerandage* (undeveloped bunches, high in sugar and extract, low in water). Michel keeps some stalks if he can because they help aerate the pulp and thereby ensure a gentle, regular start to fermentation, and also for their tannins, which strengthen a wine's resistance to ageing.

The Domaine's *cuves* are variously cement, wood and glass-fibre. According to Michel Gros, their insulation is of greater significance than their precise composition. He personally prefers cement to wood because the latter is so time-consuming to maintain – it takes one man, working full-time, a week to prepare the Domaine's four wooden *cuves* for use, and even then, there is a risk of damage if they are hydrated or dried too quickly.

Since the process of fermentation adds an almost invariant 15 centigrade degrees to the temperature of the pulp, Michel starts his vats off at about 16–18°C, aiming to arrive at a maximum of 35°C. Too many vignerons, he complains, don't worry about the temperature of their vats until it is too late; so he prefers to be cautious. The action of the screw-pump taking the grapes to the vats crushes about half of them – but only lightly, just to liberate the juice and give access to the yeasts. This, together with the ensuing foot-*pigéage*, helps to ensure as long and slow a fermentation as possible.

With all this tradition, it is curious to find that Michel is against the use of natural yeasts for fermentation. Instead, he uses a starter culture, of selected, rehydrated dried yeasts to inoculate each vat. This is no whim: cultured yeasts, he claims, are a cleaner strain and thus give better results, particularly producing alcohol levels nearer to theoretical expectations than natural yeasts. Moreover, by eliminating the bad elements of the natural population, one avoids the bad by-products. Thirdly, by choosing when to inoculate, he can ferment when it suits him – and the rest of the harvesting programme.

So, following just 24 hours of *maceration,* the *cuves* are inoculated and fermentation starts within 12 hours. Then 4–5 days later, they are covered with plastic lids, to minimise oxidation and the loss of alcohol and aromas and left for a further 3–4 days of *maceration* – a *cuvaison* of 10–12 days.

A light pressing of the pulp gives a rich press-wine which is added to the free-run wine and allowed to settle for 24 hours before being transferred to cask.

The Grands Crus, plus the Vosne-Romanée Premier Cru Clos des Réas are lodged in 100% new wood, whilst the Village Vosne, Nuits and Chambolle have about a third depending on the style of the vintage. The wines are only racked once – just after *malo* – otherwise, remaining in cask until the following spring when the different lots of each are unified by pumping, with moderate aeration, into tanks. Here they are fined with albumen, left for 1–2 months, finely filtered through a mixture of Kieselguhr earth and cellulose, and bottled. Before 1987 the wines were plate filtered, but this was dropped in favour of Kieselguhr, which was found to give greater finesse.

Michel's methods are deliberately conservative – he seeks to stray as little as possible from traditional winemaking chiefly because he realises that the Domaine's customers are used to its style and he sees no reason to change what is obviously successful.

The 'point de départ' for his entire philosophy is the observation that Vosne-Romanées are by nature 'tendres et parfumés'. Since the taste of a wine is also the consequence of the method of making it, he is able to use his influence to give some extra muscle to the wines natural qualities, adding structure and longevity. The instruments he chooses to exert this influence are a combination of longish *cuvaison*, fermentation at a high temperature, plenty of new wood, low yields, and the use of new clones which also add tannin,

Madame Gros in her office

force and structure to the wines.

There is no doubt results justify the theories. Tasting a range of Gros wines is invariably a pleasurable and rewarding experience. In the curious way that these things happen, the wines seem to know their masters and to mirror their qualities – the muscle of Michel combines perfectly with the elegance and charm of Madame Gros – sinew and style working harmoniously together.

The Gros wines do not have the exuberant silkiness of Jean-Nicolas Méo's, nor do they flex muscles to the same extent as those of Michel's cousin Bernard Gros. Somewhere in between there is a firm, rich charm which never fails to seduce.

The Vosne range provides an overview of the Domaine's style. Michel's own Clos de la Fontaine – from young vines below the Clos

des Réas – is 'tendre' and attractive but lacks the concentration yet for extended ageing. The Jean Gros Vosne has more depth and complexity – hints of *fruits rouges* on the nose in the 1993, good acidity, round tannins with elegance and richness underneath. The Premier Cru Clos des Réas, a *Monopole,* from 25-year-old vines has more depth and length, with a dollop of new oak from heavily charred casks. Here, in 1993, a fine deep colour, with more dark than red fruits on the nose and altogether more complexity waiting to emerge; a meaty wine, without being coarse in any way.

The Richebourg, from 45-year-old vines, is yet more complex and concentrated. Very much in the same style as the Clos des Réas, its overriding characteristics are those of great breed and distinction. The slightly charred, toasted undertone is there, supporting a rich layer of ripe, classy fruit and the power and poise one expects from this great Grand Cru. In short, the epitome of vinosity and finesse.

Age brings out the elegance in these superb wines. They need time, above all, and cannot be hurried. Unfortunately, too many are drunk long before they can begin to show the true craftsmanship which has gone into their making. Although the 1990s are barely beginning to emerge from their shells it is clear that the Richebourg, in particular, is a masterpiece. A fine, still youthful tone, a ripe, abundantly promising, velvety nose, with hints of leather and resin, with good acidity and ripe, soft, tannins encasing an immense concentration of flavour, complex, long and of great nobility. A wine indeed for the next generation. A 1976 Richebourg, opened in early 1996, was sumptuous, complex, perfectly poised and *à point.*

This fine Domaine is in careful and conscientious hands as it strives constantly to improve on its already undoubted excellence.

VINEYARD HOLDINGS

Commune	Level	Lieu-dit/Climat	Area	Vine Age	Status
Vosne	GC	Richebourg (MG 0.18)	0.40	45	P
Vosne	PC	Clos des Réas (MG 0.31)	2.12	25	P
Vosne	V	Les Réas	2.19	20	P
Vosne	V	Clos de la Fontaine (MG)	0.36	7	P
Vougeot	GC	Clos de Vougeot	0.20	8	P
Nuits	PC	La Perrière Noblot	0.17	15	P
Nuits	V	Les Athées	0.20	25	P
Chambolle	V	(5 different climats); (MG 0.27)	0.48	15	P
Morey	V	———————— (MG)	0.23	5	P
Vosne	R	(Bourgogne Rouge)	1.36	25	P
Arcenant / Marey-les-Fussey	R	(Htes Ctes de Nuits Rouge) (MG 7.25)	2.25	15	P
Arcenant / Marey-les-Fussey	R	(Htes Ctes de Nuits Blanc) (MG 1.50)	0.23	5	P

Totals: (Michel Gros: 10.1 ha) **9.07 ha**

Domaine Lamarche

VOSNE-ROMANÉE

Sandwiched myopically between the Domaines Mugneret-Gibourg and François Gros, in a long unassuming street known as the rue des Communes, is Domaine Lamarche. François Lamarche, a short, taciturn man, runs the estate with his pleasant, forceful wife, Marie-Blanche from Metz, whom he married in 1975. At that time he was already working with his father, Henri, who sadly died on October 4th 1985 – a date he remembers vividly.

The Domaine and its vineyards, which belong jointly to François and his sister Geneviève, are the result of careful acquisition by 3 generations of Lamarches, preceded by two generations of viticulteurs on the female side of the family. The vineyards are almost a model compound: an impressive 4.40 ha of Grands Crus, 1.36 ha of Vosne-Romanée Premiers Crus – Suchots, Malconsorts and Chaumes – 1 ha of Vosne Village and a further 1.58 ha of Bourgogne and Passe-tout-grain.

The jewel in the Lamarche crown is undoubtedly the 1.65 ha strip of land running east–west down the fall-line of the Côte between La Tâche and Romanée-Conti – La Grande Rue. This was originally given to Henri Lamarche as a wedding present in 1933. Lying between such prestigious Grands Crus, one might be forgiven for wondering why it was only classified Premier Cru. The explanation is that when the official classification was drawn up in the 1930s, Henri Lamarche believed that there was nothing to be gained – except perhaps increased taxes – from Grand Cru status; vignerons were not prosperous then, and the price differential between Grand Cru and Premier Cru wine was small. So La Grande Rue became a Premier Cru. Now, the authorities have allowed it to absorb 0.23 ha of Les Gaudichots, at its eastern end.

In 1991 an application for reclassification was finally approved, making François one of the few single proprietors of a Grand Cru in the Côte d'Or. His Grande Rue is the second smallest of these fabled patches of land, the smallest being La Romanée (0.84.52 ha), just above Romanée-Conti.

François is an excellent winemaker with no doubt as to what he is trying to achieve. He believes that a fine wine, particularly from Vosne-Romanée, should maximise finesse rather than *matière*; that tannins and stuffing should take second place to charm and elegance. Alcohol is rarely an abundant ingredient in his wines; unlike some of his confrères, *cuves* rarely pass 13 degrees and then only in the warmest, ripest vintages.

Vinification is a matter of adjusting to what comes in from the carefully picked vineyards. If the grapes lack acidity, for example, an appropriate amount of separately harvested *verjus* is added to correct the deficiency. If, on the other hand, *chaptalisation* is required, it is done little by little to avoid raising the temperature of fermentation to high and to 'better adapt the sugar to the *cuve*'. François adds a modest dose of sulphur to the crush and lets the fermentation rise to 33°C, before settling down to an ideal 27–28°C.

Cuvaison and fermentation take place in open wooden *cuves* and last 12–15 days. Four *pigéages* daily to start with, and 3 later, ensure that the cap remains moist and maximise extraction. There are three pressings – the first two being added in total to the free-run wine, whilst the third goes into the Passe-tout-grain casks, an interesting way of adding muscle and depth and even finesse.

New Allier and Tronçais oak are used across the range – some 50% for the Villages, nearer 70% for the Premiers and Grands Crus; the rest is *élévé* in older wood. The *malo* is not provoked by heat but allowed to happen naturally. Once it is fully finished, each cask is racked and the wine left for a further year in wood. A second racking, with air to eliminate any dissolved CO_2, precedes an egg-white fining. François does not hold with filtration, which removes essential stuffing, and therefore limits it to vintages which fail to fall bright naturally (none since 1987). The Domaine bottles its wines after about 15 days *sur colle* and 16–18 months in wood.

There is then, nothing exceptional about François Lamarche's vinification. He clearly believes that with healthy, ripe grapes, from fine land planted with old vines, giving low yields, the minimum interference is necessary to produce good results.

Yields rarely rise above the *rendement de base* for each appellation. 8.52 ha produces an average of 340 hl – i.e. 3,750 cases – or 40 hl/ha. Given that this figure includes the larger distorting yields of 'ordinaires', these yields are by no means excessive. In 1994 global Lamarche yields averaged 29 hl/ha – the result of severe *triage* and an August green-pruning in La Grande Rue.

Wandering around in the maze of cellars beneath the house, one end of which abuts on to those of Jean Gros, the other on to those of François Gros, François Lamarche detaches a pipette from a pair suspended from a four-pronged meat hook in the ceiling and taps away at casks drawing off samples. Old bottles are stacked in corners, wherever there is some room, and one is sometimes momentarily taken in by what appears to be a solid wall, turning out to be a floor-to-ceiling stack of mould-covered bottles waiting presumably for an order, or perhaps maturing for sale later. Prosperity has resulted in a new bottle cellar, populated with unromantic metal cages full of unlabelled bottles.

Lamarche is not much given to casual conversation, but admits to making wines in the elegant style he prefers rather than being swayed by any reflections of his worldwide clientele.

He more than achieves his goals, with wines showing above all, finesse. The Village and Premier Cru Vosne-Romanées have mid-deep colours, always bright and invariably limpid, with that alluring robe of brushed velvet which is so typical of fine Pinot Noir.

The Vosne-Romanée Village develops an attractive smokey, crushed strawberry nose, followed up with a fine, elegant swathe of flavours, backed by firm tannin and enough balancing acidity to keep it alive for years.

Of the three Premiers Crus, Les Suchots is the most typically Vosne – coming from a vineyard situated at the northern end of the village with Grands Crus Romanée-St.-Vivant on the southern side and Echézeaux to the north. The soil contains more silica, giving distinctly greater finesse; the wine generally has a mid black-cherry hue and a nose of griotte cherries, red fruits and violets. It is ripe and stylish, with plenty of concentration – from 50-year-old vines – and a finely-tuned balance. This is quintessential Vosne.

Henri with his wife Marie-Blanche

Les Chaumes, situated just to the south of La Tâche, has more clay in its soil which gives a firmer, fuller structure. It generally takes longer to unpack, being less forthcoming at first than either Suchots or Malconsorts. By contrast, Malconsorts – sited right in the 'kidney' of the hill, along the band of Grands Crus – has a much richer soil than Suchots, which gives its wine a more rustic aspect, with distinct tones of neighbouring Nuits-St.-Georges. It has a redder colour and a discernible touch of chocolate on the nose, mixed with an attractive aroma of *fruits noirs*. To taste, it is fuller and more structured than either Suchots or Chaumes when young, opening out with age to reveal a fine spectrum of old Pinot Noir smells and flavours, typically *sous-bois,* and vegetal in character.

The Grands Crus are, not unexpectedly, slower to develop; in cask, they show their breed and style, in depth of flavour, length and overall structure though giving little on the nose. The Clos Vougeot – divided into two parcels, two-thirds at the top of the Clos, near the Château, the remaining third lower down, near to the RN74 – is by far the meatier of the quartet. François considers that one has to wait at least 15 years for a good vintage to become truly drinkable; given the muscle and weight of the 1993, this would seem to be no exaggeration.

The other 3 Grands Crus – Echézeaux, Grands-Echézeaux and La Grande Rue are finer yet. The Echézeaux is characterised by a marked acidity, which gradually melds into the wine as it ages. Roundness, finesse and *puissance* wait to emerge into a most attractive and finely structured whole. The Grands-Echézeaux is still more closed until it chooses to reveal itself and should not be considered before 8 years old in a good vintage.

La Grand Rue is generally the finest of all Lamarche wines. Its soil has broadly the same composition as that of the Grands Crus which surround it. When young it shows a promising nose of 'petits *fruits rouges*' – redcurrant and raspberry – and hints of blackcurrant. These positive, complex aromas overlay a wine of dimension and substance, with length and finesse; a complete wine without being in any way heavy. La Grande Rue has more in common with La Tâche and Richebourg than with Romanée-Conti.

Lamarche Grands Crus need at least eight years before they begin to give of their best. Even in less ripe vintages, there is no need for haste. A 1955 Grands-Echézeaux tasted at the Domaine in 1995, though fully mature, was still virile and harmonious – a magnificent panoply of *sous-bois* and sweet, ripe fruit, soft, fine and wonderfully fragrant, all of which belied its old mid-tawny colour. Lamarche is sometimes berated for his prices, which tend to be painfully above the

Harsh frosts in winter hurt nothing but the vine leaves

top end of what is being asked elsewhere in the village. This well reflects the hard-nosed economics of Marie-Blanche who obviously keeps a tight grip on the family finances.

Whether the wines are value for money must be a matter for individual judgement. François' determination to achieve low yields, and his willingness to *saigner* in dilute years, means that vintages matter less here than one might imagine. Obviously, years when everything goes smoothly and the grapes are perfectly ripe and concentrated, are justifiably more sought after, but those who neglect second rank vintages – such as 1987 and 1991 – miss much that is worthwhile and thoroughly enjoyable.

VINEYARD HOLDINGS

Commune	Level	Lieu-dit/Climat	Area	Vine Age	Status
Flagey	GC	Grands Echézeaux	0.30	1961	P
Flagey	GC	Echézeaux (Cruots + Clos St.-Denis)	1.10	1961	P
Vougeot	GC	Clos de Vougeot	1.36	1960/71/76	P
Vosne	GC	La Grande Rue	1.65	1955–88	P
Vosne	PC	Les Chaumes	0.56	1960	P
Vosne	PC	Les Malconsorts	0.50	1934	P
Vosne	PC	Les Suchots	0.37	1947	P
Vosne	PC	La Croix Rameau	0.22	25	P
Vosne	V	————	0.97	30	P
Vosne / Boncourt	R	(Bourgogne Rouge / PTG/Aligoté)	1.50	15-35	P
		Total:	**8.53 ha**		

Domaine Méo-Camuzet

VOSNE-ROMANÉE

The appreciation of Burgundy is often as much a matter of the appreciation of style as of quality. Even at the highest level, styles vary considerably as growers tend to make wine to match their own specifications rather than pandering to the whims of their customers.

There are, however, some Domaines which seem to hit a sort of universal style and yet to make wine of uncompromising excellence. One such is the Domaine Méo-Camuzet in Vosne. The first whiff of their Bourgogne Rouge is enough to convince you that you are dealing with a level of quality attained by few others in the Côte.

The Domaine underwent a significant upheaval after the 1988 vintage, when Henri Jayer, who had made many of the Domaine's wines since 1945, retired. At the same time, though not in compensation, the vineyards he farmed en metayage from the Méo family reverted back to them.

The reason for Henri Jayer's regency was that Jean Méo, who inherited the Domaine from his childless uncle, Etienne Camuzet in 1959, had neither inclination nor time to run his inheritance, preferring to pursue his career as a petroleum engineer, at one time being a member of General de Gaulle's cabinet, and more recently as President of l'Institut de Pétrole, in Paris.

Although Jayer remains an advisor, the Domaine is now in the hands of a younger generation. Christian Faurois, the son of one of M. Camuzet's vignerons, joined the Domaine in 1973 from the Lycée Viticole in Beaune, first working in the vineyards and then in the cellars. Jean Méo's son, Jean-Nicolas, arrived in 1989, with Paris business-school, a Dijon diploma and a spell at Domaine Chandon in the USA, under his belt. Together, Christian and Jean-Nicolas are responsible for the day-to-day running of the Domaine, Christian being concerned more with vineyards and day-to-day matters and Jean-Nicolas with winemaking and sales.

Etienne Camuzet left his nephew a magnificent legacy: nearly 7 ha of excellent land in Nuits, Vosne, Vougeot and Corton, with no less than 2.3 ha of Grands Crus. Many of the vines are now over 60 years old, which adds an extra dimension of concentration and depth to the wines. Much of the land was rented en metayage to Henri Jayer, Jean Tardy, Jean Faurois and Jacques Faurois; however, as these tenants retire and their agreements expire, the vineyards are reverting to the Domaine.

Christian and Jean-Nicolas are striving to be as organic as is compatible with keeping the vines healthy. Efforts are also being made to encourage natural predators of spiders and grape-worms but Christian admits that this is problematic in very parcelled vineyards when your neighbour insists on using insecticides. Better product knowledge and more precision application have made for great strides in vine care in recent years.

Individual plant replacement is considered better than grubbing up entire parcels of vines – the Domaine loses around 1% of its vines each year. It is hoped to reintroduce sélection massale for plant material – a policy which had been discontinued. Replanting is on to 161/49 rootstock, generally regarded as the best adapted to soils and vines in this sector of the Côte.

It is essential to remove excess production before it can sap strength from the vine. So, every year, just before the flowering, much effort is directed at selecting what is to be excised, especially among the young vines in the Vosne-Romanée and Richebourg vineyards. Since 1991 all the Domaine's vineyards have been inspected at veraison and most green-pruned – young plants among old ones still produce excessively. The thrust of this work is to master the vine's natural vigour, encourage each to ripen a consistent, sensible yield, rather than trying to compensate later.

When the grapes are finally harvested, strict control both in vineyard and cuverie ensures that only the ripest, healthiest fruit goes into the vats. Deliberately high summer foliage – to encourage greater development of vegetation and thus of sugar – requires a particularly sharp eye later to minimise the cutting of verjus – the second, less ripe crop. Fortunately, most verjus appears at the top of the vine and would normally be removed during routine summer prunings.

At the cuverie all the stalks are removed and the grapes lightly sulphured to eradicate any promenading bacteria. Without crushing, the fruit is cooled to 15–18°C and put into wood or cement cuves and left for 5–6 days during which an intracellular extraction removes colour and aroma compounds from the skins.

Jean-Nicolas Méo and Christian Faurois – the new generation running the Domaine

Only indigenous yeasts are used for the fermentation – 'There are enough on the grapes,' says Christian, 'to avoid the need for cultured yeasts.' In years of great dilution, the vats are bled and the juice removed used to make sparkling wine for the family. During 15–18 days of *cuvaison*, temperatures are allowed to rise to 34–35°C. The level of *pigéage* depends on the vintage and the *cuvée*, but tends to be concentrated in the later stages of fermentation.

The pulp is then lightly pressed in a horizontal press and the press-wine assembled with the free-run wine. After 12 hours settling, the new wine is run into casks where it spends some 18 months – more or less depending on the vintage. The Méo policy is for 100% new oak for Premiers and Grands Crus, 50% for Villages and Bourgogne Rouge, while the Passe-tout-grain goes into second-year casks. This indicates serious dedication to quality – most growers who are content to use high proportions of new wood for their better wines would not stomach the expense for their Régionales. Jean-Nicolas and Christian prefer Nevers, Tronçais and Allier oak with a less heavy char than in Henri Jayer's day, giving the wines a less obviously toasted character.

The *malos* are left to take place naturally, without heating. Some finish early, others late, but generally by the following summer the wines are ready to be racked cask-to-cask. The 1992 *malos* were so violent that many vignerons panicked and suphured heavily, thus fixing an already significant colour loss. Jean-Nicolas admits that half his casks had been so treated before he called a halt; after a short delay, the remainder had regained their proper hue. Now, he prefers to let things happen in their own way, favouring long, slow *malos* for better equilibrium, and tends to delay racking for a few months for the same reason.

The following November – the timetable can vary by up to 2 or 3 months – the wines are racked off their lees and unified in tank, five casks at a time. They used to egg-white fine but now, after long consideration and some obvious difficulties, this has been discontinued. According to Jean-Nicolas: 'In the years when we need it, it doesn't work (i.e. the wine won't clarify), and when we don't need it, it does; in any case, it takes substance from the wine.' So now, they have either to wait, or – the least preferred option – to filter.

The Méo style has barely changed from that of Henri Jayer's regency. The overriding hallmarks are profound concentration, combined with exquisite delicacy; wines which are both ample and fat, but with a firm grip and immense charm. 1989, 1990, 1991 and 1993 are classic vintages for this elegant, round style of winemaking.

The basic Pinot Noir, with its 6 months in new wood followed by a further year in older oak, betrays its Vosne origins. Attractively perfumed, it has a good concentration of fruit and a sound structure which will develop and soften with time; a very good wine for its class.

The Vosne Village *cuvée*, mainly from the Barreaux *climat* just above Richebourg towards the Combe de Concoeur, is generally attractive and well perfumed, with its larding of new wood showing through. On the palate it has length and power with plenty of almost sweet fruit in ripe vintages. A wine of some distinction – which needs a few years to integrate and show its best.

The two Nuits Premiers Crus have considerably more Vosne-ish finesse than one normally expects from Nuits. For Les Boudots, this is not entirely surprising, since it is on the Vosne side of the appellation and has a finer soil. The 1993 had an extra dimension of concentration, from a high proportion of *millerands*, with soft supporting tannins and, in common with many 1993s, considerable aromatic potential. The Les Murgers is generally richer, with a lively acidity and notable finesse, perhaps more typically Nuits than the Boudots, but these are fine distinctions.

There are three separate Vosne Premiers Crus; Les Chaumes, with similar soil to adjoining Nuits St.-Georges, is a deep, round, quite complex and tightly-structured wine with enough, but not excessive tannins. Les Brulées is similar in style, with a touch more acidity and softer tannins – the 1993 was tight-packed, with finesse balancing the wine's natural *puissance*.

The Cros Parantoux, with a north-north-east exposition, has a slightly higher acidity than the other Vosnes, but balances this with considerable power and mouthfilling fruit. Unquestionably the best of the Premier Crus.

At the top of the Méo pyramid, sit a superb trio of Grands Crus. The Corton, made from 65-year-old vines in the Clos Rognet at the northerly, Ladoix sector of the appellation, has a broader, powerful flavour, with a dis-

tinct ripe cherry component on the nose (in the 1993) – a stylish, but very different Grand Cru to the others. The Clos Vougeot – again from 65-year-old vines, at the top of the Clos to the south of the Château – has a powerful, muscular structure. The fruit tends to amortise the effect of the tannins, giving the feeling of opulence rather than brute strength. This is very much a Vosne interpretation of Clos Vougeot – and probably the better for it!

The Richebourg has a concentration and profundity for which mere description is inadequate. From these 40-year-old vines comes a wine of complexity, length and balance with myriad nuances and immense charm, which is rather like one might imagine the feel of sipping liquid silk.

While the Méo 1990s and 1993s are yardstick wines, the 1992s are less consistent and generally on the pretty side with lowish acidities for relatively early drinking; even the Nuits Meurgeys has shed muscle to reveal an uncharacteristic feminine charm. The underrated 1994s are somewhat fleshier and rather better balanced.

Taking the ensemble, it would be difficult to find fault with what Jean-Nicolas and Christian are producing. The wines have, above all, great harmony and richness, and unmistakeable class. These are rarely big, over-extracted wines, but fine, more delicate expressions of their individual origins. This is a first-class Domaine.

VINEYARD HOLDINGS

Commune	Level	Lieu-dit/Climat	Area	Vine Age	Status
Vosne	GC	Richebourg	0.35	40	P
Vosne	PC	Les Brulées	0.70	65	P
Vosne	PC	Les Chaumes	2.00	15–40	P/F
Vosne	PC	Au Cros Parantoux	0.30	40	P
Vosne	V	Les Barreaux + 2 others	1.30	25	P/F
Vougeot	GC	Clos de Vougeot	3.00	40% 75	
				60% 15–30	P/F
Ladoix	GC	Corton (Clos Rognet)	0.45	65	P
Nuits	PC	Aux Boudots	1.04	45	P/F
Nuits	PC	Aux Murgers	0.75	25–30	P
Nuits	V	Au bas de Combes	0.57	40	P
Vosne	R	(BGO/PTG/Bourgogne Rouge)	1.15	11–25	P/F
Flagey	R	(Htes. Côtes de Nuits Blanc)	3.60	1990–92	P
Total:			**15.21 ha**		

Domaine Mugneret-Gibourg

VOSNE-ROMANÉE

It is refreshing, in this era of equality, to find Domaines of excellence, throughout the Côte, run by women. This, not from merely anti-sexist sentiments, but for the less hard-headed feelings of pleasure at being received, now and then, by a fragrant, well-groomed woman, instead of a hoary old man of the soil, usually with much of it on his boots.

At the Domaine Mugneret-Gibourg, that pleasure is likely to be trebled, since following the death in 1988 of Dr Georges Mugneret the Domaine is run by his charming widow, Jacqueline, and her daughters, Marie-Christine and Marie-Andrée. These are no lightweights – the one obtained a Doctorate of Pharmacy with a thesis entitled 'Is Wine a Medicine' and the other has an oenology diploma from Dijon University.

Apart from being one of France's leading ophthalmologists, Georges Mugneret was 'passioné du vin'. In 1930, at the height of the depression, he materialised this passion with the purchase of a substantial house in Vosne-Romanée together with parcels of Bourgogne, Vosne-Romanée and Echézeaux. Having his career to provide income for the household, he kept the Domaine afloat at a time when a full cask sold for little more than an empty one.

The Domaine today is, in reality, two separate exploitations: the original Mugneret-Gibourg vines bought with the help of Georges' mother in the 1930s and still marketed under that name, and the land added subsequently by Georges himself, sold as Domaine Georges Mugneret. These divisions are, however, no more than Chinese walls, since the ensemble of vineyards are tended and the grapes vinified under the care of mother and daughters.

In 1982, when it was clear that Georges was seriously ill, Marie-Christine began to take time off from her work as a pharmacist – she is also married to one – to understudy her father. She and her mother took more and more on their shoulders, so, when he died, 'we just had to get on with it'. As Marie-Christine explains, it was rather like the moment of one's first solo in a car – you can do it perfectly well, but the reassurance has gone. Even now she finds herself asking quietly: 'Would he have done this?', and generally erring on the side of caution.

Georges was clearly a man of shrewd judgement, building up a small Domaine spread across five communes at all quality levels. In addition, the vines are all 25–45 years old – so there is no need for concern about serious replanting for some time yet.

Whilst Mme Mugneret is occupied with the Domaine's clients and administration, it is to Marie-Christine and her sister, both now full-time at Vosne, that the task of vinification falls. Their training engenders an inquisitiveness which banishes inflexibility and, although the spirit of their father still guides the broad outlines, there is nothing routine in their approach. In fact, it is the difficult, most challenging vintages (e.g. 1994) which give them most pleasure to vinify.

Since Georges' wines were fine, and the customers liked them, they see no reason to change style. Receiving the children, grandchildren and even great-grandchildren of his original clients – he started selling direct in bottle just after the 1939–45 War – is proof of customer satisfaction and maintains a pleasant continuity with him.

Of their 8.51 ha, all but the Clos Vougeot, Ruchottes-Chambertin and Chambolle Les Feusselottes are share-cropped, half the fruit going to the *metayeurs*, with whom they work closely to ensure that the vineyards are properly maintained.

Over the years it has been a rare vintage in which the Grands Crus did not need *chaptalisation*. The need for this, especially in the Grands Crus, may seem surprising, but it must be remembered that their unique qualities derive not from high alcohol but from a particular site, soil and micro-climate. These vineyards are often on poor soil and poorly exposed, making ripening difficult. In addition, Grand Cru wines tend to need more alcohol to balance out their natural power and structure and thus more sugar. If the requisite natural grape-sugar is absent, it must be added at fermentation, bearing in mind that if you want to end up with say 12.8% actual alcohol in a wine, you probably have to start off with a potential – in sugar – of 13.5%, to compensate for expected loss on the way.

To minimise *chaptalisation*, the Domaine and their vignerons have striven to increase natural sugar levels. During the summer excess foliage is regularly trimmed off to expose as much of the canopy as possible to sunlight. High pruning of this sort has been found to add a degree or more to potential alcohol levels. The Mugnerets consult with their vignerons on the date of the harvest, in order to maximise ripeness, without risking over-ripeness, which can detract from the purity of a wine's flavour.

Another useful expedient for maximising grape sugar concentration is to remove part of the crop in August. The theory that this channels the vine's energies into the remaining bunches is borne out by Marie-Christine's experiments during 1990 which showed that green-pruned vines – compared with rows in the same vineyard which were not – gave 1.5–2.0 degrees higher potential alcohol – a significant difference. Moreover, they also ripened sooner and, although having a touch of surmaturity in that exceptionally hot summer, gave distinctly more concentrated juice. At the Domaine this operation is confined to the younger vines, which tend to be the culprits at over-producing. In some vintages (e.g. 1990) the older vines, which flower later than the rest, are caught by rain which destroys some of the flowers, and thus irrevocably reduces the crop.

If getting sufficiently ripe and healthy fruit is one side of the vineyard equation, limiting yields is the other. *Répiquéage* to maintain a high average vineage and low fertilisation, have helped keep the Domaine's yields at below 35 hl/ha over the years. Between 1988 and 1990 they only needed to replace 500 individual plants, although the severe frosts of 1985 destroyed larger parcels of Vosne-Romanée which then had to be replaced. Unexpectedly and, as time may perhaps show, unwisely, they replant systematically on SO4 roots. This tends to promote early ripening, but is known to have a relatively short life and needs an ultra-clean vineyard environment to thrive.

The Domaine's wines are above all stylish; not blockbusters, but with concentration and undoubted breeding. The vineyards may supply fruit of great potential, but that is easily destroyed in the cellar.

There is nothing radical about the Mugneret vinification, except for a firm and, in Burgundy, iconoclastic belief that natural yeasts are not the best. Thus, each year, selected yeasts are used because, Marie-Christine will tell you, they tolerate higher alcohol levels and thus prolong fermentation, which add up to more alcohol and glycerols in the final wine.

Long fermentation is felt to give better extraction and greater complexity. So any *chaptalisation* is made in several stages, towards the end of fermentation. Grape sugars – glucose and fructose – ferment quite rapidly, so a late addition of cane sugar (sucrose) can be propitious.

Marie-Christine and Mme Jacqueline Mugneret

The extent of destalking depends on the vintage. Generally, the riper the stalks the more that can be safely left in the vats, up to a maximum of 20%. Interestingly, older vines have less wood then younger plants, so a higher proportion of old vine stalks can be considered in riper vintages. Expert thinking on this subject changed radically during the 1980s; the tendency to leave most of the stalks shifted to the present practice of removing most of them.

Otherwise, vinification is relatively straightforward: a 24–36-hour pre-fermentive *maceration* at 16–18°C with enzymes added to assist clarification, is followed by fermentation, in either cement *cuves* for larger lots or wood vats for smaller lots, at up to 34°C for about 18 days. The initial cold soak makes for a later, slower *malo*, producing far better aromatics in the finished wine.

Fermentation is a sequential process – unstable colour is leached out in aqueous solution, to be fixed later by tannins which are only extracted in the presence of alcohol. The important middle phase serves to extract aroma compounds – if you lift the cover of the vats you will notice a different odour each day.

Gentle pressing, even when low yields might tempt some to press harder to extract a few francs' more juice, gives 'an honest quantity' of softish press-wine which is blended back before the wine is run off into cask.

For new barrels, the Mugnerets are more attached to their tonnelier than to the precise provenance of the wood. Marie-Christine thinks their oak comes from the Tronçais, but is unsure. Whatever, the Grands Crus see some 80% new wood, the Premiers Crus up to 70% and the Villages 40–50%. Even the Bourgogne has a touch of new oak.

The time the wines spend in cask before first racking depends on when the *malos* finish. In years such as 1989, when fermentation temperatures tend to soar, the wines have a higher risk of *volatile acidity* which,

above a certain concentration, is unpleasant both in aroma and flavour; so they are racked, cask-to-cask, as soon as their *malos* have finished, with a shot of sulphur to neutralise bacteria which might attack any residual sugar.

After a second racking some 6–8 months later, the wines return to cask until the following February, when they are assembled in tanks, fined with dried albumen and bottled 2 months later – a total *élevage* of some 18 months. Of the annual production of around ninety *pièces* of 300 bottles each, half goes to export and half to French and passing trade, much of it Swiss.

In the cellars, built around 1750, there is an air of timelessness and tradition, of a quiet dedication to quality. Nothing seems to be hurried or forced – the wines simply work at their own pace and take their time.

The range starts with an excellent, fruity, Bourgogne Rouge, which is usually worth keeping for a few years to soften out. The Village Vosne usually has all the elegance and depth one would expect – again a wine to cellar for several years, especially in the better vintages.

The Nuits Premier Cru, Les Chaignots – a semi-sloping vineyard on the Vosne side of Nuits with thin, stony, topsoil – produces a wine of highish natural acidity which has both the elegance of Vosne and a touch of the rusticity of Nuits. The 1993 has aromas of red fruits, plenty of power, with the constitution for medium-term ageing.

The Chambolle-Musigny Premier Cru Les Feusselottes – of which the Mugnerets normally have 4 casks, 3 new wood – is quite different; the 1993 has an intense colour with a nose showing hints of spice, tar and liquorice. The deepish, rich high clay soils in this relatively flat vineyard next to the village, give a broad wine, fusing Chambolle finesse with more than a nod towards neighbouring Vosne.

The Mugneret Clos de Vougeot – from a 0.34 ha plot in the Vosne section at the top of the Clos, next door to Lamarche, Méo and Engel – is distinctly more 'sauvage' than the Nuits. Both the 1990 and 1993 are big, spicy wines, with more than a touch of elegant rusticity and plenty of richness and depth.

The Echézeaux, from two separate plots (Rouges du Bas and Quartiers de Nuits) is, with the Clos de Vougeot, the most backward of the range, needing a long time to express itself, but worth the wait. The 1987 is a fine example of what can be done in a less opulent vintage – deep mid-red in colour, a thoroughly attractive nose of *sous-bois* and *fruits noirs* and a deliciously long, ripe complex flavour.

The Ruchottes-Chambertin is probably the Mugneret's finest wine. Invariably long and attractive, it seems to have that inspiring combination of great richness and great complexity. Not a wine, in top vintages, to touch for 5–10 years, but to put away, if you have the patience, to await maturity. The 1983, tasted at the Domaine, was just starting to lose some of its austere envelope of tannins and to exhibit flashes of charm and quality. An irredeemable touch of dryness at the edges is the only dissonant note on an otherwise perfectly healthy wine, now *à point*.

This then is a Domaine of great quality and style. Mme Mugneret, Marie-Christine and Marie-Andrée make a formidable, intelligent team of which Dr Georges would have been immensely proud.

VINEYARD HOLDINGS

Commune	Level	Lieu-dit/Climat	Area	Vine Age	Status
Vougeot	GC	Clos de Vougeot	0.34	40	P
Gevrey	GC	Ruchottes-Chambertin	0.64	40	P
Vosne	GC	Echézeaux	1.05	40	P
Vosne	V	(Various *climats*)	3.64	45	P
Chambolle	PC	Les Feusselottes	0.46	35	P
Nuits	PC	Les Chaignots	1.27	40	P
Nuits	PC	Les Vignes-Rondes	0.26	25	F
———	R	(Bourgogne Rouge)	0.85	30	P
		Total:	**8.51 ha**		

Domaine de la Romanée-Conti

VOSNE-ROMANÉE

The status of the Domaine de la Romanée-Conti as the leading producer of red Burgundy – the white Crown is more controversial – should be questioned by no-one. There may be arguments over this or that wine from this or that vintage, but year on year the Domaine has turned out wines of supreme excellence with that balance of power and finesse which both seduces and excites the senses.

The vineyards are magnificent. Although they own 1.6 ha spread across 5 different Vosne Premiers Crus, and 17.46 ares of Batard Montrachet, these are never sold publicly. What appears, in depressingly small quantities, is the produce of 25 ha of Grands Crus – six in Vosne and one, Le Montrachet, in Chassagne; a total of some 7,500 cases in a good year. The summit of this great range is Romanée-Conti itself, 500 cases of fabulous, highly prized and expensive wine from Burgundy's greatest single vineyard.

The Domaine is owned, equally, by two families, the de Villaines and the Leroys, each providing one manager. Until 1992, the Leroys were represented by Mme Lalou Bize-Leroy. However the Domaine's governing council withdrew her mandate over marketing irregularities – an ignominious dismissal from which she continues to smart. Her sister Pauline Roch's elder son, who replaced her, was sadly killed in a road accident; in 1993, his place was taken by his brother, Henri Roch. The de Villaine family have for many years been represented by Aubert de Villaine.

Much has been written about the history of the Domaine – the ownership of the Prince de Conti and the long-time renown of the Romanée vineyard as a site of special viticultural significance. What, surprisingly has not been much detailed is the way the Domaine works to extract the best from its land – the traditions of management and vinification which contribute ineluctably to the quality of wines, so highly prized and so much discussed throughout the wine-loving world.

The present custodians share with their predecessors the conviction that quality begins in the vineyards. Fine wine is not, as some still seem to think, a matter of the winemaker's art alone; the skills required to tend the vines and the soil in which they are planted is of equal – if not greater – importance. It is the individuality of these small plots of land which find their unique expression in the grapes grown there, and thereby in the wine made from them.

Quality potential is determined by the quality of the fruit, not by the wizardry of the winemaker who then takes charge of it. As one wine-grower put it: 'The vineyard gives the maximum potential – one can either diminish or equal this in the cellar; but not augment it.'

Apart from the infrequent occasions when the topsoil in the Romanée-Conti vineyard is renewed – fertiliser is rarely added. Annual soil analyses provide the Domaine and its 'chef de culture', Gerard Marlot, with continuous monitoring of the soil and the equilibrium of its constituents. Apart from small readjustments of magnesium in the lower part of La Tâche and Grands Echézeaux, nothing more than occasional applications of organic fertilisers have been needed in recent years. The Domaine suffers particularly from soil erosion – especially the southern section of La Tâche, and also the land between Richebourg and Romanée-Conti. The topsoil washed down has then to be put back again. The installation of special open cement drainage should mitigate erosion over the coming years.

Romanée-Conti itself, despite a slope of only 3%, has suffered erosion and occasionally needed soil replacement. In 1786–7 Grimelin, the régisseur of the Prince de Conti ordered 800 cartloads of 'terre de montagne' to fill in depressions.

More recently, in 1980, an unfortunate mistake led to the infilling of some depressions in Romanée-St.-Vivant with 'terre blanche', an earth wholly out of keeping with the existing topsoil. At the request of the INAO, the Domaine replaced it with more appropriate soil from hillsides near Gevrey. The Domaine's vineyard aims to retain the micro-climate of the soil and vines. It is not expressly an organic policy, but rather oriented towards the minimum use of synthetic products and towards traditional viticulture.

The soils – particularly around young vines – are worked with a tractor-mounted hoe, to aerate the earth. This provides a better environment for natural micro-flora to flourish and helps drainage. The soils round the roots are ploughed up each winter and down again in spring.

Pests and diseases are treated as traditionally as possible – Bordeaux mixture and sulphur for *cryptogams* (*botrytis, oïdium* and mildew) preceded by the protective copper-based 'Cuivrol' early in the season. Sulphur treatments also discourage red and yellow spiders which are particularly virulent on the Côte. Conscious effort is made to avoid systemics, unless there is really no alternative.

Apart from dealing with the grape-worm and using copper-based products to harden the skin and thus make penetration more difficult, no specific anti-rot treatments have been used since 1986. The Domaine prefers to excise any rotten material at harvest than to spray needlessly.

A rigorous policy of low yields brings a remarkable dimension of extract and concentration to the wines which is indeed one of the Domaine's hallmarks. Average yields are generally well below the *rendement de base* for Grands Crus of 35 hl/ha, or 1,848 bottles per acre. A 10-year average shows yields of 25 hl/ha, at 10,000 vines per ha; in other words it takes the grapes from 3 vines to make a single bottle of Domaine wine.

Such low yields are achieved by a combination of factors of which short pruning and a deliberately high vine age are the most significant. An old vine produces less, but of better quality and natural equilibrium, especially in acidity. This is important for ageing a wine, particularly in very ripe years such as 1989 when natural acidity levels throughout the Côte tended to be low.

Pruning is undertaken with scrupulous care by dividing the vineyards (notionally that is) into plots and then allocating to each pruner a plot. Tending the same plot each year engenders a feeling for each vine and its growing characteristics, so pruning can be adapted accordingly. For many years the pruning of Romanée-Conti itself was the personal undertaking of Mme André Noblet, the wife of the then cellar-master.

Much work is done to promote the most concentrated fruit. Apart from a very strict *évasivage* and *dédoublage*, there is a passage, normally in June after the flowering, to remove either excess embryo grape clusters or sometimes excess wood, which might sap valuable energy from the principal bunches.

When it is considered that there are still too many bunches, there is a further green-pruning. In 1990, for example, a team was sent to remove 7–8 bunches per vine. It is essential that this operation is performed relatively late in the growing season to ensure that the sugar levels remain high and that the plants do not compensate for their loss.

In addition to this, several leaf prunings are carried out to increase foliage exposure. There is a tendency to prune higher now, since this has been found to increase photosynthetic efficiency and thus ripeness.

One of the hardest decisions for the

Domaine was taken in 1945 when Romanée-Conti needed replanting because production from its ancient vines, still on their original roots had become uneconomic. Before grubbing it up, plant material was taken to reconstitute La Tâche, 75% of which is now based on Romanée-Conti grafts. After the 1993 vintage, 15 ares of Romanée-Conti were grubbed up. The land remains fallow – undisinfected because to do so would destroy the soil's natural microbial life which has taken so much hard work to preserve. Instead two cover-crops, whose roots are known to kill virus-bearing pests were sown. After detailed soil analyses, the ground will be appropriately composted – not fertilised – and replanted with clones produced from mother vines in La Tâche and Romanée-Conti itself, grafted on to 161/49 rootstock. Altogether a complex, meticulously detailed exercise – entailing, apart from anything else, the loss of 7–8 vintages' production on 1/10 of what is already minuscule.

Nowadays, vines are replaced individually if they are younger than 30–40 years old, otherwise they are replanted as part of the Domaine's programme – one 'journal' (= 1/3 ha) per year. Plant material comes from a population of 50 Romanée-Conti vines selected for small berry size. Cuttings are treated like clones and virus-indexed at Colmar's research station before being grafted on to 161/49 or riparia. Riparia,

though excellent, is especially sensitive to any excess of lime in the soil, which yellows leaves and affects the plant's photosynthetic mechanism. So great care is taken to ensure maximal adaptation of a young vine to its soil.

The attention to detail continues at harvest: *prélèvements* – 'très, très serieux' – at the rate of one per week per vineyard start 3 weeks before the anticipated vintage date. The results determine the order of harvesting. Once started, a vineyard will be finished before the team moves on to the next. The date of starting is considered more significant than the order of picking. Generally, the harvest takes no more than 8 days, so there is less urgency to start early.

In fact, the Domaine prefers to harvest late, to maximise concentration and ripeness. This is a distinct risk, but one which Aubert de Villaine believes any conscientious vigneron should be prepared to take. If an occasional loss from adverse weather is the price of quality, then so be it. Whilst a high proportion of older vines greatly reduces the risk of unacceptably low acidities, grapes so concentrated and over-ripe that they impart a 'figgy' taste are equally undesirable.

The pickers are skilled, and well supervised. No effort is spared to ensure that only the very ripest, intact fruit reaches the *cuverie*. In fact, so great was the concern in 1983 after the June hailstorms, that a small team was despatched early into Romanée-

Conti, La Tâche and part of Richebourg, armed with typesetter's tweezers to remove individual hailed berries. This saved the wine from an ineradicable taste of hail. Damaged berries readily spread the enzyme laccase to healthy fruit, increasing the extent of premature oxidation. So the earlier they are removed the better.

Once cut, bunches are put into straw baskets which are emptied on to a table where a further scan for ripeness is made. When they reach Vosne, they pass into the hands of André Noblet's son Bernard, a quiet, courteous man – 'un type enorme' – and his team in the cellars.

For a short period after André Noblet's retirement, the Domaine enlisted the services of a professional oenologist. This arrangement soon foundered – oenologists tend to work by the book rather than vinifying in sympathy with each vineyard. No doubt the imposing presence of Aubert de Villaine (a skilled winemaker in his own right) and a few hundred years of history proved too intimidating. Ruining a vat of Romanée-Conti is no short-cut to enhancing one's personal standing – certainly not in the close-knit circles of Burgundian oenology.

The philosophy behind the Domaine's winemaking is to achieve 'l'expression le plus pur du terroir'. The vigneron is no more than an intermediary between the soil and the wine and should interfere as little as possible.

Romanée-Conti with Romanée-St.-Vivant and the village of Vosne-Romanée beyond

As Aubert de Villaine somewhat cryptically puts it: 'Nothing is more difficult than to act simply; the ideal is to do nothing,' adding, 'but that is impossible.' Trying to reduce a Grand Cru to a certain number of 'savoir-faires' is like attempting to define Bach's music by analysing its counterpoint.

Translated into more tangible terms, vinification is ultra-traditional – no destalking, even in the leanest years, a smallish dose of SO_2 and a light crushing by foot.

Thereafter, the wines come to life in a series of old open wooden *cuves* of various shapes and sizes which line the walls of the neat *cuverie*, in a side street a short walk from the Domaine's offices. No two are the same shape – one is oval, another tall, some conical and at least one straight on one side and tapering on the other. Collectively, they give the appearance of an overfed, pot-bellied, and decidely misshapen, wooden chorus. Romanée-Conti itself, is invariably fermented in *cuve* number 17, a splendid vessel made in 1862.

There have been trials with stainless-steel *cuves* for at least 20 years but since these give no appreciable difference in quality there are no plans to demolish the 'ultra-traditionelle' wooden *cuves* – 'plus ca change. . .'

Where the precautions taken in the vine-yards fail to prevent an excessively dilute harvest, a *saignée de cuve* precedes alcoholic fermentation. This is a last resort – not even in 1982 was there the need to *saigner*.

Under ideal conditions, the pulp would arrive at 15°C – the temperature at which Burgundian grape yeasts begin to ferment grape sugars. In years like 1989, when the grapes are picked in great heat, attempts are made to cool the pulp by natural means. As Aubert de Villaine points out, pulp is far less easy to cool than juice. Fortunately, the *cuves* are equipped with internal heat-exchangers which will cool the pulp if all else fails. Only natural yeasts are used for fermentation, with a *remontage* at the beginning to get them working. Two or three times each day, the cap is broken up by compressed-air pistons, which are more effective than the traditional expedient of human feet. Their power means that they can be used earlier, further maxi-mising extraction and minimising the risk of acetification from a dry cap.

The temperature is allowed to rise to 33–34°C, with cooling where necessary. Since the aim is to have the longest possible *cuvaison* – on average 18–21 days – any nec-essary *chaptalisation* is performed in several small doses towards the end of fermentation. This must be done with care, since the added sugar must be fully fermented out to alcohol – it is not wanted in the wine.

The *vin de goutte* is run off as soon as the cap starts to fall, indicating that there is no more CO_2, and thus no further fermentation.

The remaining pulp is pressed in a pneu-matic Bucher press, tasted, and added to the free-run wine. The pressing is very light, yielding about 5–10% of the total volume.

No *débourbage* is considered necessary, since the care taken to excise unripe or rot-ten fruit leaves only fine, healthy lees. These will nourish the wine and help the *malolactic* fermentation to proceed smoothly.

The casks in which these precious wines spend the rest of their upbringing are com-pletely renewed each year, a policy started in 1975. It is felt that the advantage of eliminat-ing any possible problems from older casks, which might impart off-flavours, justifies the considerable expense. Since 1979, when the surge in demand for French oak caused widespread doubts about the authenticity and quality of casks, the Domaine has secured its own supply of wood from the forest of Tronçais which is delivered to its coopers to be air-dried.

This is a massive investment – 300 new casks are needed each year and the Domaine has two harvests in cask at any one time. Since the wood takes three years to dry, pro-vision has to be made for five years' supply. This ties up the cost of 1,500 casks at around £300 sterling each.

Although there is no fixed policy on rack-ing, Aubert de Villaine admits that bottling without racking incurs risks which are best avoided. Provided the lees are clean, there is little chance of *gout de lie*, *gout de reduit* or unpleasant hydrogen-sulphide. At present, they are examining the variables which determine the best moment to rack.

There is never more than one racking which, tradition dictates, occurs in early spring, after the *malos* are complete. Clean lees allow the Domaine to delay this to give the wine more fat and complexity. The wines are racked cask-to-cask, by gravity (all cellar movements following fermentation are by gravity), some 2–3 months before bottling. The length of this interval is under discussion.

The Domaine's red wines are fined, but not 'since a long time' filtered. Although not completely excluded, Aubert de Villaine is strongly disinclined to filter. In advance of fining, Bernard Noblet is despatched to a local farm to fetch 900–1,200 fresh, free-range eggs – the fresher the eggs, the better the fining. The chickens having delivered, the whites are added 3–4 per cask and allowed to settle for 1–4 weeks.

The Domaine used to bottle cask by cask. However, variation between different casks of the 'same' wine and even between first and last bottles from the same cask was significant enough to be unacceptable. Since 1982 the wines have been unified in five-cask lots – by gravity but with access to air – and assembled in stainless-steel vats before being bottled.

The Domaine's only white wine, a meagre

Aubert de Villaine

3,000 bottles from old vines on a precious 0.67.59 ha of Le Montrachet – is vinified with equal care. According to Aubert de Villaine, 'The fruit from this vineyard is of very high quality,' to which, no doubt, vine age and a deliberately late harvest both contribute. The Domaine generally harvests the Montrachet after its other vines, and is often the last to pick in that fabled vineyard.

The Chardonnay grapes are brought directly to Vosne-Romanée, pressed and the juice immediately sulphured to prevent oxi-dation. After the lightest possible overnight *débourbage*, the juice is put into new Tronçais oak casks to start its fermentation (never, as has been widely reported, in stainless steel).

There is no attempt to intervene to control the fermentation temperature – which rarely rises beyond 21–23°C. The wine is 'roused' 2–3 times each week, to keep the lees evenly distributed and add richness and flavour. Following the *malo*, the wine remains on its fine lees for about 9 months or until the time is deemed right for racking. This is per-formed by gravity, cask-to-cask. It is then fined with fresh, unpasteurised skimmed milk – Bernard Noblet being again despatched to a nearby farm to choose and collect this – 'almost direct from the cow'. After 3–4 weeks *sur colle* – 'Not too long on milk, it isn't good,' – the wine is racked clear and unified before being bottled. If neces-sary, it is first lightly plate-filtered.

The Domaine de la Romanée-Conti is sur-rounded by much myth and some absurd speculation. The intense, almost quintessen-tial Pinot-extract of its wines has led some to the malicious and groundless conclusion that the fermentation is stopped – it was even rumoured, with vintage Port! The rarity and price of its wines has made them collectibles

– Romanée-Conti and Montrachet above all. Recently there has even been fraud. One unsuspecting Japanese collector apparently paid $5,000 a case for 5 cases of Montrachet, only to find that it was counterfeit. His wine merchant refunded him, but the Domaine had the headache of tracing the source. Curiously, the alarm would not have been raised were it not for a simple mistake on the labels. Instead of 'Appellation Montrachet Contrôlée', the ignorant tricksters had put 'Appellation Romanée-Conti Contrôlée' – nonsense of course.

Few would contest the claim that the Domaine's wines are among the world's finest. Their hallmark is an extra-ordinary finesse and complexity allied to a great concentration. The care that goes into their making results in virtually impeccable typicity and balance, and fabulously seductive richness.

Each Cru has its own characteristics. The Montrachet is among the finest from that appellation with an old-vine concentration and a magnificent complexity which takes ages to develop. When fully mature, the profundity and completeness of flavour is stupendous. What leaves such a lasting impression is the combination of mighty power and thoroughbred class. If in lesser vintages, the wine needs time to evolve, in great vintages it seems to need as long as its red stable-mates. For example, the 1978 Montrachet tasted in 1989 was still in its infancy – just beginning to show the honey and grilled almonds trademarks of its origins, but in reality far from full throttle. The 1993, tasted in 1995 was explosively opulent – gorgeously intense, yet inherently complex, floral aromas, with an equally multi-faceted spectrum of flavours and extraordinary power, length and persistence. Unmistakably Grand Cru, unmistakably Montrachet.

There was unfortunately no 1992 DRC Montrachet, a fact which attracted much wine-press attention. The facts, widely misrepresented, are simple: as with many 1992 whites, alcoholic fermentation was unusually slow and reluctant to finish. Aubert de Villaine added yeast to complete it. The resulting wine is without technical fault, in fact well up to the quality of which other Domaines would be happy to sell as Montrachet. The nose is expressive with an exotic fruit element, attributable to a long, cool fermentation, and the palate round and complex with an enriching hint of botrytis. The wine is somewhat hollow and lacks the power and class which people have come to expect from a DRC Montrachet. It was on this relatively marginal palate imperfection that the decision not to release the wine was taken. The wine is not, as has been suggested, a disaster, nor in any justifiable sense was the vinification mismanaged. It is curious that when a Domaine which is some-

times pilloried for releasing wines which are not, in the view of the critics, worthy of their pedigree, decides not to release a wine for just such a reason, the circumstances are sensationalised to the point of scandal.

The 200 cases of the Domaine's Montrachet made in each normal year are fiercely fought over at ever soaring prices. As with any rarity, price bears no relationship to quality – a Chevalier Montrachet from Leflaive or a Montrachet from Ramonet would probably give DRC's Montrachet a good run in a blind tasting, at a fraction of the price.

For the Domaine's red wines, however, there is less contest. The Echézeaux and Grands Echézeaux might find peers worthy of comparison, but in great vintages, the Richebourg, La Tâche and Romanée-Conti stand above all others. Their individuality is difficult to characterise – especially in youth when they can range from the depth and pepperiness of a young Syrah, to deceptively lean-framed liquids with mouth-puckering acidity. It may not always be easy to forsee what will emerge after a decade or more in bottle but one is rarely disappointed.

The Domaine's wines are generally characterised by individual aromas and flavours of spice – especially cinnamon – violets, sometimes liquorice, and often by almost, but not quite, overripe sweetness. This great concentration results in wines which take a long time to develop. After many years, often twenty or more, they lose their youthful awkwardness and transform into seductively ripe, silky mouthfuls – with the texture of slightly worn velvet. A 1953 La Tâche drunk in 1988 was a yardstick example of what fine Burgundy is all about – a deep, limpid, slightly singed black cherry colour, with a massive, yet understated, complex nose of *sous-bois* and overripe wild fruits and a complete flavour from front to back of the mouth which simply went on and on, ending in the famous Romanée-Conti trademark – a peacock's tail. Lesser vintages often provide pleasant surprises – a 1956 Romanée-Conti tasted at the Domaine in 1995 was quite remarkable – light tawny, with a refined nose of old tea-rose and muscat and still plenty of fruit holding together a soft, elegant palate; oxidative flavours, indeed, but still a power-

ful, complex and finely-poised Grande Dame.

Romanée-Conti itself takes this 'expression le plus pur du terroir' a stage further. Perhaps – although trying to describe these wines brings one perilously close to pretention – a touch more elegant than La Tâche, but always with that supreme aristocracy. There is nothing obvious or showy about these wines – just essence of quality.

Their fame and scarcity makes the Domaine's wines more tasted than drunk for pleasure as they were intended to be. It also makes them controversial. American critics pilloried the 1992 reds, with no justification whatsoever. The wines are all sound, well-coloured and constituted, with the individuality of their Crus – not as massive and extracted as the sensational 1993s, but pretty wines which, after a decade or more, will give much pleasure.

The care that goes into these wines provides a yardstick for vignerons along the Côte who may be tempted to think that it is enough to have Grand Cru land, some old vines, and a competent cellar. The Domaine's policy is that there are no short cuts.

For Aubert de Villaine, the monks who 'invented' the Côte, and planted a mosaic of vines on its precious soil, are his inspiration. Those who try to imitate come in for some mild mirth – 'the gimmicks of winemakers' who believe, as did the unfortunate frog in the Fable de la Fontaine, that they can mimic something greater. Putting 'Montrachet' yeasts to ferment a New World Chardonnay will not turn it into a Montrachet.

Aubert de Villaine would be the first to admit that the Domaine's wines fall short of the perfection that is his constant goal. His, and Henri Roch's contribution is 'the most attentive, but also the most humble and invisible', to ensure that their wines are free from faults and that this matchless *terroir* expresses itself with the utmost purity. The intrinsic qualities and personalities of their wines rest, not on them, but on the mysterious fusion of soil, micro-climate and 'that genie of *terroir*', of which they are merely 'the modest and obliging servants'. If anyone is in a position to defend the primacy of *terroir* in the production of great wine, it is the Domaine de la Romanée-Conti.

VINEYARD HOLDINGS

Commune	Level	Lieu-dit/Climat	Area	Status	Av. Prod.
Vosne	GC	Romanée-Conti	1.80.50	P	450 C/S
Vosne	GC	La Tâche	6.06.20	P	1500 C/S
Vosne	GC	Richebourg	3.51.10	P	1000 C/S
Vosne	GC	Romanée-St.-Vivant	5.28.58	P	1500 C/S
Vosne	GC	Grands-Echézeaux	3.52.63	P/F	1000 C/S
Vosne	GC	Echézeaux	4.67.03	P/F	1340 C/S
Chassagne	GC	Montrachet	0.67.59	P	250 C/S
Total:			**25.53.63 ha**		**7460 C/S**

NUITS-ST.-GEORGES AND PRÉMEAUX-PRISSEY

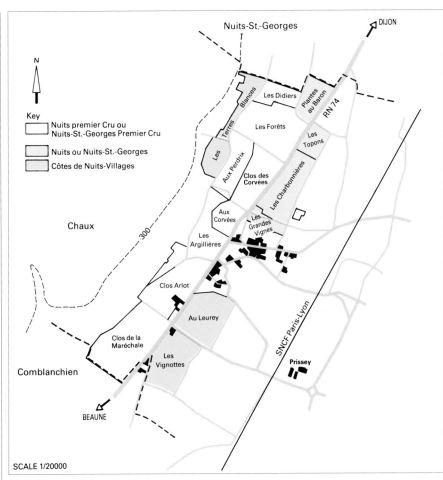

and offices, trading and dealing and much besides. Here are a great diversity of restaurants, several excellent patissiers and a 16th century bell-tower covered in ivy which marks the passing quarters with a pleasant, musical chime.

Away from the tourist's gaze, the town also boasts an attractive older quarter, with some remarkable cellars hidden beneath unremarkable façades. The square, opposite the Mairie has been renamed Place de la Cratère St.-Georges, since the Apollo XV astronauts christened one of the Moon's craters 'St.-Georges', after Jules Verne's Captain Anders who chose to toast his moon-landing with a bottle of Nuits. Then there is Rue Fagon named after Napoleon 3rd's doctor who prescribed a cure consisting, apparently, entirely of Nuits, and the usual run of Avenue Pasteur, Place République and Rue Egalité. So far the town council has resisted General de Gaulle, Winston Churchill and President Kennedy.

After much lobbying in the 1970s, the Nuitons managed to persuade the builders of the Lyon-Mulhouse autoroute to put in an interchange at Nuits. This keeps away unnecessary traffic and has generated a sizeable industrial zone on the town's eastern edge.

The mischievous river Meuzin bisects the vineyards. To the north, Côte Vosne, at altitudes of between 240 and 340 m, lie Village land and 11 Premiers Crus. Here the soils closely resemble those of Vosne, dominated by limestone and pebbles with varying but small amounts of clay. The wines tend to have less of the *charpente* and earthiness of southern Nuits, rather more of the finesse and elegance of Vosne. Nonetheless, they are well-structured and need plenty of bottle-ageing to give of their best.

On the Prémeaux side of the Meuzin valley are a further 16 Premiers Crus, including that cluster generally regarded as the cream – Les Cailles, Les Vaucrains and Les St.-Georges. These vineyards are also on hillsides, with soils which are generally deeper and browner than those nearer Vosne, with a more even mix of clay and limestone. Les Porrets St.-Georges, Les Cailles and Les St.-Georges are planted on deep brown limestone, on a band of rock and pebbles which continue the marble quarries of Comblanchien to the south. Les Vaucrains, above Les St.-Georges, has a shallower, mainly red-brown soil, with a proportion of fine sandy particles and white oolite

Nuits-St.-Georges though not the largest commune in the Côte d'Or, is the longest. Extending for some 5 km, it joins Vosne-Romanée to the north and Prémeaux to the south, where it finally peters out at the Clos de la Maréchale, marking the southern extremity of important vineyards in the Côte de Nuits.

Together – for Prémeaux has only the appellation Nuits-St.-Georges or Nuits-St.-Georges Premier Cru – there are some 175.32 ha of Village land and 144.79 ha of Premiers Crus. Nuits itself has no fewer than 33 different Premiers Crus, Prémeaux contributing 8, including 4 Clos. In 1987, following strong lobbying by growers, the Terre Blanche vineyard was promoted from Régionale AC to full Premier Cru – they had only requested a Village upgrade!

Nuits is an ancient settlement – recent excavations unearthed the site of a Roman villa – which developed during the Middle Ages into a substantial fortified town. In 1366 Philippe-le-Hardi, Duc de Bourgogne, estab-

Prémeaux-Prissey

lished a wine-tax to help pay for fortifications, but these were destroyed by the Protestant Duc Casimir in 1576.

Like many small wine towns Nuits is built on a river. No raging torrent, the Meuzin, which still tumbles down from the hills and runs through the towncentre, has been tamed since it managed to burst its banks in August 1747, repeated in January 1757, flooding the surrounding vineyards and generally wreaking havoc on both occasions. Perversely, in 1788 it, and all the local wells, dried up completely.

Today, Nuits is the commercial entrepôt of the Côte de Nuits – known as 'the kidney of the Côte' for its prodigious throughput of wine. The diligent tourist is not kept idle: here are the large négociant houses, many selling much ordinary wine at extraordinary prices; here is one of France's largest fruit-juice factories; here is the 'fons et origo' of the Cassis and sirop trade; here are shops

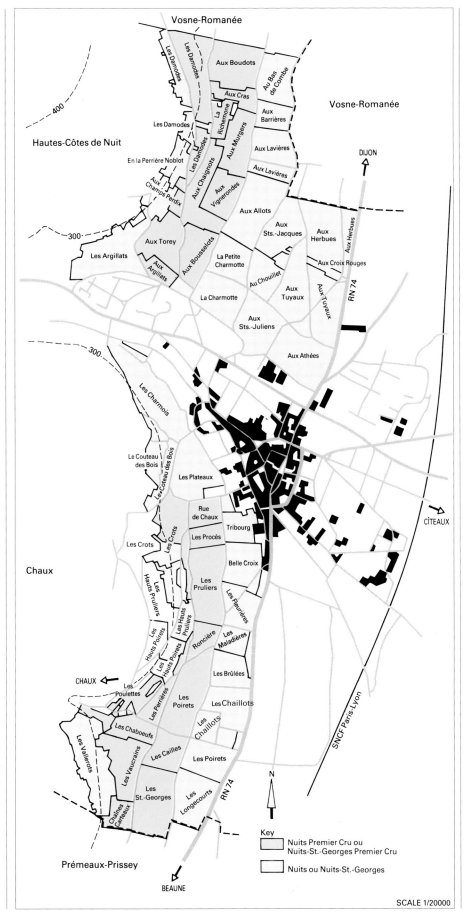

Vosne-Romanée

Les Damodes
Les Damodes
Aux Boudots
Au Bas de Combe

Aux Cras
Vosne-Romanée

Les Damodes
La Richemone
Aux Murgers
Aux Barrières
DIJON

Hautes-Côtes de Nuit

En la Perrière Noblot
Les Damodes
Aux Laurières
Aux Champs Perdrix
Aux Chaignots
Aux Vignerondes
Aux Laurières

Aux Allots

Aux Torey
Aux Bousselots
Aux Sts.-Jacques
Aux Herbues
Aux Herbues

Les Argillats
Aux Argillats
La Petite Charmotte
Aux Croix Rouges

Au Chouillet
Aux Tuyaux
RN 74

La Charmotte
Aux Tuyaux

Aux Sts.-Juliens

Aux Athées

Les Charmois

Le Couteau des Bois
Les Coteau des Bois
Les Plateaux

Chaux

Rue de Chaux
Tribourg
Les Procès

Les Crots
Les Crots
Belle Croix
CÎTEAUX

Les Hauts Pruliers
Les Pruliers
Les Fleurières

Les Hauts Poirets
Ronciere
Les Maladières

CHAUX
Les Hauts Poirets
Les Brûlées

Les Poulettes
Les Perrières
Les Poirets
Les Chaillots

Les Chaboeufs
Les Chaillots

Les Vallerots
Les Cailles
Les Poirets

Les Vaucrains
SNCF Paris-Lyon

Les St.-Georges
Les Longecourts
RN 74

Chaînes Carteaux
N

Prémeaux-Prissey

BEAUNE

Key
Nuits Premier Cru ou Nuits-St.-Georges Premier Cru
Nuits ou Nuits-St.-Georges

SCALE 1/20000

limestone, which outcrops as 'têtes de moutons'.

The 8 Prémeaux Premiers Crus occupy a narrow band of gently sloping ground between the RN74 and the woods. Here are the Clos des Forêts St.-Georges, the Clos des Corvées, Clos Arlot and the Clos de la Maréchale, all capable of producing superb wine. The soils vary with altitude becoming particularly fine and thin between the Clos des Forêts and the Clos Arlot with a limestone subsoil. Nearby Comblanchien is known for its marble – often given a pink tinge from veins of dolomite.

There is a trickle of Nuits-St.-Georges Blanc from a handful of producers. Jean-Pierre de Smet makes a delicious wine from Chardonnay and a touch of Pinot Beurot from 2 ha in the Clos de l'Arlot and the Gouges extract an unusual wine from a Pinot Noir blanc in Les Perrières. They are very different in style, the Clos de l'Arlot having greater finesse than the Perrières, which is sometimes rather flabby. Robert Chevillon also makes a delicious, mouthfilling white Nuits from old Pinot Blanc vines.

The appellation caught the international imagination after the war – doubtless because it was large enough to supply a thirsty, wine-starved Europe. Much of what passed for Nuits was deep-coloured, gutsy, hearty fluid cut with Rhône Grenache if you were lucky or with sunburnt Algerian if you weren't. The particularly privileged got a dollop of Port added at bottling, giving the wines, and the post-war British squirearchy, the comforting sensation of liquid central heating.

Nowadays, although a disturbing quantity of dreadful 'Nuits-St.-Georges' still manages to seep on to the market, the true quality of the commune is widely recognised, thanks to a coterie of excellent, conscientious growers. Anyone foolish enough to rely on the growers' maxim that 'a glass of night (Nuits) prepares yours', will at least be relieved to know that they are not tuning themselves up with the vintner's equivalent of 'electric soup'.

A profusion of indifferent, recipe-book wines fostered the belief that quintessential Nuits-St.-Georges is elusive. With great variation between producers and the commune's wide geographical spread, even the genuine article has reinforced this impression. Many tasters, some pejoratively, characterise Nuits as 'earthy' or 'rustic'. There is often a granular feel about fine young Nuits, beyond its adolescent tannins, which some consider detracts from its class, but these qualities rarely appear, at least in wines from the best Domaines, without a concomitant measure of complexity and finesse. Nuits may have a touch of the maverick, but the robust charms of leather and denim are often no less alluring than the soft elegance of silk and satin.

Domaine de l'Arlot

PRÉMEAUX-PRISSEY

The Domaine de l'Arlot was created in 1987 by the French insurance company Axa, with the purchase of buildings and land from the Domaine Jules Belin – a decaying entity which had pottered along unhindered since it was put together by its founder, the son of a local Notaire, in 1891.

To oversee this, the first of their Burgundian interests, they appointed Jean-Pierre de Smet, who had arrived in Burgundy in 1977 to help in Jacques Seysses' cellars in Morey after seven years running his own accountancy practice in New Caledonia. Jean-Pierre, an ex-University skier and a passionate yachtsman, met Axa's Chairman Claude Bebéar by chance and, discovering that he was searching for suitable Burgundian vineyards, mediated the purchase of Jules Belin.

The Domaine is run from a fine late 17th–early 18th-century building – now completely restored – on the RN74 at Prémeaux, 3 kms south of Nuits. The Clos de l'Arlot itself was created by Jean-Charles Vienot, a Nuiton vigneron, at the end of the 18th century, by enclosing 4 ha of vines with a wall. During the 19th century his son enlarged and reconstructed the buildings and laid out a splendid park, complete with a maze, on land just behind the house.

The vineyards consist principally of two *Monopoles* : the splendid 7 ha Clos des Forêts St.-Georges, and the 4 ha Clos de l'Arlot, a contoured block of vines bordering the RN74. There are also a 2 ha block of Côtes de Nuits Villages – the Clos du Chapeau – 0.25 ha of Romanée-St.-Vivant (first vintage 1991), and 0.85 ha of Vosne Premier Cru Les Suchots, acquired in 1992.

The Clos de l'Arlot was originally planted in 3:1 Pinot Noir: Chardonnay (including an important touch of old white Pinot Beurot). However, so successful was the Arlot white that a hectare of badly virussed Pinot, was grubbed up and replanted to Chardonnay in 1995, making the current proportion 2:2.

The marriage of de Smet and l'Arlot has borne rich fruit; not however, without great effort. The estate was in need of much internal and external restoration, extensive replanting, among young and old vines alike, and careful soil nutrient adjustments. Apart from the 1986 vintage still in cask, all that remained in the cellars were a few bottles of Belin's Marc. Fortified, no doubt, by this meagre legacy, Jean-Pierre set about the vineyard reconstruction, with the help of Christophe Morin, Jacques Seysses' talented 'chef de culture', while stonemasons worked

Old vines in the Clos de l'Arlot and a glimpse of Prémeaux

to uncover original brickwork in the *cuverie*.

Jean-Pierre is a positive, intelligent man, firmly focused on quality. He is absolutely convinced that fine wine is made – or lost – in the vineyard. This means very low doses of organic fertilisers – the Belins dosed low from parsimony, Jean-Pierre from conviction – and investigations into the new 'biodynamie' – a viticultural homeopathy which uses only natural products in minimum dose, with the aim of restoring each plant's equilibrium with its surroundings and strengthening its resistance to disease.

Much time is spent pruning for low yields while bunch counts in July often result in pickers being despatched to thin the crop. The reward, if the vines do not compensate – as they will if the operation is badly timed – is a low yield (in 1990, only 32 hl/ha – well below average for this abundant vintage).

Great attention is paid to harvesting. Jean-Pierre oversees picking personally for the first day or two, checking that any substandard fruit is excised. Rot – 'sec' and 'humide' – is the greatest problem; pickers

prefer not to trouble to remove patches of rotten grapes from within a bunch, so they tend to get left to the vigilance of the Domaine's regular porters. Meanwhile, Jean-Pierre's wife, Lilo, copes with the task of feeding 30–40 people 5 times a day – including a wine-based *casse-croute* at 9 am! – and the welfare of the 20 or so housed at the Domaine.

Concern for top-quality raw material is matched by equal care in vinification. The foundation of Jean-Pierre's philosophy is that the more one knows the less one interferes. Ideally, vinification should be 'le plus naturelle que possible'. So, virtually all the stalks remain in the vats; minimum doses of SO_2, only natural yeasts; a maximum temperature 32°C and 15–22 days *cuvaison*.

Although fermentation does not in fact start for 2–5 days, cold *maceration* is not expressly sought. Cooling the harvest merely establishes the base point which ultimately determines the maximum temperature during active fermentation. With an invariant 15 centigrade degree differential, it is important to start low. Any pre-fermentive *maceration* is an aid to temperature control, not a means of colour extraction. In his first three vinifications, including the abnormally hot 1989, Jean-Pierre did not need to cool a single vat; so the theory seems to work.

The high proportion of whole grapes encourages an intra-cellular fermentation, with CO_2 gas in the vat degrading the grape skins round it, extracting greater complexity, colour and aroma compounds.

After the new wine has been decanted and that from the first light pressing added, it is left to rest for 24 hours before being put into oak casks to age. In company with many enlightened vignerons, Jean-Pierre buys the cask wood he needs three years in advance. It is inventoried, numbered and delivered to their barrel-maker to be dried in the open before coopering. Although he prefers Allier, he contends that the manner and extent of charring each barrel is a more decisive determinant of quality than its provenance. A light, gentle, charring is his ideal.

Into these carefully crafted new casks go 40–50% of the Premiers Crus and Romanée-St-Vivant, and some 20% of the Côte de Nuits Villages, where they remain for 15–18 months before bottling. They are racked twice, cask-to-cask, without pumping and kept on their fine lees, provided these are clean, until the second racking. The precise timing of racking depends on taste. If a particular cask tastes *reduit* – a curious smell allied to a stale, flat taste – then it is summarily racked, by gravity, but with air, to restore the normal smell and flavour.

Fining is only made when necessary and then with fresh egg-white, before unification and bottling, without filtration. Clarification is increased and the need for filtration consequently diminished, by the addition of pectolytic enzymes during fermentation.

Jean-Pierre's approach is considered, but flexible – heuristic rather than didactic and the results are striking. The white Clos de l'Arlot is a remarkable effort – a 'vin blanc' from 'terre à rouge' – classy, with richness and florality from its touch of Pinot Beurot and a distinct hint of *terroir*; something of an over-cosseted duchess who has taken a holiday in a mine and come out a trifle dusty, with a bit of refinement knocked off.

This battered aristocrat is achieved by a broadly classic vinification. Once fermentation is heard to begin, the wine is racked off into cask. A proportion of fine lees is added and the *must* fermented naturally, enriched by 2–3 rousings a week until around Christmas. The following autumn, after fining and a light plate filtration the wine is bottled. Jean-Pierre has tried both fish and bentonite fining and seems to prefer the former.

Recent releases of the white Clos de l'Arlot

show how consistently fine this wine is. Five years on, the 1990 is just starting to show its paces, deep and characteristically earthy whilst the 1991 is marginally leaner. The 1992 is packed tight with firm, opulent fruit, and is likely to prove a slow developer. The 1993 has an explosive nose, with a strong note of candied peel – often found in this wine – strongly redolent of Viognier (Jean-Pierre swears there's none in the vineyard!), a full, sturdy flavour and plenty of fat. Though each reflects its vintage, a noticeable thematic continuity traverses the years: aromas of exotic fruits – especially of pineapple and banana – and an attractive minerally *goût de terroir*, deep and complex. The wines' fine balance and complete lack of tired, flabby structure of many whites grown on inappropriate soils, lead one to surmise that this part of the Clos has more limestone. Its 'terre à rouge' parentage gives the Clos de l'Arlot Blanc the foundation for longish ageing. If you can't wait, then decant the wine a good two hours in advance of drinking it.

The Pinot Noir section of the Clos de l'Arlot is a mixture of limestone and clay. The vineyard is, in fact, just below a rock quarry in the park behind the house, and the earth consequently shallow, giving its reds a brightish flavour aspect. Jean-Pierre confesses that the Clos provides him with the greatest challenge – probably because these older plants, many from *sélection massale*, have rootstocks less well-adapted to their soils. The wine generally has interest and depth, sometimes with a note of greenness, flavours of *fruits rouges* rather than *fruits noirs* – and the capacity to develop in bottle over the medium term.

The Clos des Forêts St.-Georges, has a mixture of young and older vines. In 1992, different *cuvées* were released to reflect this fact, declassifying the produce of younger vines into AC Nuits St.-Georges (without naming the Clos). In 1993, there were three *cuvées*: young vines (labelled Nuits St.-Georges), vines up to about 15 (labelled Nuits St.-Georges Premier Cru), and the Clos des Forêts St.-Georges, labelled as such, from vines averaging around 30. The wines differ markedly in concentration and potential – all good at their quality level, with the Clos producing the finest, most powerful and complex

Jean-Pierre de Smet

result. Complicated maybe, but logical.

The Vosne Suchots (first appearance 1992), from vines adjoining Grand Cru Richebourg, provides a change of register from Nuits. The 1993 showed a fine, deep garnet hue, marvellous aromatic potential and a deep, succulent base of firm, ripe fruit, encased in rounded tannins – with a touch of bright grippiness. In short, all the class one seeks in this pedigree Vosne Premier Cru planted with 38-year-old vines.

The Romanée-St.-Vivant – a Grand Cru which combines at best power and finesse with the accent firmly on finesse – is a further step towards Elysium. Jean-Pierre's Formula One debut – the 1991 vintage – tasted at the Domaine in 1995 had all the hallmarks of great Burgundy. By no means an easy vintage, this wine showed a depth and class which many would be happy to acknowledge in better vintages; no rough edges, ripe fruit, enough and well-integrated tannin, and a long, delicate raft of magnificently silken flavours.

In just a decade, Jean-Pierre de Smet has crafted a five-star Domaine which continues from strength to strength.

VINEYARD HOLDINGS

Commune	Level	Lieu-dit/Climat	Area	Vine Age	Status
Vosne	GC	Romanée-St.-Vivant	0.25	18	P
Vosne	PC	Les Suchots	0.85	38	P
Nuits	PC	Clos des Forêts Saint-Georges	7.00	25	P
Nuits	PC	Clos de L'Arlot	2.00	38	P
Nuits	PC	Clos de L'Arlot (Blanc)	2.00	1-30	P
————	V	Côte de Nuits Villages	2.00	20	P
		Total:	**14.10 ha**		

Domaine Daniel Bocquenet

NUITS-ST.-GEORGES

It was in 1913 that Daniel Bocquenet's grandmother, the widow Baudot, bought her first vines. Marriage to Albert Bocquenet brought further acquisitions and a son, Marcel, now nearing retirement and, seemingly, thoroughly content with his life. At 13, he was sent as apprentice cork-maker to Geisweiler, where, as well as making corks for Domaine de la Romanée-Conti – he can still tell the origin of a cork by looking at it – he learned the trade of *éleveur*. Three years with the Hospices de Nuits taught him vinification, which he then practised on his own account until his son, Daniel, joined him in the 1970s. His daughter, Monique, also works with them, in the vines and cellars – helped occasionally by their dog Fanny, whose party trick is to open the cellar door for visitors.

The Domaine operates out of what appears to be a large shed, recessed from one of Nuits' back streets, with vines behind, and the trickling Meuzin in front. There are two *cuvées* of Nuits plus one, depending on the vintage, for the négoce. The 'engin de

The commercial entrepôt of the Côte de Nuits

bataille' is a good Village Nuits, well-structured with plenty of fruit – a fleshy, but not feminine interpretation. The top Nuits bottling Aux St.-Juliens, comes from old vines planted in a Village vineyard on the edge of Nuits, Côté Vosne, which used to be a chapel before being destroyed in the wars of religion. Here, rocky ground gives a tight, firm wine, with concentration and power. 'We like our wines tannic,' Marcel explains. In fact the tannins, from 2–4 year old casks in the case of the Nuits and Vosne village *cuvées*, 100% new wood for the Echézeaux – are rarely excessive – even the 1992 had enough balancing richness.

The Bocquenets make consistently good wine. The 1993s are excellent, not overpoweringly dense, but with plenty of interest

and class. The Vosne, from a parcel bordering Nuits Premier Cru Les Lavières was well-structured and yet quite supple – very similar in character to its Nuits cousin. The Echézeaux – 'our 3-star, but not an industrial quantity,' Marcel confides, adding '30 hl/ha', is a very fine example, softish, silky in character with nicely-tuned oak, interesting palate aromas and the power, length and complexity expected from Grand Cru.

The much decried 1992s are also most attractive here – quite open and fleshy but direct and complex. The prices are also remarkably reasonable – 120 Francs pre-tax for a 1989 Echézeaux in mid 1995 and around 70 for a 1991 Aux St.-Juliens. This is not a spectacular, high-profile Domaine, but one of careful, consistent quality.

Daniel Bocquenet

VINEYARD HOLDINGS

Commune	Level	Lieu-dit/Climat	Area	Vine Age	Status
Nuits	V	(32 different *lieu-dits*)	3.50	10–50	P
Vosne	V	(Parcel touches Nuits Lavières)	0.40	1902/1970	P
Flagey	GC	Echézeaux	0.60	35–40	P
		Total:	**4.50 ha**		

Domaine Michel Chevillon

NUITS-ST.-GEORGES

The Chevillon family has two branches, both in Nuits. Michel, Georges' son, and his wife Pascale form one; his cousin Robert, son of Georges' brother Maurice, the other.

Michel, a large, smiling, generous-spirited man, operates from a modern house in one of the town's many broad backstreets. Some of his vines, notably those in Nuits and Vosne, are *en fermage* from his father; the rest, all Nuits, is either rented or share-cropped. Whites are represented by an Hautes Côtes de Nuits (Chardonnay).

Michel worked with his father from 1963 until taking full charge in 1987, and has now been joined by his daughter Claire. One gets the impression that, apart from a touch of modern technology to assist in difficult years, little of significance has changed here over the generations. The old wooden *cuves* have given way to cement, although one large oak vat remains on emergency standby in a corner, and destalking has been mechanised. A heat exchanger has appeared, but 'we use it very little,' says Michel smiling. These minor revolutions apart, the broad lines of vinification and style of wine have scarcely altered since the war.

Although Michel infinitely prefers his own *sélection massale* to clones, which he tried in the early 1980s and rejected for excessive yields, since 1991 all replanting has been with a mix of clones – selecting plant material and making grafts just took too long. Average vine age is modest because they had to replace many degenerate vines, on SO4 roots, over the last twenty years. Short pruning and careful husbandry keep yields moderate and up to 3 weeks *cuvaison* and plenty of *pigéage* ensure that the wines have firm enough structures.

For years salesmen tried in vain to persuade Michel to replace his 1957 press – 'the first Vaslin in Nuits,' he claims proudly. 'They say I can get 4–5 percent more juice from a modern press, but – what juice!' he expostulates, screwing up his face. Michel's sales resistance finally crumbled and a new pneumatic press now graces the *cuverie*.

Although his wines spend up to 22 months in cask, irrespective of quality level or vintage, Michel is no partisan of new oak – 'I like casks, but not new casks,' he confides. So, Premiers Crus are *élevés* entirely in 1-year-old wood, the rest in 10% year-old and older casks.

In years when fining is deemed necessary the wines are racked, Kieselguhr filtered and

A Côte d'Or village well

then returned to bulk for two weeks before bottling. Otherwise, they are simply filtered and bottled directly – until 1987, by hand, now on a small bottling machine shared with Gouges, Remoriquet and others, which speeds up the process no end.

The style of wine is unashamedly old-fashioned, what Michel calls traditional; 'A bit hard to start with, but ages well.' A common firm structure makes early tasting difficult but a lower percentage of stems (20–25% now, against 50% before) has greatly increased suppleness and accessibility. A few years' bottle-age does wonders for wines which initially seem over-tannic and stemmy, so premature judgements should be tempered with caution.

The best *cuvées* are excellent. Where deficiencies appear these are generally in

depth and finesse, to which high yields may well contribute – the 1990 crop averaged 50–52 hl/ha. Michel claims that he is entirely prepared to *saigner* where overall balance would benefit, but this is no real remedy for over-cropping in the first place.

The pick of this cellar are the Nuits Premiers Crus Les Porets and Les St.-Georges and the excellent, old-viney Village Nuits St.-Julien. Second-rank vintages are often well worth considering and surprisingly good, given the generally tannic style. The 1992s were starting to taste well in 1995 whilst the 1991s were more backward. For the rest, the 1989s and 1990s are progressing and should be most attractive, given time. The Chevillon 1987s were particularly successful – a fine Nuits Villages and an even better Premier Cru Les Porets. Those who so prematurely wrote down the 1987 vintage made a serious error of judgement.

Michel Chevillon does not have the sheer flare of his cousin Robert. The wines have benefitted enormously from their ration of newish wood and would benefit still further from shorter *élevage* to preserve fruit and suppleness. Nonetheless this is a good source, albeit one from which it pays to be selective.

VINEYARD HOLDINGS

Commune	Level	Lieu-dit/Climat	Area	Vine Age	Status
Nuits	PC	Les St.-Georges	0.45	1948	F
Nuits	PC	Les Porets	0.59	1954/57	M
Nuits	PC	Champs Perdrix	0.34	1972	F
Nuits	PC	Crots + Bousselots	0.78	1936/73/82	P
Nuits	V	St.-Julien	0.98	1957/63/69	P/M
Nuits	V	(6 different climats)	2.37	1954–89	F
Vosne	V	Croix Blanches	0.30	1949–64	F
Nuits	R	(Bourg. Pinot Noir / PTG)	2.03	1947–86	P
Chaux	R	(Htes. Ctes. de Nuits Chard)	0.65	1989	P
		Total:	**8.49 ha**		

Domaine Chopin-Groffier

COMBLANCHIEN

Daniel Chopin is one of the Côte's finest winemakers. Yet his wines seldom appear on the international market. For almost 40 years this friendly, reticent man has been beavering away in his modest cellars, up a back alley in Comblanchien, producing superb wines to satisfy a band of faithful customers, mostly private individuals from Paris and elsewhere. Yet, it is only now that the fine quality of his wines is becoming known outside France.

When he took over the holdings from his father in 1959 there were both vines and cereal crops – a true Burgundian post-war polyculture, which produced enough to keep a family and, by diversity, ensured that they were not totally at the mercy of the weather.

With Daniel's marriage in 1957 to a Mlle Groffier from Vougeot came some Village Chambolle-Musigny and Vougeot and in 1964 he added the Nuits-St.-Georges and the Clos de Vougeot. Now approaching retirement, Daniel is gradually handing over the harder vineyard work to his son-in-law, Hubert Chauvenet-Chopin – who has a small Domaine on his own account, in Nuits, although he continues to vinify and bottle his share of the fruit.

There is nothing iconoclastic, nothing revolutionary about Daniel's methods – just a determination to produce the best he can. He is a Tartar for fruit quality; securing the quantity and quality of the vintage – 'C'est primordiale, ça,' he declares. The key is a rigorous *évasivage* and uncompromising selection at harvest time. 'I don't use the *PLC* often,' he adds. In that super-abundant year 1990, his vineyards averaged 45 hl/ha, with the *PLC* only needed in a few parcels.

It has taken time to persuade Daniel that there might be some benefit in clones. Although he largely changed over in the early 1980s, he still clings on to his splendid *sélection massale* by constant *répiquéage*, at least until the vines reach 40.

He definitely dislikes *surmaturité* and is never the last – nor the first – to harvest. 'We don't throw ourselves in at the Ban de Vendanges, but pick when the degrees are there.' In the cellar, vinification is simple and broadly standard. 70–90% of the crop is destalked, the exact proportion depending on the state of the grapes and the style of wine Daniel is trying to make. Alcoholic fermentation lasts some 15 days in total – including 3–4 days *maceration* beforehand. The temperature of the *cuves* rarely exceeds 31°C and any *chaptalisation*, is carried out after it

has peaked to ensure a long and even cycle. 1989, 1990 and 1993 were generally rich enough in natural sugar to need only the minimum of addition. Of 1990 Daniel was moved to remark: 'I would sign a contract to have a vintage like this to end my days.'

As soon as fermentation is over the wine is run off the *marc*. All but the final press-juice is added and the *cuves* are left for a couple of days to settle before the wine passes into cask. Everything of Village quality and above goes into barrel, whilst the *régionales* are vinified in large volume up to *malo*, and kept thereafter in old oak.

Daniel Chopin has strong views on wood, the chief of these being that a wine must already be naturally well-structured to benefit from the addition of further *charpente* from new oak. He allows no more than 40–50%, with a preference for Allier, adding cynically 'but the barrel-maker puts in whatever wood he wants'. He also berates those who try to bee-fup a weak wine by keeping it in new wood.

His own wines have 15–18 months in cask, being bottled no later than one year after their *malo*. Timing of rackings and bottling depends as much on tasting as on intuition or habit. Since most *malos* are finished by February, a second racking in November or December is followed by fining in bulk or in cask (for smaller lots) and bottling 2–3 months later. Having the magnificent 1989 Clos Vougeot without filtration, only the Bourgogne is filtered nowadays.

Daniel Chopin's wines are consistently among the most compelling to be found anywhere. Deliberately low yields and patches of venerable old vines combine with his marvellous winemaking touch to produce sumptuous quality from a richly concentrated, complex *Régionales* to a masterly Clos de Vougeot. The Côte de Nuits-Villages is a splendid example of what of the nobility is inherent in a humble peasant if you treat him

like a duke. The 1993 had both depth and finesse, fine aromas and a fullish, elegant flow of flavours supported by just the right amount of structure. A wine for 5–10 years' keeping. The 1994 wasn't far behind.

Daniel's small production of Vougeot – as distinct from Clos de Vougeot – comes from the Petits Vougeot vineyard, just next to the Chambolle Amoureuses of his distant cousin Robert Groffier. Here, forty-year-old vines on meagre soils with a predominance of limestone and pebbles, give a fine, concentrated wine. The 1993 is deeply coloured with well-developed aromas of *fruits noirs*, splendid palate-richness and plenty of soft, sexy, supple fruit – a real mouthfiller.

The Chambolle and all but 0.50 ha of the Nuits Villages have gone to Hubert now, leaving the fine Nuits Chaignots as principal witness to Daniel's skill in extracting finesse from Nuits-St.-Georges. Both 1993 Village and Premier Cru were truly magnificent.

The Chopin Clos Vougeot is very special. The 1989, 1990, 1993 and 1994 – all tasted recently – are each, in their own way, remarkable. These lovingly tended old vines, next to the Ch. de la Tour, give an extraordinary richness of deeply coloured, mouthfilling fruit, complex, yet near-perfectly balanced. What makes this wine so exciting, in all these vintages, is its sheer density of flavour. The 1990 and 1993 will need at least 5–10 years to mature and will continue developing for as long again. Sadly it is soon sold – the UK allocation being a mere 12 bottles.

If the classic vintages are superb, the others are no less remarkable: finely-crafted 1987s of real finesse and interest, and well above average 1991s and 1992s.

Daniel may be slowly relinquishing the reins he has so capably held for so long, yet his touch is as bright as ever. His Paris doctors and notaires are indeed people of good taste – and good fortune.

VINEYARD HOLDINGS

Commune	Level	Lieu-dit/Climat	Area	Vine Age	Status
Vougeot	GC	Clos de Vougeot	0.35	55	P
Vougeot	V	Les Petits Vougeots	0.40	40	P
Nuits	PC	Les Chaignots	0.40	40	P
Nuits	V	———————	0.50 3	5	P
		Comblanchien + Corgoloin +Prémeaux			
Premeaux	R	(Ctes de Nuits Villages)	0.50	40	P
	R	(Bourgogne Rouge)	1.50	35	P
		Total:	**3.65 ha**		

Domaine Jean-Jacques Confuron

PRÉMEAUX-PRISSEY

Jean-Jacques Confuron and his wife – he, the son of Mme Bouchard-Pagani who owned vines in Prémeaux at the end of the 19th century, she the grand-daughter of Charles Noëllat of Vosne-Romanée – worked vineyards inherited from both sides of the family until 1980. Now, their daughter Sophie and her husband, Alain Meunier, have taken over and are enhancing the Domaine's reputation.

Alain met Sophie in 1986 when he was employed maintaining equipment for the Beaune Lycée Viticole where she was a student. They married and returned to the Domaine two years later. As both are winemakers, responsibilities are shared.

Since 1991 'culture biologique' has ruled to restore the vineyards' micro-flora; so, no synthetic chemicals, only Bordeaux mixture and sulphur, with deliberate steps to encourage natural predators for red spider, grape-worm and the rest of the insidious army of micro-fauna which cause vignerons annual headaches.

Curiously, half the Domaine – the older plantings – are trained *en gobelet* rather than in the conventional *guyot*. Although this reduces productivity, an annual scan is made to determine the need for additional green-pruning. Also, the entire Domaine is *en sélection massale*, though clones are now presumably used for replacements.

The only peculiarity in an otherwise modern-traditional vinification is the use of 100% new oak – at the insistence of their importer – for all wines destined for the USA. It is a pity that vignerons lack the courage to resist such pressure and to maintain their preferred style.

For Alain – an open, *sympa* individual – *Grand Vin* means, above all, fruit. 'The fruit you harvest must appear in the bottle.' Having said this, he vehemently dislikes tannic wines and abhors modern techniques which contribute to the extraction of bitter flavours and harsh tannins. This means that, chez Confuron, the absolute quality of a wine takes precedence over typicity or *terroir*.

Alain's approach requires top quality fruit: 'Once the grapes are vatted, it's too late.' So an early *saignée,* if necessary, to balance solids and liquid and 6–8 days of *maceration*, with a relatively hefty dose of sulphur to extract colour and fruit aromas, are essential to his vinification.

This shows in the wines, which tend to be dark in colour and soft and fleshy on

Spraying near Aloxe-Corton

both nose and palate – not jammy or cooked in any way, but just exuberantly fruity, with structures (from 15–18 months in wood) for medium term evolution.

Each vineyard has its character. The Chambolles, for example, are on the rich side of what one expects, especially the Premier Cru *cuvée*, an *assemblage* of ⅔ old-vine fruit from Chatelots and ⅓ from Feusselottes. Aux Boudots is the better of a pair of Nuits Premiers Crus, although there is an excellent Village *cuvée* from Les Fleurières, a vineyard which was formerly gardens for Nuiton houses. On this fertile soil, limiting yields is hard work – Alain reckons that this should be more expensive than the Premiers Crus because he has to spend so much time in the vineyard.

At the top of the Confuron range are a fine Vosne Beaumonts, sound, but unexciting – at least in 1993 – Clos Vougeot, and an excellent Romanée-St.-Vivant, from vines planted in 1920. These all enjoy 100% new oak and are bottled unfined and unfiltered as the rest of the range. The Romanée-St.-Vivant follows the house style; the 1993, dense, almost opaque black cherry, a restrained but most promising nose and voluptuous, very silky flavours, tight and persistent, but lacking a touch in length. It should flesh out well over a decade or so and make a fine bottle.

A Domaine in the ascendant, and clearly one to watch.

VINEYARD HOLDINGS

Commune	Level	Lieu-dit/Climat	Area	Vine Age	Status
Prémeaux	R	(Bourgognes Aligoté, Pinot Noir, Côte de Nuits-Villages)	2.28	20	P
Nuits	V	Les Fleurières	1.24	20	P
Nuits	PC	Les Chaboeufs	0.48	45	P
Nuits	PC	Aux Boudots	0.30	45	P
Vosne	PC	Les Beaux-monts	0.29	50	P
Chambolle	V	————	1.14	32	P
Chambolle	PC	Les Châtelots and Les Feusselottes	0.35	50	P
Vougeot	GC	Clos de Vougeot	0.52	35	P
Vosne	GC	Romanée-St.-Vivant	0.50	60	P
Total:			**7.10 ha**		

Domaine Robert Chevillon

NUITS-ST.-GEORGES

Robert Chevillon is one of the most conscientious winemakers in the entire Côte d'Or. The succession of Nuits-St.-Georges which emerge from his cellar are among the finest in the commune; not the dark, lumpy, rustic concoctions which often appear under this over-exposed appellation, but wines of real depth and complexity, classy and stylish.

A tall, grey-haired and dignified man, Robert has the aloof air of someone completely secure in his own convictions about how things should be accomplished. 'A job well done' is what he likes to see. He is not someone who appears to court publicity – but seems to attract it despite himself – with an impatient manner which gives the impression that visitors in general, and those who might want to buy something, in particular, are a diversion he could well do without.

He lives with his somewhat over-protective wife, Christine, in an ordinary house in one of the many backstreets of Nuits. Their sons, Bertrand and Denis have recently joined the team and now work with Robert full-time. They rarely leave, certainly not for anything as frivolous as a holiday, content rather for the world to come to them.

That this happens is evident from a miscellany of press cuttings, in various stages of disintegration, fixed to a piece of pegboard on the wall of the packing room. Wherever the family name appears, it is carefully highlighted, although the import of much of the comment probably escapes them, being mostly in English, Swedish, Dutch or German, languages none of which they understand.

Although Robert stoutly claims that his Domaine has no history, he has produced an excellent pamphlet setting out what there is. This document consists of a map on one side, showing the *climats* in Nuits in which they have vines and, on the inside, a list of the various medals obtained since 1976 at the annual Paris wine fair. The middle page contains a resumé of traditional measures of surface and volume, together with some delightful Burgundian proverbs relating to the vine: 'With good wine, good bread and good flesh one can pack off the doctor on his travels'; 'Hailed vine, smoky wine'; 'If there are more apples than pears, drink your wine, if more pears than apples, keep it', etc. The final page is devoted to Chevillon history.

The atmosphere of stability and changelessness which pervades the Côte is attributable, at least in part, to the fact that it is virtually impossible to find a vigneron whose forbears have not been resident in it for less than a couple of centuries. If by chance one does stumble across someone without this ancestral crust, then there is invariably an elaborate 'histoire' prominently featuring an in-law or other respectable relative to fill the gap.

As far as can be understood, it would appear that the current branch of Chevillons materialised from a largely undocumented mist of Chevillons, all vignerons somewhere along the Côte in the late 19th century. From this primordial genealogical plasma there emerged Symphorien Chevillon who exploited vines for himself, whilst working as a vigneron and caviste for a local négociant. His land consisted of 30 ares (>⅓ ha) comprising AOC wine, vin de table and cassis.

Symphorien died at Nuits in 1926. His only son, Eugène-François, born in 1887, worked mostly part-time for local vigneron-proprietors up to 1912 before two years of military service, marriage in 1914, then five years of war as a bandsman. Returning in 1919 he took over the family Domaine, such as it was, and started buying small parcels of Nuits Premier Cru and share-cropping others.

Up until 1940 sales of wine were so poor that Eugène-François, a competent musician, formed his own orchestra which played at local functions to supplement the family income, needed to support his wife, Marthe, and five children.

Upon his sudden death in 1943, Marthe and the children were forced to carry on making wine and looking after the vines. In 1946 the vineyards were divided between the two sons of the house, Maurice and Georges (father of Robert's cousin, Michel). Following his marriage in 1937, Maurice continued to add to his share of the vineyards – principally Premiers Crus – acquiring along the way a couple of mobile stills to augment his income.

Robert was born in 1938 and married Christine in 1961. The two stills continue to function during the winter for the production of 'Marc de Bourgogne' and 'Eaux de Vie'.

The Domaine presently extends to 12.88 ha, all in Nuits, apart from some *régionales* and 10 ares of Aligoté. The list includes 8 Premiers Crus, 3.25 ha of Nuits *tout court* and 17.50 ares of white Nuits. The vines belong principally to the family, but some are worked on a half-fruit share-cropping basis.

Whilst much of the vignoble is between 25 and 40 years old, reflecting the degeneration from poor rootstock and low disease resistance of post-war plantings, there are three magnificly old plots still in production: 1.18 ha of Les Cailles averaging 77 years; 1.55 ha Les Vaucrains averaging 78 with 0.25 ha over a century old; and 0.63 ha of Les St.-Georges of 76 years old.

An integral part of Robert's scheme is to let vines go on producing as long as possible, replacing individual plants as they give in. With 10,000 plants per ha and 13 ha in production, some 600 individual vines need replacing annually.

New plantings are on a mixture of standard clones, with young vines being trained *en gobelet* for the first 7 years or so to restrain their natural vigour. A strict *évasivage* and green-pruning, when necessary, both before and at *veraison* also help reduce yields.

Robert sets great store by an intimate knowledge of his vines. He will tell you that the Roncières and the Pruliers always ripen first and that those vineyards nearest to Vosne have a tendency to rot, particularly lower down the hillsides, so that they must be picked first.

When one grower in a commune makes markedly better wine than most of his neighbours with comparable land, it is natural to ask, 'Why, how does he manage it?' Intriguing as the questions may be, Robert Chevillon can think of no obvious answer – no gross differences in viticulture or vinification to which he can point in explanation.

One practice does set him apart from most of his Nuits colleagues – a markedly longer and slower fermentation. Believing that the extracts obtained in alcoholic solution – in other words towards the end of fermentation – are better than those obtained in aqueous solution – at the beginning – he allows his *cuves* to *macerate* for three to four weeks, or longer as in 1990. Pre-fermentive *maceration* he regards as no more than a passing fashion – rather like nouvelle cuisine.

There is not much restraint on temperature either – it is allowed to rise to 35°C before serpentine heat-exchangers are put into action to cool things down. Undoubtedly the removal of up to 70% of the stalks contributes to naturally higher temperatures; however Robert likes to leave some in the vats: 'They are there for something,' he muses.

The wines remain on their fine lees until a second racking, without air, just before the

Chevillon Père et Fils – waiting for the flag to drop?

next vintage. They are then fined, in cask, left a further 4–6 weeks *sur colle* before being reunified in bulk, lightly filtered and bottled – a total *élevage* of some 18 months. Robert has a horror of contract bottlers – 'when I see the froth on a Chambertin . . .'

Asking Robert Chevillon to account for the great finesse he manages to achieve in his Nuits merely provokes a verbal shrug of the shoulders. Perhaps it comes from the long *cuvaison*, perhaps from the slow, natural *malos*; there again, it may be the relatively small proportion of new wood (about one third in rich vintages, less or none at all in others) or the policy of leaving a proportion of fine lees to nourish the wine throughout its *élevage*. Equally, the contribution from the sprinkling of white vines in each vineyard (about 0.8% by volume) cannot be discounted. Whatever the explanation for the exceptional Chevillon quality – there it is, year after year.

Before 1984 all the produce of the white vines went into the red *cuvées*. Now, Robert makes about 1,000 bottles of an excellent Nuits-St.-Georges Blanc from 20–30-year-old Pinot Blanc vines. The *must* is fermented in cask – no more than a third new wood – and bottled without filtration after 14–15 months. The result is a wine of attractive golden colour, with a nose of honey and almonds and a firm, tightish structure; delicious after a few years in bottle, it ages well. No doubt Robert has kept back a few bottles of the first few vintages to follow their evolution.

The Nuits-St.-Georges *cuvée* comes from

vineyards on both sides of the village. The wine from the Prémeaux sector has slightly less finesse but a touch more richness than that from the Vosne sector; the two well complement each other, producing a harmonious blend with a finely judged balance of fruit, acidity and tannins.

Les Chaignots and Bousselots, both bordering Nuits on the Vosne side, are a notch up in concentration and personality – the former with less natural acidity, but sufficient compensatory tannins to see it through.

The Les Roncières is a wine which develops slowly from a base of rich fruit, with moderate levels of round, ripe tannins. The soils here are quite light and high in limestone, in a semi-sloping setting. Les Perrières, just above Roncières on the Prémeaux side of the village, gives a wine with marginally more

structure than its neighbour which is always marked by its finesse. Les Cailles, which adjoins Prémeaux, has a deep, clay-limestone soil, which gives long-lived, solid wines. From Robert's 78-year-old vines, the elements of structure are accentuated – producing wine of considerable depth and richness, with a buttress of firm, but not aggressive, tannin.

Just above Les Cailles is Les Vaucrains, which has a similarly deep soil; however, its high ironstone content seems to impart a hardness in the form of pronounced tannin and a big, angular structure. A good Vaucrains is relatively austere in its youth, without the round charm of Les Cailles or the finesse of Les Perrières. However, a decade or so in bottle sees these constituents integrate into a less awkward, more polished item, which is well worth waiting for, especially in good vintages. A quarter of a hectare of Robert's holding is planted with century-old vines, which give his Vaucrains a magnificent, craggy depth.

The finest of the Nuits Premiers Crus, Les St.-Georges, adjoins Les Cailles, at its northerly boundary. Although broadly similar in soil type to Vaucrains, the wine has a much more soft, fleshy character, with plenty of plump fruit from 75-year-old vines. Robert's Les St.-Georges is usually as good a Nuits as you can hope to find – a big, fleshy item, with bags of fruit, great concentration and overriding class. Not perhaps the unbridled aristocracy of a Vosne-Romanée Premier Cru, but rather a well-covered courtesan who has gone in for a little body-building – and all the more attractive for it!

The Chevillons produce yardstick Nuits-St.-Georges with care and devotion. Robert is not a man given to hyperbole or self-aggrandisement, but an industrious vigneron who thoroughly merits his exalted reputation. Perhaps, one day, he will allow himself the luxury of a short holiday; meanwhile he has retiled his cellar steps – to replace those worn out by four generations of Chevillons, not to mention phalanxes of unwanted visitors.

VINEYARD HOLDINGS

Commune	Level	Lieu-dit/Climat	Area	Vine Age	Status
Nuits	PC	Les Roncières	1.09	30–45	P/F
Nuits	PC	Les Perrières	0.53	25	P
Nuits	PC	Les Cailles	1.18	77	M
Nuits	PC	Les Vaucrains	1.55	75–100	M/F
Nuits	PC	Les St.-Georges	0.63	75	F
Nuits	PC	Les Chaignots	1.53	30–35	P
Nuits	PC	Les Pruliers	0.61	30	P
Nuits	PC	Les Bousselots	0.64	35	P
Nuits	V	(Various *climats*)	3.27	25–45	P/M
Nuits	V	(Blanc)	0.18	25–35	P
————	R	(BGO/PTG/Bourg. R.)	1.57	17–40	P
————	R	(Aligoté)	0.10	35	P
		Total:	**12.88 ha**		

Domaine Faiveley

NUITS-ST.-GEORGES

Domaine Faiveley, with 115 ha split between an estate of 75 ha in Mercurey and 4 ha in the Côte d'Or, claims to be the largest vineyard owner in Burgundy. Until recently, its wines were not widely known outside France; however, critical acclaim, especially for the 1985s and 1990s, brought it into the forefront of that select handful of top-quality land-owning négociants who dominate the export market.

François Faiveley, who took over from his father Guy in 1976 as head of the house, is the sixth generation of Faiveleys to follow the Joseph Faiveley who laid the firm's foundation stone in 1825. Successive generations have each added 'leur pierre à l'édifice' both literally and figuratively, to make the Domaine what it is today.

François is also Chairman of Faiveley Industrie, an engineering enterprise responsible, among other things, for manufacturing the automatic doors for France's high-speed train, the TGV, a connection of which he is justifiably proud.

He is an urbane man, of inquiring mind, who brings careful deliberation to a consuming passion for his wine. His wife Anne, will confess with mock sorrow that for François, wine comes first, sailing next, 'et puis moi et les enfants'. Whilst he indeed spends considerable time away representing the Domaine and on his boat, his heart is firmly at home in Nuits and his close-knit family an emotional anchor point for his various wanderings.

Despite ruling an estate, the size of which might drive others back into the comfort of their padded offices, François takes as active an interest in the vineyards as in the cellars. A fundamental tenet of his approach is that the material you plant is of critical importance to the quality of the wine it will eventually produce – 'If you completely bungle a vintage, it's not dramatic, but if you bungle the choice of rootstock you're stuck with it for 50 years.' Thus everything starts with rigorous soil analyses. Samples from different levels in each vineyard, down to 1 m. deep, are sent to different laboratories for analysis. The results determine any adjustments in base minerals which may be necessary (they have used nothing other than organic fertilisers for the past 14 years) and also the rootstock that is best adapted to each vineyard.

Each year, one-thirtieth of the total vineyard surface is replanted. François is a strong defender of clonal selection. His somewhat picturesque analogy is that if it is acceptable, by selective breeding, to combine the flanks

François Faiveley – head of this top-flight Domaine and Négociant House

of a horse which won the Arc with the heels of another which won the Derby, why not for vines fuse resistance to disease with proven fruit quality and low yields? Having struck his position, he will then admit that he continues to use two-thirds *sélection massale*, the remaining third being a multi-clonal mixture.

In order for the vine to give of its best, it requires adequate nourishment. Like most educated vignerons, François Faiveley endeavours to strike a balance between famine and excess. There is no gain in stressing a vine to the limit at which it ceases to work and expires; nor is there any sense in overfeeding it to the point at which it becomes lazy. The fulcrum is not easy to find, especially in the Côte's marginal climate and among its multiplicity of unique *terroirs*.

In the mid 1980s, he consulted Guy Accad on the management of the Domaine's vines. Extensive soil analyses resulted in the complete cessation of fertilisation in *climats* found to be too rich in nutrients, (excessive amounts of manure were used, without proper analyses, in the 1960s and 1970s).

The program of soil analyses continues.

Low yields are another obsession. Measures are taken, in particular a green-pruning carried out as near to *veraison* as possible, with exemplary care: first the number of bunches per vine is counted, then the average number of berries per bunch. This indicates not only how many bunches to remove, but which ones. The ideal is to remove the fruit least well exposed, generally that furthest from the trunk. These efforts result in yields near, or below the *rendement de base*.

Harvesting is no less precise. At one time, substandard fruit was eliminated in the vineyards; however, experience proved this to be of limited value, since pickers are less than thorough in poor weather, the conditions in which most care was needed. So now the picking boxes are covered and taken to the *cuverie* for triage. Up to 12 sorters, including François, pick over each batch for rotten or unripe material as it comes past on a conveyor. An impressive drying tunnel removes excess surface moisture – only a step away from concentrating the juice!

François' natural anxiety at harvest time is augmented by the practical problems of looking after 200 pickers. In the evenings they are well fed and watered, before retiring to mixed dormitories: 'I feel as though I am populating France,' he groans, 'c'est l'horreur!'

In the *cuverie* it is François' obsession with aroma which drives vinification. He would cheerfully have been a career perfumier if the Domaine had not got in the way. For him, Burgundy is capable of the greatest aromatic diversity in the world and it is essential to preserve this uniqueness. He adds, as an afterthought, that 'if it smells good in the *cuverie*, that's a great misfortune; you make a wine for the nose of the drinker not for the nose of the person who ferments it.'

To extract and preserve aromas, the bunches are first destalked and the pulp moderately sulphured. A long, slow fermentation is mediated by indigenous yeasts, without pumping-over. Regular *pigéage* helps increase extraction, but otherwise, the juice is touched as little as possible.

Red fermentations are conducted on the principle that it is better to simmer gently for longer than, as it were, to microwave. If temperatures exceed 26°C, cooling is applied through a splendid system of external sprays. As the *cuverie* was originally used for cider making, the old cider vats are invaluable as water-reservoirs, in case of shortage.

Cuvaison is deliberately long – the aim being 3 weeks, the average about 2 and the reality often longer – and *débourbage* short. Thereafter, the wine is passed into cask. The Domaine needs plenty of new wood: its Grands Crus have 50–66% and the Premiers Crus 33%. François is healthily cynical about the putative provenance of wood – 'If everyone who claims to use Tronçais actually used it, the forest would stretch from Lille to Bordeaux.' To minimise the uncertainties, new Vosges oak is bought at auction and carefully dried. In this way, he knows that it is properly treated – cut when the sap is receding and dried in air rather than in kilns.

The wines are first racked and the SO_2 adjusted, just after *malo*. Candlelight is still used in the Faiveley cellars, as the wines are racked cask-to-cask – new-to-old, to ensure an evenness in the final wine. After about 16 months the contents of each cask are tasted and any gross disparities corrected by racking and unifying in bulk – all by gravity. The wines are then egg-white fined and left *sur colle* for 1–2 months before bottling.

The Domaines Grands and Premiers Crus are always bottled direct from the cask, by hand, without filtration, at the stupendous rate of 900 bottles a day; in a good vintage, as many as 60,000 bottles may be filled in this way. Lesser wines are cartridge-filtered at a very high porosity, 'to avoid stones getting into the wine'. Care here is essential and François' crisp analogy: 'No good chef tells you that 90% of his food is fresh.'

Those who talk of 'the taste of the vintage' are roundly castigated: 'This means nothing, it could perfectly well be the taste of rot' (as in 1983). What really matters is acidity, the 'vertebral column' of wine of any colour. In François' view it is better to harvest with good acidity then *chaptalise*, than to wait for maximum sugars and then have to acidify. He recalls a striking demonstration of the value of acidity by a Dijon Professor, who acidified a 1929 Clos Vougeot which François had brought in for tasting. Its light, browning colour immediately transformed into a vibrant red. 'If harvest sugar is the criterion of a fine wine, then the best would come from Spain and Morocco,' he adds, mischievously.

François' concern with aroma – his favourite book, is on perfumes – is no less scrupulous for the Domaine's whites than for its reds. Vinification in new (Vosges and Allier) oak and in stainless steel precedes blending of the two components just before bottling. He has been experimenting with vinifying Bourgogne Blanc in new Acacia-wood, a revival of traditional Burgundian practice.

François regards the production of wine as an amalgam of hundreds of details, each contributing to quality. He has undisguised admiration for Henri Jayer, generally regarded as one of the most important influences on post-war winemaking. 'The trick is that there are no tricks – just well tended vines, small yields, cool vinification and not destroying the wine with filtration. What matters is the wine in the glass.'

Once in bottle, the Domaine's wines are stored in a magnificent network of cool, ancient galleries underneath the firm's modern-fronted offices in the Rue de Tribourg. Everywhere piles, some small, some larger, of this and that, await release stacked in bins of various sizes. When the time comes, the selected bottles are loaded on to a Dickensian system of individual buckets on an overhead tramway and conveyed upstairs for dressing and packing.

The Domaine owns some 35 different appellations. Its sole white wine of significance, a Corton-Charlemagne from a parcel of vines at the very top of the hill in Aloxe-Corton, is vinified in new Vosges oak, with a single racking before bottling. Since François dislikes the practice of *batonnage* – 'a fundamental error – it oxidises the wine' – the lees are roused instead by giving each cask a periodic rolling. The wine tends to be well coloured from the new oak, with plenty of extract and highish initial acidity. Rich in fruit, powerful and firmly structured but austerely masculine, it needs years to integrate and open out. A top flight Charlemagne – the 1989, 1990, 1992 and 1993 are all magisterial. At 18.4–26.0 hl/ha yields are pitiful, resulting in 125–200 cases per year – hardly a glut!

François' love of 'parfum' shines through out the consistently stylish range of reds, expressing itself in elegant, seductive, complex aromas of great distinction. From Mercurey to Gevrey, the wines are beautifully crafted. The Gevreys are splendid – especially the Premiers Crus Cazetiers and Combe aux Moines – and the gamme of Nuits invariably top class, with a particular soft-spot for Aux Chaignots, Les St.-Georges and Clos de la Maréchale (which last will revert to its owner, Frédy Mugnier around 2009). Of the Domaine's 7 red Grands Crus the Mazis-Chambertin, Corton, Clos des Cortons and Chambertin Clos de Bèze stand out – wines, in the best vintages, of masterly build, extraordinary concentration and immense style. At the top level, the 1990s and 1993s were spectacular successes (those who damned the 1993s should be thoroughly ashamed of themselves), with some particularly fine 1991s filling the gap.

As the Domaine's vineyards only provide 70–80% of requirements, grapes are bought in to augment the range. Whilst not so fine as the Domaine wines these *cuvées* are usually sound examples of their appellations.

François Faiveley has worked tirelessly since his father deposited the cellar keys abruptly on his desk in 1976, and left him in charge. That this is a no-compromise-on-quality, top-division Domaine is a tribute to his skill and stewardship. Faiveley is one of the best and most consistent sources of fine Burgundy and one which should continue to set the standards for both négociants and growers into the next century.

VINEYARD HOLDINGS

Commune	Level	Lieu-dit/Climat	Area	Vine Age	Status
Gevrey	GC	Chambertin, Clos de Bèze	1.29	35	P
Gevrey	GC	Mazis-Chambertin	1.20	40	P
Gevrey	GC	Latricières-Chambertin	1.21	25	P
Gevrey	PC	La Combe aux Moines	1.20	30	P
Gevrey	PC	Les Cazetiers	2.05	25	P
Gevrey	PC	————	0.55	17	P
Gevrey	V	Les Marchais	1.08	33	P
Chambolle	GC	Musigny	0.03	51	P
Chambolle	PC	La Combe d'Orveau	0.26	38	P
Chambolle	PC	Les Fuées	0.19	50	P
Vougeot	GC	Clos de Vougeot	1.29	25	P/F
Flagey	GC	Echézeaux	0.87	41	P
Nuits	PC	Clos de la Maréchale	9.55	30	F
Nuits	PC	Les St.-Georges	0.30	35	P
Nuits	PC	Les Porets St.-Georges	1.70	35	P
Nuits	PC	Aux Chaignots	0.73	35	P
Nuits	PC	Les Vignerondes	0.46	37	P
Nuits	PC	Aux Athées	0.50	27	P
Nuits	PC	Les Lavières	1.07	43	P
Nuits	PC	Les Damodes	0.82	17	F
Nuits	V	Les Argillats	0.53	20	F
Nuits	V	Les Damodes	0.70	22	F
Nuits	V	————	1.22	30	P/F
Ladoix	GC	Rognet et Corton (Clos des Cortons Faiveley)	2.97	35	P
Ladoix	R	Les Lievrières	3.06	37	P
Aloxe	GC	Corton-Charlemagne	0.62	27	P
————	R	(BGO/PTG/etc. . .)	14.13	–	P/F
————	R	(Bourgogne Aligoté)	0.77	40	P
Total:			**50.35 ha**		

Domaine Henri Gouges

NUITS-ST.-GEORGES

Henri Gouges is one of the seminal names in 20th century Burgundian history. It was he who, with a small coterie of dissatisfied growers, decided to challenge the monopoly of the mighty négociants by bottling his wine at the Domaine and selling it direct to his customers. The first bottles were sold in 1933 and the stir that this caused brought a measure of enduring fame which seems to have done the Domaine's reputation no noticeable harm.

Their 14.5 ha include the original Henri's 9, which effectively created the Domaine in 1925. Profiting from the 1920s financial slump, which decimated vineyard prices, he bought advantageously, many small growers being forced to sell to raise cash to keep their families alive.

Henri was a shrewd buyer, confining his interest entirely to the commune of Nuits-St.-Georges, with a spread over 6 well-sited Premiers Crus plus 1.3 ha of Village land. Recently, Michel and Marcel Gouge, the present generation's parents have retired, ceding their own vineyards to the Domaine. Its kernel is undoubtedly the 1.08 ha of Les St.-Georges, generally regarded as the 'primus inter pares' of the Premier Crus, closely followed by the 3.5 ha *Monopole* Clos des Porrets St.-Georges.

The supremacy of Les St.-Georges was recognised at the end of the 19th century when Nuits, with no Grand Cru, tacked on the name of its finest vineyard to give it standing among its illustrious neighbours.

The Gouges make very fine wine. Although their supremacy among Nuits growers is not unchallenged, it remains one of Burgundy's best known names. An unfortunate dip in quality in the late 1970s badly dented their reputation, but this seems to have been no more than an aberration, and the Domaine is long-since restored to form.

When Henri died, Michel and Marcel took over the Domaine. Since 1970, their respective fathers having retired, it is the third generation – Michel's son, Christian and Marcel's son Pierre – who are in control. Although they take joint responsibility for whatever is produced, Pierre is in charge of the vineyards whilst Christian looks after the vinification and commercial aspects of the Domaine.

Pierre has a deep feeling for his vineyards, and a strong interest in the commune's geology. The depth of his knowledge is crystallised in a booklet on the soils of each of the 33 Premiers Crus of this extended and heterogeneous commune.

He will tell you that one of the significant difficulties faced by Nuits vignerons is the constant soil erosion in the steeper vineyards. When it rains the water tends to wash down the more friable topsoil which must then be taken back up again. Because the replacement is, perforce, somewhat arbitrary, the structure and composition of these vineyards is gradually changing.

In an effort to combat this, Pierre started experimenting in 1977 with a special grass. Planted between the vine rows, this Ray-Grass is designed to hold the soil together and to provide a physical barrier to soil movement in wet weather. Apart from limiting erosion in this way, Pierre found that there were other advantages: such a grass-covering stifles other undesirable weeds and grasses, virtually eliminating the need for herbicides; it controls the vigour of the vines, especially the young ones, by competing with their proliferous lateral surface roots for soil nutrients, forcing the important tap roots to dig deeper for their nourishment. Grass also removes excess humidity, thereby reducing the incidence of rot.

The disadvantage is that, being perennial, its presence in the vineyard in spring brings an increased risk of frost damage, since the grass tends to hold the frost longer than bare earth. On balance, however, the Gouges consider that the advantages outweigh the disadvantages, and Ray-Grass is now a permanent fixture in a large part of their steeper Premiers Crus.

Pierre clearly enjoys finding new ways to tackle old problems. Studying the treatments which they normally apply to their vines, and being ecologically inclined, he found that by determining precisely the right moment to spray or treat any given malady, he could significantly reduce the number and dose of each type of treatment. In 1990 he needed 4 fewer treatments – advantages both to the environment and also no doubt to the Domaine's bank balance.

The proximity of some of the Gouges vines to woodland, away from neighbours' drifting pesticides, enabled Pierre to experiment with the use of predators to deal with pestilential red and yellow spiders. He distributed predators' eggs and measured the reduction in spider populations compared with untreated vines. The results so far seem encouraging.

An approximately 50:50 mixture of clones and *sélection massale* is used to replant, since Pierre is uncertain how clones planted now will develop over the next generation. Although striving to limit yields by pruning short – to 6 eyes – he fears both over-production and possible premature degeneration. Beyond this, a strict *évasivage* within a couple of weeks of budburst removes any unwanted growth – shoots and buds – above and below the graft. Later on there is a 'taille en verte' to remove unwanted vine wood round the ripening bunches. This operation clears space for air circulation and sunlight, concentrates the vine's vigour where it is most needed and strengthens the wood which remains for the following year. As the branches trailing near the ground are also removed, it helps to reduce humidity and thus the risk of *botrytis*. It also acts as a sort of pre-pruning, saving a great deal of time the following winter.

Once the fruit is picked, Christian takes over. To start with, he is very particular that the bunches are completely destalked, believing strongly that stalks in the vats bring more bad than good qualities to the wine. The destalking machine also removes unripe and rotten grapes before crushing, particularly important in years with significant rot or unripeness, since crushing such material before removing it would contaminate the juice. A 'crusher-destemmer' is different from a 'destemmer-crusher'!

Fermentation, chez Gouges, is a somewhat individual process. Henri considered that more subtlety, finesse and fruit resulted from starting fermentation with his cement vats closed and thus full of natural carbon

Christian and Pierre Gouges sharing a bottle – and, it appears, a glass

dioxide. He tried this in 1947 and the practice has stuck. This is not a full-blown *carbonic maceration* as all the grapes have been crushed before vatting, but rather a species of semi-*carbonic maceration*, lasting a couple of days and is designed to extract colour. Thereafter, following a 'pumping-over' with air to get the indigenous yeasts working, fermentation proceeds normally, rising to a maximum of 28–30°C, with one pneumatic *pigéage* and one *remontage* daily. The *must macerates* for 10–12 days more at 20–25°C, to fix the colours and to extract tannins.

Interestingly, one side-effect of the Ray-Grass regime is an improvement in acidity levels. It is likely that the grass roots are munching up some of the potassium excess from over-fertilisation in the 1960s which dramatically reduced acidities.

When necessary, the vats of younger vines, particularly in Les Chaignots and in parts of the Clos des Porrets, are 10–20% *saignéed*; the older vines produce a more concentrated juice, so it is unnecessary to *saigner* them.

Once fermentation is over, Christian Gouges tastes the free-run wine and then tailors the strength of his pressing of the pulp to its tannin level. After adding the press-wine and 2–3 days *débourbage* to remove the gross lees, the wine is put into cask where it remains until 3 months or so after its *malo* has finished.

The Domaine does not attach great importance to new wood. Only 10% of the casks are renewed each year – one of the smallest proportions in the Côte. Nor is the provenance of the wood of particular interest to Christian – 'People pay more attention nowadays to the origin of the wood than to the grape variety.' Fortunately, their barrel-maker, whose firm has been supplying them since Grandfather Henri started, is a relation, so they are content to take whatever he delivers.

The first racking is cask-to-cask, leaving some fine lees to continue nourishing the wine. The following December, half a dose of egg-white fining is used and the wines left for 2–3 months *sur colle*, to soften the tannins. Each cask is then racked – by candlelight – into a tank, to unify the different casks of each wine, and then bottled.

The Domaine also makes a minuscule quantity of white Nuits from the Premier Cru La Perrière. This is a rarity as well as a scarcity, since it is made not from the usual Chardonnay, Pinot Blanc or Pinot Beurot, but from a white mutant of Pinot Noir. One has to imagine Henri Gouges wandering through Les Perrières admiring his grapes, one warm summer evening in the late 1940s, when he comes across a few vines on which both red and white grapes are growing. Being curious, he cuts a single branch and propagates from it. The result is an unusual

and delicious white wine.

Christian vinifies La Perrière Blanc traditionally, fermenting started in *cuve* and proceeding in cask at 18–20°C, on its fine lees, with 20% new oak. The following summer it is casein-bentonite fined and bottled after a polishing filtration.

A young white Perrière tends to have a deepish yellow-green colour and aromas variously of dried orange-peel and subdued exotic fruits. On the palate it is noticeably structured, in fact quite tannic for a white wine, with plenty of old vine fruit (45-year-old vines), complexity and length. In particularly ripe vintages, however, it can become flabby and lacking in nerve. With age it often develops flavours more typical of a red wine – difficult as this is to imagine. Finding the wine to taste – be it young or old, is difficult since each vintage produces only 120 cases.

The Gouges reds are fortunately more plentiful – around 3,000 cases per year. The Village Nuits is usually attractive and well-made – far superior to what generally passes for the appellation. The Premiers Crus, whilst retaining their Nuits characteristics, reflect the differences between the soils and expositions of the various *climats*.

The Chaignots, from the Vosne-Romanée side of the village, tends to have a distinctly Vosne touch about it – more 'tendresse' and finesse with less tannin than quintessential Nuits.

The Clos des Porrets, a *Monopole* from Prémeaux, produces wines of a more 'animale, sauvage' character – quite spicy and high in acidity and tannins when young, evolving *sous-bois* and wild fruit aromas after half a decade in bottle. It seems to start all in fruit, but finishes with a more typically Nuits rusticity.

The Les Pruliers, from 45-year-old vines is characterised by very mineral flavours – *corsé*, full, with sweet fruit and fine long beautifully balanced flavours – as with most of Gouges wines, long keepers in the best vintages.

Les Vaucrains, in the heart of the Premiers Crus just above Les St.-Georges, is almost the most typically Nuits of all Gouges wines –

small yields from 50-year-old vines generally giving a deeply coloured wine, dense and limpid in the glass – a level up in concentration and nuance from Les Pruliers.

Les St.-Georges produces a wine of yet more completeness and complexity than the Vaucrains. Tannic, plenty of *charpente* and muscle to start with, developing ripe complexity as it ages in bottle. If Nuits were ever to have a Grand Cru, it would be Les St.-Georges.

Pierre and Christian have responded to the justified criticisms of their wines from the late 1970s and early 1980s, which were thoroughly uninspiring. Unfortunately, one US critic persists, in face of the facts, to accuse the Gouges of overproduction and excess filtration. It is a matter of public record that the Domaine's yields are among the lowest in Nuits (only once in 20 or more years have they demanded the *PLC* – for the 1992 Clos des Porrets). Certified yields for recent vintages, across the entire estate are as follows (hl/ha): 1992: 31.48, 1993: 31.72, 1994: 22.43. As to filtration, they only filter when they consider it absolutely necessary and then only at plate porosity 5 or 6 – a widely used coarse level of polish. There was none at all in 1988, 1992 and 1993. Continuing to promulgate such malicious, ill-informed nonsense, is an unwarranted slur. It is small wonder that journalists are so little respected by the vignerons of the Côte.

With wines of the quality of recent vintages – especially the 1990s and 1993s – it is not surprising that Christian feels unjustifiably victimised by these criticisms. 'We try to do the best we can and to make wines we like. Yes, we use very little new wood and don't vinify to make fruity, *framboisé* wines, but this is not to say the wines aren't good.' Critics should respect the validity of different approaches – one can appreciate that a wine is fine without necessarily liking its style. Fortunately, the Gouge's US clients manage to rise above such critical rubbish and sales there have multiplied. That this is a first-class Domaine, turning out first-class wine, is something of which no-one should entertain even the slightest doubt.

VINEYARD HOLDINGS

Commune	Level	Lieu-dit/Climat	Area	Vine Age	Status
Nuits	PC	Les St.-Georges	1.08	40	P
Nuits	PC	Les Vaucrains	1.00	45	P
Nuits	PC	La Perrière (Blanc)	0.39	45	P
Nuits	PC	Clos des Porrets St.-Georges	3.50	25	P
Nuits	PC	Les Pruliers	1.63	40	P
Nuits	PC	Les Chaignots	0.43	13	P
Nuits	V	————	4.20	30	P
Nuits	R	(Bourgogne Blanc)	1.00	5	P
Nuits	R	(Bourgogne Rouge)	1.00	20	P
		Total:	**14.23 ha**		

Domaine Machard de Gramont

PRÉMEAUX-PRISSEY

This, the larger of two similarly-named Domaines, is the product of a rather turbulent recent history, consisting chiefly of two brothers and a quantity of pressure cookers. The brothers, Arnaud, Xavier and Bertrand Machard de Gramont, are sons of a career civil servant who, returning to Paris from Morocco in 1959, decided to help his father-in-law, M. Dufouleur in his *négociant* business. His wife ran Dufouleur until 1964 when she sold out to her nephews.

They then established a modest 5 ha Domaine in their own name. This grew until 1970 when Arnaud and Bertrand took over. However, in 1975 the petrol crisis intervened and threatened to ruin them – prices plummeted to the point at which a cask of Nuits-St.-Georges barely made 800 Francs.

Fortune then intervened, literally and figuratively, in the form of Xavier's new wife, Mme Lescure, a lady endowed with considerable capital, founded entirely upon the sale of 'cocottes minute', a species of pressure-cooker without which no worthy French housewife appeared capable of surviving.

She injected capital into the Domaine, allowing some very advantageous land purchases – especially just before the disastrous 1975 vintage. In 1983 however, Xavier divorced, whereupon his wife extracted her large share of the Domaine and departed. The problems mainly arose because Arnaud and his brother wanted income, whilst his wife and Xavier sought capital appreciation.

Dissolution of the enterprise left the brothers with some vines but no buildings. Bertrand went off with his 2.5 ha, which he still farms in Nuits, and Arnaud took his older brother, Xavier, into partnership and embarked on the work of reconstruction. Cellars, in the form of à dilapidated set of farm buildings in Prémeaux, were bought from the négociant Charles Viénot, and a cellar-master, Louis Poignant, installed. The vineyards, owned by Arnaud, his wife and Xavier, now extend to some 19 ha, and things at last seem comparatively settled.

Despite these vicissitudes, Arnaud is a cheerful, optimistic and talkative man. His disarming bonhomie conceals a nose for quality; he knows well what fine wine is about and will settle for nothing less. Rooted firmly in his own tradition – 'I made my first vintage in 1963 and haven't stopped since' – he is critical of those who compromise, deploring, for example, market-driven colleagues who make a Nuits-St.-Georges which is ready to drink in three years.

Apart from those in Nuits, the vines are tended by contractors (*tâcherons*), although Arnaud admits that 'it's difficult to have good workers especially in the Côte de Nuits', describing the entire system as 'very middle-aged', and bemoans the standard contract under which 'by April you've paid half a year's salary for one quarter of a year's work'.

His own wines reek of tradition – wines with muscle, to be kept for the future; 'We want to keep what is traditional and what is proven.' For example, the old wooden *cuves* are still in use – although Arnaud laughingly admits that if he won the French lottery he would buy a 5,000-litre circular stainless-steel *cuve*, with a double jacket for cooling – 'the Rolls-Royce,' he explains, smiling.

For all that, his wines are lovingly tended. The grapes are more or less destalked – a recent and the only concession towards less tannin – and then dosed with SO_2 – about twice the usual level. The pulp is not cooled, but the SO_2 produces a similar result by anaesthetising the yeasts which delays fermentation for a few days. During this period, colour and aroma are extracted into the juice.

The practice of heavy sulphuring was introduced between 1973 and 1975, by the Domaine's oenologist Michel Bouchard, who incidentally manufactured and sold some 90% of the SO_2 used in Burgundy. Then he used up to 3 litres of SO_2 per tonne of grapes – triple the usual dose. This was well before Guy Accad appeared in the Côte.

Cuvaison lasts 17–21 days, with temperatures rising to 34°C and yeasts added towards the end to prolong fermentation and to ensure that all traces of sugar have been fermented out. Plenty of '*pigéage* à la main' maximises extraction and enzymes are added to help clarification – a process with which Arnaud is highly satisfied since it produces wines which are 'très brillant'.

The 18–24 months of cask maturation help to minimise later manipulations. Fining is rare – 'you can kill a tender vintage with fining' – and only the lightest of polishing filtrations is used when unavoidable.

Depending on the Cru and the vintage, up to 50% of new oak is used with the balance composed of third and fifth year wood. Arnaud does not care unduly for barrel-makers – 'You must first mistrust your tonnelier' – and reproaches them for kiln-drying their wood. Fortunately, Louis Poignant is an ex-barrel-maker, so the Domaine's cooper can hardly argue if a cask or two is returned.

Although there is a common stylistic thread of opulent silkiness running through the range, the wines are individual and their quality uniformly high. Arnaud is a vociferous partisan of late harvesting, claiming that, when he picks his Nuits-St.-Georges, many of his colleagues have already made their wine. This, and the extent to which each *cuve* is destalked will influence to its final character.

There are 3 principal whites – a Savigny

VINEYARD HOLDINGS

Commune	Level	Lieu-dit/Climat	Area	Vine Age	Status
Vosne	PC	Les Gaudichots	0.25	20	F
Chambolle	V	Les Nazoires	0.30	1966	P
Nuits	PC	Vollerots	0.78	1969	P
Nuits	PC	Les Damodes	1.00	1955/60/66	P
Nuits	PC	Les Poulettes	0.15	12	P
Nuits	PC	Les Hauts Pruliers	0.50	45	P
Nuits	V	Les Damodes	1.10	1973	P
Nuits	V	En la Perrière Noblot	0.76	1974	P
Nuits	V	Les Hauts Poirets	0.64	1980	P
Nuits	V	Argillats + Fleurière	0.25	1981	P
Aloxe	V	Les Morais	0.76	1964	P
Chorey	V	Les Beaumonts	2.00	1945/58	P
Savigny	PC	Les Guettes	1.00	1945/74	F
Savigny	PC	Les Vergelesses (Blanc)	0.25	1983	P
Savigny	V	Les Roichottes	0.45	1974	F
Savigny	V	Vermots + Picotins+ Planchots	0.75	1955/79/80	F/P
Beaune	PC	Les Chouacheux	1.00	1935/76	F
Beaune	PC	Les Coucherais	0.42	1957	F
Beaune	V	Les Epenottes	0.40	1950	P
Pommard	PC	Le Clos Blanc	1.80	1914/82	P
Pommard	V	Vaumuriens	0.35	1955	F
Puligny	V	Houillères (Blanc)	1.00	1964/68	P
	R	(Bourgogne Rouge and Blanc)	3.00	1955–1985	P
Total:			**18.91 ha**		

Premier Cru Les Vergelesses – made from a mix of Chardonnay with 3% Pinot Beurot on marls which strongly resemble the soils of Corton-Charlemagne – a Puligny and a Bourgogne. Together, these account for 10% of the Domaine's production.

Despite the occasional disappointment, the reds are usually excellent and worth seeking out. They need keeping, but are thankfully somewhat less massive than 20 years ago. Retasting a range of 1990, showed the quality of this estate, especially the Nuits Perrière Noblot and Beaune Epenottes.

The most interesting wine in the stable is undoubtedly the Vosne Gaudichots. This is sandwiched between Grands Crus Romanée-St.-Vivant and La Grande Rue to the north, and La Tâche, of which it once formed part, to the south. The true La Tâche (1.80 ha) was sold in the 1930s, leaving Les Gaudichots with 4 owners: Moillard Grivot, Régis Forey, Mme Suzanne Thomas (wine made by Thierry Vigot) and Arnaud de Gramont.

It is to be hoped that the Domaine is now out of its period of flux and on unshakeable foundations. In Arnaud de Gramont's hands it has a deservedly promising future.

Downtown Nuits-St.-Georges – the vignerons' source of necessities and nightlife

Domaine Alain Michelot

NUITS-ST.-GEORGES

There are few who make Nuits-St.-Georges as well as Alain Michelot. Apart from a touch of Morey-St.-Denis and a patch of Bourgogne in Prémeaux, his Domaine consists entirely of Nuits, with 2.5 hectares of Villages and no fewer than 7 different Premiers Crus.

By Burgundian standards, the Domaine is relatively young, having been assembled by Alain's father between 1920 and 1939, especially just after the 1929 depression, when good land was cheap.

Sadly Michelot senior died in an accident in 1966, leaving the young Alain, fresh from military service and viticultural school, in charge. The Domaine, of course, had to be divided between Alain and his many sisters who, fortunately, gave him their vines *en metayage*, so the partimony remained intact. Being the only brother, he was the natural choice to keep things going. He has since added 0.5 ha of Village Morey, 22.5 ares of Premier Cru Les Charrières and 28 ares of Nuits Village.

The Michelot cellars, along with the Michelot 'esprit', are in the heart of Nuits-St.-Georges. An impressive arch, next door to the grand Mairie, gives on to a spacious courtyard, off which lead various offices and cellars. Nothing, except 'Les Toilettes' is signposted, so pressing bells at random you might get either Alain's cheerful old mother, still in her dressing-gown at mid-morning or Alain, who lives in one corner. He obviously has enough customers without wasting money on signs, which might bring more.

Sitting in Alain's orderly little office, one is aware of a man who is tuned into detail and is convinced that this is the only reliable route to quality. Although getting an appointment with him is one of the more taxing tasks in Burgundy, once received, he gives generously of his time and expertise. A large, bear-like man, he enjoys discussing his own philosophy in particular, and the folly and wisdom of the region in general.

Once warmed to his theme, Alain's mildly scholarly manner occasionally cracks and gives way to cynical impishness. His intelligence and depth of knowledge make him one of the most articulate and well-informed sources of comparative information on Burgundy.

As one would expect, he tends his vines with loving care. He believes, to a limited extent, in individual vine replacement – as the state of each vineyard permits – but undertakes a systematic annual programme

The Pinot Noir grape

of replanting, dividing each parcel into three notional pieces to avoid unduly diluting the average vine age.

When it comes to the subject of yields, (there have been mutterings that he sometimes over-crops) Alain becomes positively voluble. He readily acknowledges that in 1988, 89 and 90, his vines averaged 50–55 hl/ha and disgorged 'le plein' (i.e. 48 hl/ha) in 1993, forcing him to send good wine to the distillery. In justification of this apparent excess, he brings out colour photographs to show how many bunches he green-pruned, but is adamant that figures by themselves are misleading. In the 1930s, when yields were laid down, only a proportion of the vines in any vineyard produced in any given year. Now, with clones producing almost predictable annual quantities, yields per hectare have perforce risen.

What really matters, in Alain's view, is the yield per vine. If each of 11,000 vines per ha produce 8 bunches, one has a total yield of 54.72 hl/ha. Whilst by no means excessive, this is well above both the permitted 40 hl/ha *rendement de base* and the additional 20% *PLC* which increases this to 48 hl/ha in particularly productive years. In short, he believes that to evaluate yields it is essential to consider how, and with what the vineyard is planted. In a growing season free of *botrytis, coulure, millerandage* and other quantity-reducers, fine, concentrated and complex wines can be produced from what might at first seem an excess.

Whatever the quantity of grapes harvested, meticulous care is taken in turning them into wine. An impeccably tidy cellar, generally a good sign – although the converse is not always the case – betokens an obsession with hygiene.

The bunches are 90–95% destalked – the stalks that remain help drain the juice through the cap – given a normal dose of SO_2, cooled if necessary, and then put into cement *cuves* for 2–3 days pre-fermentive maceration. Alain invariably adds enzymes which help both colour extraction and later clarification, but does everything he can to encourage the natural yeast population. If fermentation is slow to start, he uses a heating apparatus to generate 3 or 4 hot points in the *cuve*, which usually provokes the desired result.

His aim is a long, slow fermentation, with no obvious *coup de feu*. To achieve this it is necessary for the temperature to rise slowly to about 30°C. So, any *chaptalisation* is made in several small doses, to avoid a sudden leap in temperature. As he eloquently puts it: 'When you cook, you don't put some ingredients in at the hottest moment.'

Each of Alain's 15 *cuves* are *saignéed* if needed, otherwise the pulp is left for between 18–21 days of *cuvaison*, to extract the maximum matter from the skins into the wine. When there is no sugar left, the wine is run off, the pulp pressed and the resulting press-wine assembled with it. There then follows a *'débourbage* assez importante' for 'a good month'. If the vat has a mobile ceiling it is put in place, if not a layer of protective liquid paraffin is poured on to the wine's surface. This long period of settling is not so much a matter of improving quality, as of buying time. Alain has only one worker to help him, and has neither time nor space to deal with all 15 *cuves* at once.

Sooner or later, the new wines are transferred into cask. The preference is for a mixture of wood from several provenances – in 1989 the cocktail was Allier, Nevers and Limousin; in 1990 the Nevers was eliminated – 'too rustic' – leaving Allier and Limousin, plus a touch of Tronçais. Vosges was tried but abandoned as it made too discrete a contribution; however, he intends to use some Vosges for the Chardonnay he planted in 1991 in the Perrière Noblot vineyard.

The precise proportion of new wood depends upon the vintage. Generally it turns around 30–40%, although for some of the Premiers Crus, where there may be only a couple of casks, the level perforce rises to 50%.

After such a long *débourbage*, Alain reckons the wines can stand twenty months in cask without racking – to refine tannins. Any residual carbon-dioxide gas dissolved in the

Alain Michelot – vigneron and bon viveur

wine after *malo* will keep it fresh and prevent premature drying out, and the absence of large lees minimises the likelihood of off-flavours. Alain dislikes fining – 'I am not looking to excoriate my wines' – restricting pre-bottling preparation to a simple polishing filtration.

As well as his passion for his wines, Alain is dedicated to good food, and his conversation is seasoned with simile from the kitchen. As his figure suggests he is not a willing customer of 'la nouvelle cuisine' – thankfully now on the decline in France – but values the return to clearly stated, primary flavours. Thus it is with his wines – unmistakably Pinot, but with a rich aromatic panoply and plenty of guts.

Central to understanding Alain's winemaking is his view of what constitutes *Grand Vin*: in the first place, *Le Grand Vin* can be very good drunk young, very good at 10 years of age and still going at 30. Youth, of itself, is not a defect. Secondly, *Grand Vin* should be unmistakable, even though it is too young to drink. Thirdly, there is little hope that a wine which is poorly constituted in youth will turn into *Grand Vin* simply by keeping it – Mozart was clearly a genius at the age of seven, and the 1977 Burgundies will never be fine.

When wine and cooking are under the microscope, women are never far away. Alain firmly believes that they, like the Pinot Noir, have their individual charms in youth and age. When pressed, he is forced to admit that, stretched-out on his holiday beach, he prefers to enjoy the firmer beauty of youth, with all its inexperience, than to contemplate the maturer contours of sagging sagacity.

Tasting, chez Michelot, is a veritable 'tour

de force' round the commune of Nuits-St.-Georges. The individual characteristics of the various Premier Cru *climats* are very marked, and a striking education for anyone who presumes to doubt the importance of *terroir*.

The vineyards on the northerly, Vosne-Romanée, side of the village: Aux Chaignots, La Richemone, Aux Champs Perdrix and the Premier Cru section of La Perrière Noblot have a highish proportion of clay in their soils. The Richemone, whilst by no means lacking in depth and structure, has more finesse and precision of flavour than nearby Chaignots, the higher clay content of whose soil gives a more densely-packed, rounder wine, with more *charpente*, greater vinosity and finer tannins. Perhaps the difference is also accounted for by the higher gravel content and elevation of La Richemone. Both these wines share a Vosne-ish elegance which combines with an underlying Nuits richness to give them a schizophrenic, but most attractive, balance of characteristics. The Champs Perdrix is even more Vosne-ish, with all the flesh and intensity of vines planted in 1937 – deceptively accessible young, but in reality a wine to cellar for a decade in fine vintages.

On the southerly, Prémeaux, side of the town are Les Vaucrains, Les Poirets, Les Cailles and Les St.-Georges. These have more ferruginous soils and produce wines which are distinctly more typically Nuits. Often a touch rustic, with plenty of tannic muscle and youthful power, they go supremely well with highly flavoured game and red-meat dishes and develop well over 10–20 years.

Whilst the Les St.-Georges is probably the finest of all the Nuits Premier Crus, the Poirets, Vaucrains and Cailles are masterly wines in Alain Michelot's hands. Poirets, between Cailles and Roncières, just below Perrières, has a relatively deep bed of clay soil, giving a tannic and powerful start, with

less obvious harmony than its Côte Vosne brethren. It needs plenty of time to integrate and blossom.

Les Cailles – from land which varies from grey, heavier soil to stonier patches, is the most accessible of all Alain's Premiers Crus; opulent, almost flatteur young, it exemplifies the generous side of Nuits – an ideal starter wine for anyone wanting to understand Nuits individuality. Despite this precocity, Cailles evolves no faster than the rest, nor has less potential longevity, but merely becomes ready earlier.

Les Vaucrains has plenty of depth and really warming concentration in a good vintage. Its soil is predominantly stony with red clay but with a low iron content. Hail damage in 1989 meant replanting, reducing the average vine age; the 1993 showed a touch of hollowness, lacking something of the exuberance and density of the others.

The *primus inter pares* of the Nuits Premiers Crus, and of Alain Michelot's range, is undoubtedly Les St.-Georges. Here, from the relatively young vines (planted in 1978) comes splendidly concentrated wine, quintessential Nuits – with a deep, velvety bluish-tinged, garnet hue, discreet, confident flavours, with tannins, acids, fruit and alcohol all in balance; power, length and complexity all fused into one magnificent whole.

Alain exudes 'joie de vivre'. He eats and drinks well and occasionally hunts for the pot. One sphere, however, in which he has had no influence is on the eventual succession: he has three daughters ranging in age from 19 to 25. Apparently there is a Michelot gene which favours girls – his cousin Bernard Michelot has three daughters and he himself was the only boy among several sisters.

If you do feel like jumping the Michelot queue, it is worth noting that he tastes widely, and has a particular weakness for Sauternes and Syrah – alternatively, you could marry one of the daughters!

VINEYARD HOLDINGS

Commune	Level	Lieu-dit/Climat	Area	Vine Age	Status
Nuits	PC	Les St.-Georges	0.19	1978	M
Nuits	PC	Les Vaucrains	0.69	1971/83/90	P
Nuits	PC	Les Cailles	0.88	1938/1968	M
Nuits	PC	Les Poirets	0.55	1935/1983	M
Nuits	PC	Aux Chaignots	0.38	1960/1980	P
Nuits	PC	La Richemone	0.56	1930/72/80	M
Nuits	PC & V	Aux Champs Perdrix	0.53	1936	P
Nuits	PC & V	En la Perrière Noblot	0.50	1991	P
Nuits	V	(Various; Côte Vosne)	1.85	1957–1989	P/M
Nuits	V	Les Belles Croix	0.62	1944–1978	P/M
Morey	PC	Les Charrières	0.22	1982	P
Morey	V	Les Cognées	0.28	1964	p
Nuits/ Prémeaux	R	——————	0.90	1968/71/83	P/M
		Total:	**8.15 ha**		

Domaine Fernand Lecheneaut et Fils

NUITS-ST.-GEORGES

Fernand Lecheneaut was Chef de Culture at Morin in Nuits, but lost his job when it went under in 1980. Fortunately, he had 2.5 ha of vines, mainly reconstituted *friches* and patches inherited from his parents. He only lived until 1986, and on his death, his sons, Philippe and Vincent, took over his vines. Addition of Philippe's *metayages* and more recent acquisitions brought the Domaine up to 9 ha, which provides about enough income for their two families plus Fernand's widow, who although officially retired, still helps out with the wines.

Vincent is bearded and talkative; get him going and you'll learn all about the family and the Domaine. Philippe, the elder of the pair, just has a moustache, and is somewhat more reserved. They make a good team, as Vincent is more interested in vinification and Philippe in the vineyards.

Fernand sold his wine to the négoce; now everything is Domaine-bottled, and half is exported. The brothers have raised the quality and brought the place up to date: lower yields, a *table de trie*, destalking, cool pre-fermentive maceration, *saignées*, some new oak, and bottling where possible without filtration or fining – its all there; modern practices for a modern market.

The wines are very good, from the fresh, earthy Bourgogne Rouge, through an attractive Hautes Côtes de Nuits, Village Morey, Vosne, Chambolle and Nuits (the Damodes Village bottling in fact contains mostly Premier Cru) to a couple of Nuits Premiers Crus – an excellent Les Cailles, in particular – and one in Chambolle. At the top of this pyramid, a very fine Clos de la Roche, from 8 ares of 35-year-old vines at the Latricières (Gevrey) end of the *climat*.

There is absurdly little of this – just one *piéce* and a *feuillette*. However, what there is, is beautifully made – competing in quality with Ponsot, Dujac and Rousseau. The 1993, nearing the end of its 18-month sojourn in cask in June 1995, had a virtually opaque, dense, dark cherry hue, an almost exotically ripe *fruits noirs* nose, leading to a vast, suffusing mouthful of voluptuous, sensuous, extracty fruit, sustained by very round tannins and good acidity; a complete wine of great *puissance* and exemplary length. This is first-division Grand Cru quality. The Lecheneauts certainly know how to make wine.

Vincent Lecheneaut

VINEYARD HOLDINGS

Commune	Level	Lieu-dit/Climat	Area	Vine Age	Status
Gilly-les-Cîteaux	R	(Bourgogne Aligoté)	0.40	6	P
Nuits	R	(Bourgogne Rouge)	1.30	20	P/M
Arcenant	R	(Hts. Côtes de Nuits Rouge)	1.00	30	P
Arcenant	R	(Hts. Côtes de Nuits Blanc)	0.30	7	P
Nuits	V	(12 parcels)	2.65	30	P/M
Nuits	V	Les Damodes	0.78	31	P
Nuits	PC	Les Damodes and Les Bousselots	0.38	20	P/M
Nuits	PC	Les Cailles	0.42	35	M
Vosne	V	Les Raviolles	0.41	35+	M
Chambolle	V	(5 parcels)	0.40	45	P
Chambolle	PC	Les Borniques	0.17	45	P
Morey	V	Pierre Vivant and Charrières	0.70	17	P/M
Morey	GC	Clos de la Roche	0.08	35	P
Total:			**8.99 ha**		

Domaine Thomas-Moillard

NUITS-ST.-GEORGES

Of the vineyards owned by this family Domaine, one is struck both by their breadth and by the size of some of the individual plots. There are no fewer than 7 Grands Crus, nearly 3 ha of Vosne Premier Cru Les Malconsorts, 4.12 ha of Nuits Premier Cru Clos de Thorey and 2.2 ha of the choicest Beaune Premier Cru – Grèves.

This is the enviable property of the Thomas family who married into the Moillards in the late 1800s. The Domaine was founded by Symphorien Moillard in 1850, with vineyards owned by the family since before the Revolution. When he was killed in Algeria in 1870, the Domaine came to his sister Jeanne Thomas, since when there have been Thomas's at the helm in Nuits.

The current head of the house is Denis – eldest son of Yves Thomas, himself the grandson by marriage of Symphorien Moillard. At an age when most people would be contemplating retirement, Yves remains actively involved in the company. Forthright and determined, he combines a lively mind with a distinct enthusiasm for inventing things, a trait probably derived from his father, whom he credits with the invention of fruit-juice. Indeed, the family fruit-juice company next door to the Moillard offices has shaped many of the Domaine's wine-handling techniques; after all, wine is at least, although not thankfully at most, a refined form of fruit-juice. No doubt, fruit juice is also a useful cash source to finance acquisitions.

On top of the Domaine's 17,000 case annual output, a sister négociant business produces some 7–8 million bottles, all vinified by the same team. Moillard has recently invested in the Domaine St.-Paul, near Beziers in the Languedoc, planted to Pinot Noir, Chardonnay, Syrah and Voignier.

Unusually, most of the vineyards are cultivated on a 'share-cropping' basis, which Yves Thomas is convinced means they are better tended than would be the case with directly employed vignerons, because the *metayeur* has a financial interest in the crop. Such high grade vineyards attract the Côte's finest vignerons to take share-cropping contracts.

Although in theory each vigneron is entitled to half the crop, Moillard usually buys out his share – at top prices – thus retaining all the production.

Apart from 6.5 ha of Hautes Côtes Blanc, the Domaine also has 0.5 ha of Savigny Blanc and some Corton-Charlemagne. This latter is fermented in cask, of which 30% is new oak, at 18–21°C with plenty of *batonnage* to give it

'gras' and resistance to oxidation. The wine spends one year in wood before bottling.

The white generics and Hautes Côtes are bottled in one go, the rest early in the second year, to conserve youthful aromatic and fruit qualities. This is partly a marketing decision: 'People want a wine with the aromas of youth but an old vintage on the label.'

Some years ago, Yves instituted experiments to evaluate the contribution of stalks to red wine and concluded that they add nothing except greenness. Systematic destemming is now the rule!

Yves claims to be the inventor of the revolving *cuve*, which is used for all Domaine wines exceeding 3,500/4,000 litres of juice – not just for the *Régionales*. This device, as distinct from the *cuves* which actually turn – 'they are no good', says Yves – remains still but contains arms which rotate at 2–3 turns per minute, uninfluenced by the volume of pulp. Two turns per day give maximum extraction without loss of alcohol from evaporation.

The wines vinified in the classical manner have *cuvaison* of 10–11 days, compared with 3–4 days for 'roto' wines.

Yves Thomas concludes that it is the number of *pigéages,* not the total duration of *cuvaison* which counts. Although the occasional 'roto' wine is refused its Appellation, as atypical, Yves seems enthusiastically happy with his invention.

He tried vinifying grapes from a single vineyard by different methods – classical, 'roto', heating etc.; the 'roto' wines were ad-

judged best, especially for colour and tannins.

The Domaine's reds are reared in cask, using 30% new oak. Yves becomes highly animated: 'They are a waste – casks,' he exclaims, thinking of the precious forest needed to make a Burgundian barrel – one cubic metre of wood for 3 casks – which is discarded after a few years' use. Reflecting on the problem, he has resolved this intolerable waste with . . . a square cask, squarrels, not barrels! As the inaccessible corners would present cleaning problems, these would only be used once, and then dismantled and sold – as parquet flooring. So the wine lover, having consumed his Chambertin or Clos de Vougeot, would, under Yves' scheme, be able to have it in his sitting-room as well.

Although this particular brainchild may not have got very far, Yves is unstoppable. He has developed a stainless-steel cubic *cuve*, containing an internal pump operating a system of virtually constant *pigéage*.

However vinified, Moillard reds spend 18 months in cask before bottling, then undergo two separate finings with, unusually for reds, fish fining, chosen because it takes out any particles without removing too much tannin.

The Moillard reds are good, stylish wines – generally on the masculine side of their respective appellations. Their tannins are sometimes aggressive and would benefit from further refinement. Nonetheless, this is a reliable source of Burgundy, which deserves greater recognition.

VINEYARD HOLDINGS

Commune	Level	Lieu-dit/Climat	Area	Vine Age	Status
Vosne	GC	Romanée St-Vivant	0.17	35	P
Vosne	PC	Les Beaumonts	0.94	55	P
Vosne	PC	Les Malconsorts	2.94	45	P
Gevrey	GC	Chambertin	0.05	35	P
Gevrey	GC	Chambertin Clos de Bèze	0.24	25	P
Vougeot	GC	Clos de Vougeot	0.60	30	P
Aloxe	GC	Corton, Clos du Roi	0.84	25	P
Aloxe	GC	Corton-Charlemagne	0.23	52	P
Chambolle	GC	Bonnes-Mares	0.15	35	P
Beaune	PC	Les Grèves	2.20	25	P
Nuits	PC	Clos de Thorey	4.12	45	P
Nuits	PC	Clos des Grandes Vignes	2.12	35	P
Nuits	PC	Les Porrets St.-Georges	0.54	40	P
Nuits	PC	La Richemone	0.91	30	P
Nuits	PC	Les Murgers	0.17	20	P
Nuits	V	Aux Saints Julien	0.58	35	P
Nuits	V	Les Charmottes	0.75	35	P
Savigny	V	(Blanc – Chardonnay)	0.5	20	P
Concoeur	R	(Htes. Ctes. de Nuits R)	10.45	10	P/F
Concoeur	R	(Htes. Ctes. de Nuits W)	4.00	10	P/F
Villars	R	(Htes. Ctes. de Nuits W)	2.50	10	F
		Total:	**35.00 ha**		

Domaine Prieure Roch

As nephew of Lalou Bize-Leroy and, since her dismissal in 1990, co-administrator of the Domaine de la Romanée-Conti, Henri Roch started with advantages not enjoyed by others who launch out on their own account. He has made good use of them.

Now in his 30s, he has the confidence derived from his position at Romanée-Conti, but the hesitancy of someone who has yet to prove himself as a solo operator. He began in 1988, and three years later was joined by Philippe Pacelet as winemaker – a partnership clearly beginning to bear fruit.

Having financial resources enabled him to buy vineyards, rather than rent or share-crop. First came some Vosne Villages vines, near to the RN74; in both 1993 and 1994, these produced an elegant, soft wine — sold as Les Clous. Next, a *Monopole*, though it isn't labelled as such: Clos Goillotte, from well-sited vines just above Vosne's Mairie – a wine of typically broader frame with firmer tannins and spicy overtones.

One grade up is Hautes Maizières, which adjoins the Les Suchots – a vineyard rated highly by Duval-Blochet, in his personal 19th-century classification of the Crus of Vosne. A full, quite meaty wine, with underlying elegance, but evolving more slowly than Clos Goillotte or Les Clous. In 1994 there came Les Suchots itself – firmer and denser still, but retaining that marvellous amalgam of power and elegance which makes the wines of Vosne so fascinating.

In 1994 there also appeared Chambertin Clos de Bèze, from 45-year-old vines. Philippe Pacelet managed a wine of depth and elegance, with considerable underlying class – a magnificent debut.

Perhaps the most interesting wine is the Clos Vougeot – from a plot at the top of the Clos by the prominent small tower. This is one of the few which regularly approaches Grand Cru quality – Hudelot Noëllat and Grivot are others. To the vineyard's characteristic broad-framed earthiness, Pacelet adds an attractive, and rare, dimension of elegance and complexity. The 1994, 1993 and 1991 are all successes whilst the 1992, now showing the secondary aromas and flavours of maturity, though acceptable, is somewhat dilute.

Vinification is uncontroversial, save for the policy of leaving all the stems in the vats. Provided you don't pump or press fiercely, Henri Roch believes you can avoid extracting stemminess. Although some of the 1993s were astringent – in particular the Clos Goillotte – this is generally submerged by the overall structure and unlikely to unbalance the wine in the long term. They should experiment with different levels of stems and be prepared to be more flexible.

The Domaine is headquartered in a soulless warehouse winery in Nuits-St.-Georges – recently a garage – a priory in bygone times, hence the 'Prieure'. The street front – a curious vertical section through a vast wooden vat with curved glass windows – is dusty and uninviting, pounded by the constant flow of traffic to and from Beaune. Within, a cavernous space gives on to excellent, cool cellars – in Burgundy, even garages and priories have them – embellished upstairs by a small office and tasting bar.

In 1995, Henri Roch acquired the entire 5 ha Nuits Premier Cru Clos des Corvées, formerly belonging to Charles Viénot. Fine as this may be on his vineyard portfolio, marketing 2,000+ cases of a single wine will take considerable business acumen.

This is a fledgling enterprise, but one which promises well. The wines are good, often very good – although there have been rumbling criticisms of premature oxidation. It is to be hoped that Henri Roch contrives to balance his role as co-gerant of DRC with managing his own Domaine. The best chefs invariably remain firmly in their kitchens.

Domaine Remoriquet

Gilles Remoriquet, a tall man with an open manner, expresses a preference for 'vins bien structurés', by which he means abundant, ideally unaggressive, tannins. His wines must therefore suit him well, with little left to sell they clearly suit his clients.

His great-grandparents, who were vineyard workers, started the Domaine in the 1890s and his father Henri developed their smallholding during the middle 1900s. Gilles arrived to help in 1976, fresh from Lycée Viticole and Dijon Oenology faculty. Now there are 8 ha, spread across four Nuits Premiers Crus, a couple of Nuits Villages and some red and white generics.

The Remoriquet style makes little concession to markets which seem to want instant drinking and ageing potential rolled into one – a hopeless demand. There is an aura of uncompromising tradition about the place, a cluster of buildings in one of Nuits' quieter back streets, only a little compromised by a large stainless-steel rototank, sandwiched in a corner next to a fine, old open wooden *cuve* which stares at it with a superior air. The cellars were fine when there were 4.5 ha, but with 8 they are distinctly cramped. Plans are afoot to move the *cuverie* across the road to make some space – much less tiring than wheeling heavy vats around at vintage time.

Despite Gilles' preferred style, his wines are carefully balanced, with plenty of aromatic complexity and finesse. Not perhaps recommended for young drinking, especially in naturally high acid and tannin vintages such as 1993, but ones to buy and keep for a few years. There has been criticism from the USA for lack of finesse – but this doesn't bother Gilles, confident that his wines just need time to show it.

Cuvaisons lasting up to 20 days, with plenty of *pigéage,* are followed by 18–22 months' *élévage*. This, coupled with Nuits' natural tendency to firmness, makes a fair amount of tannin hardly surprising. However, Gilles is careful not to push extraction too far – you can over-extract as well as under-extract. Using the rototank for part of the Nuits Village *cuvée*, which is then blended with that vinified traditionally, adds an element of suppleness. Wood is limited to around 15–20% for the Premiers Crus to avoid marking the wine with oak.

For Gilles *Grand Vin* must above all have fruit and be true to its *terroir*. In Nuits, this means 'wines which live for 15–20 years'. In addition, he likes wines 'which carpet the mouth', big sturdy mouthfuls.

The Village Nuits Les Allots is tight, with a noticeably soft centre. Still, not a wine to be broached too soon; the 1993 will need half a decade to unpack, and will go on slowly revealing itself for many years thereafter.

Of the three Premiers Crus, the Rue de Chaux, just below Château Gris, is the most accessible. The 1993 was succulent, mouthfilling and quite powerful, something you could contemplate within a few years of the vintage, but which has all the ingredients for an extended lifespan.

The Damode is more typically Nuits – earthy, tannic, broad-framed – from lightish sandy, pebbly soils. Les St-Georges (and Rue de Chaux) have more and harder clay, with heavier coagulations, which imparts good acidity and plenty of sinewy flesh. The 1993's sturdy, yet fine, concentration endow it with the potential to last for a generation.

With all this good wine in the cellar, the Remoriquets' black and white rabbit, which roams freely round their house, occasionally being fed a lettuce leaf to keep it going, is clearly in daily peril from the oven. Meanwhile, those who talk about lack of finesse might do well to keep out of Gilles' way also. His wines may be a touch *sauvage*, but their finesse is in no doubt.

Domaine Daniel Rion

PRÉMEAUX-PRISSEY

Patrice Rion's house

Daniel Rion started in 1955 with 2 ha inherited from his father. Marriage to a girl from Prémeaux added a further 0.5ha of Nuits, and parcels of Nuits Premiers Crus and Chambolle followed. His first harvest was in 1959 and he retired in 1995. Now the Domaine is run by his sons – Patrice, Christophe and Olivier.

The high international profile of this Domaine is largely due to Patrice, a quiet, soft-spoken man, who has made the Domaine's wines since 1979.

These do not invariably attract adulation, inspiring detractors as well as acolytes. They can lack charm and grace – with an individual spicy style, too burly and rustic, and short on finesse. Notwithstanding, the care which goes into their making is beyond doubt.

Traditional *sélection massale* from grandfather's Les Chaumes vines provides excellent material for *répiquéage*. There has been no major replanting for 16 years except for 2.5 ha of Hautes-Côtes Chardonnay, planted in 1991 with an experimental mix of 5 clones.

Down on the Côte, vine foliage is pruned high for maximum exposure to the sun by fitting the tractor with extra-large wheels. In drought years this is most important; in wetter years, they can trim tighter. Copper sprays are used on the flowers to control excess, and work well, especially when the flowering coincides with a period of dry heat, as in 1988.

Knowing his vines enables Patrice to fine-tune his harvest. Although he looks for maximum sugar levels, he regards over-maturity to be as undesirable as under-ripeness.

Vinification incorporates one or two idiosyncrasies. For example, in order to achieve a period of cool pre-fermentive *maceration,* to extract colour and aromas, the pulp is not cooled, as normal; rather Patrice relies on ultra-clean vats to delay the onset of fermentation should the grapes arrive too hot. Also, yeasting only occurs towards the end of fermentation as Patrice reasons that indigenous yeasts are fine for the initial phases, but lack the power to control the process to the end.

In contrast to earlier years, the crop is now virtually 100% destalked. Stalks are useful anti-oxidants, as their acids fix the oxidases naturally present in grape pulp.

An important factor in deciding how long to vat is the ratio of solids to juice in the *cuves.* The ideal is about 25% solids to 75% liquid; this can support some 18 days *cuvaison* whereas less favourable proportions (e.g. the 40:60 solids:liquid of 1990) perform better with only 11 days. Any natural imbal-

ance is adjusted by a *saignée* – in Patrice's view 'the last chance to concentrate'.

Although the amount of new wood has increased slightly in recent years, the proportions allocated (Villages 20%, Premiers Crus 30–40% and 50% for the Clos de Vougeot) vary little with the vintage, since Patrice believes that these are, in some way, absolutely right for each wine. It seems unusual to find such a supremely cerebral winemaker not adapting the amount of new oak to the style of the vintage. This may account for a certain dryness in Rion's wines in less opulent years.

After *malo* the wines remain on their lees for 2–3 months. Although this risks increasing volatile acidity, Patrice is confident that it adds complexity. An unacceptable level of VA is corrected by a filtration straight after the *malo.* One doubtful vat of 1983 thus treated was pronounced to be among the best of the vintage. The wines are bottled 16–18 months after harvest, fined, but unfiltered.

Tasting wines, both old and young, shows

a wide variation in quality – some fine successes and some good, but rather dull efforts which just don't sing. This is not a matter of occasional underperforming, or of mediocrity in less good vintages – simply a lack of stylistic pattern. If there is a theme, it is a tendency towards masculinity and dryness. Patrice's preference for greater suppleness has signalled a welcome shift towards more obvious fruit and less austerity.

There are certainly some fine 1990s and 1993s. The 1993 Nuits Vignes Rondes is tight and powerful, but with higher apparent acidity and less flesh than either the Hautes Pruliers or Argillières; definitely in the old Rion style. The Clos des Argillières, yielding 22 hl/ha, is altogether softer and fleshier, with a hint of Rion smokiness on the nose – quite succulent but a touch four-square.

The 1993 Vosne Beaux Monts, from 1930 vines, is more in finesse than size – an elegant, restrained wine; quite promising, but somewhat lacking in concentration.

From the 1990s, the Nuits Les Argillières stands out – a concentrated, tannic wine. Patrice considers this his finest Argillières.

In 1991, Patrice and his wife Michelle set up their own Domaine, with 0.62 ha of Bourgogne Rouge 'Bons Batons' and 0.46 ha of Chambolle Village, Les Cras. These receive the same treatment as the rest.

Recent years have seen a distinct improvement – and the appearance of an excellent white Nuits Premier Cru, Terres Blanches, from Pinot Blanc vines. Rion's wines are conscientiously made but remain something of an acquired taste. A Domaine to taste carefully and to follow, if the style appeals.

VINEYARD HOLDINGS

Commune	Level	Lieu-dit/Climat	Area	Vine Age	Status
Vougeot	GC	Clos de Vougeot	0.73	1945	F
Chambolle	V	Les Beaux Bruns	0.33	1975/78	P
Chambolle	PC	Les Charmes	0.41	1945	P
Vosne	PC	Les Chaumes	0.42	1930	P
Vosne	PC	Les Beaux Monts	1.08	1970	P
Vosne	V	Les Hauts Beaux Monts	1.16	1971/72	P
Vosne	V	Les Ravioles	0.70	1956	P
Nuits	PC	Les Vignes Rondes	0.46	1945/1972	P
Nuits	PC	Clos des Argillières	0.72	1955	P
Nuits	PC	Les Hauts Pruliers	0.42	1962	P
Nuits	PC	Terres Blanches (Pinot)	0.66	1959	P
Nuits	PC	Terres Blanches (Chard.)	0.38	1990	P
Nuits	V	(Various *climats*)	2.50	1940/45/65	P
Nuits	R	(Côtes de Nuits-Villages)	2.29	1950/1966	P
	R	(Bourg. Htes. Ctes de Nuits, Chard)	2.35	1989	P
Nuits	R	(Bourgogne Pinot/PTG)	2.73	1955-1980	P
Nuits	R	(Bourg. Chard/Aligoté)	0.88	1985/1991	P
Total:			**18.22 ha**		

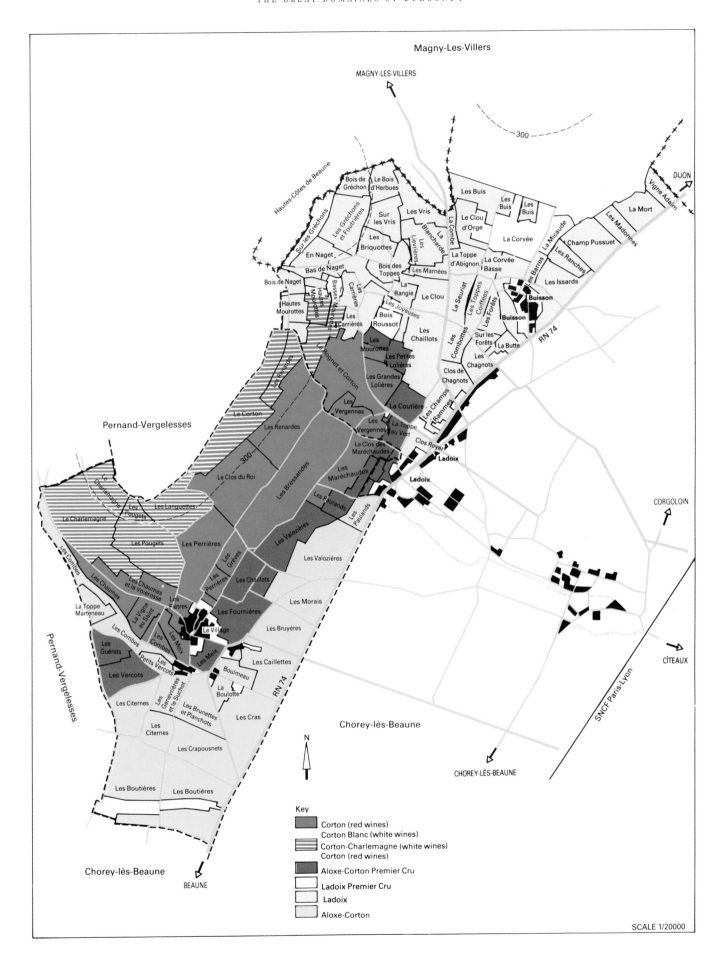

Magny-Les-Villers

MAGNY-LES-VILLERS

300

DIJON

Vigne Adain

Hautes-Côtes de Beaune

Bois de Gréchon

Le Bois d'Herbues

Les Buis

Les Buis

Les Buis

Les Buis

La Mort

Les Madonnes

La Corvée

Champ Pussuet

Sur les Gréchons

Les Gréchons et Foutrières

Sur les Vris

Les Vris

Le Clou d'Orge

La Corvée Basse

Les Ranches

En Naget

Les Briquottes

La Blancharde

Les Lievrières

La Combe

La Toppe d'Abignon

La Corvée Basse

Les Issards

Les Barres

La Micaude

Bas de Naget

Bois des Toppes

Les Marnées

Le Seuriat

Les Toppes Coiffées

Buisson

Bois de Naget

Basses Mourottes

La Rangie

Le Clou

Les Joyeuses

Les Forêts

Buisson

Hautes Mourottes

Les Carrières

Bois Roussot

Les Chaillots

Les Combottes

Sur les Forêts

La Butte

RN 74

Hautes Mourottes

Les Carrières

Les Mourottes

Les Chagnots

Les Roignet et Corton

Les Petites Lolières

Les Grandes Lolières

Clos de Chagnots

Pernand-Vergelesses

Le Corton

Les Vergennes

La Coutière

Les Champs

Les Renardes

Les Vergennes

La Toppe au Vert

Rammes

Le Clos des Maréchaudes

Clos Royer

Le Charlemagne

300

Le Clos du Roi

Les Bressandes

Les Maréchaudes

Ladoix

Les Languettes

Les Pougets

La Charlemagne

Les Perrières

Les Paulands

Ladoix

Les Valozières

CORGOLOIN

Les Combes

Les Pougets

Les Grèves

Les Chaillots

Les Valozières

Les Chaumes

Les Chaumes et la Voierosse

Les Perrières

Les Paulands

Les Valozières

La Toppe Marteneau

Les Fiètres

Les Morais

La Vigne au Saint

Les Fournières

CÎTEAUX

Pernand-Vergelesses

Les Combes

Le Village

Les Bruyères

Les Meix

Les Combes

Les Guérets

Les Meix

Les Caillettes

SNCF Paris-Lyon

Petits Vercots

Boulmeau

Les Vercots

Les Genevrières et le Suchot

La Boulotte

RN 74

Les Citernes

Les Brunettes et Planchots

Les Cras

N

Chorey-lès-Beaune

Les Citernes

Les Crapousnets

CHOREY-LÈS-BEAUNE

Les Boutières

Les Boutières

Key

Corton (red wines)

Corton Blanc (white wines)

Corton-Charlemagne (white wines)

Corton (red wines)

Aloxe-Corton Premier Cru

Ladoix Premier Cru

Ladoix

Aloxe-Corton

Chorey-lès-Beaune

BEAUNE

SCALE 1/20000

ALOXE-CORTON AND LADOIX-SERRIGNY

The quiet village of Aloxe-Corton (population 250) has a reputation far out-stripping its size. Nestling beneath the magnificent Corton hillside, it is home to the largest swathe of Grand Cru land in the Côte d'Or. From 160.19 ha come the sole red Grand Cru of the Côte de Beaune, Corton, white Corton-Charlemagne, a little Corton Blanc and the usual gamut of Premiers Crus and Village wines.

Aloxe has a long history. In 858 it was cited as Aulociacum, which evolved into Alossia, then Alussa; in 1577 it became Alouxe, finally Aloxe. Corton – a corruption of Curtis d'Orthon after an eponymous Emperor – was added in 1862.

Roman artefacts attest to Aloxe's importance as a strategic outpost on the third century Roman road from Marseilles to Autun. Wine from these vineyards, already known and respected from an early date, took on legendary status when the Emperor Charlemagne acquired the land which, in 775, he ceded to the Abbey of Saulieu in compensation for its destruction by the Saracens.

The commune is unusual in having no fewer than 3 Châteaux within its boundaries: the magnificent 18th-century Ch. Corton-Grancey, belonging to Domaine Louis Latour; the 19th-century Ch. de Corton-André, showpiece of the large firm La Reine Pedauque, and the Ch. d'Aloxe-Corton. Their green, yellow and russet enamelled tiles give the appearance of a chameleon who poked its head up above the vines one day to see what was going on, and got stuck there.

The vineyards pack tightly round the village, precluding any expansion beyond perhaps a telephone box. Their division into *climats* and appellations has evolved in a haphazard and confusing fashion. Part of the problem is that the neighbouring communes of Pernand-Vergelesses and Ladoix-Serrigny both have vineyards which are entitled to some of Aloxe's appellations, including Corton and Corton-Charlemagne.

These administrative contortions are further complicated by rules which entitle both red and white wines to be made from certain specified vineyards, but according them different appellations. There are 15 *climats* in Aloxe (71.94 ha), and 6 in Ladoix (16.37 ha) designated Corton for both reds and whites. A further 89.14 ha – 71.88 in Aloxe, 17.26 in Pernand-Vergelesses – supply Corton-Charlemagne, if white, Corton if red. There are also 89.71 ha of Aloxe Village land, and 14 Premiers Crus, of which 9 (29.13 ha) are in

Aloxe and 6 (8.46 ha) in Ladoix.

It should be stressed that red wine produced from Corton-Charlemagne vineyards is not red Corton-Charlemagne, but, e.g. Corton 'En Charlemagne' (rouge), and that white from Corton vineyards is not Corton-Charlemagne, but Corton (blanc). The reason for this latter is that the authorities are endeavouring to discourage the production of white wine from essentially red soils.

Understanding Aloxe-Corton is further complicated by the Grands Crus having over 200 owners, although only 26 growers and 1 négociant operate from Aloxe itself, with the remainder scattered throughout the Côte.

This results in a wide diversity of style and quality. The best Charlemagnes come from Bonneau du Martray, Louis Latour, Coche-Dury, Rapet, Remoissenet, Champy, Faiveley, Jadot and Tollot-Beaut. These last three, together with Chandon de Briailles, Philippe Senard and Prince Florent de Merode produce the finest red Cortons and Chandon de Briailles a particularly fine Corton blanc. There are also worthy wines from Maurice Chapuis, Michel Voarick and the skilled, enthusiastic Franc Follin-Arbelet.

A few Domaines continue to produce poor wine from excellent vineyards: Bouchard Père et Fils (who own nearly 7 ha of Le Corton) and La Reine Pedauque are notable examples. Even in great vintages their offerings are frequently unbalanced and uninspiring. Added to these peaks and troughs there is much over-cropped, over-*chaptalised* fluid from other growers, which seems to find a gullible market at Grand Cru prices.

The hill of Corton is a magnificent saddle of land. Expositions through almost 270 degrees vary from east-facing Ladoix through due-south to west-facing Pernand, where part of the En Charlemagne vineyard actually faces north-west. Westerly sectors tend to ripen later and produce wines of less obvious richness than those more favourably exposed.

Here, more than anywhere else on the Côte, the permutations of heat, cold, sun and shadow significantly influence vegetation and ripening. North-east facing vines receive

early morning sun, but it is cold; to the south it is both hot and sunny; to the south-west it is hot, but for much of the day in shadow whilst the west is both cold and shaded.

Unsurprisingly in so large a vineyard, the soil-profile is complex with a wide variation on both axes – from top to bottom of the hill and around it, from Ladoix to Pernand – to which millenia of erosion have contributed. Higher up, limestone predominates, contrasting with more scree, iron, clay and ammonite fossil material lower down in the Village land. Each *climat's* geology is reflected in its wine.

It is no accident that white grapes – Aligoté, later Chardonnay – were planted on the upper sections, beneath the Bois de Corton, where the clay topsoil gives way to oolitic limestone, with more marl and pebbles. This ideal terrain produces wines of masculine elegance – entirely different from those of Meursault and Puligny – which, given time, develop a magnificently austere, aristocratic quality.

In the middle of the slope, brown limestone emerges and the proportion of clay increases – excellent territory for Pinot Noir. Here are to be found the best Corton *climats*: Clos du Roi, Bressandes, Perrières, Poujets and Le Corton. Soils vary: Perrières has only 25 cm of soil on top of hard rock, while Bressandes is planted on an old quarry.

Attempts to characterise a typical Corton beyond the broadest brush-strokes are doomed. The best are powerful and tannic with an overlay of finesse – a touch sauvage, with rather less self-restraint than the equally intractable Clos Vougeot. Cortons are capable of great longevity: a half-bottle of Jadot's 1928 Pougets was still strong, almost spicy, and rich over 60 years on.

As usual quality depends more on the grower than on the vineyard. This said, there is a strong case for reclassifying this over-extended Grand Cru, with a view to eliminating vineyards on colder, less favoured sites. Until this (politically unimaginable) event, yields and the integrity of the grower will continue to count.

GRANDS CRUS OF ALOXE-CORTON			
Lieu-dit	Area	Props.	Prod.
Corton (Rouge – all *climats*)	160.19.26	200	61,000 c/s Red 450 c/s White
Corton-Charlemagne	71.88.34	75	27,500 c/s White
Totals:	**232.07.60**	**275**	**88,950 c/s**

117

Domaine Daniel Senard

ALOXE-CORTON

In espousing the controversial methods of Lebanese oenologist Guy Accad, Philippe Senard has radically changed the direction of his Domaine and propelled it into Burgundy's top flight.

Before taking over from his father's 'chef de cave', in 1971, Philippe spent five years working as commercial director in the family factory in Beaune, making chips for casinos (only one of two in the world, apparently). Realising he knew little about making wine, he sent himself to Beaune's Lycée Viticole for some formal training.

Philippe's Domaine is an amalgam of two separate estates: the Domaine du Comte Senard, founded by his grandfather, Jules Senard, in the middle of the 19th century, comprising nearly 9 ha in Aloxe, Chorey and Beaune, belonging to members of the Senard family. A further 6.34 ha of Savigny, Beaune and Côte de Beaune make up the Domaine des Terregelesses, an estate created in 1984 by an anonymous 'lover of Burgundy'. Philippe's father, Daniel Senard, who did much to establish the Domaine's identity, has now retired, but continues to take a keen interest.

After sixteen years at the Domaine, Philippe found himself becoming stale and de-motivated. Travelling outside France, especially in Oregon, California and in Spain, Philippe was persuaded that whilst other viticultural regions were progressing, Burgundy was under-performing and failing to emulate the really great winemaking of the past. His instinct that there was need for change was reinforced by his own 1982 and 1986 vintages, where he sensed that the grapes had the potential for *Grand Vin*, but felt himself incapable of extracting it. The turning point came in 1986 when he first tasted wines made by cold-*maceration* and was impressed with the results. Accad's engagement lasted from 1987 until after the 1993 vinification.

A great deal of nonsense has been promulgated in recent years about the so-called 'méthode Accad'. He, and those who espouse his philosophy, have been criticised for both destroying Burgundy's unique typicity and for making wines which are unlikely to last. Now that the vintages of the late 1980s are maturing, it is patently clear that both claims are false.

Guy Accad's principal concern is to establish the best possible soil equilibrium, since he believes that the soil's capacity to nourish the vine is limited by the extent to which it is in balance. The 'larder' is there, but you have to find the natural key to unlock its nourishment. Adding fertilisers merely encourages higher productivity. What is needed are regular, precise adjustments in the soil's base elements to promote a natural balance; this in turn helps ripen fewer grapes earlier and to a better degree.

Philippe Senard's soil-care regime minimises the use of strong, synthetic treatment products, which can easily unbalance the soil and destroy valuable micro-flora. Thus only Bordeaux mixture, sulphur and insecticides are used – 'we haven't much choice' he argues. His thinking is increasingly oriented towards 'biodynamie' – an organic treatment system based on precisely timed, homeopathically dilute, doses. However, in Burgundy's heavily subdivided vineyards, it would need an inconceivable consensus to introduce this successfully on a large scale. Philippe does not view things with unremitting gloom: 'This isn't altogether bad – it permits us to evaluate the results of different policies.'

Philippe admits that one of Accad's strongest influences was on the date of harvest. 'I have put back my vintage by 3 weeks – it's obviously a risk; the drama of Burgundy now is that people unfortunately aren't prepared to wait for proper maturity – they won't take the risk to really ripen the grapes.' In this, they are egged on by officials who set the *ban de vendange*, the earliest permitted harvesting date. For 1990, in Aloxe-Corton this was the 15th September: 'Absolutely scandalous,' shouts Philippe, 'it should have been at least ten days later.' He waited to start picking until 25th September and did not harvest his Cortons until 1st October.

The ten days' difference was striking: for example, his machine-harvested 3 ha of Chorey, on flatter land, showed 11.2 degrees potential alcohol on 2nd October whereas the final batch, picked from the same vineyard on 12th October, came in at 13.2 degrees – a full 2 degree gain in ripeness. 'We were entitled to harvest on 15 September – this is the whole problem!'

Although Accad no longer consults here, vinification continues on modified Accad guidelines of which 'the great principle' is to vinify as cool as is compatible with the extraction and, as important, the retention, of the maximum aroma and colour. The use of only one single, large dose of SO_2 to delay fermentation caused problems, as it selected out a highly resistant strain of yeast which remains active well after fermentation is over and can attack the SO_2, producing unpleasantly aromatic mercaptans. Philippe's solution is to heat his vats to 32°C at the end of fermentation which kills any residual yeasts, without destroying aromas. He is now working to finding the balance point to maximise the one and minimise the other.

The 'slow and cool' principle parallels the difference between simmering and boiling a soup – one way you keep the aromas, the other way you lose them. In an Accad *cuverie* there is little ambient aroma, whereas a traditional one reeks of fermentation.

The bunches are first destalked to a degree determined by the ripeness of the wood and the general state of the crop – 50% in 1988 and 75% in 1989 and 1990 – then given a calibrated dose of liqud SO_2 as the grapes emerge from the crusher. This contrasts with the traditional practice of waiting until a vat is full before adding sulphur. The dose, 3.5–4 litres per tonne of harvest depending on the fruit, (healthier grapes getting marginally less than otherwise) compares with a traditional dose of 1 litre/tonne.

The crush is then cooled to 5–10°C and put into open *cuves* to *macerate* for several days (8–9 in 1993) before the yeasts start to work. The sulphur neutralises the feebler yeasts, leaving the more resistant population to ferment the *must*. This is a bonus, as these yeasts are more likely to remain active as the alcohol level increases, thus ensuring complete transformation of the sugars.

During fermentation there are regular, rapid *pigéages*, and heating if a vat seems sluggish. The temperature is allowed to rise no further than 25°C – although Philippe admits to becoming anxious at around 20°C having left a *cuve* contentedly fermenting at 19°C one evening only to find it bubbling away at 30°C next morning.

Cuvaison now lasts around 15–20 days, instead of Accad's more usual 25, after which the output of the first two pressings of the pulp is added and 2–3 days allowed to settle out the gross lees. The wines then pass into cask – the Cortons into a mixture of new and old wood – 25–30% new, 20% one year old and the rest older. The Villages and Premiers Crus have somewhat less new wood as this is not a flavour Philippe likes – 'It's artificial, not a natural aroma,' he declares.

The wines spend around 2 years in wood – some 6 months longer than traditional *élévage* – with 2 rackings to aerate and unify the different casks of each Cru. Given healthy lees, the first racking is delayed until

Philippe Senard tasting with clients

September after vinification, but the wines are now given a small dose of sulphur at bottling.

The addition of pectolytic enzymes helps clarification but, as this vinification produces strong tannins, Philippe generally fines his wines, not to clarify, rather to soften them. There is, however, no filtration. He is scathing of some of his colleagues who 'bust their guts to make great wine and then filter it all out', and agrees with Accad on the desirability of correcting any faults during the early stages of vinification, instead of making adjustments later on.

The results of Philippe Senard's first collaboration with Accad – the 1988 vintage – are now starting to emerge from their shells. Both 1988s and 1989s tasted at the Domaine in the mid-1990s, had everything necessary to last well into the 2000s.

The 1989 Corton 'En Charlemagne' – a red Corton, and not, as one misinformed American commentator described it, a red Corton-Charlemagne, had a limpid black-cherry hue, an attractive open, rather aged 'sauvage' nose and opulent, mouthfilling, quite feminine flavours with an angular, marginally unbalanced tannic edge. A red wine from 'white' soil perhaps, but still fine.

The Corton *tout court* from the Paulands vineyard, just below Bressandes, is very typical Corton, 'sauvage', powerful and distinctly visceral. 'Hare's intestines,' Philippe chortles. Only a Frenchman would know. He recalls a Belgian customer who finally plucked up the courage after 15 years visiting the Domaine to confess that he had never managed to track down 'Corton *tout court*' or find it on a wine list.

The Bressandes is tighter and less expressive than the others with aromas of very ripe, almost overripe *fruits noirs*, warm and fleshy on the palate rather than massively powerful.

The Clos des Meix is more sizeable, more tightly structured with softish tannins and a shade less complexity. The fifth member of the Corton quintet, the Clos du Roi is finer still – richer, fuller, more masculine. These are an impressive and classy range of yard-stick Cortons.

The 'méthode Accad' is often accused of effacing *terroir*, standardising wines, and of producing wines which lack staying power. The standardisation claim is one which Philippe Senard vehemently rejects, with good justification; even from the cask, his wines (the splendid 1993s for example) show marked and systematic differences between the various Corton *climats*. In any case, even without Accad, what is a typical Corton or Clos de Vougeot? Being able to describe differences between *climats* or communes in general terms, is not the same as resolving the question of typicity. As for durability, the wines clearly speak for themselves.

In addition to his excellent reds, Philippe makes about 900 bottles of white Aloxe-Corton – a rarity – from a plot of 70-year-old Pinot Beurot (Pinot Gris). This is sold almost entirely to the Domaine's privileged Michelin-starred restaurant customers. Such is the demand that 43 ares of the Clos des Meix were replanted with white grapes in 1995.

Philippe Senard suffered much personal criticism for his espousal of Accad from critics who barely stopped to ponder whether a highly intelligent, thoughtful man would risk his Domaine and reputation on a mere whim. So far, his 'new' wines have enjoyed considerable success among his clientele and attracted unprecedented attention from customers and the media.

Given the quality of Philippe's mature wines, the Accad debate should now cease. It is, however, probably too much to expect that critics will admit their mistakes and apologise for the damage done to both spirit and wallets of their hapless targets. Fortunately, this is a Domaine making fine wine with consummate care, a fact not lost on Philippe Senard's fellow vignerons or on his contented customers.

VINEYARD HOLDINGS

Commune	Level	Lieu-dit/Climat	Area	Vine Age	Status
Aloxe	GC	Corton Clos du Roi	0.64	45	P
Aloxe	GC	Corton Bressandes	0.63	38	P
Aloxe	GC	Corton (Les Paulands)	0.83	50	P
Aloxe	GC	Corton Clos des Meix	1.52	40	P
Aloxe	PC	Les Valozières	0.70	18	P
Aloxe	V	————	3.32	27	P
Aloxe	V	Caillettes (Blanc)	0.21	65	P
Aloxe	GC	Clos des Meix (Corton Blanc)	0.43	Pl.1996	P
Pernand	GC	Corton en Charlemagne	0.40	22	M
Beaune	PC	Les Coucherias	0.29	25	M
Chorey	V	Les Champs Longs	0.51	18	P
		Total:	**9.48 ha**		

Domaine Jayer-Gilles

MAGNY-LES-VILLERS

Life is definitely leisurely up the 'arrière Côte' – that peaceful gently undulating stretch of land behind the Côte d'Or. Nothing much seems to stir in these quiet little working villages, beyond the occasional passage of a tractor or the strident klaxon announcing the arrival of the mobile grocer.

However, wine is made here. Although much is sound, modest stuff, destined for the négociant market, a few enlightened vignerons are making valiant attempts to build up a bottle trade and thereby to establish a reputation for themselves.

Among the best of these pioneers is Robert Jayer-Gilles. A man of military mien, tall and broad, with a pair of luxuriant handle-bar moustaches and a gravelly voice, he exudes the confidence of a freshly-minted British sergeant-major as he surveys his private army of casks ranged in impeccable review order in his immaculate cellar.

Robert is a native of Vosne and a cousin of the great Henri Jayer. He started his career in 1948 as an apprentice working for André Noblet, the then cellar-master at the Domaine de la Romanée-Conti. In 1955 he left to marry a Mlle Gilles, daughter of a viticulteur whose family had owned vines at Magny-Les-Villers for centuries. Her vines and his inheritance of Echézeaux and Nuits Premier Cru Les Damodes remain the kernel of the Domaine.

Further parcels of Hautes Côtes, Nuits and Beaune, both red and white, Côte de Nuits-Villages, some Aligoté and Passe-tout-grains were added later, giving a current total average production of 5–6,000 cases.

The wines are made with infinite care and are much sought-after, even sometimes by other top growers needing some more Bourgogne for their clients. Robert clearly enjoys the rewards which his efforts have brought and like his neighbour, Claude Cornu, the physical manifestation of his prosperity is a magnificent new push-button cellar, featuring, among other novelties, an illuminated well, to show visitors the water table just below, and an opulent spitoon surmounted by a large stone gargoyle.

Despite the cellar's brash modernity, vinification is largely updated traditional. Although Robert dislikes destalking, a respect for his clients' wish for more supple wines means that 80–90% of stems are now removed. He still leaves 7–8 harvesting boxes of uncrushed grapes in each *cuve*, to prolong the maceration, though he believes his clients are mistaken: 'They won't keep

bottles for 10–15 years – they're wrong!' he expostulates.

Pushing the button to irrigate the spitoon, he explains that he has no means of cooling his *cuves* – 'I don't like pressing buttons' – but relies on a moderate dose of SO$_2$ to delay the onset of fermentation long enough for a reasonable extraction of colour. When the temperature rises above about 36°C, the *must* is simply decanted from its own *cuve* to a cooler one. Robert used to tread the cap personally. Now, with advancing years, he has installed a pneumatic plunger with which he seems happy.

The red wines generally spend some 15–17 months in new Allier oak – the Echézeaux also has a touch of Tronçais – in the luxurious surroundings of the new cellar. Robert started using new wood in 1977 for all except his Passe-tout-grains. His Romanée-Conti training has led him to use 100% irrespective of vintage or appellation. This can easily over-power a less naturally structured regional wine or even a better appellation in a weaker vintage. He should review this policy. The reds are normally bottled without fining, but with a light Kieselguhr filtration.

The Hautes Côtes – red and white – are excellent wines. The whites are fermented in 50% new wood and 50% stainless steel to provide a final blend of freshness and structure and bottled after the second winter – some 18 months old. Of these, the Aligoté, from 50–70-year-old vines and the Haute Côtes whites, the Beaune from 70% of Henri Gouges' famous white mutant of Pinot Noir and 30% Chardonnay and the Nuits from the reverse proportions, are particularly successful – delicious and individual.

For the reds plenty of attractive flavours and a firm structure come from a vinification

with a 5-day pre-fermentive *maceration,* that high fermentation temperature, some 15 days' *cuvaison* and a *malo* which can last up to 14 months. These are reds of military proportions, sometimes rather four-square – but definitely not fashioned for the faint-hearted looking for a fruity picnic wine.

Whilst the Côtes de Nuits Villages is a fine example, it is with the Nuits-St.-Georges Hautes Poirets and Damodes that one begins to see the foundations of Robert's reputation. The former, with a fine nose redolent of bitter chocolate (1993), is relatively accessible, fleshy and classy. The latter, from the Vosne side of Nuits and 50-year-old vines, is equally dense. Dark cherry on the nose, more floral than the Poirets, still fine, with notes of chocolate and a generous layer of succulent ripe fruit; underneath, it has firm tannins which need time to soften. A distinctly Vosne-ish Nuits.

The Echézeaux is yet another quantum away – a deep, limpid wine of almost black-cherry hue; completely unforthcoming on the nose, but with a vast, mouthfilling panoply of sweet, ripe fruit. A wine of considerable depth and flavour with superb length. A gentle giant from a gentle giant and one of the best from this variable Grand Cru.

Robert Jayer is not a vigneron who leaves his cellars for long. In fact he rarely takes a holiday, probably in case an important client turns up in his absence. 65% of his wine is exported, to all the usual places; the 35% remaining finding its way into the cellars of private individuals and on to the lists of restaurants. 'I supply all the great restaurants – over one hundred Michelin stars.' It would be a pity if he were on the beach sunning himself – an almost unthinkable prospect, in any case – when one of these culinary luminaries arrived for his annual tasting.

VINEYARD HOLDINGS

Commune	Level	Lieu-dit/Climat	Area	Vine Age	Status
Flagey	GC	Echézeaux	0.54	45	P
Nuits	PC	Les Damodes	0.11	50	P
Nuits	V	Les Hauts Poirets	0.30	45	P
Corgoloin	R	Côte de Nuits-Villages	1.31	25	P
————	R	(Hautes Côtes de Beaune Rouge)	1.02	20	P
————	R	(Hautes Côtes de Nuits Rouge)	2.37	20	P
————	R	(Hautes Côtes de Beaune Blanc)	1.01	30	P
————	R	(Hautes Côtes de Nuits Blanc)	1.22	30	P
————	R	(Passe-tout-grain)	0.44	20	P
————	R	(Bourgogne Aligoté)	2.62	50–70	P
		Total:	**10.94 ha**		

Domaine Prince Florent de Mérode

LADOIX-SERRIGNY

Florent, Prince de Mérode, a 64-year-old nobleman, lives in the splendid Château de Serrigny, bought by his ancestors in the 1700s. It came to him, complete with moat, a 500-metre-long canal, and a splendid 'parc à l'anglaise' via his family's maternal line; each child was given one property, this was his. He is a reserved, quiet man, full of old-world courtesy and a respect for the land he has inherited. The eighth generation, he came to live in Serrigny in 1954, on his marriage to the sister of Comte Alexandre de Lur-Saluces, owner of Ch. Yquem.

The Domaine has nearly 12 ha of fine land, including almost 4 of Grand Cru Corton. From 1953–1990 the winemaking was entrusted to Pierre Bitouzet, a grower from Savigny, and the Domaine was clearly not fulfilling its potential. The wines were pleasant enough, but deliberately made for early drinking, lacking substance and depth even in good vintages.

Now, however, under the aegis of Jean-Louis Burelle, who has worked at the Domaine for years, and with the help of an oenologist, things have improved dramatically. Low yields, complete destalking, longer *cuvaisons* (17 days for the 1993s, rather than Bitouzet's 10–12), *saignée de cuve* when necessary, fractional *chaptalisation*, and plenty of *pigéage* have transformed weak-kneed Cortons into wines of presence and interest.

After fermentation in fine, old, open wooden *cuves* and addition of the press-wine, the new wine is settled for 3–4 days before being transferred to cask. The Cortons have around 25% of new oak, the rest less. Two rackings, the first after *malo* and the second, cask-to-cask, after fining, precede bottling at 15–18 months. Since 1990 there has been no filtration – a welcome improvement.

The Domaine's sole white is a Premier Cru Ladoix, Les Hautes-Mourottes, made from Chardonnay and fermented in cask (33% new wood) with *batonnage* for up to a year to give it fatness, and bottled relatively early – after 10–12 months – to retain freshness. This can be pleasant and interesting – full, sappy and classily rustic, with a distinct *goût de terroir* – a bit of a dark-haired gypsy.

The junior reds – the first two from the Domaine's largest holdings – consist of a Ladoix, Les Chaillots, a Pommard Clos de la Platière and an Aloxe-Corton Premier Cru; all well-made, especially the Pommard which has depth and an elegance infrequently found in this commune.

The church at Aloxe

One then jumps straight to the quartet of Cortons: a Marechaudes, quite full and broad-shouldered, from oldish vines planted in predominantly clay soil; then Renardes, with more obvious aromatic complexity and highish acidity – quite gamey in character from 35 cm of soil, giving directly on to rock; greater ageing potential here. The Bressandes fuses Renarde's elegance with Marechaude's *puissance*; a most attractive wine which is accessible at a relatively early stage but in vintages such as 1993 will certainly last a decade or more. The Clos du Roi is the most typically Corton of all, firm yet elegant, powerful yet supple – a combination of fruit from ferruginous and marly soils and vines which are nearing their half century. Its inherent balance makes it an abundantly satisfying wine, even in youth, but this same quality endows it with longevity.

The Prince has taken the reins of his Domaine firmly back into his own grasp and the results are increasingly impressive. It is heartwarming to see such a thorough transformation. Although still a touch inconsistent for top class, his wines are well on the way there. His wife's connection enables him to exchange wine with his brother-in-law: 'a little Yquem against a lot of Corton'. No doubt the proportions will balance more in his favour; if not now, then in the near future.

VINEYARD HOLDINGS

Commune	Level	Lieu-dit/Climat	Area	Vine Age	Status
Aloxe	GC	Corton, Clos du Roi	0.57	47	P
Aloxe	GC	Corton, Bressandes	1.19	35	P
Aloxe	GC	Corton, Renardes	0.51	40	P
Aloxe	GC	Corton, Marechaudes	1.53	42	P
Aloxe	PC	Les Marechaudes	0.69	44	P
Pommard	PC	Clos de la Platière	3.73	20	P
Ladoix	PC	Les Hautes-Mourottes (W)	0.31	48	P
Ladoix	V	Les Chaillots (R)	2.84	25	P
		Total :	**11.37 ha**		

PERNAND-VERGELESSES

The little village of Pernand – the Vergelesses was added in May 1922 – sits at the foot of the hill of Corton, about 3 km from Aloxe-Corton itself. It is a friendly, attractive, peripheral place, largely bypassed by tourists who see no particular reason to go there, with a maze of narrow streets radiating from the Church up and down the hillside. The absence of a hotel,

and the presence of only one small restaurant is an effective disincentive for casual travellers.

Pernand is architecturally interesting, consisting principally of six large 19th-century mansions, distributed like sentinels round its periphery. Each has its own park, many planted with magnificent, and important, mature trees, and its particular Clos of vines.

In the last century these *maisons bourgeoises* housed the grand employers for whom the rest of the village worked – de Grossets, Rameaus, Chansons, Copeaus, Ponnelles and Moreys. For the rest, rows of ancient village houses are huddled together cheek-by-jowl, befitting the scale and style of feudal dependents.

Time, however, has reversed the roles and

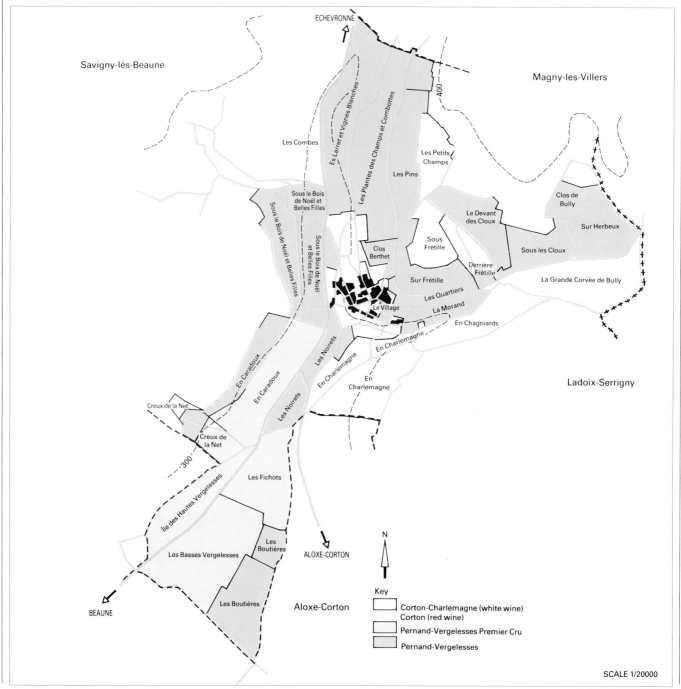

clipped the feudal wings of the great landowners. No descendants of the original families remain in possession, each house now belonging to someone from the village, as if time had turned social history on its head and the village inside out.

Pernand's 35 growers and population of under 350 make red and white wine from 137.63 ha of Village land and 56.51 ha spread over 5 Premiers Crus. There are also 17.26 ha – just over a fifth – of the Corton-Charlemagne appellation – in a single swathe of land, known as 'En Charlemagne', which sits at the northern end of the Corton hill, on the outskirts of the village. It is believed that it forms much of the original land gifted by Charlemagne to the Abbey of Saulieu in 775 AD, although this attribution is by no means certain.

In 1978 the local growers' association successfully applied for several important changes to their *vignoble*. Firstly, the area of Grand Cru was extended to incorporate several small parcels of land which were formerly within the appellation but had since lapsed; secondly, the Grand Cru designation was altered to allow production of Corton (red) as well as of Corton-Charlemagne (white), and thirdly, the right of growers to use the appellation Aloxe-Corton for red wines from certain of the commune's vineyards was rescinded.

The wines of Pernand are among the least known of the Côte. This is largely because growers often don't bother to market 'Pernand-Vergelesses', preferring instead to sell much of their red under the alternative appellation of Côte de Beaune-Villages. The problem might also be due, in part, to the awkwardness of the name – 'Pernand-Vergelesses' is hardly the kind of snappy, punchy brand name likely to motivate a modern marketing department.

Low profile as the appellation may be, there is much to commend it, especially in good vintages, when the best wines are well worth buying and keeping for a few years. This said, it is necessary to choose with care, since, although the growers are a conscientious bunch, there is much wine which is frankly meagre and uninspiring.

The difficulties faced by Pernand's *vignerons* derive mostly from the poor exposition of their vineyards. Looking at the map, one can see that most of the *vignoble* is situated at the northern end of the valley, in the direction of Echevronne. This means that much is in shade for the greater part of each day, screened from direct sunlight by the hill of Corton. It is no accident that the best of the Premiers Crus – Les Basses Vergelesses and Ile des Hautes Vergelesses – are on the flatter, more open section of the valley floor, where they receive the most sunshine. Although some of the Village vineyards face

Pernand – one of the many unspoilt villages of Burgundy – nestles beneath the northerly end of the Corton hillside

south-east, much, including En Charlemagne, faces west or even north-west, which considerably delays ripening. Those who compensate by harvesting late, risk grapes being destroyed by autumnal storms.

The soils, however, are good, especially for white grapes – which is curious since nearly 75% of the vineyards are planted with Pinot Noir. En Charlemagne is mainly of hard limestone composition – with significant rock outcrops in places; these 'têtes du loup' can destroy ploughs and hoes, so some of the Domaines concerned have recently brought in special machinery to excavate and pulverise them before returning the result to the vineyard as manageable, ground-down topsoil. In addition, new walls in the lower end of the Pernand section of the Corton hill have been built to help retain topsoil washed down by rain.

Elsewhere, there is a diversity of soils, most being based on various forms of limestone. In Les Vergelesses, Les Fichots and the Ile de Vergelesses, the ground is significantly more clay-bearing and ferruginous. Apart from reddening the earth, this latter provides ideal terrain for red grapes, giving the wines breadth and structure.

The commune also produces a modest quantity of white Pernand-Vergelesses which may be made from either Chardonnay or from Pinot Blanc; at present, this seems to be undergoing something of a revival. Bernard Dubreuil – with his excellent village *Monopole* Clos Berthet – Roland Rapet and the de Nicolays at Chandon de Briailles in

Savigny, make their white Pernand from 100% Chardonnay, although a few growers still retain a small proportion of Pinot Blanc in their blends.

In good vintages, such as 1983, 1985, 1988, 1989, 1990 and 1992, the Blanc has a green-gold appearance and is marked by an aroma of peach-kernels and a strong, flinty *goût de terroir*. These wines have the capacity to develop over several years, but are probably best drunk young for their uncomplicated, sappy fruit.

The red wines are frequently – and in many instances justifiably – criticised for a rusticity and lack of finesse. The better Domaines have realised that destalking helps to remove an extra element of raw tannin which contributes to the problem, especially in unripe years which are naturally somewhat angular. In good vintages, on the other hand, Pernand reds, especially from Les (Basses) Vergelesses and the Ile des (Hautes) Vergelesses are wines of weight and structure, capable of ageing for 20 years or more. As usual, quality depends on the grower.

Apart from the 'hors classe' Domaine Bonneau du Martray for Corton-Charlemagne, the best wines come from the growers already mentioned. There is also a competent *cuvée* of Ile des Vergelesses from Louis Latour and a village Clos de la Croix de Pierre, from Louis Jadot. All these wines are well worth seeking out, not only for their quality but also for their modest prices. If you taste carefully, Pernand-Vergelesses represents some of the best value in the Côte.

GRAND CRUS OF PERNAND-VERGELESSES

Lieu-dit	Area	Props.	Prod.
** En Charlemagne	17.25.89	35	6,600 C/S

**N.B. Wine from this vineyard is entitled to the Appellation Corton if red, Corton-Charlemagne or Charlemagne if white.

Domaine Bonneau du Martray

PERNAND-VERGELESSES

The white wines from Corton have a special place in the Burgundian mosaic. Whether or not one accepts the lore attributing the planting of white grapes on the hill of Corton to the desire of Liutgarde, Charlemagne's empress, to satisfy her bibulous Lord's thirst for Corton with a white wine, to avoid undignified red stains on his light-coloured beard, the production of a great white wine from this predominantly red hillside is an enduring curiosity, another expression of the Chardonnay grape to delight and stimulate the palate.

Although it owns 1.5 ha of red Corton, Bonneau du Martray is best known for its great Charlemagne, produced from 9.5 ha sited in the choicest parts of this magnificent hillside. From 1969, when the Countess inherited it as chosen legatee of her god-father and uncle, René Bonneau du Martray, until 1993, the Domaine was managed by the Count and Countess Jean de la Morinière.

On taking possession, the de la Morinières found 4.5 ha of their vineyards leased out to an assortment of tenants; it took them five years to negotiate the repurchase of the land and to put the totality back into proper order.

Although Jean le Bault administered the Domaine's commercial activity from Paris, he spent as much time as possible in their house in Pernand – particularly at weekends and during the vintage. This smallish 'maison de vigneron' is simply but beautifully furnished; one entire wall of the sitting-room is devoted to a superb Aubusson tapestry; Jean de la Morinière's brother has its twin.

Jean le Bault spared no expense to make the best possible wine – enjoying a walk through his vineyards, looking at the condition of the vines or examining the soil to see how it was reacting to whatever rainfall there had been. He knows each plot of vines intimately, how it behaves and what it needs.

In 1993, following illness and the death of Comte Jean's adored wife Alice, his eldest son, Jean-Charles, took over day-to-day running of the Domaine, moving himself, his family and the administration to Pernand-Vergelesses. A career architect, with a successful private practice, he is now firmly in charge 'for a minimum of 25 years'. In that same year, Henri Bruchon (affectionately known as 'Monsieur Henri'), the Domaine's regisseur since 1963, handed over to his sons Bernard and Jean-Pierre, who had worked with him for several years. So sons succeed fathers in this close-knit family team.

The vineyards are in a single piece – a rarity in Burgundy for such a large parcel. The half-century-old red Corton vines are in Aloxe-Corton, at the base of the hill, following the road from Aloxe to Pernand. Here the soil is moderately deep, ferruginous in character with hard limestone rock underneath. The 9.5 Charlemagne hectares, although contiguous, are split about equally between the communes of Aloxe and Pernand but are higher up the hillside, where the soil contains more clay and limestone and is more suitable for white wines.

Soil erosion is a constant problem. Rainstorms rapidly wash down the fine, valuable topsoil which Monsieur Henri and his team regularly collected and took back up to the top again. Jean le Bault solved this problem in characteristic fashion, installing water conduits to trap the soil, which, once recovered, he restored to the vineyards by mechanical harvester. He clearly enjoyed shocking traditionalists by telling them that he used a harvesting machine.

In 1993, he shocked the entire village by bringing in a helicopter to dry off wet vines. With meticulous planning to avoid simply blowing water from one plot to another, it flew 2 metres above the vines and saved one degree of potential alcohol. 'The results were excellent – but everyone laughed and joked: Bonneau du Martray needs publicity,' Jean-Charles recalls, adding: 'In 1994, it was not only us who brought in helicopters.'

Jean le Bault and Jean-Charles are perfectionists, who enjoy doing things properly and, thanks to a factory making a significant proportion of the bottles used by the French perfume industry, have the necessary means to implement their ideas. 'Nothing is too fine, for Mon Seigneur the wine,' Comte Jean avows, adding, with a twinkling smile, 'It's a labour of love.'

In 1990, following an unsuccessful quest for larger cellars, a magnificent building with a splendid classical pediment – designed by Jean le Bault himself – was constructed on the outskirts of Pernand. This facility can store several vintages of the Domaine's production or be used as independent négociant premises, should future expansion go in that direction. Its top floor, lit by natural daylight, is designed as a tasting and reception room.

Jean-Charles, who has inherited all his father's charm and quality, is in no hurry to instigate change. He is taking time to examine every aspect of the Domaine's wine-producing process to understand why things work as they do and to identify areas needing refining or improvement.

In their search for perfection both Comte Jean and his son recognise that, whilst their Corton-Charlemagne has gained wide critical acclaim, their red Corton falls far short of what others are achieving. Tasting a range of vintages, it is clear that, even in good years such as 1985 and 1990, the wines lack the depth of extract and concentration expected from a Grand Cru.

It is not easy to pinpoint precisely what is going wrong. There is no material difference in vine age or viticulture between the red and white vines. Yields may play a part in explaining the relative dilution of the Corton. Experience indicates that above about 35 hl/ha the Pinot Noir loses concentration of flavour, whereas the Chardonnay can tolerate up to 45–50 hl/ha without such consequences. Pinot yield has now been reduced to at, or below, the *rendement de base* of 35 hl/ha – and it shows, in a better-structured, better-balanced and richer 1993.

An over-cautious outside oenologist, who dictated Domaine practice for many years, was unwilling to prolong *cuvaison* beyond 6–8 days; this is too short for proper extraction, particularly of aromas and tannins. Under the new regime, *cuvaisons* have been extended to 8 days+, and there are now 3–4 days of pre-fermentive maceration, both significant improvements. There remains the

The late Comtesse Jean le Bault framed by an Aubusson tapestry in the house at Pernand

élevage to be tackled. To date this has consisted of just under a year in cask and a further 5–6 months in *cuve* 'to reclaim space and casks for the next crop' – curiously penny-pinching for a Domaine which is not short of resources. A great Corton merits 16–18 months in cask (some would say 20) and then just the lightest (if any) filtration rather than the present double Kieselguhr and plate processing. Jean-Charles is determined that his Corton will rival the finest. The 1993 – nicely oaky, with plump, concentrated fruit, good length and underlying power – is an attractive wine and represents a significant step in the right direction.

There are no such quibbles with the Corton-Charlemagne. This, in vintages both great and small, is a wine of presence and distinction; not designed to be drunk young – although most invariably is – but for ten years or more cellaring to shed its youthful austerity and to show its breed and finesse.

The vinification for this aristocrat is a species of 'modified classical' – the principal modification being that fermentation is started in stainless steel to enable the temperature to be kept at a maximum of 18°C; after 5–6 days when there is no longer a significant risk of overheating, the *must* is passed into cask.

One third of the wood is new – the remainder being equally second and third year barrels. This used to be Limousin oak – 'it's less strong,' was Monsieur Henri's curious explanation – but, after trials, Jean-Charles has opted for Allier and Nevers; 'Vosges is no good.' He works closely with several tonneliers – 'we put our noses in everywhere' – to obtain wood with the tightest grain and a medium to light toast. These factors impact on the wine, especially on its aromatics.

The Bonneau du Martray Charlemagne seems oblivious of this, generally absorbing its measure of oak without difficulty. Once all the casks have finished *malolactic* fermentation, the wine is racked off its lees and unified in tanks. It then returns to casks, until just before the new vintage when it is re-racked and left in bulk to await bottling, some 15–18 months after harvesting. This, preceded by both a Kieselguhr and a sterile plate filtration, is deliberately early to retain maximum freshness and youthful fruit.

Whilst, according to Comte Jean, you are the servant of your wine whilst it is being produced, the reverse is the case when the time comes to drink it. Then you have the right to demand from it nothing short of perfection.

Unfortunately, the majority of great white Burgundies are consumed long before reaching maturity – the result either of the exigencies of holding stock, especially for restaurants, or of natural curiosity 'to see how it's developing'. Fortunately, or perhaps unfortunately, young Charlemagne is by no

Jean-Charles de la Morinière flanked by Bernard and Jean-Pierre Bruchon: the new generation at Bonneau du Martray

means an unpleasant drink although, like Puligny's Grands Crus, it gives its optimum performance after a decade or so in bottle.

The Bonneau du Martray Charlemagnes are yardstick examples. They tend to start out with the youthful, rather masculine reserve, which so often marks this appellation. Sometimes the early aromas are citrus-based (1994), in other vintages (1989) with a peely, dried apricot character reminiscent of Condrieu. Often the nose has a strongly floral component (1990, 1992) which transforms with bottle age into aromas of acacia, nuts and orange-blossom.

These are wines which need time to integrate and unpack; their youthful qualities are scant guide to the magnificence awaiting those prepared to wait. Not only in top-class vintages, but also in leaner years, they contain the seeds of an enriching development which cannot be hurried.

The 1987 is still evolving – quite a stony, steely, peachy sort of wine, with a fine nerve of that vintage's acidity, yet plenty of depth and weight and flashes of the mature lime-blossom and hazelnut nose which so often characterises fine mature white Burgundy. Here is a wine which is barely ready, yet much of the 4,000 or so cases produced have probably already been sunk by the importunate and the impatient.

To get a line on to the real potential of a Bonneau du Martray Corton-Charlemagne, one must go back to the 1979, which is now at full power. A brilliant green-gold, with a fine, steely nose of almost smoky nuts and lime-blossom and a flavour which, although tight, fills the mouth with its richness and complexity. Do not expect opulence of a Bâtard or a Pucelles, but more intellectual charm – wits rather than flesh, Bach not Brahms.

While lesser vintages will stand up to plain fish and possibly light poultry, the grander bottles can take on something 'plus cuisiné', although anything too heavily spiced or sauced would destroy everything that Comte Jean, Jean-Charles, Monsieur Henri and his sons have striven to create.

VINEYARD HOLDINGS

Commune	Level	Lieu-dit/Climat	Area	Vine Age	Status
Pernand	GC	En Charlemagne (Blanc)	4.50	48	P
Aloxe	GC	Le Charlemagne (Blanc)	5.00	48	P
Aloxe	GC	Le Charlemagne (Rouge)	1.50	46	P
		Total:	**11.00 ha**		

Domaine Dubreuil-Fontaine

PERNAND-VERGELESSES

Bernard Dubreuil runs one of Pernand's more substantial Domaines. Largely created by Bernard's great-grandfather, a Monsieur Arbinet, in the late 1860s, and continued by his son-in-law, Julien Dubreuil, it was further enlarged by Bernard's father, Pierre, who married a Mlle Fontaine. Bernard, who started with his father in 1957, married a Mlle Bidot from Pommard and then proceeded to make his own contribution to the estate – 0.75 ha each of Corton-Bressandes and Clos du Roi in 1966, 0.16 ha of Les Petits Epenots in 1969, the *Monopole* of Savigny Clos Berthet in 1971 – 1 ha of white and 0.5 ha of red, just below the village – and finally 0.25 ha of Aloxe-Corton Village and a further 0.25 ha of Corton Clos du Roi, in 1985.

Bernard is a courteous family man, a touch reserved, with a deep love of his vineyards and a feel for fine wine. The family lives in one of Pernand's original Manor Houses with cellars scattered round the village.

Innate caution causes Bernard to start his harvest with the Grands Crus. Although these are normally the first to flower, shoot buds and ripen fully, he admits that this policy reflects more his unwillingness to take risks than any natural phenomenon. If rain comes, then at least the valuable Grands Crus are safely gathered in.

Until recently, growers were allowed to make table wine from vines too young to be declared for appellation. In 1987, the rules changed giving young-vine production the appellation a year earlier – after their third flowering. As *quid pro quo*, Vin de Table from these vines was outlawed; so young-vine production is now thrown out or distilled.

Bernard destalks up to 90%, preferring new wood tannins to those from stalks. Following family tradition, he used to leave both reds and whites unsulphured until first racking – an unusual, and curiously risky procedure, especially with white grapes which demand supreme hygiene to prevent premature oxidation. Now his oenology-trained daughter Christine insists on adding SO_2 before fermentation, which seems over-cautious; 'She's attached to sulphuring and although she listens to her father, I won't say she obeys,' Bernard explains, adding ruefully: 'You must let the young have their head.'

The reds ferment at 28–32°C, with around 12 days' *cuvaison* followed by a further 5 days maceration with the vats sealed to extract the maximum from the fruit. This deliberately longer vatting time has added a richness and

flesh without compromising the finesse which Bernard and Christine seek in their wines.

Of the Domaine's Pernands, the Ile des Vergelesses, which has a markedly argilo-calcaire soil with a high iron-oxide content, has more structure and thus greater ageing-potential, though less elegance than the straight Pernand. In many ways it is a scaled-down Corton, but with more obvious finesse. The Corton Bressandes, *élévé* in 50% new oak, typically starts life with a deepish colour and firmer structure than most Dubreuil reds, taking several years to show its qualities. If anything, the Corton Perrières has even more colour and complexity, tight to start with but with plenty of elegance underneath.

The 1978 Bressandes and the 1969 Clos du Roi show how well Bernard Dubreuil's wines age. The 1978 had distinctly visceral aromas, mingled with that gorgeous *sous-bois* which so often characterises mature Pinot Noir. When Bernard suggested to some customers – surgeons – tasting the same wine that it seemed to him redolent of viscera, the rebuke came back that it wasn't nearly strong enough for that. Nonetheless the wine does hint at raw meat, with an excellent ripe substructure which makes for a satisfying and most attractive mouthful. The 1969 was, surprisingly, even more youthful – very different in style to the 1978 – slightly *surmature* with quite firm almost tarry undertones – still a relatively immature wine.

The best of the whites are undoubtedly the Clos Berthet (100% Chardonnay) and the Corton-Charlemagne. The Clos, being better exposed than the Domaine's Pernand Village vineyards, has a notch more concentration

allied to old vine fruit. In good vintages Pernand whites tend to develop a hallmark *goût de silex* from the soil, which shows up as an earthy, slightly peachy flavour. The Corton-Charlemagne, from Pernand vines on the Aloxe border, is usually a masculine example of that generally masculine wine – tight, austere in youth, developing a complex nose of charred almonds and lime-blossom with 5–10 years' bottle-age. Bernard laments the fact that so much of this is consumed before it has begun to open out.

Neither whites nor reds are marked by new wood – the Grands Crus never see over 50% and the Villages and Premiers Crus much less. The whites start fermentation in bulk at 20–22°C and are then decanted into cask to finish the transformation.

As for the reds, no SO_2 is added until the first racking when the different casks of each wine are unified. Sulphur levels are further adjusted at second racking and, again, at bottling. All Dubreuil's wines are both fined – egg albumin for the reds and casein for the whites – and plate-filtered.

This is a serious house. Bernard Dubreuil and Christine, who speaks fluent Californian and is also qualified in business studies, are careful vignerons and winemakers. Some of the wines – especially the reds – would benefit from a touch more concentration and Christine might beneficially throw a little of her father's natural caution to the winds, especially in the matter of early, safe, harvesting and systematic, safe filtration – 'a client might return a bottle with a slight deposit'.

Nevertheless, for all its prudence, this is a high-quality Domaine, but one from which it is necessary to pick and choose.

VINEYARD HOLDINGS

Commune	Level	Lieu-dit/Climat	Area	Vine Age	Status
Aloxe	GC	Corton Bressandes	0.75	50	F
Aloxe	GC	Corton Perrières	0.60	45	F
Aloxe	GC	Corton Clos du Roy	1.00	35	F
Aloxe	PC	Les Vercots	0.50	30	F
Aloxe	V	Les Combes/Les Cras	0.50	40	F
Pernand	GC	Corton-Charlemagne	0.76	38	F
Pernand	PC	Ile des Vergelesses	0.73	41	F
Pernand	V	(Several *climats*, W)	1.90	40	F
Pernand	V	Clos Berthet (R and W)	1.50	25	F
Pernand	V	Les Fichots (R)	3.00	45	F
Savigny	PC	Les Vergelesses	3.72	45	F
Beaune	PC	Les Montrevenots	0.30	15	F
Volnay	V	(Several *climats*)	0.50	35	F
Pommard	PC	Les Epenots	0.40	55	F
Pommard	V	(Several *climats*)	0.59	30	F
————	R	(PTG/R/W/Aligoté)	5.44	10–40	F
		Total:	**22.19 ha**		

A stone shelter hut amidst summer vines near Savigny-Lès-Beaune

SAVIGNY-LÈS-BEAUNE

Anyone wanting to escape the waves of determined, eager summer tourists whose loud and incessant babble fills the hotels and restaurants of Beaune, could do worse than make their way a few kilometres north to the pleasant green village of Savigny-lès-Beaune.

Sandwiched in the opening of a peaceful, wooded valley – La Combe de la Fontaine Froide – Savigny offers the visitor tranquil walks, a few small shops, a rather dismal bar/café, modest restaurants and a small hotel, in addition to a splendid 17th-century Château, a Church with a remarkable clock-tower and a clutch of friendly growers.

The settlement of Villa Saviniaco is Gallo-Roman in origin. By the 12th century this had become Savigniaci – sounding like a cross between an exotic pasta dish and an Italian lyric-tenor – whilst further refinements led to Savigny-près-Beaune and Savigny-sous-Beaune before the place finally made up its municipal mind on Savigny-lès-Beaune in 1863.

Two Roman roads, parts of which are still visible, traverse the village, whilst the newer A6 autoroute provides superb elevated views across the vineyards to the distant Bois de Corton from one of its most picturesque stopping-places, which according to a wall-plaque, marks the halfway point between Lille and Marseilles.

The Savigny Village AC covers both red and white wines. The former are also entitled to the AC Côte de Beaune-Villages although, as Savigny becomes better known, this alternative is seldom used by top producers. The AC Savigny vineyards cover some 238.58 ha, a further 144.02 ha being divided into 18 Premiers Crus. The village's 1,500 inhabitants include over 90 growers and 5 négociants, the largest and best known of this quintet being Henri de Villamont and Doudet Naudin.

The river Rhoin – a feeble, half-hearted watercourse – neatly bisects the vineyards. On its northern side, beneath the Bois Noël, lies most of the Village land and a narrow band of 12 Premiers Crus. These latter include: Les Guettes, marked by a distinctive castellated tower, built as a hunter's lookout by Leonce Bocquet who ruined himself restoring the Château de Clos Vougeot; Les Lavières, so called because of the high proportion of 'laves' or shale in its soil; Les Serpentières – probably so named because of the small water-runs which

wriggle through the vineyard and Les Vergelesses (near to Vergy).

The soils vary markedly between *climats* – the flatter, lower slopes are deeper and richer, whilst the sloping hillsides have less generous, but finer soils. The Bois Noël vineyards' privileged southerly exposition ripens grapes a week or more before those on the opposite side of the valley.

There, under the Mont-Battois, lie a further 6 Premiers Crus – including Les Marconnets, Les Peuillets, Les Jarrons and Les Narbantons, marked by a rather functional workers' hut. Here, a less advantageous north-easterly exposure is compounded by some patches of heavy, wet soil, especially around the flatter Les Peuillets.

Savigny is unusual in having two small *Monopole* vineyards, each part of a larger Premier Cru: Albert Morot's La Bataillère – a 1.81 ha plot of 28–45-year-old vines in Les Vergelesses and a Clos until one wall collapsed – and Champ Chevrey, 1.47 ha of 40-year-old vines in the westerly corner of Les Fournaux, belonging to Domaine Tollot-Beaut of Chorey.

Savigny occupies an important place in Burgundian history, thanks chiefly to the innovative Comte de la Loyère, who ran the Côte d'Or Viticultural Society from 1854 to 1879. He is credited with planting vines in straight rows, rather than *en foule*, and with introducing the vineyard plough. He also invented the grape-destalking machine, an early version of which can be seen on the ground floor of the Château, and presided over the prototype straddle-tractor and the first Burgundian vineyard map in 1862. He also entertained at Savigny Dr. Guyot, creator of the now famous pruning system.

Savigny's white wines – on average 3.3% of Village and Premier Cru output – come mainly from Chardonnay vines on limestone and marl soils on the Bouilland side of the commune. Some growers consider that the marls on the upper slopes resemble the soils of Corton-Charlemagne. Pinot Blanc is also allowed, but most goes to make Bourgogne Blanc, growers preferring Chardonnay for its finesse and staying power. Notwithstanding, Domaine Ecard produces a *cuvée* of white Savigny from 100% Pinot Blanc, and Patrick Bize a fine clutch of Bourgogne Blancs, including one from one-third each Chardonnay, Pinots Blanc and Beurot. In general, whites made from vines on *terre à rouge* are altogether less fine and more rustic

than those from more appropriate soils.

Savigny Blanc is underrated. From a decent grower, it can be a delight – with a touch of *goût de silex* and plenty of ripe, fat fruit. Better vintages repay a few years in bottle, emerging to a nutty, rather individual, middle age.

The reds need careful choosing. Whilst lean years can be charmless and rather angular, good vintages from the right Domaines can be finely perfumed, plump and seductive. Styles vary from Tollot-Beaut's pure crushed strawberry Champ-Chevrey and slightly more muscular Lavières, to Doudet-Naudin's thicker, slow evolving 'méthode ancienne' bottlings.

Between these bookends are finely-tuned, mid-weight offerings from Chandon de Briailles, especially attractive in riper vintages, the excellent La Dominode from Bruno Clair (of Marsannay), made predominantly from 90-year-old vines and an overstructured Narbantons from Leroy. The Savignys, and everything else, of Henri de Villamont are overrated, although they have superb vineyards capable of producing fine wine. The finest Savigny of all is Françoise Choppin's Clos la Bataillère, a stylish wine of great class, which ages wonderfully.

Anyone with time to wander should peer through Chandon de Briaille's gates in the Rue Soeur Goby, to admire this fine example of a small 18th-century gentleman's residence, encrusted with the most unusual horticultural sculpture, and its elegant, walled park, laid out by Le Nôtre.

Nearby is the Château, part 13th but mainly 17th-century, sitting in its park flanked incongruously by a squadron of assorted war-planes. In the early 1970s, it was acquired by an English company which immediately removed all its antiques, mostly museum-pieces, to England, without export licences and auctioned them before the French could intervene; a thoroughly shameful episode. It has recently undergone a complete restoration at the hands of its new Japanese owners.

When you have finished visiting, make for the Combe de la Fontaine Froide – either for a picnic in the water-meadows by the Rhoin, or else for a good meal and a fine bottle at the Vieux Moulin in Bouilland. If you have any surplus energy, you could always try scaling one of the vertical limestone overhangs opposite the restaurant.

SCALE 1/20000

Key

Savigny-lès-Beaune Premier Cru

Savigny-lès-Beaune

N

LYON

BEAUNE

Chorey-lès-Beaune

CHOREY-LÈS-BEAUNE

DIJON

RN 74

Les Ratosses

Les Petits Picotins

Les Planchots de la Champagne

Les Planchots du Nord

Grands Picotins

Chorey-lès-Beaune

Les Prévaux

Les Bourgeois

Aux Champs des Pruniers

Les Pimentiers

Aux Champs Chardons

Pré Vaux

Aux Fourches

Les Narbantons

Moutier Amet

Moulin Gombaut

Aux Boutières

Aux Fournaux

Ez Connardises

Aux Grands Liards

Les Bas Liards

Les Lavières

Aux Petits Liards

Moulin Moyne

Les Saucours

Aux Crotots

Pernand-Vergelesses

Basses Vergelesses

Les Charnières

Petits Godeaux

Aux Serpentières

Aux Pointes

Aux Gravains

Les Lavières

Les Lavières

Les Talmettes

Aux Vergelesses

Les Godeaux

Roichottes

Aux Guettes

Aux Clous

Le Village

Pernand-Vergelesses

Combe d'Orange

Aux Guettes

Le Village

Dessus de Moncheneyoy

Guettes

Les Dessus les Vermots

PERNAND-VERGELESSES

Les Goudelettes

Dessus les Goliardes

Les Vermots

Dessus les Vermots

Le Village

Les Vermots

Les Goudelettes

Les Goliardes

BOUILLAND

BEAUNE

BEAUNE

A6

Les Peuillets

Les Peuillets

Bas Marconnets

Les Hauts Marconnets

Les Jarrons

Hauts Jarrons

Redrescul

Les Rouvrettes

300

Beaune

PARIS

300

400

Domaine Simon Bize et Fils

SAVIGNY-LÈS-BEAUNE

Patrick Bize with his new van rouge

Among these is the Domaine Bize. Patrick
Bize, a mildly serious man in his thirties,
with a wry sense of humour and quietly
forceful opinions, is a member of that band of
talented young winemakers who have so
enhanced Burgundy's quality image.

Despite several generations of Bizes at
Savigny, the Domaine really started with
Patrick's grandfather who owned both vines

Until comparatively recently, the status
of a Burgundy Domaine depended
more on the grandeur of its land than
on its winemaking. Today, by contrast, the
estates which excite most attention are often
those making superlative wine from relatively modest vineyard holdings.

and the local butcher's shop – the Savigny
butcher is still 'A. Bize'. His winemaking
skills have been passed from father to son.
Patrick admits that he was a reluctant
vigneron – disliking wine and with no desire
to work in the vineyards or the cellar.
Fortunately, by degrees, he came to like
what he was doing – and almost changed
without noticing it. Neither he nor his father
had any formal training, and the only
members of his immediate family who did –
two uncles who spent some time at the
Lycée Viticole – gave it up after the war as a
bad job.

An intimate knowledge of the characteristics of his 5 Savigny Premier Crus and his
various Village plots, enables Patrick to adapt
his viticulture to the way he feels each will
behave. He paints a strong contrast between
his own attitude and that of wine-growers in
the USA where the winemaker is seen as
determining the quality of the bottle: 'It's
nonsense, just publicity; it isn't Monsieur
Gadget or Madame Machine who makes the
wine, it's the Appellation and the grape; one
should never forget this.'

This 'esprit' suffuses everything he does –
from the flexibility in controlling pests and
diseases – 'we treat as the vine demands,
there are no formulae' – to the way the vines
are pruned and trained: for young vines – up
to 20 years old (!) – *taille en royat* to reduce
yields; after that, the classic *Guyot Simple*.
Practical experience also helps keep the
vines healthy and yields down to 30–40
hl/ha. Knowing the productivity of each plot
enables its regime to be tailored accordingly.
This is not simply a question of reducing
yields but of optimizing the balance of constituents within the grapes themselves.
There is a strict *évasivage* each spring, but
no green-pruning, Patrick prefers controlling
production with his secateurs in March
rather than removing grapes in July, or even
performing a *saigner de cuve* at vinification.
The order of harvesting is critical. Patrick
generally starts with the oldest vines which
tend to be on the more precious rootstocks (Aux Vergelesses) and works backwards – except in 1990 when the opposite
was the case, the young Marconnets vines
having matured more rapidly than the
others.

In the cellars the main concern is to retain
the typicity of each vineyard and vintage.
Each Premier Cru has its own style which
must be preserved along with the character
of the vintage.

The grapes are foot-crushed to liberate the juice and vinified in open wood or enamelled *cuves*. These receive a mixture of whole bunches with stalks from the older vines and partially destemmed grapes from the younger vines. The aim is as long a *cuvaison* as possible – late *chaptalisation* helps here – with a pre-fermentative maceration of some 3–5 days, minimal sulphur (30 cl. of 5% solution per barrel) and a maximum temperature of 32–33°C. 18 days' vatting is not unusual here, in marked contrast with other growers in the commune. This shows in the Domaine's style. Patrick trusts to the indigenous yeast population for the depth and complexity of his wines.

Each *cuvée* is tasted to decide when to decant the free-run wine off the pulp. Patrick distrusts analysis to make decisions for him: 'Numbers are interesting but . . . with numbers you would make a classic, stereo-typed wine – straight from the oenology laboratory; if you want class, you must taste'. In fact, he decants with some 5–6 grams per litre of sugar remaining to further lengthen fermentation.

There is no *débourbage* – 'except in very rich years; it depends on the quality of the vintage'. Contemplating the use of pectolytic enzymes to settle gross lees, Patrick remembered that he had kept some unused in a cupboard for five years, and finding them there decided to use them on the 1990 vintage. This was exceptional as he only normally uses enzymes when a high level of rot threatens clarification and thus the health of the lees.

The Domaine buys its own Nevers wood from 'the best grower in the forest' and dries it at Savigny. It is then delivered to 'the best tonnelier' for coopering. Bize casks are medium charred to avoid excessive toast flavours. Patrick's policy is to use the maximum new wood between decanting from the vat and first racking, ideally after a year on lees. So 50–100% of the Premiers Crus start their *élevage* in new wood (100% in 1988) and the proportion is adjusted after tasting at first racking, sometime between March and September following the vintage, depending when the *malos* finish.

Preparation for bottling follows no routine but is a matter of tasting the wine and deciding what suits best. In general, the wines are unified before fining or filtration, and bottled about 14–18 months after the vintage.

Patrick's excellent whites are fermented in cask – 15% new wood – fined with either fish fining or a mixture of casein/bentonite and bottled after 12–14 months to retain freshness and aroma. His Bourgogne Blanc Champlains is somewhat particular in that it comes from roughly equal proportions of Pinot Blanc, Chardonnay and Pinot Beurot, vinified separately. 20% or so new oak imparts a touch of butteriness and structure,

VINEYARD HOLDINGS

Commune	Level	Lieu-dit/Climat	Area	Vine Age	Status
Savigny	PC	Aux Vergelesses	2.20	40	P
Savigny	PC	Les Fourneaux	1.00	35	P
Savigny	PC	Aux Guettes	0.48	30	F
Savigny	PC	Les Talmettes	0.80	23	P
Savigny	PC	Les Marconnets	0.60	23	P
Savigny	PC	Les Serpentières	0.35	36	F
Savigny	V	Les Grands Liards	1.57	1939–82	P
Savigny	V	(Several climats)	5.20	25	P
Savigny	V	(Blanc, several parcels)	1.00	10	V
Aloxe	V	Le Suchot	1.00	10	F
Savigny	R	Les Perrières (Bourg. R.)	2.00	25	P
Savigny	R	Les Perrières (Bourg. W.)	1.00	30	P
Savigny	R	Les Champlains (Bourg. W.)	2.30	12	F
Gevrey	GC	Latricières-Chambertin	0.32	35	F
Total:			**19.82 ha**		

whilst the Pinots Beurot and Blanc give a distinctly floral element to the aroma. A second Bourgogne Blanc, Les Perrières, from older Chardonnay vines planted on stony ground, produces a wine of greater weight and matter, although with somewhat less obvious elegance.

The Savigny Blanc *cuvée*, from the Les Pimentiers vineyard, is 100% Chardonnay. Its characteristic is an earthy *goût de silex* – a variety of silica – often found in white Savignys. Generally quite fresh and sappy, it is perhaps something of an (easily) acquired taste.

The Domaine produces a fine range of red Savignys – six Premier Crus, one individual Village *lieu-dit*, Les Grands Liards, and a standard Village. In general the style is for quite meaty, structured wines which mature well over a decade or so in good vintages. The Talmettes is probably the most forward of the range – soft, fruity and attractive.

The Vergelesses (Savigny, not Pernand) comes from seven different parcels spread over 2.20 ha of poor, rocky vineyard which produces a wine with greater lightness and finesse than the other Premiers Crus. A plot of 40+-year-old vines adds weight and *charpente* to the ensemble. The 1993 vintage, tasted in 1995, had the fine deep colour so characteristic of the vintage, a nose which, although relatively closed, promised well, and a marvellous, rich silkiness on the palate, sustained by a layer of ripish, balanced tannins; not massively structured, but a fine, confident wine, needing 5 years plus to deliver its riches.

The Village Grands Liards is often deliciously soft and seductive with plenty of succulent, plump fruit and in good vintages an element of almost creamy richness, which is most attractive. Premier Cru quality in 1985, 1990 and 1993 – a wine to lay down in magnums for 5–10 years.

The Savigny Marconnets vineyard lies just beneath the Autoroute lay-by (for the wine-loving motorist, one of the most appealing places anywhere to pause and picnic).

Separated from Beaune Marconnets by only these few metres of tarmac, it shares its geology. The result is a wine more in style and structure Beaune than of Savigny – aromas of *fruits rouges*, quite fat and round on the palate with plenty of grip and length.

The Les Guettes – from the opposite end of the Appellation – is different in character – more in finesse, almost lacy in texture, though not lacking in fruit and depth. Its portion of new wood gives it a harmonious scaffolding of creamy oak. Les Fourneaux, which adjoins Les Lavières at the Pernand end of the vignoble, is the most forward of the Premiers Crus and shares something of the style and rondeur of Les Guettes.

A sixth Premier Cru, Serpentières, was added to the collection for the 1993 vintage. This, just below Guettes, combines the broad Corton-ish shoulders of Marconnets and the finesse of Guettes, with 36-year-old vines contributing to overall concentration. Stepping well off habitual Bize rails, a goodly patch of Grand Cru Latricières-Chambertin arrived for the 1995 vintage.

There have been unjustified rumblings recently about uneven quality and suggestions that the Domaine's size is incompatible with real control. It should be remembered that Savigny lies at the foot of a combe and to the west, disadvantages which show in marginal vintages when both reds and whites can lack depth. This is not a criticism of Bize, rather a comment on Savigny's geographical situation which even the most talented of winemakers is powerless to influence. Also, the house style is for finesse not size (if you want that, Maurice Ecard is the right shop) – something which many critics seem to have forgotten.

Patrick and his father have recently bought the house next door, destined to become the *cuverie*. Although this has to be paid for, the Bize's prices are more than reasonable, so anyone searching for sound quality, rather than grand Appellations, should visit this fine Domaine.

Domaine Capron-Manieux

SAVIGNY-LÈS-BEAUNE

This is an exciting small Domaine of high quality, created in 1974 by Jean-Marie Capron and his attractive, rather shy, wife Nicole Charcousset. After renting vines in Savigny, they made their first land purchase in 1977 – pine forest, which they felled to plant vines. Now, with some Aligoté in nearby Bouze-lès-Beaune, some Pommard and additional Savigny, taken as inheritance from Nicole's parents in exchange for their house which went to her late sister, Madame François Tollot, the Domaine has reached 6.88 hectares.

Jean-Marie admits to an ignorance of viti-culture when he arrived in Burgundy: 'I had-n't touched a vine in my life.' With no career plan, apart from a liking for the outdoor life, he enrolled at Beaune's Lycée Viticole, emerging in 1965 with a Diploma and a strong desire to begin on his own account. Before embarking upon any such commit-ment, he spent four years gaining practical experience, one with Michel Pont in Volnay and three with Michel Voarick in Aloxe-Corton.

Jean-Marie's wines have great delicacy in both colour and nose, coupled with firm, ripe, almost mouthwatering fruit and con-siderable style. His desire – to emphasise fruit and finesse – leads him to prefer, for example, Corton Bressandes to Clos du Roi, for its accentuated perfume, although techni-cally, the latter is probably the greater.

In the cellars proceedings are traditional: there is no destalking, rather the bunches are sulphured and lightly crushed by foot. The stalks aerate the pulp and thus help to keep the fermentation temperature within sensible bounds, since the Domaine has no cooling apparatus to deal with *musts* which threaten the desired 35°C maximum.

The secret of the great elegance of Jean-Marie's wines lies partly in the short *cuvaison* – just 8–10 days – including two days of pre-fermentive maceration. When the tempera-ture falls to about 28°C, the wines are *débourbés* for 2–3 days and put into casks, (20% new) with no special preference for oak: 'It's the tonnelier who chooses,' Jean-Marie admits with a cynical laugh.

15–18 months after the harvest, the wines are racked again and lightly plate-filtered be-fore being bottled. Those in new wood remain there only up to the first racking (after 1 year) to preserve freshness and avoid marking the delicate fruit with excessive wood characteris-tics; this also releases casks for the new crop. The white wines also have 20% new oak.

and 18 months in cask before bottling. To finance the two vintages always in the cellars, Jean-Marie sells most Aligoté and some Savigny and Pernand Blanc *sur pressoir* to négociants. These latter, from 100% Chardonnay, are delicious, best young or else after 5-8 years when they become quite fat and somewhat rustic, accompanying simply cooked dishes to perfection.

Of the 1.63 ha of Savigny Rouge, the grapes from hillsides and plain are fermented separately before unification into a single *cuvée*, whilst those from Pimentiers, acquired in 1989, are also vinified separately.

Deceptively light colours – the Pimentiers is a shade deeper than the straight Savigny – should fool no-one into thinking that the wines lack substance: far from it. They have abundant, mouth-watering fruit and finesse, the Pimentiers having the slightest hint of white pepper, or 'Piments'!

The Premier Cru Les Peuillets – a vine-yard half Village and half Premier Cru – expresses its gravelly, sandy subsoil in a firmer structure (20% or so of new wood here) than Pimentiers, with aromas of *fruits rouges* and wild berries – generally quite powerful and attractive. Les Lavières is gen-erally reckoned among the Savigny top Premiers Crus – a wine from predominantly rocks (laves), hardish to start with but with greater longevity than the Peuillets which sets out with more obvious fruit.

Jean-Marie and Nicole Capron's wines are not for early drinking. Even in good vintages (e.g. 1993) they taste austere and unflattering – inclusion of all the stems doesn't make for youthful charm. But, given half a decade or more in bottle, they transform – red and white alike – into beauties.

A decade on, the 1985s are only just begin-ning to show their real character with deli-cious layers of ripe, soft fruit setting off spicy, vegetal and chocolate flavours and old vines adding an extra note of concentration. Sadly, in 1985 February frosts wreaked disaster here, as elsewhere along the Côte, with temperatures plummeting to minus 27°C for several days. The vineyards on the flatter land nearer the village suffered most; in Les Peuillets, which marches with the Paris-Lyon autoroute, Jean-Marie harvested only 600 out of 15,000 vines and had to grub up over half the vineyard.

Nicole and her husband work their small Domaine without help – except at harvest time. They are dedicated to quality and con-sequently spend little time away. Even their only daughter had to wait to make her appearance until they were established enough to have time to spare to look after her. Their 12,000 bottles are eagerly snapped up by a loyal following of importers and private customers. A top-notch Domaine.

The colourful Caprons – Jean-Marie and Nicole – among their unpruned vines above Savigny

VINEYARD HOLDINGS

Commune	Level	Lieu-dit/Climat	Area	Vine Age	Status
Savigny	PC	Les Lavières	0.18	15	M
Savigny	PC	Les Peuillets	0.28	7 and 40	F
Savigny	V	Les Pimentiers	0.31	35	P
Savigny	V	(Various climats)	1.55	15-50	P/M/F
Savigny	V	(White)	0.66	5-50	P/M/F
Pernand	V	Les Belles Filles (W)	0.39	9 and 10	F
Pommard	V	En Boeuf	0.11	5	P
Savigny/ Bouze	R	(Aligoté)	2.58	35-45	P
Bouze	R	(Hes. Ctes. de Beaune Chard.)	0.26	5	P
Savigny	R	(Hes. Ctes. de Beaune Rouge)	0.18	14	P
Savigny	R	(Hes. Ctes. de Beaune Chard.)	0.38	5	P
Total:			**6.88 ha**		

Domaine Girard-Vollot

SAVIGNY-LÈS-BEAUNE

As with other communes of the Côte d'Or, Savigny has a multiplicity of vignerons producing wines in a variety of styles. Of these, Domaine Girard-Vollot falls somewhere between the elegance of Capron-Charousset and the more structured, denser offerings of Pavelot and Bize. This is a sizeable Domaine. From a total of 18 ha, 8.5 are dedicated to Savigny Rouge, with the remainder spread across Savigny Premiers Crus Peuillets, Rouvrettes and Narbantons, with a little Savigny Blanc, some Pernand-Vergelesses Premier Cru and Aloxe-Corton, with some baseline Aligoté, Bourgogne Rouge and Blanc.

The Girards are one of Savigny's oldest vigneron families – tracing a founding Jean Girard back to 1529. Today, the Domaine is run by Georges Girard and his sons Philippe and Jean-Jacques, who started work at the formative age of 16, and of whom Georges is wonderfully proud. Girard Père is a charmer with infectious good humour and short grey hair which stands on end as if connected to an electricity supply of opposing polarity. Now in his late sixties, he exudes contented energy as he rolls out of the courtyard on his gleaming new tractor.

Clones, which came late to Girard vineyards, in 1985, are viewed by Georges with undisguised misgiving, although he believes they will probably make very good old vines. Faced with their vigour, he prunes very short indeed – 3–5 eyes – and prefers to ébourer strictly rather than to saigner his cuves. 'That is the essential principle, take off the grapes at the beginning,' he affirms. The Girards are clearly paying much more attention now to fruit quality than a few years ago.

Vinification proceeds in cement with about one third of the stalks at up to 32–33°C. Cuvaison is shortish – 10–12 days in total and for no articulated reason the cuves are yeasted to avoid any pre-fermentive maceration. According to George, long cuvaison extracts too much tannin, produces more bad tastes than good, and masks the fruit underneath. 'We don't want wines which won't be drinkable for 30 years.' The Girard style is for vins de garde which start with firm structures and thereafter age well over 10–15 years.

The wines spend some 18 months in cask – 25–33% new Allier or Nevers oak for the Premier Cru reds and Vosges for the white Savigny. The provision of new casks 'depends on what we have'. The economics of providing new casks for a modestly priced wine differ from those governing the élevage of Grands Crus. As Georges Girard sagely puts it, 'The casks for Chambertin are the same price as those for Savigny.'

The cold cellar means that malos can take up to a year to complete – 'we let nature do its work.' A low ambient cellar temperature also means that traditional fining is unlikely to work – 'then we have to filter again' – so the wines are just given a single Kieselguhr filtration to clean them up before bottling. Reflecting increased demand, there are now four very respectable white wines – some more Savigny and a fine, minerally Pernand Blanc having been recently added to the Bourgognes Chardonnay and Aligoté. These are fermented in bulk at low temperature (22°C) and spend about a year in cask (20% new wood) before bottling.

The Savigny Premiers Crus, Rouvrettes, Peuillets, Narbantons and most recently Serpentières and Lavières, vie for top billing in the Girard cellar. The sandy soils of Les Peuillets give its wine more stuffing and finesse than the straight Savigny, but a shade less structure than either Rouvrettes or Narbantons, with a nose of coffee which blossoms out into a ripe open wine after 5–10 years of age. This is generally bottled last, to encourage its tannins to soften out.

Rouvrettes, on steeply sloping land with poor soil, tends to have more acidity and greater finesse, when young – more typically Savigny than Peuillets. The Narbantons, just below the excellent Les Dominodes, is somewhere in between in style – more corsé than Les Peuillets, with a deeper colour and tighter structure, but with somewhat less finesse than the Rouvrettes.

The Serpentières comes from half-century-old vines, and a vineyard full of springs – the serpentine water rivulets give the name. It is generally one of the more elegant and finely structured Savigny Premiers Crus. Les Lavières, from 45-year-old vines on rocky ground, combines delicacy with acidity and a solid structure; a wine which needs keeping at least 5 years – 10+ in 1990 and 1993.

These are wines of structure and interest. The Girards dislike large yields – their own average 40–45 hl/ha – arguing that Burgundy is not made for that. However, even with moderate cropping, their 10 ha of Village land produce far too much for them to handle in bottle, so half is sold to négociants. The Premiers Crus are all Domaine-bottled and marketed.

Contrary to general belief, there is no undue hurry to drink Savigny Rouge – or Blanc. If they are made 'à l'ancienne', as with Girard-Vollot, they will keep well for a decade or more. The advent of Jean-Jacques and Philippe has seen an increase in quality. These wines are carefully made and well worth investigating.

The Mairie and town fountain at Savigny are guarded by a regiment of pollarded trees

VINEYARD HOLDINGS

Commune	Level	Lieu-dit/Climat	Area	Vine Age	Status
Savigny	PC	Les Peuillets	1.98	25	P
Savigny	PC	Les Rouvrettes	0.47	45	P
Savigny	PC	Les Narbantons	0.40	20	P
Savigny	PC	Les Lavières	0.33	45	P
Savigny	PC	Les Serpentières	0.50	50	P
Savigny	V	(Several climats)	8.40	5–40	M/P
Savigny	V	(Blanc)	0.81	15	F
Savigny	R	(Bourg. R./Perrières)	0.87	20	P
Savigny	R	(Bourgogne Blanc)	0.61	10	P
Pernand	PC	(Rouge)	0.45	65	P
Pernand	V	(Blanc)	0.80	8	P
Aloxe	V		0.39	35	P
Pernand	R	(Bourgogne Aligoté)	1.00	15	P
	R	(Bourgogne Rouge)	0.80	17	P
Total:			**17.81 ha**		

Domaine Chandon de Briailles

SAVIGNY-LÈS-BEAUNE

R arely in Burgundy can one honestly say of a Domaine that the beauty of its architecture matches that of its wines. Chandon de Briaille is a notable, and welcome, exception.

By itself, the Rue Soeur Goby, tucked away at the back of Savigny, is not by any stretch of the imagination picturesque. However, halfway along, a gap in the buildings makes room for a modest pair of stone pillars giving on to a splendid courtyard, at the far end of which is an imposing and finely-proportioned Manor House. Built at the beginning of the 18th century and now classified as a historical monument, this is pure Louis XIVth. Classical in proportion, simple of line, it was once described as 'an 18th-century extravagance'. As it stands there surveying its visitors, it seems to be saying: 'Voila, here is style, here is elegance, here is a fine Gentleman's residence'.

The only note of ill-proportion is struck by two tall asymmetrical brick chimneys grafted on to either side of the house. They seem like later additions, being far too large for their apparent purpose and give the impression of an immense pair of utilitarian handles by which the entire house might be lifted and rotated for an occasional change of view.

Behind the house is a small park laid out by the famous landscape designer, Le Nôtre – creator of Versailles and other important French gardens. Pleasantly wooded for shade in the summer, and with low-cropped box hedges interspersed with narrow gravel paths, its air of formality is perfectly in keeping with the house itself. Until recently, the far end of the park was the province of the family pony, but its proclivity for further cropping the hedges and eating the vegetables caused it to be stabled elsewhere.

In contrast to the clean classicism of the house itself, the front pillars, park walls and every conceivable parapet and lintel are decorated with a curious, but attractive, species of ornery. Consisting of collages of rough-hewn stonework, this gives the appearance of ancient sandstone statuary which has haphazardly eroded away over the centuries. The family for whom all these delights are laid out are the de Nicolays who have owned the Domaine since 1834. Count Aymar-Claude de Nicolay, a Paris-based property dealer, inherited it from his grandmother, Countess Chandon de Briailles. The Count, though proud of his Domaine, is not especially interested in wine. The passion that is currently driving the estate to new peaks of quality is that of his wife Nadine, who left Paris to take charge in Savigny in 1984, when it became clear that the Domaine was badly in need of attention, and of her slim, dark-haired daughter, Claude.

Nadine, who knew next to nothing about viticulture or vinification applied herself assiduously to her new task. According to Claude, her mother, having finished with the kids, needed something to occupy herself. Vinifying her husband's wine and looking after the vineyards came as an ideal solution. Between them, Claude and her mother have completely transformed a mediocre estate into a top-class property with wine to match. Claude, with an oenological and viticultural Diploma at Dijon, finished her studies with 'une année sublime' in New Zealand and Oregon. Since returning to Savigny, she has put a great deal of intelligent thought into the Domaine's wines and is becoming a fine winemaker in her own right. Day-to-day care of the wines and cellars is in the indispensable hands of Jean-Claude Bouveret, a short, completely bald man in his forties, known to everyone, including himself, as Kojak.

The vineyards cover 13.6 ha. The Savignys consist of Village and Premiers Crus Fournaux and Lavières. In Pernand, there are Premiers Crus Basses Vergelesses and nearly half the entire Ile des Vergelesses, which produces both red and white wine. The Aloxe is mainly Grand Cru including some rare Corton Blanc. Altogether a fine, medium-sized estate.

The vineyards are carefully tended. Nadine and Claude spend much of their time outside, and it is not remotely surprising to

The Domaine's impressive headquarters in the Rue Soeur Goby

find one or both wrapped up in old clothes, cheerfully pruning on a freezing winter's morning. The de Nicolays prefer to prune when it is humid, since the wood is easier to bend and there is thus less risk of breaking a shoot and losing a year's fruit.

Since Nadine de Nicolay took charge, much greater emphasis has been put on replacing individual vines to maintain a high average vine age, rather than larger scale replanting, with a preference for *sélection massale* over clones. A parcel of Bressandes on 10 cms of topsoil, replanted as recently as 1984, was found to have a disturbingly high incidence of *eutypiose* and had to be grubbed up and replanted anew. This disease is virtually undetectable for six years or so, and once infected, vines rarely survive.

During the spring and early summer the vines are stripped of any double shoots and excess buds. Just after *véraison*, usually in August, any excess bunches are removed to further limit production.

To complete the green work, the vineyards are summer-pruned two or three times to limit leaf production and to clear space round the ripening bunches. If the foliage is left to grow high, it improves sugar production and thus reduces the need for *chaptalisation*. In most years summer-pruning also removes *verus* – the second growth of grapes. In 1990 the quantity of *verus* almost equalled that of the first sortie, so removal was essential to avoid the vine dissipating energy in useless grape-production.

A brochure produced by the de Nicolays tells you that the heart of the Domaine is located in the 'fermenting rooms, winemaking plants and cellars'. These annexes flank the house on both sides of the courtyard, and being of contemporary construction, blend unobtrusively with it. The 12th-century cask cellars are particularly fine, being of rare, low pillar-vaulted design. Here the wines mature in perfect tranquillity.

The vinification which precedes this is relatively straightforward, with the sole peculiarity of a 5–6 day intra-pellicular pre-fermentive maceration at 18°C for the red grapes to maximise glycerol extraction. Although only the young-vine fruit is destalked, there is no deliberate crushing, in order to keep the maximum amount of whole bunches. In prolific years, the *cuves* are *saignéd*. Thereafter, fermentation proceeds with temperatures peaking at around 30°C, and with two pump-ings-over and two human *pigéages* each day. Towards the end, the *cuves* are blanketed

with nitrogen and ferment for 2–3 days at 25°C to macerate and ferment out any remaining sugar. *Cuvaison* thus totals 15–20 days.

In 1990 Claude decided to ferment a *cuvée* of Ile des Vergelesses at 25°C to see what a below-average temperature produced. The result was a wine of great finesse – light, stylish but lacking in real depth and stuffing. Nadine intends her pre-fermentive maceration and low temperature fermentation to produce wines which emphasise elegance rather than tannic robustness. She argues that if you ferment at too high a temperature you extract harsh, herbaceous tannins, especially if you don't destalk.

The reds spend 18–24 months in cask, entirely in wood – from Méo Camuzet (qv) – which has already been broken in with red wine. There used to be up to 50% new oak but this was felt to compromise the wines' purity and typicity: 'We're in the Côte de Beaune,' Claude reminds you.

The *malos* tend to happen slowly in these cold cellars – 10–12 months is normal – with first racking only occurring just before the new vintage. Claude sees the delay as beneficial, in that it refines the wine's aromas and structure. The lots are then assembled Cru by Cru, pumped from their casks with or without air, depending on their development, and returned to cask for a further 8–12 months. The Premiers Crus are normally kept for 18 months, the Grands Crus for 22–24 before bottling which takes place after – if necessary – egg-white fining and Kieselguhr filtration; the ideal is neither. Since 1980, all Chandon de Briaille production is sold in bottle, and recent years have seen a considerable improvement in overall quality and consistency. The red wines, whilst often deceptively light in colour, are never heavily structured. One might be tempted to suppose that they lack fruit; nothing could be further from the truth.

The Savignys and Pernands are wines of considerable finesse. As one would expect, the Premiers Crus have more depth than the Village wines, although not necessarily more depth of colour. The Savigny Les Fourneaux from heavier, limestone soil, is usually more *corsé* than the Lavières, which comes from less profound soil containing more rock and stone. On the palate, the Lavières has a distinctively mineral flavour with a good concentration of fruit from its 40-year-old vines. The 1993, from just 15 hl/ha, is exceptional – so little and so good that Claude intends to bottle it entirely in magnums.

The two red Pernands present a striking contrast: clay soils make the Basses Vergelesses distinctively tannic – the de Nicolays refer to it as their 'petit Corton'; a wine to keep for several years in better vintages. The Ile des Vergelesses, from white soils (60:40 limestone:clay), has much

greater finesse and considerable aromatic intensity – strongly fruit-based, sometimes almost floral. This *terroir*, and its mainly 60-year-old vines, give abundantly rich, silky fruit, with a characteristic seasoning of Pernand spiciness – more accessible and less of a keeper perhaps than the Basses Vergelesses. According to the Domaine, this wine is particularly appreciated by the female gender'. Generally, the Chandon Pernands evolve more slowly than its Savignys. A 1959 Ile des Vergelesses was still gloriously ripe and generous in early 1991.

The Domaine's Corton vines are all relatively young, that is to say under 30. However, the wines they produce rarely lack concentration or depth of flavour. The Maréchaudes – from 16- and 21-year-old vines – tends to evolve more rapidly than the other Grands Crus. The 1993, ready for bottling in 1995, had a definite aroma component of new oak (although, of course, none was used), and an exuberantly expressive amalgam of vanilla and *sous-bois*; a broad, full-flavoured wine on a firm tannic base although somewhat lacking in acidity – yard-stick Corton.

The Clos du Roi's finer, more limestone-based soil is reflected in a wine with greater delicacy than one normally expects from a Corton; in fact, more Pernand than Corton. In good vintages this comes through as a crushed *fruits rouges* tone with muscle and power; a wine needing ten years to mature.

The Bressandes is the most powerful of all the Cortons – a wine of depth and presence. Deeply coloured for a Chandon de Briailles wine, with a nose of *fruits sauvages* when young which slowly develops a marvellous complexity of truffle and *sous-bois* aromas. The young wine tends to a lean backbone of tannins and acidity which ensures it considerable longevity. Claude admits that Cortons' tendency to absorb oxygen rapidly and to become volatile makes them difficult to handle. Both susceptibilities result from low acidity, in turn the consequence of an excess

of acid-munching potassium in the soils.

At present, there are only two Chandon de Briailles whites: a Pernand Blanc, made from 11- and 12-year-old vines in Les Vergelesses, and a rare Corton Blanc, from three parcels of 15- and 30-year-old vines in *climats* Chaumes and Bressandes. (This latter is not Corton-Charlemagne, being made from Chardonnay planted on red wine soils.) A patch of Corton-Charlemagne – 11 ares of young vines in the Ladoix *climat Renardes* – was bought in 1995. Until the vines are old enough, the fruit is being amalgamated with the Pernand. The grapes are pressed in a new Bucher pneumatic press – as different from the old Vaslin as 'day from night', without any *maceration pelliculaire*. The juice is fermented in 50% new oak – pre-washed with hot water and coarse salt to remove the most aggressive tannins – and 50% in second-year white Pernand casks, at 20°C for 10–15 days. *Élevage* has been extended from 15 to around 20 months and fining and filtration eliminated, where possible; the 1990s and 1993s had neither treatment, the 1991s and 1992s were simply fined.

The Pernand blanc is a ripe, fat, peachy, greengagey sort of wine, slightly rustic perhaps, but with an attractive and marked *goût de terroir* and plenty of guts and style. It is best drunk young or else kept till after its fifth birthday.

The Corton Blanc is equally individual, showing more aromatic complexity, acidity and power than the Pernand. It has the feel, structure and length of a Corton-Charlemagne, balanced by a splendid overlay of mildly exotic ripe fruit. There are only some 2,000 bottles of each.

Not content with a slow, deliberate, evolution in winemaking, Claude has changed the colour, size and style of the Domaine's labels – nothing flash, but nonetheless a Domaine de Briailles, a minor revolution. She and Nadine de Nicolay have made remarkable strides in the last decade. Chandon de Briailles is now making top-class Burgundy.

VINEYARD HOLDINGS

Commune	Level	Lieu-dit/Climat	Area	Vine Age	Status
Aloxe	GC	Corton Chaumes (V)	0.12	1980	P
Aloxe	GC	Corton Clos du Roi	0.46	1961/86	P
Aloxe	GC	Corton Bressandes (Pinot)	1.76	1962/75/84	P
Aloxe	GC	Corton Bressandes (Chardonnay)	0.14	1980	P
Aloxe	GC	Corton Les Maréchaudes	0.40	1975/80	P
Aloxe	PC	Les Valozières	0.29	1988/89	P
Pernand	PC	Ile des Vergelesses	3.33	1938–1986	P
Pernand	PC	Les Basses Vergelesses	1.27	1954	P
Pernand	(Blanc)	Les Vergelesses	1.00	1988	P
Savigny	PC	Les Fourneaux	1.60	1956/61	P
Savigny	PC	Les Lavières	2.61	1955	P
Savigny	V		0.50	1955	P
Ladoix	GC	Corton Charlemagne (Renardes)	0.11	1990	P
Total:			**13.59 ha**		

Domaine Maurice Ecard

SAVIGNY-LÈS-BEAUNE

Maurice Ecard is a large, cheerful character whose Domaine, with five red and one white Premiers Crus, is an ideal starting point for exploring the *terroirs* of Savigny. Moreover, his wines are among the best in the commune – traditionally vinified, quite solid to start with, but with plenty of stuffing and structure and thus, excellent ageing potential.

The Domaine operates out of a large, rambling set of 19th-century buildings in Savigny's main street – Rue Chanson-Maldant. This is home to Maurice and his maternal aunt (97) – all, apparently, in the pink of health and living proof of the restorative powers of hearty red and white Savigny. Ecards have been in Savigny since the Revolution (1789) and are set to remain, as Maurice has three adult sons who have now joined him in the Domaine. 'It's hard work, you know,' he explains, leaning pleasantly on a cask at the end of a day's spraying, 'we can't knock off at 5 – the vines keep us all there until late evening, and then there's the housework to do.'

Life is made no easier by the self-imposed policy of making all their own grafts. These are a *sélection massale* from a Savigny Village mother vine, itself selected from Tollot-Beaut vineyards at Chorey by Maurice's father. With a highish average vine age, yields are reasonable (42 hl/ha in 1993, 35 hl/ha in 1994). In 1993, Maurice, seeing the prospect of a large crop, took the risk of putting copper-based Bordeaux mixture on his vines just before flowering to encourage *coulure* and *millerandage*. 'It worked,' he admits with a broad grin, 'but it could have been disaster. My Serpentières is black, black – you'll see.'

Indeed it is, as are several other of the 1993s. Not content with small, naturally concentrated berries, Maurice likes a highish fermentation temperature (35°C) for colour, some stems and some whole bunches in the vats, and plenty of *pigeage*: 'Oh là!, I really believe in that. He used to jump into the vats himself, but now his sons do the treading. 'It's very tiring, and there isn't much oxygen around.'

The house style follows Maurice's preference for relatively sturdy wines – the expression of *terroir* comes first, with vine age and yield playing their part. 'Then add the sun.... and the vigneron: don't forget him.'

Despite its atypical colour, the triple black Serpentières is the most typically Savigny of the Premiers Crus. Tightly structured and quite toughly tannic, it has an underlying suppleness and potentially greater aromatic complexity than the others. It comes from a band of vineyards on the Pernand-Vergelesses side of Savigny which are generally considered to produce wines which emphasise elegance, whereas those nearer Beaune show more breadth and muscle.

Maurice Ecard's Peuillets, Jarrons and Narbentons (unusually, he spells it with an 'e'), are both *côté* Beaune. The first is the broadest in flavour, the second has a marginally firmer, more obviously tannic structure and the third (apparently named after the original planters, who came up the Rhône from Narbonne), has a more solid, concentrated base. Each is fine, in its own way, but distinctively individual.

Apart from a bottling for the Dutch – 'who want something cheaper' – the Savigny Villages is sold *en négoce* to give Maurice time to concentrate on his four 'stars' and his sought-after Savigny Haut Jarrons Blanc. This unusual wine comes entirely from old-vine Pinot Blanc, originally selected from Henri Gouge's Nuits La Perrière vineyard. In 1994 it ripened to 13+ degrees of potential alcohol, giving a blockbusting, but low-acid wine – fortunately, atypically blowsy. Not perhaps a wine for the 90-year-old Ecard generation! This is a top-class Savigny.

Maurice Ecard (right) relaxing with a client after a day's pruning

VINEYARD HOLDINGS

Commune	Level	Lieu-dit/Climat	Area	Vine Age	Status
Savigny	V	(Pinot; Several parcels and *climats*)	2		
Savigny	PC	Les Serpentières	3	40	P
Savigny	PC	Les Narbentons	2	40	P
Savigny	PC	Les Jarrons	2	50	P
Savigny	PC	Les Peuillets	2	35	P
Savigny	PC	Les Cloux	1	30	P
Savigny	PC	Les Hauts Jarrons (Blanc)	0	50	P
Savigny	R	(Bourgogne Rouge)	0	18	P
Total:			**13.00 ha**		

Domaine Jean-Marc Pavelot

SAVIGNY-LÈS-BEAUNE

Savigny-lès-Beaune

Jean-Marc Pavelot's wines have improved considerably in recent years and are now in Savigny's top league. They used to be so tannic and stalky that it was difficult to discern what, if anything, was underneath – wines which needed years of maturing to come back into any sort of balance. Now, things have changed: there are less stalks (up to 25% for the Premiers Crus depending on the wine and vintage) and a few days of cool pre-fermentive maceration. It also appears that *pigéage* has been reduced and that there is less, but better, press-wine. All this makes for finer, better balanced, readily accessible wines.

The only Pavelot white is a peachy, minerally, Savigny Blanc, from vines partly on river alluviums which give structure, and partly on limestone (near Bouilland) which imparts nerve and acidity. The juice is mainly fermented in cask and left on its lees until bottling at around 11 months – any longer and it would start to dry out. This is a wine to buy in vintages for its ripe plump fruit, balanced by a good fresh zing – for drinking young or moderate ageing.

The rest of the range comprises a straight red Savigny, one Pernand and five Savigny Premiers Crus. A high average vine age and modest, but not exaggeratedly low yields (average 35–40 hl/ha in the Premiers Crus), makes for well-structured, concentrated wines. A touch of cold maceration, then 12–15 days' vatting at highish temperatures followed by 12–15 months in wood (10–25% new for the Crus), result in attractive wines which start out quite hard and firm but develop well with a few years in bottle.

The heart of the Savigny Village *cuvée* is the produce of 50–70-year-old vines, assembled from three separate parcels. Only 10% of stems are left in the *cuves*, giving an open, supple wine with real depth and a firm, balanced structure.

The Savigny Premiers Crus start with Les Peuillets – from a flattish band of stony soils under the Autoroute du Soleil. In character, this reflects its proximity to Beaune – acter, plenty of *fruits rouges*, good acidity and altogether quite a broad and muscular feel. This is perhaps the least typically Savigny of the six and one to avoid in drought years, as its efficient drainage tends to over-stress the vines. Jean-Marc usually bottles this before the following vintage to conserve its softer, open fruit.

The Narbantons – also from the *secteur* Beaune – is equally broad and fleshy, but is more *fruits noirs* in character, with greater elegance, more grippy *mâche* and a firmer, tannic structure (up to 20% of stems left in these vats). In good vintages it has an attractive depth and a touch of spice.

Two Premiers Crus come from the 'classic' band above Jean-Marc's house on the Pernand side of the village – Guettes and Gravains. It is this sector which is generally considered as producing the most typical wines of the Appellation. Here, the vineyard is steep, with thin stony limestone soils giving onto rock, a *terroir* producing livelier, more aromatic and noticeably less-structured wines than Narbantons or Peuillets. Both the 1990 and 1993 Guettes showed length and class, with good acidity and firmish tannins supporting a substantial layer of ripe fruit. The 1990 was beginning to open out – a softish, rich wine with length and complexity and just a touch of stem tannins to absorb.

Gravains is an unusual Premier Cru in that its soils are mostly scree-derived, eroded from the Combe d'Orange above. In style and quality it approaches Guettes, with an emphasis on aroma and palate finesse, soft tannins and high acidity.

Although situated in the *secteur* Beaune, La Dominode is capable of producing some of the finest Savigny. In fact, it forms part of the Jarrons vineyard named after an erstwhile owner, Monsieur Domino, and has five other principal proprietors apart from Jean-Marc Pavelot: Bruno Clair (q.v.), Louis Jadot (q.v.), Leroy (q.v.), Chanson and Maurice Écard (q.v.). The soil is mainly sandy clay which produces well-constituted grapes with excellent colour, aroma and flavour potential. The result is a complete wine, with good concentration and plenty of *charpente*, needing longer than the rest to reach maturity.

Jean-Marc Pavelot's Savignys are true *vins de terroir* rather than simply *vins de fruit*. The Pinot Noir is there, but it is the individuality of each *climat* which makes this range of wines so interesting. Different from Bize, Écard or Capron – but fine nonetheless.

VINEYARD HOLDINGS

Commune	Level	Lieu-dit/Climat	Area	Vine Age	Status
Savigny	V	(Several climats)	5.07	10–50	P
Savigny	PC	Aux Guettes	1.48	30	P
Savigny	PC	La Dominode	2.21	40	P
Savigny	PC	Les Narbantons	0.36	60	P
Savigny	PC	Les Peuillets	0.45	50	P
Savigny	PC	Aux Gravains	0.60	50	P
Savigny	V	(Blanc)	0.83	30	P
Pernand	PC	Les Vergelesses	0.61	20	P
Total:			11.61 ha		

The vineyards in springtime

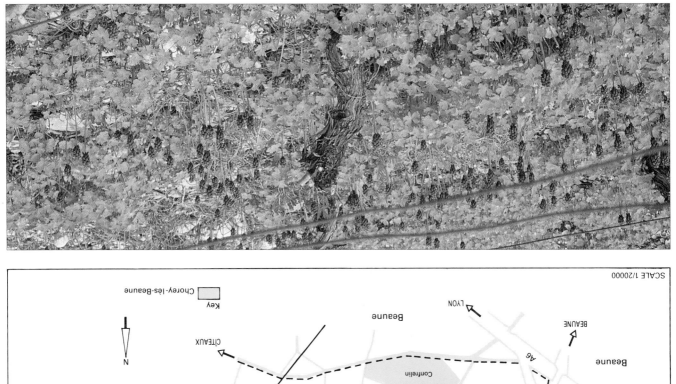

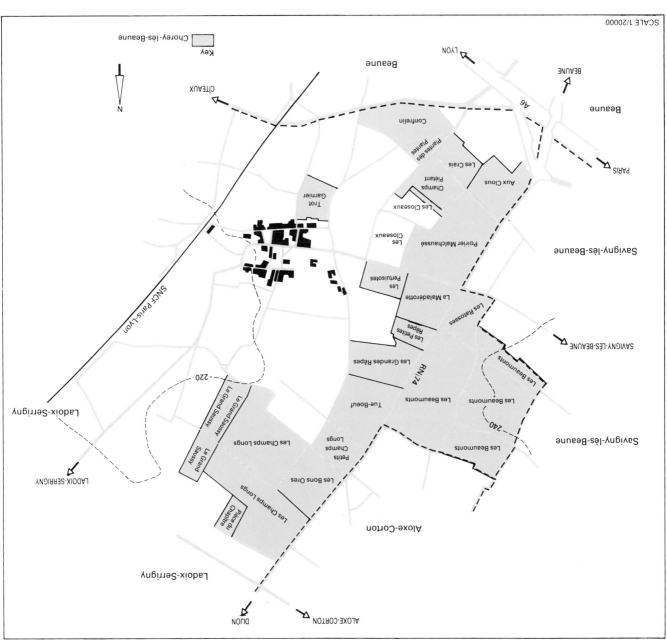

SCALE 1/20000

Key

Chorey-lès-Beaune

N

CÎTEAUX

Beaune

LYON

BEAUNE

Beaune

A6

PARIS

Ladoix-Serrigny

SNCF Paris-Lyon

Trot Garnier

Confrelin

Plantes des Plantes

Les Crais

Aux Clous

Champs Piétant

Les Closeaux

Savigny-lès-Beaune

Les Closeaux

Poirier Malchaussé

LADOIX-SERRIGNY

Les Pertuisotes

La Maladerotte

Les Ratosses

220

Le Grand Saussy

Le Grand Saussy

Le Grand Saussy

Les Petites Répes

Les Grandes Répes

RN 74

Les Beaumonts

SAVIGNY-LÈS-BEAUNE

Tue-Bœuf

Les Beaumonts

Les Beaumonts

Les Champs Longs

Petits Champs Longs

240

Savigny-lès-Beaune

Les Champs Longs

Les Bons Ores

Les Beaumonts

Place du Chapitre

Aloxe-Corton

Ladoix-Serrigny

DIJON

ALOXE-CORTON

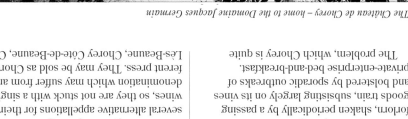

CHOREY-LÈS-BEAUNE

Chorey is a place which has got itself on to the wrong side of practically everything. Sandwiched between the main Paris–Lyon railway line and the RN74, on the wrong side of the road, it is a heartless little village, neat and tidy, but perpetually aware of the fact that, unlike its neighbours on the right side of the road, it was ignored when the appellations were being dished out, and had to wait until 1974 before it was granted one of its own. Even then, it missed out, ending up without a single Premier Cru. Kept in the limelight by a handful of fine Domaines, Chorey languishes somewhat forlorn, shaken periodically by a passing goods train, subsisting largely on its vines and bolstered by sporadic outbreaks of private-enterprise bed-and-breakfast. The problem, which Chorey is quite powerless to solve, lies in its land, much of which is flat and low-lying. Although parts of the commune sit on well-drained sandy soils, much consists of water-retentive clay. Moreover, some of the vineyards to the east of the RN74 are renowned frostpockets. There is a better section, on the western side of the road, which comprises two vineyards – Les Beaumonts and Les Ratosses – squeezed into 45.61 ha between the adjoining communes of Aloxe and Savigny. These produce some good wine, particularly those sections farthest from the main road.

Fortunately, Chorey's 40 growers have several alternative appellations for their red wines, so they are not stuck with a single denomination which may suffer from an indifferent press. They may be sold as Chorey-Les-Beaune, Chorey Côte-de-Beaune, Côte de Beaune-Villages or be declassified to Bourgogne, Bourgogne Grand Ordinaire, or Bourgogne Ordinaire. In theory therefore, a vigneron desperate to create an impression of diversity, could market his single red under six different appellations.

Chorey's history is, unfortunately, no more exciting than its wines. Like many other communes along the Côte, it took a few centuries to fix its present name: Hauriaco, in 667, became Caracum in 1004; followed Cherriacum in 1150 and Chartre in 1207. Thirty years later came Charvey, which gave way to Cherrey in 1304. Finally Chorey (sic) in 1437, which more or less settled it for the next five-and-a-half centuries. Chorey's only moment of fame came in May 1658, when it was chosen by the burgers of Beaune as the site to welcome Louis XIV, who happened to be passing. From then on, however, things deteriorated. The place was shaken by earthquakes in 1681 and 1783. Despite this, it was not until 1851 that the local fire brigade was formed. In 1688, Chorey's crops were ravaged by wild boar which descended on the wretched village from the woods of Cîteaux. Thereafter, Chorey enjoyed a period of calm and relative prosperity. Religious foundations owned one sixth of the vineyards, and the village was renowned as an unusually healthy spot, perhaps helped by its proximity to the river Rhoin, which makes a muted, fitful appearance on its southern side. The Beaunois liked to use Chorey as a refuge from the plague and reciprocated that facility by granting its wines privileged rights of access to the favoured markets of Beaune.

The principal architectural interest lies in the Château. Originally built in the 13th century as a 'maison fortifiée', it was destroyed several times between then and its most recent reconstruction, in the late 1660s. An impressive building, with imposing gates, surrounded by a deep ditch which has been known to contain both water and fish, it is presently owned by François Germain who offers accommodation (at a price).

Chorey's wine is nearly all red, although a little white is made from Chardonnay. Generally sound but uninspiring, in good vintages they can be pleasant and well-balanced for inexpensive drinking. The best come from Domaines Tollot-Beaut and Jacques Germain in Chorey itself and from Domaine Daniel Senard in Aloxe-Corton. They are reasonably priced and so, when good, usually represent excellent value.

The Château de Chorey – home to the Domaine Jacques Germain

Domaine Tollot-Beaut et Fils

CHOREY-LÈS-BEAUNE

The Tollot family are unusual – 3 brothers each with one offspring, all working together, making and selling wine. Jacques and Alain Tollot each have a son in the business whilst François Tollot's daughter, Nathalie, manages the office and receives the clients. The whole enterprise seems remarkably harmonious; the wines are excellent and the business, no doubt, successful.

The present trio of brothers are the fifth generation to vinify at Chorey. The original Tollot was their great-great-grandfather who apparently successfully combined the rather heterogeneous callings of musician and vigneron. His son continued the exploitation and started buying vineyards on his own account, at the same time working as a vigneron for the Prince de Mérode. The 'Beaut' arrived with the present older generation's grandmother. Clearly something of a forceful lady, she started selling wine in bottle, under her own label in the 1920s, which must have brought not a little négociant wrath down on her head – as the négoce then enjoyed a virtually uncontested monopoly of the market.

Careful acquisition has gradually enlarged the Domaine, which now comprises some 22 ha spread over good Village and Premier Cru sites in Beaune, Savigny and Aloxe, and régionales in Chorey and a trio of Cortons to top off the pyramid. François admits that they would, collectively of course, like to add a few ares of Grand Cru but 'you know what the prices are like,' he shrugs.

Somehow, the Tollots have managed to avoid the fragmentation of their vineyards, suffered by most family Domaines, by ensuring that, whilst individual ownership might change through death and division, the land was always kept in the same exploitation. This requires exceptional family cohesion – one wonders what the secret is. A sister who left to marry a vigneron at Auxey was presumably bought out.

Collectively, the Tollots recall to mind Dickens' Cheeryble brothers: kindly, warm-hearted models of courtesy, charm and charity, vying with each other to help the needy and brimming over with generosity of spirit. Their wines mirror their progenitors – characterised by soft appealing flavours, with much finesse and charm. The reds are vinified to mature in the medium term, with a shortish cuvaison of 7–10 days to conserve the more evanescent aromatic elements.

François believes that concentration and extract should properly come from old vines and low yields, rather than from prolonged maceration, whether pre- or post-fermentation, which is positively discouraged. So keen are the brothers not to delay fermentation a moment longer than necessary, that they use a quantity of grapes picked three days before the main harvest to make a pied de cuve, 20–30 litres of which serves to activate each vat, so that it ferments without delay.

Grape health and cellar hygiene are matters on which the Tollots lay great stress. For the former, they strive to keep treatments to minimum dose, following the advice of the Service des Végétaux 'without exaggerating'. Precise soil analyses in each vineyard enable them to adjust any deficiencies in base elements – chiefly nitrogen, phosphorus, potassium or magnesium – to maintain an equilibrium of nutrients.

If they do have to replant – for example, in 1982 they grubbed up a plot of Beaune 'Blanche Fleurs' planted in 1926 – the soil is rested for at least two years before the new grafts are planted. No herbicides are used, just constant hoeing to keep the soil aerated and the weeds down.

As for hygiene, the Tollot cuverie is a model establishment. Neat as a new pin, its open cement cuves, each painted in a light wash with the name of the wine that goes into it picked out in large wine-coloured capital letters, seems like so many private front doors in a rather self-conscious surburban street – just another gesture of Tollot friendliness – a sort of vinous good-neighbour scheme.

Everything is spotless. As a result of obsessional cleaning, the painted vats, installed in 1949, look almost new. At the start and end of each harvest all the pipe-work in the cellar is connected together and water pumped through it under pressure – presumably with a supervisory Tollot at either end and a few more in between.

Forty years' expansion has seen the business outgrow the space by the row of front doors. Packing materials, filters, this or that apparatus are stored there and the vats have started to complain. So a new bottle cellar and shipping hall have been built to simplify working and get rid of the clutter.

If hygiene is paramount in the cellars, then yields drive work in the vineyards. Up to 35 years old, vines are replaced individually, on low-vigour rootstocks, to keep average vine age as high. There was much replanting in Beaune and Corton in the 1970s, but elsewhere the vines are considerably older. Feuillage is taken very seriously: in 1990, for example, three separate passages were made through the vines to remove excess buds and shoots. However, there is no green-pruning since the collective Tollot belief is that excisions are better done before mid-June, rather than leaving later. François is scathing of the much-publicised August green-prunings: 'it is good for photographs for journalists,' but not of much serious value, since, done properly it involves removing unripe material from the middle of the vine, rather than making random excisions around the edges.

The timing of harvesting – crucial to grape quality – is determined both by prélèvements and by the risk of waiting. In 1988 they decided that the risk is worth taking, although the feeling is that it is better to pick slightly unripe then make suitable adjustments in the cuverie, than to delay unduly and risk a completely spoiled crop. When they do decide to pick, the bunches are subjected to three separate scrutinies – as they are cut, by the porters on the carts, and again by 8 people manning a sorting-table at the cellar.

The Beaunes, the earliest to ripen, usually begin the harvest which always ends with the whites – Bourgogne Blanc, Aligoté and Grand Cru Corton-Charlemagne.

The whites, though a small proportion of production, are something of a Tollot speciality. The Bourgogne Blanc is usually excellent – plenty of ripe fruit, good acidity, round, complex and mouthfilling. It is not cheap but, crafted with Tollot thoroughness, invariably outclasses itself.

The top rung of the ladder is occupied by the Corton-Charlemagne, made from a plot of

The Tollot family – at work in their vineyards. Recognise them?

VINEYARD HOLDINGS

Commune	Level	Lieu-dit/Climat	Area	Vine Age	Status
Aloxe	GC	Le Corton (Charlemagne)	0.24	29	P
Aloxe	GC	Corton Bressandes	0.91	41	P
Corton	GC	Les Combes	0.60	50%:65 50%:11	P/F
Aloxe	PC	Les Vercots	0.79	66	P
Aloxe	PC	Les Fournières	0.88	20	P/F
Aloxe	V	(Several climats)	1.89	15	P
Beaune	PC	Grèves	0.59	23	P
Beaune	PC	Clos du Roi	1.10	14	P
Beaune	V	Les Blanches Fleurs	0.28	8	
Savigny	PC	Les Lavières	0.98	50	P
Savigny	PC	Champ Chevrey (Monopole)	1.46	40	P
Savigny	V	Les Ratosses	0.26	37	P
Savigny	V	Aux Champs Chardons	0.40	1992	P/F
Chorey	V	(Several climats)	7.82	28	P/F
Chorey	R	(Bourgogne Rouge)	1.20	30	P/F
Savigny/ Chorey	R	(Bourgogne Blanc)	0.68	28	P
Chorey	R	(Bourgogne Aligoté)	1.20	24	P
Total:			**21.28 ha**		

30-year-old vines in Le Corton, exposed due east. Its fermentation starts in stainless steel and finishes in cask with sulphur and manipulations kept to the minimum. The wine is generally fine rather than overly muscular – an attractive Charlemagne best drunk while still showing the succulent fruit of youth, rather than waiting for the uncertainty of old age. Not a top example, but almost there in vintages such as 1993.

All the white wines have a touch of new wood – 25% or so for the Charlemagne – with a preference for the Tronçais. 'I know the forest of Tronçais and the wood – lovely wood, impeccable; that's what I would like to have in the cellar.' Whatever preference François Tollot may confide to his tonnelier, he is wisely sceptical about what may eventually turn up: 'There's no Appellation Contrôlée for wood,' he laughs, 'so it is probably better to buy the planks from a friend, dry them for three years yourself and then stand over the tonnelier while he makes the casks.'

Tollot barrels are described as 'assez brulés' – but not by express order: this imparts a noticeably toasty flavour to the whites. Unusually, Tollot whites are not bâtonnés, because they only consider this sound practice with wines which are long in fermenting to high alcohol levels. It is simply not their style.

In compensation, they have extended lees contact, being racked twice, once 'well after the malo', which avoids early yellowing, and again just before bottling, at relève de colle.

'We have much to learn about white wine vinification,' chuckles François. 'Highly gifted amateurs!'

Red vinification is 'très classique'. The bunches are 66–75% destalked and crushed before being transferred to their allotted front-door. The régionales are kept in stainless steel. Fermentation is started as soon as possible and cuvaison is deliberately short, with temperatures not permitted to exceed 30–35°C and the vats saignéd, if necessary. The wine is decanted when a match lit in the cuve fails to extinguish – i.e. no more CO_2, and thus no further fermentation.

Assemblage of press- and free-run wine is followed by 2–3 weeks of débourbage, with the cuves covered to prevent oxidation and loss of aroma. This seems an excessively long period of settling without the prospect of much gain in quality.

The wine then passes into casks – 'one-third new wood for Grands and Petits Crus alike – we're very socialist here,' muses François. There are three rackings in all – the first, in early spring, cask-to-cask with aeration by spraying over an umbrella-shaped contrivance to maximise air contact.

Some fine lees are left to keep the wine nourished until the next racking around four months later. Here the wines are unified and pre-filtered with Kieselguhr before being returned to cask where they remain until the day before bottling, when they are lightly plate-filtered. Up to 1974 they were fined, but decided that this battered the wines more than a gentle second filtration.

For the Tollots, the production of truly fine wine is an amalgam of a multitude of small interrelated details. Their reds are highly individual in style, accentuating the ripe, succulent, almost sweet flavours of which the Pinot Noir is deliciously capable. 1985 and 1989, for example, are vintages which well complement this style, whilst the high tannins and firmer structure of 1993 is somewhat less typically Tollot.

The 1993 Chorey – an appellation deserving of better currency – is unusually muscular, marginally deeper than the excellent Bourgogne Rouge, from Chorey vines. Of the two Savignys, the Lavières, from less humid soils than Champ Chevrey, has more power and muscle, with, in 1993, aromas of fruits rouges, highish acidity and tight, dryish tannins. The Domaine's Monopole, Champ Chevrey, a road's width away but on stonier soil, is denser and better structured – with greater depth of flavour and more vinosity. However, when these wines age, the

Lavières, from vines planted from sélection massale by Tollot Père in 1945, usually develops more complexity than its sibling.

The pair of Beaune Premiers Crus, although from relatively young vines, have good depth and finesse. The Clos du Roi is not the easiest of vineyards, containing large limestone boulders which tend to absorb moisture. Thus, in dry years, such as 1990, maturity can be a problem. The 1993 has a deep garnet colour, good aromatic potential and underlying finesse – not dissimilar to the Domaine's Village Beaune Blanches Fleurs which it adjoins. Any slight lack of concentration and complexity will be corrected as the vines mature. The Grèves, probably the best of all Beaune's Premiers Crus, from older vines, invariably shows its class – with a bit more of everything, longevity included.

The two Aloxe Premiers Crus – Les Vercots and Les Fournières – separated from the Aloxe Village cuvée in 1993, differ markedly in character. The Vercots from 1929 vines in Aloxe's westerly, Pernand sector, is the meatier and less flatteur of the pair, the Fournières, south-east of the village, the more elegant. A high percentage of iron in the vineyards – an Aloxe-Corton characteristic, deriving from both the soil and from small brown stones – contributes an earthy depth which takes time to round out.

The two red Grands Crus – Corton and Corton Bressandes – are both substantial, powerful wines. The Corton, whilst good, is generally eclipsed by the Bressandes, which generally has more subtlety and finesse. With age, the sheer class, greater breed and vinosity of the Bressandes comes through, making it more sensual than the Corton, which is more direct, more intellectual.

The Tollots are a fine team, and a reliable source of delicious wines – individuals, made collectively, of course.

Not all, but a selection of Tollots

Domaine Jacques Germain

CHOREY-LES-BEAUNE

This is one of those medium-sized self-taught Domaines which one comes across from time to time, which if not quite top-class, is capable of exciting quality. The setting is perfect: a fine, if marginally crumbling, 17th-century Château surrounded by a deep moat containing a modicum of water and some fish, all enclosed by an ancient stone wall and screened by an attractively wooded park. The 13th-century Château, built by Migieu, who was also responsible for the Ch. de Savigny, was unfortunately destroyed and rebuilt several times, so little remains of the original. Modern disintegration is more credibly attributable to creeping noble rot than to warriors storming the drawbridge. The expense of the Château's upkeep is partly defrayed by 6 bedrooms, offered as a *chambres d'hôte* to visitors looking for elegant surroundings.

This is the home of François Germain and his family. François, a cheerful, excitable middle-aged man and one of two brothers in a family of 5 children, took over on his father's death in 1968. His training covered both the commercial side of his father's négociant business, and, because he valued practical experience, vineyards and cellar work. In addition, he spent a few years in a larger establishment, chiefly remembered for its policy of filtering red wines through Kieselguhr, then plates and finally a membrane, doubtless leaving precious little of the wine for the customer.

François draws his policy guidelines with firm, uncompromising strokes: 'You must extract the best – *Grand Vin*; it's not always easy.' He is sharply critical of vignerons who, driven by what their customers can afford, make wine to a price and not to a standard. An ebullient extrovert, whose own enthusiasm shine through, he confesses a passion for good food and fine wine and makes no secret of his search for perfection.

He seems to be more than master of his 17 ha Domaine. Apart from *régionales*, this consists of Pernand Blanc, a 5 ha slab of Chorey Village and no fewer than 6 different Beaune Premiers Crus. François feels this is a comfortable size for him to oversee, with the help of his son Benoît and a handful of workers. In the vineyards healthy, ripe grapes and low yields are the aim. 'With Pinot Noir,' he explains, 'you must not exceed 30 hl/ha for the Premiers Crus and 40 hl/ha for Village appellations. To this end, good quality clones, short pruning and an *'écusvage très sérieuse'* are all germane. Although

he dislikes green-pruning in principle, in 1990 an entire month was spent in removing excess buds and there were further excisions later – 'exceptionally, I haven't done this since 1973'.

François has also worked to optimise the training for his vines. Whilst most viticulteurs are content to use the *Guyot simple* pruning – a single *baguette* with up to 10 eyes on it and a spur for next year's wood, since 1988 François has trained *en cordon de Royal*, using a one metre cane with just three eyes and a spur with just one. This gives both lower yields and higher sugars – a whole degree more of potential alcohol. 'Even with the best clones, classically trained, you get too much fruit. The Guyot *baguette* was invented first to lower the level of the fruit and secondly to increase yields, not to reduce them.'

Vinification is conducted on modified classical lines: 'I start from the premise that stalk tannins are hard and skin tannins are fine, but difficult to extract.' The solution, introduced in 1983, is complete destalking and a good week of post-fermentive *maceration* to leach out these fine tannins and to fix the colours extracted before fermentation. Once vatted, a larger than normal dose of SO_2 is administered, both to minimise volatile acidity produced during *malo* and to allow 2–3 days pre-fermentive *maceration* to maximise extraction of glycerol and aromas. If fermentation is sluggish, François simply borrows a bucket of ferment from a friend and inoculates.

After fermentation at up to 32°C in a varie-gated rank of well-kept, open wooden *cuves*, housed in a newly acquired cellar in the village, the wine is left to macerate with the *cuves* firmly closed. The lighter, relatively rapid-maturing Chorey, has only 10–12 days total *cuvaison*, the Premiers Crus have 18–22 days.

Thereafter, *élevage* in cask – 50% new oak for the Premiers Crus and 25–30% for the Chorey – is followed by two rackings and a Kieselguhr filtration. François is bowled-over with delight by the Kieselguhr system – it excoriates the wine much less than fining, which, in any case, is ill-adapted to his cold cellar. *Élevage* is rounded off with a light plate-filtration to remove any Kieselguhr left in the wine and bottling after 18 months for the Premiers Crus and 12 for the Chorey.

The result is a range of well-made wines of reasonable depth and sound structure. The Beaune Premiers Crus make a particularly interesting group – showing how much *terroir* varies within the appellation. The Boucherottes and Cent-Vignes, from moderately sandy soils are the lightest, generally quite soft and supple. The Vignes Franches, from 45-year-old vines on a higher clay soil, is more solid – broader with more structure and depth. The Les Cras and Les Teurons are the most *charpenté* of the group – much more of Pommard than of Savigny in style. The Cras was at one time considered as a 'Tête de Cuvée' among Beaune's Premiers Crus and its heat-retaining, stony soil usually ripens grapes well giving a wine of very typical Pinot character.

François Germain's whites are particularly interesting. In contrast to his reds, they get only minimum SO_2, and are fermented in cask (15% new Vosges oak), using a selected strain of Montrachet yeast. The Pernand Blanc, from 3 ha of south-facing land near Echevronne is quite masculine in character with a pronounced *goût de terroir* and a characteristically crisp acidity. The vineyard, to François' eye, has much the same soil as the Pernand sector of Corton-Charlemagne but, despite his animated protestations that 'it's exactly the same, exactly the same – that

VINEYARD HOLDINGS

Commune	Level	Lieu-dit/Climat	Area	Vine Age	Status
Beaune	PC	Les Boucherottes	1.00	25	P
Beaune	PC	Les Vignes Franches	1.00	45	P
Beaune	PC	Les Cras	1.30	45	P
Beaune	PC	Les Teurons	2.00	45	P
Beaune	PC	Sur Les Grèves	0.12	45	P
Beaune	PC	Les Cents Vignes	0.60	8	P
Chorey	V	(Several climats)	5.00	25	P
Pernand	V	Plante Des Champs + Combottes	3.00	25	P
	R	(Bourgogne Rouge)	2.00	45	P
	R	(Bourgogne Blanc)	0.50	9	P
Total:			**16.52 ha**		

makes superb wines' – the wine is not of Grand Cru quality. The Beaune sur les Grèves Blanc has greater richness – sometimes with an almost exotic-fruit quality – a good solid wine, needing around 2–5 years to reach its peak.

In 1989 there was a third, rather unexpected white produced when François abandoned a few rows of Bourgogne Chardonnay,

from the walled vineyard opposite the Château gates, believing them to be hopeless. Returning from holiday in November, he found perfect *noble rot*, picked the grapes and made a couple of casks of 'sélection des grains nobles'. He had to telephone a vigneron friend in Alsace to find out how to handle the juice, which had 50 grams per litre of residual sugar. The result: a remark-

ably attractive wine with good natural acidity, from a blocked *malo*, sweetness which does not cloy and plenty of enriching *botrytis*. An attempt a repeat performance in 1990 was a failure – the rain came in October and washed his hopes away.

This is an interesting Domaine; one from which to pick and choose, but certainly well worth watching.

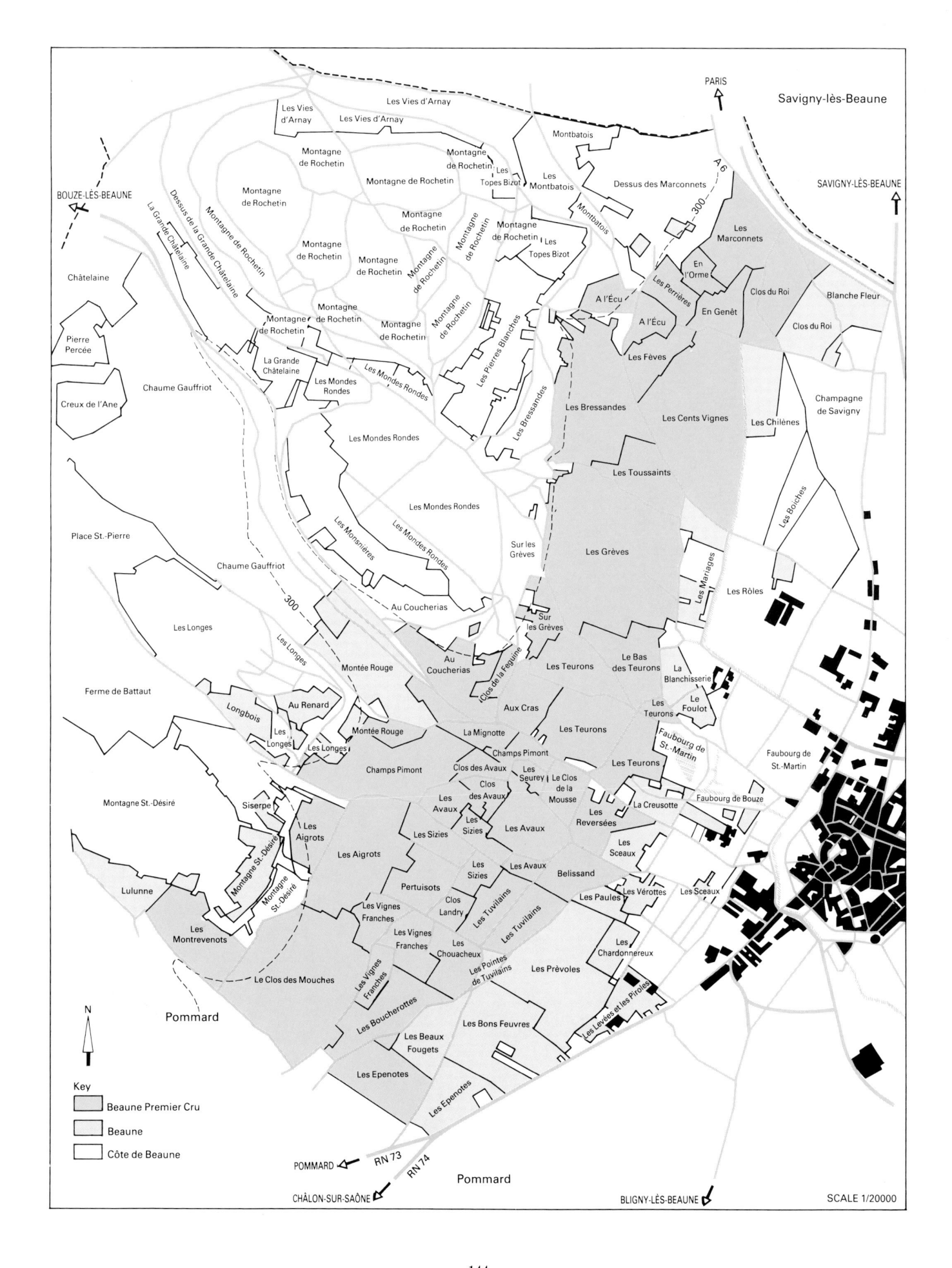

PARIS

Savigny-lès-Beaune

SAVIGNY-LÈS-BEAUNE

BOUZE-LÈS-BEAUNE

Les Vies d'Arnay

Les Vies d'Arnay

Les Vies d'Arnay

Montbatois

Montagne de Rochetin

Montagne de Rochetin

Montagne de Rochetin

Montagne de Rochetin

Les Topes Bizot

Les Montbatois

Dessus des Marconnets

Montbatois

Les Marconnets

Châtelaine

Montagne de Rochetin

Montagne de Rochetin

Montagne de Rochetin

Montagne de Rochetin

Les Topes Bizot

En l'Orme

Les Perrières

Clos du Roi

Blanche Fleur

La Grande Châtelaine

Dessus de la Grande Châtelaine

A l'Écu

A l'Écu

En Genêt

Clos du Roi

Pierre Percée

Montagne de Rochetin

Montagne de Rochetin

Les Pierres Blanches

Les Fèves

Chaume Gauffriot

Montagne de Rochetin

La Grande Châtelaine

Les Mondes Rondes

Les Mondes Rondes

Les Bressandes

Les Bressandes

Les Cents Vignes

Champagne de Savigny

Creux de l'Ane

Les Mondes Rondes

Les Bressandes

Les Chilènes

Les Mondes Rondes

Les Toussaints

Les Boiches

Place St.-Pierre

Les Mondes Rondes

Les Monsnières

Les Mondes Rondes

Sur les Grèves

Les Grèves

Chaume Gauffriot

Au Coucherias

Sur les Grèves

Les Mariages

Les Rôles

Les Longes

300

Les Longes

Montée Rouge

Au Coucherias

Clos de la Féguine

Les Teurons

Le Bas des Teurons

La Blanchisserie

Ferme de Battaut

Longbois

Au Renard

Montée Rouge

Aux Cras

Le Foulot

Les Teurons

Les Longes

Les Longes

La Mignotte

Les Teurons

Faubourg de St.-Martin

Faubourg de St.-Martin

Les Longes

Champs Pimont

Champs Pimont

Les Teurons

Montagne St.-Désiré

Siserpe

Champs Pimont

Clos des Avaux

Les Seurey

Le Clos de la Mousse

Les Teurons

Faubourg de Bouze

Les Aigrots

Clos des Avaux

La Creusotte

Les Avaux

Clos des Avaux

Les Reversées

Montagne St.-Désiré

Les Aigrots

Les Sizies

Les Sizies

Les Avaux

Les Sceaux

Lulunne

Montagne St.-Désiré

Pertuisots

Les Sizies

Les Avaux

Belissand

Les Vérottes

Les Sceaux

Les Montrevenots

Les Vignes Franches

Clos Landry

Les Tuvilains

Les Paules

Les Vignes Franches

Les Tuvilains

Les Tuvilains

Les Chardonnereux

Le Clos des Mouches

Les Vignes Franches

Les Chouacheux

Les Pointes de Tuvilains

Les Prévoles

Pommard

Les Vignes Franches

Les Boucherottes

Les Bons Feuvres

Les Levées et les Piroles

N

Les Beaux Fougets

Les Epenotes

Key

Beaune Premier Cru

Les Epenotes

Beaune

Côte de Beaune

POMMARD ← RN 73

RN 74

Pommard

CHÂLON-SUR-SAÔNE

BLIGNY-LÈS-BEAUNE

SCALE 1/20000

144

BEAUNE

If Dijon is the administrative capital of viti-cultural Burgundy, then Beaune is its geographical, commercial and historical capital, as well as its spiritual home. Encapsulated inside its medieval ramparts is Burgundy's history from Beaune's beginnings as one of Julius Caesar's encampments in 52 BC, whilst the periphery is devoted to the late 20th-century industrial sprawl, stimulated by the opening of the Autoroute du Soleil in 1970. With some 22,000 inhabitants, it serves as both tourist and wine centre for the Côte d'Or.

The heart of Beaune is an amalgam of smart shops, restaurants and wine houses, compacted into a maze of narrow streets and attractive squares. This is principally the territory of the large négociants – Jadot, Drouhin, Bouchard Père et Fils, Bichot, Patriarche and more. These vary in style, the grander hidden discreetly from public gaze behind high walls, in elegant old houses, whilst the less sensitive deploy prominent 'dégustation' signs, netting coach-loads of visitors to taste and buy. Below the tourists' tramping feet winds a honeycomb of quiet, cool, cellars full of bottles, casks and cobwebs.

Each November, Beaune becomes the focus of the Côte, when the Hospice auctions the 1,000 or so casks of new wine made from its vineyards. Since its foundation in 1441 by Chancellor Nicolas Rollin and his wife Guigone de Salins, the Hospice has used donations of money and land to fund a Charitable Hospital. Today, the grounds of the magnificently preserved medieval Hôtel-Dieu are occupied by a modern, well-equipped medical centre, which depends on the wine sale for its income. Some 34 *cuvées* are offered, from a dozen different communes; the wines are variable in quality and invariably expensive. Those who buy are motivated more by charity and publicity than by any expectation of a bargain.

Beaune's commercial development has spawned acres of brick houses and corrugated warehouses round its outskirts, swallowing up much good vineyard land on the way. What is now the Lycée Viticole is partially built on the former Clos Maire, requisitioned just after the war, though the old airstrip has now been returned to vines. Whilst the town planners are making valiant efforts to preserve a feeling of tradition, visitors passing on the Autoroute might be forgiven for concluding that industry has won.

The vineyards, dispersed widely over a band of gently sloping ground in the north-west quadrant beyond the town, comprise 51.97 ha of Côte de Beaune, 128.13 ha of AC Beaune and 321.66 ha of Premiers Crus, numbering 39–45, depending on how one counts the various Clos. Bisected by the N470 meandering towards Bouze-lès-Beaune, they are mostly well-exposed to the southeast and, although the soils vary, the Premiers Crus are generally on a mixture of clay and limestone, which becomes thinner and more ferruginous as the slope increases. Those in the western section – Aigrots, Pertuisots and Vignes-Franches in particular – have lighter soils, whilst those on the old Pommard road – Boucherottes, Chouacheux and Tuvillans and the lower-lying Village land – are damper, with more clay, which increases the risk of spring frost damage.

The cream of the Premiers Crus lie beneath Les Mondes Rondes, a hill to the north-west of the town. Whilst individual fine Beaunes can be found from the westerly sector, it is these dozen or so vineyards which produce the deepest, richest and most complex wines. This was recognised during the 19th century, with the designation of 7 vineyards as 'Têtes de Cuvée': Champs Pimont, Clos des Fèves, Perrières, Bressandes, Grèves, Marconnets and Clos des Mouches (the only one from the westerly section).

A small quantity of Chardonnay is produced – in particular, Drouhin's excellent Premier Cru Clos des Mouches and an attractive, characterful Beaune du Château from Bouchard Père et Fils. White Beaune accounts for only 6,000 cases per year, some 5% of red output.

The 132,000 annual cases of red vary widely in style, both between vineyard and producer. Outside Beaune itself, excellent examples can be had from Tollot-Beaut and Jacques Germain in Chorey, Faiveley and Arnaud Marchard de Gramont in Nuits, Michel Ampeau in Meursault, the Lafarges in Volnay and André Mussy in Pommard.

Where Beaunes do lack depth and complexity this, more often than not, reflects overproduction rather than any deficiency in the quality-potential of the vineyards. Sadly, although long known and appreciated, Beaune's are Burgundy's Cinderellas, with a seemingly unshakeable collective reputation for dull neutrality. Wines from Domaines with well-sited old vines, low yields and long *cuvaison* give the lie to this image; a mature example from Drouhin, Jadot or Albert Morot should be enough to convince anyone.

Unfortunately, the wines of a number of prestigious houses continue to keep the old criticisms alive. Bouchard Père et Fils, the largest owner of Beaune Premiers Crus, turn out a lacklustre range although their Beaune Vigne de l'Enfant Jesus, from Les Grèves, can be excellent. In 1995 Bouchard was bought by Joseph Henriot (of Champagne Henriot). Poor wine was cleared out and some Clos Vougeot and Bonnes-Mares land added. With the old wine making team in place, Henriot is determined to realise the full potential of Bouchard's land.

Others producing mediocre wines from good vineyards are Chanson, Jaboulet-Vercherre, Patriarche and, their Domaine Clos Frantin in Vosne excepted, Bichot.

Perhaps the high proportion of Beaune vineyards in the hands of a relatively small number of producers contributes to the commune's poor consumer image. Fortunately, the handful of top Domaines make enough fine wine to more than redress the balance.

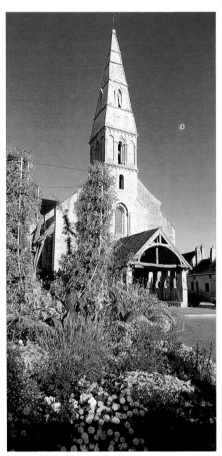

Beaune is often festooned with flowers

Domaine Joseph Drouhin

BEAUNE

Until recently, the great négociant Houses of Beaune and Nuits dominated the international Burgundy market. The volume they commanded, and the limited exposure of growers' wines, generated the belief that what they produced represented the best that could be had. For many, négociant Burgundies were their introduction to the region's wines.

However, the advent of a more sophisticated market, Domaine bottling, and marginally tighter controls has gradually transformed the picture. The négociant stranglehold is now broken – their original sources of supply, the small growers in each commune, are bottling and selling more of their own wine, so what is left for the négociant buyers is frequently of indifferent quality. Some of the best growers continue to sell to the négoce as a matter of financial expediency, but what fine wine there is, is fiercely fought over and prices are high.

At the top of the ladder, a handful of quality-conscious négociants have striven to maintain quality, and ensured their supplies by taking the only realistic course open to them – buying their own vineyards. In fact, these Houses now compete on equal terms with their erstwhile suppliers, the growers, who are generally seen by international markets as setting the yardsticks for quality.

Drouhin is one of Burgundy's top-level négociants. More importantly, it is also one of Burgundy's finest Domaines, owning some 25.9 ha of vineyards from Puligny to Gevrey. Founded by Joseph Drouhin in 1880, as a general négociant, it is not an old House, at any rate by Burgundian standards. After the 1914-18 war Joseph's son, Maurice Drouhin decided to specialise in Burgundy and started to buy vines. The exigencies of working with horses confined his purchases to the locality of Beaune where he acquired the 13.7 ha Beaune Clos des Mouches, which remains the kernel of the Domaine.

Much of what Maurice bought was *en friche* – land entitled to appellation status, but which, for one reason or another, was not planted. In 1938 he added 0.9 ha of Clos de Vougeot 'pour le plaisir' – although Vougeot was rather far from his usual ambit and probably not then a viable proposition.

The Domaine is now run by Joseph's grandson Robert, a tall, rather reserved man in his early sixties. Although intended for five years of oenology training, he was pitched into the deep end in 1957, aged 24, when his father suffered a stroke. An education in Germany, England and France, and 30 months' military service in Africa, prepared him well for his international role as an Ambassador for his own and Burgundy's wines.

His lack of formal training is compensated for by a formidable tasting experience, not only of post-war Burgundy, but of wines from every corner of the globe. You are just as likely to come across him in Alsace, on the banks of the Douro or in California, as in Beaune. An articulate, knowledgeable and courteous man, he is a media favourite.

Robert's reign has seen great change. Between 1959 and 1962 he extended the Domaine's holdings, particularly in Chambolle-Musigny and in 1968 he bought 37.7 ha of unplanted land in Chablis. The most significant purchase was 40 ha in Oregon's Willamette Valley – 'on the same latitude as Burgundy, at the same altitude and with broadly similar climate', although with soils which are higher than ideal in acidity. He put his daughter Véronique in charge of the project and seems satisfied with the early results. Unfortunately the multi-million dollar cost of this foreign foray, coupled with economic recession, overstretched Drouhin's finances. In 1994 they were bailed out by their Japanese importer, Snow-Brand, whose core business is dairy products. As with Jadot and Kobrand, the parent is content to vest a large measure of autonomy in its subsidiary.

Care of the Domaine's vineyards – including those in Chablis and Oregon – is in the hands of Robert's son Philippe. One of his first acts on taking charge in 1988 was to inform his father that there were no worms or lizards on their land – the result of overuse of chemicals. Disbelieving, Robert went out with a spade and indeed found none. So, now the policy is more ecology conscious – plenty of hoeing and fewer chemicals.

Robert attributes much of the increase in quality he has achieved to his ability to control viticulture. A vine, in his view, produces well for around 35 years, so the quality of plant material is of prime importance. For the grafts, experience led to the conclusion that clones are less good than his own *sélection massale*: 'They seem to give less complexity, but I can't prove it.' Now some 66–75% of replantings are generated from a 1935 *vigne mère* in Clos des Mouches, the rest coming from a mixture of selected clones.

The Domaine's vineyards are managed on the overriding, quasi-homeopathic principle that the physiology of the vine must be seen as a whole, not merely as an amalgam of leaves, roots, wood, bunches, etc. Foliage control, short-pruning, fertilisers and treatments should not be considered in isolation from their effects on the rest of the plant.

Part of the equation relating fruit to wine quality is plant density – in the Côte d'Or usually 10,000 vines per ha with 8 buds per vine. Many growers, among them Drouhin, are experimenting with denser plantings in the belief that this will produce improved fruit quality all round. Now the Domaine plants 12,500 vines per ha – one of the highest densities in Burgundy – which encourages root-systems to delve deeper to compete for nutrients.

In 1976, a serious fire, which destroyed their new bottling plant, was something of a watershed, causing Robert Drouhin to rethink his winemaking philosophy and to admit that many of his wines were of less than top quality. A period of reflection resulted in longer *cuvaison* for the reds – from 10–18 days – and a lower fermentation temperature for the whites (now 18–22°C). His natural prudence distrusts trends and fashions which lead people to imitative folly. 'What may seem to be an improvement may turn out not to be one' – faults may only become apparent after many years.

Whilst overall direction is the responsibility of Robert, and increasingly, Philippe, Frédéric and Véronique, winemaking is in the talented, and widely respected hands of

Philippe Drouhin in the vineyards – here the soil is ploughed up round the vine roots for frost protection

Laurence Jobard. Installed in the Domaine's new *cuverie* and cellars, just outside Beaune, she reigns over the firms large array of red and white wines and superintends their vinification and *élevage*.

Included in her charge is the precious produce of 2.05 ha of Le Montrachet – the largest plot in single ownership – and 2.5 ha of white Premier Cru Chassagne-Montrachet Morgeot, both belonging to the Marquis de Laguiche. Following a long tradition, the Morgeot is simply labelled Chassagne-Montrachet. Drouhin has been entrusted with making these wines since Maurice and the Marquis became friends in the 1940s – a faithful stewardship as both are among the finest in their respective appelations.

The task of Drouhin and Jobard is to ensure that each wine reflects its origin as closely as possible. Robert knows the *climats* of the Côte inside out, and is thus well aware of what to expect from each. During vinification much emphasis is laid upon tasting, to decide for example, the right moment to rack, or the appropriate proportion of new oak for a given *cuvée*. The well-equipped laboratory is there to provide analyses, but in the end it is the palate which decides.

The white wines are fermented in cask, after a light pressing and 8–12 hours *débourbage*. Only natural yeasts are used and each cask is roused periodically, especially towards the end of fermentation, to ensure that all the sugar is fermented out. Racking is delayed until early summer to extract maximum finesse and richness into the wines.

Depending on the vintage and Cru, the whites receive 10–20% of new oak, much less than before: 'I became tired of excess new wood.' The Grand Crus see none, only one-year-old casks, which impart a much more subtle, and supple, tannin. Drouhin buys oak and dries it outside where rainwater takes out much of the gross, aggressive tannins. Robert is convinced that careful natural drying impacts more on wine quality than the particular provenance of the wood.

Elévage is dictated by constant tasting though, in general, the white wines are bottled after 7–15 months. The Montrachet, Corton-Charlemagne and Bâtard-Montrachet, being naturally richer and more powerful, tend to be bottled last, without cold stabilisation, but with a minimum bentonite fining and a Kieselguhr filtration.

The red grapes are partially destalked – Robert Drouhin holding the somewhat heterodox belief that without stalks a wine lacks complexity. 33% of stalks give wines which, although a touch raw at the outset, have an ultimately better evolution than those without them. The unstemmed grapes are vatted as whole bunches, to promote more regular fermentation and colour stability. The *cuves* are cooled to 14–15°C for 48 hours of pre-fermentive maceration after which fermentation temperature rise, to a maximum of 35°C – 'then we start to worry,' admits Laurence.

In addition to traditional wood and double-jacketed stainless steel, there is an impressive battery of *cuves auto-pigéantes*. Encouraging trials with rotating *cuves* in the early 1980s generated an enthusiasm for the method which both automates vinification and enables an extended maceration. Laurence is emphatic that these should not be considered as a means of shortening fermentation nor as a substitute for traditional *cuvaison*, but as a modern means of achieving the same end. Drouhin's reds used to be criticised for a lack of extract – a charge which would be difficult to sustain today.

The Premiers and Grands Crus spend 12–18 months in cask – depending on their evolution. Natural richness and level in the hierarchy determine the proportion of new wood – maximum one-third – and trial finings decide the appropriate dose and fining agent. As a neat concession to information technology, each cask is bar-coded, so that its contents can be readily identified; at least they don't have to worry about where they last left the chalk.

The Domaine produces some 20 wines from its own vines, and a vast range from juice and grapes it buys and vinifies; it also buys young wine for *élevage*. In common with most top-rank négociants Drouhin treats *négociant* wines with the same care as those from its own vineyards. Robert Drouhin claims equal pride in being a négociant as in being a winemaker, although he is well aware that for many, 'négociant' has pejorative undertones. For him, all his wines are important, from the humblest Aligoté to the greatest Musigny or Montrachet.

If there is a wine which is perhaps a shade closer to his heart than the rest, it is undoubt- edly the Clos des Mouches. This vineyard produces both red and white wine from vines planted on several small plateaus. Interestingly, there is no attempt to determine parcels which might better suit Pinot or Chardonnay, both appearing at each level. For each variety, the produce of young and old vines is vinified separately so that any substandard casks can be weeded out and sold as Beaune Premier Cru.

In good vintages the Clos produces fine wines – which develop well over the medium term. Never blockbusters, they have breeding and finesse above all, backed by solid fruit, some from very old vines. This sits with the Domaine's overall style, which tends to emphasise elegance rather than brute size.

Drouhin's wines are generally excellent. The reds, in particular, have improved significantly over recent years, with better structure and greater concentration – the result of higher fermentation temperature, more *pigéage* and longer vatting – but without compromising finesse. They still emphasise the 'feminine' elegance so close to Robert's heart of which Pinot Noir is the supreme exponent. He insists on the importance of tasting the wine itself, not this or that method of vinification: 'Of course the interpreter matters, but you don't listen to Menuhin, you listen to a Bach Sonata.'

Robert Drouhin relies much on his experience, which he defines as 'the sum of past mistakes. I don't know whether I am a man of experience,' he confesses, 'but I've certainly made enough mistakes.' Nonetheless, experience has led him well and he has every reason to be proud of his achievements. His unremitting quest for quality has rubbed off on his children, other producers and those around the world who owe to Drouhin their discovery of really fine Burgundy. Those who love the Côte and its wines have much to thank him for.

VINEYARD HOLDINGS

Commune	Level	Lieu-dit/Climat	Area	Vine Age	Status
Beaune	PC	Clos des Mouches (W)	6.90	32	P
Beaune	PC	Clos des Mouches (R)	6.80	29	P
Beaune	PC	Grèves	0.80	12	P
Beaune	PC	(Several *climats*)	1.60	21	P
Volnay	PC	Clos des Chênes	0.30	27	P
Chorey	V	————	2.70	41	P
Aloxe	GC	Corton-Charlemagne	0.40	16	P
Aloxe	GC	Corton-Bressandes	0.30	25	P
Chambolle	GC	Bonnes-Mares	0.30	29	P
Chambolle	GC	Musigny	0.70	21	P
Chambolle	PC	Les Amoureuses	0.60	35	P
Chambolle	PC	————	1.50	22	P
Flagey	GC	Echézeaux	0.50	30	P
Flagey	GC	Grands Echézeaux	0.50	23	P
Vougeot	GC	Clos de Vougeot	0.90	15	P
Vosne	PC	Les Petits Monts	0.39	35	P
Gevrey	GC	Chambertin Clos de Bèze	0.10	23	P
Gevrey	GC	Griotte-Chambertin	0.50	15	P
Puligny	GC	Bâtard-Montrachet	0.10	50	P
Total:			**25.89 ha**		

Maison Louis Jadot

BEAUNE

The fusion of Domaine and négociant is nowhere better manifest than in Maison Louis Jadot. Since its foundation in 1859, by the man whose name it bears, this house has grown both into one of the largest proprietors of Premier and Grand Cru land in the Côte and into one of Burgundy's handful of utterly reliable sources, from Chablis to Beaujolais.

Its heart, however, is firmly in the Côte. Here, over the years it has carefully acquired and tended land to produce wines which exemplify at a uniformly high level, the typicity and character of their origins.

This did not happen all at once; in fact, Jadot's development was distinctly fitful. Louis started with a parcel of vines in the Clos des Ursules bequeathed to his uncle by his father – a local négociant – who had bought it in 1826. With this, and a broad, paternal education, he built up a successful négociant business. Purchases of vines in Beaune Theurons and Clos des Couchereaux followed. On his death the business was taken up 'enthusiastically' by his son Louis-Baptiste who reinvested his profits in Premier and Grand Cru land, including Chevalier Montrachet 'Les Demoiselles'.

Louis Baptiste died in 1939 leaving the firm to his eldest son, Louis-Auguste, who had assisted his father since 1931, opening up significant export markets, including those of the USA, UK, Holland, South America and New Zealand. In 1954, he took on a young assistant, André Gagey, then working in his father-in-law's négociant business. Gagey had qualified in commerce and business administration in Dijon, before marrying Marie-Hélène Tourlière in 1947. In those days, the alliance of someone from nearer to Dijon with a girl from Beaune was rather frowned upon, but her father clearly minded sufficiently little to give him experience in viticulture and cellar work which stood him in good stead when he joined Louis-Auguste.

On Louis-Auguste's death in 1962, his widow asked André Gagey to take responsibility for the firm's operations, until her son, Louis-Alain, should come of age. Sadly, Louis-Alain was killed in a car crash in 1968 at the age of 23. André Gagey was then appointed General Manager, and subsequently Managing Director. In 1985 the Jadot family sold out to the Kopf family, owners of their American importers, Kobrand. Now, André's son, Pierre-Henri, is in charge, with complete discretion to continue the policies of development begun in 1962.

An integral part of André's plan was the acquisition of land, to give the firm control over at least part of its requirements. Now, in addition to négoce activities, Jadot manages 4 separate viticultural estates, as well as having long-term vinification and marketing contracts with 3 others. These are:

1.Domaine des Héritiers Louis Jadot – 15.65 ha of Premier and Grand Cru land in Corton, Beaune, Pernand-Vergelesses and Puligny – including Corton-Charlemagne and Chevalier-Montrachet 'Les Demoiselles'.

2. The 26.89 ha owned by Maison Louis Jadot, comprising the Domaines Clair-Däu in Marsannay, purchased after Clair family quarrels in 1986 precipitated its sale, and the smaller Champy, purchased in 1989 – for its vineyards and marvellous collection of ancient Burgundy dating back to the 1820s. Its splendid cellars adjoining those of Jadot beneath the Couvent des Jacobins in Beaune were sold on to the Meurgeys, with the name Champy (q.v.). These Domaines added a superlative portfolio of vineyards including important parcels of Musigny, Bonnes Mares, Chambertin Clos de Bèze, Chapelle-Chambertin, Gevrey-Chambertin Clos St.-Jacques, Chambolle Les Amoureuses, Clos Vougeot and much besides.

3. Domaine André Gagey – consisting of 3.67 ha of Premier and Grand Cru land from Puligny to Morey.

4. Domaine Robert Tourlière – 2.87 ha of 4 well-sited Beaune Premiers Crus and some Clos de Vougeot.

In consequence, the firm now has under its direct control 49 ha of the Côte d'Or, of which 8 are Grand Cru. In addition, it makes and markets 80% of the wines of the Duc de Magenta which includes fine parcels of Puligny, Chassagne and Auxey-Duresses,

Pierre-Henri and André Gagey enjoying a glass of their own Burgundy

90% of the Clos des Corvées in Nuits-St.-Georges, share-cropped by Michel Thomas, and the 7 ha Santenay Clos de Malte.

André Gagey, a charming man, full of the gentlest of old-fashioned courtesy and worldly wisdom, has now handed over control of the house to Pierre-Henri, who was trained, not as a winemaker, but as an engineer and business administrator. André will tell you proudly how, despite a notably successful education, he refused his son employment in the firm until he had gained wider experience elsewhere. Returning from his banishment, suitably broken in, he is now following in his father's distinguished footsteps. According to André, Pierre-Henri is 'passioné du vin' and 'un très bon dégustateur' to boot.

Technical direction is in the capable hands of Jacques Lardière, who joined André Gagey in 1970 to understudy him in that role. He in turn is supported by an oenologist, Christine, and a team of Chefs de Culture to look after the 4 Domaines. Lardière, who might easily be mistaken for Vladimir Ashkenazy, is an articulate and highly competent winemaker who believes that his mission is to interfere with nature as little as possible; consequently pumps, filters, and the rest of the technical impedimenta of the inept are, as far as possible, kept out of the way. Above all, he strives to retain the typicity of each appellation and *lieu-dit* in its wine. 'Le *terroir*, c'est une mémoire,' he explains, waving his arms round galvanically, at a bank of casks, as if they were instruments in some sort of private vinous orchestra he was engaged to conduct.

The Domaine wines are indeed forceful expressions of their respective *terroirs*. The négociant wines, however, when they come from less specific origins, a commune or region, for instance, will express a different, broader typicity. A Jadot Meursault, for example, being an *assemblage* of the wines of twelve or so different proprietors, will sink the individual style of each within that of the generality. With 300 casks of Meursault, or 90 of Chassagne Village, it can only be so.

Over the years, the Gageys have built, and carefully nurtured, close relationships with the growers who provide them with grapes, juice or wine. These are based firmly on 'gentlemen's agreements' – and trust. By and large, a Jadot grower, once his quality and competence are proven, is left to get on with his job. If he needs advice it is there, but otherwise there is no more than a watching brief over his activities. The House is under no obligation to buy anything that is not up to its own standards, which growers well understand; equally, the grower is not obliged to sell to the House, if he feels that he can do better elsewhere. However, as Pierre-Henri points out, Jadot's policy of buying grapes or juice at finished wine prices together with the certainty of payment and the freedom of such an arrangement, puts the balance of financial advantage with the grower as well as ensuring Jadot continuity of supply. A secure network of this sort is a fundamental part of any successful négociant – even one with 49 splendid hectares of its own.

The great price increase in the 1983 and 1985 vintages, especially for Côte d'Or whites, temporarily kinked the supply lines. According to Pierre-Henri, a fragile equilibrium has now been restored and the focus has shifted to the Grand Crus, where the pipes appear to be showing signs of spluttering. However, as he optimistically adds, 'There is progress to be made in areas where the wines are not as good as they should be.' Whether this Delphic pronouncement is meant to reflect the need to improve the quality of winemaking in poor Domaines with otherwise good land, or the desire to bring out the inherent qualities of the Côte's lesser-known communes is unclear. Either way, increases in demand will require négociants like Jadot either to increase the flow through the existing pipes or else to find somewhere else to pipe from.

For the present, supply and demand seem precariously balanced – except perhaps for the rarer Grands Crus, where rationing is the inevitable consequence of scarcity. In this climate, there is ample room for diversity – for example, Jadot market 5 different Beaune Premiers Crus and 7 different Gevrey Premiers Crus. This strong desire to bring into consumer consciousness the individuality of each *lieu-dit* thrives on an increasingly sophisticated trade and public, who are increasingly interested in what others might regard as distinctions without differences, and is a cornerstone of Jadot policy.

In the cellars, Jacques Lardière watches over his 62 *cuves* and a veritable batallion of casks with infinite care and patience. He knows each village, and each *climat* intimately – its soil, exposition, vine age and ripening characteristics. He knows the way each lot of grapes behaves in the fermenting vats – whether they lose acidity or work better at this or that temperature – and takes pride in letting each wine express to the fullest extent, the character of its origin.

His philosophy is courageously simple: the less you intervene, the better the expression of typicity. 'Men are afraid; they don't dare follow nature,' Jacques remarks – a pungent imprecation on many viticulteurs who interfere too much with their *cuves* and casks. For him, the lightest of sulphuring, neither heat-

The engaging Jacques Lardière, at work in the tasting room

ing nor cooling, and a pre-fermentive maceration of 4–7 days – until nature is ready for the yeasts to work – is ideal.

Jadot's reds invariably need time to blossom. Jacques Lardière is not a man dedicated to short *cuvaison*: a remarkable 25-33 days in *cuve* to extract the very maximum of colour and aroma is about average, where everyone else is content with half that time probably fearing volatile acidity and excess tannins. Jacques regards this, and his almost 100% destalking (except for the smaller parcels such as Chambolle Les Amoureuses and Musigny where a small proportion of stalks are left) as important elements in making a fine, long-lived wine. 'Tiens,' he exclaims, with yet more orchestral gesturing, 'aromas come from the dynamics of yeasts and bacteria; *cuvaison* is like charging a battery – the longer you charge it, the more aromatic and gustatory power you will have at the end.'

Undaunted by a month or more of *cuvaison*, he is proud to announce that he generally ferments at 35–40°C. Most vignerons would break out in a muck sweat at the thought, and warn that beyond 32°C you are courting disaster – fermentation might stick, volatile acidity may rise and heaven knows what else may befall. Jacques is quite content: he has fermented some 1,500 *cuves* in 25 years of winemaking and not one has 'stuck'. In any case, if one day it happens, then 'c'est facile', you simply decant the wine off its solids, press the pulp, re-vat the whole lot and off it goes again. 'There is no danger in the *cuves*,' argues Jacques, 'the potential danger is in the imbecility of man.' There are many estimable vignerons who would not subscribe to this radical view of things.

As you might expect with this disarming traditionalist, cultured yeasts have no place in his scheme of vinification; that would be unwarrantable intervention. It is pretentious to interfere with nature. 'Selected yeasts,' says Jacques scornfully, 'selected for what, why? Selection means nothing at that level since we don't really know what the micro-

organisms are.' There are more than 500 different aromas detectable in wine and the extraction of the maximum possible from this great diversity is so important, and only achievable with indigenous yeasts.

Tasting with Jacques Lardière is an education. Wine as he sees it has a definite role to play in people's lives – to bring a little imagery, a little magic. People buy a fine bottle not simply to spend money but to have a far off, shaded window opened – a glimpse of something magical, of something special. 'We are working with the imagination, the emotions, the unconscious' – a pointed stab at those who spend their time nit-picking over sterile descriptions, instead of enjoying what is in their glass.

Jacques' wooden *cuves* are *pigéed* twice daily to keep the cap moist and to help extraction – but there is no *remontage*; this deprives the yeasts of oxygen and thus lengthens fermentation. The wines are then put into cask – about 15% new wood for the Premiers and Grands Crus and older casks – 'des bons' – for Villages and *Régionales*. Traditionally, Jadot wines were racked 2 or 3 times before bottling; Jacques has reduced this to one single racking, 11–14 months after harvest. The racking is carried out cask-to-cask within the same population of casks for each wine. Whether the wine is racked new to old or new to new etc. depends entirely on tasting; there are no fixed rules.

After 18–22 months in wood the wines are racked clear of their lees and unified. 2–3 weeks later they are bottled with neither fining nor filtration. The regional wines are in fact very lightly filtered – 'It is less tiring for the wine than a racking,' argues Jacques.

The Domaine's white wines are fermented in cask direct from the presses. No time is allowed for the juice to settle since Jacques is convinced that once you clarify a juice you remove something from its aromatic organisation which has an impact on typicity; you end up making a wine rather than producing it. The wines spend anything between 12 and 20 months in cask with only one racking. In naturally leaner years (e.g. 1987/88/ 91) some 15–20% of new oak is used and cask ageing is prolonged to add fat to the wine. In better years (e.g. 1985 and 1992) – the whites have no new wood at all since they are considered to have enough natural structure without adding more. A skimmed-milk fining and a plate-filtration precede bottling.

The results of all Jacques' conducting are stunning – a range of wines with individuality and depth and of consistently high quality. From the attractive, sappy, regional Bourgognes, through the ripe, earthy Auxey Duresses to the heights of Chevalier-Montrachet Les Demoiselles and Montrachet itself, Jadot's whites combine finesse and depth of fruit. Whilst the négoce wines are well-made and correct, the Domaine wines equal what one might expect to find in growers' cellars. The Duc de Magenta's Chassagnes are impeccable, with considerable vinosity and depth, whilst the Grand Cru whites have a complexity and power which need years of cellaring to develop but which are well worth the wait. A Chevalier Les Demoiselles 1978, tasted from a magnum a decade on was everything one might expect from a wine of such pedigree – a deepening golden colour with a fully developed, highly complex, honey and grilled almonds aroma and a superb spectrum of flavours which kept one sniffing and sipping with fascination and pleasure.

The range of reds is no less impressive. Long *cuvaison* inevitably results in a deep colour – more or less dense Victoria plum in youth – evolving into a lighter garnet 'tuile' with progressing age. Each Village wine admirably evinces the typicity of its origins – from a somewhat rustic Marsannay and Fixin in the north to a Santenay Clos de Malte of some depth and finesse in the south.

From the vast range of the Domaine's Premiers and Grands Crus the Beaunes stand out – not just for their overall quality, but for the differences between the various individual *climats*, spread throughout the commune. The *Monopole* Clos des Ursules – part of the Vignes-Franches vineyard originally owned by the Ursuline Convent at Beaune in the 17th century – is the Jadot flagship; its wine is generally quite perfumed and relatively forward, never a blockbusting Premier Cru but one which has no difficulty ageing. Of the others, the Grèves and the remarkably deep Les Avaux, from the Champy Domaine excel. In good vintages, Les Avaux is almost opaque black-cherry in colour; the very old vines clearly contributing to its huge concentration of fruit – wholly atypical of most young Beaunes one is ever likely to encounter; a wine destined to last a quarter of a century without turning a hair.

The range and overall quality of the Grand Crus from the Domaine's own vineyards is impressive. Of the 1993s and 1994s (some excellent *cuvées* here) some are more concentrated, others more elegant – but there are none which would cause one to question for a moment their ranking as Grands Crus. In 1993, the Bonnes-Mares, Clos de Bèze (made entirely in *cuves auto-pigéantes*) and the supremely silky, aristocratic Musigny stood out for sheer balance and excitement. Undoubtedly with the 1990s the finest of recent vintages.

Louis Jadot is a firm of uncompromising quality. As with any Domaine not everything is invariably wonderful, but competence and integrity make it a thoroughly trustworthy source of yardstick Burgundy.

VINEYARD HOLDINGS

DOMAINE GAGEY :

Commune	Level	Lieu-dit/Climat	Area	Vine Age	Status
Beaune	PC	Les Chouacheux	0.67	23	P
Beaune	PC	Les Cents Vignes	0.42	15	P
Beaune	PC	Les Grèves (Blanc)	0.84	7	P
Nuits	PC	Les Boudots	0.50	18	P
Chambolle	PC	Les Baudes	0.27	40	P
Chambolle	V	————	0.40	25	P
Morey	GC	Clos St.-Denis	0.17	37	P
Puligny	PC	Champ-Gain	0.40	30	P
		Total:	**3.67 ha**		

DOMAINE ROBERT TOURLIÈRE :

Commune	Level	Lieu-dit/Climat	Area	Vine Age	Status
Beaune	PC	Les Grèves (Rouge)	0.65	18	P
Beaune	PC	Les Grèves (Blanc)	0.13	43	P
Beaune	PC	Les Toussaints	0.89	28	P
Beaune	PC	Les Tuvilans	0.56	38	P
Vougeot	GC	Clos de Vougeot	0.64	30	P
		Total :	**2.87 ha**		

DOMAINES DES HÉRITIERS LOUIS JADOT :

Commune	Level	Lieu-dit/Climat	Area	Vine Age	Status
Aloxe	GC	Corton	0.19	N/A	P
Aloxe	GC	Corton-Charlemagne	0.88	23	P
Aloxe	GC	Corton Pougets	1.54	28	P
Pernand	PC	Clos de la Croix de Pierre	1.59	18	P
Beaune	PC	Les Bressandes	1.03	17	P
Beaune	PC	Les Theurons	1.03	15	P
Beaune	PC	Clos des Couchereaux	1.93	25	P
Beaune	PC	Les Boucherottes	2.74	33	P
Beaune	PC	Les Chouacheux	0.39	20	P
Beaune	PC	Clos des Ursules	2.74	33	P
Puligny	PC	Les Folatières	0.24	18	P
Puligny	GC	Chevalier-Montrachet Les Demoiselles	0.52	40	P
		Total:	**15.65 ha**		

DOMAINE LOUIS JADOT :

Commune	Level	Lieu-dit/Climat	Area	Vine Age	Status
Gevrey	GC	Chambertin Clos de Bèze	0.42	42	P
Gevrey	GC	Chapelle Chambertin	0.39	33	P
Gevrey	PC	Clos St.-Jacques	1.00	33	P
Gevrey	PC	Les Cazetiers	0.12	23	P
Gevrey	PC	La Combe aux Moines	0.17	25	P
Gevrey	PC	Lavaux St.-Jacques	0.22	31	P
Gevrey	PC	Estournelles St.-Jacques	0.38	38	P
Gevrey	PC	Les Poissenots	0.19	26	P
Beaune	PC	Les Avaux	1.43	28	P
Beaune	PC	Les Theurons	0.38	13	P
Savigny	PC	La Dominodes (Rouge et Blanc)	2.01	28	P
Morey	GC	Bonnes-Mares	0.27	8	P
Chambolle	GC	Musigny	0.17	33	P
Chambolle	PC	Les Amoureuses	0.12	8	P
Chambolle	V	————	0.04	33	P
Vougeot	GC	Clos de Vougeot	2.20	13	P
Santenay	V	Clos de Malte (Rouge)	4.88	30	P
Santenay	V	Clos de Malte (Blanc)	1.65	30	P
Pernand	PC	Clos de la Croix de Pierre	1.88	1	P
Savigny	PC	Les Narbantons	0.40	27	P
Savigny	PC	Les Vergelesses	0.53	25	P
Savigny	PC	Les Lavières	0.85	28	P
Puligny	PC	Les Referts	0.45	15	P
Marsannay	V	(Blanc)	0.56	1	P
Marsannay	V	(Rouge)	1.91	30	P
Marsannay	V	(Rosé)	2.78	30	P
————	R	(Bourgogne Aligoté)	0.91	31	P
————	R	(Bourgogne Passe-Tout-Grains)	0.42	33	P
————	R	(Bourgogne Rouge)	0.16	30	P
		Total:	**26.89 ha**		
		Grand Total:	**49.08 ha**		

Champy et Cie

BEAUNE

Henri and Pierre Meurgey (father and son) are longtime *courtiers* (brokers) who sell wine on behalf of Domaines but – as distinct from négociants – do not hold stock. In 1990, they bought the goodwill and cellars of Champy Père et Cie from Louis Jadot, who in turn had bought the business a few months earlier, for its vineyards. Their aim is to build up a quality négociant house adding contracted vineyards, should viable opportunities present themselves.

The Meurgeys are a strong team. In addition to his skill as a winemaker, Henri's 35-years' broking give him an unrivalled knowledge of the Côte d'Or and its vignerons, and both of them a valuable entrée to the best sources of supply. Their broking house – DIVA – trades alongside Champy, in Beaune's quiet Rue Grenier-à-sel.

At a time when many non-vineyard-owning négociants are in difficulties – mainly because their traditional suppliers, especially the better Domaines, are bottling more of their own wine and only need the négoce as an outlet for inferior *cuvées* – one might sensibly question the prudence of starting out in this market. Pierre Meurgey, a cultured, 20th-century man, looking somewhat incongruous seated in the time-warp of his 19th-century office, justifies the investment with the optimistic belief that even top Domaines will continue to sell a few casks *en négoce* to help their cash flow. Also, their relationship with growers should assist them to lever a more advantageous split between better and less good *cuvées* – a few barrels at a time.

Pierre and his father insist they are in business for quality, not volume: 'We are not hectomaniacs.' Their aim is to bottle modest-sized lots of decent wine – even different *cuvées* of one wine if blending would detract rather than enhance the components. 'For instance,' Pierre explains, 'Meursault Clos du Cromin is fuller and Les Chevaliers more elegant, so we should bottle these separately to preserve their identities.'

Production is currently running at around 30,000 cases – including Chablis, the Mâconnais and Côte Chalonnaise – and the wines fully justify the Meurgeys' faith in the buying power of their special relationship. 'If you select the wine right at the start, there isn't much to do' – indeed, but many manage to do it wrong. New wood – the nemesis of much good Burgundy – is kept at around 15%, with Grands and Premiers Crus being mainly matured in second-year casks from Hospices purchases. *Elévage*, fining and filtration are dictated by the needs of each wine and, where merited, casks are bottled individually.

The whites (1992s) – from a fresh, floral generic Chardonnay through a most attractive, substantial Auxey Duresses to a full range of Meursaults, Chassagnes and Pulignys – are sound and well composed. Bottling is deliberately late (20 months), reflecting the Meurgeys' view that 'typicity comes from keeping the wine in cask'. This requires somewhat higher sulphur levels than normal, which initially flattens the wines; however, the underlying quality is there, needing only time to emerge.

The reds veer towards the masculine, with firm, but not aggressive, tannins. In some cases, this comes through as an element of rusticity and an impression of lacking the purity one finds with growers' bottlings. This is particularly so in Appellations whose early hallmark is finesse – e.g. Vosne-Romanée and Volnay; in those with greater natural structure – e.g. Clos Vougeot, Clos de Bèze or Corton, the results are more obviously successful.

The Meurgeys' first Champy vintage was 1990. Now, with a few years under their belts, Pierre and Henri are much surer of what they need. They prefer buying wine to grapes, which is racked from growers' casks to their own, after *malo*. These are then transported to their magnificent 15th-century cellars, under the offices, for maturation. Here, in a small, grimy corner, lie a few bins of old Champy stock, going back to the 1858 vintage.

The investment has clearly been enormous. Burgundy needs négociants of the quality of the Meurgeys, as a bridge between the small, often unobtainable, Domaine lots and the oceans of indifferent quality offered by the hectomaniacs. They deserve to succeed.

Eating chez Champy

Domaine Louis Latour

BEAUNE

Louis Latour, one of Burgundy's most respected and traditional Domaines, is, in fact, an amalgam of two distinct, but closely related enterprises. The older arm of the business, Maison Latour, represents the development of an established wine négociants, Lamarosse, founded in 1797, and acquired by Louis Latour III in 1867. It buys both grapes and juice from growers throughout Burgundy, making and marketing a complete range of wines, and was responsible for bringing more modest appellations such as Mâcon-Lugny and Chardonnay de l'Ardeche to the international wine-list.

The younger part of the business is the Domaine Louis Latour which started when Latours, a family of vignerons since the early 17th century, arrived at Aloxe-Corton in 1768. Plying their trade as schoolteachers, vignerons and coopers, they retained their handful of hectares until Louis III (1835–1902), whose business acumen increased it from 4 to 10, in the 1860s.

The Lamarosse négociant business thrived to the extent that in 1891 Louis Latour had amassed enough capital to profit from the family squabbles of the Comtes de Grancey and buy their magnificent 35-ha Domaine in Aloxe-Corton. Since then each successive Louis Latour has been Mayor of Aloxe, which remains the Domaine's physical and spiritual heart.

Until the appearance of Louis Latour IV (1874–1941) a series of only sons had ensured an unproblematic succession. However, not content with adding vines to the Domaine by marrying some, Louis IV broke the rules and sired six children. In the 1960s when five decided to withdraw their vineyards, the Domaine was unable to buy them out, so by 1970, it found itself some 15 ha the poorer.

Nonetheless, impoverishment is relative, and the Domaine still owns some 46 ha of vines, the majority being Premier and Grand Cru. Apart from 0.8 ha each of Chambertin and Romanée-St.-Vivant, bought in 1898, all the land is in the Côte de Beaune.

The succession continues – the Domaine is now directed by Louis V's son Louis-Paul Latour VI (b.1931), who has recently been joined by his son Louis-Fabrice VII (b.1962) as finance director. Louis V's brother, Jean Latour, now 85, who managed the Domaine for nearly half a century (1925–1974) continues the living link with the past.

The Domaine's day-to-day fortunes are in the hands of the lean, intense Denis

The Domaine's Château de Grancey at Aloxe-Corton gives its name to the firm's finest Corton

Fetzmann, a qualified agronomist and oenologist, who heads a small technical team overseeing vineyards and cellars. His formidable expertise ensures maximum care throughout production and provides an element of cross-fertilisation between the different responsibilities.

In the vineyards, the Domaine has a history of being innovative. During the late 19th century *phylloxera* epidemic, it was the wit of Louis III who realised that one could bypass the disease by grafting on to resistant U.S. rootstocks, which prompted him to buy vineyards cheaply, whilst most vignerons despaired. In the 1890s he planted 17 ha of the Grancey Domaine on to new roots and encouraged other vignerons to use the technique. He was also instrumental in planting Chardonnay, in place of Aligoté and Pinot Noir in limestone-dominated sections of the southern slopes of the Corton hill, which remarkable insight paved the way for the appellation Corton-Charlemagne.

Denis Fetzmann and the Chef de Culture, Michel Magnien, take the care of their vineyards seriously. 'Culture traditionelle' is the policy, which means resting soils for 2–3 years before replanting. As the Domaine is replanted in total every 47 years, this represents a permanent sacrifice of several years' production on 1 ha of vines.

Whereas the Domaine's Pinot Noir is a mixture of *sélection massale* from their own vineyards plus one-third clones to preserve, as far as possible, the 'originality' of each *climat*, new Chardonnay plantings are exclusively in clones. The difference reflects the

difficulty of finding suitable indigenous Chardonnay plant material with low disease risk. In this respect, Pinot is less problematic. Where clones are used, their progress is closely monitored, from vineyard to bottle.

Soil erosion, especially in the steep vineyards behind the *cuverie* at Aloxe-Corton, presents a constant problem. Constructing special drainage conduits to collect rain-eroded soil is one line of attack, whilst a full-time worker to maintain the Domaine's kilometres of stone walls is the other. Eroded soil may not be reconstituted with earth from anywhere – especially in a Grand Cru – so keeping what is already there is essential.

Since the vine is a naturally rambling plant, health by itself will not produce high quality fruit – one has to limit its yield. Denis Fetzmann takes pride in a 20-year average yield of 30 hl/ha in the Domaine's Corton vineyards; hardly excessive against a permitted maximum of 35–42 hl/ha. The keys are well-known: old vines, careful *sélection massale* from low-yielding vines, short pruning and minimum fertilisation.

To this formula, Denis Fetzmann adds a green-pruning of bunches when he considers it is necessary. In 1990, despite restricting each vine to some 6–8 bunches, a perfect flowering presaged a huge harvest. Between the 20th July and 15th August, a team removed half the crop from 12 ha. In 1989, 15 ha were scoured to remove a second generation of grapes, which threatened to sap sugar production and would have added unwelcome acidity. Recently, there have been successful trials with a product which aborts imperfectly set flowers; this is a precise operation with a treatment window of a few days.

The wines are vinified by Jean-Pierre Jobard; the reds in their superb vaulted *cuverie*, built in 1830 in Aloxe's Les Perrières vineyard. The grapes are destemmed and crushed, then transported by a system of large shiny copper bowls on overhead rails (another Louis III innovation) to the vats, each representing a particular parcel of vines – selected by age, Appellation or plant origin.

There is no pre-fermentive maceration but *cuvaison* has now been 'gently prolonged' to around 10 days. This follows the principles of Dr Guyot, set out in the 1850s, which counselled a rapid fermentation which did not pass 30°C. Temperature is controlled by heat-exchangers, whilst frequent *pigéage* – 'a bit more' now than before – keeps the cap of skins broken up and moist.

The press-wine, expressed by an ancient pneumatic membrane press, used for both red and white grapes, is added to the free-run wine; this is followed by 24 hours *débourbage* before the new wine is transferred to casks in the magnificent cellars below.

Such abnormally short vinification has attracted its share of criticism. It is said that one cannot extract enough matter in eight days to give sufficient structure and typicity. The defence is both that this is no more than traditional Burgundian practice, and moreover, that what is sought is finesse rather than sheer size. After ten days *cuvaison*, says Denis Feztmann, you extract tannin at the expense of finesse. In any case, Jean Latour vinified the Hospices de Beaune wines from 1925 to 1975 in exactly the same way, and no-one complained about those.

The red wines remain in cask – 20% new oak only – for about 18 months. They are racked after the *malo* – cask-to-cask – and again before the vintage, when a selection is made for each *cuvée*. Fining depends on the vintage; however, there are two filtrations – one after the second racking and one two months or so later, just before bottling.

In between, the Domaine's red wines are subjected to a process which has caused considerable controversy – they are flash-pasteurised for 3 seconds at 72°C. This practice, instigated by Louis IV at the end of the 19th century, is intended to protect colour and aroma, to increase stability and to guard against bacterial spoilage. It does not, according to the Domaine, 'prevent wines ageing, improve poor wines or make all wines taste the same'. It is felt to be the gentle option – less tiring than a harsh filtration or fining.

Whilst pasteurisation may not prevent a red wine from ageing, it may change the way in which it does so. Wine contains a host of naturally volatile elements – so it is not inconceivable that even as little as 3 seconds at

72°C might dramatically alter their balance. Louis Latour has not, as far as can be ascertained, followed the evolution of the same wine bottled with and without pasteurisation – it would be a simple experiment and would kill the controversy once and for all. Commentators have too often noted rich, opulent fruit in cask and rather less excitement in bottle, for the controversy to be quelled with a colour pamphlet. The Domaine doth protest too much.

Latour's explicit preference for finesse and their shortish *cuvaisons* result in wines which generate controversy. For many, their Corton-Grancey – a brand representing the best of each vintage's Cortons – Chambertin and Romanée-St.-Vivant, represent the apotheosis of fine red Burgundy; for others the wines simply lack guts. Argument is superfluous, in the end it is a matter of taste.

Whilst the Village wines and some of the Premiers Crus have often seemed pleasant but lacking in precision, the Grands Crus in great years can make fine bottles. However, although not expressly designed for longevity, with age these wines often become dull – just flat and uninspiring.

It remains to be seen whether the increased *pigéage* and longer *cuvaisons* will make any significant difference. Tasting recently bottled 1993s in mid-1995, the wines, although retaining the normal Latour mid-ruby colour – seemed richer and better structured than usual; but 1993 was an exceptional vintage. Only with bottle-age will any real change become apparent, so their evolution will be followed with interest.

Whatever the doubts about the Domaine's red wines, there can be none about its whites, which represent some of the finest

Burgundies available. These wines are vinified at the Domaine's new *cuverie* in Beaune; the grapes from Montrachet and from Corton-Charlemagne are pressed at Aloxe-Corton and the *musts* transported to Beaune.

There, the juice is put into tank, controlled at 29°C until fermentation has begun when it is transferred to cask. Latour are very particular about their casks – all are made from their own Allier oak, selected for its fine grain and dried naturally at Aloxe. Whilst the reds only see 20% of new wood, the whites are fermented in about 80% new casks.

After a minimum of four months on their fine lees, the wines are racked, cask-to-cask, followed 9 months or so later with a fining and light filtration, before being bottled.

The 3,000 cases of Corton-Charlemagne and the pitiful 180 cases of Chevalier-Montrachet Les Demoiselles represent the totality of the Domaine's white wine output. The grapes are deliberately harvested late, ripeness, not acidity, being the principal consideration. Invariably great, they start life tight-budded, but, with age, blossom into supreme aristocrats.

The common denominator of immense power and complexity hides very different characters. The Charlemagne tends to more masculine elegance and slightly reserved austerity, underpinned by firm, ripe fruit, whereas the Chevalier shows the plumper, more feminine charm one associates with Puligny. There is also an equally fine Montrachet, but not from Domaine vines.

As a substantial Domaine and négociant, Louis Latour's reputation stands high. Controversy over its red wines should not detract from its achievements in bringing fine Burgundy to a much wider public.

VINEYARD HOLDINGS

Commune	Level	Lieu-dit/Climat	Area	Vine Age	Status
Aloxe	V	——————	3.00	11	P
Aloxe	PC	Les Chaillots	5.30	19	P
Aloxe	GC	Corton Bressandes, Perrières, Pougets, Grèves, Clos du Roi, Clos de la Vigne Au Saint, Chaumes	17.00	24	P
Beaune	PC	Vignes Franches	2.70	25	P
Beaune	PC	Les Perrières	30.00	31	P
Beaune	PC	Clos du Roi	0.42	8	P
Beaune	PC	Les Cras	0.54	27	P
Pernand	PC	Les Caradeux	0.76	43	P
Pernand	PC	Les Caradeux (Blanc)	0.81	4	P
Pernand	PC	Ile des Vergelesses	0.75	41	P
Pernand	V	(Rouge)	0.44	6	P
Volnay	V	——————	0.47	41	P
Volnay	PC	Mitans	0.27	10	P
Pommard	PC	Les Epenots	0.41	21	P
Aloxe	GC	Le Charlemagne (Blanc)	6.70	20	P
Aloxe	GC	Les Languettes (Blanc)	1.95	25	P
Aloxe	GC	Le Corton (Blanc)	0.88	32	P
Puligny	GC	Chevalier-Montrachet	0.51	35	P
Gevrey	GC	Chambertin	0.81	26	P
Vosne	GC	Romanée-St.-Vivant	0.76	36	P
		Total:	**45.78 ha**		

Domaine Albert Morot

BEAUNE

A chance bottle with a friend in Chablis 30 years ago provided the spark for an introduction to the Domaine Albert Morot. Having tasted what was excellent wine, the first visit was something of a shock. The Domaine's headquarters, the whimsically neo-gothic Château de la Creusotte, on the periphery of Beaune must rank in the top flight of Burgundy's architectural curiosities. It appears to represent no particular style but bears a strong resemblance to the sort of 'hatter's castle' mixture popular with wealthy industrialists in the north of England at the turn of the twentieth century.

Whilst probably the last word in modernity and fashion when it was built in 1890, the Château has clearly been subjected to the sternest of test any building might be expected to undergo – neglect. For the past century or so, bits have been falling off it: chimney pots missing, shutters hanging at rakish angles – rather as if the house had made the mistake of opening an eye to the sun one day and then finding it couldn't shut it again; tiles missing off the roofs; plants sprouting out of water-hoppers long unkempt, and a veritable snakes-&-ladders of a guttering system which cascades water in every conceivable direction; in short, a museum of bad maintainence. The guttering has now been dealt with, but the shutters still look precarious.

However, this is not a Domaine to be judged on appearance. Whilst it is rarely mentioned in books and its wines seldom seen at tastings, the quality is uniformly high and its Beaunes among the finest in the Appellation. This is due largely to the enthusiasm and dedication of the Choppin family who have owned and managed the Domaine for over seventy years.

The present generation comprises Guy and Françoise Choppin, grandchildren of Albert Morot, a late-19th-century Beaune négociant. Guy, who looked after things so competently from 1952, sadly became ill in 1984, suffering from a progressive malady which has left him housebound and withdrawn. Fortunately, his younger sister, Françoise, a charming and efficient lady, now in her sixties, stepped in and took charge of both Guy and the Domaine.

She is a remarkable person – short, wiry and energetic, with a passion for her wine and a deep feeling for quality. With the help of a vigneron for the vines, an 'ouvrier' for the heavier work and the part-time services

Françoise Choppin watching casks being topped up in her cellars

of a couple of ladies, she now runs the entire operation – vineyard, cellar and business. Françoise does not drive and virtually never leaves the estate – 'in case a customer calls – they even come on Sundays, you know'. In some years, her furthest excursion is to her barrel-maker in Meursault; 'abroad' probably means Santenay.

A visit here is always an eccentric delight. A dilapidated, cock-eyed sign propped up against a tree on the edge of the walled park which surrounds the Château extends a permanent invitation to 'visite et dégustation'. The courtyard is generally presided over by a large, harmless, hyperactive dog which makes a lot of noise and seems to be everywhere at once – almost as if he felt personally obliged to represent a small canine army, the remainder being temporarily absent.

The cellars, reached from a raised ground-level *cuverie*, are old and exceedingly cold. Tasting raw, young wine from the cask here on a January afternoon, is likely to impact more on one's feet than on one's teeth. However, it is worth the discomfort, for the hundred or so old oak *pièces,* neatly stacked along the main cellar aisle, contain the results of a tradition that has no intention of compromising on quality.

For Françoise everything begins with the vine. She is fortunate, in that 80% of the Domaine's wine comes from its own vineyards, acquired between 1893 and 1894, principally from the then owners of the Domaine de la Romanée-Conti and the Domaine de la Pousse d'Or. These consist of a patchwork of almost seven ha comprising six of the finest Beaune *climats,* scattered around the southern, classier end of the Beaune vignoble, and the 1.81 ha *Monopole* Savigny Premier Cru Clos la Bataillère. These produce fewer than 3,000 cases annually – all Premier Cru.

The Morot Pinot Noir vines are allowed to

reach an advanced age. Françoise Choppin has no doubt that, even though the yield is commensurately reduced, the quality of fruit improves dramatically with increasing vine age. Even with rigorous pruning to further reduce yields and increase concentrations, this is sometimes not enough. In 1990 a woman was employed for the entire holiday month of August, to green-prune much of the Domaine. This resulted in substantially reduced yields, and a 'very contented' worker.

It is fair to say that one can learn much about a vigneron's attitude to quality from their attitude to vine age. Those who are too ready to grub up vines before their 50th birthday, or who think that a vine produces its best quality fruit when it is 30 years old, say more about the quality of their own wines than they might ever imagine. The unmistakeable contribution to taste of very old vines is a hallmark of Françoise Choppin's wines.

Vinification is thoroughly traditional: since 1926 the grapes have been completely destalked. 'Stalks, they're bitter, they fill up the *cuves* every year, that's all; they bring nothing good to the wine,' is her uncompromising statement on the matter. *Cuvaison* lasts up to three weeks – with plenty of *pigéage* to prolong fermentation and to maximise the extraction of colour and flavour compounds. No cultured yeasts here: 'One tries to be as natural as possible.'

The press-wine is normally added to the free-run wine. A new Vaslin press, acquired in 1982 presses gently, leaving a rich pulp for the distillery to make into the Domaine's excellent Marc (one of the best in Burgundy). The wine is then put into cask and taken down to the depths of the cellars.

Françoise is not blindly enamoured by new wood. However, in 1990 her new bottling-machine broke down whilst bottling the 1989s, resulting in a shortage of casks, so she had to buy new ones. Thus the 1990s had 50%, rather than the usual third new oak: 'easily, easily – I made a very great effort, I had to find a place for those wines,' she chuckles, surveying the line of bright new barrels with evident pleasure. Subsequent vintages benefited from this, and 50% seems now to be the rule.

Bottling used to be early 'to keep the perfumes, the freshness'. Now, for no apparent reason *élévage* has been extended from 12 to 18 months. This may refine tannins, but one wonders what will be the effect on the richness and elegance which have always characterised these wines. This seems a distinct change of style – although if the 1993s are anything to go by, it may also be an improvement.

For all her experience, Françoise Choppin is not an oenologist, so has to rely for advice on experts and journalists, to whom perhaps she listens rather too attentively. All the wines are fined, with albumin. 'Some tell you "no fining" – those are the people from the Côte de Nuits who like tannic wines – others tell you 10% or 20% fining, or half' – a laugh and a shrug of the shoulders. Since 1991 there has been no filtration – a welcome change. But what does it matter, the results are magnificent.

Bottling used to be by hand, but in 1986, seeing the travails of the man bottling the large 1985 harvest, Françoise took pity and bought a small bottling machine. As she tells you this, she adds, in case you might be assailed by doubt, 'This is not a factory you know, we take our time to do things.'

The results are impressive – wines with plenty of depth and flavour, each expressing the individuality of its *climat* and which, above all, age superbly.

The Savigny Bataillère, apart from being the most delicate of the range, is also something of an oddity. It is not in fact a designated vineyard site, but rather a triangular enclave at the base of the Hautes-Vergelesses (Savigny, not Pernand). It has, as far back as anyone can remember, always been known as Savigny-Vergelesses 'dit Bataillère'. Up to recently it also carried the designation 'Clos', being enclosed with a wall on two sides, the third being the track dividing the Haute from Basse Vergelesses. However, the authorities took exception to this, hotly contested, of course, possibly because part of the wall had collapsed. So, for the moment it is simply 'Savigny-Vergelesses, la Bataillère'. In 1987 the officials had another go and tried to suppress the 'Bataillère', but Françoise was on the telephone straight away: 'Ecoutez !'. . . She won her point.

The Clos la Bataillère is generally harvested late, the vines being relatively young (planted 1958, 1972 and 1992; they had finally to grub up the 1945 vines). In character it has great perfume and finesse and plenty of extract – almost a junior Beaune Cent Vignes. 'It's a ladies' wine, this,' remarks Françoise with a smile. Maybe, but it is also the best Savigny.

The Cent Vignes itself tends to be deeper in colour than the Bataillère, with plenty of stuffing on the palate and an attractive nose which develops early. The vineyard was replanted during 1958–9 so the vines are approaching an age of interesting quality.

The Toussaints, replanted in 1969, is often rather tight to begin with, with a good natural acidity and plenty of firm fruit. Often quite a meaty wine, it needs a decade or more to show its true colours, in vintages such as 1985, 1988, 1990 or 1993.

The Marconnets – half planted in 1950 and the rest in 1958 – is rather more Pommard or Corton in style than Beaune. It has the finesse of Corton but the depth and breadth of Pommard. It can be quite soft (e.g. 1989) with an individual nose of more animal character, and is particularly long-lived.

If Marconnets is Corton, then the Teurons is decidely Gevrey – a masculine, firmly-structured wine, with overtones of meat-extract and a distinct hint of *fruits sauvages* on the nose. It keeps especially well in great vintages.

The last two of Françoise's remarkable range of Premiers Crus, Grèves and Bressandes, are, in great vintages, among the best wines to be found in the Côte de Beaune. The Bressandes typically starts off closed up like a clam, giving nothing much for five years, and then gradually emerges from its shell to reveal a silky opulence of aromas and flavours of great distinction. The major part of the vineyard was last replanted in 1946, so there is no lack of delicious, concentrated old-vine fruit. A 1971, 'Tête de Cuvée', tasted in 1995, was still seductively youthful, but with a richness and depth which made one think of a mature Vosne-Romanée or even an Echézeaux.

The Grèves, from a mere 12.53 ares of vines planted in 1948 is sensationally good. Sadly, the vineyard was grubbed up after the 1990 harvest, so the supply dried up until 1993. The wine is usually among the deepest in colour of the range, with a nose of *fruits sauvages*, liquorice and almost sweet fruit. On the palate it manages to combine the depth of the Bressandes with the finesse of the Cent Vignes.

This is fine winemaking (and consistent) by any standards. If the great vintages are excellent, the 'in betweens' are no less successful in their own way. In 1992, 1987, 1982, 1979 and 1967, for example, the wines are more delicate but at the same time full of nuances and lingering flavours, with, invariably, a touch of tannin and enough acidity to keep everything alive. Wines to enjoy whilst

The Château de la Creusotte's newly restored exterior

waiting for the grander vintages to mature.

However, it is the five-star vintages which really put this Domaine at the top. For Françoise, 1971 is, so far, the real vintage of the century. Her 1971s have a dimension of ripe complexity and breed which puts them into the same league as the best of the Côte de Nuits. There were 'Tête de Cuvées' in this vintage for Marconnets, Bressandes and Grèves. Guy Choppin certainly knew what he was doing. Françoise's magisterial 1990s and 1993s seem set to follow suit.

It is difficult to understand why Beaune has always been something of a Cinderella among cognoscenti. Given the choice between Premiers Crus from Volnay and Beaune most would choose Volnay. This implied indictment is unjustified, particularly when one has wine from properties such as Albert Morot to testify in Beaune's favour. Also, Françoise's policy of very modest pricing make it an ideal source for anyone looking to stock a cellar without contracting cirrhosis of the wallet.

The succession has been the subject of some speculation since, sadly, neither Guy nor Françoise has children. In time, the reins will pass to 'nos petits cousins' from Le Havre; what this will mean for the Domaine's wines is a matter of conjecture. One thing, however, is certain: as long as Françoise is in charge, there will be no concessions on quality.

VINEYARD HOLDINGS

Commune	Level	Lieu-dit/Climat	Area	Vine Age	Status
Beaune	PC	Les Teurons	0.99	1963	P
Beaune	PC	Les Grèves	0.13	1991	P
Beaune	PC	Les Toussaints	0.77	1969	P
Beaune	PC	Les Bressandes	1.27	1946/60/82	P
Beaune	PC	Les Cent Vignes	1.28	1958/59	
Beaune	PC	Les Marconnets	0.68	1950/58	P
Savigny	PC	La Bataillère	1.81	1958/72/92	P
		Total:	**6.93 ha**		

POMMARD

The vineyards of Pommard begin at a fork in the road, two kilometres south of Beaune. Branching to the right the road follows the wall of Les Epenots for a further half kilometre, passing the solitary disused railway station and the imposing Clos of the Château de Pommard on the left, before reaching the village itself.

Here, in a small square, a couple of pleasant 'routier'-style bars/restaurants, one on each side of a small bridge, and a smarter new enterprise represent the complete extent of the village's gastronomy. Beneath the bridge meanders l'Avant-Dheune, a dispirited little watercourse which descends from the Combe high above the vineyards, regularly overflowing, flooding houses and cellars and causing general inconvenience. Pommard is further animated by a dress shop, a patisserie and a newly-opened wine shop, offering the ware of its owners – a consortium of local growers.

For many years, Pommard enjoyed the reputation of producing big, heavy, heart-warming brews, a sort of comforting alcoholic soup, with plenty of guts and not much finesse – wines which Harry Yoxall aptly characterised as 'pleasant drinks without much authority'. Producers, both inside and outside the commune, climbed on to this gallopingly profitable bandwagon, with wines which were either dismally dilute, or else cut with something distinctly unBurgundian, to satisfy a seemingly insatiable demand for Pommard.

This was known and noted in the 1930s and continued, despite the introduction of AC 'controls' in 1936 until well into the 1960s. The runaway popularity, and prices, have now abated and Pommard has settled down. Now, several top-class Domaines produce affordable wines of excellent quality.

The vignoble, much reduced since the early 19th century, now covers some 337 ha, of which 211.62 ha are designated AC Pommard and 125.19 ha Pommard Premier Cru.

The Village wines, from vineyards either on higher ground above the village or else on the flatter land between the RN73 and RN74, encompass a broad spectrum of styles and qualities. The rockier, thinner soils of the upper slopes give wines with more finesse but less depth than those from the heavier, clayier soils lower down. The vineyards at the commune's eastern end, which continue Les Epenots, have stonier, better drained soils giving commensurately finer wine.

However, it is with the 24 Premiers Crus that the wines of Pommard become serious. These are sited on a belt of hillside, flat at the bottom and steep at the top, on either side of the village.

On the Beaune side of Pommard, the best are Les Pézerolles, L'Argillière, and Les Epenots which is divided into Les Grands and Les Petits Epenots. Straddling these last two is Comte Armand's Clos des Epeneaux (sic), whilst the section of Grands Epenots closest to the village contains the 2.92 ha Clos des Cîteaux, which belongs to Jean Monnier of Meursault.

In this sector, a south/south-east exposure combines with stony, red clay-limestone soils to produce wines of power and muscle. They tend to have noticeably more tannin and less delicacy than the Premiers Crus of adjacent Beaune, and the best need keeping for 10 years or so to fully develop their potential.

On the Volnay side of the village lie Les Rugiens, Les Jarollières and Les Fremiers (which becomes Les Fremiets in neighbouring Volnay). Often among the richest wines of Pommard, Les Rugiens is divided into the excellent Rugiens-Bas and the less good Rugiens-Hauts, although the distinction is never made on labels. The vineyards here are steeper, on rockier soils, and well-exposed to the south-east. The wines have more finesse and less rustic muscle – often with hints of the silky delicacy of the best Volnays about them. If there were a reclassification, then Les Rugiens-Bas and parts of Les Epenots would be credible candidates for elevation to Grand Cru status.

Here is a handful of exciting Domaines, including that of François Parent, whose wife, Anne-Françoise, makes wine from vines owned or *en fermage* from her parents – Jean and Jeanine Gros of Vosne-Romanee.

One third of Pommard's gastronomy – the bridge Café

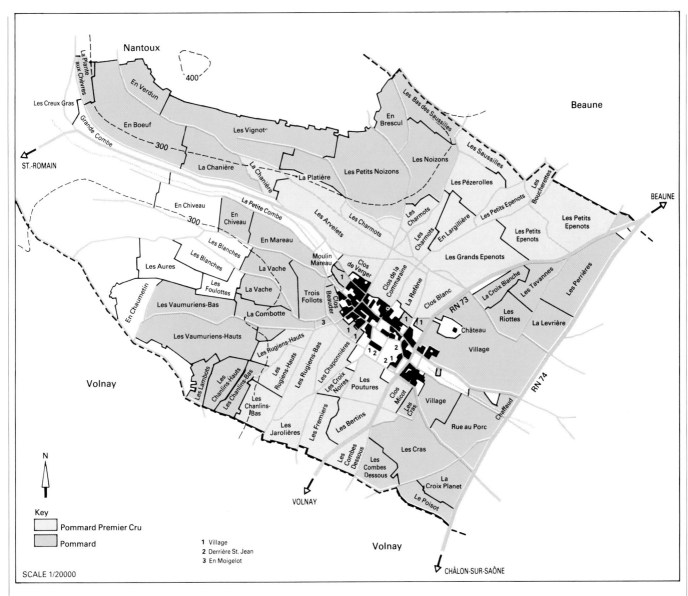

Key

Pommard Premier Cru

Pommard

1 Village
2 Derrière St. Jean
3 En Moigelot

SCALE 1/20000

The kindly André Mussy – now well into his 80s produces good to excellent Pommard Premiers Crus Epenots, Pézerolles and Saucilles, a pair of Beaunes (Epenottes and Montremenots) from his 6 ha. Having vinified successive vintages since his first, 1928, he now shares the work with his son-in-law. This is a reliable source.

Outside the village, Hubert de Montille's Pézerolles and Rugiens are wines of great distinction and Madame Armande Douhairet's Pommard Chanlins is often excellent, especially in ripe vintages such as 1990 and 1993. The Château de Pommard makes a respectable wine from its 20-ha Clos – the largest in single ownership in the Côte – matured in 100% new wood. Drouhin and Jadot both produce good *cuvées* of Les Epenots, and Arnaud Machard de Gramont a fine Pommard Le Clos Blanc. Many vignerons in Volnay are also good sources of Pommard – Joseph Voillot, Regis Rossignol, Jean-Marc Bouley and Yvon Clerget in

particular – albeit on a small scale.

Apart from the attractions of the dress-shop and the patissier, Pommard boasts no fewer than three separate Châteaux, and a fine 18th-century Church with a 32-metre-high bell-tower. This, the centrepiece of the quiet tree-lined main square, is surrounded by fine Domaines – Parent, de Courcel, Gaunoux, Clos des Epeneaux – and the village school.

Of the Châteaux, two, the 18th-century Château Micault and the 1802 Château de Pommard, both belong to the family of Jean-Louis Laplanche, professor of Psychology at the Sorbonne. The third, on the north-eastern side of the village, is the Château de la Commaraine, which, with its 3.75-ha Clos, is the property of Jaboulet-Vercherre. The wine is good, but uninspiring.

For the rest, Pommard has a quiet, monastic history. Probably named after Pommone, the goddess of fruits and gardens, its best *climats* were owned by a variety of religious

orders from the 13th century onwards.

A cross at Pommard used to mark the site of a muddy ford until a bridge was built in 1670. Here, between the two Routiers, the 'diligences' would stage, and passengers would have to traverse on foot. If successful, a hole in the base of the cross – still there in the replica – was provided for a suitable contribution. For most visitors, however, the vineyards and growers are the main attraction and here, there is increasingly enough to justify an exploration. The place has an air of increasing self-confidence and a caucus of excellent growers, which augurs well for its future.

Domaine du Clos des Epeneaux

POMMARD

This Domaine originally belonged to the Marey-Monge family, one of the greatest of 19th-century Burgundian proprietors. When in 1855 one of the Marey-Monge daughters married Comte Armand, the Domaine, being part of her dowry, passed into the 'patrimoine' of the Armands.

Being not by tradition vignerons, they employed *régisseurs* to manage the estate. This system, quite common among grander Burgundian landowners, was open to abuse, especially if the *régisseur* had his own vineyards to tend and the landlord was frequently absent. In January 1985, the present Comte Armand, a Paris-based international lawyer, appointed a young French Canadian, Pascal Marchand, to sole charge of his estate.

The choice of Pascal was an unusual one. Already 'passioné du vin' he had arrived to explore Burgundy in 1983 from Montreal. 'I had never seen a vineyard or *cuverie*,' he confesses, 'but wanted to visit Burgundy because it was the region I knew least.' After helping to vintage the 1983 and working for a few months in the cellars, Pascal returned home.

In June 1984 he went to work for Bruno Clair in Marsannay, and whilst there met, by chance, his future employer. He enrolled for a viticulture and oenology course in Beaune and returned in November of the following year to take up his place.

Quite what inspired the Comte to put this inexperienced young man in sole charge of his precious Domaine is not clear, but he did, and the result has been eminently successful.

The Domaine Pascal took over was unusual in that it consisted of one 5.2-ha slab of vines – the Clos des Epeneaux. In a region where a broad portfolio of small holdings is the norm, a single plot represented a weather risk that many hardened vignerons would contemplate with trepidation. It was also 'a bit faulty'. Whilst the vineyard was acceptable, the cellars needed tidying up and much of the cask stock needed renewing. Apart from looking after the ripening 1985 grapes, there was still the entire 1983 and 1984 vintages in cask to be seen to.

When the 1985 vintage was out of the way, Pascal started to work out policies for maintaining the vineyard. Without the luxury of a fragmented vignoble as an insurance against frost, storm or disease, innovative plans had to be tempered with a degree of caution.

To keep vine age high and to maintain a sensible level of production, *répiquage* is preferred, although limited to vines less than 40 years old since digging individual holes into solid rock is very hard work. Replanting larger parcels of the Clos is also kept to a minimum – since 1985 only one ha has been grubbed up. Pascal chose to replant this on a mixture of selected clones but, seeing the results, decided that the next substantial planting will use a *sélection massale* from the Domaine's own vines.

The current vine population ranges from 5 to 56 years in age. Whilst the older plants are mostly on SO4 roots, apparently defying the conventional wisdom that they are short-lived, newer plantings are on the fashionable 161/49 – well-adapted to its moderate lime content.

The soil profile of the vineyard – studied with care by Pascal – shows a rather meagre topsoil, with a high stone content, which gives on to a substantial bedrock of Marne Calcaire. Curiously for Pommard, the iron content of the soil is not especially high; however, it is well drained, which is important on this flattish ground.

Pruning is kept short. Young vines are trained *en crochet* up to 6 years old, making a gradual transition to the conventional adult *Guyot* training by adding one eye each year.

Much reflection has gone into developing a strategy for treating the vines during the growing season. Pascal admits that in this respect he is still feeling his way. The main problem is the grape-worm, a miserable, useless insect which fractures the skin of the berries and renders them prone to rot through the open wound. The vigneron's dilemma is that if he simply blankets the vines with effective, but perforce, strong insecticides, he kills the insects at the expense of problems later on – spray resistance, alterations in the soil micro-flora etc.; however, not treating the vines risks extensive rot resulting in low yields and a possible reduction in quality.

The solution may lie in new sprays which destabilise the grape-worm's reproductive cycle by destroying the odour compounds upon which it relies to attract and thus to reproduce. Although much less harmful to both soil and vine, these products do not seem to eliminate the worms entirely. They can breed, but are invisible and do not puncture the grape skins. To detect them, one has only to put a grape into warm water when they materialise quite rapidly.

As for other treatments, Pascal is more sure of his ground. He has banished all systemic products and is considering putting an embargo on all *pénétrants*. This will only leave contact sprays – which are effective until the next shower washes them off the leaves. These exclusions include herbicides – so the soil has to be worked by hoe and pick to uproot grass and weeds.

Until there is more information on how synthetics affect the vine and on their patterns of degradation in the soil, he is happier working without them.

Of equal importance to healthy vines are low yields. Here, fertilisers are the key. Growers these days, Pascal admits, are rich, they can afford to buy whatever they want to put on the soils. However, he limits himself to 'very careful' doses of organic fertilisers, simply to adjust trace-elements when necessary. The plants must suffer – 'it is necessary to understand the soil and the needs of the vine. Sometimes, when you see the leaves green until November, you know that there is too much nitrogen in the soil.'

The point Pascal makes is important. In Burgundy, the uniqueness of each small vineyard is a function of its soil. For the wine it produces to express that uniqueness, it is necessary for the vine to nourish itself, not from artificially enriched surface soils, but from deeper down, where trace elements are leached into the water table. For this to happen, growth of the naturally proliferous lateral roots must be restricted, so that the main tap roots are encouraged to seek sustenance further down. To achieve this it is necessary for the vine to have enough vigour of its own, with adequate surface nutrition, provided largely by a balanced cocktail of well-known essential elements – phosphorus, magnesium, potassium, nitrogen, etc. This is why the use of fertilisers is critical. The temptation to overfertilise, producing masses of healthy green foliage and kilos of juicy, ripe grapes, is too much for many Burgundian vignerons, who no doubt feel their coin-laden trouser pockets sagging in sympathy with the pendulous vine branches. The dilute wine such grapes produce, even if the grower bothers to *saigner* the *cuves*, pleasant though it may be, does nothing to express the typicity and character of its origins, of which most Burgundians, with all their 'réunions' and 'confréries' constantly swear to uphold.

Whatever his decision about treatments and fertilisers, there is one misfortune from which Pascal's vineyard seems to be miraculously immune – hail. Hail is by no means uncommon in Pommard – from May to August the risk is there. However, the Clos des Epeneaux, situated at the northern end

Pascal does most of the work on his own

of the commune, usually escapes when its more southerly neighbours suffer. The storms seem to drive from the south-east across the village and then turn sharply north-west, funnelled by the Combe behind. This is indeed a stroke of fortune for what, until recently, was a single vineyard Domaine.

When it comes to harvesting, there is another advantage – the Epenots (of which the Clos des Epeneaux is a part), invariably ripens early. Other viticulteurs, with several plots in Pommard and nearby, tend to harvest their Epenots first if they have any. With this principal plot, Pascal Marchand waits until the grapes are fully ripe – but not over-ripe, before picking.

The vinification sequence is broadly traditional. The grapes are entirely destalked, given a moderate dose of SO_2 in *cuve*, homogenised with an anaerobic pumping-over and then left to ferment on their own yeasts. Pascal tries to mix cooler morning grapes with the hotter afternoon harvest to avoid artificial cooling. Fermentation usually starts after 3–4 days; a further *remontage*, this time with air, helps to multiply the yeasts and start the process off. Fermentation temperatures rise to 33°C, with a total *cuvaison* of 10–17 days, depending on the speed of fermentation and on the vintage. Four separate lots are made from the Clos, reflecting the different vine ages.

Following a 2–3 day *débourbage* in tank – 'clarification problems,' contends Pascal, 'come from what one puts on the vines' – the wine goes into casks, 30% of which are new. Pascal prefers a mixture of Allier, Nevers and Vosges wood to any single oak, but believes

that 'the provenance . . . says nothing, it is the quality of the barrel-maker which is most important.' His casks are medium charred – having tried a very strong charring and found that this tended to lock in any *goût de reduit* the wine might have.

In any case, he does not want to mark the wine too much with wood flavours, so after the first racking, at the end of the first year, the wine in new casks is assembled with that in older casks – the original four Clos *cuvées* now becoming two – and then put back entirely into 3–5 year-old casks. The two lots are reunified at the second racking and then left for three weeks in tank before bottling by gravity, since 1989, with neither fining nor filtration, although these are not excluded *a priori*.

It is worth stressing that the Clos des Epeneaux is a wine made from an assemblage of different wines from vines of different ages grown on a single plot of land. The grapes are harvested by vine age and vinified in three lots – young vines, that is to say, less than 12 years old; 12–20 year-old vines and finally vines older than 30 years. The point of this is that, when the wine is finally

assembled, there are three or more individual palette-colours available which can be used, in greater or lesser proportion, to enhance the complexity of the Grand Vin. Until 1994, any wine not used for the Clos *cuvée* was sold off in bulk. Now Pascal is Domaine-bottling this for sale as Pommard *tout-court*.

In specially good vintages, there may be a Cuvée Vieilles Vignes, made exclusively from the older vines. However, fine as this is, using the best wine on its own inescapably detracts from the concentration of the standard blend.

Tasting cask samples of each 'lot', the differences are striking. The younger vines (9–13) give a wine of greater delicacy – aromas of *fruits sauvages* – with goodish concentration, quite a firm structure, and almost tarry flavours. Wine from the 20–25 year vines is more intensely coloured, with a layer of aggressive tannins dominating the ripe fruit underneath. The older vine lots (35–45 and 55–65) produce the best-integrated and most opulent wine of all – less obviously delicate but disarmingly soft.

The style of finished wine tends to be very structured, even for Pommard which is often regarded as the Nuits of the Côte de Beaune. The natural balance of old vine fruit contributes significantly to the wine's depth, especially in vintages of the quality of 1993, 1990, 1988 and 1985, imparting less aggressive tannins and notably better acidities. Although the earlier vintages are good, the 1988 in particular, they lack complexity. Pascal is working on this and, in particular, on refining and softening the tannins to make the wine more accessible. The results are evident in an excellent, forward 1992 and in the components of a magisterial 1993.

There is clearly a bond of mutual confidence between Pascal Marchand and Comte Armand. In 1994 and 1995 the Domaine bought and contracted vineyards in Volnay, Meursault and Auxey-Duresses, effectively doubling its size, and also giving Pascal his first white wines to vinify. It will be interesting to see what this talented red-winemaker achieves with them.

VINEYARD HOLDINGS

Commune	Level	Lieu-dit/Climat	Area	Vine Age	Status
Pommard	PC	Clos des Epeneaux	5.20	9–65	P
Volnay	PC	Les Fremiets	0.40	0 and 35	P
Volnay	V	Les Famines	0.30	10	P
Meursault	V	Les Meix Chavaux	0.75	2/3 80;	
				1/3 10	M
Auxey	PC	Les Duresses (R)	1.00	10–70	M
Auxey	PC	Les Breterins (W)	0.50	(Various)	M
		Total:	**9.15 ha**		

Domaine Jean-Marc Boillot

POMMARD

Jean-Marc Boillot's considerable talents were honed working with his grandfather from 1967–1984 and then as winemaker for Olivier Leflaive from 1985–1989. Without formal training, he has turned himself into a skilled hand at both red and white wine, which is fortunate because he possesses eleven Appellations of the one and ten of the other.

The Domaine's nerve centre is a fine old house, La Pommardière, adjoining the Château de Pommard, which Jean-Marc rents from his grandfather's legatees. Here the red grapes are destemmed, cold-macerated for 4–5 days, then heated to start fermentation, using selected yeasts, which gives better more regular results – especially with the all-important aromatics. This happens in closed vats, which are only opened for *chaptalisation* and *pigéage* – to conserve aromas. A further period of maceration, brings total *cuvaison* to 18–20 days. The wines remain in cask on their fine lees until the following June to prevent them drying out and are bottled after 14–18 months *élevage*, always with filtration and sometimes with fining.

Jean-Marc's system of allocating new wood is thoroughly democratic: 'Nothing is privileged, it all gets 20–25%,' he explains, adding, as an afterthought: 'except the Pommard Rugiens and the Bâtard-

Montrachet, which have 50%.' Quite why the Bourgogne Rouge merits as much as a Premier Cru is not entirely clear.

The white grapes are pressed, the juice cooled to 14°C, *chaptalised*, yeasted and put into casks. Several different yeasts are used – 3 casks of Puligny, for example, might each have a different variety. Instead of having a *maceration pelliculaire* to enrich his whites, Jean-Marc prefers traditional *batonnage*: 'Maceration makes heavy wines, with heavy aromas and takes away finesse; we leave our whites on lees without racking, but with *batonnage*, for one year; this gives fatness and fine fruit aromas.'

Jean-Marc is a short, close-cropped, rather serious individual, whose conversation shows an occasional, perhaps involuntary, vein of cynicism. Talking animatedly about filtration, he lambasts the current fashion for unfiltered wine, berating into the bargain those ('including some very well-known Domaines') who filter clandestinely, on Sunday, then announce on Monday that they don't. In any case, Jean-Marc believes that properly executed, the delicate operation of filtering can enhance aromatic purity – especially in reds where even the slightest deposit can create dissonant, reduced and gamey aromas.

Both his reds and whites testify to Jean-Marc's desire for 'explosive aromas, great

Jean-Marc Boillot

purity, and maximum fruit'. The reds have 'rich, round and noble tannins, and enough structure; vinification is the same for all – so that the *terroir* comes through'. Democracy means that Pommards are not vatted for longer to produce their hallmark muscle, nor Volnays less for finesse and elegance. 'Pommard can be fine and round, Volnays can be robust.'

For the whites, the florality and fruitiness of Chardonnay is paramount; the wines must be 'opulent, round, fat; I hate whites which are too dry' – faults which generally come from excess racking and too long in wood.

In 1993, Jean-Marc inherited four Puligny Premiers Crus and some Puligny and Chassagne Village whites from the Etienne Sauzet estate; his sister, Janine, is married to Sauzet's Gérard Boudot and his brother, Henri Boillot, makes wine with their father at Volnay. According to Jean-Marc, the widely reported family feuding over the break-up of the estate was no more than press sensationalism. His 1993 versions of the wines are excellent.

With such a wide range, there are inevitably more and less successful *cuvées*. Nonetheless, the standard is uniformly high and the wines thoroughly meritorious.

VINEYARD HOLDINGS

Commune	Level	Lieu-dit/Climat	Area	Vine Age	Status
Volnay	R	(Bourgogne Rouge)	0.54	20	P
Volnay	V	(Various *climats*)	1.23	30	P
Volnay	PC	Ronceret	0.33	15	P
Volnay	PC	Carelle Sous La Chapelle	0.27	36	P
Volnay	PC	Pitures	0.44	45	P
Pommard	V		0.40	25	P
Pommard	PC	Saucilles	0.41	45	P
Pommard	PC	Jarollières	1.31	60	P
Pommard	PC	Rugiens	0.16	80	P
Meursault	V	(Blanc)	0.23	30	P
Chassagne*	V	(Blanc)	0.30	55	P
Puligny*	V		1.44	30	P
Puligny*	PC	Combettes	0.48	35	P
Puligny*	PC	Champ Canet	0.59	40	P
Puligny*	PC	Referts	0.61	46	P
Puligny*	PC	Truffière	0.25	38	P
	R	(Bourgogne Blanc)	0.20	5	P
Beaune	V	(Blanc)	0.10	30	P
Beaune	PC	Montrevenots	0.41	50	F
Beaune	PC	Montrevenots (Blanc)	0.25	3	F
Puligny	GC	Bâtard-Montrachet	0.20	25	F

Total: **10.15 ha**

* Vines from the Sauzet *partage*; first vintage, 1993

Domaine A-F Gros/Domaine Parent

POMMARD

These Domaines, an amalgam of 11 Parent Beaune ha of Côtes de Beaune and 4 Gros ha of Côtes de Nuits, were effectively united when Anne-Françoise Gros, daughter of Jean and Jeanine Gros of Vosne (q.v.) married François Parent in 1976. He had taken over vinification from his father, Jacques, in 1974, as the 12th generation of Parents – the earlier five in Volnay from 1650, the later scions in Pommard where the Domaine has its epicentre in a fine house on the southern side of the Place de l'Eglise. Their son, Mathias, born 1990, is the 13th in direct line from the original François, born 1615.

The Gros wines, all *en fermage* from various relations, include Vosne Village Aux Réas – a vineyard adjoining Mme Gros' fine Clos des Réas, Vosne Maizières, 20 ares of Grand Cru Richebourg and 55 ares of Echézeaux and 2 ha of Hautes Côtes de Nuits – 'my father's folly', comments Anne-Françoise, referring to the years the Gros brothers spent exchanging land at Arcenant to have 6 ha in one single plot and the effort needed to have the authorisation to plant and then to break up and prepare this rocky land. For the Gros family, the Hautes Côtes represents a symbol of liberty from the rules and restrictions of the Côte itself. The Richebourg is vinified and bottled, along with his own and that of their mother, by Anne-Françoise's brother Michel. Thus appear three identical Richebourgs bearing different labels. The tentacles of the Gros clan are complex – they don't always work the land they own and what they own, they don't always work.

The Parent vines are mainly concentrated in Beaune and Pommard – with outposts in Aloxe and Ladoix. These are a mixture of acquisitions and inheritance, built up over centuries, with a touch of *metayage*.

Since March 1995, sales of wine from all five Gros Domaines – Jean Gros, Gros Frère et Soeur, Anne et François Gros, Michel Gros and Anne-Françoise Gros – are entrusted to a family friend, Bernard Mounier. This leaves each Gros – and François Parent – free to concentrate on their vineyards and winemaking.

Quality has been steadily improving here. Parent wines of the late 1970s and early 1980s were too often unduly tannic and lacking in elegance; now, much greater effort is going into fine-tuning the balance of tannin, fruit, alcohol and acidity, and the wines are noticeably better for it.

François – a tall, somewhat reserved, sandy-haired man – has thought deeply about what he is trying to achieve. For him vinification is directed towards the extraction of aromas and typicity and to ensuring that the wines are sufficiently round when they arrive in the bottle. Aromatic intensity and complexity are of prime importance: 'I have to find the relationship between the *must*'s density and the (fermentation) temperature necessary to have maximum aroma.' This depends both upon the speed at which fermentation starts and the length of *cuvaison*. The temperature of $33^{0}C$ seems to be critical: if the density is too high here (i.e. too much sugar unfermented), 'you won't get aromas'. Thrice daily manual *pigéage* up to the middle of fermentation, *remontage* throughout and fractional *chaptalisation*, help ensure a long, slow, even cycle.

Elévage lasts 20–24 months and uses 30–50% of new wood. Fining is generally avoided – except for the smaller volumes of Echézeaux and Corton – and filtration depends entirely on the amount of pectins in each *cuvée*.

The sole major white wine (Parent) – a Corton Blanc (not Charlemagne) – from young vines is quite rich and distinctive; a curiosity rather than a true Grand Cru.

The reds, however, more than merit their status. The Gros include an excellent clutch of Vosne-Romanées, fullish, finely aromatic and with characteristic Vosne elegance, and a powerful, fleshy Echézeaux – from the excellent Champs Traversin *climat*, which adjoins Grands Echézeaux above Clos Vougeot. The Parent camp contributes a fine Beaune Epenottes from 30-year-old vines and Pommards, with a dazzling array of eight Premiers Crus, topped off with Pezérolles, Epenots and Rugiens. This last comes from both Haut and Bas sectors of the vineyard, very old vines in the Haut compensating somewhat for the better intrinsic quality of the *secteur* Bas. François' desire for aromatic intensity generally comes shining through.

Anne-Françoise and François Parent will tell you that the 8th Parent, Etienne, struck up a lasting friendship with the US Ambassador, later President, Thomas Jefferson, when he visited Burgundy. This resulted in the DoN"ine becoming the first accredited Burgundy supplier to the White House. Now, some 80% of Parent-Gros production is exported. No doubt the occasional bottle retraces the route of its 18th-century precursors and ends up in the cellars on Pennsylvania Avenue.

Commune	Level	Lieu-dit/Climat	Area	Vine Age	Status
Vosne*	V	Aux Réas	0.70	25	F
Vosne*	V	Maizières	0.28	15	F
Vosne*	V	Chalandins	0.34	40	F
Vosne*	GC	Richebourg	0.20	5/8/50	F
Flagey*	GC	Echézeaux (Champs Traversins)	0.26	55	F
Arcenant*	R	Bourg. Htes. Ctes. de Nuits (R)	2.02	20	F
Arcenant*	R	Bourg. Htes. Ctes. de Nuits (W)	0.23	5	F
Pommard	V	Croix Blanche	0.45	20	F
Pommard	PC	(Several *climats*)	0.22	35	F
Pommard	PC	Pézerolles	0.34	25	F
Pommard	PC	Les Arvelets	0.31	15	F
Pommard	PC	Les Chanlins	0.35	35	F
Pommard	PC	Les Chapponières	0.60	28	F
Pommard	PC	Les Epenots	0.58	15	F
Pommard	PC	Les Argillières	0.30	3	F
Pommard	PC	Les Rugiens			
Beaune	PC	Les Epenottes	2.00	35	F
Beaune	PC	Boucherottes	0.30	30	F
Aloxe	GC	Corton (Blanc)	0.28	5	M
Aloxe	GC	Corton Renardes	0.30	25	M
Ladoix	PC	Corvée	0.39	25	M
Ladoix	V	(Ladoix, Côtes de Beaune)	0.37	25	M
Gros Vines	R	(Bourgogne Rouge)	4.57	30	F/M

* Gros vineyards		**Total:**		**15.39 ha**	

Domaine de Courcel

POMMARD

Unusually for Burgundy, Pommard has two high quality Domaines not directly operated by their owners: Clos des Epeneaux and Domaine de Courcel.

This latter has been in the de Courcel family for four centuries. Its present owner, Gilles de Courcel, a Paris banker, 'passioné du vin', took over in 1976 having worked in wine in Beaune, Reims and Bordeaux.

Since 1966, the Domaine has been in the capable hands of Yves Tavant, a slender, galvanic, jockey-like man in his late forties. The third generation of his family to run the cellars he takes justifiable pride in the Domaine's wines. Unfortunately, his son is developing more literary than oenological tendencies, so Yves may be the last Tavant at Domaine de Courcel.

The Domaine's heart is 5 ha of the Grand Clos des Epenots, whose vines average 45 and range from 5–60 years old. For the rest: Pommard Premiers Crus Rugiens, Fremiers and the rarely seen Croix Noires, Pommard Villages and Bourgogne Rouge.

There is no evidence of things falling into the rut which elsewhere is usually referred to as 'tradition'. Gilles de Courcel is bent on quality and clearly flexible enough to espouse beneficial innovation.

He is finding, as are many other Domaines, that *cordon* training reduces yields and produces smaller berries. Experimental rows in Les Epenots produced better fruit than those trained conventionally.

The separate treatment of younger vines, especially in the Grands Epenots, is integral to the Domaine's search for quality. They are picked later and vinified separately from older vines, only being amalgamated if judged to be of suitable quality. Otherwise, their produce is sold to the local négoce.

In the vineyards, soil erosion is a continuing problem, particularly in the steeper parts of Les Rugiens. Yves Tavant remembers his grandfather struggling with hods of earth on his back to replace topsoil washed down by heavy rains. Yves himself did not escape – in 1969 he spent 15 days carting soil back to the top of the vineyard.

Harvesting generally starts with old Grands Epenots vines, followed by the steeper Rugiens, then the 35-year-old Epenots and so on.

In parallel with the vineyards, there is evolution in the cellars. Yves used to leave 30–50% of stalks in the vats; however, in the huge 1990 harvest, exigencies of space forced a complete destalking to reduce volume, a practice which has continued.

1990 was a year of experiment for Yves Tavant and Gilles de Courcel. Yves also wanted to try a short, cold pre-fermentive maceration to extend *cuvaison* beyond its usual 14–15 days. Despite adding 50% more sulphur than usual, the super-healthy yeasts started working at 14°C. This cooler, slower fermentation extracted more 'fat and glycerol', so this, given a healthy harvest, is now Yves' practice.

In 1975 all the Domaine's wines were sold *en négoce*. Now at least half is Domaine-bottled, and the proportion is growing – not fast enough for Yves who seems locked in an interminable struggle to increase it.

He believes that his methods are reverting, with modifications, to what his father and grandfather did 'dans le temps', although some things have changed, for better. 'Dans le temps', they used to heat the cellars to start *malos* – bacteria work better in a warm environment; now, they just put the casks downstairs and leave the bacteria to their own devices. *Elévage* used to last upwards of two years; now, the realisation that wines, especially from lighter vintages, dessicate rapidly with too long in wood, has reduced maturation to a more fruitful 15-18 months.

Another common practice 'dans le temps' was excessive, excoriating filtration. Now there is only a light plate-filtration (at the behest of their US importer) which Gilles de Courcel is striving to eliminate altogether.

De Courcel's wines are carefully crafted, abundantly characterful and fashioned to be kept. At the back of Yves' mind is the precept that the Pinot Noir is not highly coloured, so there is no attempt to extract unnatural depths by exaggerated fermentation temperatures or unduly long *cuvaison*, although their 14–15 days' vatting is longer than generally found in Pommard or Volnay.

The range opens with a Bourgogne Pinot Noir from 33-year-old vines, matured entirely in old wood. More Volnay in style than Pommard, this has a clean, ripe strawberry nose and plenty of solid fruit. In some vintages it starts off rather raw and four-square, but rounds out after a year or two in bottle.

The lightest of the Pommard Premiers Crus is Fremiers, made from vines planted in 1970 and 1974. The wine is elegant with hints of cherry on the nose, and often, something of a dryish edge to its tannins, although succulent and *puissant* underneath.

The Epenots and Rugiens are in a different class. The former – from 30 hl/ha in 1993 – is intense, in colour, on the nose and palate and, whilst not exceptionally concentrated, is characteristically beautifully perfumed – violets, red fruits, liquorice – with notable length. The Rugiens has a deeper hue and is firmer and more structured. The soil, although not deep, is richer in clay than the Epenots, giving a broader, more typically Pommard profile which takes longer to evolve. 25% of new oak enhances its natural structure, without dominating. A wine to keep for 10–20 years.

Like much of the best of Burgundy, de Courcel wines are made to be kept and should definitely not be finally judged until after several years in bottle. In 1990, the 1985 Rugiens was just beginning to show itself: not deep in colour reduced but a superbly opulent and complex nose, starting to emerge from its slumber, turning from primary, fruit-based aromas, to the distinctive Pinot *sous-bois*, with violets and spice. On the palate, delicate for a youngish Pommard, but with fruit and tannin to keep it going for several years, and supreme finesse. A Côte-Rôtie which appeared similarly forward at so young an age might cause anxiety, but for a Pommard, this is nothing untoward.

The great vintages from this Domaine are fine and elegant. By 1995, the 1978 Epenots had developed an opulent, magnificent visceral, gamey nose, with a hint of vegetal *sous-bois* and equally complex flavours. A wine of ripe, fat fruit, with a thin sustaining line of tannin. A marvel, but not surprising from only 20 hl/ha and the talented Yves Tavant.

VINEYARD HOLDINGS

Commune	Level	Lieu-dit/Climat	Area	Vine Age	Status
Pommard	PC	Grand Clos des Epenots	5.00	45	P
Pommard	PC	Rugiens	1.00	45	P
Pommard	PC	Fremiers	0.65	23	P
Pommard	PC	Croix Noires	0.60	13	P
Pommard	V	Vaumuriens	0.35	7–19	P
Pommard	R	(Bourgogne Rouge)	0.70	12–35	P
		Total:	**8.30 ha**		

Domaine Michel Gaunoux

POMMARD

Madame Gaunoux is a lively, articulate lady, who has battled for her Domaine since her husband, Michel, died suddenly in 1984. Her legacy was 7 ha, principally Pommard, but with some Beaune and Corton, founded by Michel's grandfather in 1895. He arrived having met (and later married) a local négociant's daughter at a wedding at the Ch. de Volnay. Michel took over from his father in 1960. Fortunately in addition to his capable wife, he left a son and daughter who will eventually inherit the Domaine.

Although she sold their wine, Mme Gaunoux knew little more than the broadest details of how Michel set about producing it. Rather than giving up and selling, she decided to build on what he had achieved. Replacing Michel brought only 'no-hopers', so she elected to go it alone, appointing their long-time 'caviste' as winemaker. As long as he could tell her that 'Michel would have done it like that', she was content.

This single-minded lady has indubitably succeeded, with wines of a quality and consistency others might do well to emulate. Part of the secret lies in the high proportion of 40–60-year-old vines: 'These have proved themselves over half a century, so we don't want to change them.'

When yields dwindled to unviable levels, some replanting became inevitable. In 1990 they dipped their toes in the water, replacing 0.25 ha of Les Arvelets – with 4 different clones: 2 selected for quality and 2 for productivity. This seems a curious compromise, rather like buying two separate trouser legs – one chosen for crease resistance, the other for colour-fastness; you could still end up looking like a discoloured concertina.

Now, much useful technical input comes from 'Domaines Familiaux de Tradition' – a federation of top Côte d'Or estates, which organises seminars, expert lectures and study visits to keep its members informed of technical advances. Treatments follow the advice disseminated by the local co-operative, run by a retired French Colonel.

In the cellars tradition reigns: 14 large open wooden vats stand in a well-disciplined row (they probably know about the Colonel), any stainless steel sitting disconsolately in corners, no doubt trying to pretend that it's traditional too. Vat number 4 is an impostor, being stainless steel camouflaged with wood.

Vinification is 'the most intellectual part of our work; each year, everything is re-examined.' Although Mme cheerfully discussed her *cuvaison* – a traditional 15–17 days – she was somewhat coy about her fermentation temperatures. 'Everyone has their own methods; you have to take risks'; then, under gentle pressure – 'let's say 32–34°C'. The true figure is probably much higher, but it seemed ungentlemanly to press the point.

Mme Gaunoux dislikes push-button vinification. 'Each cask behaves differently – like a patient who is ill, they must be treated as individuals. It's no good just pressing a button and going off to bed – you have to be prepared to get up at 3 a.m. if necessary.' So every night during fermentation, each vat – even number 4 – is carefully tucked up with a plastic lid, to conserve aroma and alcohol.

The wines remain in cask for 18–24 months – with 30–50% new Allier oak – 'plus a little Tronçais'; less structured years see more, better years less. 'We are not particularly in favour of new casks, it's fashion, snobbism.' Once unified and fined, the wines are filtered 'à plaques Suisses'. Whether Swiss filter-plates are superior is obscure, but Madame clearly considers them so.

Minimum sulphur is used and Mme Gaunoux confesses herself flabbergasted by what goes on in the Côte de Nuits: 'I won't say the names, but some people put in 6 litres per tonne!' This, she is convinced, has nothing to do with real Burgundy.

Madame stoutly refuses to bottle any vintage which she considers indifferent: 'The consumer must never be disappointed by a bottle of our wine,' she argues. Thus, not a single Domaine bottling was produced in 1970, 1975, 1980, 1986 or 1991, and precious little in 1977. In a region where everyone professes the undying pursuit of quality, it would be encouraging to see a few more producers making a similar sacrifice.

The Domaine's marketing is decidedly idiosyncratic. Tasting in cask is not allowed, nor is anything released with less than two years in bottle. Madame never lists fewer than five vintages, and keeps back stocks for later sale to her regular clientele. Great vintages such as 1993 present their own problems: 'I've had so many people asking for 1993s – but I don't like working like that.'

If her marketing is charmingly eccentric, her sales are no less so. From 1983–93, not a single bottle was sold to the USA, nor (surprisingly) has she a UK importer: 'We have enough clients in France.' She faces her absence on Burgundy's two greatest export markets with pragmatic equanimity. 'We don't go out looking for clients, they come to us,' is the essence of her strategy.

Mme Gaunoux is proud and clear-headed, and is suspicious of anyone she considers won't appreciate what she is trying to achieve. She need have little anxiety – her wines are of very fine quality; nothing blowsy, just discreet class and exemplary complexity.

The Pommards are impressive. In style, deliberately *vins de garde*, they accentuate the expression of individual *climats* rather than youthful Pinot flavours. The Grands Epenots tends to a rich, almost *figué* aroma in vintages such as 1983, but typically Pommard spiciness in vintages such as 1985 and 1990. Underneath is ripe, sturdy, old-vine fruit and a breed and length seldom seen in this commune.

In Mme's view, lesser vintages need 10 years to reach maturity, greater years at least 15. The 1987 Grands Epenots, for instance, is concentrated, developing quietly seductive, almost Provençale pine and garrigue aromas. The 1990 (45 hl/ha) fills the mouth with powerful *fruits noirs* flavours – yet is delicate underneath – a 10-year bottle, at least. These wines may lack the strength of Vintage Port, but seem to demand similar ageing.

Mme Gaunoux deserves greater recognition. She is a redoubtable lady who probably cares more for acclaim than she will readily admit. Her distaste for publicity may have contributed to her low profile, but anyone seeking fine Pommard should stroll up the Place de l'Eglise and investigate the high wall in its north-eastern corner.

VINEYARD HOLDINGS

Commune	Level	Lieu-dit/Climat	Area	Vine Age	Status
Pommard	PC	Les Rugiens (Bas)	0.69	45	P
Pommard	PC	Les Grands Epenots	1.76	50	P
Pommard	PC	Les Arvelets	0.26	1990	P
Pommard	PC	Les Charmots	0.26	40	P
Pommard	PC	Les Combes	0.25	55	P
Beaune	PC/V	(4 *climats*)	2.04	40–45	P
Aloxe	GC	Corton Renardes	0.65	35–40	P
Pommard	R	(Bourgogne Rouge)	1.00	35	P
Total:			**6.91 ha**		

Domaine Le Royer-Girardin

POMMARD

Beneath the Côte's grandest ranks, toils a band of less prestigious, but no less hard-working estates which provide those drinkers and merchants who are not quite so mesmerised by labels, with excellent wine at affordable prices. These are the engine room which keeps Burgundy's wheels in motion and cost-conscious consumers supplied with what they need.

The Girardins are one such Domaine – an exploitation of 6.47 ha spread wisely across Pommard, Beaune and Meursault, with a little Aligoté and rather more Bourgogne Pinot Noir included for good measure. No fewer than seven different red Premiers Crus – two in Beaune, five in Pommard – form the kernel of the estate.

This is a truly family enterprise. Henri and Hélène Girardin, now not far off retirement, and their talented and knowledgeable daughter Aleth (one of five children of which four survive), work hard to keep the vineyards healthy, vine age as high as possible and to bring up their wines in the cellars beneath their respective family houses, which stare at each other across the dangerously fast road leading out of Pommard towards Volnay.

Aleth's marriage in 1988 to actor Michel Le Royer, and the subsequent arrival of children, temporarily put her out of action. However, she is now back at the helm and is quietly teaching her interested, but as yet not entirely tutored husband, the manifold mysteries of wine in general and of Pommard in particular.

Unlike larger establishments, financial stringencies ensure that the ideal rarely matches the actual. Until recently, when they finally acquired a destalking machine, they struggled on with an ancient crusher, which, according to Aleth 'swallowed everything'. The essential *pigéage* is done by human feet; folkloric and charming as this may seem, the hard cake of stems and skins make the going 'like concrete', especially to start with. Pressing, with a 1906 vertical press which grinds away, but takes all night about it, is equally 'artisanale'.

Undaunted, they soldier on. Only the Premiers Crus are given a ration of new wood, and then only 10%, probably because the casks cost so much. After some 18–20 months in barrel, a contractor (the ubiquitous Ninot of Beaune) is summoned – they can't possibly afford the investment in even the smallest of bottling machines for one week's work a year – and the wine

Pommard from its vineyards

Kieselguhr filtered and bottled.

For the American market things are slightly different: their importer requires them to put everything he buys into 100% Allier oak – a policy which the Girardin's would never dream of employing for their own wines, even assuming they could afford it. Unfortunately they are not at present in a position to refuse a good order, but when they have established a broader client base they should insist on the wine being made in the way they want and not to the fashionable recipe of this or that market. As might be expected, the new wood *cuvées* completely dominated by the oak, effectively stifling much of the rich fruit underneath – hardly an encouraging sign for their future development.

These *cuvées* apart, the wines are generally excellent, sometimes superb, especially now that the occasional stalkiness of pre-*egrappoir* vintages is a thing of the past. A high average vine age and 10–12 days of *cuvaison* at up to 35°C results in limpid Victoria-plum or black-cherry hues and plenty of densely packed, structured, fruit; wines of impressive depth and concentration.

Whilst the Village Pommard, from a vari-

ety of *lieus-dits*, is invariably authentic and well-made, it is the Beaune and Pommard Premiers Crus which constitute the pick of this cellar, with the Rugiens and the Grands Epenots being, as it were, the 'Crème de Tête'.

The Rugiens comes from 35 ares of vines planted in 1910 in the vineyard's late ripening lower section where the soil is deep and high in red iron oxides – hence the name 'R(o)ugiens'. This generally starts out intensely and virtually opaque, with tannins which vary from quite firm (1990 and 1993) to rather rounder (1989, 1992) but invariably well covered by concentrated, sweet, old-vine fruit. The common denominator is great length and finesse, which amply reward long keeping.

The Grands Epenots comes from 53 ares of vines planted a decade earlier than the Rugiens, in a section of the vineyard between Comte Armand's Clos des Epeneaux and Monnier's Clos de Cîteaux. The rootstocks are divided between rupestris and riparia, both in wide use at the end of the 19th century – and in some years the vines fail to produce anything at all, so yields are very low indeed. The wine is yet denser than the Rugiens, with even more guts and stuffing and an appealing nose of *fruits noirs*, especially blackberries. In vintages of the calibre of 1993, 1990 and 1989, the Girardin Rugiens is of exceptional quality, one of the best *cuvées* to be found in Pommard, with an impressive concentration and richness of extract which show remarkable promise.

This is a very fine small Domaine; no pretension, no self-aggrandizement, just unremitting hard work and great attention to detail.

VINEYARD HOLDINGS

Commune	Level	Lieu-dit/Climat	Area	Vine Age	Status
Pommard	PC	Les Rugiens	0.35	86	P
Pommard	PC	La Reféne	0.40	15	P
Pommard	PC	Les Charmots	0.47	75	P/F
Pommard	PC	L'Argillière	0.08	45	F
Pommard	PC	Les Epenots	0.53	80	P/F
Pommard	V	(Several *climats*)	1.40	60	P/F
Beaune	PC	Clos des Mouches	0.35	40	P
Beaune	PC	Les Montrevenots	0.41	70	P
Beaune	V	Les Bons Feuvres	0.09	30	F
Meursault	PC	Les Poruzots	0.26	1990	F
————	R	(Bourgogne Pinot Noir)	1.91	50	F
————	R	(Bourgogne Aligoté)	0.30	60	P
Total:			**6.47 ha**		

VOLNAY

The wines of Volnay are the Chambolle-Musignys of the Côte de Beaune – elegant, full of finesse and lacy delicacy, but with a depth and structure which can keep them alive for decades.

If the wines of Pommard sometimes seem like a truck-driver's interpretation of Pinot, then those of Volnay are a ballerina's.

As usual, this has more to do with the soil than with any quirk of winemaking. Much of Volnay's vignoble sits on slopes underneath which runs a band of Bathonian limestone, overlaid with either marls of various geological origins or with stony, well-drained scree material. Even the lower, Village vineyards contain significantly less clay than those of Pommard, so the broad character of finesse is maintained.

The village itself is a compact little borough, tightly encircled by its vines, leaving no room for trendy architects to scar the view. Many of the houses have an uninterrupted vista over the vines to the plain and hills beyond. Even the telephone box on the terrace outside the rather drab Mairie enjoys this pleasing prospect.

The name Volnay derives from Volen, the god of water, worshipped, for some obscure reason, by the Gauls. In 1195, just before the Dukes of Burgundy started to use Hugues IV's Château as a summer retreat, this became 'Vollenay' – the form still preserved on the Marquis d'Angerville's elegant labels.

Royal patronage continued into the 16th century, when Louis XI took a particular fancy to the Volnay, acquiring several of the best vineyards – including Champans, Frémiet, Bousse d'Or, Caillerets and Taillepieds. He even despatched a royal official to make an inventory, presumably to verify that they were all still there. The Sun King (Louis XIV) is also recorded as an amateur of Volnay, perhaps because the Faculty of Medicine of the period extolled its qualities.

With all this exalted hype, Volnay became something of a cult drink, and prices rose accordingly. When the time came to classify the Côte, in 1860, those responsible were 'very generous' (Henri Cannard) in their treatment of Volnay, 'probably for reasons of commerce'. This might explain why 54% of the commune's land is designated Premier Cru, significantly more than other communes, with the exception of Beaune, the home of the Committee looking into the matter.

Volnay's vineyards extend to 213.27 ha, of which 98.37 ha are AC Volnay and the

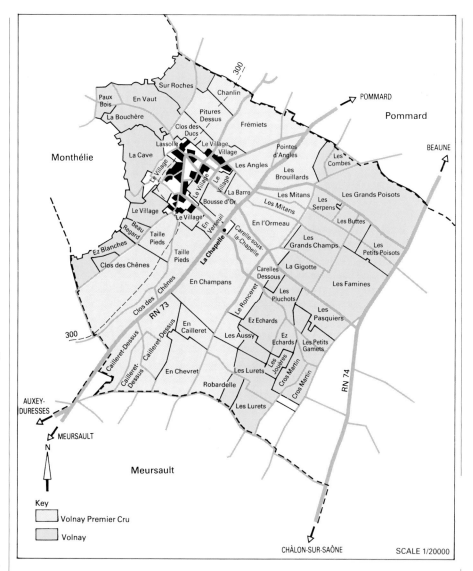

remaining 114.90 ha Premier Cru, comprising thirty-three individual *lieus-dits*.

As at Pommard, the Village vineyards are either on the higher, more exposed slopes, or else on the lower and flatter land between the RN73 and the RN74. These form the upper and lower bounds of the Premiers Crus, which occupy a narrow band below and to either side of the village itself.

These can be broadly classified into five geologically distinct sections: firstly, those in the village centre – Clos des Ducs, Bousse d'Or, Le Village, Carelle-sous-la-Chapelle and Taillepieds are planted on hard marls, with a high proportion of white chalk admixed. This gives wines of both vigour and finesse; in fact some of the best in the commune.

The second section lies due south of

Volnay – Champans, Caillerets, Ronceret and En Chevret. Here the vines are on moderately steep slopes, well-exposed to the south and south-east, with stony soils and rusty topsoils giving on to a vein of quite friable Bathonian limestone. Further down these vineyards, away from the RN73, the rock disappears and the soil deepens.

Third, the Clos des Chênes, just above the RN73, consists of pure limestone soil, very thin and stony, with the terrain becoming steeper the further from the road one gets, making soil erosion a recurring problem.

The fourth section comprises the Premiers Crus to the north-east of the village adjoining Pommard – Frémiets, Chanlins, Pitures Dessus and Les Angles. Here the limestone is less evident, and the soils are stony, with a covering of loose shale which detaches itself and washes away in the rain. These wines, Frémiets in particular, tend to emphasise finesse rather than structure.

The final section, the 29.07 ha of Premier Cru Volnay-Santenots, is something of a peculiarity, being located entirely in the commune of Meursault. The soils vary widely, from limestone to 'terre rouge', stones to no stones, slopes to flat, giving wine which is least typical of Volnay. Its situation is one of those administrative abberations which cause needless confusion. The vineyard is divided into five individual *lieus-dits*, each of which is entitled to the appellation Volnay-Santenots (Premier Cru), provided the wine is red. If however, white wine is produced, then the relevant appellation becomes Meursault, or Meursault Premier Cru depending upon the *lieu-dit* from which it emanates. This gobbledygook must keep several important officials in Dijon permanently on their administrative toes.

Some 85 individual growers and 11 larger Domaines operate from Volnay and, whilst numbers by themselves are no indication of quality, the standard of winemaking is high. Although the Domaines profiled here excel,

there are several other consistently reliable sources for anyone in search of good wine.

Yvon Clerget, with five separate Premier Cru Volnays in his 5.10 ha, produces wines which are agreeable to drink young but structured for age. The Volnay Santenots, from 57-year-old vines, the Caillerets from 58-year-olds and a fine Carelle-sous-la-Chapelle deserve special mention.

Jean-Marc Bouley turns out rather more overtly muscular wines, with plenty of stuffing from his 12 ha spread principally between Pommard and Volnay. Late harvesting and long slow fermentation, followed by light filtration but no fining, results in concentrated, well-defined wines of depth and style. His use of 60% new oak seems to have spawned him a particular following in the USA. The Volnays Clos des Chênes and Caillerets and the trio of Pommard Premier Crus – Pézerolles, Frémiets and Rugiens – are the cream of this cellar. The quality can be excellent but is uneven, so it is essential to taste carefully.

Regis Rossignol, a short, animated man with dark, swept-back hair, distantly related to the Rossignols of Gevrey, manages to combine a passion for excavating cellars and other do-it-yourself activity with skilled wine-

making. His policy of not destalking produces tannic wines which need bottle-age, but his meticulous attention to detail and his willingness to keep back wines which are unduly hard amortise the effects. A Pommard Village and a Volnay Premier Cru are the best *cuvées* here.

Finally, Joseph Voillot, a charming older vigneron, steeped in the traditions of the land, produces a near-exemplary range of Volnays and Pommards from some 10 ha of 25–35 year-old vines. 8–12 days *cuvaison* of 30–100% destemmed bunches and a 15–18 month *élévage* in up to one-third new wood results in wines which are complex and characterful. In good vintages, his Volnays Frémiets and Champans and the Pommards Pézerolles and Rugiens (this deliciously rich in good vintages) would hold their own against examples from grander Domaines.

Great Volnays, from the hands of such as Michel and Fred Lafarge, Jacques d'Angerville, Pousse d'Or or Hubert de Montille are inspirational wines. In their own way essence of Pinot Noir, they admirably reflect their noble origins and the skills and qualities of which this corner of the Côte de Beaune is eminently capable.

Volnay and its vines, looking south towards distant Meursault

Domaine Marquis d'Angerville

VOLNAY

D'Angerville is among the greatest names of Burgundy. It became so in the late 1920s when the father of the present Marquis became dissatisfied with the négociants, who then controlled virtually all Burgundy sales, and began to openly criticise them for their corrupt blending practices. Getting nowhere, he and a few other courageous growers, including Henri Gouges, decided to distance themselves from the négoce and started to bottle and sell their own wine. Others joined them, and thus was Domaine bottling born.

The present Marquis, Jacques d'Angerville, does not pretend to such iconoclasm. He is content to enjoy the peace and quiet of his delightful 18th-century home, and to produce superlative Volnay for the world to share his pleasure.

The family house, which came into d'Angerville hands in 1804, when Baron du Mesnil, then Vice-Governor of Autun, bought vineyards in 'Vollenay', is a handsome country manor situated on a small elevation at the northern end of the village. Whoever built chose the site with care: a broad terrace faces south and east over the vineyards, and, together with the more recent swimming-pool, enjoys sunshine, when there is any, all day long. Indeed, the Marquis will tell you that in high summer he can swim in the evening sunlight until eight o'clock.

The vineyards, comprising 13.5 ha, have remained intact since the days of Baron du Mesnil. They include no fewer than 8 Volnay Premiers Crus, some Meursault Santenots and Pommard Les Combes. The pearl in the oyster is the 2.40-ha Clos des Ducs – a *Monopole* – which abuts the northern wall of the house, effectively forming part of the garden. The wine is ripe, smoky, and in great vintages, capable of long ageing.

The Marquis is uncompromising in his quest for quality. As he sees it, the keys are low yields – generally 27–33 hl/ha and a significant proportion of old vines. Since he came to work with his father in 1950, he has never asked for a *PLC*. Of course, yields see-saw naturally: in the disastrous 1975 they sank to 18 hl/ha, peaking at 43 and 40 in 1990 and 1993. Equally, he rarely grubs up vines; the last occasion was in 1984 when a small, very old parcel ceased to be viable. Only this, or severe soil erosion, would cause him to replant to any significant extent. Otherwise vines are simply replaced one by one as they die or are enfeebled by age.

In the steeper vineyards the soil is systematically worked rather than treated with herbicides. The Marquis believes that hoeing aerates the earth which encourages the penetration of any surface water, thus holding the soil together and so minimising erosion. This contradicts the usual view, namely that hoeing the soil makes it more friable and thus more prone to erosion.

The vineyards are tended on the principle of minimum interference – yields being kept down by using only 'plants fins' – a *sélection massale* of his father's, short Guyot pruning and severe *évasivage* when the growing season begins. In 1990, for the first time, grapes were removed in August – at *veraison* – to further reduce yields. There is, however, some doubt in the Marquis's mind as to whether this really produces the desired results – the timing is so precise: 'Too early and the vine catches up, too late and, well . . . it's too late and the operation is useless.'

Otherwise the viticultural regime is fairly classical but adaptive to circumstance. Treatments, both preventive and curative, especially for the grape-worm, tend to be administered together. *Court-noué* – the dreaded fan-leaf virus endemic in Burgundy – is dealt with by using specially vaccinated clones from Alsace's Colmar research sta-

tion. *Eutypiose* is also becoming a serious threat – in one of the d'Angerville vineyards, a count recorded the incidence to have already reached 1.34%. Given its destructiveness and its 7-year incubation period, it is, not surprisingly, under constant surveillance.

There is no systematic order of harvesting, picking depending entirely on the maturity of each 'Cru'. In 1976, for example, the Meursault Santenots was so ripe that it was harvested in August. Of all the Volnays, the Clos des Ducs is generally picked last, because the vines on this harder, limestone-rich soil require a longer ripening cycle.

Vinification is as traditional as the Marquis: 'The less one puts this and that in the wine, the better. I don't do anything – just wait for the fermentation to start.' In other words, don't interfere with nature. So, once completely destalked, lightly sulphured and vatted, the grapes are left to ferment.

There is, unusually, virtually no standard *pigéage*, rather twice daily *remontages* using powerful jets to break up the hard cap. For the 1990 vintage the Marquis tried out a couple of *cuves auto-pigéantes* for the Volnay Champans – something of a break with tradition! He considers that the results of this *essai* more closely resemble a lesser than a great year, so the experiment has not been repeated. However, he does admit that these new-fangled *cuves* give better extraction and tannins but warns that one has to know how to use them: 'You mustn't turn them round and round like coffee mills – just a couple of minutes each way, twice a day will do.'

Jacques d'Angerville is not in favour of *saigner* – although he did *saigner* a little in 1984 and again in 1990. He will tolerate a maximum of 10% if really necessary, but considers that it brings no real benefit, removing both sugars and aromas as well as the intended water. He is, however, following closely trials at nearby Pousse d'Or, of an apparatus which extracts water by evaporation. Although perfection of this technique would spell the end of widespread *chaptalisation*, Jacques d'Angerville has yet to be convinced: 'Concentration is *géniale*, but in years when you need it, you are more likely to concentrate what is bad; that's no use.'

The 'less you put things in the wine . . .' principle precludes the use of enzymes. However, as *chaptalisation* is inevitable in Burgundy's marginal climate, sugar, when needed, is added in several small doses during the active phase of fermentation, rather than the widely regarded optimum

Jacques, Marquis d'Angerville – one of Volnay's and Burgundy's most respected vignerons

period, towards the end.

The temperature is allowed to rise to 35°C during the 8–10 days of *cuvaison*. After press- and free-run wine have been assembled, the *cuves* are covered and left for 2–3 days for the gross lees to settle out before the wine is transferred to cask.

For a Volnay, whose finesse might easily be submerged under new wood, Jacques d'Angerville defends his decision to use 'never more than 35% new oak – one shouldn't abuse it'. Moreover, the wine only remains in its new barrels until it is racked and unified after the *malo* some 3–10 months later. The remainder of its *élevage* – 15–24 months in total – is spent in older oak. In preparation for bottling, each cask is fined, without further unification, and given a light plate-filtration.

The Marquis has no more dealings with the négociant fraternity than did his father; the entirety of the Domaine's 100–200-cask production is sold in bottle – either to export markets, which take some 65%, or within France, particularly to the great restaurants which lap up all they can get. No doubt he comes across his bottles in the course of his long-distance peregrinations, of which he is especially fond.

Jacques d'Angerville worked closely with his father until the latter's death in 1952. This experience and the years that followed have turned him into a fine winemaker with a sure touch. Strolling round the neat rows of bar- rels in the cellars under the house, one becomes aware of his passion for the estate and its wines – undiminished after nearly half a century. He pronounces a preference for wines which are 'distinguished and long; unc- tuous and ripe', wines which, unlike the general misconception about the Côte de Beaune, are generally more rewarding after ten years than after five.

Of the Premiers Crus, the Clos des Ducs stands out, followed north to south by the Frémiet, Taillepieds, Champans and Cailleret. The Frémiet vines are planted in a poor, thin topsoil on 'lave calcaire' – a Marne limestone – and being on the Pommard side of the village, tend to produce a quite broad and muscular wine.

In contrast, Taillepieds (so named because the sharp stones used to damage workers' bare feet) lying on the same band of whitish limestone soil as Frémiets and Clos des Ducs, but with a more southerly exposure and at the other end of the village, 'Côte Meursault' has greater length and distinc- tion. It also tends to be considerably more concentrated, often showing a classy 'smoky bacon' nose, with oldish vines contributing firmness and intensity.

The Domaine's mouthwatering 3.98 ha of Champans, just below the road to Meursault, is divided into two separate strips running

north-east to south-west at either end of the vineyard. The wine has greater *charpente* than the other Premiers Crus with more sinew and drier tannins. In 1993, Champans played true to form – noticeably deeper and meatier than Frémiet or Taillepieds but still showing length and class underneath.

The Marquis refers to the Champans, together with Frémiet and Cailleret as 'Têtes de Cuvée'. The Cailleret, planted in the top, 'dessus', section of the vineyard, abutting the Meursault road, is arguably the finest of the trio. It seems to combine the power and strength of the Champans with the exuberant finesse of the Frémiet. A 1964 Frémiet, tasted in 1989, was still in great form – plenty of ripe, old-vine fruit with a marvellous, thor- oughly seductive mature Pinot nose. It com- bined delicacy with power and considerable length – a complete and most enjoyable wine.

Among this magnificent array, the Clos des Ducs stands out for its unbridled distinc- tion and that extra touch of class and concen- tration. In character, it combines Taillepieds' depth with Champans' tannins. The 1993 showed a fine, deep colour, a reduced yet complex nose, firm, masculine richness and wonderful length; a distinct notch above the rest – fine as these are.

The Clos des Ducs, from that much and unjustly criticised vintage, 1987, was still closed up in December 1990 – not a block- buster (these wines rarely are) but plenty of wine nonetheless, with a touch of raw tannins to lose. It has both depth and vinosity and will make a good bottle for the mid-90s.

The 1983 Clos des Ducs was, in contrast, beginning to release its aromas – with a touch of *sous-bois* and a distinct point of *sur- maturation* which shows as a slight figginess on the nose. The ripeness comes through on the palate – a deep wine, with incipient com- plexity and a slightly dry edge; hint neither of rot nor of the excessive dryness which marked some wines of this patchy vintage.

The time will come, perhaps in the next decade, when this kindly nobleman will seek to extend his travels and to let go of the reins which he has held so capably for nearly half a century. Sadly, his most likely successor of

The entrance to the 18th-century Domaine

his three children, a daughter in her early forties, died recently, a tragedy which has left a very deep wound. Fortunately, as the next Marquis is a merchant banker in London and, apart from enjoying the occasional ship- ments he presumably receives from Volnay, seems unqualified to replace his father, her husband now works at the Domaine. His third child, a daughter, lives in Paris and does not appear to be interested in the estate.

Such is the anatomy of one of Burgundy's great estates. It is a shame that many people who buy fine Burgundy seem to confine their purchases to the Côte de Nuits, in the mis- taken belief that the Côte de Beaune does not produce wines capable of ageing. Whilst the soils in the Côtes de Nuits tend indeed to produce longer-lived wines, there are many estates in the Côte de Beaune producing wines of distinction and longevity.

Jacques, Marquis d'Angerville, is a man of great quality and one of Burgundy's finest winemakers. His wines are marked by exem- plary typicity and exceptional elegance – Volnays which may be equalled, but rarely bettered.

VINEYARD HOLDINGS

Commune	Level	Lieu-dit/Climat	Area	Vine Age	Status
Volnay	PC	Clos des Ducs	2.40	30	P
Volnay	PC	Champans	3.98	30	P
Volnay	PC	Frémiet	1.57	30	P
Volnay	PC	Cailleret	0.45	30	P
Volnay	PC	Taillepieds	1.70	30	P
Volnay	PC	L'Ormeau	0.65	30	P
Volnay	PC	Les Angles	0.53	30	P
Volnay	PC	Pitures	0.31	30	P
Meursault	PC	Santenots	0.50	30	P
Pommard	V	Les Combes	0.38	30	P
Total:			**13.47 ha**		

Domaine Michel Lafarge

VOLNAY

Michel and Frédéric Lafarge produce some of Burgundy's most precise and penetrating wines. From their base in Volnay – a neat but unpretentious house in a quiet backstreet hiding some splendid 13th-century cellars – they tend and vinify the produce of just short of 10 hectares, over half in Volnay. Although the Domaine dates back to the early 19th century, its present size is largely attributable to Michel and his father who added parcels of land whenever suitable opportunities came their way. Michel's own contributions were the small plots of Premiers Crus Beaune Teurons and Pommard Pézerolles.

This tall, grey-haired and thoughtful man has been running the family estate since 1960, for the last ten years with his equally tall son, Frédéric. For years he combined winemaking with the Mayoralty of Volnay, a function demanding both tact and diplomacy; he retired from that office in 1995.

From their house, perched on one of the highest points in this pleasant little village, the Lafarges can see right across the vignoble. It is here that they believe the quality of wine is made or lost. Listening to Michel discoursing on his vines and their care, it is clear that, despite his advancing years, he has not become embedded in any of the tradition or dogma which vignerons so often use as excuses for sloppiness and incompetence. Although he places high value on the traditions of transmitted experience, he likes to think things through afresh, with an open mind.

Michel and Fred are convinced that the initial selection of plant material is one of the most important decisions a vigneron has to make. For themselves, they continue to use a *sélection massale*, although sometimes mixed with a few different clones in a row or two to see what they will give. Hesitancy about clones stems from the feeling that too much about their performance remains unknown. Also, even if one prunes short, debuds severely and takes all the usual steps to restrict yields, clones still overproduce.

This overproduction is an amalgam of two factors: firstly, the health of modern plant material means that each vine in the row produces regularly – unlike the pre-war pattern of, say, seven out of ten. Secondly, each plant is more prolific than its predecessors. The result: higher yields, and the only sensible remedy: less productive clones.

Whilst waiting for these to appear, the Lafarges are content to observe their own

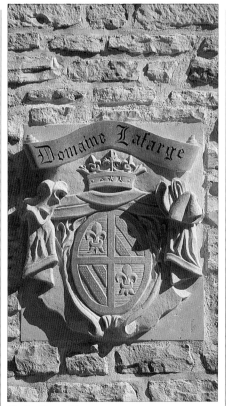

The family escutcheon

plants producing reasonably, but rarely excessively. In passing, Michel observes that the same clone, planted on the same rootstock will produce differently, both in quality and in quantity, in different vineyards. He concludes that there is an urgent need for a much wider variety of roots and clones to suit Burgundy's multifarious *terroirs*.

The Lafarge vineyards are tended with expert care. There has been what Michel refers to as a 'twinge of conscience' among vignerons in recent years, towards the fauna of their soils. A more ecological attitude has led to the use of less noxious products in smaller doses and to individual vines, rather than blanket blitz-spraying. Their own policy is 'to observe, see what is happening, then work parcel by parcel'.

Michel and Fred pursue their own ideas wherever feasible. For example, they are passionately in favour of *cordon* pruning – a system which consists of a single spur from which several shoots are trained. This has distinct advantages: it limits the harvest, by producing more grapes, but these are much smaller and more concentrated; also, by spreading out vegetation and bunches – not possible with traditional *Guyot* pruning – it

both reduces rot and makes any outbreak easier to handle. Finally, it facilitates winter 'pre-pruning' but makes the essential spring *ébourgonnage* much harder.

Given their ecological stance, it is not surprising to find the Lafarges using only organic fertiliser, and as little of that as possible. His mistrust of advice, especially from product salesmen meant that Michel was one of the few vignerons not to overdose their vines with potassium in the 1960s. 'You must never throw yourself at once into everything they tell you,' is wisdom kept permanently in the background and dusted off from time to time, particularly, no doubt, when fertiliser salesmen appear at his front door.

On treatments of the vine, policy is succinct: 'You should always be careful – if you can't, then at least limit it as much as you can.' The Lafarges have used traditional remedies, based on copper and sulphur, for as long as Michel can remember and have no intention of changing without a very good reason. Not satisfied with the standard product, they make up their own Bordeaux mixture – a laborious procedure – which is worth it because 'it has a better action'.

One of the greatest problems in Burgundy is the *verjus* – that second crop of unripe grapes which appear from time to time, especially in hot years, and which must be kept out of the vats at all costs because they would only contribute green acidity and dilution. They are hard for pickers to distinguish from ripe bunches since their skins may be equally black, so the Lafarges weed them out at the *cuverie*. Growers who are not so careful just add volume at the expense of quality.

When necessary, there is a green-pruning, although they are not entirely convinced of its value: at present, only young vines and clones which are affected, but timing is critical if the remaining bunches are not to compensate with large, dilute berries.

If the vineyards are worked on the principle of 'watch then act' vinification is no different; nothing is systematic. The broad guidelines allow for 80–100% destalking – the less the better for the health of the bunches, since stems lengthen fermentation. There is a short pre-fermentive maceration in good years, whilst in poor vintages fermentation is started immediately with a *pied de cuve*. Commercial yeasts are never used because they give a much more fragile fermentation.

As for the fermentation itself, Michel and Fred 'ask themselves the same question every year' – how long and at what temperature? The answer is reached by scrutiny of the charts for previous vintages and trying to reconcile what they did then with the results, before deciding how to ferment this year's crop. 'The only way of improving quality is to review what has been done and achieved before.' Generally, a longer, cooler fermentation is preferred to something shorter and hotter – an expedient reserved for rotten or unripe years. Michel admits that the decision process is most enjoyable – working closely with his son.

Avoiding pumps and enzymes is also a matter of policy. 'Every pump is bad,' Michel declares roundly, adding that the need for enzymes indicates a problem in clarifying the wine which in turn indicates poor raw material, which in turn indicates 'above all, poorly maintained vinification equipment', excessive pressing or the presence of spray residues in the *must*. 'No one had enzymes thirty years ago,' he argues.

There is a vigorous dislike of automation – not just because its untraditional, but because it can so easily destroy the precious raw material. For example, many vignerons use a pump to transfer the pulp left in the *cuves* to the presses. Chez Lafarge it is removed by hand. 'Don't forget, the harvest is fragile,' one is reminded.

Cuvaison lasts up to 14 days, with a temperature bracket of 28–33°C. Although prepared to bleed up to 10–15% if really necessary, as in 1990, Michel and Frédéric are no great partisans of *saignée*, believing that it unbalances a wine. 'It's not a panacea, but it can help from time to time.'

Looking at the vignerons around him, Michel finds that many are constantly being surprised by the quantity of grapes arriving at their *cuveries*. He thinks that they would do better if they took the trouble to match their harvesting to their style of vinification and the capacity of their *cuves*. For him, it is better to reduce the number of pickers and spend a few more days harvesting, than to have to speed up or shorten vinifications because you are constantly being knocked down with yet another load of grapes.

Having exercised themselves forking the pulp from the vats, the Lafarges are not going to compromise that effort by using an automatic press. For them a manually driven extraction is best – since they see too much possibility of prolonged or excess pressure with the modern machines. 'If you go away and leave a manual press for two minutes, it is still in the same place when you return,' explains Michel, 'with the automatic ones . . . it may have gone beserk and crushed the pulp to death.'

Once the result of the first, gentle, pressing has been amalgamated the wine is run into cask. Generally, Lafarge wines have 25% of new wood, perhaps a little more for the

Premiers Crus, but Michel is somewhat bemused by those who declare a policy on this matter. 'When you order your casks,' he observes, 'you know neither the quantity nor the quality of the crop, so it is almost impossible to match new casks to the harvest.'

What happens to his wines thereafter depends entirely on how they evolve and in particular on how they taste. 'Laboratories are all very fine, they provide control, but you can't vinify by numbers,' chants Michel, adding, 'Yes, oenologists are precious, but they are never very good vinificators.'

If the lees are healthy the first racking may be delayed by a month or so. The second racking will depend on the date of the *malo* and on the type of wine. The Lafarges like to bottle their Volnays before the second summer, even earlier in less structured vintages, so *élevage* typically lasts 15–20 months. Filters are used as little as possible – they prefer to fine instead.

The results of the Lafarges' skill are stunning – wines of a concentration and purity which exemplify 'par excellence' the spirit and style of Volnay. Their basic Bourgogne Pinot Noir, from old Volnay vines, vinified and *élevé* in exactly the same way as the rest, is one of the best in the entire Côte. It has a raspberry-ish, Volnay-ish nose which invites one to taste, and although a touch rustic on the palate, given a few years in bottle softens out into a delicious, complex mouthful.

The Lafarge wines are characterised by a finely-tuned combination of refinement and structure. Whatever the vintage, the balance is always there; in the greater vintages, 1985, 1988, 1989, 1990 and 1993 (even the much-maligned 1994), for example, although the nuances differ, there is a distinct thematic continuity, a house style almost, which emphasises the delicacy of Volnay, or the meatier genre of Pommard or Beaune.

The Pommard Pézerolles is more lively than either the Beaune Grèves or the Volnays – supple with a firmish structure and great finesse. A Volnayish Pommard, as it were.

The Beaune Grèves, from 50-year-old

vines, is altogether different; never aggressively structured, but opulent, spicy and powerful, with plenty of fruit supported by round tannins, a fine balance and long finish; a wine for medium-term cellaring.

The Volnay Village *cuvée* is an assemblage of the produce of 8–9 different parcels of vines. In good vintages, this has a medium-deep colour and crushed strawberry hue, aromas of violets and a touch of liquorice, with a lively yet soft flavour, good depth of fruit and sufficient acidity to keep it for several years. Not a big wine, but one that is nevertheless fine and interesting.

There are three different Volnay Premiers Crus to choose from. The 'Premier Cru' itself is an amalgam of Chanlins and Mitans from 20 + 40-year-old vines. The Clos du Château des Ducs – a Lafarge *Monopole* – comes from 57 ares of 16–55-year-old vines planted in some 40 cm of red soils on a layer of gravel. This gives a wine of great finesse – violets and *fruits rouges* on the nose, harmonious tannins and complex, tender flavours. The Clos des Chênes, from 12–50-year-old vines in much poorer soil, on rock, is usually the more complete of the pair, with spicier overtones than the Clos du Château des Ducs, exemplary concentration and considerable length; in vintages of the calibre of 1990 and 1993, a ten-year bottle.

Michel and Frédéric Lafarge make very fine wines. They also make a formidable team – working together to refine and transmit a tradition, as three generations before have done. Michel values their partnership: 'We can have two different ideas and take the best bits of both; in Burgundy, so many people have to work alone,' he explains, sitting at the larger of two scholastic wooden desks, with Frédéric nodding agreement from his smaller post alongside. They can be relied upon to turn out interesting wines in almost any vintage – wines which give immense pleasure when young and plump, but which turn into something more subtle and interesting if you can bear to keep them for half a decade or more. This is a five-star Domaine.

VINEYARD HOLDINGS

Commune	Level	Lieu-dit/Climat	Area	Vine Age	Status
Volnay	PC	Clos des Chênes	0.90	12/30/50	P
Volnay	PC	Clos du Château des Ducs	0.57	16/55	P
Volnay	PC	Mitans + Chanlins	0.36	20/40	P
Volnay	V	(Several *climats*)	2.48	(Various)	P
Pommard	PC	Les Pézerolles	0.14	30	P
Beaune	PC	Les Grèves	0.38	50 +	P
Beaune	V	Les Teurons	0.20	35	P
Meursault	R	(Côtes de Beaune Villages)	0.28	12	P
Meursault	V	(Blanc)	1.00	36	P
Volnay	R	(Bourgogne Pinot Noir)	1.21	20/35	P
Volnay	R	(Bourgogne Passe-Tout-Grain)	1.20	20/45	P
————	R	(Bourgogne Aligoté)	1.05	40	P
Total:			**9.77 ha**		

Domaine de Montille

VOLNAY

Hubert de Montille combines the dual callings of lawyer and vigneron with apparently effortless ease. From his cellars come some of the finest Pommards and Volnays, wines which exemplify both a dedication to quality and supreme skill in producing it.

De Montilles have lived in Volnay since before the Revolution and despite the inevitable expansions and contractions that the inheritance laws have wrought, successive generations have managed to maintain a viable viticultural Domaine.

Hubert was born into wine in 1930, just after his grandfather had divided his land between his children. In 1947, his father died and he was pitched into managing the Domaine with his mother and an uncle. The years spent shadowing his father in the vineyards and cellars stood him in good stead when, in 1954, a year after his uncle's remarriage, his aunt gave birth to a son during the vintage, and he was left alone to make the wine.

However, wine was not as profitable then as now, so a vigneron had to supplement his income where he might. After completing his studies, Hubert followed the family tradition of advocacy, developing a thriving general practice in Dijon. His children, who both work part-time at the Domaine, also have twin careers: Alix (married to Jean-Marc Roulot) is a lawyer and Etienne works for accountants Coopers and Lybrand.

The family often get together round the kitchen table in their spacious, shady house in Volnay. In early summer, the furniture is dusted off and Hubert and his wife move in for the season. After the Hospices sale in November, the place is shuttered up and left in the custody of the couple responsible for the vineyards and routine cellar work. Hubert repairs to Dijon to work his law practice, making no more than occasional visits to Volnay to taste and keep an eye on his estate.

Hubert de Montille's inheritance consisted of just 3 ha of vines. Careful acquisition has more than doubled this into a fine spread across Volnay and Pommard. In 1993, a splendid half-hectare of Puligny Les Caillerets was bought from Jean Chartron 'for the children'. Not for Alix the more usual apprenticeship struggling with Bourgogne Blanc or Aligoté, but a debut vinifying fruit from vines twenty metres from Montrachet!

In the 1950s, before clones were available, vignerons used to select their own plant material from the best in their vineyards –
sélection massale – which was then grafted on to phylloxera-resistant rootstocks. Hubert de Montille remembers marking some 2,000 plants for possible selection in his own vineyards. Eventually, he became persuaded, although he can't remember how, that clones were an improvement on tradition, and started planting them in 1978, together with a touch of massale, for insurance and variety. This early plot of clones was one of the first trial plantings in the Côte. Now all new plantings are with clones, predominantly on rootstock 161/49.

Hubert de Montille does not share the legal profession's collective insensitivity to reality, and is well aware of the practicalities of the theories he expounds so eloquently. For example, although in favour of a selective green-pruning, he realises that this should only be performed by highly skilled workers, and in August, when everyone is on holiday. So, for purely practical reasons, the operation is out of the question.

Maître de Montille is at his best when there is a problem to solve. The care of his vineyards is a constant challenge, which he tackles with relish and urbane intelligence. Much as he might prefer to run a wholly organic regime for dealing with pests and diseases, he realises that in the Côte's fragmented environment, preferences have to be tailored to reality. Nothing is achieved, from up-to-the-minute 'biodynamics', for example, if your neighbours drench their vines in a constant shower of systemic sprays and powerful synthetic insecticides.

The aim of each year's vineyard work is to achieve the ripest, healthiest grapes. To this end, the de Montilles invariably take the significant risk of a late harvest – 'compared to others'. Whilst each additional day of sunshine adds to a grape's quality potential, a few hours of a Burgundian autumn storm can mean a rapid dilution of the juice, or worse still, rampaging rot.

Turning even the finest Pinot Noir into wine presents an annual challenge. The Domaine's philosophy is that it's better to try and extract noble, softer tannin in the first place, than to go for maximum extraction and then try to inject refinement later on.

At present there is a distinct vogue for a period of cool maceration before fermentation starts – said to extract both colour and aroma from the skins into the juice. Hubert de Montille is sceptical, admitting that maceration adds power and aroma, but believes these to be ephemeral: 'I'm not persuaded,' is
his verdict. His preference is for 2–3 days' maceration, then fermentation at a relatively high temperature (up to 34°C) and 6–8 pigéages daily. This, together with a cuvaison of 15-17 days, will give maximum extraction of durable colour and aromas.

'According to the type of vintage,' 70–75% of stalks are removed before vatting, a higher proportion being retained in years when the wood is riper.

Since 1964 Hubert de Montille's principal 'bête noire' has been excessive alcohol in wines which he considers are, above all, delicate. For him, above 12 degrees, the subtlety of a wine risks being masked by the alcohol. Chaptalisation, a necessity in most Burgundy vintages, is therefore kept to the minimum compatible with Appellation requirements and balance. He vividly recalls the wisdom of an old vigneron: 'You haven't understood – you can't compensate for lack of sun with beetroot.' This worthy went on to explain to the young de Montille that chaptalisation leads to two separate tastes: 'Armagnac and then your wine behind'.

In this regard, he is watching with particular interest trials being carried out at Pousse d'Or and Ch. Leoville Lascases (whose wine he admires greatly) – of an apparatus which removes water from grape-juice by evaporation. Whilst it remains to be seen whether concentrating sugar by extracting water is the converse of adding it, there is hope that such means might reduce chaptalisation, if not eliminate it entirely.

Elévage is traditional, although tailored to reflect a dislike of 'solid' wines and a corresponding desire to retain maximum natural delicacy and purity. Hubert abhors the vogue for over-concentration and new wood, both of which banalise wine, and rails at American critics who 'make us make oaky, tannic, competition wines; look at the guru-driven Bordeaux of the 1980s, they haven't aged well.' For him, 20–30% new wood each year plus a cocktail of 1–3-year-old casks for the rest is enough. The preference is for Nevers, Chatillonais and especially Vosges which gives an element of 'finesse and distinction'. 'If our wines were Chambertin or Richebourg, we would put them all into new wood, but for Volnay the wood would dominate the wine.'

The Domaine buys its own wood and leaves it at Volnay to dry for 18 months. The barrel-maker gives it 'a touch of steam' to further dry it ('15 minutes of steam saves four months of natural drying'), before fashioning it into casks.

Maître Hubert de Montille dwarfed by a large oak tree in his park

By and large, nature is left to work on the wines at her own pace. The reds are *batonnés* up to Christmas – 'we've been doing this for fifteen years' – then remain on lees until racking the following August. *Malos* happen slowly and naturally, finishing around flowering the following June; 'The later they are the less I am displeased.' A year later, another racking is followed by fining in cask. The wines remain *sur colle* for 3–4 months and are bottled, generally without filtration – a total *élevage* of 20–24 months. There have been occasions when a light plate filtration was deemed necessary but 'that is not my cup of tea,' Hubert confesses.

Hubert and (since 1990) Etienne's wines are yardstick Volnays and Pommards. Although temptingly concentrated in flavour and beautifully 'parfumé' in youth, these are not designed for early consumption.

Of the Volnays, the Village *cuvée* is, as one would expect, the least complex. Nonetheless, it is a serious wine and repays keeping in all but the lightest vintages. There is a Volnay Premier Cru from a mixture of the produce of several different small plots, none large enough to justify individual bottling. This is usually quite a rich, firm wine, with plenty of meat under a positive, well-developed nose.

There are three separate, named, Premiers Crus. Taillepieds, situated opposite the Champans on the southern, Meursault

side of the village produces a wine of great finesse, generally more supple and less tannic than the others. The Champans is invariably much fuller and more powerful, with almost Pommard-ish muscle, yet with hidden finesse. The Mitans comes somewhere in between, with attractive plump fruit and considerable delicacy, especially when it has the chance to mature.

The Pommard Premiers Crus are a superb trio: the Pézerolles shows the depth and complexity derived from its *terre rouge*, whereas the Rugiens, also on *terre rouge*, seems to combine this structure and depth with notable finesse, from the relatively poorer soils of its more sloping situation. The

Epenots is fatter and firmer than the Pézerolles, but can't quite match the Rugiens for length and harmony.

It is, however, with age that de Montille's wines really show what they are made of. After a few years in bottle, the 1985s are just beginning to open out – still young, but starting to show the transition between youthful fruit-based aromas and more mature, ripe, liquorice, *sous-bois* and vegetal character.

The 1972 Taillepieds and the 1971 Pézerolles, tasted at the Domaine in January 1991 were both very fine wines. The 1972, picked on the 10th October – the latest in Hubert de Montille's memory – has blossomed from its virtually untasteable early years (by virtue of its overwhelming acidity), into a magnificently distinguished mature Pinot, with a hint of faded flowers, which Hubert particularly likes, and a soft, stylish complexity which is most attractive. Incidentally, 1972 would have undoubtedly been written off by modern critics – a striking lesson in the inadvisability of premature judgement which many have still to grasp.

The 1971 Pézerolles is even more alluring, with an almost creamy ripeness preceded by an attractive touch of *surmaturité* and offset by a layer of fine, delicate aromas. Its depth and complexity of fruit well covers its 13 degrees natural alcohol. A very fine bottle by any standards.

The Taillepieds from the vintage which convinced Hubert de Montille of the folly of chaptalising to over 12° alcohol (1964), was still supreme in 1995 – barely mature to look at, with a magnificent old tea-rose nose, and a ravishing depth of sweet, ripe fruit which suffused the palate through to a long, lingering finish. A wine to seduce and inspire.

Hubert and Etienne de Montille's Volnays are sometimes criticised for being rather too plump for typicity. Maybe, but for a Domaine capable of producing such consistently fine bottles, does it really matter ?

VINEYARD HOLDINGS

Commune	Level	Lieu-dit/Climat	Area	Vine Age	Status
Volnay	PC	Les Champans	0.66	1/15/30	P
Volnay	PC	Carelles Sous Chapelle	0.20	5	P
Volnay	PC	Les Brouillards	0.38	3/4	P
Volnay	PC	Les Angles	0.15	2	P
Volnay	PC	Le Village	0.15	30	P
Volnay	PC	Les Taillepieds	0.79	11	P
Volnay	PC	Les Mitans	0.73	13	P
Volnay	V	——————	0.15	13–25	P
Pommard	PC	Les Rugiens	1.01	8/15/30	P/M
Pommard	PC	Les Pézerolles	1.09	10/25/50	P/M
Pommard	PC	Les Grands Epenots	0.23	5	P
Pommard	R	(Bourgogne Rouge)	0.75	20	P
Pommard	R	(BGO – Les Sorbins)	0.60	50	P
Puligny	PC	Les Caillerets	0.52	45	P
		Total:	**7.21 ha**		

Domaine Bitouzet-Prieur

VOLNAY

Vincent Bitouzet-Prieur

Vincent Bitouzet, now in his forties, took charge here in 1981 – the fifth generation, since Simon Bitouzet arrived in Volnay in 1860. Marriage to Hubert Prieur's daughter added 3 ha of Meursault and 1 ha of Beaune to his seven. A charismatic, thoughtful man, he approaches winemaking with an untrammelled openness which reflects a determination to express the various *terroirs* through the grape and to put the stamp of each vintage on its white wines. In Burgundy, where *terroir* is its own recipe; no complex *cuisine* is required of the vigneron who has cropped low yields and tended his vines properly.

For Vincent, *Grand Vin* is a matter of finesse above all. In his excellent reds this comes from temperatures below 35⁰C and twice daily *pigéage* to extract aromatics, colour and tannins, but without overdoing it. For Volnays and Beaunes, bottling is latish – after 15–18 months in cask – allowing the wines to gain in richness from deliberately extended lees contact. He dislikes prefermentive maceration, preferring to destem and crush, leaving the yeasts to work naturally. 'We have no sophisticated cooling equipment,' so Vincent's vigil at vintage time doesn't respect office hours: 'Accidents happen and the night is long.'

His Volnays – a Village and five Premiers Crus – are splendidly stylish. Of the latter, Clos des Chênes and Pitures are more powerful and less elegant at the outset, a fact attributable to heavier soils, which tend to impart breadth and tannins. Pitures, just above Frémiets, develops finesse with time, to match a refined Taillepieds and the little seen Aussey.

In 1993, the Aussey fermentation blocked, leaving unfermented sugar. So Vincent ran off the wine, pressed the pulp and waited patiently for fermentation to resume. The result was a virtually black wine, full of sumptuous sweet fruit – rather resemblng a young Australian Shiraz. Tasted blind, one would never imagine it as Volnay, let alone Pinot Noir. One important US critic found it 'fabulous', which puzzled Vincent.

The Caillerets is best of all, fusing power and finesse. The 1993 packed a mouthful of intense, pure fruit, excellent tannins and a nice touch of oak (Vincent only buys enough new oak to renew his cask population, not to influence his wine). Not quite in the class of de Montille, d'Angerville or Lafarge, but a fine wine nonetheless.

Presumably so they can feel at home, the Bitouzet whites are vinified at Vincent's father-in-law's house, opposite Dominique Lafon in Meursault, whilst the reds are vinified in the family cellars next to the Lafarge's in Volnay's Rue de la Combe.

Vincent's continuing practice is to simply Kieselguhr filter his wines and he harbours an abiding distrust of importers who try to influence him in this respect: 'I'm in charge here.' In 1987, tiring of his US importer's insistence on unfiltered wine, he separated one red *cuvée* into two – part bottled only fined, the rest just filtered. To start with the fined wine tasted better, but later the reverse. His US importer hasn't asked for unfiltered wine again.

Vincent Bitouzet is a careful, classy winemaker as skilled with reds as with whites – a rare talent – and an excellent source of both Volnays and Meursaults. At present about half his production is sold in bulk, but with an increasing coterie of appreciative customers that is doubtless destined to change.

Commune	Level	Lieu-dit/Climat	Area	Vine Age	Status
Volnay	PC	Clos des Chênes	0.55	14	F/M
Volnay	PC	Caillerets	0.15	14	P
Volnay	PC	Taillepieds	0.71	19	M
Volnay	PC	Pitures	1.01	34	F/M
Volnay	PC	Aussey	0.51	37	F
Volnay	V	———	2.34	17	F/M
Volnay	R	(Bourgogne Rouge)	0.90	25	P
Volnay	R	(Bourgogne Passe-Tout-Grain)	0.63	34	F
Beaune	PC	Cent Vignes	1.25	8	F
Meursault	PC	Perrières	0.28	12	F
Meursault	PC	Charmes	0.52	25	F
Meursault	PC	Santenots	0.20	24	F
Meursault	V	Clos du Cromin	0.84	17	F
Meursault	V	Les Cabrins	0.66	20	F
Meursault	V	———	0.38	34	F
Meursault	R	(Bourgogne Aligoté)	0.30	42	F
Total:			**11.23 ha**		

Domaine de la Pousse d'Or

VOLNAY

This Domaine comprises the southern portion of the original 100 ha Duvault-Blochet estate, of which the northern arm included Romanée-Conti and Clos de Tart. In 1964 it was acquired by a small consortium, including Jacques Seysses' father and Jean Ferte – 'un amateur averti'. A close friend of Seysses, and Ferte's nephew, *ingénieur agronome* Gérard Potel, who lived in Champagne, was invited to take charge. He remains the Domaine's *gérant* and winemaker owning 50% of the equity, the other half now belonging to a group of Australians.

Although not without charm, and much respected for his skill and innovation, Potel is not an easy man to deal with. He gives the impression, rare in Burgundy, of someone whose ideas have been cast in the hardest, least flexible of metal and who is not to be gainsaid. Conversation rapidly becomes a lecture, with his views marshalled as so many logical cannons, for the immediate and summary destruction of any opposition.

Whatever his infelicity of manner, Potel's wines are invariably a joy. Pommards, even Santenays, but above all Volnays, of exemplary purity and definition. These are *vins de terroir*, produced from low-yielding old vines and designed for 'elegance and finesse'.

To preserve each *cuvée*'s origins, M. Potel operates a 14–20 day vatting: 'To make *Grand Vin*, you mustn't be afraid of long *cuvaison*.' This is essential to extract the right sort of tannins, from the two main species: short-chain, smaller molecules which are hard and astringent, and larger molecules which are only present to any significant extent in riper years and, unfortunately, less readily extracted. A balanced wine demands careful management of the three phases of *cuvaison*: pre-fermentive *maceration*, fermentation itself and post-fermentive *maceration*.

Gérard Potel has tried a variety of vinifications, including part whole bunches for slower fermentation, roto-tanks and a 'pseudo-Accad' method. 'I don't want to die an idiot,' he explains, adding that although the grape contains the power and pigments of its growing season, you spoil a wine by overextraction. He professes a strong dislike of 'gurus': 'Look at Bordeaux – the gurus are too powerful and the wines too standardised.' For him, structure is not a wine's most important attribute, rather finesse and length he considers first.

He also has firm views on gurus from outside France – critics whom he regards as having too much power and too little taste. 'The problem of Burgundy is the difficult vintages; these people want you to make a monster every year. It's like saying that if a woman is not blonde with such and such measurements, she's no good.'

Gérard Potel expounds on wood, filtration and concentration, to all of which he has devoted much work and thought. His Santenays only see year-old Volnay casks, whilst the Volnays and Pommards have always had 20% new Alliers or Nevers oak – 'I don't like Vosges very much.' In his view, if new wood is used, is essential that the wine has it before *malo* – 'I know vignerons whose wine stinks of wood, after ten years.'

Filtration, he regards as one weapon in the vigneron's armoury – not a procedure to be included or excluded *a priori*. 'In 1966, the Americans wouldn't tolerate the slightest deposit; now it's all changed.' For him, filtration is perfectly acceptable, provided it's done carefully – 'It's like pushing someone through a door – if you do it gently, there is no damage'; the pressure used makes all the difference. He dislikes the modern tendency to taste the method of production rather than the quality of what appears in the glass. 'When I eat in a restaurant, I don't ask what goes on in the kitchen; if it's good, it's good.'

Gérard Potel has pioneered work into mechanisms for removing water from *must* to bring the liquid:solids ratio nearer to the 60:40 which most top-class winemakers agree is ideal. The authorities allow him to use, on an experimental basis, an apparatus which evaporates water from *saignéed* juice, concentrating what remains. This, he stresses, is corrective, to be used sparingly. It is an essential control that what is evaporated is added to the final yield calculation.

Tasting, in Pousse d'Or's cellars, beneath its prominent, long, white shuttered, headquarters – part 13th-century, part Napoleon I – is a lesson in consistency. Here, the 1994s have a richness, balance and finesse that many would be proud of in their 1993s – yet the vintage is derided. The 1993s are, of course, yardstick wines, from a delicious, complex Bourgogne Rouge, from 50-year-old vines just above the Château de Pommard, through a Village Pommard and a pair of excellent Premiers Crus Santenays – Clos Tavannes (part of Gravières, on the Chassagne Montrachet border) and Gravières itself, to a truly remarkable array of Premiers Crus Volnays.

The Clos d'Audignac in the middle of the village, below the Domaine – part of which was reclaimed from garden in the 1960s – has a fine, deep colour, and an elegant, gently oaky nose, followed by rich, opulent fruit with enough structure and acidity to see it through a decade of maturity. The vineyard is exposed due north, which means lateish ripening and less natural structure than either Caillerets or Clos des Chênes.

Les Caillerets (*secteur bas*) has better structure, medium density and noticeably more *fond*, yet remains essentially *tendre*; a fine wine, for longish ageing. The Clos des 60 Ouvrées (an ouvrée is 1/24 of a hectare and was reckoned as a day's work for one man) is part of Les Caillerets (*secteur dessus*). Here, thin soils, giving onto hard rock, impart acidity and depth to the wine which has a lighter structure, more obvious finesse and a finely-judged balance.

The Pousse d'Or, long and complex, is somewhat Pommardish in style, more mouthfilling perhaps, but less precisely focussed than either the Caillerets or the 60 Ouvrées. Good, but not best of the bunch.

The quality of his wines is perhaps reasonable excuse for Gérard Potel's aggressive self-confidence. After all, it is his skill alone which has turned Pousse d'Or into a top-flight Domaine.

Commune	Level	Lieu-dit/Climat	Area	Vine Age	Status
Volnay	PC	Clos de la Pousse d'Or	2.14	35	P
Volnay	PC	Clos des 60 Ouvrées (Caillerets)	2.40	30	P
Volnay	PC	Les Caillerets	2.26	40	P
Volnay	PC	Clos d'Audignac	0.80	30	P
Pommard	PC	Les Jarrollières	1.45	35	P
Santenay	PC	Clos Tavannes	2.10	46	P
Santenay	PC	Les Gravières	1.83	40	P
Pommard	R	(Bourgogne Rouge)	1.20	50	P
		Total:	**14.18 ha**		

MONTHÉLIE

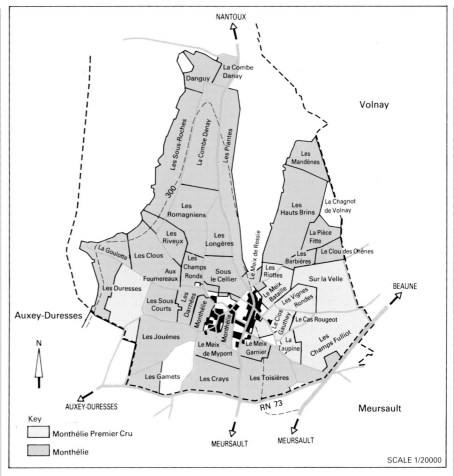

Tucked away behind Meursault, at the top of a hill, is Monthélie, one of the most underrated communes of the Côte d'Or. It is odd that this delightful, picturesque little village, perched above its vines, as though it were keeping some sort of perpetual eye on them, should be so neglected. This may have something to do with the fact that until recently, much of its excellent red wine was sold in bulk to négociants, finally reaching the market as Côte de Beaune-Villages rather than as Monthélie. The time has come for a revival.

Although overlooking them, Monthélie lives in the shadow of Meursault and Volnay, which bound it to the south and east respectively. As if to ensure that it has no chance whatever of expanding, and thereby regaining the pre-eminence it enjoyed between the 11th and 16th centuries, when it belonged to the Abbey of Cluny, the siege is completed by hills to the north and Auxey-Duresses to the west. Thus are the 200 inhabitants of Monthélie and their vines ineluctably encased.

Fortunately what they have is good: their village, a maze of steep, narrow streets and alleys, some leading somewhere, others going nowhere, has barely changed since much of it was built during the 18th and 19th centuries. Wandering these quiet byways, one would not be entirely surprised to encounter a sedan-chair ferrying a noble de Suremain back to his splendid Château, or a crier in frock-coat and stove-pipe hat announcing Napoléon's defeat at Waterloo.

Monthélie has recorded history dating back to the 9th century when the Gauls occupied the land, and unrecorded history back to the Romans. The remains of a Roman encampment are to be seen on the west side of the village, and an assortment of Roman artefacts have surfaced over the years to embellish the story.

Recent times have been relatively tame. Apart from the phylloxera which devastated Monthélie, as it did the rest of the Côte in the last quarter of the 19th century, nothing much happened until 1913, when a parish war broke out with Auxey-Duresses over the provision of water, from which Monthélie, having only three small wells, suffered particular deprivation. The arguments were somehow settled and a permanent water supply finally established in 1919.

In September 1944, a squadron of French troops, sent to liberate Monthélie, ran out of petrol. It took them several days to find any

and when they came to leave, they departed with many enduring friendships and plenty of wine. Every two years since, veterans have returned to the village to renew the ties – and to replenish their cellars.

With under 200 inhabitants, Monthélie is one of the smallest communes of the Côte, second only to Vougeot. 42 individual growers are listed, together with two Domaines, for a total of 172.21 ha of vines. Of these, 108.72 ha are AC Monthélie and 31.18 ha are Monthélie Premier Cru, whilst the remaining 42.31 ha are *régionales*.

Monthélie has the distinct advantage that most of its vines are on more or less steep slopes, to the north, south and west of the village. These hillsides are equally varied in exposure, but are well-drained and do not have the heavier soils found elsewhere.

There are 11 Premiers Crus. Of these, 3 account for two-thirds of the total surface: Sur la Velle (6.03.01 ha), Les Champs-Fuillot (8.11.22 ha) and Les Duresses (6.71.34 ha). The finest – Sur la Velle and Les Champs-

Fuillot – are due east of the village, contiguous with Volnay's Caillerets and Clos des Chênes. The soils, as those in this sector of Volnay, are mainly Bathonian limestone, with an admixture of marls and iron-bearing rock, particularly in the higher sections, giving the ground a reddish tinge.

The only Premier Cru outside this section is Les Duresses, situated in the Auxey valley and oriented on a north-south axis. This gives an exposure to both the east and west, far less favourable than that of the Volnay sector. The soil contains markedly less limestone, which makes for wines with more structure, but commensurately less finesse.

Although there is a tiny quantity of Monthélie Blanc, made from 100% Chardonnay – on average some 660 cases each year – it is on the reds that Monthélie's reputation is founded. From the best Domaines, these are wines of depth and structure, with reasonable longevity. In a good vintage, they tend to start off rather austere, with high acid and tannins, but with plenty of ripe, fleshy, fruit underneath. In character, the best combine the finesse of Volnay with the body and structure of Auxey.

The finest Monthélies come from the de Suremains, Didier Darviot and from the engaging nonogenarian, Mme Armande Douhairet; elsewhere, there are excellent *cuvées* from Jadot in Beaune and from Jean-François Coche in Meursault.

Monthélie deserves wider recognition, both for its wines and for its pretty village. The Château, with its magnificent wrought-iron gates and splendid carriage-sweep, is well worth a look. Although slightly faded, it exudes a noble, crumbling defiance, with the air of a building which is saying: 'I've seen it all and had enough; if you don't look after me, I reserve the right to fall down altogether.'

Elsewhere, there is La Ferme du Majorlet, between Monthélie and Volnay, which also belongs to the de Suremains. This has a curious place in the village's history. In 1765, as Henri Cannard recounts, the farmer's wife, driven next door by a leaking roof, gave birth to a child. Unfortunately her neighbour's house being in the commune of Volnay, there followed an epic struggle between the Priest of Volnay and the Seigneur of Monthélie, for the soul, and taxes, of this brand new parishioner. It took 25 years to resolve the matter . . . in favour of Monthélie.

Monthélie's wines are undervalued and underpriced. Anyone seeking to buy sound, often excellent, sensibly-priced red Burgundy could do worse than investigate this friendly, attractive commune.

Monthélie – a quiet, picturesque village surrounded by its vines

Château de Monthélie

MONTHÉLIE

The Château de Monthélie is one of the few substantial buildings of the Côte d'Or. Principally of early- and mid-18th-century construction, it sits on the edge of an escarpment, perched above Monthélie's southerly extremity. Though once fine and noble, the building, through decades of neglect, has degenerated into a state of slightly scuffed aristocracy.

This eccentric establishment originally belonged to the de Monthélie family, who built it. Handed down through the years, it finally came to Robert de Suremain just before the last war. Since 1983, his grandson, Eric de Suremain has run the estate.

With an oenology diploma from Beaune, preceded by a short spell at Chalone in California in 1976, Eric is well qualified to look after his future inheritance, and his 3 ha in Rully, where he and his wife live.

After extensive replanting in the late 1970s, every endeavour is being made to keep vines as long as is practicable. In the 3 ha of Premier Cru Sur la Velle, for example, nearly 0.75 ha were planted in 1928.

Yields are kept down by widespread use of the low-vigour rootstock Riparia Gloire, and by leaving grass untreated between the vine-rows, using only spot herbicide applications directly beneath each plant. The apparently untidy state of the Suremain vines causes some derision among their neighbours, but then, as Eric points out, he is not a gardener.

In the cellar, the orientation is firmly traditional. Well aware of the latest techniques, Eric is sceptical of much that passes for progress. He eschews automation, preferring personal contact to get the feel of each *cuve*; so, twice daily, he strips off, jumps in and starts treading. 'Pigéage gives one the aspect of the *cuve*,' he explains.

In advance of Eric's immersion, the bunches are completely destalked and lightly crushed. Following his grandfather's practice, he adds between 2 and 5% of whole bunches to each vat, although he does not seem quite certain what this might achieve.

The pulp is cooled to control both the speed and temperature of fermentation, which normally rises to 35–37°C. In 1990 one *cuve* rocketed to 41°C, luckily without blocking. A trial cold maceration in 1993 'smelt of the pharmacy', so that's that for the present.

Cuvaison – five days in 1988, a couple more in 1990 and 1993 – is surprisingly short for the depth of extract achieved. However, as *décuvage* occurs before all the sugar has been converted – which gives more finesse –

Part of the enamel-tiled roof of the de Suremains' Château de Monthélie

this figure is illusory. Four further days *débourbage* finish off the fermentation.

Neither Eric nor his predecessors have favoured new oak; indeed, there used to be none. When new plantings became productive the proportion of new wood inevitably increased – to about 20%; but this is now declining. 5% is seen as ideal – but Eric is still tinkering with the problem.

In the cold, dripping cellars beneath the terrace (the roof leaks) the *malos* proceed slowly, until midsummer when the wines are racked, unified and returned to cask. Thereafter the time they spend in wood is determined by the vintage; the shortest total *élevage* was for the 1984/86 and 87 vintages which were bottled after 16 months. The longest – for most of the 1985/1988/1990 and 1993 Premiers Crus – is 2 years. The wines are 'never, never' fined but, since 1984, both Kieselguhr and plate-filtered. Eric is trying to eliminate these and experimented with cartridges for his 1989s. A trial with Kieselguhr filtration, just before the *malo*,

gave 'spectacular results with the wine's colour' which stimulated further *essais*.

The Domaine's wines are individual, and fine. In youth, they tend to a deep, impenetrable appearance, almost the black-cherry aspect of a young Syrah, which lightens quite rapidly. Low yields (27–40 hl/ha in Village and 30–37 in Premier Cru) and old vines endow even the Monthélie Village with a ripe, almost sweet concentration, overlaid by a tarry, velvety texture.

Exceptionally, the Château recorded lower yields in 1990 than in 1989 and both its 1990s have matured beautifully. The Village, still deep in colour, is deliciously 'tendre', although quite big-framed, with generous rich, spicy, almost *confit* fruit. The Premier Cru Sur la Velle has a dimension more of everything – gorgeously concentrated, powerful and long. Neither shows the slightest sign of the rusticity one sometimes encounters in Monthélie. The 1993s seem set to develop in much the same style, although with a somewhat lighter touch.

It is with age that their true qualities emerge. Although Champs Fuillot is generally regarded as the commune's finest Premier Cru, Sur la Velle is not far behind. Eric's version of the latter ages well, gradually developing secondary and tertiary aromas of *sous-bois* and strawberries. While the 1987 was reaching maturity in 1995, the 1985 was almost fully mature – with fine aromas of *sous-bois* and game leading to a rather less evolved palate, still rich and elegant, tight and powerful, long, complete and very persistent. No loss of grip here and a few more years to go.

These wines are among the best in Monthélie, an achievement Eric attributes to low yields and to his habit of finishing the fermentation off the skins. If he follows Robert de Suremain's precept: 'there are no petites années – it is just the balance which counts', the Domaine cannot but progress from strength to strength.

VINEYARD HOLDINGS

Commune	Level	Lieu-dit/Climat	Area	Vine Age	Status
Monthélie	PC	Sur la Velle	3.00	1928/60/80/84/90	P
Monthélie	PC	Le Cas Rougeot	0.16	1972	P
Monthélie	V	En Remagnien	0.88	1972/85	P
Monthélie	V	Les Hauts Brins	0.51	1976	P
Monthélie	V	Les Clous	0.72	1987/91	P
Monthélie	V	Les Barbières	0.37	1984	P
Monthélie	V	Les Sous Courts	0.36	1985	P
		Total:	**6.00 ha**		

Domaine de Monthélie-Douhairet

MONTHÉLIE

The fortunes and style of this 300-year-old Domaine are entirely in the hands of the delightful nonagenarian Mme Armande Douhairet. This personable, chatty lady, the last surviving member of the family, presides over her Domaine and the reception of visitors, from her cosy first-floor apartments opposite the cellars. Known affectionately by everyone in Monthélie as 'Le Miss', she continues to taste, preferring mature vintages now to newer ones, and takes a lively interest in whoever passes through the arch into her courtyard. Apparent frailty hides indomitable courage – she recently put a hand into a ventilator fan and laughed it off: 'c'est rien'. Then she broke her leg, and was found, grounded, chuckling away in much the same vein. A tribute to the noblest spirit of old age.

She took over, after her uncle's death in 1945, 12 ha, reduced to the current 7 when her sister sold her share. Although known principally for red and white Monthélie, these account for only half total production.

Day-to-day vineyard and cellar work is in the hands of Francis Lechauve, who learned his skills with André Mussy and Bernard Fevre. Since 1990, overall winemaking policy has been the responsibility of André Porcheret, now winemaker at the Hospices de Beaune, who has made a considerable impact on the quality of Mme Armande's wines, which went through an uneven patch in the late 1970s and early 1980s.

The Domaine's vineyards are mostly on hillsides – especially in Monthélie, where the half-slopes are considered to produce the best wine. Careful selection of 'plants fins' ensures sensible yields and a favourable solids:liquid balance in the grapes. Yields have been significantly reduced since 1990 when, despite rigorous *évasivage*, a second passage through the vines was deemed necessary just before *veraison* to remove bunches from overcharged vines. Village appellations now produce 40–45 hl/ha, and Premiers Crus 30–35 hl/ha – 'often less,' adds Madame, 'with 35 hl/ha we can make something fine.'

Red vinification is 'revised classical' – the principal revision being the systematic introduction of some 17% whole bunches into the otherwise destalked pulp. These prolong fermentation whilst the stalks help make the *chapeau* less jammy and easier to work.

The pulp is cooled to 14°C, which delays the onset of fermentation by 3-4 days, during which colour is extracted. Before the advent

A living testimony to the benefits of good wine – 90-year-old Mme Armande about to enjoy something from her personal reserve

of controlled cooling, the gradual filling of the wooden vats with fresh cool grapes kept fermentation from starting, so there is some historical precedent for pre-fermentive *maceration*. Fermentation proceeds with natural yeasts peaking at 33°C – above this, there is significant loss of aroma. In pursuit of better balance and extract, André Porcheret has lengthened vatting from 8 days (1989) to 15–20 days.

Red *élévage* lasts some 18 months with 40% of new oak for the Premiers Crus, and little or none for the Villages. Two rackings are followed by the minimum fining and filtration – none in 1993 – then bottling.

The Domaine has always made *vins de garde*. The Monthélies generally start out quite deep and succulent, with enough tannin to keep them going, but with a measure of

finesse – in part the contribution of the whole bunches. This contrasts with the softer, more elegant style of Ch. de Monthélie down the road. Of the Domaine's two Premiers Crus, Le Meix Bataille tends to have more finesse than the Duresses; its clay-limestone soil and its situation on the Volnay border seems to impart roundness and delicacy. The Duresses, on the border of Monthélie and Auxey-Duresses, is quite the opposite in character – greater rusticity, more closed up and tannic – a wine which in good vintages must be kept for at least 5 years to integrate and begin to show its paces.

Mme Armande's Pommards and Volnays are also excellent. The Pommard Frémiets – which touches its Volnay namesake – is more typical of Volnay than Pommard; more lively, more finesse, but less structure; a wine of lace not muscle. The Pommard Chanlins, which adjoins Rugiens on the Volnay border, has more obvious depth and structure. The 1990 Chanlins is a remarkable wine – with real profundity, backed by a layer of well-integrated tannins. This, from nutrient-poor soil, is a wine to keep for a decade or two.

The Pommards are deliberately given more new oak than the Volnays. Whilst the Volnay Village is good, the Champans is significantly better, combining Volnay's delicacy and finesse with elements of the structure of Pommard. This is the *cuvée* the Domaine holds back most of – since it ages best of all – no doubt, the 45-year-old vines play a part here.

The quality of Mme Armande's wines may have varied in the past, but this indomitable, charming old lady and her Domaine seem at last set on course for a bright future. She is well assured of some magnificent drinking on her hundredth birthday.

VINEYARD HOLDINGS

Commune	Level	Lieu-dit/Climat	Area	Vine Age	Status
Monthélie	PC	Les Duresses (R)	0.21	24	P
Monthélie	PC	Les Duresses (W)	0.26	8	P
Monthélie	PC	Le Meix Bataille (R)	0.43	22	P
Monthélie	PC	Clos de Meix Garnier	1.00	¾ 50; ¼15	P
Monthélie	V	————	2.05 (R)	25 and 40	P
Monthélie	V	La Combe D'Année (W)	0.17	8	P
Meursault	PC	Les Santenots (W)	0.30	38	P
Meursault	V	————	0.17 (W)	30	P
Volnay	PC	En Champans	0.94	30 and 45	P
Volnay	V	————	0.13	30	P
Pommard	PC	Les Frémiets	0.17	30	P
Pommard	PC	Les Chanlins	0.30	35	P
————	R	(Bourgogne Grande Ordinaire)	0.22	45	P
————	R	(Bourgogne Aligoté)	0.51	45+	P
		Total :	**6.84 ha**		

Domaine Darviot-Perrin

MONTHÉLIE

Didier Darviot really wanted to be a wood craftsman. He trained for it, but then veered towards the vine. In fact he couldn't help it – wine was in his blood; his Beaunois family had owned vines for generations and his father had sold wine to the likes of Jadot, Drouhin and Latour. Then there were his in-laws, the Perrins, who had vines on both sides – grandmother in Chassagne and father in Volnay. No escape really.

Didier and his wife Geneviève – blonde, petite and vivacious, for some unexplained reason known to everyone as Julie – installed themselves in his uncle's house in Monthélie in 1986. This spacious residence on the edge of the village is strategically placed, equidistant from Beaune and Chassagne, the outposts of their empire. From 1989, they sold progressively less in bulk and began to bottle wine. Now, there are 30,000 bottles – 'it grows every year' – from excellent Bourgognes to white Meursaults and Chassagnes (3 of each), a Monthélie, Chassagne, Pommard and Beaune in red, with two *cuvées* of Volnay assembled from seven different *climats* to round things off.

With little formal training, taught mainly by his father since 1978, Didier has achieved a good deal. His wines are skilfully put together, with minimum preconceptions, and a sound feel for quality.

He has the sensitivity and enquiring nature of an artist; indeed, with his mass of greying hair flourished back, he looks the part. His manner is thoughtful, confident yet reflective – quite serious underneath a natural charm. His paternal apprenticeship has ingrained wise practice.

Deciding how to look after plants and soils is not easy. If you work the soil, then you risk spreading airborne nematodes and thus increasing disease – especially the endemic *court-noué*, which has been destroying Côte de Beaune vines in particular, since 1945 when there were no clones and much genetically infected material was planted.

Vinifications are relatively straightforward, with 90–95% destemming and 'great care over *pigéage*' for the reds, and 90% cask fermentation for the whites. Didier likes a short temperature peak for his reds, to extract aromas and adapts *cuvaison* to the vineyard – Chassagne gets around 8 days, whilst Volnays 'need long *cuvaison* for extract' and are consequently left for 15–17

days. Wines of both colours are bottled after 18 months or so, by a contractor. 'To bottle yourself, you need top quality equipment,' he admits, dismissing the meccano-like small fillers many growers use as 'folklorique'. Some red *cuvées* are, however, bottled cask by cask. Which? – 'Ça dépend', is the reply, with the cynical rider that one should beware of *vignerons* who bottle one cask unfiltered and then filter the rest – labelling the totality 'vin non-filtré'. Darviot reds are fined, more for brilliance than to soften tannins, according to need (less in 1993, more in 1990/1 and 2) and only filtered if they haven't fallen bright naturally.

For the whites, *batonnage* is the most crucial operation, especially towards the end of fermentation. In 1993, like many growers, Didier managed to flesh out naturally lean, acidic wines with extra lees-stirring. White *élévage* consists of a single racking after 10–11 months, then returning the wine from casks to larger *foudres* for a further 8–9 months before fining, membrane filtration and bottling.

Both reds and whites are excellent. Fine Meursaults – a tight, fleshy La Velle from vines adjacent to Bernard Michelot's house, a classy young-vine Tessons and a couple of

Premiers Crus (Charmes and Perrières). Then come a worthy pair of white Chassagnes – a Village *cuvée* from 80+ -year-old vines and a Premier Cru Blanchots Dessus from 80 rows right against the wall of Le Montrachet, vinified with the Rebichets. The reds' flagships are undoubtedly the three Volnays – Les Blanches, Les Santenots and a generic wine assembled from the smaller parcels. The former, a Village vineyard which touches the Clos des Chênes is hillside land, overlaid with white stones which reflect back the heat. This is harvested late, giving low yields and fullish wine, with plenty of concentrated fruit. The Santenots, from older vines, generally heavily *millerandé*, is altogether broader, deeper flavoured and more muscular with oak tending to show in its structure. An interesting and contrasting pair.

Didier and Julie Darviot are a conscientious team. When not at home looking after their two children, you might come across them cross-country cycling, eating in a new restaurant, or in Avignon at the theatre or listening to music. 'Our tastes are eclectic, everything from Baroque to Beethoven' – presumably no Berio or Blush; but then this is a traditional establishment!

VINEYARD HOLDINGS

Commune	Level	Lieu-dit/Climat	Area	Vine Age	Status
Chassagne	PC	Les Rebichets (W)	0.09	30	P
Chassagne	PC	Les Blanchots Dessus (W)	0.29	25 and 35	P
Chassagne	V	La Bergerie (W)	0.46	80+	P
Meursault	PC	Les Charmes	0.31	25 and 35	P
Meursault	PC	Les Perrières	0.29	35	P
Meursault	V	Les Tessons, Clos la Velle, Les Clous, Vireuils	2.17	10–30	P
Monthélie	V	Les Craies (R)	0.19	10	P
Chassagne	PC	Les Bondues (R)	0.32	25	P
Beaune	PC	Bellisands	0.45	40	P
Pommard	V	Les Vaumuriens	0.19	20	P
Volnay	PC	La Gigotte	0.27	20	P
Meursault	PC	Volnay Santenots	0.58	35 and 45	P
Volnay	V	Les Blanches	0.52	40	P
Volnay	V	Les Petits Gamets	0.05	30	P
Volnay	V	Les Petits Poisots	0.18	20	P
Volnay	V	Les Pasquiers	0.16	40	P
Volnay	V	Les Pluchots	0.17	20	P
Meursault	R	Les Maguys (Bourgogne Blanc)	0.21	30	P
Meursault	R	Les Maguys (Bourgogne Rouge)	0.14	30	P
Meursault	R	(Bourgogne Aligoté / Passe-Tout-Grain)	0.80	15/30/50	P
Total:			**7.84 ha**		

AUXEY-DURESSES

Auxey from the slopes of Montagne du Bourdon – with its best-known Premier Cru, Les Duresses, in the foreground

Pommard etc., but rather that the consumer's ignorance allowed duplicity on an egregious scale.

Despite its erstwhile role of compliant understudy, Auxey is a pleasant, elongated little village sitting peacefully in the valley between a pair of gentle, green hills. Here the roads from Beaune, Meursault, Saint-Romain and Autun converge, which gives the place an air of bustle and commerce which belies the reality.

This strategic location made it an ideal site for ancient settlers, of which prehistoric encampments on Mont-Mélian and a Druid Temple at nearby Petit-Auxey are evidence. Petit-Auxey – 'Hauxiacum' – is thought to be the earlier settlement, since it controlled not only the traffic along the valley, but also essential water sources.

Vines have been planted on these hillsides for centuries. The monks at Cluny owned land and here between the 10th and 14th centuries, until the Abbey of Maizières took over. A contemporary inventory shows them as proprietors, in 1692, of most of the *climats* which are still considered the finest.

Auxey is not a large vignoble. Some 169.63 ha of Village and Premier Cru land are spread out over three geographically

Auxey-Duresses is another of the small communes of the Côte de Beaune which is deservedly undergoing something of an image transformation.

Until relatively recently, its vignerons provided an excellent source of Côte de Beaune-Villages and Bourgogne Rouge and Blanc for the main négociant houses. However, with escalating prices of the better known Appellations, buyers have been sniffing round in Auxey and elsewhere for sound red and white Burgundy at sensible prices. Today, whilst more Auxey is being bottled and sold by growers directly, under the Village label, merchants are making a well overdue reappraisal and a distinct air of prosperity abounds.

The village has long had a reputation for honest, no-nonsense wines, which are straightforward but without a great deal of character. Post-*phylloxera*, and until the AC system arrived in the late 1930s, much of Auxey's red output went to augment the insatiable thirst for 'Volnay' and 'Pommard', whilst the whites no doubt stood in for 'Meursault'. Given the difficulty of finding the genuine article, the conclusion must be, not that Auxey was considered as good as

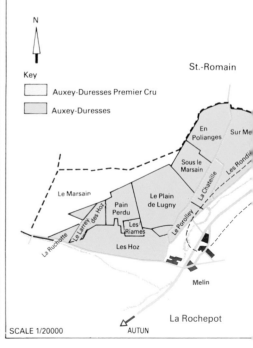

separate areas: Mont-Mélian to the south-east, Montagne du Bourdon and Montagne du Tillet to the immediate north and west, and the Hameau de Melin, a kilometre or so down the RN73 towards Autun.

Although red and white wine is produced on each site, most of Auxey's white output – approximately 25% of the total – comes from grapes grown on the Mont-Mélian. Until the Chardonnay took over, this cluster of ten vineyards was planted extensively with Pinot Blanc and Aligoté. What Aligoté there now is, comes predominantly from lesser, *régionale* land round the base of the hill.

The vineyards of Mont-Mélian face north or north-east which makes ripening difficult. However, being a continuation of Meursault their soils add an element of class in years when the grapes do ripen fully. Underneath a few centimetres of stony, thin, topsoil, there is a layer of easily dislodged shale. There is virtually no Pinot Noir in this sector.

On the northern side of the village, adjoining Les Duresses of Monthélie, on a swathe of 31.76 ha of moderate and steep-sloping ground, directly beneath La Montagne du Bourdon, lie Auxey's seven Premiers Crus. Apart from its protective properties this hill faces almost due south, giving an excellent chance of fully ripening Pinot Noir.

A charming feature of these vineyards are the little 'clochetons' – small wrought-iron fretwork follies with painted white roofs, which serve as shelters in hot weather from where owners can both admire their vines and oversee their workers.

The soils here are generally deep, with varying proportions of limestone. Much of the topsoil is stony scree, which makes soil erosion a constant problem, especially in the steeper sections of Duresses and Reugne. Several growers are experimenting with sowing selected grasses to help retain the soil, which otherwise they must take back up the slopes after rain has washed it down.

The third section of 13 vineyards lies just above the hamlet of Melin, on the Autun road. From a mainly easterly exposure come both reds and whites, in about equal quantity.

In 1961 Auxey took to the viticultural leading-edge. Under the auspices of the *INAO*, a couple of vignerons planted an experimental area in vines trained on the high, spread, Austrian Lenz-Moser system. This was modified into a 'Lyre' configuration in 1965, and there are now some 20 ha, planted thus. Spreading the vegetation in this way promotes better photosynthesis, and therefore higher sugar levels, particularly valuable in this marginal climate.

As the wines of Auxey continue to become better known, vignerons sell more in bottle at better prices and are thus able to invest more in vineyard maintenance and vinification equipment. Whilst the wines of lesser vintages suffer from a lack of roundness and charm and are best avoided, those from riper years can be excellent. The whites might almost be taken for junior Meursaults, with aromas of hazelnuts and lime-blossom and often a pleasant, fat flavour with a noticeable *goût de terroir*. The reds tend to muscular

robustness, with aromas of 'petits *fruits rouges*' and plenty of guts. They benefit enormously from a few years' cellaring – ten or more will do no harm in top-notch vintages.

Apart from the galvanic Jean-Pierre Diconne, profiled here, the best wines come from the estate of the Duc de Magenta which are both vinified and marketed by Louis Jadot in Beaune. These are invariably yardstick wines of high quality – the white, especially, is usually ripe and fat – setting the standards for the rest of the commune's vignerons and admirably demonstrating the class of which Auxey is capable.

In addition, Domaines Michel Prunier, Leroy and Roy Frères are excellent sources, and there are fine white Auxeys to be had from Michel Ampeau, and reds from Jean-François Coche, François Jobard, and André Pernin-Rossin in Vosne.

The village is not bereft of humour: in 1971 the chef-patron of the local restaurant, La Cremaillère, Jean Camilleri, and some German customers, founded La Confrérie du Pot au Feu, to mimic a more illustrious and older Burgundian organisation, the Chevaliers du Tastevin. There are now over 400 members in several countries, presided over by a Grand Sénéchal, swearing undying and constant allegiance to the Pot au Feu. Since this estimable dish is probably accompanied, to perfection, by copious quantities of Auxey-Duresses, what started as a prank is doubtless helping the commune to market its increasingly good wares.

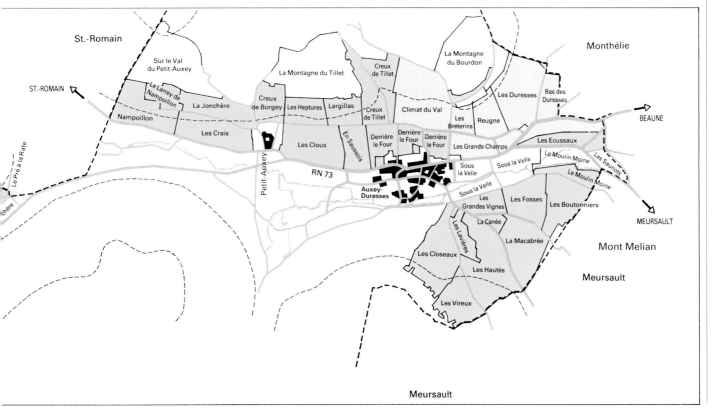

Domaine Jean-Pierre Diconne

AUXEY-DURESSES

Of the few producers of note in Auxey-Duresses, Jean-Pierre Diconne is the most individual. An angular, rather animated and galvanic Burgundian, he took over the family vineyards from his father in 1972, having worked with him from 1960 when he was 15. His parent, in turn, had worked as a paid employee at Meursault before moving to Auxey to work for the proprietor of some vines which were bequeathed to him in 1927.

Jean-Pierre is not a man to be influenced by what goes on around him. He operates on the belief that knowing your vines is the best route to quality, and is clearly cynical of much of what currently passes for progress. He likes to have old vines – his oldest is a patch of Chardonnay in Les Duresses, planted in 1927. When the time does come to grub up a parcel, there is no question of replanting straight away; rather he follows his father who believed in allowing the land to rest before putting it to work anew. Jean-Pierre recalls one plot of Auxey-Duresses which was finally replanted in 1955 after some 25 years fallow, and he recently replaced a parcel which had been without vines for 14 years. Decisions here are clearly not taken with unseemly haste.

The trick of keeping vines into old age is apparently to stress them and make them suffer. Low yields are strongly favoured, although Jean-Pierre remarks dryly that you get the lowest crop of all when part of the vineyard is not planted. Nonetheless, his 1893 Chardonnay vines in the Meursault Les Luchets vineyard are still going strong, so they must be doing something right.

When all else has failed to restrain yields, Jean-Pierre sends his wife into the vineyards to remove excess bunches. In 1990, however, even though 'the wife had taken off 6 bunches per vine', the yield was still very large. The trouble appeared to be that Mme Diconne was despatched on her mission too early – if she had waited until August instead of going out in July, the vines would probably not have been able to compensate for their loss. Jean-Pierre grumbles that he is not at all sure that the large berries he harvested were as well structured as the smaller ones he normally gets. 'The journalists, the writers, the media believe it works, but, in the end, its more complicated,' he comments.

Since his vines in Meursault ripen a few days before those in Auxey, he usually starts picking there. However, 'one can make a mistake', he admits somewhat ruefully, recalling

that in 1990 'everyone harvested too early'. The problem, in his eyes, is that in calibrating the date of full maturity, people erroneously count 100 days from the start of the flowering, instead of waiting until at least half the flowers have developed.

The Domaine's production is divided about equally between red and white. Jean-Pierre works to a limited extent with négociants – especially Ropiteau and Olivier Leflaive – whose *cuvées* are generally separated out before the wines are transferred to cask.

· The white wines start their fermentation in bulk and once the temperature is stable, are put into cask – 25% or so new Allier and Tronçais oak. Cask hygiene is of great importance to Jean-Pierre, especially since his whites spend a minimum of 15 months in wood, on their lees, without being racked – 'our *malos* are slow to happen,' he explains, with unaccustomed understatement. If the casks are not cleaned thoroughly, the wines can develop off-flavours and, as he has noticed with certain of his neighbours' wines, can dessicate and lose their fruit. After this abnormally extended sojourn in cask, the wines are unified in tank, bentonite-fined and, six weeks or so later, Kieselguhr filtered and bottled by a contract bottler.

Wandering around tasting among the rather disorganised honeycomb of cellars scattered around the Diconne Domaine provides a salutory experience in not judging by appearances. Although order does not appear to be one of Jean-Pierre's highest priorities, the wines are, by and large, excellent.

The Auxey Blanc is generally an excellent example: ripe and spicy with excellent acidity, a touch of oak on the palate and deliciously long and stylish, needing 3–5 years in bottle to give of its best.

The Meursault Les Narvaux, extracted from its original cask and proffered for tasting after Jean-Pierre had drawn the pipette across his nose and approved a modest sample squirted directly into his mouth, is bigger and burlier than its Auxey cousin. The vineyard, on the Puligny side of the village is composed of a thin limestone topsoil giving on to almost impenetrable rock, which imparts finesse and acidity to the wine. The Meursault Clos des Luchets is entirely different: much finer, leaner showing more race and style and, typically, very mineral in character. This vineyard is situated a mere 500 metres from the Auxey boundary, and consists mainly of mountain scree material, relatively deep red earth, with a high proportion of stones and 'lave' – a type of porous rock.

The red wines are equally individual in their vinification: a strong dose of SO_2 (1.5–2.0 litres per tonne) is given to delay fermentation by 3 days. There is no destalking and 12–15 days' *cuvaison* at high temperatures – often above 35°C. 'Temperatures are getting lower,' comments Jean-Pierre ruefully on 'the advice of all these prestigious oenologists.' He prefers not to *piger* but to work with a *chapeau immergé*: 'only one good *pigéage*, just up to my elbows'.

The press wine is tasted before being added, or not, to the free-run wine which is then transferred to cask to spend at least one year on its lees. Having tried Nevers oak and wood from Buxy and the Morvan, Jean-Pierre has settled on Allier as 'beaucoup plus fin'.

The *malos* proceed very slowly in the ice-cold cellars – 'In 1988 some casks took two years to complete their *malos*,' remarks Jean-Pierre by way of illustration. If on completion of the *malo* he is not ready to rack the wine, each barrel is given a half dose of SO_2 and

VINEYARD HOLDINGS					
Commune	*Level*	*Lieu-dit/Climat*	*Area*	*Vine Age*	*Status*
Auxey	PC	Les Grands Champs (R)	0.42	1962/67	P
Auxey	PC	Les Duresses (R)	0.42	1927	P
Auxey	V	Les Grandes Vignes/ Les Vireux / Les Heptures (R)	1.23	1945/67/ 71/75	P
Auxey	R	Les Grandes Vignes / Les Clous Les Closeaux/Les Fosses (W)	1.70	1927/55/59/71/91	P
Auxey	R	Les Closeaux (Bourgogne Rouge)	0.20	1972/73	P
Meursault	V	Les Narvaux Dessous	0.77	1970/81/86	P
Meursault	V	Les Luchets	0.71	1893/1930/1950	P
Meursault	R	(Bourgogne Aligoté)	0.92	1930/52/88	P
Meursault	R	(BGO – GAMAY)	0.62	1932/36	P
Meursault	R	(Bourgogne Blanc)	0.34	1954	P
Meursault	R	(Bourgogne Passe-Tout-Grains)	0.62	1932/38/73	P
Total :			**7.95 ha**		

184

left until he has the time. In principle, each *cuvée* is racked once – into a bulk container. On rare occasions the wine is fined it needs a second racking; it is never returned to cask. The last fining was in 1985.

Unlike the white wines, the reds are filtered by Diconne himself, not by the bottler. A light pre-filtration precedes a second, tighter plate-filtration. The entire process from vat to bottle usually exceeds two years: 'On a une vinification longue, nous,' remarks Jean-Pierre phlegmatically.

As one might expect from wines given cold maceration, 15 days *cuvaison*, fermented on a submerged cap containing plenty of stems, the Diconne reds are neither shrinking violets, nor ideal for early consumption. The Auxeys tend to be quite raw and unapproachable for the first few years, opening out slowly over a decade or so to reveal their real qualities. The excellent Auxey Premier Cru *cuvée* is a mix of Les Duresses and Les Grands Champs.

Sadly, people do not generally think of

Auxey-Duresses as producing *vin de garde*, so much of the Domaine's wines are drunk too soon. All Jean-Pierre has to say is: 'We don't change what works.' This doggedly old-fashioned style of winemaking, albeit modified to suit Jean-Pierre's own perceptions of Auxey, produces distinctive, but interesting wines, although less successful in leaner than in riper vintages. If you like the style, then this is as good a source for red as for white.

Golden slopes – autumn vines at nearby Monthélie

Domaine Leroy

AUXEY-DURESSES

Not least because of the personality of its owner and chief publicist, Leroy is Burgundy's most vehemently discussed estate. A chic, slender, blonde dynamo in her early 60s – Mme Lalou Bize-Leroy seems to attract (and sometimes provoke) controversy. In 1992, following a much publicised row over sales, she was removed – by the vote of her own sister, Pauline Roch – from her position as co-administrator and principal distributor of the Domaine de la Romanée-Conti (of which the Leroy family continues to own half). The evident rancour in her attitude towards the Domaine and its wines suggests that this public disgrace bit deep.

Her own Burgundian activities are substantial and invariably high-profile. Apart from Domaine Leroy, she and her *sympa* husband Marcel own the Domaine d'Auvernay which produces exemplary Bourgognes Rouge and Blanc and a clutch of Villages, Premiers and Grands Crus. Leroy itself is both négociant and wine-producer, with 22.42 ha of prime vineyards mainly acquired since 1988. These cover 30 different Appellations from Régionale to Grand Cru (of which there are nine).

From an elegant house in Auxey Mme Bize-Leroy distributes what many regard as the finest Côte d'Or Burgundies to a voracious worldwide clientele, at prices that provoke amazement, admiration, and often thinly-disguised jealousy, among her competitors. In her cellars, if hearsay is to be believed, mature over a million bottles of Burgundy dating back to the 1920s – a unique collection which has been compared to Paris' Bibliothèque Nationale and to the Louvre for its depth and completeness.

Despite an abortive attempt to sell Leroy (to the Japanese) in the late 1980s, this is an estate which exudes wealth. Top prices (some say 'over the top') are paid for vineyards, and entire estates are bought when their land is considered of sufficient quality (e.g. Remy in Gevrey-Chambertin and Charles Noëllat in Vosne-Romanée). The policy of expanding vineyard holdings is a considered reaction to the difficulty of finding suitably high quality wine for the Leroy négociant label – a problem faced by all major négociants. Substantial financial resources also enable it to operate with yields which, in terms of the capital employed, most Domaines would consider unviable. However, with selling prices which outstrip comparables by a multiple of five or more,

Auxey

the economics may be less marginal than some suppose.

Controversy engendered by the personality of Mme Bize-Leroy herself (many consider her arrogant) extends to her wines. Expensive they may be, but are they genuinely great Burgundy? Are the yields as low as are claimed, and is the policy of 100% new wood for everything a credible way to express *terroir* or does it stifle the purity of Pinot Noir, especially in lesser Appellations? These debates are not confined to the international cognoscenti, but are conducted with equal vigour amongst growers and merchants throughout the Côte.

Lalou Bize-Leroy's personality undoubtedly contributes to all this. She has business acumen, a strong flare for publicity and is capable of turning on considerable charm. However these attributes are compromised by an overwheening concern for the cash-value of her actions and an apparent streak of vengefulness which many find unattractive. People also comment on her tendency to be openly dismissive of other growers' wines whilst being noticeably oversensitive to criticism of her own.

Above all, it is her wines which generate the most heated controversy. There are powerful forces, especially in the USA, whose glowing commentaries have led to runaway sales at sky-high prices and spawned a coterie of admirers. Elsewhere, the wines are far from universally lauded, others finding them over-tannic and lacking in typicity.

All Domaine Leroy wines are vinified at Les Genevrières, an elegant building opposite the Clos des Réas in Vosne. Until 1993, when he left to return to his old job of mak-

ing the wines of the Hospices de Beaune, the cellar was in the charge of André Porcheret. Now the wines are made by Mme Bize-Leroy herself.

She takes considerable care over the quality of the grapes that arrive at the *cuverie*. From the beginning, she was convinced that chemical sprays and artificial fertilisers were disastrous for the long-term health of the vineyards. Since 1989 speedy progress has been made towards biodynamic viticulture, on whose precepts the entire estate is now cultivated. In contrast to 'culture biologique', which only cares for plants when their health is threatened, biodynamics restores the vines' equilibrium with their environment. It also gives a vine its own force, enabling it to better resist disease as well as producing more anthocyanins, better aromatics and naturally lower yields. 'It's all plus.'

Terroir is of supreme importance to Lalou Bize-Leroy: 'Fruit has identity, not just as Pinot Noir or Chardonnay, but as Bâtard, Criots, or Corton-Charlemagne.' So much so, that she claims the ability to identify the provenance of grapes merely by tasting them: 'In two years I've never been wrong.' In pursuit of top-class raw material, much time is spent outdoors: 'I'm always in my vineyards – my friends tell me I have *oïdium* and mildew in my head.'

Vine age is deliberately kept high and yields are pitifully low. In 1993, Mme Bize-Leroy reported harvesting only 6 hl/ha in Romanée St-Vivant and Nuits and 9–10 hl/ha for the remainder. Her refusal to breach her biodynamic code and treat rampant mildew was seen by many as irresponsible obstinacy. It is this which precipitated André Porcheret's departure: 'One has no right to lose a harvest; I would have treated,' is his crisp comment on the matter.

Such low yield figures, whilst impressive, need putting into context, as in some of the vineyards many vines are missing. One grower, whose own Grand Cru plot adjoins Leroy's, reports 30% 'manquants'; if so, this automatically increases the true yield commensurately. Even accepting these yields as coming from fully productive vineyards, it is debatable whether reducing output beyond a certain point brings any genuine gain in quality. Some feel that you can over-concentrate and over-extract, which is as undesirable as the converse.

Concern about yields is backed by a thorough *trie* – 'very, very important, I want to have the most natural wine possible.' In 1993, with already minuscule yields, the sorters refused to discard anything more – Madame had to persuade them to remove the *verjus*, a second generation of grapes which look ripe, but are not. 'We've never made wine like it.'

The overriding aim of vinification is to extract the individuality of each *terroir*. This means leaving in the *cuves* as much as possible of what the *terroir* brings. So, all the stalks remain, not only for their physical drainage properties, which facilitate the management of fermentation, but for their indigenous yeasts ('phenomenal!') and for what Mme Bize-Leroy calls 'the ambience of the *cuve*'.

Low yields also bring natural concentration, which eliminates the need for *saigner*. If you bleed off juice, you risk too strong a concentration of tannins, which leads to an imbalance. Maceration, of whole, uncrushed fruit proceeds naturally, with neither cooling nor heating, which alter the character of the vintage. 'I like to feel each *cuve* – living.' *Cuvaison* lasts for 18–20 days, with as little *chaptalisation* as possible – 'just half a degree' – but twice daily foot *pigéage*. Fermentation over, and with press-wine incorporated, the new wine is then transferred to cask, without *débourbage* so as to retain the lees, which have 'their own life'.

To ensure perfect hygiene, both red and white wines are matured entirely in new oak for the complete duration of their *élevage*. 'I don't know whether wood brings anything to wine – I don't think so,' is Mme Bize-Leroy's current verdict, although she admits that her ideas on this may change. In André Porcheret's view a 1992 Savigny Village, for example, is perfectly capable of supporting 100% new oak 'provided the Savigny is made properly' and the casks prepared thoroughly. For him, and thus for Leroy wines, including the 1993s, this means leaching out unwanted tannins in advance. 'The wine must eat the wood, not vice versa,' is how he sees the process of *élevage*.

Following *malo*, the wines are racked off lees which 'don't bring anything further', cask-to-cask, by candlelight. Just before bottling, the reds are assembled, four casks at a time, and fined (if absolutely necessary), but never filtered: 'Filtering a red wine is barbarous.'

Young Leroy reds are thoroughly untypical of mainstream Burgundy. Generally virtually opaque and impressively intense they are unusually dark in colour and, whatever the wine or the vintage, massively tannic. In appearance and structure they have more in common with Syrah than with Pinot Noir. Mme Bize-Leroy counters that this is to be expected with old vines and low yields, and that in any case, Pinot Noir should never be identifiable, being merely the vehicle through which *terroir* expresses itself. However, she freely concedes that such concentration of fruit and tannin will initially mask *terroir* and aroma – a revealing admission in view of respected commentators' frequent reference to the intense Pinot character and typicity of young Leroy Burgundies.

Tasting through the range, even from a lesser vintage such as 1992 which one would expect to find more open, it is difficult to distinguish one Cru from another, so heavy are the wines' structures and so completely unforthcoming their aromas. Differences, when you do find them, are nuances rather than clearly delineated traits of character. If *terroirs* differ so strikingly, this is far from evident across a row of young Leroys.

Maybe such typicities simply require time to emerge. Possibly, but the structure and sheer size of Leroy reds mean that it will be decades before any real distinctiveness becomes apparent, by which time the wines will have been long sold and the controversies long forgotten.

For those who admire these wines, the air resounds with superlatives – 'Brilliant!', 'Stupendous!', 'Mind-blowing!' and so on. Nothing will lead the faithful to entertain even the slightest doubt over their actual quality or inherent potential of the highly-priced treasures in their cellars. However, there are doubters – not people who seek to criticise Mme Bize-Leroy through her wines, but experienced Burgundy-lovers who, try as they will, cannot see in these the seeds of either great Burgundy, or even ultimately, of great wine.

Whilst no competent taster could credibly dispute the depth of extract or tannin in these wines, they can, and do, argue about what is underneath. The clear, pure fruit to be found in, for example a Dujac or Rousseau Clos de la Roche, does not seem to be there in the Leroy version. For those accustomed to rate a wine by its sheer size, Leroy's score highly; others, concerned more for the building than for the scaffolding, who expect subtlety and balanced tannins, are less enthusiastic. There is, however, no serious dissent from the view that these are wines structured for very long ageing, although there must be considerable doubt as to what will emerge when the corks are eventually drawn.

Lalou Bize-Leroy is unlikely to react to such criticisms – apart from condemning them as unjustified. A determination to produce what she sees as top-quality, and an unswerving dedication to her principles, will continue to guide her; both are to be applauded. It seems unfortunate that a potent cocktail of exaggerated hype, high prices, and a passing fashion for massively over-extracted wines, has led to an excess of uncritical adulation for which, for the time being, it is difficult to imagine any convincing justification.

VINEYARD HOLDINGS

Commune	Level	Lieu-dit/Climat	Area	Status
———	R	(Bourgogne Grand Ordinaire)	0.92	P
———	R	(Bourgogne Rouge)	0.76	P
Pommard	V	Les Trois Follots	0.07	P
Pommard	V	Les Vignots	1.26	P
Nuits	V	Au Bas de Combe	0.15	P
Nuits	V	Aux Allots	0.51	P
Nuits	V	Les Lavières	0.68	P
Vosne	V	Les Genevrières	1.23	P
Chambolle	V	Les Fremières	0.35	P
Gevrey	V	———	0.11	P
Volnay	PC	Les Santenots	0.35	P
Savigny	PC	Les Narbantons	0.81	P
Nuits	PC	Les Vignes Rondes	0.38	P
Nuits	PC	Les Boudots	1.19	P
Vosne	PC	Aux Brulées	0.27	P
Vosne	PC	Les Beaux Monts	2.61	P
Chambolle	PC	Les Charmes	0.23	P
Gevrey	PC	Les Combottes	0.46	P
Aloxe	GC	Corton-Charlemagne	0.43	P
Aloxe	GC	Corton Renardes	0.50	P
Vosne	GC	Romanée St-Vivant	0.99	P
Vosne	GC	Richebourg	0.78	P
Vougeot	GC	Clos de Vougeot	1.91	P
Chambolle	GC	Musigny	0.27	P
Morey	GC	Clos de la Roche	0.67	P
Gevrey	GC	Latricières Chambertin	0.57	P
Gevrey	GC	Chambertin	0.50	P
Total:			**22.38 ha**	

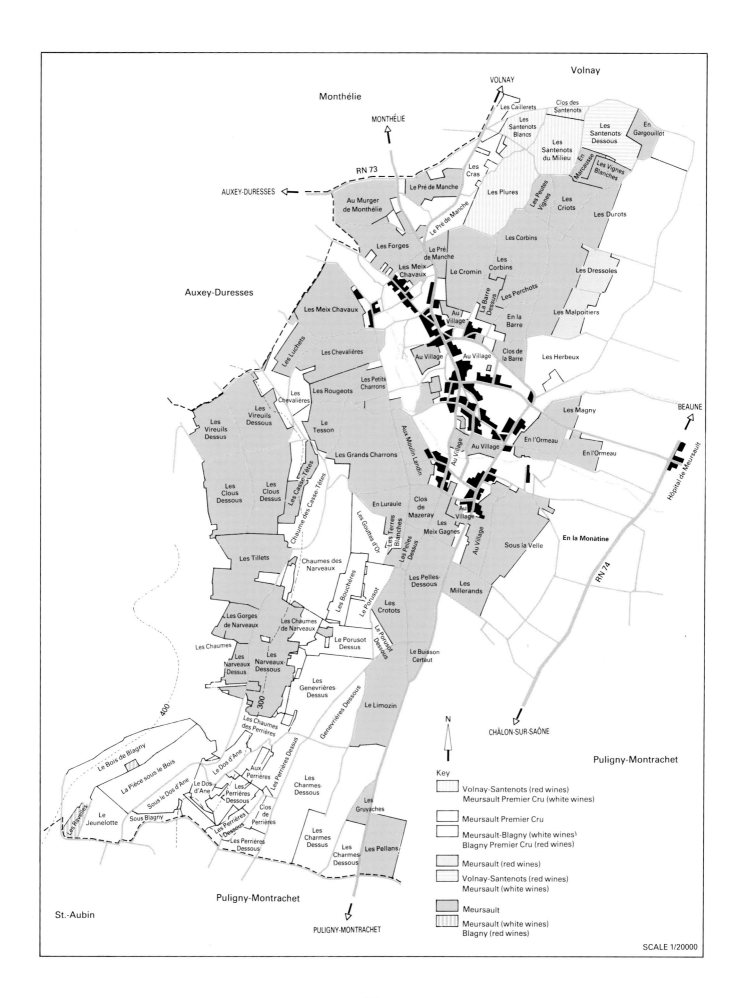

Monthélie

Volnay

VOLNAY

Volnay

MONTHÉLIE

RN 73

AUXEY-DURESSES

Auxey-Duresses

Clos des Santenots

Les Caillerets

Les Santenots Blancs

Les Santenots du Milieu

Les Santenots-Dessous

En Gargouillot

En Marcausse

Les Vignes Blanches

Les Cras

Le Pré de Manche

Les Plures

Les Peutes Vignes

Les Criots

Les Durots

Au Murger de Monthélie

Le Pré de Manche

Les Corbins

Les Forges

Le Pré de Manche

Les Corbins

Les Dressoles

Les Meix Chavaux

Le Cromin

Les Perchots

Les Meix Chavaux

Au Village

La Barre Dessus

En la Barre

Les Malpoitiers

Les Luchets

Les Chevalières

Au Village

Au Village

Clos de la Barre

Les Herbeux

BEAUNE

Les Magny

Les Rougeots

Les Petits Charrons

Les Chevalières

Au Village

Au Village

En l'Ormeau

En l'Ormeau

Hôpital de Meursault

Les Vireuils Dessus

Les Vireuils Dessous

Le Tesson

Aux Moulin Landin

Les Grands Charrons

Les Casse-Têtes

Chaume des Casse-Têtes

En Luraule

Clos de Mazeray

Les Meix Gagnes

Au Village

Au Village

Sous la Velle

En la Monàtine

Les Clous Dessous

Les Clous Dessus

Les Gouttes d'Or

Les Terres Blanches

Les Pelles Dessus

RN 74

Les Tillets

Chaumes des Narveaux

Les Bouchères

Le Porusot

Les Crotots

Les Pelles-Dessous

Les Millerands

Les Gorges de Narveaux

Les Chaumes de Narveaux

Le Porusot Dessus

Le Porusot Dessous

Le Buisson Certaut

Les Chaumes

Les Narveaux-Dessus

Les Narveaux-Dessous

Les Genevrières-Dessous

Genevrières Dessous

Le Limozin

N

Les Chaumes des Perrières

CHÀLON-SUR-SAÔNE

400

Le Bois de Blagny

La Pièce sous le Bois

Sous le Dos d'Ane

300

Les Perrières Dessus

Le Dos d'Ane

Aux Perrières

Le Dos d'Ane

Les Perrières Dessous

Clos de Perrières

Les Charmes-Dessous

Les Gruyaches

Puligny-Montrachet

Key

Les Ravelles

Le Jeunelotte

Sous Blagny

Les Perrières Dessous

Les Charmes Dessus

Les Charmes Dessous

Les Pellans

Volnay-Santenots (red wines)
Meursault Premier Cru (white wines)

Meursault Premier Cru

Meursault-Blagny (white wines)
Blagny Premier Cru (red wines)

Meursault (red wines)

Volnay-Santenots (red wines)
Meursault (white wines)

Meursault

Meursault (white wines)
Blagny (red wines)

St.-Aubin

Puligny-Montrachet

PULIGNY-MONTRACHET

SCALE 1/20000

188

MEURSAULT

About halfway between Beaune and Santenay lies Meursault. Radiating outwards from the main square on top of the hill, roads lead to Monthélie and Volnay, to Auxey and Saint-Romain, through vineyards to nearby Puligny or by more arterial connection to Autun and Chalon.

Immobile, at the centre of all this to-ing and fro-ing, is Meursault's solidly gothic town hall with its multi-coloured enamelled roof, from where the affairs of the commune's 1,700 inhabitants are administered, vineyards bought and sold, harvests declared and marriages solemnised.

The village reeks of prosperity, mostly derived from wine, but tangentially from the services it provides – shops, a cluster of hotels, a basic but welcome public lavatory, and several restaurants await the tourist or weary buyer. Meursault is a place for wandering; attractive narrow streets leading to small courtyards, or into the vineyards, contrast with broader thoroughfares syphoning off heavier traffic to more exotic destinations.

The imposing Château de Meursault, standing among its own vines, is also worth visiting, especially as the entry fee allows you to amble through its splendid cellars and to taste *ad volente*.

With some 170,000 cases to dispose of annually, not surprisingly many of the village's 170 vignerons rely heavily on 'vente directe' – proclaiming their existence with elaborate signs.

The commune, divided into Village land (304.94 ha) and Premiers Crus (131.88 ha), is the largest producer of fine white wine in the Côte. The standard is generally high, with a handful of top growers producing superlative wines.

Pinot Noir accounts for about 6,000 cases per year from 3 separate ACs: Meursault Rouge (and Premier Cru), Blagny (and Premier Cru) and Volnay-Santenots. Each has its designated vineyards – Blagny's two vineyards surrounding a picturesque hamlet which is divided between Meursault and Puligny, and the Volnays coming from an administrative hiccup of six vineyards at Meursault's northern boundary. In ripe years, the reds are fleshy, soft and attractively perfumed, with those who destalk invariably more successful than those who do not.

Administrative buffoonery extends its confusion to Meursault's whites. Chardonnay planted in Volnay-Santenots makes Meursault Santenots (Premier Cru) or plain Meursault, whilst that from Blagny becomes Meursault-Blagny (Premier Cru) or straight Meursault, depending upon its precise provenance.

Several of the village *climats*, while not Premiers Crus, are becoming sufficiently known to appear on labels. Among the best are: Clos de la Barre, Limouzin, En Luraule, Charrons, Narvaux, Tillets, Rougeots, Luchets, Chevalières, Casse-Têtes, Vireuils and Meix Chavaux. Whilst these vineyards extend almost from top to bottom of the limestone escarpment, bounded below by the RN74 and above by woods, the principal Premiers Crus lie on south-east-facing slopes to the south of the village. A lone pair – Les Cras and Les Caillerets – stare across the Volnay border, above Les Santenots Blancs.

Of the 6 principal Premiers Crus, four – Charmes, Poruzots, Genevrières and Perrières – are subdivided into two or more *climats*, the quality and qualities of each differing enough to justify a distinction. Dramatic soil variation within this narrow band, and experience, has evolved what amounts to an informal hierarchy. With the constant proviso that the vigneron's contribution can submerge that of the vineyard, the dominant character of each Premier Cru can be broadly described.

At the northern extremity, Bouchères (4.41 ha) and Gouttes d'Or (5.33 ha) produce wines of less finesse but fuller structure than the rest. They last well, without developing the complexity of, for example, a great Genevrières or Charmes.

Next in rank, Charmes, the largest Premier Cru, at 31.12 ha, occupies most of the slope's vertical extent. Effectively in three sections, the lower two – Charmes-Dessous – have richer soil and make broader, fuller wine, whilst the upper 14.27 ha, Charmes-Dessus, produces wine of complexity and *rondeur*, often with a curiously soft, minerally undertone. The wine exemplifies its name.

Poruzots (11.43 ha) is also tripartite: Poruzots, Poruzots-Dessus and the tiny Poruzots-Dessous – are all on sloping stony soil, giving wine with a strongly flinty bouquet and relatively high natural acidity.

Genevrières (16.05 ha), divided into Dessus and Dessous, is quintessential Meursault – lime-blossom, honey and nuts on the nose, long and subtle on the palate.

Finally, Perrières (12.91 ha), divided into Perrières Dessous, Clos des Perrières, Aux Perrières and Perrières Dessus, and adjoining, like Charmes, the commune of Puligny, sits on limestone, with an overlay of heat-reflecting stones. From here come the finest Meursaults – steely, yet rich and elegant, full of body and backbone, less forthcoming when young but with time, developing a majestic aristocracy. More of the understated Puligny, than the warm Meursault accessibility, a mature Perrières is a fine experience.

Although home to a wealth of fine winemaking, Meursault's vignerons vary widely in style and competence. An apparently insatiable demand in the 1970s and 1980s led many to overgenerous pruning and excessive yields. Unfortunately, far too many dilute, weedy wines still appear as Meursault and Premier Cru – flat, flabby, over-sulphured and cardboardy wines which discredit this noble Appellation. A fine Meursault should have concentration, grip and backbone, in addition to its natural open, 'peaches and oatmeal' tones, characterised by Harry Yoxall as 'ingratiatingly soft'.

On the Côte's broader canvas, Meursault is renowned for the feast it provides each November during Les Trois Glorieuses, on the Monday following the Hospices auction. The Paulée is a magnificent lunch, to which the commune's growers invite friends and customers. No wine is provided, but 'according to tradition . . . each brings his bottle'. This amounts to a gargantuan bottle party, lasting well into the afternoon, with venerable wines passing from table to table as guests and hosts taste each other's offerings. The Paulée is by far the most relaxed gathering of the entire Burgundian year and a splendid tribute to the spirit and purpose of wine.

Meursault from Les Grands Charrons; the colourful roof of the Mairie is clearly visible

Domaine Robert Ampeau et Fils

MEURSAULT

Domaine Ampeau is one of the few establishments in the Côte d'Or where the quality of red-winemaking approaches that of the white. Most growers in Meursault and Puligny will tell you that they have more difficulty crafting their reds than their whites, and even the best seem to be mildly baffled by the intricacies of destalking and *cuvaison*, variables peculiar to red vinification. However, because they are talented people, most manage to make a respectable shift of things and although the Pinots are distinctly less consistent and interesting than the Chardonnays, red Pulignys and Meursaults are by no means to be written off wholesale.

Ampeau is a noteworthy exception; a Domaine where the quality of their reds – from Volnay, Blagny, Pommard, Beaune, Savigny and Auxey – has reached the point at which it might almost rest its reputation on them. Nonetheless, it is with their Meursaults that the Ampeaus have made their name and continue to excel.

By Burgundian standards the Domaine is not old, having been created by the grandfather of the present manager, Michel Ampeau, at the turn of the century with the acquisition of a few vines in the locality: Village Meursault, Premiers Crus Charmes and Perrières and a parcel of Volnay Santenots. Michel's father, Robert, took charge in the early 1940s and added significantly to the Domaine's holdings, firstly by marrying a Mlle Bobey who brought with her vineyards in Beaune and Savigny, and then by careful purchases as suitable land came up for sale.

The parcels of Puligny Combettes, Pommard, Auxey-Duresses (rouge) and some more Volnay Santenots were added during the early 1950s, and the 1.6 ha of La Pièce Sous les Bois in 1973. Robert remained firmly at the helm until Michel took over in 1985, and both he and his wife live at the estate to make sure Michel continues the traditions of two generations. In 1980 a Société Civile was created to exploit the vineyards, although the vines themselves continue to belong to Robert.

Whilst the wines are made in a separate *cuverie* in Meursault, the Domaine's headquarters are in the Rue du Cromin, one of the many narrow feeder roads skirting the village. Here, behind a line of white-painted posts fencing off a small courtyard, are the offices and principal cellars, adjoining a row of sheds and garages along one side.

Michel Ampeau where he most enjoys being – among his vines

Beneath the house, rather like a lopsided mouth waiting to be fed, gapes a ramp leading down to the cool vaulted cellars.

This is the charge of the young-looking mid-fifties Michel, a lean, energetic bachelor, whose infectious humour masks an intensity and single-mindedness which, combined with his passion for his vines, are the talk of his peers. On winter days of an inclemency which would drive even the most conscientious of growers indoors to their paperwork or their firesides on the pretext of a bout of stock-control or urgent tasting, you may, more often than not, find Michel muffled up and hard at work in his vineyards – pruning, ploughing or whatever needs doing.

Not only is he a fanatical viticulteur, but also a highly skilled one – not a man to cut corners or to espouse the soft option. His way of looking after his vineyards is direct, careful and labour intensive. When it comes to replacing vines, every effort is made to adapt clones and rootstocks to the microclimate. Only the finest clones are used, several in each vineyard for complexity and equilibrium, as Michel believes that selection has

honed them to a fine pitch of excellence, unmatched by any possible *sélection massale*. 'It's like running a race,' he explains, 'if you have trained athletes they will finish in say two hours and still be fit; but if you asked the growers of Meursault to run, they would take all day and some would still be going.' Unnatural selection, perhaps, but one Michel prefers.

The Ampeau viticultural regime has one point of particular interest; namely, that each July Michel carefully sows seeds of Ray-Grass in between each vine row. Along with a handful of other growers, the Ampeaus have been doing this for 25 years. The belief is that the grass – which reaches a height of 10–12 cm by harvest time – serves the dual functions of opening up soil compacted by the passage of machinery or by geological adhesion, and of stabilising it against erosion in especially wet or windy years. The grass remains until December and is then destroyed with a herbicide treatment. Any still *in situ* in January becomes stubbornly tenacious and virtually ineradicable.

Michel is as attentive to detail in the

cellars as he is in his vineyards. What he is after are wines which will keep. This is not simply a matter of high initial acidity for the whites and brutally aggressive tannins for the reds, but the more difficult achievement of an equilibrium which will hold and not fracture because one constituent happens to dominate the rest.

Built-in longevity is an integral part of Michel and Robert Ampeau's philosophy, since theirs is one of the few Domaines on the Côte which does not release its wines until they are deemed ready to drink. Not a bottle, of either colour, is generally sold until it is five years old – and many are kept even longer. In 1995, for example, small quantities of 1979 Meursaults were still being offered to their regular clientele, whereas the 1990s remained 'in reserve'.

Vinifications are broadly traditional, with natural yeasts and plenty of *batonnage* to extract maximum richness and complexity into the wines. Although only 10–25% of new wood is used, to avoid an excess of oak flavours, Michel believes that fermenting his whites in new rather than old oak casks harmonises wood-derived flavours with the wine more successfully than would be the case if the wine was put into new oak after fermentation. In addition, fermentation in casks, old or new, produces wines which age more slowly than those fermented in bulk.

He also considers it important to leave any necessary *chaptalisation* until the last practicable moment to prolong fermentation and to extract greater finesse and complexity, whereas most vignerons add their sugar either at the beginning or just after the moment of highest temperature. *Chaptalising* in this way requires considerable precision of judgement and carries the attendant risk of unwanted residual sugar remaining in the wine after the yeasts have given up working. While he is fully aware of the dangers, Michel believes that the rewards more than outweigh the risks.

After the *malolactic fermentation*, around May following the vintage, the new wine is racked into casks which are then moved to a cellar at 13°C. A month later they are bentonite-fined and given a light plate-filtration (a pity, because it is unnecessary and because filtration, however delicate, cannot help but remove some of the natural guts and acidity from the wine) before being bottled by a small bottling machine. *Elévage* of only 9–10 months seems unusually short; however Michel Ampeau considers that early bottling helps retain the youthful fresh grape aromas and flavours and, above all, the acidity so necessary for the long period the wines are destined to spend maturing in the cellars.

The Domaine's wines are highly individual in character. Tasting a range spanning eight different vintages, one is struck by a distinct

house style – lean, taut Chardonnays and Pinots, not immediately flattering to the palate but rather endowed with an intellectual austerity which it takes a little time to appreciate. Ampeau wines give one the impression that they are busy cogitating in their bottles and will decide for themselves how much they are prepared to reveal. If you are discourteous enough to interrupt them at the wrong moment, then you cannot expect much by way of response. If, on the other hand, you tap into an Ampeau bottle whilst it is in a state of relaxed communicativeness, then you may expect, and get, much.

Especially interesting are the so-called 'off-vintages'. Not only do Ampeau's 1974s, 1977s, 1980s, 1984s, 1987s and so on, last long after practically everyone else's have been consigned to the vinegar jar, but they often provide interesting and delicious drinking. Because of this, trying to guess the vintage of an Ampeau Meursault can reduce the most experienced of tasters to despair; so well are they made that the vintage identity markers are frequently nowhere to be found, leaving the taster fog-bound. This is the result of infinite pains to put only the healthiest, ripest fruit into the fermenting vats.

However fine the lesser vintages, they are naturally overshadowed by the well-known great ones. The high initial acidity of Ampeau wines means that even longer is needed to soften and harmonise them, especially with vinifications which emphasise not fat and flesh, but the lean and intellectual form where acidity long remains obtrusive.

By refusing to sell their wines young, the Ampeaus avoid the danger that premature consumption will lead to their wines being misunderstood or tasted in an incomplete state. However, keeping back every vintage, good and less good, apart from having a devastating effect on their cash flow, runs the concomitant risk that one wine or another will fail to develop as expected, especially in less good years where the balance of constituents in a wine tends to be more fragile.

Michel seems unconcerned – he knows his wines and has a good idea of how they will age in bottle; he also benefits from an impressive track record to bolster his confidence, should his nerve start to wobble.

Whilst tradition plays its part in his thinking, Michel is not averse to a little modernisation when it seems appropriate. For example, the Domaine used to press with a Mabille press, which tended to give a rather murky juice requiring long settling before fermentation started; now a pneumatic Willmes press, incorporating a relatively new internal drainage system for running off juice, has been installed, which Michel considers gives a much clearer *must*. Balanced against this benefit is the greater time (2.25 hours) taken to process a pressful of grapes which brings an attendant risk of oxidation. Again, Michel is prepared to accept this in the cause of quality.

Red wines now account for some 60% of the Domaine's total production. Over the last decade Michel's meticulous winemaking skills have greatly improved their quality which, although perhaps not quite as consistent or exciting as the whites, imparts typicity and substance and makes them well worth seeking out, especially in good vintages. It would seem that, at last, Mlle Bobey's dowry is coming into its own.

Michel Ampeau's Meursaults are gloriously austere and delicious wines, which characteristically develop flavours and aromas of lime-blossom, acacia and *noisette*. Tasting a range of Premier Cru Perrières showed how the vintage plays variations on the overall theme. The 1983 – rich, almost overripe, with mouthfilling fruit and yet good sustaining acidity – contrasted with a leaner, tighter 1980. In between, more or less substantial 1981, 1982 and 1984, a much finer, better balanced and altogether more complex 1979 and a deep, golden, surprisingly floral and honeyed 1976. Here are wines which would partner to perfection a plain, or even a strongly sauced dish of sea-bass or sole not to mention a noble crustacean.

VINEYARD HOLDINGS

Commune	Level	Lieu-dit/Climat	Area	Vine Age	Status
Puligny	PC	Les Combettes	0.75	40	P
Meursault	PC	Les Perrières	0.60	40	P
Meursault	PC	Les Charmes	0.40	45	P
Meursault	PC	Volnay Santenots	1.51	30	P
Meursault	PC	La Pièce Sous Le Bois	0.80	40	P
Meursault	V	Les Crotots	0.45	17	P
Meursault	V	Sous la Velle	0.42	30	P
	R	(Bourgogne Blanc)	0.40	35	P
Pommard	V	Les Vaumuriens	1.10	30	P
Beaune	PC	Clos du Roi	0.32	25	P
Blagny	PC	La Pièce Sous Le Bois	0.80	40	P
Savigny	PC	Les Lavières	0.55	40	P
Savigny	PC	Les Fournaux	0.80	30	P
Auxey	PC	Les Ecusseaux	0.90	25	P
		Total:	**9.70 ha**		

Domaine Coche-Debord

MEURSAULT

Alain Coche lives with his family not far from his cousin – Jean-François Coche-Dury – in Meursault's La Velle quarter. He is a short, stocky man, with greying hair and a slightly harassed manner, giving the impression of being generally dragged along by events. He runs the Domaine with his son, Fabien; both play the saxophone – as does Jean-François, with *his* son, Rafael, completing the quartet, on drums. Meursault has life beyond wine.

The Coches' house, of post-war construction, does not have the air of prosperity of those of other growers. One gets the feeling that life has been unfair to Alain and his wife – the deaths of both his parents within a few years brought heavy inheritance taxes and only a timely bank loan enabled them to carry on without selling vineyards. Nonetheless, Alain seems more cheerful and relaxed nowadays.

Getting to know him is not easy; a reserved manner makes initial conversation rather stilted but, as he warms to his subject, a distinctly mischievous twinkle and an impish sense of humour emerges from underneath the austere exterior. It is rather like watching a closed-up Meursault open out.

Alain's father, Julien, was not originally a viticulteur. He bought a single hectare of vines, just after the last great war and this, with subsequent purchases and divisions, has grown to its present size of 8 ha, the most recent acquisition being a small parcel of Bourgogne Chardonnay in the village. Some 60% of his vines have seen their 60th birthday and the average is 30–40.

Harvesting is as late as possible: 'I usually pick a week later than the others!' The grapes are pressed in a Vaslin press, sulphured, then given 24 hours to settle, whether or not the lees are clean 'because if the wine is to spend two years in cask then only the fine lees are needed'. A long and slow cask fermentation ensues – sometimes lasting up to three weeks. There is no attempt at temperature control, although any necessary *chaptalisation* is delayed until the last moment to prolong fermentation and help maintain a low ambient temperature.

The Meursaults are then put into cask, the lesser Appellations into larger wood. Twice a week they are *batonnéd* – a process which is continued for as long as necessary. For the 1988 vintage *batonnage* lasted one and a half years, until the spring of 1990! 'I am the King of *batonnage*,' Alain explains. adding that stirring is not equivalent to using a 'dodine' – a

scythe-like instrument – which has holes and thus degassifies the wine, removing aroma and freshness.

Unusually, the whites are not racked after *malo* but kept on their fine lees until fining, with bentonite, during the second year. Shortly afterwards, the wines are racked, left for about a month and then bottled with a light plate-filtration. This amounts to a total *élévage* of two years – which is at the extremity of what most would regard as prudent, especially in less ripe vintages.

Red wines, some 50% of production, used to be heavily overtannic and stemmy. Now, Alain has bowed to pressure and destems – although he can only bring himself to 25–40%, leaving 75–60% in the vats.

His red vinification is more Bordelais than Burgundian and the use of a heavy dose of sulphur and cold maceration is reminiscent of the practice of Guy Accad. Alain still appears to be experimenting to find out what works best. He is highly cynical about changing fashions, especially the current 'no filtration' fad: 'Fifteen years ago, clients wanted nothing in the bottle (i.e. no deposit) – almost not even wine! Now they won't accept the slightest filtration.'

Tasting in one of Alain's several cellars, scattered round the village – he has recently bought a bicycle to get round them all – surrounded by unlabelled bins of old vintages, it was instructive to see how stalks and long maturation affected the structure and overall balance of a range of red 1989s. Those, such as an Auxey-Duresses matured without new oak, were supple, with reasonable length and soft, ripe fruit. Those kept in

new oak seemed over-balanced with tannins. Unusually ripe grape-wood in 1989 may help bring these wines back into some sort of equilibrium, but the combination of new wood, stalks and two years *élévage* in vintages such as 1987 and 1988 will require owners of Alain's reds to keep them for 20 years before, if ever, they soften out. Perhaps realising the problem, he keeps the reds for a few years before releasing them.

The best reds are a soft, fleshy Meursault, a firmer, substantial Monthélie Les Duresses and the Village Pommard La Platière, which contains the produce of a patch of Premier Cru, insufficient to produce a *cuvée* of its own. This, plus Alain's 45-year-old Platière vines, adds a touch of extra finesse and concentration to its firmish structure. Even with greater destemming, Coche reds bear more resemblance to all-in wrestlers rather than to prima ballerinas.

The Domaine's white wines are kept in another building at the top of the village, near the Chevaliers vineyard. These are decidedly masculine, with firm acidity and plenty of sappy sinew. Alain wants his wines to last '10 years at least for a Meursault to start drinking well', observing, with a sigh, that most of his colleagues in the village make 'vins primeurs'. Goutte d'Or, Limouzin and Charmes are the best of the bunch, with Chevaliers and l'Ormeaux close behind.

Alain Coche puts much thought into his wines. They are, in truth, highly individual in style, but nonetheless, for those prepared to be patient, represent excellent examples of their origins, which, after all, is what great Burgundy is about.

VINEYARD HOLDINGS

Commune	Level	Lieu-dit/Climat	Area	Vine Age	Status
Meursault	PC	Les Charmes	0.29	55	P
Meursault	PC	Goutte d'Or	0.19	55	P
Meursault	V	Les Chevaliers	0.31	35	P
Meursault	V	Les Limouzin	0.25	55	P
Meursault	V	l'Ormeau	0.37	35	P
Meursault	V	————	1.00	35	P
Meursault	V	————	0.40	40	P
Auxey	V	(White)	0.21	15	P
Auxey	R	(Auxey Côte de Beaune)	0.40	40	P
————	R	(Bourgogne Blanc)	0.80	30	P
————	R	(Bourgogne Aligoté)	0.79	35	P
Pommard	V	La Platière	0.26	45	P
Monthélie	PC	Les Duresses	0.30	20	M
Monthélie	V	————	0.23	20	M
————	R	(Bourgogne Rouge)	1.50	20	P
————	R	(Passe-Tout-Grain)	0.64	20	P
Total:			**7.94 ha**		

Domaine Michel Bouzereau

MEURSAULT

This is a thoroughgoing Meursault estate. Michel Bouzereau, now in his 50s, learnt his trade with his father Robert, erstwhile *metayeur* for Albert Grivot, and brother Pierre, and is a self-confessed empiricist. His son, Jean-Baptiste, who joined him in 1991, has a winemaking diploma and part of the Domaine's vineyards; Michel is proud of that learning and that his son tastes widely with other young Meursault *vignerons*.

Apart from patches of Volnay, Pommard, Beaune and Puligny, all their 12 ha are in Meursault. Winemaking gives no concessions to modernity; there is no *macération pelliculaire* – 'I'd like to see the results,' Michel admits – just fermentation in cask after a day in *cuve* to set it off, plenty of *batonnage*, and lees contact for 9 months or so before fining, filtration and bottling. A horror of the taste of new wood limits its presence to around 5% for the Bourgogne Blanc and 20% for the Villages and Premiers Crus. The Bouzereaus consider it indispensable for vinifying fine white wine, but are concerned that in excess of these proportions aromas and flavours are masked, origins obliterated and a measure of unattractive hardness imparted to the taste. 'You must only smell the wine, not the wood.'

Although Michel has had problems with the oak for his reds – 'too charry, we made the wrong choices' – and is striving to improve this, he is more confident about his selection for the whites: Allier and Vosges.

The wines reflect a desire for suppleness. In general soft and *flatteur* with good aromatics and overriding elegance, there is a feel of underlying class running throughout the range. Despite low yields – averaging 35–40 hl/ha for the whites – there is sometimes an impression that elegance has been achieved at the expense of richness. Perhaps, after all, a touch of *macération pelliculaire* might help.

Nonetheless, the wines are good. There is a pair of fine Pulignys – the Champ Gain, from higher land with poor, red soils, has more finesse, while the Champ Canet, from much older, rocky limestones on a *demi-côteau* more *puissance* and length. Then a clutch of Village Meursaults – Tessons, Blagny, Grand Charrons, straight Meursault from several parcels and, since 1995, Limouzin – all from respectably old vines. The Grand Charrons is soft and fleshy, sometimes with an almost peely, Voignier character (e.g. 1994), balanced out

Michel Bouzereau

with around 13% alcohol, but no hint of that distasteful raw burn which ruins so many otherwise well-made Meursaults. The Tessons is altogether finer and more stylish, with better acidity and greater complexity – approaching Premier Cru in quality.

Michel and Jean-Baptiste's trio of Premiers Crus are well worth seeking out. Genevrières, quite rich and elegant from clayey soils, Charmes (Dessous) just below

Perrières and a solitary cask of Perrières itself, with its tight structure and noble *puissance*. An air of permanent experimentation pervades the reds – apart from getting the oak right, there have been essais with bought yeasts which turned out well in 1992, but less so in 1990 and 1991. The wines are pleasantly softish, perfectly acceptable but no more. This is definitely a finer source for whites.

VINEYARD HOLDINGS

Commune	Level	Lieu-dit/Climat	Area	Vine Age	Status
Meursault	PC	Les Genevrières	0.50	12	P
Meursault	PC	Les Charmes	0.22	20	P
Meursault	PC	Les Perrières	0.05	40	P
Meursault	V	Les Tessons	0.50	40	P
Meursault	V	Les Grands Charrons	2.00	28	P
Meursault	V	(Several *climats*)	2.00	28	P
Puligny	PC	Les Champs Gains	0.30	40	P
Puligny	PC	Champ Canet	0.13	40	P
Meursault	V	Blagny (W)	0.50	7	P
Meursault	R	(Bourgogne Aligoté)	2.00	30	P
Meursault	R	(Bourgogne Blanc)	1.50	20	P
Volnay	R	(Bourgogne Rouge)	0.70	—	P
Volnay	V	————	0.30	20	P
Pommard	V	————	0.40	15	P
Beaune	PC	Les Vignes Franches	0.50	25	P
Beaune	V	Les Epenottes	0.50	40	P
		Total:	**12.10 ha**		

Domaine Coche-Dury

MEURSAULT

It would be inconceivable to discuss the important Domaines of Meursault without, in almost the same breath, uttering the words Coche-Dury. For two decades, this estate has been widely considered to epitomise the finest of which the appellation is capable.

This runaway success has been the personal achievement of Jean-François Coche who took over from his father in 1972. On first acquaintance he gives the impression of a dedicated, thoughtful scholar who happens to find himself in a *cuverie* rather than in a library, although he would probably be equally happy in either. Closer scrutiny reveals, beneath the apparent scholarship, real scholarship, allied to a quietly confident devotion to quality.

Jean-François is the third generation of his branch of the family to run the Domaine. The first generation Coche, his grandfather, acquired six parcels of vines after the First World War: Bourgogne Chardonnay Les Belles Côtes, Meursault Blanc in the *lieus-dits* Les Vireuils and Les Petits Vignes, Auxey Duresses Blanc Les Boutonnières, Monthélie Les Crays and a very small parcel of Bourgogne Pinot Noir. Initially, grandfather Coche employed vignerons to make the wine, but later started to do it himself, selling wine in bottle, as well as *en négoce*.

Jean-François' father took charge in 1964, remaining at the helm until 1972 and finally admitting to retirement in November 1989. During his custodianship a further sixteen individual parcels of vineyards were added to the Domaine's holdings bringing the total up to almost 9 ha. These augmentations, most notably in the Volnay Premiers Crus Clos des Chênes and Taillepieds, and in Meursault Premier Cru Les Perrières (Dessus), added significantly to the Domaine's commercial viability.

On assuming responsibility Jean-François set about buying outright the parcels of vines which were *en metayage* – that is to say those being share-cropped for other owners. This system – well established in Burgundy, where vineyard holdings tend to be small, and frequently commercially unviable by themselves – allowed owner and farmer to divide the crop in an agreed proportion, usually 50:50. Sometimes the rent is paid in wine, sometimes, as with M. Coche, in fruit.

The most recent acquisitions are a parcel of Meursault Chevaliers bought in 1986 to supplement an adjoining holding and 0.5 ha of Puligny Les Enseignères. Although soar-

Jean-François Coche, his wife and their daughter Marie-Hermine; as usual young Rafael was out on his bicycle

ing land prices preclude significant expansion, Jean-François is keen to snap up any available vines which happen to abut his own.

It is hardly surprising to hear that here, quality begins in the vineyard. Jean-François is emphatic that, to give of their best, vines must be severely pruned. Traditional *Guyot* pruning, even with a short fruiting cane, tends to produce larger and less concentrated grapes than those from vines trained *en cordon*. Some 30% of his vines are trained *en cordon de Royat* – with three fruiting canes off the main *cordon*, pruned to two buds each. This system regularly produces smaller grapes, reducing yields by up to half that of *Guyot*. Which vines are treated in which way is up to the pruner, who will take into account the natural vigour of each vine. Jean-François feels that this balance is about right.

As with any conscientious grower, vine age is also a critical quality factor. Coche's policy is to replant as and when individual vines die rather than grubbing up a designated area each year. He has novel views on the effect of vine age on wine: 'You can make a good wine with young vines, but you must be severe in limiting the number of bunches you leave on each plant.' Wine from younger vines tends to evolve more rapidly and to have a shorter life, but can be very *flatteur* to begin with.

Rigorous pruning also encourages a sound, deep, root system – a key to drought-resistance and wine complexity. To this end, his young vines are hoed throughout the year to plough in grass and weeds, whilst the older ones are hoed twice, each spring, and then given a dose of herbicide to keep them weed free during the growing season. 'This way we are free of worry through the

summer, when there is so much else to do.'

His pursuit of quality has engendered a dislike of commercially produced clones – they are over-selected, 'too uniform, too little finesse'; instead, Jean-François selects plant material from his own vineyards, which is then delivered to the nurseryman who prepares the grafts. This *sélection massale* leads to a greater diversity in the vineyard, and thereby to greater complexity in the wine.

Whilst normal vine afflictions are easily controlled, there is much concern over a new malady which is making its presence felt in most wine-growing areas of France, not least Burgundy. *Eutypiose* is an insidious infection, since after the early, visible symptoms, outward manifestation can disappear altogether for up to seven years, by which time the vine is irrecoverable and the disease has probably spread to other parts of the vineyard. Two randomly selected parcels in the Coche vineyards studied in 1990 by the local research station showed 4.48% of Chardonnay with symptoms of *eutypiose* in one and 0.45% in the other. Jean-François can only speculate on this difference: the most affected parcel, Meursault Les Luchets, is on a hillside with dry, stony and rocky soil, whereas the untouched vines are on flat land, with richer, more humid soil. This latter was badly affected by the great frosts of 1985, which Jean-François believes killed off the disease, whereas the sloping vines escaped frost damage, possibly allowing the fungus which spreads *eutypiose* to live on. Vigilance, and instant removal and incineration of affected vines, is the only hope.

In Jean-François' modest, modern cellar, vinification for both reds and whites proceeds along broadly traditional lines. He believes in adding sulphur to the grapes as soon as they are picked to avoid any possibility of oxidation. American experiments showing that this procedure protects the final wine less against eventual oxidation than not doing so, is dismissed with a disbelieving shrug which recognises the contradiction without being able to account for it.

Alcoholic fermentation, with only natural yeasts, used up to 50% new Allier oak for the whites. The precise fraction is determined both by wine and vintage – no formulae here! Jean-François is adamant that the longer the fermentation the finer, and richer, the wine; so he is delighted when some casks continue fermenting well after the usual 10–14 days – often up to 3–4 weeks. The *malolactic* fermentation is relatively unproblematical.

On the rare occasions when a cask fails to start its *malo*, it is given an inoculation of fresh lees from a cask which has just finished – a trick which usually has the desired result.

Another tradition which Coche believes enriches a wine is that of rousing the lees in a cask by stirring its contents with a stick. In higher acid vintages such as 1993 the wise *batonner* more than in fatter years such as 1992 or 1994. The lees may indeed nourish the wine, but excess can produce undesirable off-flavours, so care has to be taken to avoid over-feeding.

Coche's whites spend some ten months on their lees until their first racking in July following the vintage. A second racking four months later and fining with bentonite to deposit smaller particles is followed by a further six months of rest. After some 20 months in cask, the wines are bottled by hand, without filtration, direct from their fining.

Apart from his magnificent and much-sought-after whites, Jean-François Coche produces some of the finest examples of Meursault and Auxey-Duresses Rouge. Here, the main problem is finesse, since in his experience, and somewhat contrary to common belief, Pinot is more susceptible to loss of aromas than Chardonnay. So, 'To have finesse in a red wine is difficult . . . very difficult.'

Being a talented man, he manages it. His Pinot Noir is completely destalked (others please note!) and fermented for 10–12 days before being transferred to cask, of which 20% are new. In contrast with his white wines, only one pressing is used, instead of two, and the first racking is in spring, 2–3 months earlier. The wine remains on its fining throughout the following winter and bottled directly from cask after some 18 months *élevage* with neither further racking nor filtration. All this, and scrupulous topping up of casks, helps keep oxidation at bay, and retains freshness and finesse in the wines.

From a well-structured, concentrated Bourgogne Pinot Noir from six different *lieus-dits* in Meursault, through a ripe, succulent Meursault Rouge, a Monthélie and an Auxey-Duresses, to a fine pair of Volnay Premiers Crus, the reds are beautifully crafted wines, well worth seeking out.

Remarkable complexity and richness characterise Jean-François' whites. From a superlative Aligoté (vinified in second- or third-year oak) to a noble Meursault Perrières (50% new oak) the wines have a depth and structure which are, sadly, all too rare. Ask him what really matters in the achievement of quality and he will tell you that one must start with a fair proportion of old vines, severely pruned for low yields: '45 hl/ha is ideal for making a *Grand Vin*,' reflects Jean-François, although 40 hl/ha is more often the reality – except in 1990 where yields rose to 60 hl/ha. Thereafter it is a matter of putting a cool juice into the fermentation casks and allowing as long a transformation as practicable. Then, providing you disturb things as little as possible – you have a fair chance of making fine wine.

There is no doubt as to the quality of the Coche product. The Meursaults are characterised by great richness with a firm backbone of harmonious acidity which ensures them longevity. The wines have flesh but it is taut rather than flabby which gives them athletic charm rather than fragile elegance – Betjeman's Joan Hunter-Dunne rather than Dickens' Dora Spenlow.

Even the humble Aligoté is here ennobled with an uncommon, but most attractive, veneer of finesse. Coche's only Premier Cru, Les Perrières, is a delight, from colour to nose to aftertaste – honey and flowers when young, developing into hazelnuts and toast with age. In style it is more redolent of Puligny, next to whose northern border it lies, than of Meursault, where there is more clay in the soil. Some claim to smell the stones, from which the vineyard takes its name, but this smacks of pretension. In addition to his Meursaults, Jean-François produces 385–450 cases of a magisterial, firm-framed Corton-Charlemagne – one of the best in the Appellation.

All these wines are intended to be kept, even in lesser vintages. In late 1990, Jean-François was heard advising a Swiss customer that the 1984s were just beginning to approach their rightful drinking age, and that the 1985 reds might also be started upon.

As with the wines, so with their creator: an understated, quiet complexity and dependable firmness, with much beneath the surface for those who care to search for it. Jean-François mirrors his Meursaults – not the fleshy, extrovert opulence of Lafon, but more restrained, intellectual expressions of their origins.

He clearly cares where his wines end up, bemoaning the restaurateurs who pass greedily from one vintage to the next, regardless of their differing maturities, without the slightest pretence at keeping the bottles a year or two before letting their uncomprehending clientele loose upon them. 'There are some who make an effort,' says Jean-François, with evident exasperation, and one has only to glance round his office shelves at menus from Girardet, l'Auberge de l'Ill, Troisgros, Lameloise and the rest to know what level of quality he's talking about.

The Domaine's clientele is faithful and fortunately, for the most part, comprehending. One third of each vintage – the same *cuvées* every year – is sold to négociants Latour and Jadot – both justifiably proud of their white wines. The remainder goes to individual customers, approved restaurants and increasingly, abroad. Buyers around the world clamour for stocks and those lucky enough to succeed know that they have yardstick bottles on their hands.

When, in the distant future, Jean-François' son Rafael takes on his father's fine mantle, it seems likely that nothing much will have changed.

VINEYARD HOLDINGS

Commune	Level	Lieu-dit/Climat	Area	Vine Age	Status
Aloxe	GC	Corton-Charlemagne	0.34	1960	F
Meursault	PC	Les Perrières	0.23	1947	P
Meursault	PC	Les Perrières-Dessus	0.29	1960–74	F
Meursault	V	Moulin-Landin	0.43	1972	P
Meursault	V	Chevalières	0.12	1956	P
Meursault	V	Les Rougeots	0.65	1943/62/74	P
Meursault	V	Les Dressoles	0.44	1930	F
Meursault	V	Les Narvaux	0.38	1965/85	F
Meursault	V	Clos des Ecoles	0.51	1973	F
Meursault	V.	Les Vireuils	0.61	1947–84	F
Meursault	V	Les Luchets	0.32	1930/73	F
Meursault	V	Les Peutes-Vignes	0.19	1938	F
Meursault	V	Les Durots	0.12	1961	F
Meursault	V.	Les Malpoiriers (red)	0.14	1981	F
Meursault	V	Les Caillerets	0.18	1937/71	
Puligny	V	Les Enseignères	0.50	40	P
Volnay	PC	Le Clos des Chênes	0.16	1960	F
Volnay	PC	Les Taillepieds	0.21	1989	F
Auxey	V	Les Fosses (red)	0.27	1982	F
Auxey	V	Les Boutonnières (white)	0.23	1928	F
Monthélie	V	Les Crays	0.28	1987	F
Meursault	R	(Bourgogne Pinot Noir – 5 different parcels)	1.21	1954–72	F
Meursault	R	Les Pacriots (Aligoté)	0.39	1951	F
Meursault	R	(Bourgogne Chardonnay – 4 different parcels)	1.23	1972–75	F
		Total:	**9.43 ha**		

N.B. The vineyards marked F are *en fermage* to Jean-François Coche from his father.

Domaine des Comtes Lafon

MEURSAULT

The Domaine des Comtes Lafon is, without doubt, the finest estate in Meursault. It has the advantage over most of its competitors of a litany of land-holdings which warms the heart to read: 12.7 ha of superbly sited vineyards including no fewer than 4 Meursault Premiers Crus, over 3 ha of Meursault Villages, some of the most favourably located plots of Volnay and Volnay Santenots, a hectare of Monthélie Premier Cru and 0.33 ha of Le Montrachet. Not only these vineyards, but a talented winemaker whose consummate skill, year on year, extracts from them something exceptional.

Dominique Lafon is the latest in a line of an interesting family. His great-grandfather, Comte Jules Lafon – who incidentally founded the annual Paulée at Meursault, the final feast on the Monday after the Hospices de Beaune sale – was an unusual man. A lawyer by profession, he amassed a great fortune, marrying on the way a Mlle Boch from Meursault who probably had vineyards, and certainly had no money. A man of spirit, *bon viveur*, member of the Club des Cents in Paris, he enjoyed eating and drinking well, and collected everything from fine paintings to fine china. He circumnavigated the globe twice before finally dying in 1940.

In the meantime, being only interested in the best parts of the best vineyards, he had sold off the less good parts of his wife's land to buy better parcels. Thus today the Domaine has vines among the choicest parts of Meursault Perrières – generally regarded as the cream of the Premiers Crus – Meursault Charmes and a large chunk of the kernel of Volnay Santenots, the Santenots du Milieu – a vineyard Lavalle referred to in 1855 as a *Tête de Cuvée*. In 1935 Jules acquired some Montrachet, in the Chassagne section, between the holdings of Baron Thenard and Romanée-Conti. The fine house in which Dominique's parents still live, with the magnificent 2.10 ha Clos de la Barre for a garden, was in all likelihood, part of the Boch patrimoine.

Jules had two sons – Pierre and Henri. Pierre who died in 1944 never had charge of the estate, which was taken in hand by Dominique's great-uncle Henri in the early 1940s. Unfortunately, Henri had an aversion to work, and soon sold much of his inheritance – priceless paintings, furniture, china, land, farms and houses all went to subsidise his extravagant lifestyle. Fortunately, the Domaine remained intact, although Henri preferred to sell the grapes because he

could not be bothered to vinify them.

In 1954 matters came to a head when uncle Henri and Jules' wife – an indomitable old lady – decided to sell the estate. Dominique's father, René, intervened to stop the sale, undertaking to manage the estate despite being put under an injunction neither to make capital expenditure nor to borrow against the assets. Clad in this extraordinary pecuniary straitjacket, he set about putting the Domaine back into good order. At that time, much of the land was let out to two families – the Bouleys of Volnay and the Moreys of Meursault – so it was possible to oversee the upkeep of the vineyards without having day-to-day care of them. In addition René, an engineer by profession, was living in Paris and unable to spend much time in Meursault, although he somehow managed to vinify his own wines, with the help of an employee. Gradually the vineyards were restored to their proper condition.

In 1967 René moved back from Paris to live in the family home, with his wife and four children, Dominique, then aged 9, his younger brother Bruno, Jean-François and Anne, and began to take full charge of vinifying the grapes arriving under the 50% share-cropping agreement.

In 1978 Dominique was sent to Beaune to study viticulture and oenology and a year later started to be involved in the estate, helping out during the vintage. After graduating, he worked for the courtier Becky Wasserman, in nearby Bouilland, saving his holidays to be at the Domaine during the harvest. During the early 1980s, he became progressively involved with decision-making, being partly responsible for the 1981 and 1982 vintages, finally taking full responsibility for the 1984s. The same year, his brother, Bruno, arrived to help with matters financial and administrative, remaining until after the 1989 harvest.

Meanwhile, the Domaine had become a Société Civile, the shareholders being René Lafon, Jacques Lafon and Marie-Thérèse d'Armaille, respectively Dominique's father, uncle and aunt. In April 1988, Dominique married Anne Roumier, sister of Christophe of Domaine Roumier in Chambolle (he had to consult his engraved wedding band for the year and date – such is the hierarchy of importance to a dedicated vigneron) and now has a daughter, Lea, and a son, Guillaume. His parents still live in the fine house in the Rue de la Barre, whilst he and Anne live 'two minutes away' in the village.

Dominique has worked indefatigably to create the worldwide reputation for excellence that the Domaine presently enjoys. Much of what he learnt at viticultural college was useful, although he subsequently found out that theory and practice do not always coincide. None the less, he learned to recognise what was valuable and to discard what was of little use, and that discipline has stood him in firm stead.

This Domaine not only produces exemplary wines but is a model of how such an estate should be run. The overriding impression here, and indeed from most top-class producers in Burgundy, is that there are no formulae. Each decision is taken on its merits against a background of experience of possibilities and consequences. One also gets a strong sense of flexibility – winemaking not ossified in unquestioning tradition but undertaken with at least one eye on new ideas which might improve quality.

In technical matters, Dominique is immensely able. He discusses winemaking techniques and innovations with friends of his own generation up and down the Côte d'Or. Given a problem he will make a dozen telephone calls to get some advice on how to set about solving it – a refreshing readiness to admit difficulties, far less evident among the older generation. Equally, he is always willing to help friends with problems of their own – a difficult fining, stuck fermentation, how to fine, whether to filter – all important decisions needing careful consideration.

His own vineyards are expertly tended, with a distinctly organic orientation. Traditional products – chemical sprays, herbicides etc. – are no longer used, and Dominique has shifted as much towards organic materials as possible. A new state-of-the-art tractor has appeared which enables more precise targeting of sprays to the parts of the vine where they are most needed.

He is very aware of rot, and considers it important to try and eradicate this early, instead of waiting until the harvest to excise affected grapes. He attributes much of the incidence of rot to the grape-worm, which punctures the skins and opens the berry to *botrytis* infection. Among a number of interesting experiments he has on hand, is one of introducing specially bred flies known to feed on grape-worms. They have no detrimental effect themselves but have to be introduced annually, in egg form.

The viticultural thrust is firmly aimed at maintaining healthy vines to an old age and at reducing yields. The latter is achieved by short pruning, low fertilisation and by planting carefully selected clones on to low-vigour rootstocks (predominantly 161/49). Training is *Guyot simple* with a small amount of *cordon de Royat* for older vines.

When replanting, the preference is to replace individual vines in vineyards which are in basically healthy shape; otherwise, where an entire parcel has to be grubbed up – as in Goutte d'Or which had old vines badly degenerated by *court noué* when it reverted from the farmer who had share-cropped it – replanting is made with four or five different selected clones. Chardonnay clones show less quality variation in taste than Pinot Noir, so there is less need for a wide variety.

Choosing Pinot Noir plant material is a complex process, since there are numerous strains available. The two main subspecies are the Pinot Fin (also called Pinot Tordu), used by all good growers, and the Pinot Droit, growing taller and straighter, which one often sees in the 'arrières Côte'. Although Droit is much easier to work with, can be trained high and mechanically harvested, its quality is greatly inferior to that of its twisted brother.

The Domaine uses two sources of Pinot Noir – firstly the newest and finest low-cropping clones available (113/115/667 and 777) and secondly, a *sélection massale* from a plot of 65-year-old Volnay Champans vines. Dominique has started trials with a few vines from friends he respects – the Lafarges in Volnay, Patrick Bize in Savigny, Christophe Roumier in Chambolle and Etienne Grivot in Vosne – to see how they work in his soil.

Lafon usually harvests later than his neighbours. The order of picking each parcel is determined by ripeness – and seems to change every year. Unlike other growers in the village, he is not especially concerned with acidity levels – 'a green apple is not as good as a ripe apple' – but with maximising sugar. He claims that he rarely has problems with acidity because his viticultural regime keeps vigour low and restricts yields. Only those with high yields have acid deficiencies, especially in riper years. The pH, in finished wines, which he regards as the most useful measure of acidity, settles near 3.5 for his reds and 3.35 for the whites. As for yields, 45–50 hl/ha is regarded as an acceptable maximum for Meursault Village, 40 hl/ha for Premier Cru and 35 hl/ha for the reds.

On arrival at the *cuverie*, the hand-picked grapes are pressed slowly and gently in a pneumatic Bucher press for 2–2.5 hours. The maximum pressure is 2 bars, but Dominique programmes the press cycle so that the minimum time is spent at this pressure to avoid extracting harsh tannins from stalks and pips.

The juice is then given a sanitising dose of

SO_2 at the lower end of the normal level – a maximum of 5 gm/hl for whites and 7 gm/hl for reds. Excision of rotten fruit in the vineyards obviates the need for excessive sulphur. The juice is then left to settle and eliminate gross lees. The length of *débourbage* depends on the vintage; in clean years, (e.g. 1985/1988/1989/1990/1992) 12 hours is allowed; in less healthy years, longer. Dominique has been refining his *débourbage* to recoup as much wine as possible, as lees account for around 5% of total volume.

After cooling to 12–14°C, the *must* is put into barrels for fermentation. Premiers and Grand Crus go into 100% new oak – a mixture of Vosges and Allier, from three barrel-makers, where they remain for six months; the Village Meursaults are put into second-year wood from the previous vintage.

Once a week, each cask is *batonné*, to give a better extract and richness; this process also helps the *malo* and aids final clarification of the wine. *Batonnage* usually ceases, during February or March, when tasting indicates that the flavours are correct.

Six or seven months after harvest, the first racking occurs. At this stage the wines are assembled, and a *cuvée* made up in tanks from the various lots of each wine. The fine lees are retained and the wines then pass by gravity into casks in a yet cooler cellar. There they remain until the following spring when they are racked clear of their lees.

Fining is a matter of considerable concern to Lafon. Realising different finings can have noticeably different impacts on aroma and flavour, he is very careful to find the most suitable fining agent. In addition, since he has found that unfiltered wines taste better than filtered wines, special care is needed in fining to obviate the need for filtration. The system is simple: samples of all the wines are taken and sent to a specialist laboratory where they are analysed for proteins and other matter in suspension and subjected to sample micro-fining. Three or four days later Dominique and his oenologist assess the results for both clarity and for taste. Provided the wine is reasonably clear, taste quality takes preference over clarity. These results determine which wines require which finings. The options are usually: 1. Casein and bentonite – casein adjusts undue yellowing in the colour and rounds out the wine, especially if it contains undue harsh wood tannins, while bentonite aids in precipitating suspended proteins; 2. Isinglass and bentonite – isinglass is a fish-fining with neutral taste impact and just clarifies the wine; 3. Bentonite alone – for proteins and 4. Isinglass alone – a polishing fining. Thus after 20–24 months of cask age, the Lafon Meursaults and Montrachet are finally bottled.

In 1990 Dominique decided to leave a plot

The Domaine's residence seen from its garden – the Clos de la Barre

of Meursault Village 'En la Barre' – just below the Clos de La Barre – to harvest late. About three weeks after the general harvest he induced some friends – with the promise of a good lunch and some interesting bottles – to help him pick. They worked well during the morning, but after lunch experienced some difficulty focussing. They tottered around harvesting – 'quite well', recalls Dominique – and the Domaine's first late harvest Meursault was born.

Lafon's red wines are also models of their kind and therefore worth considering more closely. The aim is to harvest as ripe as possible to avoid the need for additional stalk tannin. After 90–100% destemming and a light crushing, in a machine designed to simultaneously eliminate dry rot, the pulp is cooled to 16°C in tanks and then left to ferment with natural yeasts. Dominique denies that this is a deliberate pre-fermentive maceration but prefers to consider the process as a development of the traditional belief that cooler grapes make better wine. Cooling the pulp delays fermentation by 3–4 days, since yeasts function very slowly at lower temperatures, giving time for better extraction of fruit components. The final aim is to ferment the red wines at anywhere between 16°C and 30–32°C, and a heat exchanger is on hand to lower temperatures a second time should they rise too far.

The theory of fermentation is complex, but it is known that an important element of coloured pigments, the anthocyanins, are soluble in water, so are most effectively extracted by a maceration of skins and juice before fermentation (grape juice is about 95% water and of course contains no alcohol at this stage). However, these anthocyanins, essential to the continued colour development of a red wine, are chemically unstable. Fortunately, they are made stable by tannins; but tannins are only extracted in sufficient concentration by alcohol. Dominique Lafon considers that the higher temperatures of fermentation further aid extraction of both tannins and colour pigments. Artificially heating the pulp before fermentation was an option to maximise colour extraction, but this did not fix or stabilise the colour thus extracted – they rapidly degenerated and browned.

Finally, Dominique concluded that his regime of cooling the red pulp and allowing it to rise gradually to fermentation temperature both aided the extraction of water-soluble colours and, by slowing down the onset of fermentation, extracted better fruit flavours and finer, less harsh tannins, which helped stabilise the inherently unstable anthocyanins.

Once the free-run wine is run off, the remaining pulp is pressed for ¾ hour at a gentle 1.5 bars to extract a relatively supple press wine which is then added to it before removal to tanks for 48–72 hours to sediment out unwanted gross lees. The wine is then transferred into casks – 33% of which are new – for 20–24 months. They are racked once in the following spring after *malo* – less fine lees being retained than for the white wines – and again after egg-white fining a month or two before bottling.

The yields are small – on average 35 hl/ha for the whites – a reflection of the deliberately severe pruning and the high proportion of old vines. With the return of share-cropped vines, average annual production is increasing steadily towards an anticipated maximum of 60,000 bottles.

The Domaine seems to have cellars everywhere: two under the house, one under the *cuverie* and a new cellar, for palletised bottle storage, recently excavated to connect these all together. Interestingly, the digging revealed a splendid six vertical metres' soil profile of the Clos de la Barre, which abuts the south-eastern side of the house. Beneath barely a metre of rocky soil lies a bed of solid calcareous rock. Through this seemingly impenetrable foundation, thick, healthy vine roots were clearly visible. It is the natural ability of this rugged plant to penetrate such terrain that gives the produce of its fruit such

absorbing yet inimitable qualities.

Dominique Lafon aims at no particular style. His view is that you obtain a wine's power and extract by working conscientiously in the vineyards and work on its elegance in the *cuverie*. If his wines have a common thread it is a remarkable concentration and plump succulence which makes them most attractive when young and an exemplary length and well-nigh impeccable balance which give them longevity. Long fermentation and lees contact gives a softness and complexity to even the Meursault Village and Clos de la Barre which make them quite seductive and approachable from an early age. The Clos contains two-thirds of 40-year-old vines which helps concentration and its clay, rocky soils give the wine a mineral character and a nose often redolent of citrus fruits. The Meursault Désirée (a *lieu-dit,* not a Premier Cru) is characterised by aromas of exotic fruits – mangoes and pineapples – and of dried apricots. Dominique refers to this as his Viognier, and enjoyed presenting it as such to Marcel Guigal who makes one of the finest Condrieus from that unusual grape.

The Charmes is a notch up the quality ladder, with a much tighter, more energetic structure and generally greater power than the Désirée; it is fatter and richer than Clos de la Barre, often with a hint of *fruits exotiques* on its nose. The second Premier Cru, Genevrières, from light, finely-divided, yellow ochre soils on a steep slope, is very different, with less obvious power and far greater elegance – all in finesse, never in force. It tends to be somewhat closed up for the first couple of years and shows less attractively than the Charmes to start with.

The Perrières, acknowledged as the finest of the Premiers Crus, would be upgraded to a Grand Cru if the authorities could work out how to do it without too much fuss. As its

name suggests, the soils are predominantly stony – although with a significant marne/clay content. In its Lafon interpretation, it fuses Charmes' structure and power with Genevrières' elegance and finesse. With more style and complexity than either, it is also longer and more concentrated.

These are, of course, generalisations; the style of each wine varies from vintage to vintage and changes with age. Lafon wines are made to be kept and indeed, repay patient cellaring. The Domaine's Montrachet is without doubt its finest wine. According to Dominique, the wine is never big or powerful, but a wine of finesse, elegance and above all astonishing length. If you are looking for power choose a Bâtard-Montrachet, not Le Montrachet. Lafon's Montrachet is a stylish, powerful and above all, complete wine supported by a line of firm, harmonious acidity. What sets it apart from the Meursaults, in almost every vintage, is an extraordinary concentration and persistence combined with a multi-dimensional finish which remain on the palate long after the wine itself has left.

Montrachet matures slowly and needs patience. The Domaine's 1981 and 1989, tasted in the French Alps in 1996, though fine, were still young. While the 1981 showed obvious aromatic development and was reaching maturity, the 1989 was still shut tight although its greater power and eventual quality was very evident.

The Domaine is now at full throttle, having finally reclaimed the last of its vineyards from their *metayeurs*. It is a pleasure to see Dominique's confidence and single-mindedness succeeding against what, when he took over, must have appeared as insuperable odds. It is also encouraging to find a supremely talented winemaker showing many of his less able peers what can be done with meticulous care and considerable dedication.

VINEYARD HOLDINGS

Commune	Level	Lieu-dit/Climat	Area	Vine Age	Status
Chassagne	GC	Montrachet	0.33	30/50	P
Meursault	PC	Les Charmes	1.75	40/70	P
Meursault	PC	Les Perrières	0.75	40	P
Meursault	PC	Les Genevrières	0.55	45	P
Meursault	PC	Goutte d'Or	0.33	1990	P
Meursault	V	Clos de la Barre	2.10	35	P
Meursault	V	En la Barre	0.60	40	P
Meursault	V	Désirée	0.50	25	P
Meursault	PC	Volnay Santenots-du Milieu	3.75	33/40	P
Volnay	PC	Clos des Chênes	0.33	25	P
Volnay	PC	Champans	0.50	⅔:70 ⅓:8	P
Monthélie	PC	Les Duresses	1.00	9/20	P
Puligny	PC	Champ Gain	0.25	35	F
Total:			**12.74 ha**		

Domaine Jacques Prieur

MEURSAULT

This Domaine, based in Les Herbeux – a fine house just below the Clos de la Barre, surrounded by a splendid park – has nearly 13 ha of magnificent vineyards stretching from Gevrey to Puligny and including 8 Grands Crus. Until recently the wines have been thoroughly mediocre as the shareholders – Jean Prieur and his sister – pursued a policy of maximising income rather than investing for quality. Then in 1988 Jean decided to take off round the world to indulge his passion for sailing.

Fortunately, he had already formed an association with the Mercurey-based firm of Antonin Rodet to inject technical and commercial expertise into the Domaine. Rodet and four associates own 50% of the Domaine and the four branches of the Prieur family the other half – the Labruyères in wine, the Neyrats in umbrellas, the Clayeux in bonnets and the Pochs in Paris.

As the Flying Dutchman, Jean, continues his ceaseless voyage, the Domaine is now managed by his son Martin, representing the Prieurs, and Bernard Devillard, representing the Rodet interests. Happily Jean Prieur and Bernard agree 'totally' on long-term aims: to make the best wine possible, compatible with a sensible return on their investment. As the wines improve and the firm comes back into profit, the shareholders are content.

Meursault

Although major decisions are taken jointly, Martin oversees the daily routine and the Domaine's vineyard team. The driving force behind the vinification is Rodet's Nadine Gublin, who shares the responsibility with Martin.

A great deal of work has been done to put the vineyards back into order – pruning, replanting, increasing trellis and *ronage* height to improve sugar levels, reducing treatments to need (*lutte raisonnée*) rather than blanket spraying and detailed *prélevements* to refine the order and timing of picking.

In the cellar a *table de trie* has appeared, as has a Willmes pneumatic press. A great deal of old wood has been thrown out and small new casks brought in. The Village and Premiers Crus now enjoy 30–60% new wood, the Grands Crus 60–100%.

Although there is still an air of 'feeling the way', these changes have wrought a dramatic effect on the Domaine's output. Wines lacking concentration seemed to owe little to their origins – flat, dilute Montrachet, weak Chambertin and lumpy Clos de Vougeot – are now tight and well-crafted.

The whites have real grip and presence – fermentation in cask (part started in bulk), enough *batonnage* and, most importantly, maturation periods tailored to each *cuvée* rather than to economic considerations (around 16 months' *élévage* now) or the need to liberate cask space. Some *malos* were blocked in 1994 to retain acidity. The reds have greater typicity and depth – with a few days pre- and post-fermentive maceration giving total *cuvaisons* of 15 days. *Elévage* of 14–20 months is primarily geared to refining the tannins produced by this longer vatting. The Domaine is working with 6 different *tonneliers* and several origins of wood as a route to gaining complexity, and fining and filtration are on the decline. 'We have no doctrines although we try to intervene as little as possible; but don't promise our wines aren't filtered.' Bernard Devillard sums up the new approach: 'Our conviction is that quality is a matter of lots of little details, but none of them alone is sufficient.' First results are distinctly encouraging. For the rest, let's wait and see.

Commune	Level	Lieu-dit/Climat	Area	Vine Age	Status
Chassagne	GC	Montrachet	0.59	20	P
Pulingy	GC	Chavalier-Montrachet	0.14	15	P
Puligny	PC	Les Combettes	1.50	15	P
Meursault	PC	Les Perrières	0.28	12	P
Meursault	V	Clos de Mazeray Monopole (W)	1.80	15.	P
Meursault	V	Clos de Mazeray Monopole (R)	1.32	6	P
Volnay	PC	Clos des Santenots Monopole	1.19	20	P
Volnay	PC	Champans	0.35	20	P
Beaune	PC	Clos de la Feguine Monopole (W)	0.27	4	P
Beaune	PC	Clos de la Feguine Monopole (R)	1.48	20	P
Beaune	PC	Grèves	0.51	50+	F
Aloxe	GC	Corton Bressandes	0.73	10	F
Ladoix	GC	Corton Charlemagne	0.22	50+	F
Vougeot	GC	Clos de Vougeot	1.28	35	P
Chambolle	GC	Le Musigny	0.77	25	P
Chambolle	PC	La Combe d'Orveaux	0.05	25	P
Gevrey	GC	Chambertin	0.84	8	P
Gevrey	GC	Chambertin Clos de Bèze	0.15	10	P
	R	(Bourgogne Rouge)	0.46	12	P
	R	(Bourgogne Blanc)	0.50	8	P
		Total:	**14.43 ha**		

Domaine François Jobard

MEURSAULT

François Jobard is a difficult man to pin down. He works his 5 ha virtually single-handed with the help of one occasional labourer, his wife and a state-of-the-art straddle tractor and never seems to be at home. This machine, which arrived in his courtyard in 1990, was forced upon him because, although his old open tractor was still in good working order, he could no longer stand the ravages on his face and eyes of the chemicals which he had to spray on his vines. He was, justifiably, not prepared to keep the vines in good health at the expense of his own. Now, with a bright sky-blue covered cab – it even has air-conditioning – he is clearly a much happier viticulteur.

The estate about which he drives this expensive piece of modern farming hardware is itself a model of a high quality small Domaine. The land, although almost entirely in Meursault, comprises a good, varied spread of some dozen different *climats* divided between 5 Premiers Crus, Meursault Village, Aligoté and some Bourgogne Blanc and Rouge. However, with so little help, it is hardly surprising that François' neighbours regard him as a workaholic.

He is a man of thoughtful, rather shy demeanour. Talking to him in the dining room of his spacious house, just below the Clos de la Barre, communication was at first rather one-sided. However, avowing a reasonable acquaintance with his wines as a London wine merchant resulted in a noticeable thaw in the temperature, monosyllabic responses giving way to virtually complete sentences. Once François realised that the sacrifice of two hours of his precious time was to result in something other than just another magazine article, conversation positively buzzed along.

François' shyness hides a great depth of understanding of wines and the intricacies of their creation. Brought up in the house in which he now lives, surrounded by wine and its trappings, he is imbued with a devotion to what he has. A man whose instincts are for traditional practices, he looks with some suspicion on those of his colleagues, both young and old, who 'rush off to their oenologist every five minutes'. It is this same tradition which dictates that science should be kept firmly in its place – at the service of the vigneron; technologists may have designed and built his new tractor, but on no account should they be allowed to drive it.

The land he farms is, with the exception of two small plots, all his own. His great–grandfather, or great-great-grandfather – he can't remember which – started the whole enterprise going in the 1860s and on the way constructed the house he now lives in (with convenient modifications). His wife looks after him and their three children – two girls aged 21 and 25 and a boy of 18. The elder girl is studying pharmacy and doesn't, at present, seem interested in the vineyards; perhaps now her father's swollen eyes and blistered face have abated, her perception of the vigneron may become more favourable.

François' style of wine is individual. His aim is to do as much as possible naturally, without interfering. 'Let nature do the work; co-operate with nature, don't try to fight it,' is his guiding principle. In practice this amounts to as near an organic regime as he can get; although he still uses standard chemical treatments these are stopped six weeks before harvest to ensure that no trace of product finds its way into the wines.

Since 1975 he has used virus-indexed clones instead of *sélection massale* – less risk and less labour. Nowadays, replanting is parcel by parcel, letting the soil rest for 3–4 years in between. Wherever possible, soil adjustments are made organically, with a

François and his colourful tractor

dose of natural, powdered manure added for good measure.

Young Jobard vines are pruned very severely – only half a baguette – until their fourth flowering. 'If,' says François, 'the charge on the young vine is excessive in relation to its strength, it gives nothing interesting.' Pruned thus, the fruit is of excellent, usable quality. Of the mature vines about half are trained in the classic *Guyot simple* and half in the less seen *cordon de Royat* which is better suited to feeble, less productive vines and tends to produce smaller berries. Which vines are trained *Guyot* and which *Cordon* is a matter for instinct, the aim being to restrict yields and maximise fruit quality.

When to harvest – one of the vigneron's most important decisions – is also a matter of feel. François discounts the value of *prélèvements*: 'These,' he tells you, 'give the barest of indications of maturity, which are usually wrong,' and, in any case, maturity levels can alter dramatically in 48 hours, so they have little value. His own method is to walk through his vineyards to see when the grapes are ready. This is a time when he is delighted to subjugate technology to instinct.

Although he vinifies traditionally, there are a couple of interesting nuances of technique which illuminate the style of wine produced: a long, slow pressing – some three hours in a Willmes press; no *débourbage* – he is against it; rather a vigorous *batonnage* before the wine is transferred to a mixture of casks and larger *foudres* for fermentation, to ensure an even distribution of lees.

The rest is deliberately traditional: no cultured yeasts; no control of fermentation temperature – the key is to press the grapes immediately they are received, which avoids the need for temperature-control afterwards, and *chaptalisation* as late as possible to prolong fermentation and to keep down the ambient temperature in the casks.

A Jobard wine spends a long time in the cellar before being allowed out in a bottle dignified with a Jobard label on it. François' policy is to keep wines on their original lees for 12–18 months, when they are racked and unified. In his experience, any *goût de lie* disappears at racking and, in any case, 'wines without lees won't keep well'.

They are then returned to cask for a further period of maturation of up to 3 months, after which they may be fined with casein (to clear up any colour defects) and bentonite (to precipitate out any suspended proteins). There follows a further 1–2 months' settling before they are given a final polishing filtration and bottled on the small, rather ancient Jobard bottling line. François is trying hard to suppress fining as it tires the wine, so there was none in 1990/91/92/93 and 1994.

The result of this absorbing mixture of tradition and instinct is an impressive range

Bottles maturing undisturbed in the cool Jobard cellars

of wines. The House style tends, if anything, to a rather refined rusticity and a certain dryness – presumably from the time the wines spend in cask. New wood is deliberately underplayed, with no more than 15–20% new Vosges oak, which François finds most discreet and least violent in its impact.

Set against this slightly austere component, Jobard's wines have an amplitude on the palate and, with age, develop superb aromas – particularly the Genevrières and Charmes – to which long fermentation and extended lees contact undoubtedly contribute. This is distinctly old-fashioned Meursault, muted with considerable finesse – but none the worse for that.

The 1993s and 1994s show great promise – the former having the leanness of the vintage and the latter being rather more fleshy, in the restrained Jobard style. Of the Premiers Crus, the Poruzots (from high-iron-bearing, pebbly soils) tends to be plumper than the Genevrières which in turn is finer and longer. Genevrières, however, suffers more in dry years, having well-drained, very thin, stony soil. The Charmes is generally more obviously *flatteur*, quite long and mouthfilling, but with less life-giving acidity.

Having offered a remarkable, honeyed, decadently overripe 1983 Genevrières, François disappears into a small mycelium-wreathed bin in a corner of the cellar and carefully extracts a black candy-floss-covered bottle. The wine emerges a bright green-tinged gold with an immediate and attractively rich honeyed nose, redolent more of lime-blossom and spices than fruit or flowers. Guessing the vintage was a challenge; as wines develop, they tend to lose their more obvious, youthful, vintage markers and to present themselves with tertiary aromas of mushrooms, undergrowth and spices. The wine, a 1979 Charmes, was all too easily mistaken for a 1978. We were all told how wonderful were the 1978s, and how less fine, by comparison were the 1979s – a large, dilute, crop. The passage of time has proved these judgements premature. Jobard was proud of his 1979 Charmes, and with good reason.

The Domaine's 2,000 or so cases are avidly snapped up by its restaurant and private clientele. François could so easily increase his yields and give himself more to sell, but that would never be his way. This is one of the best Domaines in Meursault, run by a man who inspires confidence.

VINEYARD HOLDINGS

Commune	Level	Lieu-dit/Climat	Area	Vine Age	Status
Meursault	PC	Les Charmes (Dessus)	0.16	32	P
Meursault	PC	Les Genevrières	0.54	21	P
Meursault	PC	Les Poruzots (Dessus)	0.77	20	P
Meursault	PC	La Pièce Sous le Bois	0.21	8	P
Meursault	V	En la Barre / Corbin	1.28	33	P
Meursault	V	En la Barre	0.13	30	F
Meursault	V	Les Tillets	0.74	40	M
Blagny	PC	La Pièce Sous le Bois	0.29	38	P
Meursault	R	(Bourgogne Blanc)	0.32	20	P
Meursault	R	(Bourgogne Aligoté)	0.19	9	P
Meursault	R	(Bourgogne Rouge)	0.38	25	P
Puligny	V	Le Trezin	0.17	38	P
Total:			**5.18 ha**		

Domaine Joseph et Pierre Matrot

MEURSAULT

Thierry Matrot always wanted to be a vigneron. Having absorbed all his father's knowledge, he took himself off to Beaune to study oenology and then to Mâcon to learn the commercial aspects of running an estate. In 1976, aged 21, he returned to the family Domaine in Meursault, where he is now in full charge.

His philosophy is simple: 'Wine is made in the vineyards – and far less than people think, in the cellar.' However talented an oenologist, if his raw material is poor then he's lost before he's even started. With 21 ha of quality vineyards, Thierry has ample scope for putting his theory into practice.

Although Joseph Matrot, his grandfather, founded the Domaine, around 1909, it was his son Pierre who seeded its current reputation. He was among the first to realise the value of clones, especially in vineyards badly affected by *court noué*, following success with plantings as early as 1955. Walking through Côte d'Or vineyards provides ample evidence of unhealthy and unproductive vines.

Thierry speaks passionately on yields. Some of his colleagues believe that 50–60 hl/ha is compatible with top quality; he does not. In his view, ideal yields are 35 hl/ha for Pinot Noir and 45 hl/ha for Chardonnay and his own ten-year averages are 30 hl/ha for Pinot, 40.5 hl/ha for Village Meursault and 38.5 hl/ha for Premier Cru.

According to Thierry, the relationship between yield and quality is not the simple inverse correlation that most believe: his own theory is that, up to a certain yield, quantity does not affect quality. Beyond this there is a caesura and quality plummets. Although the precise rupture point depends on vintage, vineyard etc., the critical level for Chardonnay is higher than that for Pinot. This hypothesis obviously confronts difficulty with vintages such as 1973, 1979, 1988 and 1990 where naturally large yields produced exemplary quality.

Thierry harvests at optimum ripeness, defined as about 13.2 potential alcohol. He dislikes the taste of over-ripeness, especially in Chardonnay, preferring to maximise maturity without risking the *botrytised* richness which can result from too late a harvest. 1983, a vintage considered great by many in Meursault and Puligny, was, for Thierry, the worst of the 1980s, combining clumsily high alcohol with excessive over-ripeness.

The grapes are pneumatically pressed – 40 minutes at low pressure then 40 at higher pressure. Settling follows to remove gross

lees before the juice is cooled to 15–16°C and transferred to casks for fermentation.

The Aligoté is dosed with bentonite to eliminate not only the gross lees but also one of the two usual rackings. This accelerates its progress into bottle for earlier sale and is gentler for the Aligoté's more fragile juice.

Apart from eliminating a deleterious pumping, cooling in bulk ensures that fermentations do not rise much above 20°C. Thierry is cynically disbelieving of vignerons claiming to ferment at a specific temperature – the magic number usually turns out to be their ambient cellar temperature, so their 'policy' reflects nothing more than necessity.

The aim is to start fermentations quickly and to keep them active for as long as possible; the first to avoid oxidation and the second to maximise extract and flavour. Cultured yeasts are used to get the pot boiling, both because speed is essential and also because anti-rot sprays destroy much of the micro-flora, including the natural yeasts essential to fermentation and, many believe, to wine complexity – a further spur to those seeking to reduce chemical treatments.

Thierry unconventionally refuses to use a single new cask, vinifying and maturing entirely in second-year or older oak. New casks are broken in with Bourgogne Chardonnay, which is then sold in bulk. He thus retains control of his casks, whilst avoiding the oak flavours he so dislikes.

He also dislikes *batonnage* which 'stirs up good and bad lees alike', making the wines too powerful, heavy and lacking in finesse. He does, however, like extended lees contact, and therefore only racks once – a month

or so before bottling, just before the next vintage comes round.

Matrot's winemaking, if not revolutionary, is certainly iconoclastic. Tasting in the cellar allows him to articulate what he is trying to achieve in a fine Meursault. His aim is to maximise fruit, to assist the *terroir* in expressing itself through the grape and to retain maximum elegance.

The wines are well-balanced – and although some may at first appear to lack acidity, it is there, masked by a rich overlay of ripe (but not overripe!) fruit. The Meursaults are fine, though deliberately restrained – intellectuals rather than chorus-girls. Interestingly, although Thierry vinifies each Meursault Village *lieu-dit* separately, the results are blended into a single *cuvée*. There is no obvious house-style, common threads being understated class and good ageing potential.

Although Thierry is no great amateur of very old white wines, he reported that a 1947 Matrot Meursault tasted recently was still attractive and vigorous. His own wines are definitely not designed to be drunk young; it would be infanticide to tackle the 1992 Meursault Premiers Crus, for example, before their fifth birthday although you might be forgiven for going at a bottle of the ripe and succulent Premier Cru red Blagny, 'La Pièce sous le Bois', while waiting.

Fortunately, Thierry's taste in rock music and blues – 'It's my generation' – does not pervade the cellar. His wife, Pascale, shares his taste but his three daughters apparently prefer the television, which worries him somewhat – he might have to join them!

VINEYARD HOLDINGS

Commune	Level	Lieu-dit/Climat	Area	Vine Age	Status
Meursault	PC	Les Charmes	0.92	30	P
Meursault	PC	Les Perrières	0.53	35	P
Blagny	PC	La Pièce Sous le Bois (Blanc)	1.78	30	P
Meursault	V	(Several *climats*)	5.83	30	P
Meursault	PC	Volnay-Santenots	1.39	30	P
Blagny	PC	La Pièce Sous le Bois (Rouge)	2.35	35	P
Puligny	PC	Les Chalumeaux	1.31	30	P
Puligny	PC	Les Combettes	0.31	30	P
Meursault	V	(Rouge)	0.41	25	P
Auxey		(Rouge)	0.57	25	P
Monthélie	V	(Rouge)	0.45	20	P
————	R	(Bourgogne Chardonnay)	1.98	30	P
————	R	(Bourgogne Aligoté)	2.04	30	P
————	R	(Bourgogne Grand Ordinaire – Gamay)	0.62	30	P
Total:			**20.49 ha**		

Domaine Michelot-Buisson

MEURSAULT

Bernard Michelot, now well into his 60s, presides over 22 ha of well-sited vineyards, and one of the largest estates in Meursault, with aimiable geniality. This, as many Burgundian Domaines, originated at the end of the last century when the devastation wreaked by *phylloxera* and *oïdium* drove vignerons from their polluted land in search of more profitable pursuits.

The Domaine operates from modest buildings in La Velle, at the end of a row of houses with a triangular corner pointing directly towards Puligny. A brand new office in the courtyard has replaced the old, cramped back room fronting the small family-owned Clos St.-Felix. Bernard sits uneasily at his allotted desk in this clinical, electronic environment, shielded by a transparent partition. A computer finally arrived in 1995, although Bernard is not convinced that it will bring anything other than trouble. His distaste for office work is evident: 'I'm a manual worker, not a bureaucrat,' he protests.

Fortunately he is assisted in keeping the paper at bay by his three daughters – Chantale, not yet married, her sister Geneviève, divorced, and Odile, married to Jean-François Mestre, who has declared his allegiance by hyphenating Michelot to his name. As Bernard explains, no-one has heard of Mestre, but the adjunct 'Michelot' brings recognition and not a little lustre.

Bernard radiates 'joie de vivre' and sees his mission as bringing conviviality to those around him. Wisely, given 100–180,000 bottles to shift, his thoughts are firmly focussed on the consumer. He aims to make wines at once 'sec' and 'moelleux', evincing the true character of *cépage* and *terroir* which are, above all, a pleasure to drink – wines for the soul not the intellect. However, great Meursaults need time, and Bernard is severe with those who draw their corks prematurely.

Michelot's 50–55 hl/ha average yields have given rise to mutterings of excess. Confronted with this, he replies that he does not set out to maximise yields by generous pruning but, on the contrary, prunes severely; it is rather the weather which is the final determinant. What matters is the quantity of grapes per vine, rather than the yield per ha. He compares his vineyards with the Bordelais: he has 11,000 vines per ha, Bordeaux has 5,000, so there must be fewer grapes per vine in Burgundy to give the same gross yield per ha as in Bordeaux. He concludes that his yields are entirely compatible with *Grand Vin* and points out that in eight

Bernard Michelot tasting in his cellars; note the ceiling light – bottles (one hopes not full of Meursault)

vintages in ten it is those with higher yields which produce the finest quality. 'Look at 1973 – splendid wines harvested at 12.5 degrees alcohol – and 80 hl/ha.'

Another historical argument is wheeled out in support of greater yields in modern vintages: with mechanisation, replanting is considerably easier – a tractor makes 150 holes in the time it takes to dig 10 by hand. So, vines were replanted less often then than now and were thus less productive. In a modern vineyard, 98% of vines regularly crop, whereas 40 years ago it was nearer 80%; ergo, greater gross production. Whilst he may have convinced himself, Bernard still has to explain how he regularly manages 5–10

hl/ha more than his colleagues.

Vinification is traditional: 2–3 pneumatic pressings are followed by fermentation in oak – about 25% new. The remainder of the casks are under five years old – 'You can't make good wine in 10–15-year-old casks.' There is no attempt at temperature control since, according to Bernard, 'fermentation directs itself'. The presses are filled quickly – a white Michelot grape waits no more than 2 hours – and the casks filled up as soon as the tumultuous phase is over, all of which helps to prevent premature oxidation. The wines are bottled just before the new vintage.

Underneath the house, substantial cellars, parts dating from the 15th century, house the Domaine's production. In an inner room, the visitor is invited to taste bottled wines, sitting on a four-legged stool, surrounded by a cob-webbed library of older vintages.

Bernard's Meursaults are interesting, well-made wines, individual in style but usually powerful and fleshy. They are not designed for long ageing, but generally best within a decade or so. Although the Premiers Crus are the pick of the crop, the Villages wines are good, particularly the Grands Charrons which Bernard, with an illustrative shaping of both hands and a mischievous laugh, likens to 'a well-built 16-year-old girl – volcanic!' The advent of Jean-François Mestre seems to have wrought a change towards fresher flavours. These wines can be bought with confidence, and are particularly well worth looking for in second rank vintages, at which the team seems to excel.

VINEYARD HOLDINGS

Commune	Level	Lieu-dit/Climat	Area	Vine Age	Status
Meursault	PC	Les Perrières	0.20	14	P
Meursault	PC	Les Charmes	1.60	24	P
Meursault	PC	Les Genevrières	1.65	29	P
Meursault	V	Les Narvaux	1.30	31	P
Meursault	V	Les Tillets	0.83	45	P
Meursault	V	Les Grands Charrons	0.85	38	P
Meursault	V	Clos du Cromin	0.98	24	F
Meursault	V	Clos St.-Felix	0.82	35	P
Meursault	V	Les Limozins	0.68	36	P
Meursault	V	Sous la Velle	1.98	45	P
Meursault	V	(Various *climats*)	2.40	40	P
Puligny	PC	Les Folatières	0.16	25	P
Puligny	PC	La Garenne	0.12	23	P
Puligny	V	Les Grands Champs	0.28	39	M
Santenay	PC	Les Gravières	0.41	N/A	P
Santenay	PC	La Comme	N/A	N/A	-
Pommard	V	————	0.13	N/A	-
————	R	(Bourgogne Chardonnay)	5.56	25	P
————	R	(Bourgogne Aligoté)	0.75	45	P
————	R	(Bourgogne Pinot Noir)	0.58	37	P
		Total:	**21.23 ha**		

Domaine Pierre Morey

MEURSAULT

Pierre Morey has a smallish estate of his own in Meursault, and in 1989 was awarded the ultimate accolade of being invited to succeed Jean Virot as wine-maker at Domaine Leflaive in Puligny. He will tell you that the omens were not good – he was born in a relatively poor vintage, 1948, but mercifully conceived, as he may cheerfully add, at the end of the exceptional 1947 harvest. His family was copious – one brother and six sisters.

The Moreys, established in Meursault, are only tenuously related to the Moreys of Chassagne. They arrived in Meursault under somewhat unorthodox circumstances during La Terreur in 1793. During the Revolution, though the Meurisaltiens' republican distaste for the clergy deprived the village of its priest, there was an equally strong popular desire to remain good Catholics. The problem was solved by Alexis Morey – from Chassagne – who persuaded a priest to make night-time visits to Meursault to celebrate mass in wine-cellars there. Whilst on these nocturnal peregrinations, Alexis met and fell in love with a Mlle Millot. They married, had several children, and built up a small viticultural estate.

Unfortunately, frequent subdivisions under the Napoleonic inheritance laws left virtually nothing of the original family 5 ha when Pierre's father, Auguste Morey-Genelot came to inherit in 1930. He abandoned life as a viticulteur in 1934 to become a travelling representative for a pharmaceutical company. During this wilful absence the little land remaining was run by his father – Pierre's grandfather. Being an old soldier, wounded in the First World War, he soon became physically and spiritually tired of keeping the show going and issued an ultimatum to Auguste to return or see the estate abandoned. Auguste returned in 1936.

In those days, it was common practice to either rent vineyards or farm them on a share-cropping basis. Auguste refused to buy land because he regarded the prevailing prices as exorbitant, and therefore set about finding suitable vineyards to share-crop. He ended up in 1937 with 4 superb hectares including Meursault Premiers Crus Perrières, Charmes and Genevrières and 35 ares of the Grand Cru Le Montrachet, all of which belonged to the Domaine des Comtes Lafon. Sadly for Pierre, the tenancy has now expired and the vineyards returned to Lafon. To compensate for the loss – 'I couldn't survive without Genevrières, Charmes and

Montrachet in the cellar' – Pierre has started a 1,000-case négociant business, called Morey-Blanc (not a pun, Blanc is his wife's maiden name). He buys in *must* – only white wine – 'so I am virtually the vigneron', and has managed to find acceptable sources of the Meursault Narvaux, Montrachet and St. Aubin Premier Cru.

Although he and his wife have moved to a rather grand, large house on the westerly edge of the village, with a good piece of garden for their two children, for most of his life Pierre and his family lived in a pleasant, but unpretentious, house in Meursault's so-called Quartier Neuf. These were built just after the twin miseries of *oïdium* and *phylloxera* at the turn of the 20th century. Money being scarce, building started then stopped in something of a hurry.

The First War was followed by the great depression of the late 1920s and then the Second War. These momentous events left little cash for building grandiose houses, hence the Quartier Neuf of 1890 was little changed by 1945. Today Meursault is considerably expanded and it would probably be the grand custom-built mansions up on the hill behind the camping site which would be entitled to the designation 'Quartier Neuf' – if anyone bothered any more.

Pierre is a tall, dark man, whose manner combines a university professor with an incipiently mischievous schoolboy. Confident in his ability to make and judge fine wine, he has the humility to be aware of the tightrope a conscientious vigneron is expected to walk. Brought up surrounded by vineyards and wine, his art is second nature. Although he and his brother were both expected to join in at vintage time, he recalls that his brother's cooperation was only forthcoming with considerable reluctance, whereas he could not wait to help.

For Pierre, as for most great winemakers, nothing is dogmatic; everything has its reason and is thoroughly thought through. If tradition is upheld it is because it coincidentally produces the best results, not because it is tradition. He admits that his methods have changed little from his father's day. There is more technical insight into why things work as they do, and help is available to put them right if they go wrong, but these only serve as backup for instinct and experience, for which there is no substitute.

Since much of the family land has usually belonged to someone else, and merely farmed on their behalf, Pierre admits to no

great expertise in matters of viticulture. Regimes of treatment for the vines, replanting policy, clonal selection or *sélection massale* were all questions which were ultimately decided by the landowner, not the farmer. He will shortly have to make such decisions himself, since vines originally planted by Auguste now require replacing.

In general, herbicides are discouraged in favour of hoeing, because they tend to proliferate lateral roots on the vine thus discouraging the important tap root from seeking nutrients and water further down in the soil; because they encourage rot in wet or humid years; because they change the natural development of the vine and, because they infect and destroy the structure of the soil. In addition – just in case any of the pro-herbicide lobby are still standing after this sustained battery – herbicides are the progenitors of other, more resistant, weeds and grasses than those you started with. One has the distinct impression that herbicide salesmen are among the least successful tradesmen calling at Domaine Pierre Morey.

Controlling yields is of supreme importance to Pierre, who believes that vignerons should not have economics at the back of their minds when deciding how severely to prune or how many excess buds and shoots to remove each spring. Additional measures include removing excess grapes after the flowering, outlawing the vigorous SO4 rootstock and using 161/49 on hillside vines and riparia gloria on plains and flatter land. Since 1992, Morey's vineyards have been tended biologically, with no synthetic products. As he gladly confesses: 'The vineyards no longer smell of chemicals.'

His inevitable involvement in Leflaive's experiments with biodynamics, tempt him to try this in his own vineyards. This system relies on the ability to apply treatments to vines and soil at precise times of the day. The doses are of relatively high potency, in the homeopathic sense in which greater potency accompanies greater dilution of the original reagent. An experimental hectare was tried during the 1990/1991 growing season. Preliminary results with red grapes particularly interest him, as these seem to show a much more supple, finer quality of tannin than that in wine made from traditionally treated vines.

On yields, Pierre's views are unexpected: Chardonnay and Pinot Noir yields of up to 60 and 45 hl/ha respectively are compatible with Grand Vin 'without enormous risk',

Pierre Morey in front of his little summer-house – in search of divine inspiration?

provided one is prepared to *saigner* red vats in vintages which are naturally dilute (e.g. 1982, 1992, 1994). He now regards 45 hl/ha as sufficient yield for Chardonnay; his own are around 40. Perhaps having to defend somewhat larger yields at Leflaive with rather less at his own Domaine gives him some unease.

As far as vinification goes, nothing is skimped. According to Pierre, 'The only great decision is to choose the right day to pick.' In practical terms, it is of course necessary to decide on the vintage date in advance, firstly to have enough pickers on hand, and secondly so as to move quickly should weather conditions suddenly deteriorate. Morey visits each vineyard several times in the days up to harvesting to determine the exact ripeness of the grapes. What is sought is not maximum ripeness, but that elusive equilibrium between sugar and acidity which will put balance and finesse into the final wine.

Apart from the decision on when to pick, one of Pierre's greatest responsibilities is to decide the order of harvesting the various parcels. This decision is always taken with an ear to the weather forecasts – which reflect the one element of the equation over which no one has control. Whilst a late harvest is not his policy, he does admit that 'we are not among the first to pick'.

With Leflaive taking ever more of his time, Pierre has completely reorganised his home team to ensure that everything runs smoothly whilst he is in Puligny. He has a couple, M. et Mme Lete, who live in the old Morey house – she looks after visitors and deliveries, whilst he helps care for the vineyards and works in the cellars. In 1992, Pierre engaged a young Angevin, Christophe Chauvel – an earnest fellow with a National

Oenological Diploma – to understudy him. However, since Domaine Leflaive is but five minutes by car, and the telephone has now reached Puligny, there is no real risk of things going awry in Meursault.

Morey vinification is robustly classical. The grapes are pressed in a new pneumatic press, a recent change which doesn't seem to have unduly antagonised Pierre's old father, who used to operate the family's ancient Vaslin, and remains a valued member of the workforce. Pierre's brother, an engineer with the French aircraft company Aerospatiale is a reformed character as far as wine and wine-making are concerned, and now appears eagerly at vintage time.

As the juice runs from the presses it is given a dose of SO_2. If it is *botrytised*, or not reasonably clean, it is allowed to settle, before being run into casks for fermentation. The cellar is constructed on three levels, so that the wine can be moved from press to fermentation to maturation casks without being aerated by a pump. The casks used for the regional appellations are all second-year or older; the Village wines go into 25% new oak, and the Premiers and Grands Crus have 33%. Experiments have led to the conclusion that Vosges is better for Meursaults whereas Pulignys harmonise better with Allier. Given sufficient volume of any single *cuvée*, Pierre prefers a contribution from each type of oak in the final *assemblage*.

The wines are *batonéed* three times each week up to the winter equinox, as lees contact is valuable for the development of a young white Burgundy. Thus, at first racking, after the *malolactic* fermentation, only the gross, heavier lees, are racked off, leaving the fine lees to nourish the wine during the summer. At second racking, in September, the wines are drained completely clear of their lees.

After tasting and analysing each wine, a decision is made on whether to use fish or bentonite fining. In some vintages one works markedly better than the other. Wines which are unduly yellow may also require casein to be added to the bentonite to clarify them properly.

After a light cartridge filtration, the wines

are bottled early in the second year – some 18 months after the vintage. This *élevage* is relatively long compared with what happens elsewhere, but Pierre believes that these additional months in cask give the wines a much better evolution, adding a structure and richness which make for longevity. He tried bottling at 11 months, but the results were manifestly inferior.

As one tastes at the third, deepest level of this quiet, cold cellar, with bins of mycelium-covered bottles tucked into obscure corners, the value of all the care and thought that goes into a Morey white wine becomes apparent. Their overriding characteristic, from the Aligoté made from a patch of 35-year-old vines now partly replanted, to the Bâtard-Montrachet, is aristocracy. The wines have ineffable breeding, backed up by firm, fleshy fruit. Nothing lean or ascetic here – but glorious opulence, evident especially in the young wines, still in cask in October, when most of their contemporaries at other Domaines are beginning their evolution in bottle. Pierre believes in waiting : 'You need great patience in the *élevage* of a wine,' and moreover, 'You often need the courage to do nothing'.

Every stage in the production of these marvellous wines is approached with skill, care, and above all, diligence. As so often with quality, it is details which make the difference between magic and mediocrity. From the simple expedient of filling each cask up as soon as the first tumultuous phase of fermentation is over to keep a slow fermentation going for as long as possible, to delaying bottling until that precisely chosen moment, nothing is left to chance or undertaken thoughtlessly.

Pierre Morey is a consummate artist and his wines are a fitting tribute to the co-operation between man and the land.

VINEYARD HOLDINGS

Commune	Level	Lieu-dit/Climat	Area	Vine Age	Status
Puligny	GC	Bâtard-Montrachet	0.48	30	M
Meursault	PC	Les Perrières	0.52	27	P
Meursault	V	Les Forges/Les Tessons	1.00	29	P/M
Meursault	V	Les Durots (Red)	0.26	21	P
Monthélie	V	(Several *climats*)	0.82	30	M
Pommard	PC	Les Grands Epenots	0.43	30	M
Meursault	R	(Bourgogne Aligoté)	1.94	2–35	P/M
Meursault	R	(Bourgogne Blanc)	1.30	23	P/M
Meursault	R	(Bourgogne Rouge/PTG)	1.21	34	P/M
		Total:	**7.96 ha**		

Domaine Rougeot

MEURSAULT

Marc Rougeot was born in one of those vintage years that Burgundy, would rather forget – 1956. Through effort of will, he overcame this congenital, frosty, misfortune and is now installed as the Domaine's winemaker and the fifth generation of Rougeots in Meursault.

Landownership began with Marc's grandfather who possessed a small Domaine selling wine in bottle under the Rougeot-Latour label. Marc's father, who took over in 1955, soon realised that there was not enough land to provide a sensible living, since most of the 20 ha were situated in scattered plots of lesser appellations. He therefore decided that his viticultural activities would have to be subsidised by something more profitable, and promptly invested his business skills in founding a firm of public works contractors.

This enterprise prospered, finding rich nourishment on the autoroutes. The 'travaux publics' enabled Rougeot Père to add 3 ha of Ladoix in the 1960s and a further ha of Pommard in 1975. In addition, until the late 1980s, the Rougeots farmed vineyards for the Ch. de Meursault; 6 ha of Premiers Crus which one suspects they would dearly have liked to add to their portfolio.

When Marc took charge in 1975 much of the wine was sold in bulk. In the intervening years he has gradually weaned the Domaine off this practice and built up the private and export sales to the point that wine is now all sold in bottle under the Domaine's own label. Thus he finds himself in the fortunate position of having as much custom as stock in normal vintages and in the invidious position of having far less stock than custom in less abundant ones. The income to replant and re-equip is thus assured, and Marc is left to concentrate on producing top-quality wine.

Like many of the new wave of young Burgundian winemakers, Marc lives over the shop – in this case an elegant 17th-century village house bought by the family in 1981 – thank heavens for autoroutes! This quiet, substantial dwelling is entered from the street by a pair of solid automatic steel gates which would have given Monsieur Hulot endless scope for mishap. Within, a secluded garden with pear and apple trees adjoins a small walled vineyard – the 'Clos des 6 Ouvrées' – from which comes a soft, attractive Bourgogne Chardonnay.

Underneath the house is a maze of cellars terminating in a steel-encased library of older bottles. Browsing through this small, but growing, treasure-house you should not be surprised to find bottles of Claret and a couple of cases of Romanée-Conti walled up for future feasts, whilst a bottle of Yquem 1937 props up a little pile of older Sauternes. In contrast, there are few of the Domaine's own mature wines to draw upon, since the purchase of two Willmes presses in 1985 and major works in the *cuverie* depleted its resources. Now finances have improved, Marc is steadily accumulating a reference library.

Marc Rougeot trimming grafts for his plants

206

In the vineyards, hoeing-in weeds and grass is preferred to herbicides which can engender resistance; soil is also ploughed up round roots in the winter for frost protection. Any vines that, despite this care, manage to die, are grubbed up in the autumn and replaced the following spring. They used to use clones from an old mother vine at Ladoix, but abandoned these for more reliable and virus-indexed quality from the nurseryman.

To keep pests and diseases at bay Marc favours the traditional Bordeaux mixture – a copper-sulphate-based brew which is a proven, non-toxic anti-mildew and anti-oïdium treatment – plus specific insecticides as they are needed. He is aware that the copper tends to harden the grapes, and thus to delay maturation, since the sun penetrates harder matter less easily, so some care is taken to spray no more than necessary.

Once at the *cuverie*, the grapes are dosed with SO_2 at the rate of 0.5–1.0 litre per tonne before being pressed in the new Willmes presses. These were chosen by Marc after considerable experimentation. This involved vinifying two separate *cuvées* of Meursault in three different presses – a Vaslin which consists of a pair of stainless-steel plates which come together squeezing the grapes in between, and Bucher and Willmes pneumatic presses, which operate by blowing up an expandable balloon which gently crushes the grapes.

He then invited 'all the viticulteurs of Meursault' to blind taste the results. The Willmes press won. This also revealed that the Vaslin produced twice the volume of lees as the Willmes and that those were coarser and less easily settled. Lees are important in the first months of a wine's life, since it feeds on them, gaining in complexity and structure. It is also known that the finer the lees the more finesse in the wine.

In addition to these advantages, the Willmes press has a series of programmes which give finely-tuned control over total pressing time, maximum pressure, the time to reach, and remain at maximum pressure and the time during which the press drum turns. It is possible to have a pressing so gentle that it is like crushing the grapes in one's hand. In recent vintages, Marc has tended to give his lesser whites, especially the *régionales*, 8–12 hours of *macération pelliculaire*, to add extract.

After pressing, each *cuvée* is unified and the juice allowed to settle at 6–7°C for 12–15 hours. If necessary, dirty juice is clarified with bentonite – but this is rare.

Fermentation takes place in bulk, with twice daily *batonnage* to ensure even lees distribution. This frequency is greater than one normally finds in Burgundy, but a particularly cold ambient cellar temperature makes this necessary. After fermentation at 19°C in large oak *foudres* and at a density of about 1008, all but the Aligoté is put into small oak casks.

After much experimentation it was decided to use 35–40% of new Vosges oak. The exception is the Premier Cru Meursault Charmes which is felt has the natural power to support 100% new wood.

Elévage is designed to allow slow maturation with minimum interference. Hence, the least possible number of rackings – two: one after *malo* and the other after fining (with bentonite). Filtration is used only when absolutely necessary; and then with Kieselguhr and not plates, which would take out acidity and stuffing. Bottling takes place after some fifteen months in cask.

Whilst there are many Domaines in Meursault with a more prestigious catalogue of vineyards – only one Premier Cru here – what is achieved is impressive. Marc has a horror of Meursaults which are fat, heavy or overblown, preferring wines with 'subtlety, finesse, elegance and vinosity'.

The results show considerable style and harmony. Wood is used with care to avoid dominating the wines with oak flavours, which, by and large, exhibit good balance and finesse. Many are stored under Marc's parents' house, a modern building next to the 'travaux public' depot on the outskirts of the village. This is in the Monatine vineyard which produces one of Rougeot's finest Meursaults.

Tasting in the cellars beneath, brought to mind a magnificent bottle of Rougeot Meursault Charmes from the distinctly unmagnificent 1975 vintage. This was Marc's debut vintage and he well remembers being continually shouted at by his father whilst he was making this wine. For its first year or so it was deemed undrinkable and consigned to a corner as unfit for sale, accompanied no doubt, by further imprecations from Rougeot Père. In time, it emerged as a truly remarkable wine, not just for the vintage, but for Meursault of any vintage – a deep yellow-gold colour, an exotic fruit aroma and an almost overripe richness – immensely seductive and utterly delicious. Apologies were apparently forthcoming !

The younger wines show considerable promise. From a rather floral Aligoté – Marc claims to prefer making Aligoté than Meursault Charmes, more of a challenge presumably – through a nine-month bottled Bourgogne Chardonnay with an attractive lemony richness and a firm structure, to the Meursaults – characterised by their amplitude and length.

The reds are less inspiring, though Marc says emphatically: 'I am learning, I am learning, I am learning with reds.' His policy of using 100% new oak for his Pommard and Volnay Santenots together with 100% of the *vin de presse*, is frequently too much for the rather delicate Pinot fruit to stand. This is essentially a white Domaine.

In 1990, Marc and his wife started a separate *négoce* house, Rougeot-Dupin, which deals mainly in Grands Crus. Its principal supplier is a well-known Vougeot grower who sells them around half his crop, which is bottled *sur place*, unfined and unfiltered. The range includes Romanée St.-Vivant, Clos de Vougeot and Richebourg, plus some Vosne les Suchots and around 2,000 bottles of Le Montrachet. Marc somehow manages to handle sales and administration for this as well as for the Domaine, single-handed.

Marc Rougeot is doing an excellent job with quiet confidence. His family – an agglomeration of 12 horses, a charming wife who is descended from a quality printing business in Beaune and works there from time to time, and two children, Pierre-Henri aged 15 and Alexandre aged 11 – have every reason to be proud of him.

VINEYARD HOLDINGS

Commune	Level	Lieu-dit/Climat	Area	Vine Age	Status
Meursault	PC	Les Charmes (Dessous)	0.46	50	P
Meursault	PC	Volnay Santenots (R)	0.85	1976/82	P
Meursault	V	Sous la Velle	2.09	1969–86	P
Meursault	V	Le Pellans	0.39	1978	P
Meursault	V	Monatine	0.39	1974/75	P
Meursault	V	Les Grandes Gouttes	1.37	1974/79	P
Meursault	V	Au Village	0.33	1971	P
Meursault	R	(Bourgogne Rouge)	1.98	1967–85	P
Meursault	R	(Bourgogne Aligoté)	1.49	1980–81	P
Meursault	R	(Bourgogne Passe-Tout-Grains)	1.42	1973	P
Meursault	R	Clos des 6 Ouvrées	0.25	1973	P
St. Aubin	V	Le Banc (W)	0.26	1989	P
Pommard	V	(Several *climats*)	0.99	1950–80	P
Ladoix	V	(Several *climats* – R)	3.07	1956	P
Monthélie	V	Les Toissères (W)	0.35	1989	P
Auxey	V	Sous la Maison	0.27	1989	F
St. Romain	V	La Perrière (R)	1.96	40	F
St. Romain	V	La Combe Bazin (W)	1.09	60	F
		Total:	**19.01 ha**		

Domaine Guy Roulot

MEURSAULT

Despite a somewhat turbulent recent history, this 10-ha Domaine is among Meursault's finest. Since the premature death, in 1982, of the creator of the estate, Guy Roulot, there have been no fewer than 3 winemakers: Ted Lemon, from California, responsible from January 1983 to January 1985, was succeeded by Franc Grux, who made 1985, 1986 and 1987 vintages, leaving during the 1988 harvest to become Olivier Leflaive's winemaker in Puligny, and finally, the present co-manager, Guy's son, Jean-Marc Roulot, who assumed full responsibility in 1989.

This is a truly family affair – Jean-Marc and his sister Michèle Javouhey-Roulot run the Domaine, together with their mother, Mme Geneviève Roulot, Guy's widow, from a modern house-cum-cellars on the periphery of the town. Jean-Marc is a somewhat serious person, who regards visitors, especially writers, with a degree of caution amounting to downright suspicion. However, when one establishes one's credentials and gets to know him he is a man of warm amiability.

Although his career as a classical actor has taken second place to the Domaine, he does occasionally leave to tread the boards. His mother and sister manage the financial and office departments and wisely leave him to get on with the viticultural and cellar work. The elegant Mme Roulot senior mans her computer in the small Roulot office, whilst Michèle takes firm charge of finance, with the air of someone entirely capable of dealing firmly with recalcitrants – be they customers or bank managers.

Jean-Marc's responsibilities have recently increased, with his marriage to Hubert de Montille's daughter Alix. Now you are just as likely to find him tasting in Volnay as manning the pumps in Meursault. Alix's timing, and choice of husband, were fortunate – as she has just acquired her first plot of Chardonnay – in Puligny's magnificent Premier Cru, Les Caillerets. Further demands on Jean-Marc's time and skills come from his friend Pascal Marchand, who has cast him in the important, though unremunerated role of sympathetic counsellor for his first few white vinifications at the Clos des Epéneaux.

The Domaine is of post-war construction – built up by Guy Roulot during the late 1950s and early 1960s, with purchases of vineyards in Meursault, Auxey-Duresses and Monthélie. Jean-Marc learnt the ropes from his father and more or less continues in the fashion set at that time.

Roulot is a model of careful viticulture: short pruning and two separate spring *évasivages*, the first to remove suckers sprouting on the lower part of each plant and the second to cut off any double shoots which sap strength from the vine, limit yields and ensure that the available photosynthetic power is concentrated where it is most needed – in the young bunches.

Since 1992, all the Domaine's vines are hoed rather than treated with herbicides. Respect for the soil has led Jean-Marc to join a group of 50 estates commissioning their own organic compost from Cyril Bongiraud, an ex-Romanée-Conti employee. Spray treatments are now more precisely targeted, which reduces both the volume and concentration used. Gone is the wasteful, and highly visible, cover-all cloud of spray which destroyed useful micro-flora as well as the fungi and pests intended.

Vine replacements are carried out individually using 3 clones in each parcel replanted, giving greater complexity in the final wine. Soil is ploughed up round the roots (*buttage*) each winter only on those parcels which have been worked by hoe, rather than treated with herbicides.

Harvesting is particularly careful; vintagers are never left alone, because they tend to cut bunches indiscriminately. Instead, an experienced member of the Roulot team shadows them to ensure that only fully ripe bunches are picked and more importantly that any *pourriture sec* (dry rot) is excised. Limited amounts of *pourriture humide* are acceptable as this adds a degree or two of alcohol to the wine, and thus, especially in leaner years, a little more richness and amplitude.

Once harvested, the grapes are pressed in a pneumatic Bucher press. The pressing only lasts an hour and a half – some 20–30 minutes less than normal elsewhere in the commune, which results in less juice, but of a higher quality.

Jean-Marc also firmly believes that too long at maximum pressure extracts skin and pip tannins which are detrimental to wine quality. His press enables him to programme the total duration of each press cycle, the time taken to reach maximum pressure, and the time spent at both ends of each cycle, giving him total control. A tangential advantage is that the cake remaining after pressing is much more amenable to distillation of a quality *marc*, on which this Domaine prides itself; 'we have no wish to distil straw.'

Alcoholic fermentation is preceded by a period of *macération pelliculaire*. This, pioneered outside France, leaves the grape juice on its skins for between a few hours and several days to extract flavour and aroma compounds, many situated just beneath the grape skin and not readily detached by normal pressing. In the absence of alcohol, extraction of undesirable harsh tannins is also kept to a minimum. In addition, this process delays the onset of fermentation which Jean-Marc considers beneficial.

Another matter on which he expresses strong views is *batonnage* – rousing the lees in cask to add *gras* and complexity, using an old stick or broomhandle, if you are traditional, or a specially bent stainless-steel tool if you want to be technologically correct. Although practised elsewhere, this is a particularly Meurisaltien habit. Burgundian lore has it that 'A woman, a Puligny and a walnut tree, the more you beat them the better they be'; maybe, but there is a sight more beating in Meursault than in its illustrious neighbour. The most beneficial beatings are those administered between the termination of alcoholic fermentation and *malo* finishing.

Frequency of *batonnage* is a matter of judgement, not science. Although noticeably adds richness some, including Jean-Marc, detect a compensating loss in finesse, and contend that you rouse bad lees with good. Some growers rouse as many as 50 times during the weeks following fermentation, others twice weekly or just once a month. Jean-Marc favours the latter on the grounds that it minimises losses whilst maximising gains.

The whites are vinified in 20–30% of new oak, the proportion depending both on the character of the Cru and the vintage. Whilst fermentation proceeds more rapidly in new than in older oak, it is generally felt that the qualities imparted by new wood harmonise better with the wine when fermentation, rather than just subsequent maturation, is carried out in new oak. So there is a balance to be struck.

In February, after *malo*, the different lots are assembled, sulphur levels adjusted and the wines then returned to cask until the following June. The lees are kept for making Fine – a brandy distilled from wine – another speciality of the house. After fining and second racking the wines are plate-filtered and then bottled. Jean-Marc is anxious to have a more sensitive carton filter to min-imise the deleterious effects of filtration on flavour and acidity levels. Total *élévage* is about 10–11 months; this may seem short, especially for the better wines, but Jean-Marc considers that his cellars are not cold enough to justify any longer in cask.

There has been much experimenting with different fining agents since Jean-Marc dis-covered that traditional bentonite fining tended to give a rather broader, less brilliant, style of wine, whereas fish fining was much less violent and more aromatically true. He also found that some vineyard sites were more compatible with fish fining than with bentonite. On tasting, the 'fish' wines showed a much tighter, leaner spectrum of flavours – this was especially evident in the Vireuils and Tessons *cuvées* – whereas the profile of 'ben-tonite' wines was more diffuse – particularly for the Charmes, Meix Chavaux and Perrières. The provisional conclusion is that bentonite, although needing greater care than 'fish', is better for wines intended for long ageing. Interestingly, bentonite-casein finings are much more common in Meursault, whereas *col de poisson* is used more in Puligny. One is led to speculate on whether any similar comparisons have been made by anyone in Puligny.

The Roulot style is midway between the overtly riper wines of Dominic Lafon and the more austere, intellectual, style of Michel Ampeau. The wines have frank aromas, not masked by either oak or lees, and a marked richness, even in less opulent years, which in time develops the classic nut/honey charac-ter so often found in Meursault. However, there is a lean, cerebral quality in these wines which gives them a considerable depth and interest.

The basic Bourgogne Chardonnay, from 1 ha in Meursault, is usually excellent – plenty of richness and concentration backed by a firm structure, derived in part from con-tact with new oak, and an attractive *goût de terroir*. The *cuvées* from the various Meursault Village *lieux-dits* are well made and interesting, evincing the individuality of each *terroir*. The Meix Chavaux is generally quite rich, tight and distinctively spicy, the Vireuil – from vines on the Auxey-Duresses border – rather fatter and livelier. The Tillets, from thinner soils above Premier Cru Goutte d'Or, has more acidity and class and soft-centred, bright minerally flavours, good, fleshy richness and plenty of life-giving *puis-sance*; it is at its best in naturally ripe vintages – e.g. 1992 and 1993.

Tessons is perhaps more typically Meursault – long, warm and rich, with aro-mas of grilled nuts and acacia, and a slightly limey flavour; well up to Premier Cru quality in good vintages. This vies for Village supremacy with Luchets – a semi-sloping

Jean-Marc Roulot and his sister Michèle

vineyard which gives more finely structured, plumpish wine of arguably greater breeding than the rest.

The two Roulot Premiers Crus are invari-ably excellent. Les Charmes – open, ripe, with a broad, well balanced structure, devel-ops well over a decade or more. Les Perrières is yet finer: a powerful, complete wine, with all the richness, length and class one expects from this noble vineyard and, in vintages such as 1983 and 1990, great longevity.

The Domaine is back in skilled and consci-entious Roulot hands. Until Jean-Marc is called away for an extended run of Hamlet or Macbeth, it remains one of the finest sources of Meursault.

VINEYARD HOLDINGS

Commune	Level	Lieu-dit/Climat	Area	Vine Age	Status
Meursault	PC	Les Charmes	0.25	53	P
Meursault	PC	Les Perrières	0.25	31	P
Meursault	V	Les Tessons, 'Clos de Mon Plaisir'	0.80	34	P
Meursault	V	Les Luchets	1.02	2/35	P
Meursault	V	Les Tillets	0.48	21	P
Meursault	V	Les Meix Chavaux	0.96	2/20/40/66	P
Meursault	V	Les Vireuils	0.66	9	P
Meursault	R	(Bourgogne Chardonnay)	1.00	25–35	P
Meursault	R	(Bourgogne Aligoté)	1.00	25–35	P
Auxey	V	——————	1.50	25–35	P
Monthélie	V	Les Jouères	0.30	8	P
Monthélie	PC	Les Champs Fuillots	0.19	7	P
——————	R	(Bourgogne Pinot Noir)	2.00	25–35	P
		Total:	**10.41 ha**		

PULIGNY-MONTRACHET

The attractive, self-confident yet unpretentious village of Puligny-Montrachet lies at the foot of a band of vines 2 km wide and 1.5 km deep, from which come some of the world's classiest, most complex, and sought-after dry white wines.

Here one finds the Village, Premier and Grand Cru vineyards which make Puligny a place of pilgrimage, not just for grateful drinkers, but for frustrated Chardonnay producers from elsewhere striving, although loathe to admit it, to imitate Puligny's excellence from less propitious *terroir*.

The village exudes discreet prosperity: neat, manicured houses and cellars, hidden from view by simple glossy wooden gates, a few offering half-hearted invitations to 'visiter les caves', attest to the commercial success which Puligny's vignerons have long enjoyed. Nothing fancy, or ostentatious, however, to show for astronomic land values and high wine prices; the only flashy cars are those parked in the square next to Le Montrachet, the village's sole hotel.

Prosperity has not, however, bred laziness. Puligny's growers are hard-working individuals who dislike any distraction from their daily routine. The most extravagant frivolity to which they might be persuaded to succumb, usually at the insistence of their wives, would be a week or two's exotic holiday. Otherwise they stay firmly put, to mind their Domaines and to receive a relentless stream of international visitors.

The fief for which Puligny's 75 viticulteurs

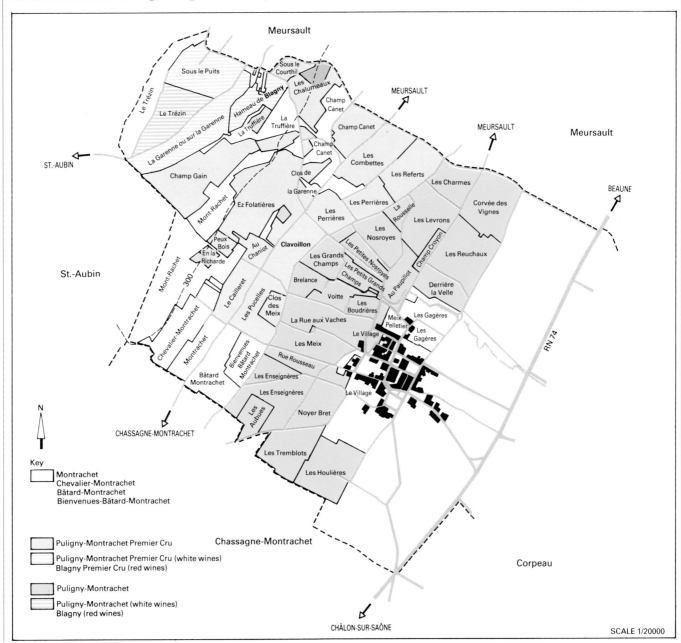

and 3 Domaines are responsible consists of 114.22 ha of AC Puligny-Montrachet, 100.12 ha of Premier Cru, and 21.09 ha of Grand Cru. These produce annually, on average, 88,000 cases of white wine and 3,200 of red. This may seem abundance, until one realises that 50% of total production belongs to négociants and a further 50% of what remains is sold in bulk; thus, around 25% of Puligny is bottled and sold by Puligny growers.

It is not, at first, easy to accept that the wines of Puligny – especially the Premiers and Grands Crus – differ from those of neighbouring Meursault or, indeed, from each other. After all, they share broadly similar soils, a common *cépage*, equally well-exposed hillsides, and equally skilled vignerons.

However, differ they do – a phenomenon largely attributable to changes in soils and subsoils, often within the space of a few metres. Stand, for example, in Grand Cru Bienvenues-Bâtard-Montrachet, where the vineyard tracks cross, facing the village: a couple of metres below is AC Puligny-Montrachet (80–110 francs per bottle); to your left is Premier Cru Les Pucelles (150–250 francs); and the Bienvenues you are standing in sells at 250–350 francs. These differences do not reflect cupidity, but soil, and are as striking a demonstration of the importance of *terroir* as can be found anywhere.

There are 12 Premiers Crus in Puligny and 3 in Blagny, the hamlet above the village which, owing to a characteristically Gallic muddle which no-one seems willing to simplify, divides its 54 ha of vineyards between Puligny and Meursault.

These Premier Crus vary in style and status. Those closest to Meursault – Champ Canet, Chalumeaux, Combettes and Referts – have thin soils dominated by scree and rock, with patches of slate; these produce lighter, more floral wines, with less power and richness than those nearer Chassagne.

In the middle of the Premier Cru band are Clavoillon, Folatières, Clos de la Garenne and Perrières, with Champs Gains and Truffière above them. These also represent a mixture of soils – varying from the deeper ground of Clavoillon through the stony Perrières to the steep, easily eroded limestone scree of Folatières. If it makes any sense to generalise, one might characterise these vineyards as producing the most masculine wines of Puligny; they begin life rather austere, but develop attractively over 5–10 years or more.

The finest of the Premiers Crus are, without question, those adjacent to the Grands Crus. Here, Les Pucelles and Le Cailleret produce wines of abundant power and concentration which, in good vintages, are of Grand Cru quality. Indeed, part of Le Cailleret is now incorporated into the Grand Cru Chevalier-Montrachet and sold as Les

Demoiselles, so-named after two Mademoiselles Voillot, who owned it in the 1880s. Domaine Leflaive owns a commanding 3.06 ha of Pucelles, producing around 1,500 cases of superbly concentrated, complex, opulent wine, which outshines many others' Grands Crus.

Puligny has four Grands Crus, all superbly exposed to the south-east, two of which are shared with Chassagne. Unfortunately, these have become heavily fragmented, with some owners having only a few rows. Apart from practical difficulties – if you only have two barrels what do you top them up with? – small volumes are difficult to work and rarely make top-class wine. Selection is therefore 'de rigeur', if one is paying Grand Cru prices.

The smallest of the quartet is Bienvenues-Bâtard-Montrachet, so christened by outside workers who farmed these vines *en metayage* during the 19th century, and were known as 'Les Bienvenues'. Although Bienvenue is no more than an administrative enclave of Bâtard-Montrachet, some claim to detect differences between the wines – the Bienvenue being allegedly more complex and feminine and less durable. In reality, any differences are more credibly attributed to vine age and vinification than to soil or micro-climate.

Of Bâtard-Montrachet's 11.86.63 ha, only 6.02.21 ha are in Puligny. The wine is characteristically more virile than either Le Montrachet or Chevalier-Montrachet but, in the hands of masters such as Leflaive and Sauzet, has great power and weight needing years to open fully. Interestingly, the Domaine de la Romanée-Conti own nearly 0.2 ha, but sell their wine *en négoce*.

Chevalier-Montrachet occupies 7.36.14 ha of sloping ground just below the Mont-Rachet. The soil is thin, with a layer of marl and scree covering seemingly impenetrable limestone. Somehow the Chardonnay's rootsystem works its way into this rock, producing wines of immense presence and concentration. The respects in which an individual Chevalier may differ from an individual Le Montrachet are best ascribed to differences other than those of soil, although being on slightly higher and steeper ground may account for the marginally less richness which some claim to detect. The best Chevaliers come from Leflaive, Latour, Jadot,

Precious vines at Puligny – looking over Les Grands Champs and Clavoillon up towards Blagny. Hot-air balloons are a popular attraction for tourists seeking a different perspective

Chartron and Niellon. Bouchard Père own a princely 2.028 ha, but produce wine which invariably manages to lack the concentration and depth one expects from a Grand Cru.

Le Montrachet, the most expensive and precious dry white wine in the world, comes from a 7.99.80 ha strip of vines, no more than 100m wide, with one end just below Chevalier-Montrachet and the other adjoining a Village vineyard in the commune of Chassagne. Puligny's 4.01.07 ha are divided among 5 proprietors, of which the largest, by far, is the family of the Marquis de Laguiche with 2.062 ha. Other important proprietors in the Puligny sector are Ramonet (0.259 ha) and Bouchard Père et Fils (0.889 ha).

Whilst the Montrachets from Ramonet, Romanée-Conti, who own 0.676 ha in the Chassagne sector, Lafon, Leflaive and Drouhin's Marquis de Laguiche, invariably outclass the rest, excellent *cuvées* are made by a number of Domaines – Marc Colin and Jacques Prieur in particular. The best of the Chevaliers are often equally fine. It is interesting to note that, apart from Leflaive's 0.08-ha patch, not a single vine of this fabled Montrachet is owned by a Puligny grower!

GRANDS CRUS OF PULIGNY-MONTRACHET

Lieu-dit	Area	Props.	Prod.
*Le Montrachet 7.99.80	17	2600 c/s	
**Bâtard-Montrachet	11.86.63	49	4400 c/s
Bienvenues-Bâtard-Montrachet	3.68.60	15	1300 c/s
Chevalier-Montrachet	7.36.14	16	1950 c/s
Totals:		**30.91.17 ha**	**10250 c/s**

*Total area; only 4.01.09 ha are in Puligny
**Total area: only 6.02.21 ha are in Puligny

Domaine Louis Carillon et Fils

PULIGNY-MONTRACHET

The Carillons are a splendid family – delightful, welcoming, enthusiastic, and moreover, producers of some of Puligny's finest wine.

They are absorbed by their family history and have recently been digging around in the local archives in search of Carillon ancestors. While they already knew of a Carillon viticulteur at Puligny in 1632, the latest bout of excavation has unearthed a Jehan Carillon, of similar calling, who worked there in 1520. Perhaps now that they have traced their history beyond the 1580 reached by the Leflaives, they will ease up on genealogy, but somehow one doubts it.

Fortunately, there are plenty of Carillons to do the digging: Louis, the present head of the house, succeeded his father Robert after the war, in turn bringing in his two sons – Jacques in 1980 and François in 1988 – to help him. Grandpère, now in his late 70s, is still much in evidence, if a neat plot of leeks and other vegetables behind one of the many Carillon cellars is trustworthy testimony.

Although the Domaine's headquarters are nominally in Puligny's Rue de l'Eglise, the village's proximity to the water-table has made underground cellars unviable, and obliged it to extend sideways. Thus the visitor is conducted out and about the locality, through a gate here, a door there, up this flight of steps, down that, to taste from tanks and barrels hidden in the most unlikely corners. Opening a door of a 15th-century courtyard, you may well find yourself facing a battery of late 20th-century stainless-steel, or an up-to-the-minute computer-controlled press. In another building one finds a confessional grille set into a wall, used during the Revolution, when religion was banned; in the event of discovery, a flight of steps enabled the priest to escape across grandfather's vegetable garden. Another small cellar was used during that period to store valuable religious artefacts from the Church opposite, and blocked with a cupboard to avoid detection.

In spite of external appearances, the Domaine is thoroughly modern. The Carillons are masters of their craft, using technology judiciously to back up tradition, and producing wines of great depth and purity. The heart of their 12-ha Domaine is in Puligny – with a patch of Bienvenues-Bâtard-Montrachet, five Premiers Crus and five ha of Puligny Village, spread over eleven separate *lieux-dits*. In 1981 a Société Civile was formed to run the vineyards for Grandfather, Louis and his two sons, who own them – a saving in administrative time and expense.

Anyone with vines in Puligny has to remind himself constantly that the soils, especially around the village where the ground is flat, are only a few centimetres from water, and thus very humid. This influences choice of clone and rootstock, and makes for greater vigilance in case of mildew or rot. On the slopes, away from the village, the risks diminish.

The soils are ploughed twice a year – once in the autumn to mulch in fertilisers and even out the ground, and again in the spring to destroy the roots of any indigenous grasses. Nourishment is calculated to ensure a healthy working vine, which will produce of its best between 15 and 50 years old.

The most besetting diseases are mildew and *oïdium* – rose-growers' nightmares – particularly for the Chardonnay, which is especially susceptible to *oïdium*. Whilst traditional copper-based treatments are preferred, they are used only at the end of the vegetative cycle since copper tends to retard the growth of a young vine and sulphur is only effective if the weather remains both hot and dry. Recent years have seen a shift towards modern products, both preventive and curative, to control pests and diseases.

Periodically, patches of vines are grubbed up and replanted to ensure a good mix of ages. Whilst older vines are more desirable, a vigneron who had only these, would sooner or later be obliged to replant and thus find himself with no wine for several years. Carillon replantings are infrequent, the most recent being in 1980, '82 and '89.

Sadly, the entire 0.47-ha plot of Combettes, originally planted by Grandpère between 1935–40, was grubbed up after the 1986 vintage; the soil remained fallow for six years, before replanting in 1992. Since the produce of young vines is not entitled to the Appellation for three years, this means a loss of nine years' production – a total of some 2,000 cases of Premier Cru Puligny – a compelling testament to their dedication to quality. 'We like it best if the soil rests a little, to re-establish structure,' Jacques explains.

Since 1982, new plantings have been 50:50 clones and *sélection massale* – with a carefully chosen mixture of clones and rootstocks. 'Only 50% of clones are any good,' reckons Jacques, adding that the widely used 161/49 rootstock is maladapted to Puligny's humid soils, so they have used less of this and more of others, such as 3309, 5BB and 101/14.

The date of harvest is carefully studied – acidity as well as sugar levels being taken into account. Unfortunately, although the *ban de vendanges* is normally calculated as 100 days from the flowering, an extended period of flowering because of rain or lack of sunshine, can result in widely different levels of maturity in a single vineyard. So, as well as noting the information given by the village *prelévements*, the Carillons make their own assessments before starting to pick, preferring in general not to harvest too late: 'We don't have grapes which are adapted to Vendange Tardive here.'

The wines are vinified in what the Domaine describes as a 'semi-traditional' manner. The 'semi' component refers to their practice of keeping the wines in cask for only 9–12 months, and then decanting them into tank for a further 3–6 months before bottling. This is more a practical expedient to release casks for the new vintage than a matter of preferred style.

After a light *débourbage* to conserve as much of the fine lees and indigenous yeasts as possible the Bienvenues and the Premiers Crus are fermented in cask, with a maximum of 20% new oak. However only 66–75% of the produce of their five hectares of Puligny Village ferments in small oak, depending on the casks available. Louis Carillon dislikes both the exotic fruit flavours produced by low temperature fermentation, and the use of too much new wood, so he ferments at around 25°C. He also believes that too much new oak dries out a wine and can destroy its typicity – 'The wine tastes delicious young, but not when it becomes older.'

The large Puligny Village *cuvée*, 100-120 casks altogether, is assembled in tank and bottled, in September, just before the harvest. The wine is fined with a 2:1 mixture of bentonite and casein, and then filtered twice, first with Kieselguhr and then through a membrane, which may or may not be of sterile porosity depending on the vintage. The aim of what might be regarded as severe filtration is to remove any risk of deposit – more visible in white wine than in red – and to ensure stability for wines destined for export to a variety of hot and cool climates.

The Premiers Crus and the Bienvenues are left in tank for a further 3–6 months before similar treatment and bottling. Quite what this extra period of ageing adds to the wine is not entirely clear, although being in tank rather than in cask risks drying out the wine less.

One-third of the Domaine's production is

3 generations of Carillons: Robert, Louis and François

red – 1 ha each of Mercurey, Bourgogne Rouge, Chassagne-Montrachet and Côte de Beaune-Villages. The Carillons destalk 80–100% and prefer a long *cuvaison* of between 15–20 days, arguing that this is necessary to unlock colour and to extract the 'more difficult' but finer tannins. They ferment at up to 35°C, with a few days' pre-fermentive maceration 'if the grapes are not too hot'.

An interesting, and sensible step is to keep the press-wine apart until the following September and then to taste it before deciding whether and in what proportion it should be assembled with the free-run wine. This latter is kept on its lees until September, whereas the press-wine, having more gross lees, is racked after its *malo*. The wines are assembled in tank just before the vintage, given an albumin fining then a light membrane filtration, and bottled between January and March of the second year.

Around 10% of the Domaine's output, notably a proportion of the Puligny Village, Mercurey and Côte de Beaune, finds its way on to the négociant market. The rest is bottled by the Carillons and sold either to one of their many export customers or to a growing band of private and restaurant clients.

The reds tend to be well-made examples of their origins, the long maceration giving a good depth of structure and plenty of concentration. The Chassagne, from vines planted

between 1955 and 1964 on the Puligny side of the commune, is undoubtedly the best of the bunch, with an attractive strawberry perfume, plenty of ripe fruit, and a soft and stylish open texture, underpinned with tannins. The Mercurey is also worth looking out for – a more 'sauvage', masculine wine, but one which will develop into an excellent bottle if it is given 5 years or more to do it.

The Carillon whites exude purity, almost extract of Chardonnay, with discreet class and complexity. The keys to their style, according to Jacques, are low yields (50 hl/ha for Premiers Crus), and minimum racking, preferably without air. They attribute the aromatic typicity of their wines

to their care in fermenting at the right temperature.

The Puligny Villages is an excellent example of the Carillon style: direct pure fruit, opening out in the mouth to show a lovely, understated richness with a hint – in 1994 – of *surmaturité*. A wine which will benefit from a few years' keeping.

All the Domaine's Puligny Premiers Crus are *côté* Meursault. Champ Canet is the most delicate, most feminine with aromas and flavours of supreme finesse, rather like intricate lace, backed by a gentle richness which imparts substance underneath the rather fragile exterior. It is always the first of the Carillon Premiers Crus to open out after bottling.

The Perrières is a complete contrast: an altogether richer, broader wine, from less stony soil from vines lower down the hillside than the Champ Canet. Its heavier skeleton make it a wine for longer keeping.

The Referts is different again: here a more stony and shallower soil gives the wine a characteristic 'mineral' flavour, with an initially marked acidity. Less round and supple, often with a nose reminiscent of dried oranges and apricots, it combines power and complexity which develop into quite a rich, fat wine with age – more perhaps of a Meursault with Puligny overtones than the converse.

The 0.12 ha of Grand Cru Bienvenues-Bâtard-Montrachet produce a characteristically firm, tight wine, but one through which can be discerned inherent power and richness. Tasting it young, one has to look for the aromas and try to guess how all the rather disparate elements will fit together, but its class is never far below the surface.

If the Carillon whites are not quite as seductive as those of Etienne Sauzet, nor as magnificently aristocratic as those of Leflaive, this is not to deny them a place in the top league. They have their own individuality and profound purity which, although different in style, is something to be prized and savoured; a tribute to this excellent family's skill and art.

VINEYARD HOLDINGS

Commune	Level	Lieu-dit/Climat	Area	Vine Age	Status
Puligny	GC	Bienvenues-Bâtard-Montrachet	0.12	1959	P
Puligny	PC	Les Combettes	0.47	1992	P
Puligny	PC	Le Champ Canet	0.55	1959/1972	P
Puligny	PC	Les Perrières	0.94	30/20/9	P
Puligny	PC	Les Champs-Gains	0.23	1964/65	P
Puligny	PC	Les Referts	0.24	1961	P
Puligny	V	(Several *climats*)	5.00	1952–1990	P
Puligny	R	(Bourgogne Aligoté)	0.25	1961	P
Puligny	R	(Bourgogne Rouge)	1.00	1955/68/70	P
Chassagne	V	–(W)	0.25	1955/63/64	P
Chassagne	V	–(R)	1.00	1955/63/64	P
St.-Aubin	PC	Les Pitangerets	1.00	1977/78	P
Mercurey	V	–(R)	1.00	1970/76	P
Total:			**12.05 ha**		

Domaine Jean Chartron

PULIGNY-MONTRACHET

Jean Chartron is a short, amiable life's man, who clearly enjoys good things and is content to be privileged enough to produce some of them.

Until 1989, when he gave up the mayoralty of Puligny-Montrachet, after 12 years in office, his life as a grower was inextricably entwined with that of the community in which he lives and works.

Now, Jean Chartron devotes his considerable energies to his fine estate, which he took over after his father died, in 1983. This was founded by his grandfather in 1860, consisting of some 10 ha of vines situated entirely in the commune of Puligny.

The jewel in the crown is not the 0.55 ha of Chevalier-Montrachet, but the 2.06 ha of Clos du Cailleret – an enclosure which forms Cailleret's northerly extension, and shares similar geology to Le Montrachet. Sadly, death duties forced the recent sale of 0.41 ha of Chevalier, 1.62 ha of Cailleret and 0.82 ha of Folatières, but what remains is still an enviable slice of magnificent vineyard and the Clos du Cailleret and Clos de la Pucelle are still *Monopoles* of the Domaine.

Jean Chartron is also an equal partner with Louis Trebuchet in a négociant business set up under their joint names in 1984. Chartron et Trebuchet's large range is mainly exported. Of their 1,000-cask output, some 200 casks are attributable to Domaine Jean Chartron.

The Domaine's wines are carefully wrought by Jean's son, Jean-Michel and its winemaker, Michel Roucher, who together with Louis and Jean Chartron take all the major decisions.

Policy is based on the overriding principle of minimum intervention – minimum additives, manipulation and filtration. The vinification is a mixture of tradition and innovation. Although he will admit that he is not a revolutionary, Jean Chartron is a born experimenter. In 1991 he decided to try 15-18 hours of pre-fermentive *macération pelliculaire* – fashionable in the New World and designed to extract greater aromatic richness and depth of flavour. The typicity, which many considered this process to destroy, was clearly evident in a range tasted in 1995, so it is likely that this will continue.

Unusually, fermentation uses an inoculation of selected yeasts. Jean Chartron insists that they provide an important element of control, both at the start and during the process of fermentation. 'Indigenous yeasts are a mixture of good and bad; bought yeasts are only the good ones.'

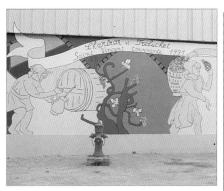

Mural painted on the cuverie for the 1991 St. Vincent tournante. St. Vincent is the patron saint of wine and villages take turns at hosting the festivities

The whites receive a maximum of 40% new Allier and Vosges oak for the Grand Cru and 30% for the Premiers Crus. A rotation ensures that no cask is more than three years old.

In general, the Premiers Crus are bottled just before the summer, to preserve their typicity and finesse and the more powerfully structured Grands Crus some 12 months after the vintage – never longer,

Preparation for bottling presently consists of a light bentonite-casein fining followed by langential filtration. The aim is to eliminate both processes completely. This consists in passing the wine several times tangentially across the filter medium rather than forcing it through a cartridge or plate. As no pressure differential is involved, less is lost in aroma and flavour.

The Domaine's wines are designed to reflect their origins as closely as possible. Although, especially in ripe vintages such as 1983, 1989, 1990 and 1992, they have undoubted power, the overall style tends to emphasise finesse rather than size.

The Puligny Premier Cru Les Folatières, at the northern, Meursault, end of the commune, has thin, limestone-rich soil. This gives steely finesse, good natural acidity and a distinctive mineral flavour; less 'flatteur' to start with than, for example the Pucelles, but delicious after a few years in bottle.

The Clos de la Pucelle is much richer and fuller than Folatières, less floral on the nose with greater fatness and power. In a good vintage this might easily be mistaken for Bâtard-Montrachet – a junior version, perhaps.

The Caillerets was originally two distinct parcels of vines until 1974 when Les Petits Caillerets, a 0.71-ha plot at the northern end of the Chevalier-Montrachet vineyard was, after some pressure on the authorities, obligingly reclassified as Chevalier.

The Clos du Cailleret produces a white wine of distinction. Although often starting out tough-edged, the class is always there, lurking underneath. Surprisingly, the Chartrons still have 0.39 ha of Pinot Noir in this quintessentially white wine vineyard – 'they must be mad' remarked one colleague. The Clos des Chevaliers (first vintage 1991) is what remained of the Domaine's Chevalier holding after the sale – 'we kept the best'. Here respectably old vines, some dating from 1948, produce a fine amalgam of power and understated elegance – a wine of true Grand Cru breed. As with all great white burgundy, this begins life as a rather compact bundle – one can see the inherent finesse and can taste the power and the fruit, but it needs a slow evolution in bottle to decode its charms.

The Domaine is improving as the years go by. In greater vintages the wines have a balance and depth which put them into the top flight; in less ripe years, however, they seem to lack an indefinable particle of the class which one finds for example, in a Leflaive or Ramonet. This should be seen as no more than a minor quibble about a fine Domaine.

VINEYARD HOLDINGS

Commune	Level	Lieu-dit/Climat	Area	Vine Age	Status
Puligny	GC	Chevalier-Montrachet	0.55	1948/74/86	P
Puligny	PC	Clos du Cailleret (W)	2.06	1944-1990	P
Puligny	PC	Clos du Cailleret (R)	0.39	1946/57/72	P
Puligny	PC	Les Folatières	0.42	1938-1989	P
Puligny	PC	Clos de la Pucelle	1.16	1950/54/ 68/80	P
St. Aubin	PC	Les Murgers Des Dents De Chien (W)	0.55.	1954/94	P
Chassagne	V	Les Benoites (W)	0.62	1947/95	P
Chassagne	V	Les Benoites (R)	0.62	1954	P
Puligny	R	(Bourgogne Blanc)	1.80	1944-1991	P
Puligny	R	(Bourgogne Aligoté)	0.59	1962/95	P
Puligny	R	(Bourgogne Rouge)	0.27	1979/80/82	P
Total :			**9.03 ha**		

Domaine Gérard Chavy et Fils

PULIGNY-MONTRACHET

Alain and Jean Louis Chavy

Although there have been *vigneron* Chavys in Puligny since 1820, it was not until a century and a half later (1986) that Chavy wines found their way into Chavy bottles. Gérard started it in 1976, and since retiring in 1994, his sons Jean-Louis and Alain have increased Domaine bottling to 90% of production.

The two brothers work well together and are establishing a reputation at home and abroad. From their 11 ha come well-made, stylish Bourgognes, a Village Meursault Les Pellans and a couple of Village Pulignys – one from the Charmes *climat*, the other from nine separate vineyards covering 4.4 ha. The cream of this range are four Puligny Premiers Crus, including a sizeable chunk (2.66 ha) of Les Folatières.

The vineyards are tended as organically as possible and spraying carried out on an 'as needed' basis. Severe pruning is supplemented by a further culling of embryo bunches before flowering, in May, and a *vendange vert* if an excess really seems likely. All this keeps yields around 45–50 hl/ha in Puligny, less in Premier Cru, which the Chavys consider compatible with top quality.

Vinification is relatively uncontroversial. One peculiarity is that part of each *cuvée* is fermented and kept in *cuve*, rather than in cask. The proportion varies from 100% for the Bourgognes, to 20% for the Premiers Crus. The wine which does find its way into cask has between 5% (Bourgognes) and 35% (Premiers Crus) of new oak – with an average of 25%, so one quarter of the entire cask population is renewed each year. The *partie cuve* is fermented at 22–24°C, to give more durable wines with less immediate aromas which need time to develop.

The following April or so, the cask-aged fractions are racked and blended together and returned to barrel on their fine lees until November when the *partie cuve* is added. The whole is then fined (with casein and bentonite), filtered and bottled (since 1993 by the Chavys themselves). For security, and for no other apparent reason, the wines are both Kieselguhr- and plate-filtered which is pity.

The range starts with fine examples of Bourgognes Aligoté and Chardonnay, both from Puligny vines. Both are top class, the Aligoté in particular being round and surprisingly fat (1994) with a nice, earthy undertone. The Village Pulignys fill the gap between these and the Premiers Crus – the undoubted picks of this good cellar. The Charmes has a marked Meursault-ish character, quite fleshy and powerful but with a noticeable breadth underneath the elegance – hardly surprising, since the vineyard lies below Puligny's Les Referts on the limit of Meursault's Charmes.

The Perrières, from young vines, shows the powerful stoniness from which the vineyard gets its name. With more latent complexity than the Charmes, it has a strong peely nose and quite firm fruit, backed by a nicely-judged touch of oak. Both 1992 and 1994 here needed a touch of acidification to correct a deficiency.

Clavoillon's 40-year-old vines contribute depth and a natural balance to its wine which is generally more in finesse than either Charmes or Perrières. The 1992 and 1994 showed excellent balance – though the former could have done with a shade more grip – and sufficient depth to ensure a decade or so of beneficial maturation.

The sizeable chunk of Folatières is in the steepest sector of this vineyard. Despite cutting the rows to break the water-fall when it rains, the topsoil still erodes and has to be collected and put back again. The wine is above all elegant – in good vintages such as 1992 and 1994 it is fat as well, but tends to lack centre in less ripe years. The 15 ares of Pucelles were replanted in 1992, and so will not come on stream until 1996 at the earliest. This, arguably the finest of all the Puligny Premiers Crus, adjoins Grands Crus Bâtard and Bienvenues-Bâtard and broadly shares their soils.

Jean-Louis and Alain Chavy are fine *vignerons* and winemakers. Theirs is a thoroughly dependable Domaine.

VINEYARD HOLDINGS

Commune	Level	Lieu-dit/Climat	Area	Vine Age	Status
Puligny	PC	Les Clavoillons	0.79	40	P
Puligny	PC	Les Perrières	0.36	1986	P
Puligny	PC	Les Folatières	2.66	25	P
Puligny	PC	Les Pucelles	0.15	1992	P
Puligny	V	Les Charmes	0.90	30	P
Puligny	V	Levrons, Corvées des Vignes, Reuchaux, Petit Grand Champ, Meix, Noyer Bret, Tremblot, Houillères, Nosroyes	4.47	30	P
Meursault	V	Les Pellans (W)	0.17	1992	P
Puligny	R	Petits Poirriers (Bourg. Blanc)	0.86	30	P
Puligny	R	Ormeau (Bourg. Aligoté)	0.63	45	P
Puligny	R	Les Bergeries (Bourg. Rouge)	0.77	15	P
Beaune	PC	Les Cent Vignes	0.33	23	P
Total:			**10.94 ha**		

Domaine Leflaive

PULIGNY-MONTRACHET

The hamlet of Blagny just visible from the vineyards at the north-east edge of Puligny, near the Meursault border

Whilst experts might argue the relative merits of one particular bottle of white Burgundy over another, there is rare unanimity over the Domaine which consistently produces Burgundy's finest white wines.

For years the Leflaives have supplied their neighbours and the rest of the world with yardstick examples of what can be done with the raw materials of prime vineyard land and the Chardonnay grape. The results are inspirational – Premiers and Grands Crus of immense depth and concentration, raw power combined with great complexity, yet with that dimension of aristocratic breed which defies description.

If the village of Puligny-Montrachet is self-effacing, no less is its greatest estate. The visitor in search of the source of its marvellous bottles will find little enough to help him. If he walks round the main square, the Place Marronnier, and heads for the western corner, he will come across a pair of black iron gates giving on to an inner courtyard. Nothing as prosaic as an identifying nameplate, nor is there a bell to ring to tell anyone

that he's there; all but the most intrepid would probably give up at this point and go off to Le Montrachet on the southern side of the square for a consolatory glass or two, or better still, for lunch.

If, however, our visitor keeps going and passes through the small white-painted postern gate, he will find himself in another, larger, courtyard facing a substantial old manor house, with doors everywhere but rarely anyone to be seen either coming in or going out of them. Having got this far, the only course is up one of a pair of stone staircases to the first floor. Whilst the right hand one leads nowhere, its twin arrives at a small, neat, paperless office, manned by a computer apparently working away in an appropriately respectful manner, all on its own.

It is fair to say that the Domaine does not encourage visitors to turn up hoping for the best. However much you love Leflaive's wines, you are more likely to succeed if you come armed with an appointment, or at least with an introduction from one of their importers, than by trying the 'I've come 10,000 miles just to be here' approach.

This is an estate with a great deal of fascinating history behind it. As an excellent booklet, produced with great flair by the late Vincent Leflaive's wife, Liliane, describes, there have been Leflaives in the area since 1580 when Marc Le Flayve (sic) turned up at nearby Cissey. However, it was not until his great-great-great-grandson Claude Leflaive who came to live in the Domaine's present headquarters, on his marriage to a widow, Nicole Vallée on the 3 February 1717, that Leflaives came to Puligny.

In 1835, his son, also Claude, divided up his 5 hectares (including a plot of Bâtard-Montrachet) among his five children. Only one of these legatees, again Claude (when you've got a good name, stick to it), kept his patrimony, and it was his grandson, Joseph Leflaive, who is the real founder of the Domaine as we know it, when he inherited the family house and a mere two ha of vines in 1905. The estate had dwindled not because vineyards had been lost, gambled or sold, but because of French inheritance laws which require all property to be divided equally among descendants, making it almost impossible to keep important Domaines intact.

Between 1905 and 1925 Joseph gradually built up the Domaine's vineyards by careful acquisitions, made possible in many cases by the desire of vineyard owners to leave viticulture after the *phylloxera* and *oïdium* epidemics of the late 19th century. As well as acquiring about 25 ha of prime vineyards, Joseph added another 25 in and around Puligny as well as numerous buildings, including the chais, and the *cuverie* in the Rue de l'Eglise.

With his régisseur and friend, François Virot, Joseph instituted a plan of systematic replanting on to selected rootstocks, taking the opportunity to replace plots of Aligoté and Gamay with Chardonnay. Having divided his vineyards between his five children in 1930, with a legal instrument which prevented them from further selling or subdividing, Joseph died at Puligny in 1953. In 1955, four of his children decided to cooperate in order to keep the Domaine intact. Of these, Anne and Jeanne, together with their descendants, are now the major co-owners of the Domaine.

Vincent and his brother Jo took over the Domaine in 1953 and ran it together until Jo's death in 1982. There being a family tradition of always having two managers at the Domaine, Jo's son Olivier was put in joint charge with his uncle Vincent in 1986. Vincent, a man of forceful zeal, died in 1993, having ceded his place to his daughter Anne-Claude in 1990.

Thus flows the history of a great estate. Now, firmly in the hands of an eminently capable younger generation, Domaine Leflaive seems set for a future no less illustrious than its past. Anne-Claude, an intelligent and articulate woman, is now in full-time charge. She is assisted by her cousin, Olivier, who also runs his own Domaine in Puligny and divides his time between that enterprise and the Domaine, receiving clients and travelling widely. There is also a monthly council of 25 of the Domaine's principal shareholders, to discuss major policy decisions and to keep everyone informed. Reports of (understandable) confusion among clients with two entirely separate Leflaive wine-producers in Puligny, and of Olivier wishing to become more actively involved in day-to-day affairs of the Domaine, have led to rumours of dissent. It would be unfortunate if everything Anne-Claude has worked to achieve were to be compromised by family argument.

Anne-Claude is backed by a formidable technical team : Pierre Morey, from Meursault, appointed winemaker on the retirement of Jean Virot (François' son) and Jean Jafflin, who replaced Michel Mourlon as Chef de Culture, both in 1987.

Leflaive's vineyard holdings are awe-inspiring: in Grands Crus: 2 ha of Chevalier-Montrachet (out of a total of 7); 2 of Bâtard-Montrachet (out of 12) and one of Bienvenue-Bâtard-Montrachet (out of 2.3). In Premiers Crus: 3 ha of Pucelles; 0.7 of Combettes, one of Folatières and almost 5 of Clavoillon, plus Puligny Village and some red Premier Cru Blagny. All this makes Leflaive the single largest owner of Premier and Grand Cru vineyards in Puligny – a total of 21 ha.

Until 1994, they owned no Le Montrachet. In that year, they bought a minuscule patch in the *secteur* Chassange, making them the first, and so far only, proprietor in Puligny to own vines in this greatest of white Burgundy vineyards. Even so, 0.08 hectares is hardly an effective presence, producing just over a cask-full – 30 cases. Fortunately, their Chevaliers – of which there are some 7–800 cases – out-distance most Montrachets.

The accession of a younger generation to the Domaine's management has brought a spirit of re-evaluation and research to its activities. Nowhere is this more evident than in the vineyards. The widespread incidence of the fan-leaf virus – *court-noué* – especially in Bienvenues-Bâtard-Montrachet and other Chardonnay plantings has remained an unresolved problem since the war. This virus, which takes many forms, degenerates the leaf and thus inhibits effective production of grape-sugars by photosynthesis. As traditional chemical treatments have ceased to work, with vines growing ever more resistant, ever stronger products have had to be developed.

Anne-Claude believes strongly that it is undesirable, both ecologically and for the long-term health of these precious vineyards, to continue with this cycle of ever more powerful chemicals. In October 1990 a trial was started on one hectare of vineyards – drawn from all levels of quality – of a treatment system known as biodynamics. This, in essence, follows the work of Rudolf Steiner at the turn of the century, and more recently Claude Bourgignon, using dilute doses of plant-based compounds to treat both vines and soil. The aim is to stimulate the vine to develop its own resistance mechanism to parasites and viruses and to treat the soil, not so much for mineral deficiencies, but in a way which maximises the activity of benevolent micro-flora.

This quasi-homeopathic treatment is relatively new in vineyards. There are growers in the Rhône and in Vouvray who have experimented successfully with it, but its long term efficacy and consequences remain uncertain.

Biodynamics requires the application treatments on precise days and at precise times, calculated in part by reference to the lunar cycle. In one case, Leflaive was asked to treat just before sunrise, which required

workers to be up and about at 5 a.m. This, in addition to asking them to mix a teaspoonful of powder to 500 litres of water, rather than the usual 5 kilos of chemical, must have come as something of a surprise. No doubt the reduction in the miserable effects of chemical spraying on their faces and eyes more than compensates for the odd early hour. As long as they are not asked to dress in white and chant mystic canticles, whilst bent double facing Mecca, little difficulty is envisaged in getting them to accept what is still something of a novelty.

Preliminary results have been encouraging – more soil microbial activity, better rot-resistance (no conventional anti-rot treatments necessary since 1993), brighter and healthier foliage and more advanced maturity with higher sugar levels, but not at the expense of acidity or pH in the wines. Interestingly, the *court-noué* in their 40-year-old Bâtard vines appears to have stabilised – no better but no worse. Tastings of 'bio' and 'non-bio' wines from the same vintage and vineyard were inconclusive. The 'bio' samples had a more oxidative and mature feel about them, whilst their 'non-bio' stable-mates showed less development and more classical lines. It will take 10–20 years to properly assess the experiment. Meanwhile, 6 Leflaive ha out of 22 are now *en biodynamie*.

Elsewhere, great effort is put into reducing yields. Pruning is *Guyot simple* – that is one branch pruned to six eyes and a spur, pruned to two eyes, for next year's wood, which Anne-Claude is trying to reduce to five eyes. In 1988 the practice of *ébourgonnage* was introduced; as soon as is practicable after bud-break, workers are sent out to remove excess buds – both on the main branch and on the spur. This reduces the number of bunches and thus limits yields.

In some incipiently prolific years, a further special passage through the vineyards is made during the summer to remove yet more bunches. This green-pruning is painful, but necessary to maximise the concentration of flavour and sugar in the bunches that finally achieve ripeness.

In the knowledge that the consequences of a mistake will last half a century or more, the choice of plant material is made with considerable care. The rootstocks on to which a Leflaive scion can expect to be grafted are those low-vigour standards used by most other conscientious growers: 161/49 for the Premiers and Grands Crus (with the exception of the Bâtard-Montrachet which is planted on 5BB), and the somewhat less common Riparia, and a little of the congenitally vigorous SO4 for the Puligny Village vineyards. The Chardonnay clones preferred are either B77 or B95 – the qualitative best of what is currently available.

The Domaine has a policy, which borders

on fanaticism, for putting only the healthiest fruit into the presses. To this end, they like to harvest just a few days after the official *ban de vendange* – the earliest permitted picking date. Since the *ban* frequently coincides with the autumn equinox, they fear that any further delay might bring an unwelcome seasonal change in the weather – rain followed perhaps by rot.

Preparations for harvest begin a couple of weeks earlier, when 200–300 individual grapes are harvested from different parts of the estate and pressed in small hand-presses. From this juice the ratio of sugars to acids is computed which enables Pierre Morey and Jean Jafflin to follow the evolution of maturity in each parcel of vines and thus, eventually, to determine the precise moment of harvesting. When the time comes, the pickers are despatched, with specific instructions to pick neither rotten fruit nor fruit which is towards the top of the vine, as this is likely to be much less ripe than that lower down.

Once the grapes reach the Rue de l'Eglise, they are immediately pressed in one of two new pneumatic Bucher presses of 3,600 litres capacity each. These give a throughput of about 40–45 228-litre barrels per day. The juice is then dosed with sulphur at the rate of 25 cl of 5% solution per barrel, to inhibit oxidation and to help settle gross lees during the 24 hours *débourbage* which follows.

When necessary, the must is then *chaptalised*, whilst still in bulk and before the alcoholic fermentation. Anne-Claude looks for a final balancing alcohol level of 13 to 13.5 degrees for the Premiers and Grands Crus, and 12.5 degrees for the Village wines.

Fermentation takes place in large wooden *foudres* for the Bourgogne Blanc and Puligny Villages lots, and in small casks for the Premiers and Grands Crus, one third of which find their way into new wood – mostly Allier, with a touch of Vosges. As far as possible, indigenous yeasts are used, to maximise typicity and complexity; however, in some vintages, for example 1987, cultured yeasts were necessary to kick-start fermentations.

Whilst a long, even fermentation is preferred, no artificial means are employed to prolong it beyond its natural limits. However, Pierre Morey has recently instituted some trials with yeast husks which are thought to give a longer, more regular cycle. Throughout, twice-daily *batonnage* ensures an even distribution of lees throughout each cask.

Following a lead from Patrick Bize in Savigny (q.v.), the Domaine is now buying its own wood. The worldwide demand for French oak casks has led to misgivings, shared by Anne-Claude, about the quality of the wood used by tonneliers and in particular about the accelerated methods of drying which often lead to green, sappy flavours. She is now buying her own oak from the

Forest of Bertranges, in the Nièvre region, and drying it naturally at Puligny for at least two years. It is then given to a small tonnelier to fashion into casks. The ability to pursue this policy makes the Domaine the envy of many growers who lack only the financial resources to follow suit.

Until 1988, the grapes from each vineyard were amalgamated and vinified as one wine. Now, each lot is vinified separately until it has finished its *malo* and been given its first racking. This enables Anne-Claude and Pierre to follow more closely the evolution of the wine from each patch of vines. There are already dividends in the form of systematic, recognisable differences between different vine ages, rootstocks, soils and locations within a single vineyard.

Although the practicalities of such a policy are daunting – many small volumes of wine to be kept apart and scrupulously recorded – the experiment has been extended to keeping individual lots apart until bottling. It is hoped, eventually, that this work will enable them to further improve quality by fine-tuning the *élevage* of each *cuvée*.

Not usually later than April, the wines are transferred from the Rue de l'Eglise to the cellars beneath the offices in the Place Marronniers. Here, in a row of pot-bellied stainless-steel tanks, with legs that appear to be far too short for them, giving the impression of a sort of overfed metallic 'corps de ballet' waiting mischievously until no-one is looking, to break into a vigorous 'pas de dix', the various lots are unified, ten casks to a tank, and left through the following winter.

The purpose of this is to conserve freshness and structure in the young wine and to release cask space for the vintage to come. A fining with casein and bentonite (fish fining was tried but found to be less conclusive) and a single cellulose plate-filtration before bottling between February and April of the second year, completes the bringing up of a young Leflaive Puligny.

There is nothing particularly revolutionary or remarkable in this vinification of some of the world's greatest Chardonnays, except perhaps for the unusual expedient of a long period in stainless steel before bottling. What shines through is the infinite care to obtain the best fruit and, with an obsession for hygiene, to respect its delicacy. A clinically clean environment – clean tanks, picking baskets, floors, hands, pipes, air, in short clean everything, leads to clean wine. In turn, clean wine requires less disturbance and handling, and above all, less sulphur. Less disturbance, less handling and less sulphur in their turn, mean that one destroys less of the delicate natural flavours and aromas of the grape. The principle may be blindingly simple but in practice demands obsessive vigilance at every stage.

Tasting a range of Leflaive wines in the small, informal tasting room off the main courtyard, is as much a philosophical exegesis on what constitutes a fine wine, as a survey of the characteristics of whatever vintage is being offered. Understanding the Domaine's 'esprit' is a prerequisite of understanding its wines, and the better they are understood, the greater the enjoyment. A Bach fugue may be appreciated for its power or sonority, but says much more to someone aware of the principles of contrapuntal construction and therefore able to appreciate what has wrought such a sublime combination of external simplicity and inner complexity.

The Leflaive concept of a great white wine stresses complexity and harmony combined with finesse. A wine may exhibit a multiplicity of aromas and flavours, but if they do not combine harmoniously, the wine is unbalanced and therefore flawed. Such deceptively easy synergy, which characterises all Leflaive's wines, belies their true nature. Even the simple Village Puligny has a structure and class that others would be content to emulate in their Premiers and Grands Crus.

What is the secret? Vincent Leflaive would tell you that there is no magical alchemy by which a bunch of ripe Chardonnay grapes are transformed into exquisite wine, although he was adamant that care and control are necessary at every stage of production – from the clonal selection and pruning in the vineyard through to deciding on the precise moment to bottle each appellation.

However, whilst they may be necessary to the production of great Pulignys, care and control are themselves by no means sufficient. A vigneron may be able to control the temperature of his fermentation vats, and may be infinitely careful in doing so, but this will not, by itself, produce the quality of a Leflaive or a Ramonet. The vigneron's art is as much one of knowing what to do as of knowing how to do it. Behind the judicious use of technology there must be a feel for what goes into a fine bottle of Puligny. This is the vigneron's true art – a talent beyond the power of teaching.

What are the results of such toil and skill? A range of wines which make one's mouth water just thinking about them. The red Blagny from the picturesquely named Sous la Dos d'Ane – Under the Donkey's Back – is a wine full of seductive, ripe fruit with, as one might expect, balancing acidity and tannin. Not a wine for great feasts or for analytical sipping, but a delicious mouthful to enjoy with simple dishes. It is reasonably priced and usually excellent value.

The Pulignys begin with the Village wine, assembled from four different vineyards whose grapes are vinified separately. It generally has bags of fruit, superb balance and for its level, remarkable complexity. Of the

*Olivier, Vincent and Anne-Claude Leflaive in the
Domaine's courtyard at Puligny*

quartet of Premiers Crus, the Clavoillon, geographically midway between Puligny and
Meursault is the most masculine – combining the nuttiness of Meursault with the
elegance of Puligny; usually ripe, stylish and
several notches more complex than the
Puligny *tout court*. The Folatières, high up
above Clavoillon and Perrières, is characteristically finer, more elegant and powerful,
than those nearer to Meursault. The
Combettes, situated two-thirds of the way up
the hillside on the Meursault border, produces wine of a different character, with a
touch more earthiness and distinct tones of
grilled almonds, peaches and honey.

Fine as these three undoubtedly are, they
are invariably overshadowed by the Pucelles
– a vineyard just below Les Caillerets and
adjacent to the Grand Cru Bâtard-
Montrachet. In a great vintage (1983, 1989,
1990, 1992 for example) this wine has a sensational depth of flavour and concentration
and a dimension of class and vinosity which
bring it into Grand Cru quality.

The Grands Crus themselves, each with
its individuality and spectrum of aromas and
flavours, are magnificent. Leflaive's have
richness and intensity, power and complexity, and so much nuance that every sniff begs
a sip and every sip is sheer delight; fine testa-
ments to the winemaker's art.

Vincent Leflaive used to say, if you gave
him the chance, that his wines were usually
drunk too young. They need time to evolve –
to unpack and show their qualities. After five
years the Premiers Crus will begin to drink
well, but one should wait eight to ten years
before making a tentative foray at the Grands
Crus. A 1979 Bienvenue drunk in 1990 was
just beginning to show its real class, and a
1983 Chevalier tasted in the same year was
still an infant. Less opulent vintages – 1991,
1987, 1982 and 1981 – invariably exhibit the
same spectrum of qualities as richer vintages, but in less degree. You should not buy
Leflaive's wines by the vintage chart – there
are no disappointing bottles here.

Great white Burgundy has the potential, if
properly stored, to keep for a long time.
Anne-Claude cites a bottle of the Domaine's
Chevalier, 1949: 'I am always a bit puzzled
over the qualities of old wines from our
Domaine; but I assure you, this was oooh! ex –
tra – ord – in – ary, with aromas of kernels
and walnuts – ex – tra – ord – in – ary.'

Pierre Morey and the Domaine are fortu-
itous partners – a talented winemaker in a
privileged environment. Anne-Claude has put
down sound roots in this magnificent her-
itage and – barring family strife – there is
reason to expect a refulgent future at this
greatest of Burgundy Domaines.

VINEYARD HOLDINGS

Commune	Level	Lieu-dit/Climat	Area	Vine Age	Status
Chassagne	GC	Montrachet	0.08	1950	P
Puligny	GC	Chevalier-Montrachet	1.91	1970	P
Puligny/ Chassagne	GC	Bâtard-Montrachet	1.91	1972	P
Puligny	GC	Bienvenues-Bâtard-Montrachet	1.16	1958	P
Puligny	PC	Les Pucelles (Clos du Meix)	3.06	1971	P
Puligny	PC	Les Combettes	0.73	1964	P
Puligny	PC	Les Folatières	1.27	1972	P
Puligny	PC	Les Clavoillon	4.80	1974	P
Puligny	V	Brelance/ Tremblots/ Houlières /Les Nosroyes	4.08	1963	P
Puligny	R	Les Houlières (Bourgogne Blanc)	1.74	1980	P
Blagny	PC	Sous le Dos d'Ane (R)	1.08	1957	P
Blagny	PC	Meursault Blagny (W)	0.55	1995	P
Total:			**22.37 ha**		

Domaine Étienne Sauzet

PULIGNY-MONTRACHET

It is not easy – nor perhaps is it necessary – to be thoroughly objective about a Domaine which, year after year, turns out superlative white Burgundies. A bottle of Sauzet Puligny rarely fails one's expectations and frequently surpasses them. If, in the greater, riper vintages, the wines exemplify that supreme combination of power and elegance for which Puligny is justly renowned, in leaner vintages, although less naturally opulent, they attain a level of finesse and breed which gives them continuing interest.

Apart from a cellar full of mouthwateringly fine wine, Domaine Sauzet has a view which most Burgundy-lovers would happily gaze at for hours; from the windows of its headquarters, on the westerly extremity of Puligny, one looks directly out on to the magnificent saddle of the Grands Crus. When the routine of 'declarations' bores her, Etienne Sauzet's granddaughter, Jeanine Boudot, can simply raise her eyes from her office desk beyond Les Pucelles towards Bâtard, Bienvenues, Les Chevaliers and Montrachet itself. In such circumstances and with a glass of Puligny in hand, a lack of enthusiasm for the authorities and their witless stream of paperwork is entirely understandable.

Scanning the vines, Jeanine Boudot could probably take in most of the Domaine's own vineyards. This is not a large estate, comprising 7.5 ha, almost all situated in Puligny.

It remains substantially that built up by Etienne Sauzet in the 1920s. He started at the turn of the century with around 3 ha and then married some more vineyards in 1924. Additions, largely of Premier and Grand Cru, followed during the 1950s, bringing the Domaine up to its present size.

In 1989, Jeanine's mother, Etienne's daughter, who owned the vineyards, decided, largely for tax reasons, to divide them between her three children. However, she failed to stipulate that the Domaine remain intact, so when Jeanine's brother, Jean-Marc Boillot, signified his intention to extract his share, the problem of equitable division arose, and with it, domestic dissension. Although resolution was not simple, it was achieved, and its impact amortised by the agreement of the other brother to contract his vines to the Domaine for 20 years.

The result was that in 1991 the Domaine lost all its Premier Cru Les Truffières, some Puligny Village, and part of Referts, Champs Canet and Combettes. Whilst this is naturally a severe blow, Gérard and Jeanine's own wine has not suffered in quality – there is just

one-third less of it; fortunately the Grand Cru holdings remain intact. In 1990, to compensate, they started up a small négociant business to buy in *must* from vignerons whose quality they knew and have managed to make up the deficiency, adding along the way Grand Cru Chevalier Montrachet, Puligny Premiers Crus Folatières and Garennes, plus more Bâtard and Bienvenues. The Bâtard is bought as grapes and vinified with their own fruit. There is also some Montrachet, bought from Baron Thenard as wine, and transferred in cask after *malo* – he won't release it sooner. Total purchases now account for around one-third of production.

Although Gérard Boudot now seems a 'natural', winemaking was not his first choice of career. He wanted to work in the open air, in the Département of Forêts et Eaux, and saw no attraction whatsoever in viticulture. However inadequate examination results and a chance meeting with Jeanine, whilst playing rugby in Beaune – her father was President of the local Club – decided him on viticulture and took him to the Lycée Viticole. After graduating and marrying Jeanine he took over the Domaine in 1974, the year before Etienne Sauzet's death.

Under his hand it has become one of the finest in the Côte. Initially great efforts were needed to re-establish the condition of the vineyards, which were what Gérard describes as 'a veritable mine of potassium' following the wild excesses of potassium-based fertilisers lavished on them in the

Gérard and Jeanine Boudot with their children

1960s. It took constant soil analyses and ten years of repeated, small doses of potassium-munching magnesium to restore some sort of equilibrium.

Also, whilst realising the necessity of using fungicides and insecticides, Gérard is anxious to avoid the vicious circle of ever stronger chemical products, which do nothing for the health of vines or soils.

As well as being an important determinant of the Domaine's fertilising programme, soil analyses are used to help decide the appropriate rootstock for new plantings. Vines die, often of old age, sometimes from hail or storm damage, but frequently from disease. Virus diseases such as *eutypiose* and leaf-roll are particularly savage, since long incubation and gradual, almost imperceptible degeneration, make early detection virtually impossible. The choice of root is critical to the maintenance of a healthy vineyard, and the adaptability of root to both soil and vine variety an integral part of that choice.

As with any quality-oriented estate, much work is done whilst the vine is growing to concentrate its vigour, in particular, a very strict *évasivage*, especially with the young vines, to remove double shoots and excess buds. Gérard considers this operation to be 'even more important than pruning', especially for the Chardonnay where a green-pruning, to cut off excess bunches, is not regarded as a credible option. The reason is that, while you may indeed end up with fewer bunches, these are likely to contain too much

juice as Chardonnay puts any additional energy at its disposal into swelling the berries, whereas Pinot Noir simply thickens the skins.

The mathematics of yields are complex; however, Gérard Boudot has no doubt that he would prefer, for example, 50 hl/ha from 15 bunches per vine, than the same yield from 8 bunches per vine; the larger the number of bunches the greater the concentration of juice and the correspondingly less loss of aromas in the final wine. 'This is very important – in fact it's fundamental.' So, there is no *vendange verte* here.

The aim is to pick at their maximum maturity, which usually means leaving the plantings on 3309 roots until last. However, delaying unduly risks overripeness, which may add an element of richness to the wine but tends to detract from its aromatic purity and thus from its typicity. This *surmaturité*, which can easily become the noble form of rot so important in the great sweet wines of Sauternes, Germany and elsewhere, tends to mask the underlying qualities of any wine it affects with its own distinctive aromas and flavours. Gérard justifiably describes choosing the right moment to harvest as a lottery.

After the intricacies of viticulture vinification is relatively uncomplicated. After dosing with just enough sulphur to kill the natural yeasts, the intact bunches are pressed in a pneumatic press and the resulting juice left for 12–18 hours to deposit its gross lees. In 1993 the fruit from vineyards damaged when a 200-metre wide band of hail swept across Puligny's Premiers Crus on 21 June, was destemmed before fermentation to remove split wood and rotten berries which would otherwise release bitterness and off flavours. The result: low yields (only 15 hl/ha in Referts) but more than acceptable wine.

Fermentation takes place in cask, provided there is space, otherwise the Puligny is fermented in tank. Experiments recently repeated, suggest that fermentation is more regular and complete with cultured yeasts than with the indigenous population. In particular, natural yeasts risk keeping residual sugar which refuses to ferment. This is a winemaker's nightmare, since if malolactic bacteria attack this sugar, the result is ineradicable 'piqure' – acetic acid – which smells and tastes unpleasant even in modest concentrations.

After fermentation, Gérard aims to leave the wine on its lees as long as possible, provided they are healthy. To achieve the finest lees, a prolonged *débourbage* of the press juice is essential. The finer the lees, the less the risk of a *goût de lie* which can so easily dominate and spoil a wine.

To get the best out of a wine's fine lees, it is important to ensure their even distribution throughout the cask by periodical *batonnage*.

This starts whilst the wine is still fermenting, when it is roused every two days. The frequency is reduced to fortnightly up to the *malo*, and thereafter monthly until the wine is first racked. Increasing *batonnage* played a seminal role in fleshing out the Domaine's 1993, which would have otherwise been lean and unbalanced.

In years with healthy lees there is a single racking – after some twelve months, and two months before bottling. The Puligny and Chassagne Villages and the Puligny Referts and Perrières are usually bottled before the following harvest; Combettes, Champs Canet and the Grands Crus are left until November.

In preparation for bottling, the wines are rack into *cuves* then fish fined for 15–21 days. Gérard has found that this particular fining retains more purity and finesse than the widely used casein. Also, 'the wines often taste better after fining than before – much finer,' so this is not just a matter of clarification. They are then Kieselguhr filtered, using the lightest earth – 'terre rose' – which Gérard has found to tire less than the traditional plate-filter.

Sauzet wines exude aristocracy and elegance. Part of Gérard's secret is the judicious seasoning of new wood which, he emphasises, is not used to impart its own qualities to his wines, but rather to support their own, natural, aromas. He prefers Vosges, Allier and Tronçais, with no more than a medium char, allowing a maximum of 50% new wood for the Grands Crus, 40% for the Premiers Crus and 25% for the Puligny Village – 'never above, but often below; the proportion must not be higher than that necessary to keep the wine consistent – that's the way to work.'

The range starts with a delicious Bourgogne Blanc, made from vines in Puligny but without its Appellation, yielding about 30 hl/ha. This generally far exceeds its official class, being full and ripe, with plenty of soft, fleshy fruit and good length.

The Puligny Village is invariably fresh and beautifully balanced with a floral elegance and Puligny power which are most attractive. Even in leaner vintages, such as 1981, or dilute vintages, such as 1982, Gérard manages to achieve a grip and balance in this

cuvée which give style and interest. Undoubtedly, lowish yields of around 45 hl/ha contribute useful concentration.

Puligny's vignerons have been blessed with some excellent vintages in recent years. In 1989 the harvest was virtually perfect: 'The best raw material I have ever seen,' volunteered Gérard, and the quality of the wines remarkable. 1990–1994 were also excellent – especially the 1990s and 1992s, with the 1991s, 1993s and 1994s not far behind, though somewhat less obviously opulent.

Referts is the most masculine of Sauzet's Premiers Crus – often quite fat to start with and somewhat more immediate than the others, yet often with a distinctive *goût de terroir* and muscle reminiscent of Meursault (whose Charmes vineyard it touches).

The Combettes is a complete contrast – with a honeyed mouthfilling panoply of fruit coupled with nuance, power and length, which brings it within a hair's breadth of Grand Cru quality – the 1989, 1990 and 1993 are unquestionably Grand Cru quality.

The hallmarks of Gérard Boudot's wines are richness and class. They seem to combine Puligny breed with an almost exotic concentration of fruit, without being remotely clumsy or overblown.

The Grands Crus evince these qualities in fine measure, although in different styles. The Bienvenues, from a patch next to Les Pucelles, more often than not, emphasises Pucelles' finesse rather than Bâtard's power and structure – more delicate, rounder and more accessible. The Bâtard, on the other hand, trades Bienvenue's brains for brawn, with noticeably greater richness and breadth – a big, masculine, virile wine, with finesse and style underneath. Both wines for keeping a minimum of 5 years – the Bâtard being the slower maturing of the pair.

The contraction of Gérard Boudot's vineyard holdings was a tragedy for the wine-drinking world – as if Ashkenazy were somehow reduced to half a piano or Perleman restricted to a two-stringed violin. Fortunately, this talented winemaker has managed to compensate, so Sauzet afficionados can continue to enjoy some of the world's finest Chardonnays.

VINEYARD HOLDINGS

Commune	Level	Lieu-dit/Climat	Area	Vine Age	Status
Puligny	GC	Bâtard-Montrachet	0.14	22	P
Puligny	GC	Bienvenues-Bâtard-Montrachet	0.12	30	P
Puligny	PC	Les Combettes	0.97	43	P
Puligny	PC	Champ Canet	1.00	35	P
Puligny	PC	Les Perrières	0.48	10	P
Puligny	PC	Les Referts	0.70	30	P
Puligny	V	————	3.10	27	P
Puligny	R	(Bourgogne Blanc)	0.52	9	P
Chassagne	V	Les Encegnières (W)	0.49	30	P
		Total:	**7.52 ha**		

CHASSAGNE-MONTRACHET

Chassagne-Montrachet – a long, straggling village, just over the old main Paris–Lyon road, the RN6, from Puligny – is by no stretch of the imagination an exciting place, but a solid, workaday commune without Puligny's compact charm or Meursault's open, commercial bustle. However, the excellence of its wine amply compensates for the somewhat pedestrian ambience.

Chassagne's origins are Roman. Human remains unearthed in Les Caillerets suggest that early settlements were probably further up the hill – beyond what is now the older part of the village. If so, then Chassagne has gradually expanded downwards to its present position, newest manifestations of which are a grand 'Salle de Réunion', a 'Caveau des Vignerons' and a large, rectangular, brick bus-shelter.

A somewhat unprepossessing exterior is relieved by occasional outbreaks of delightful little courtyards and mellow old stone buildings. Behind discreet façades live many of the families whose names have for centuries been associated with the community: Colin, Delagrange, Gagnard, Morey have rooted

SCALE 1/20000

here and spread their matrimonial tentacles. Disentangling the different affinities may drive the wine-lover to genealogical tables to verify that he is dealing with the right Domaine. The popular habit of adding one's spouse's surname often generates more confusion than it dissipates.

A widespread, but erroneous belief is that Chassagne produces mainly white wine. In fact, in an average year, only 42% of the 120,000-case production is white, the remainder being red; in the years following the last war, the red proportion was nearer 80%. This false impression probably arises from the strong international market for white wine which has enabled growers to charge considerably more for white than for red.

The change in fashion has led to extensive replanting, to meet the demand for white wine. Whilst most of Chassagne vineyards are entitled to produce red or white wine, there are sound geological reasons for preferring some *climats* for one or the other. Unfortunately, much recent planting has been on flatter land, whose high-yielding fertile soils are unsuitable for Chardonnay; resulting wines are dilute and generally mediocre.

A few years ago, Bernard Morey and others tried to draw up a Chardonnay map of Chassagne, in an effort to limit plantings to suitable soils. The initiative failed, through lack of cooperation. In the interests of their appellation's good name, the *INAO* should be asked to resuscitate and supervise this worthwhile project.

The vineyards start just over the RN6 and extend, generally with a good south-easterly exposure, for 2.8 kms before reaching Santenay and Remigny. The degree of slope varies, from the flatter land below the Santenay road to the steeper hillsides 1.5 km above, at 300–400 m. under 'La Grande Montagne'.

The Chassagne Village appellation covers 179.51 ha, almost all below the Puligny–Santenay road. Most Chassagne Rouge is produced here, although some excellent red Premiers Crus are made, particularly in Clos St.-Jean, Clos de la Boudriotte, and Morgeot. The soils designated as those best suited to Pinot Noir tend to have more depth and a higher iron-oxide content. These are concentrated below the village, mainly on Village AC land.

There are no fewer than 18 principal Premiers Crus, covering 158.79 ha; many are subdivided into 2, 3 or 4 individual *climats*, so the wine may bear either the name of the principal *lieu-dit* or else that of the *climat*, giving ample scope for confusion. The most frequently encountered are: Boudriotte, Vergers, En Remilly, Morgeot (58.11 ha divided into 22 *lieux-dits*), Maltroie, Grande Montagne, Clos St.-Jean (14.16 ha),

Fortunately Chassagne's wines are more complex and aesthetically interesting than its parochial architecture. This is the new bus shelter . . .

Chenevottes, Chaumées, Champs Gain, Caillerets, Embazées and Grandes Ruchottes.

Two of Chassagne's three Grands Crus – Le Montrachet and Bâtard-Montrachet – are discussed under Puligny-Montrachet, since they straddle the two communes. The third, and smallest of the six white Grands Crus of the Côte de Beaune, is Criots-Bâtard-Montrachet. This rather forlorn patch of land, entirely in Chassagne, extends to a mere 1.57.21 ha and produces some 550 cases per year. The largest owner, with a holding of 0.62 ha, is the Domaine Saint-Joseph in Santenay, which belongs to Joseph Belland, Adrien's brother.

Mme Bize-Leroy recently acquired a plot of some 600 sq m of Criots-Bâtard-Montrachet, in appalling repair, for what local gossip puts at 1.6 million French francs; at this rate, 1 ha of this, the least prestigious of the Grands Crus, is worth 27 million francs. One wonders whether this is commercially viable.

The cream of the white wines derives from the broad band of hillsides above and either side of the village. Here the rock is mainly oolitic limestone – a fish-fossil substance – imparting nerve and vinosity. Across this band, soils vary from *terre rouge*, with some clay in the Les Vergers and Les Chenevottes sector, though the white marls of Morgeot,

Boudriotte and Champs Gain, to the red, ferruginous earth on either side of the Santenay road and the very hard, clay and stony ground of Clos Pitois and Les Embazées, on the commune's southern border.

As with Puligny and Meursault, there is much Chassagne that is dilute and disappointing. Equally, there are excellent wines to be had from every sector of the vignoble; as usual, vine age, yields and the skill of the grower are as important as the appellation.

Apart from the Domaines profiled here, fine Chassagnes are made by Laurence Jobard for Drouhin from the Marquis de Laguiche's estate, and by Jacques Lardière at Louis Jadot, from the vineyards of the Duc de Magenta. These are yardstick, classy Chassagnes; they are expensive, but worth every penny.

White Chassagne, from top growers and good vintages, will keep for years. Wines from the 1970s and 1980s are still delicious and the best are by no means fading. The reds do not, generally, have the longevity of their white counterparts – being quite soft and plummy after 5–10 years and developing a lean, pinched character thereafter.

GRANDS CRUS OF CHASSAGNE-MONTRACHET:

Lieu-dit	Area	Prods.	Prod.
Criots-Bâtard-Montrachet	1.57.21	7	550 c/s
Bâtard-Montrachet	5.84.42	See Puligny	–
Le Montrachet	3.98.73	See Puligny	–
Totals:	**11.40.36 ha**		**550 c/s**

Domaine Blain-Gagnard

CHASSAGNE-MONTRACHET

Unlike his brother-in-law Richard Fontaine (Domaine Fontaine-Gagnard), Jean-Marc Blain comes from a family of viticulteurs; so, when, in 1980, he married Jacques Gagnard's younger daughter Claudine, whom he met whilst they were both studying oenology at Dijon, and moved to Chassagne, winemaking did not come as a complete novelty. Jean-Marc and his wife now have 7.26 ha of vines including Grands Crus Bâtard- and Criots-Bâtard-Montrachet plus five white and two red Chassagne Premiers Crus.

Jean-Marc is a shy, diffident man who works hard at his job. He strives to keep his vineyards in top condition and to maintain a high average vine age. He stresses the importance of mixing vine ages in each *vignoble*, not only to give more complex wine, but because a vineyard composed entirely of old vines will one day have to be replaced, with the consequent loss of several years' production. Separate vinification of grapes from young and old vines from his two Grands Crus indicated that the young vines gave finesse and fruit, whilst wine from older plants was noticeably fatter and richer. A mixture of the two was best of all.

Yields are maintained as far as possible at 40–45 hl/ha for Chardonnay and rather less for Pinot Noir. Apart from a careful *ébourgonnage* each spring, the method of pruning helps significantly, particularly for red vines, which are trained *en cordon*, spreading out the vegetation. Limiting the spurs to two on each of three eyes, each pruned to two buds, gives a maximum potential of 12 bunches per vine (=40 hl/ha). One curious feature of *cordon*s is that berries tend to be large at Chassagne and Santenay and small at Volnay.

The harvest is of great concern to all the Gagnard clan. Richard Fontaine is the fortunate possessor of a refractometer, which is shared during the run-up to picking for assessing sugar levels in each vineyard. Jean-Marc often starts by picking his 'tête de cuvée' reds – the Premiers Crus Morgeot and Clos St.-Jean – deliberately leaving the most important vines of all – the 'battle engines' of the Premiers and Grands Crus whites – until they are at optimum ripeness.

The Gagnard harvest tends to be a co-operative family effort, with pickers moving between all three Domaines, giving Jean-Marc ample time to ferment one vat before the next trailer-load of grapes arrives.

His aim is to make *vins de garde* – wines with sufficient depth and structure to be kept. SO$_2$ is kept to a minimum and lees contact to a maximum, with regular *batonnage*. He gives each cask a periodical sharp tap with a rubber hammer; the resulting shockwave keeps the lees on their toes, as it were, and is especially efficacious in promoting a regular *malo*. This causes mirth among his colleagues – perhaps it's the rubber hammer?

The whites are fermented in cask, 25–33% new oak, with a moderate charring. Jean-Marc tried Vosges and Cher oak but found the Nevers more satisfying. He breaks in new casks with hot water, to remove excess tannins – a practice which his barrel-maker considers akin to putting ice-cubes into a glass of Montrachet.

The wines are racked twice before fining in the autumn. The fining agent is milk or casein – bentonite takes too much out of the wine. Bottling is just before the vintage – six months earlier than his father-in-law, whose colder cellar gives a slower evolution in wood.

Jean-Marc's whites are invariably copybook Chassagnes – sharply defined wines, generally on the richer side, but with a careful balance of constituents. The best are Caillerets, Morgeot and Boudriotte. Of these, Caillerets is the most elegant and feminine – though it can start off closed and unyielding. The Morgeot, from *terre rouge*, is heavier, with a broader frame and obvious muscle. If there is a hierarchy, then the Boudriotte would probably just win; it combines Cailleret's 'primeur' aspects with Morgeot's structure – a lovely wine when young, but which soon closes up.

Of the pair of Grands Crus, the Bâtard is the more expressive, with more than a hint of Morgeot's breadth and virility. In contrast, the Criot's stony soils give something of the style and finesse of Caillerets.

If the keys to a fine white Chassagne are plenty of *batonnage*, good casks, minimal oxidation and scrupulous cellar hygiene, coupled with a well-balanced soil and small yields, fine reds are no less exacting. Jean-Marc systematically destalks his bunches before vatting; *cuvaison* of 12–14 days is the norm, peaking at 35°C. Yields are so low, that there is never the need to reduce the volume with a *saignée de cuve*, and *chaptalisation*, in small doses, as late as possible, prolongs fermentation by up to 4 days.

A peculiarity of the Blain red *élevage* is that only 10-year-old white wine oak is used. 'Chassagnes are savage enough,' remarks Jean-Marc, 'better to have finesse than adding more hardness with new casks.' Despite this concession to suppleness, his reds generally merit 5–10 years' bottle-age.

Of the two red Chassagne Premiers Crus, the Clos St.-Jean – from well-drained soil, with a lowish clay content and stony topsoil - has indubitably greater finesse. The Morgeot, from strongly red clay soil, is much harder, needing time to integrate and express itself. The 1978 Morgeot, tasted in 1991, was still young, with a nose which suggested that it might just be starting to emerge from hibernation. Although closed up on the palate, there was evidence of a long and delicious wine in prospect.

Jean-Marc Blain is a fine, conscientious winemaker who cares about quality. His wines may start life with his reticence, but they seem to end up with his smile.

VINEYARD HOLDINGS

Commune	Level	Lieu-dit/Climat	Area	Vine Age	Status
Chassagne	GC	Bâtard-Montrachet	0.37	9/20/40	P
Chassagne	GC	Criots-Bâtard-Montrachet	0.21	20/45	P
Chassagne	PC	Les Caillerets (W)	0.37	30	P
Chassagne	PC	Morgeot (W)	0.86	30	M/P
Chassagne	PC	La Boudriotte (W)	0.81	30/4	P/M
Chassagne	PC	Clos St.-Jean (W)	0.22	1987	P
Chassagne	PC	Morgeot (R)	0.49	28	M/P
Chassagne	PC	Clos St.-Jean (R)	0.22	35	P
Chassagne	PC	Les Champs-Gains (W)	0.12	15	P
Chassagne	PC	La Grande Montagne (W)	0.23	1988	P
Chassagne	V	Les Mazures + Les Chaumées (W)	0.47	30/45	P
Chassagne	V	Les Gougeonnes + Les Houilléres + Les Chaumes	1.05	35	P
Volnay	PC	Chanlin	0.37	20/65	P
Volnay	PC	Les Champans	0.36	13	M
Pommard	V	Combes + La Croix Planée	0.52	10/14	P
Volnay	R	(Bourgogne Passe-Tout-Grains)	0.59	30/55	P
Total :			**7.26 ha**		

Domaine Colin-Deleger

CHASSAGNE-MONTRACHET

While Chassagne has a less grand international image than Puligny, it makes up the deficiency – if it is sensible to describe it so – with a coterie of conscientious growers, producing wines to a high standard year on year.

Among them is Michel Colin with a judiciously spread 20 ha including a pocket-handkerchief parcel of 46-year-old vines in that curiosity, Puligny Les Demoiselles, plus a further 0.11 ha belonging to an absentee owner, for whom he also makes two Chassagnes, under the St.-Abdon label. Parcels of Morgeot, Chenevottes and Maltroie came with his wife – marriage is not just a matter of the heart in Burgundy! In 1994 he took over a small Puligny estate, adding Truffières to his range.

Michel, a serious, quietly spoken man in his fifties, the third generation of Colins in Chassagne, learned his art from his father, with whom he worked from 1964–1975.

Vinification of the whites, which form just under half the Domaine's production, is relatively straightforward: following pneumatic pressing which yields only fine lees, thus eliminating the need for *débourbage*, the smaller lots go directly into cask for fermentation; volumes in excess of 8 *pièces* start off in temperature-controlled stainless-steel *cuves* and are transferred to cask when the *must* density reaches 1020 or so.

Some 20–25% of new Vosges and Allier wood is used and the wines are kept on their fine lees until the July following the vintage – even if the *malo* has finished. Weekly *batonnage* is administered until Christmas when the frequency is doubled until after *malo*.

The wines are then racked into bulk, left on a casein fining for 1–2 months before being plate-filtered and bottled just before the new vintage, as soon as everyone has returned from their August holidays.

The policy of longish lees contact and speedy, early bottling is designed to give wines freshness both in flavour and aroma, whilst having the potential for moderate ageing.

Tasting with Michel consists of a delightful ramble through the Crus of Chassagne. Maltroie and Morgeot apart, all his white vineyards are on the Puligny side of the commune, which makes for consequently greater finesse. Quality and consistency have been steadily improving here and this is now a thoroughly reliable source.

It seems invidious to select one of the Premier Cru Chassagnes above the others; each has its own characteristics and temperament. The En Remilly is intellectually the most interesting for its situation at the top of Montrachet, at the limit of Grand Cru Chevalier, on the other side of the hill, where Chassagne meets St.-Aubin. The soil is poor, and the rock soon reached; however, being just below the summit, it suffers less from wind which tends to over-cool the St.-Aubin vines. In style, one might consider Michel's En Remilly as a junior Chevalier – it has its richness and structure, combined with power and finesse, and a dimension of class which the Morgeot, for example, sometimes lacks.

The Puligny Les Demoiselles is a curiosity, being the first small patch of vines in Premier Cru Les Caillerets – bordered on two sides by Grands Crus: Montrachet and Chevaliers; the filling in a distinctly exalted vinous sandwich! The soil is similar to that of Montrachet – clay-limestone, with a predominance of clay. The wine has both power and finesse, although with marginally lighter structure than its illustrious neighbour. None-the-less, Michel Colin's Demoiselles is a very fine wine which fills the mouth and begs to be kept for 5–10 years.

The 1993 and 1994 Colin whites are both exceptionally promising – the former some of the best produced in Chassagne in that difficult vintage. The Chassagne Premiers Crus Vergers and Chaumées have – as usual – greater finesse than Morgeot which, like the Maltroie is broader and altogether spicier. The St.-Aubin Les Charmois is a fine example – quite full and earthy, but minerally and attractively rustic underneath. 60+-year-old vines and the stony soils of the Chenevottes *climat* at the bottom of the village next to the road contribute to a characteristically concentrated, elegant wine – arguably the best of Michel's white Chassagnes. The first Colin Truffières (1994) was fine quality, full of restrained Puligny elegance and breed with good grip and nicely oaked.

The reds are less even. Like many of his colleagues, Michel seems less sure of vinifying Pinot Noir, although he seems to be doing all the right things. His reds are tough, summarised as 'Pretty tannic – ten years, no problem'. Whether this amounts to an imbalance is a matter of individual taste. The best, in the years when he makes it (1985/87/88/90/93) is the Chassagne 'Vieilles Vignes' from 30+-year-old vines.

These wines are good, the whites sometimes verging on great. Michel Colin's care and skill are rewarded with a faithful clientele, both in France and abroad. His wines find their way on to the lists of several grand restaurants where, no doubt, he sometimes eats after a strenuous day at one of his two favourite pastimes – skiing and hunting.

VINEYARD HOLDINGS

Commune	Level	Lieu-dit/Climat	Area	Vine Age	Status
Chassagne	PC	Les Vergers (W)	1.00	25	P
Chassagne	PC	Les Chaumées (W)	1.50	20	P/F
Chassagne	PC	En Remilly (W)	0.70	15	
Chassagne	PC	Les Chenevottes (W)	0.75	40	P/F
Chassagne	PC	Morgeot (W)	0.65	35	P
Chassagne	PC	La Maltroie (W)	0.40	10	P
Chassagne	PC	Clos St.-Jean (W)	0.05	10	M
Chassagne	PC	Chaumées, Clos St.-Abdon (W)	0.44	20	M
Chassagne	V	–(W)	1.50	25	P/F
Puligny	PC	La Truffière	0.50	20	F
Puligny	PC	Les Demoiselles	0.26	25 and 50	P/M
Puligny	GC	Chevalier Montrachet 'Les Demoiselles'	0.27	25	P/M
St.-Aubin	PC	Les Combes	0.20	30	F
St.-Aubin	PC	Charmois	0.34	35	P
Chassagne	PC	Morgeot (R)	0.24	25	P
Chassagne	PC	La Maltroie (R)	0.15	25	P
Chassagne	V	——— (R)	5.05	35	P/F
Santenay	PC	Gravière (R)	0.90	30	F
Santenay	V	——— (R)	1.40	35	F
Maranges	PC	(Côtes de Beaune R)	0.90	25	F
———	R	(Côtes de Beaune R)	0.40	25	F
———	R	(Bourgogne Aligoté/Bourg Bl.)	0.88	15	P/F
———	R	(Bourgogne Rouge)	0.53	15	P
———	R	(Cremant de Bourgogne)	0.50	12	P
Total:			**19.51 ha**		

Domaine Jean-Noël Gagnard

CHASSAGNE-MONTRACHET

Jean-Noël Gagnard is somewhat out on a limb, both physically and figuratively, from the rest of the Chassagne Gagnards. His house, an imposing edifice opposite Ramonet's cellars at the southern end of the village, is about as far as possible from his brother Jacques and his sons-in-law and he works completely independently of the rest of his relations.

Jacques and his attractive daughter, Caroline, are the 11th and 12th generations of Gagnards in Chassagne, and claim to trace their ancestors back to 1632. He worked with his father from 1943–1969 before taking full control and now has Caroline, a graduate of Beaune's Lycée Viticole, working nearly full-time with him, 'doing a bit of everything'.

The Domaine currently stands at 8.43 ha – beefed up with purchases of Morgeot and Caillerets between 1948 and 1950, and more recently with a further 0.5 ha of Caillerets.

Although Jean-Noël gives the impression of a rather laid-back attitude to the details of what goes on, he is a quiet, reflective person who runs his estate with care. Not an 'up to the minute' technocrat, but someone preferring a system which might accurately be described as stuck in transit somewhere between old-fashioned and traditional.

In the vineyards, rather than replacing individual vines, parcels are left until they are about 35 years old and then grubbed up. All but the steepest vineyards are treated with herbicides, after a single annual hoeing. Jean-Noël is contemplating *enherbement*, especially in the steep Caillerets, to limit soil erosion – a common struggle in Chassagne.

Regular soil analyses provide the meat for a five-year plan of adjustments in trace and base elements, and the Service des Vegetaux supplies a programme of recommended treatments for pests and diseases. However, for the worst malady of all – apoplexy – in which an apparently healthy vine suffers a sort of botanical heart attack through an excess of vigour, and dies – there is no cure.

Fortunately some of the more regular vine-pests seem to be localised. The grape-worm, for example, is much more severe in Volnay and Meursault than in Chassagne and Santenay. Nevertheless, a thorough selection in the vineyard, supervised by Jean-Noël's wife, is necessary to ensure that only prime fruit reaches the *cuverie*.

The harvesting date is also decided on the basis of advice from the Service des Vegetaux – rather than on individual *prélévements*; this is rather a rough-and-ready expedient, since maturity can vary widely between different sections of a commune, especially one so extended as Chassagne. One year, Jean-Noël reported finding differences of up to fifteen days in vegetal development on a single vine – although he reckons that it caught up by harvest time. Delaying picking beyond the cautious advice of the Service would undoubtedly benefit the wines, especially the reds.

The white juice is sulphured, given a light *débourbage* and put straight into casks, of which 20–25% are renewed annually. Although the *must* is not cooled, the cellar is

Caroline and Jean-Noël spring-pruning in Les Caillerets

air-conditioned, and so the temperature rarely rises above 22°C. There are two rackings – the precise timing depending on what other work is on hand. Generally, the aim is to rack as soon as possible after *malo*, unifying in tank, then being put back into the same casks. The same process is repeated in November, before the wine is fined, plate-filtered and then bottled 2–3 months later – an *élevage* of nearly 18 months: 'We remain traditional,' comments Jean-Noël.

Reflecting on the value of these extra few months in cask – the norm is nearer 11-12 – Jean-Noël can only offer in justification: 'I think that there is a good result – it's that which counts in the end,' adding that unduly early bottling can sometimes lead to problems with clarification.

Whilst Jean-Noël is chiefly concerned with the whites, red vinification is confided to Caroline's capable hands. It is based on total destalking and a longish *cuvaison* (12 days or so) at a maximum temperature of about 32°C. If the grapes arrive too hot, Jean-Noël throws open the cellar doors to cool them down, otherwise fermentation is left to proceed naturally. In 1988 the crop came in at 29°C – beyond the cooling powers of the widest cellar door – so a heat-exchanger was rapidly acquired; a contrast to the scorching 1947 vintage which failed to respond to bags of ice in the *cuves* and had to be flash-pasteurised at 80°C to ensure stability.

To date, with low yields and both fining and filtration, there has been need for neither *saignée* nor enzymes. Exceptionally, the red *cuves* are not *pigéed*. This is not some whimsical policy decision, but reflects the fact that the *cuverie's* two floors leave only 60 cms, clearance between the top of the *cuves* and the ceiling, making it physically impossible to introduce apparatus, human or mechanical, to punch down the cap.

After an amicable disagreement between Caroline and her father over new wood – by family tradition there used to be none at all – the reds now have 25%, which has given them rather more structure and completeness. *Élevage* mirrors that for the white wines – two rackings, the second in November, fining in cask with egg albumen and a polishing filtration just before bottling early the second year. In 1993 they tried bottling some red Morgeot and Chassagne village unfiltered. Jean-Noël would like to think that there is no difference, but it shows – the unfiltered wine has markedly more substance. For the moment, Caroline has won her point – Jean-Noël concedes gracefully.

These mild idiosyncrasies do not detract from the overall quality of the Gagnard wines. The reds tend to be quite soft and plump – not particularly long-lived wines, but attractive after five years or so. The Clos St.-Jean is marginally the better of the two

Premiers Crus – with more finesse and elegance than the Morgeot, which has greater power and breadth. This is explained, in part, by the relative richness of the Morgeot soils, especially in the lower sections of the vineyard, which contrast with Clos St.-Jean's lighter *terre rouge*.

The whites are delicious: the Chassagne Village, from the thin soils of Les Masures, just below Premier Cru Champs Gains, is quite fat and stylish, although softer, more fruity and noticeably less structured than the Premier Cru *cuvée*. This, a mixture of Maltroie and Les Blanchots, is very typical of white Chassagne, with a spicy, earthy component and quite broad in flavour.

There are six individual white Premiers Crus, of which the Clos de la Maltroie, replanted in 1989, only returned to production in 1992. The Chenevottes and Champs Gains, both first released separately in 1993, are a notch up on the Premier Cru *cuvée*. The one, from deepish, stony, iron-bearing fossil soils has greater power and richness, whilst the other has a lively, spicy, orange-peely character and noticeably greater finesse.

Caillerets and the Morgeot top the sextet: the latter from 17-year-old vines from two different parts of this large vineyard, is usually a powerful, plump wine, the characteristic depth of Morgeot plus broad finesse. The heavier ground of the La Chaume (*dit* Boudriottes), more suited to red grapes, provides depth and structure, whilst finesse comes from *terres fins* in the Petit Clos, next to the Abbey of Morgeot. Caillerets has less substance than Morgeot, but greater finesse, starting with highish acidity; altogether more complete and much classier.

The Bâtard-Montrachet is the summit of Caroline and Jean-Noël's range. This, from a mixture of 1959 and 1975 plantings in the *secteur* Chassagne, has, as expected from a well made Grand Cru, abundant power and complexity. Good acidity gives more finesse

than normal in Bâtard, with this vineyard's characteristic virility and firm flesh, Jean-Noël explains. The wine ages splendidly – the 1969 and the 1991 – tasted at the Domaine in 1991 and 1995 respectively – were both exemplary. The former had a mid old-gold hue, an attractive, fully mature, lanolin and hazelnuts nose, with fresh, powerful, complex flavours. The latter, beginning to open out aromatically, was still youthful and firm, with good fruit, power and excellent concentration.

The Gagnards' cramped, low-ceilinged cellar is another of Chassagne's several splendid sources of fine Burgundy. Caroline's arrival full-time (for how long when children start to appear is open to conjecture), has brought a fresh perspective to Jean-Noël's unquestioning tradition. In particular, a rather imprecise attitude to racking and a tendency to leave some whites a bit too long in cask before bottling, which made for some unevenness, should be reappraised. There is something disarmingly 'seat of the pants' about this Domaine – but what classy pants!

Grape set – the moment when embryo bunches become visible

VINEYARD HOLDINGS

Commune	Level	Lieu-dit/Climat	Area	Vine Age	Status
Chassagne	GC	Bâtard-Montrachet	0.36	25	P
Chassagne	PC	Les Caillerets (W)	1.01	20	P
Chassagne	PC	Morgeot (Les Petits Clos – Les Chaumes) (W)	0.80	12	P
Chassagne	PC	Clos de la Maltroie (W)	0.33	1990	P
Chassagne	PC	Chenevottes (W)	0.50	30	P
Chassagne	PC	Champs Gain (W)	0.22	30	M
Chassagne	PC	Places (W)	0.45	–	P/M
Chassagne	V	Les Masures (W)	0.75	20	P
Chassagne	PC	Clos St.-Jean (R)	0.33	30	M
Chassagne	PC	Morgeot Clos Charreau (R)	0.14	40	P
Chassagne	PC	Morgeot – Grand Clos+ Clos Charreau + Les Boirettes (R)	0.63	40	M
Chassagne	V	(Several *climats*) (R)	1.46	35	P/M
Chassagne	R	Champ Derrière (Aligoté)	0.44	–	M
Chassagne	R	(Bourgogne Rouge)	0.72	–	P
Santenay	PC	Clos de Tavannes	0.29	30	P
Total:			**8.43 ha**		

Domaine Gagnard-Delagrange

CHASSAGNE-MONTRACHET

Jacques Gagnard, a short, square man, gives you the distinct impression that he does not enjoy sitting still – someone who much prefers to be out among his vines than in his neat little office. He admits that he is a 'type indépendent' – definitely not a team man – and that 'no-one would put up with my character'. In truth, he may appear as something of a bruiser, but there is friendly charm underneath once you get to know him, not to mention a profound knowledge of the ways of the vine and the goings on of the Côte in general and Chassagne in particular.

With his brother Jean-Noël, Jacques is the head of a confusingly tentacular Chassagne family. Both his daughters are now married into winegrowing – Laurence to Richard Fontaine and Claudine to Jean-Marc Blain (q.v.). Jacques' own wife, Marie-Josephe – née Delagrange – has a sister, Andrée, who married a viticulteur, Edmond Bachelet. Each of these worthy husbands decided to award himself a 'Delagrange', further contributing to the confusion. Apart from joint ownership of some expensive machinery, these several Gagnard exploitations are totally independent and autonomous entities: none more so than Jacques'.

His declaration of independence does not extend to the vineyards, where 'We use the latest techniques of culture.' Jacques' regime derives from the idea that vines are like humans and need a balanced diet; 'If you ate a biscuit with a liter of water for a month, you wouldn't be left with much energy,' is how he explains his thinking.

Jacques' views on modernity are tempered by the transmitted intelligence of Mme Gagnard's deceased, pre-phylloxera, grandfather, another Bachelet. This acquired knowledge of traditional methods enables him to resist the more persuasive product salesmen. Instead of spraying mindlessly to treat rot, he is content to prune short, plant less vigorous clones and rootstocks and to control foliage to encourage good air circulation round the bunches. He is also closely following research to develop Pinot strains with less compact bunches; these might diminish the incidence of rot, but could also have negative taste consequences.

Like humans, vines live longer nowadays. Looking after them has become as much a matter of adapting the plant to its soil, as of a series of predetermined operations each month of the year. Whilst 'Pruning is the master-word,' the height and width of summer foliage pruning and the timing of harvest all depend upon vine vigour and the humidity and general characteristics of the soil.

Vines often die from 'infectious degeneration', a virus for which the only solution is to replant. Unfortunately, the malady remains deep in the soil, so the developing root system of a new vine, as it plunges deeper into the subsoil, will eventually become infected. In times past, the recommended treatment was gas fumigation of the soil, but the gases became trapped underground and released later damaging new plantings. Virus-free clones should overcome this problem, but success is by no means guaranteed.

Jacques makes excellent wines, of both colours. The reds, from 100% destalked bunches and an 8–10 day *cuvaison*, are soft, fruity and concentrated. The best are the Chassagne Morgeot, from his father-in-law's 65-year-old vines, which sees no new wood, and a deliciously silky Volnay Champans, from young vines and around 30% new wood.

The whites are even better. The life of a great white Burgundy, Jacques will tell you, depends on its first 24 hours in the *cuverie* – rapid pressing and plenty of water to keep pipes and working tools completely clean. There is no *débourbage*: 'What's the point, you have no lees left,' but 'we stir, we stir.' He likes his wines to gain richness from lees contact, rather than from selected yeast strains, which he considers destructive of concentration. So indigenous yeasts and plenty of *batonnage* are de rigeur in his cellar.

He also abhors new wood – 'Burgundy's major problem' – quoting approvingly Jean Hugel who answered his own rhetorical question: 'What is Meursault?', with: 'Chardonnay with new oak in it.' Not only does new oak dominate a wine and mask typ-icity, but the 'vanillin' it leaches out, being a sugar, will itself ferment and add alcohol. Although Jacques uses a maximum of 20% new wood himself, he considers that 'it is barely merited, even in a Grand Cru'; second-year casks have a far gentler and finer effect. In his view, new wood is one of the negative effects of recent prosperity – vignerons can now afford a new cask for its impact on the wine, rather than just to replace one no longer serviceable. Jacques' whites are fined in cask, lightly filtered and bottled 15–16 months after the vintage.

The Morgeot, from stony, clay soil, has good acidity, finesse and depth. With a slender bouquet to start with, it is generally quite ripe and fat. Boudriotte has less topsoil than Morgeot, tending to produce wines which are both drier and more elegantly perfumed – rather close-knit, but with noticeably greater length and finesse. There is also a small quantity of excellent Bâtard-Montrachet and even less of Montrachet.

Jacques has now ceded much of his Morgeot, Clos St.-Jean and Boudriette to his daughters, although he retains and vinifies all or part of the fruit. The Burgundian practice of clinging on to your vines till the bitter end does not appeal to him: 'It's our lot to die and also, when we do the tax authorities stick their noses into our affairs.'

His thoughts are bending towards retirement but the economics seem unfavourable – the rules only allow him the revenue from 0.32 ha of Village vines. Stirred by the inequity he growls, 'The wealthy Beaune doctors can retire and have as many vines as they like, but I can't afford to retire.' Good news indeed for everyone who enjoys his wines!

VINEYARD HOLDINGS

Commune	Level	Lieu-dit/Climat	Area	Vine Age	Status
Chassagne	GC	**Le Montrachet	0.08	31	**
Chassagne	GC	Bâtard-Montrachet	0.27	17	P
Chassagne	PC	*** La Boudriotte (W)	1.15	28	***
Chassagne	PC	Morgeot (W)	0.47	36	P
Chassagne	V	Voillenots-Dessus + Les Crais (W)	0.37	26	P
Chassagne	PC	Morgeot (R)	0.43	65	P
Chassagne	R	(Côte de Beaune) (R)	0.33	20	P
Chassagne	PC	*** Clos St.-Jean (R)	0.30	41	***
Chassagne	R	**(Côte de Beaune) (R)	0.25	46	**
Chassagne	PC	*** Morgeot (W)	0.26	31	***
Chassagne	PC	*** Morgeot (R)	0.25	28	***
Volnay	PC	*** Les Champans	0.37	16	***
————	R	(Bourgogne Aligoté)	0.15	41	P
————	R	(Passe Tout-Grain)	0.19	21	P
Total:			**4.87 ha**		

Domaine Jean-Marc Morey

CHASSAGNE-MONTRACHET

Although there are many points of similarity between the methods of Jean-Marc and his brother Bernard – hardly surprising sixteen years working and vinifying together with their father – it would be misleading to treat them as one large Domaine with two separate branches.

Jean-Marc is a bluff, friendly no-nonsense man, who lives in a commensurately pleasant house on the edge of the village. His amiable, open charm, however, hides much suffering. In 1990, his wife, who looked after all the Domaine's administration, died; added to this tragedy, one of his workers was killed in a tractor accident and the other was so shocked that he stopped working altogether. Thus, in the space of a few months, Jean-Marc had much heaped on to his broad shoulders. Fortunately, he's looking less harassed now, and rather rounder and chubbier, having acquired a 'partner', Katherine, to help him, and with the prospect of his daughter Caroline taking over in due course. Jean-Marc continues to make superb wine from his 8 ha. Albert clearly taught his sons to take infinite pains, especially in the vineyards.

Chassagne's relatively rich soils mean that without severe pruning, yields, especially for Pinot Noir, would be excessive. This explains why most Pinots here are trained *en cordon de Royat*. By limiting the number of spurs on the *cordon*, and by pruning short, yield is controlled. Whilst most of his Pinot vines are so trained, Jean-Marc admits to 1 ha of older vines *en Guyot*, somewhere in the middle of his vineyards. The *cordon* system also spaces out the vine's foliage, which increases natural sugar production and thus concentration. Jean-Marc is vociferously opposed to green-pruning to limit production. 'That isn't part of a viticulteur's mentality; people do this more for publicity than for quality; a proper *évasi-vage* is the best *vendange verte*.'

Yields average around 48 hl/ha for Chardonnay, although in 1990 they soared to nearly 57 hl/ha. He agrees with Bernard that Chardonnay will produce fine quality at yields that are disastrous for Pinot Noir.

Jean-Marc's white vinification differs little from Bernard's. They both agree about the need to use indigenous yeasts and to max-imise lees contact before the first racking, for greater richness and depth. Jean-Marc is not in favour of the fashionable *macération pellic-ulaire*. 'I spent a long time discussing this with Prof Max Leglise, at the time when he became rather obsessed with this 'truc', rec-ommending it to everyone from here to

California, but I don't think that this is really adapted to my style of wine.'

The lees are cleaner from the new pneu-matic press, so the juice is put straight into casks (15–20% new), without *débourbage* – for alcoholic fermentation. For his *malos,* Jean-Marc has tried 30 different strains of lactic-bacteria, without perceptible improvement – indigenous varieties give the best results.

The whites are always bottled in Septem-ber, to conserve freshness and, more pragmat-ically, to make room for the new vintage. The risks of drying out a young wine in cask in-crease with time, so unless you have a glacial cellar and thus a much slower evolution it makes sense to bottle sooner rather than later.

The Chassagne Village *cuvée*, from 40-year-old vines on flatter land, is generally good and 'typé'. The 1993 had a soft, broad nose redolent of lime-blossom, floral, with a hint of grilled nuts; on the palate, quite fleshy and complex with good acidity and a note of *goût de terroir;* a clean, attractive wine.

The Caillerets, although closed and some-what austere to begin with, is typically rich and *puissant* with good acidity. The vineyard is very steep, with heavy white clay soils which remained after the lighter red earth screed off down the hill. The fruit beneath the structure is quite 'tendre' – giving a wine which typically opens out after about five years in good vintages.

The other white Chassagne Premiers Crus, Chaumées and Champs Gains contrast strikingly with Caillerets. Chaumées is more 'primeur' in style, more open, but with plenty of guts and ripe fruit and lively acidity; a wine at once both *fin* and *gras*. The vines are on

the Puligny side of the village, on a steeply sloping hillside, with soil which is high in limestone which would account for a pre-dominance of finesse over structure. Champs Gains, from broadly the same band of rock but lower down the *côteau*, is somewhat more floral in character, with equally good acidity but a notch less concentrated.

Jean-Marc is clear about the style he seeks to achieve, for both reds and whites – 'I look for maximum fruit, but also for maximum keeping; paradoxical, perhaps, but my wines can be drunk young but will keep for 10, 20, 30 years without problem.'

The reds, vinified in much the same man-ner as Bernard's, are worthy examples of their appellations. The Beaune Grèves is per-haps a shade more elegant than his brother's, with plenty of 'fond' and character. There is only one *cuvée* of Chassagne Village – no Vieilles Vignes here, it all goes into the same pot. The wine is of medium weight, backed with tannins to give it longevity.

The cream of Jean-Marc's reds is unques-tionably the Chassagne Premier Cru Champ-Gains – a sloping vineyard just below Ramonet's cellars. A higher clay content at the top of the vineyard and limestone lower down combine to give the wine considerable presence and power. Both the 1990 and 1993 were deeply coloured – with aromas of black cherry and *fruits sauvages*. On the palate, the wine is invariably bigger and denser than the Village *cuvée*, with length and real depth – delicious and very stylish.

Jean-Marc is a fine and careful winemaker. The new-found stability in his life is already paying dividends and the future seems bright.

VINEYARD HOLDINGS

Commune	Level	Lieu-dit/Climat	Area	Vine Age	Status
Chassagne	PC	Les Caillerets	0.70	35	P
Chassagne	PC	Les Champs Gains	0.40	1966	P
Chassagne	PC	Les Chaumées	0.38	1951	P
Chassagne	PC	Les Chenevottes	0.22	1980	P
Chassagne	V	(Chardonnay)	0.94	35	P
Chassagne	PC	Clos St.-Jean (R)	0.19	1982	P
Chassagne	PC	Les Champs Gains (R)	0.63	1966/70	P
Chassagne	V	(Pinot Noir)	2.08	1957/68/74	P
St.-Aubin	PC	Les Charmois (W)	0.33	1979	P
Santenay	V	Les Cornières (W)	0.21	—	P
Santenay	PC	Grand Clos Rousseau	0.41	1972	P
Santenay	PC	La Comme Dessus	0.48	1978	P
Santenay	V	Chainey (R)	0.32	1978	P
Santenay	V	Les Cornières (R)	0.23	—	P
Beaune	PC	Grèves	0.65	60+	P/M
————	R	(Bourgogne Aligoté)	0.27	1985	P
————	R	(Bourgogne Rouge)	0.53	20	P
————	R	(BGO)	0.28	1975	P
		Total:	**8.25 ha**		

Domaine Bernard Morey

CHASSAGNE-MONTRACHET

The Moreys, with the Gagnards, are the most important winemaking dynasties in Chassagne. Their history is simple: Albert Morey – now in his late seventies – had two sons, Jean-Marc and Bernard. When he retired in 1981 he split the Domaine between them, retaining only his holding in Bâtard-Montrachet – partie Chassagne.

The brothers agreed that their work would be easier if the appellations rather than the vineyards were divided; so now for example, Jean-Marc has Les Chaumées, and Bernard Les Embazées. The only vineyards they have in common, apart from Village appellations, are Santenay Grand Clos Rousseau, St.-Aubin Les Charmois, Beaune Grèves and Chassagne Les Caillerets. Up to 1987 treatments and harvest were undertaken jointly but now they work entirely independently – it seems to be a question of maintaining complete independence for inheritance purposes, rather than anything disagreeable; no doubt they chat from their tractors from time to time when their paths happen to cross.

Bernard Morey is a large, friendly man, with a quiet, modern house in the centre of Chassagne. He works hard and devotes much care and thought to his task. He is one of the few vignerons who still makes his own grafts – about 10,000 in 1991 – giving him complete control, from vine to bottle. Cynical about the quality of bought plant material, he uses mother vines from Les Baudines, a vineyard replanted in clones in 1972. 'This is the only way of knowing what you're planting,' he adds with a laugh, 'this way the grafts are freshly lifted and don't spend two months outdoors before being used.'

The health aspect of clones may attract Bernard, but he does not believe that they are best for quality – 'It is heresy to try and transform a vineyard into two or three clones; they only give excessive neutrality.' So, he uses a *sélection massale* to replace individual vines. He is now trying to isolate the best qualities of each group of clones, a sort of *massale des clones*, to give diversity.

To satisfy himself on this point he vinified grapes from clones and from a traditional planting in the same vineyard separately, which confirmed that the wine was indeed of markedly lesser quality, even with a mix of clones. He staunchly contends that the clones from Les Baudines invariably taste less good than his other Premiers Crus.

What also disturbs him is the mounting incidence, over the last decade, of the virus disease *eutypiose*, especially in the Chardonnay. There is no ready cure, except to grub up the affected vines, disinfect the soil and replant. Unfortunately, because they are trained *en Guyot*, he has to pre-prune his Chardonnay vines to remove surplus wood, in the autumn while the sap is descending. This makes it much easier for the micro-organisms which spread *eutypiose* to infect. His Pinot Noir, being trained *en cordon*, can be left to be pruned until the spring, whilst the sap is rising, and is therefore less at risk.

On the matter of when to harvest, Bernard is characteristically forthright : 'I like to pick quite late; the malaise of this region is the current tendency to advance the date of the harvest.' He is in no doubt that, certainly over the last decade, the balance of advantage has been heavily skewed in favour of waiting; 'There has hardly been a year when we have not gained from waiting.'

He recalls one colleague who, in 1988, harvested his Chardonnay a full ten days before he did; the wines had two degrees less potential alcohol and a thin and weedy aspect which even prolonged lees contact failed to redeem. 'You must learn to wait.' Bernard's illuminating discourse on harvesting a friendly, but scathing attack on the over-cautious: 'It's no good falling into the trap of harvesting when the pH is right – this usually means the grapes aren't ripe and will simply result in excess acidity. The degree of sugar is more important than the acidity; you must be prepared to take risks. The last 8 days of maturity are those which give the wine more natural alcohol and power.'

Bernard's white wines are classically vinified with about eleven months of *élevage* from the moment they are put into casks for fermentation until they are removed from their fining, filtered and bottled. There are one or two concessions to the 20th century: a pneumatic press, which presses gently and gives such fine lees that there is no need for any *débourbage*; also, the juice is cooled to around 15°C so that the fermentation will not heat above 20–21°C. For the rest, the process is uncompromisingly traditional – lots of *batonnage*, no artificial yeasts and leaving the new wine in cask until the last possible moment before racking off its fining.

On casks and wood, Bernard becomes openly cynical: 'Even if you buy your own wood, you must sleep at the barrel-makers to make sure that they use nothing else for your casks.' The provenance of his oak elicits a humorously jaundiced: 'Well, we ask for Allier . . .' Whilst his casks are normally renewed at the rate of 25% each year, as he cheerfully points out, things can go wrong: in 1989 the usual quantity of barrels was ordered, well in advance; in the event, the crop was small, so using all his new wood augmented the proportion from 25% to 30%.

Bernard's whites are fine and reliable. Deliberately long lees contact and naturally high alcohol (from that late harvest) gives them an attractive richness. In his view, there is no doubt about the key to a good balance of alcohol, acidity and aroma: '*élevage* in cask, on the lees'. He confesses himself bemused by the 'Californian method', which seems to consist of first centrifuging the juice to remove yeasts and lees and then putting back cultured yeasts to start the fermentation.

The Domaine's whites are normally fined in July following the vintage and subjected to a moderately strong plate-filtration before bottling just before the new harvest. Filtration evidently exasperates Bernard: 'It's a real saga; people want unfiltered wines but, at the same time, want wines which are clear.' He concludes that this is all a passing fashion which will probably go away sooner or later, if he doesn't ponder on it too much.

Tasting in the 250-year-old cellars beneath the *cuverie*, one has a feeling that Bernard and his views are all part of a tradition, which, like the mould on the walls, is not lightly discarded.

Although there is a little generic red and white, the serious whites start with the St.-Aubin Premier Cru Les Charmois. This is usually well-structured, with good depth and a distinct *goût de terroir*. The iron-laden soils here are poor and pebbly; this, and vines planted in 1956 both contribute to the wine's concentration.

The Chassagne Village *cuvée* is usually very good – because it contains a proportion of Premier Cru Vide-Bourse – which adjoins Bâtard-Montrachet – and because it emanates from 35- and 50-year-old vines. In good vintages it starts life with a masculine charm, quite firm and 'puissant', which needs a few years to round out and open.

The Premier Cru Les Baudines – 'the famous clones,' chortles Bernard – is situated at the southern extremity of the village, on the Santenay border, just beneath Adrien Belland's Clos Pitois. In fact part clones and part *sélection massale* this, at least in recent vintages, has been more floral and rather four-square, lacking the depth of the Village wine. After all, the vines are only eighteen years old . . . barely adult!

The Embazées, of which Bernard has 1.25 ha, tends to show best when it is quite young; a charmer, but without the 'fond' of either Morgeot or Caillerets. The light, stony and red soil gives finesse, but insufficient depth and structure for long ageing.

Supremacy in this Morey cellar is between the Morgeot and the Caillerets. Both vineyards have rich soil, with significant limestone content, which makes for big, powerful wines which repay keeping. If the Caillerets can be generalised, it tends to great 'rondeur' and 'finesse', whereas the Morgeot is 'plus solide', with great richness and power. In good vintages, such as 1989 and 1990, both are heavyweights – not lumpy or out of balance in any way, but just big wines. The Caillerets has a more approachable floral side when young, whereas the Morgeot is slightly deeper in colour and a bit more obviously fleshy. Whatever the nuances, however, both are generally very fine.

Bernard Morey's reds account for 55–60% of his production. Vinification is fairly traditional: the bunches are completely destemmed and allowed to macerate for as long as possible – 'If it lasts 3–4 days I am very pleased' – before being heated to 20°C to induce fermentation. Cement *cuves* are used as they maintain temperature more evenly and are easier to look after: 'Wooden vats are all very fine for decoration, but what happens during the rest of the year – they dry out, are rehydrated, dry out again, and so on,' is all Bernard has to say on this matter.

Fermentation temperature rarely rises above 32–33°C, although cooling was needed in 1990 when it rocketed to 36°C. *Cuvaison* lasts for 12–15 days – longer than that of most in this part of the Côte – and the *cuves* are systematically *saignée* for further concentration. Enzymes are added just before transfer to cask to help eventual clarification, which is also facilitated by the traditional practice of pitch-forking the *marc* into the presses, rather than pumping it.

The proportion of new wood depends on the vintage and the wine – the Santenay, Beaune and Chassagne Vieilles Vignes usually see 25% of new Allier, the Chassagne 'jeunes vignes' having somewhat less. Two rackings later, the wine is fined and bottled, since 1993 unfiltered, usually just before the new vintage or during the second winter.

The range of reds is small, but good. The Beaune Grèves – one of the best of the spectrum of Beaune Premiers Crus – tends to be quite soft and spicy – an individual wine, a Chassagne interpretation of Beaune. The Santenay Grand Clos Rousseau is invariably of a fine colour, with a slightly 'sauvage' nose and a long, soft flavour – a wine of great delicacy and reasonable structure.

In 1980, Bernard's Swiss importer sug-

Bernard Morey – a concentrated sniff

gested that instead of submitting samples to the Chevaliers de Tastevin for the lottery which is 'Tastevinage', he should market a *Cuvée* Vieilles Vignes. Since then, there have often been two *cuvées* of red Chassagne-Montrachet – the Vieilles Vignes, made from 40–50-year-old vines, and a standard *cuvée* made from younger plants. The VV comes from 2 ha of vines, mostly on the flatter ground, part of which is on the Puligny side of the village. There is a single plot of one hectare, the other hectare being made up of three separate parcels. 'Not a single vine is missing,' says Bernard, proudly, as the pipette disappears into the cask for a sample.

In vintages where he deems the wine worthy of separate designation, it is a fine example of what red Chassagne should be – moderately deep in colour, soft, plump strawberry fruit, with an overlay of delicacy and succulence which makes you want to keep sipping. Not a long stayer, but a wine which needs time to integrate its constituents – to absorb the wood and grape tannins.

No Domaine is perfect – perhaps the Beaune and Santenay are not as exciting as one can find elsewhere. Nonetheless, the standard of Bernard's winemaking is high and his label is a guarantee of quality. Since 1970 all his production is Domaine bottled – except for the odd lot which doesn't meet his exacting standards. He also has an allocation of Albert's fine Bâtard, which he reserves for favoured customers.

Bernard's interests extend beyond the village – he skis, professes himself a good fisherman, and enjoys visiting other growers, especially in Alsace and Bordeaux, for which he has a particular affection. He adores Sauternes, of which there is a small stack maturing in one corner of the cellar. He has ensured future supplies by sending one of his sons for a *stage* to Bordeaux and the other on a similar mission to – where else –Alsace.

VINEYARD HOLDINGS

Commune	Level	Lieu-dit/Climat	Area	Vine Age	Status
Chassagne	PC	Les Embazées (W)	1.25	35	P
Chassagne	PC	Les Caillerets (W)	0.31	20	P
Chassagne	PC	Morgeot (W)	0.64	25	P
Chassagne	PC	Les Baudines (W)	0.37	18	P
Chassagne	PC	Vide-Bourse (W)	0.20	55+	P/F
Chassagne	V	———— (W)	0.68	50	F
Chassagne	V	———— (R)	3.10	35	P/M
Puligny	PC	La Truffière (W)	0.50	25	F
St.-Aubin	PC	Les Charmois (W)	0.33	40	P
Santenay	PC	Grand Clos Rousseau (R)	0.41	23	P
Santenay	PC	Passetemps (W)	0.25	30	F
Santenay	PC	Passetemps (R)	0.50	35	F
Maranges	PC	La Fussière (R)	1.00	20	F
Maranges	V	(Pinot Noir)	0.50	15	F
Beaune	PC	Les Grèves (R)	0.64	25	M
————	R	(Bourgogne Rouge/Blanc)	1.10	25	P/M
Total:			**11.78 ha**		

Domaine Fernand Pillot

CHASSAGNE-MONTRACHET

This is another of Chassagne's fine Domaines, comprising 13 ha of well-placed vines, including 6 white and 3 red Chassagne Premiers Crus. Fernand Pillot, and his son Laurent, a cheerful, uncomplicated man, fresh from the Lycée Viticole and a *stage* at Saintsbury, the USA Pinot specialists, spare no trouble to make the most of their fine land.

Short and dark-haired with a wry smile, Fernand is in no doubt as to what determines quality: low yields, minimum fertilisers and an obsession with hygiene. Years working with his father provided a thorough grounding in the vigneron's art. His preferred *sélection massale* has now given way to 'clones fins', whose vigour make him a stickler for careful pruning and thorough *évasivage* : 'We cut off masses of embryo bunches.'

Pinot vines are trained *en cordon* and Chardonnays *Guyot simple*. Fernand prunes short – especially the Guyots which are cut back to six eyes. This and the *évasivage* help to avoid the need for a green-pruning, which he believes attenuates the vine's natural vigour.

As with many producers in Chassagne and St.-Aubin, Pillot whites are of higher overall quality than reds – although the gap is narrowing. Growers here admit to having greater difficulty vinifying red grapes than white – the Nibelung hordes of fermentation, maceration, destalking and *élévage* seem to conspire against them.

The principal problem lies in managing tannin – a substance virtually absent in white wines. The naturally less structured style of red Meursaults, Pulignys and Chassagnes in particular makes achieving a balance between fruit, alcohol, acid and tannins a precise matter, since the delicacy of the fruit is easily upset by an excess of any of the remaining three constituents. Thankfully, Pillot reds are now 100% destemmed – apart from a few boxes of whole bunches included in very ripe vintages; a distinct improvement on the former 70%.

Cellar manipulations are kept to a minimum, using gravity where practicable to move the wines, rather than pumps which aerate and oxidise. Reds from Chassagne, Meursault and Puligny seem peculiarly prone to developing a flat, cabbagey taste from premature oxidation.

The red Chassagnes spend about a year in cask, the Pommards 3–4 months longer, of which 25% is new Allier oak: 'fine grained, above all'. This amounts to a total maturation of 13–17 months.

Fernand reasons that fining gives finesse and is therefore necessary. However, if you fine and don't filter you are obliged to remove the wine from its fining and leave it for a further month or so to rest – an additional, undesirable racking. Ergo, he both fines and filters. The logic may be impeccable but the argument is not: if enzymes were added at fermentation the wines would clarify naturally and could thus be bottled with a light polishing filtration in all but the most difficult vintages – a better solution altogether. There have been experiments with enzymes recently, so perhaps a change is on the way.

Working out how best to vinify the reds has become more urgent with the inheritance, in 1993, of half the Pothier-Rieusset Domaine in Pommard on the death of Laurent's father-in-law – Virgil Pothier's brother. The 1993s showed distinct signs of improvement although some fine-tuning is still needed to balance overall structures.

The whites, however, tell a different story. Here, the Pillots are clearly masters of their craft. The juice is put into either enamelled or stainless-steel vats to begin its fermentation (20–30% starts in new, strongly charred, Allier oak). When there is no longer a risk of overheating it is transferred to cask with its fine lees. Infrequent, but regular *batonnage* ensures that these lees are kept in suspen-

sion. At second racking, larger lots are fined in bulk, smaller 'more important' lots in cask.

The cream of this cellar is undoubtedly the splendid range of Chassagnes. In such an extended, diverse vineyard as Morgeot, location has an important bearing on quality. The Pillots have plots in Farandes and Petits Clos – both with relatively fine soils, in contrast to the heavier, richer ground of lower-lying sectors. The vines are a mixture of clones, which give fruitiness to the wine, and very old *sélection massale*, which contributes complexity.

The Vide-Bourse – a tiny Premier Cru adjoining Bâtard-Montrachet – gives great elegance and open fruit and, though lighter in tone than Morgeot, the vines ripen well here and produce an attractive wine.

Noblest of these fine whites is the Grandes Ruchottes, the closest of all Chassagne Premiers Crus to Bâtard-Montrachet. The Pillot version has a pronounced green-gold colour with a ripe, positive greengagey nose. In its youth this tends to evince lime-blossom and the more floral aspect of the Chardonnay grape; with a few years bottle-age, this transforms to aromas more redolent of nuts and honey. The wine is usually ripe and powerful, with mouthfilling substance and considerable length, yet greater finesse than Morgeot. In essence, this is Fernand and Laurent's junior Bâtard, and a worthy testament to their skills.

VINEYARD HOLDINGS

Commune	Level	Lieu-dit/Climat	Area	Vine Age	Status
Chassagne	PC	Grandes Ruchottes (W)	0.37	24	F
Chassagne	PC	Les Vergers (W)	0.87	27	P
Chassagne	PC	Morgeot (W)	0.52	25	P/F
Chassagne	PC	Vide-Bourse (W)	0.45	26	P
Chassagne	PC	Champs Gains + Macherelles (W)	0.05	31	P
Chassagne	PC	Champs-Gains (R)	0.33	41	P
Chassagne	PC	Morgeot (R)	0.38	31	P
Chassagne	PC	Clos St.-Jean (R)	0.10	41	P
Chassagne	V	(Various *climats*) (W)	0.98	7	P
Chassagne	V	(Various *climats*) (R)	1.67	30	P/F
Santenay	V	——————	0.32	31	P
St. Aubin	PC	——————	0.41	24	P
Puligny	V	—————— (W)	0.50	7	P
Pommard	PC	Clos de Verger	0.42	21	F/P
Pommard	PC	Les Charmots	0.30	25	F/P
Pommard	PC	La Refène	0.22	44	F/P
Pommard	PC	Les Rugiens	0.28	26	F/P
Pommard	V	Les Tavannes	0.96	30	F/P
Volnay	PC/V	(4 *climats*)	0.73	29	F/P
Beaune	PC	Boucherottes	0.23 Pl.	1996	F/P
Pommard	R	(Bourgogne Blanc)	0.43	8	F/P
Chass/Pom'rd	R	(Bourgogne Aligoté)	1.69	30	F/P
Pommard	R	(Bourgogne Rouge)	0.77	35	F/P
Chassagne	R	(BGO)	0.43	29	F/P
		Total:	**13.41 ha**		

Domaine Morey-Coffinet

CHASSAGNE-MONTRACHET

This Domaine represents the fusion of vines from two already established Chassagne estates – those of Michel Morey's father, Marc, and his father-in-law, Fernand Coffinet. Taking over the vineyards progressively since 1979, it was not until 1990 that the lean, accessible Michel, now in his 40s, began to sell in bottle. Now only 10% finds its way into négociant hands.

Tantalisingly, there is Grand Cru Bâtard-Montrachet on both sides of the family. For the moment, Marc is holding on to his, but Michel will have Fernand's vines by the turn of the century (at present the crop is sold to Drouhin).

The standard here is excellent, across a range which consists mainly of Chassagne Village and Premiers Crus, both red and white. In fact, the Domaine is split almost 50:50 between the colours, with three Premiers Crus in white and two in red.

The nerve centre of the Morey-Coffinet operation is a splendid early-19th-century mansion at the top of the village, backing on to the Clos St.-Jean, meticulously restored over the years since they bought it in 1978. Underneath, are five galleries of 16th-century cellars with magnificent honey-coloured stone vaulting – some of the most impressive in the village. Rows of casks, aligned with military precision, attest to the care and attention which characterise Michel's way of working.

With the exception of eschewing anti-rot treatments since 1987 – 'They're useless,' Michel argues – the vines are tended by traditional means. Disc-ploughed and herbicided, then mainly Bordeaux mixture and sulphur to counteract viral and fungal disease – for example, oïdium, which ran riot in Chassagne in 1994. There are neither fertilisers nor green-pruning (except for vigorous young vines), just yields kept down to 45 hl/ha for Pinot Noir and 50 for Chardonnay. Michel invites those who are told of crop levels of 30 hl/ha to walk around and examine the vineyards: 'Often, a quarter of the vines are diseased or missing, so the real yield is much higher.'

Vinifications are uncontroversial – white fermentations begin in tank and finish in cask, to avoid worries about rocketing temperatures. Bottling is deliberately early – around 11 months, since Michel firmly believes that white wine needs early bottling; this, partly because he prefers young, fresh aromas, and partly because he fears the wine will dry out if kept in cask any longer.

Michel Morey-Coffinet

His whites are fined, but not filtered.

As for wood, Michel is wryly cynical. Although his predilection is for Allier for whites and Vosges for reds, he reckons that it all depends on the quality of the cask, but realises that you can't tell whether you've got it right until later. At present, the Chassagne whites see 33% new oak (40% for the Caillerets) and the red Premiers Crus 40–50%, depending on the vintage.

Although red Chassagne is generally regarded with indifference by the connoisseur press, Michel Morey's are among the best in the village and well worth looking out for. In style, soft and supple with plenty of ripe fruit, they exude Pinot purity and have the structure to age well over 5 or so years. Wisely, the crop is largely destemmed – 80% in 1994, 100% in 1993, which gives a plump, soft mouthfeel to the wines and avoids much of the hard, green stemminess one so often finds in the southern Appellations of the Côte de Beaune. Of the two Premiers Crus, the Morgeot (from 40-year-old vines) is the firmer and better structured, although both are finely made.

The white Chassagnes are top-class, from a soft, fleshy Village wine to a midweight, elegant Caillerets, with distinct mineral undertones, and a fine, broad and powerful La Romanée. This latter is a relatively little seen Premier Cru situated at around 300 metres, below La Grande Montagne. Its mainly limestone soils – especially thin in the top, steeper section – produce a long, balanced raft of flavours and characteristic, unusual, aromas of quince. In fact, there is a quince tree in the vineyard (which has nothing to do with it) and Michel is inundated with requests from his fellow vignerons to pick some of the fruit – presumably for their wives to turn into quince jelly. His Caillerets vines, covering the entire vertical extent of the vineyard, march in a long strip alongside Jean-Marc Morey's. Wine from younger vines is sold off in bulk.

Some may consider that 11 months' maturation is insufficient for whites which should be capable of lasting years in bottle. In theory they are right. However, Michel Morey's wines are firm and well-constituted, with enough in them to age for 10 years or so. This mirrors his own preference for the aromas and flavours of youth rather than age. A conscientious, self-taught winemaker and a fine source of Chassagnes of both colours.

Commune	Level	Lieu-dit/Climat	Area	Status
Chassagne	PC	Les Caillerets (W)	0.65	P
Chassagne	PC	La Romanée (W)	0.70	P
Chassagne	V	(W)	1.50	P
Chassagne	R	(Bourgogne Blanc)	0.50	P
Chassagne	PC	Clos St.-Jean (R)	0.20	P
Chassagne	PC	Morgeot (R)	0.50	P
Chassagne	V	(R)	1.50	P
Chassagne	R	(Bourgogne Rouge)	1.50	P
Total:			**7.05 ha**	

Domaine Ramonet

CHASSAGNE-MONTRACHET

If there is one Domaine which can challenge Leflaive and Sauzet for the overall consistency and excellence of their white wines it is Domaine Ramonet in Chassagne. Although there have been eccentricities and hiccups, due to uneven bottlings rather than inherently poor winemaking, this estate regularly produces remarkable wines at every level, from superb Village Chassagnes to masterpiece Grands Crus.

By Burgundian standards, this is not an old-established outfit, being no more than a third generation parvenu. Started by Pierre Ramonet during the late 1920s, it came briefly into the hands of his son André before passing to the present custodians – André's sons Jean-Claude and Noël. Pierre Ramonet had married a Mlle Prudhon, so for a time the wines were sold under their joint names or, confusingly, as Domaine André Ramonet – only the label differed. However when the brothers created a Société Civile to exploit the Domaine's vineyards, the name was changed to Domaine Ramonet. Now, following André's death, wines are appearing labelled variously as Noël Ramonet and simply Ramonet.

Vineyards have been acquired gradually since the first purchase in 1934 – a parcel of Chassagne Premier Cru Ruchottes. The most recent acquisition was the Montrachet in 1978. Interestingly, all the Ramonet Grands Crus are in the commune of Puligny, although the Domaine itself operates from Chassagne.

The visitor to the corner of a quiet little square tucked away at the far end of Chassagne, will find no identification, just an undistinguished modern *cuverie* building, with functional cellars beneath. The office, if it can be called that, consists of a partitioned-off cubicle on an upper level, next to a grindingly noisy labelling machine. The Domaine's idiosyncratic administration is orchestrated elsewhere in the village.

Pierre Ramonet vinified his last vintage in 1983 with André; the following year Noël and his brother took control. Although both take joint responsibility for everything, the division of labour allows Noël to concentrate on the cellar work whilst Jean-Claude tends the vines and, being computer-literate, superintends the office-work. Some jobs, such as pruning and tasting are joint undertakings, which makes for an integrated operation. 'From graft to bottle – we do it all,' barks Noël; 'The patron is in the vineyard, in the cellar – everywhere!'

Noël, André and Jean-Claude Ramonet outside their cuverie

Noël Ramonet, a shock-haired, track-suited, studiedly eccentric individual in his thirties, is the more vociferous of the two brothers. Although appearing to disdain publicity, he clearly relishes the opportunity to air his views, a proceeding carried on in short, ballistic sentences from which the principal verb is frequently omitted as if, shorn of unnecessary verbiage, they might be expected to travel faster: 'No stainless-steel here; personal policy!'

In the vineyards, efforts are directed to keeping vine age high and yields low. Until they are 30, vines succumbing to frost or disease are replaced individually; thereafter the parcel is left until the time comes for complete replantation. The Ramonets consider the minimum age at which a vine will produce wine of sufficient quality for their high standards, to be of equal importance. Produce of 'jeune vignes' – i.e. vines below 18 – is not incorporated into Domaine *cuvées*.

Beyond a generalised statement of uncontentious principles, Noël Ramonet is imprecise as to the details of their vineyard regime. One gets the impression that he regards viticulture as unsophisticated outdoor farming work – a necessary but irritating step to obtaining raw material for him to work on. The starred chef may have to look after his kitchen-garden, but the interest really starts when he gets the vegetables into his pots.

The Ramonet pots produce nectar. For all his apparently bluff indifference, Noël knows perfectly well what fine wine is about and, if the 'office' is any guide, tastes whatever is finest from around the world. Apart from a scarcely-credible, anatomically record-breaking, pneumatic nude stuck on the back of the door – 'Miss December' on what appears to be a tractor-driver's calendar from a fertiliser company – the only embellishments of this spartan enclosure consist of photographs of rows of grand bottles with Noël standing behind them. Any spare shelf space is consecrated to more tangible memorabilia, in the form of empties from bygone tasting epics. These attest to an eclectic palate – Grange Hermitage, old Alsatian Vendange Tardive, 1947 Cheval Blanc, Petrus of various vintages, New World Chardonnays and so on. The finest wine almost always goes hand in hand with winemakers who taste widely outside their own region.

The Ramonet harvest generally starts with the older Pinot vines which take some two days to pick. Whilst these are fermenting – a period of some 8–10 days – they get on with picking the Chardonnay and the harvest traditionally ends with the younger red vines.

The reds tend to be supple and soft, for relatively young consumption. The *régionales* – the Bourgogne Grande Ordinaire and the Passe-Tout-Grains – are vinified in autovinificators. The results have not encouraged Noël, who finds that the wines made thus lack finesse. The Chassagne reds are vinified differently – with 50% destalking and a species of *carbonic maceration* in semi-closed cement *cuves*, with two *pigéages* and two *remontages à la pompe* daily for about 8 days. They then spend a year in cask – with 35% of new Vosges and Tronçais oak. Whether or not the *malos* are completed, the wines are then racked, unified in tank and fined with albumen. Three weeks later they are filtered through wide pore plates – which Noël does not regard as filtration – and bottled.

Both the Clos de la Boudriotte, from old vines on clay-limestone soils, and the Morgeot, from younger vines on soils with more clay, are quite ripe and stylish. Never aggressive, the tannins always seem to balance the fruit and acidity. The Boudriotte is the more concentrated of the pair, typically smelling of *fruits rouges*, griotte and Kirsch cherries. The 50% of whole bunches undoubtedly contributes to the characteristic softness of these reds, although they would profit in extract and structure from a day or two longer *cuvaison* and possibly a few more stalks in riper years.

The white vinification is started off in stainless-steel or enamelled *cuves*, where the *must* is *chaptalised* if necessary. Once fermentation is underway, the wines are transferred to cask – again 35% of new wood, but here Chatillonais and Tronçais, lightly charred – where it is completed. There are generally 3–4 days of strong fermentation at 22–25°C.

Unusually for white winemaking in the Côte de Beaune, Noël Ramonet does not *batonner*. Apart from being a 'tradition familiale', he argues that stirring risks mixing both good and bad lees together. 'If you do this, your wine won't be well nourished . . . personal policy'!

The wines remain on their lees for some considerable time before their first racking when they are assembled in *foudres*. After a total of 12–15 months in cask, they are racked again and then fined with a mixture of casein and bentonite, left a further 21 days, and bottled directly off their fining with a light plate-filtration.

The Ramonet cellars are a doubtful example of order, but this does them no apparent harm. On the contrary, year after year they nurture some of the most stylish and concentrated white wines which vineyard land is capable of yielding.

When young, the Ramonet Chassagnes have a glorious green tinge and a modestly exotic spectrum of fruit-based aromas. The Morgeot, from a part clay/part limestone soil is usually the most delicate of the 3 Premiers Crus, whilst the Cailleret, from hillside land with a higher limestone content, is richer, with greater depth and firmer underlying structure. The Ruchottes, also from hillsides,

with a higher proportion of clay than the Caillerets, is fuller and more supple, with one ha of 60-year-old vines contributing to concentration.

Noël Ramonet has scant patience with colleagues who cut corners or overcrop, especially those whose wines he finds unbalanced for want of acidity – a problem especially in super-ripe years – 1983, 1985, 1988, 1989, 1990 and 1992. 'Too much crop,' he snaps, addingand 'low yields and old vines are the only solution.'

Good as are the white Chassagne Premiers Crus, the Grands Crus are several leaps up that rocky ladder leading to the elusive chimera of absolute perfection. Quantities are pitifully small – seven 300-bottle *pièces* of Bâtard-Montrachet, nine of Bienvenues-Bâtard-Montrachet and finally, huddled together in a far corner of the cellar for mutual society, a disconsolate pair of barrels containing the riches of Montrachet itself.

Noël finds no great or systematic difference between his Bâtard and his Bienvenue – 'barely a metre between them,' he explains. Any similarity is more plausibly accounted for by the fact that the grapes from both are vinified together and only separated at the moment of transfer to cask. The Bâtard goes into Chatillonais barrels – 'more violent, masculine, hard,' chants Noël – while the Bienvenue has Tronçais – 'much finer!'

Both wines are as rich and powerful in impact as one would expect from Grand Cru and a great Domaine. They have deeper concentration, greater complexity and considerably more power than the Chassagnes, combining the seemingly immiscible characteristics of finesse and power. Perhaps the Bâtard is a shade more masculine than the Bienvenue, but there is really very little in it.

Unable to meet the demands of 35% of two casks, the Montrachet has 100% new Chatillonais oak. The wine is difficult to judge when young and although not obvi-

ously more concentrated than the other Grands Crus (Montrachet rarely is) has an extra dimension of complexity and completeness which sets it apart. The Domaine has only made Montrachet since 1979, so those fortunate enough to have some, will watch the vintages develop with interest; the results should be spectacular.

Ramonet's wines are as near to the apotheosis of Chardonnay as one is likely to get (apart from a range of uniformly disappointing, flat 1993s). They are not intended for drinking young, but to be kept for ten years or more. Ruchottes 1970 and Morgeot 1971 were magnificent, complex and elegant wines twenty years on, while the Ruchottes 1978 was still evolving.

Noël considers that the best way to enjoy his white wines is 'en aperitif' or, if you must eat, then with the simplest of dishes. He is firmly against attempts to match fine wine to fine food – neither enhances the other and there is invariably a loss of quality on both sides.

Being minor wine-media personalities has led Jean-Claude and Noël Ramonet to develop a routine of mild eccentricities. Correspondence goes unanswered and appointments (if you manage to secure one at all) are frequently unkept. On the occasions they are, the reception is likely to be gruff, to say the least. If you do go visiting, expect the unusual. One visitor, rendezvous arranged, turned up to find Noël, whom she hadn't met before, stationed outside the cellars to tell her that he wasn't in and furthermore that, in all probability he wouldn't be back for several hours. When you're involved in the all-consuming task of making great wine, the unwelcome distractions of administration and visitors inevitably take second place. In the nature of things, one discounts the discourtesies although with a sneaking feeling that they are not invariably distractedness but more correctly ascribed to . . . 'personal policy'.

VINEYARD HOLDINGS

Commune	Level	Lieu-dit/Climat	Area	Vine Age	Status
Puligny	GC	Le Montrachet	0.25	75	P
Puligny	GC	Bâtard-Montrachet	0.40	45	P
Puligny	GC	Bienvenues-Bâtard-Montrachet	0.50	45	P
Puligny	PC	Champ-Canet	0.40	1993	P
Chassagne	PC	Les Ruchottes (W)	1.03	45	P
Chassagne	PC	Morgeot (R)	0.50	30	P
Chassagne	PC	Morgeot (W)	4.00	35	P/M
Chassagne	PC	Clos de la Boudriotte (R)	1.00	55	P
Chassagne	PC	Les Caillerets (W)	0.40	30	P
Chassagne	PC	Les Chaumées (W)	0.25	5	P
Chassagne	PC	Les Vergers (W)	0.50	35	P
Chassagne	PC	Clos St.-Jean (R)	0.70	65	P
Chassagne	V	———— (R)	2.50	35	P
Chassagne	V	———— (W)	0.90	40	P
Chassagne	R	(Bourgogne Aligoté)	0.40	55	P
Chassagne	R	(Bourgogne Grande Ordinaire)	0.23	25	P
Total:			**13.96 ha**		

ST.-AUBIN

St.-Aubin is a pleasantly tranquil, compact village, nestling under a band of gently sloping limestone next to a bend in the RN6 Chalon–Avallon road. Although only a few kilometres from both Puligny and Chassagne, the visitor may well feel that he is exploring off the beaten track as he meanders through its narrow, convoluted streets. Just under 300 souls inhabit St.-Aubin, most of whom toil in the service of wine.

The origins of the village date back to the turn of the second millenium, although recent archaeological discoveries seem to confirm that the site was inhabited during the Bronze and Iron ages. Henri Cannard records that in 1890, in the Champ de la Vigne, a great number of ancient human bones were found; further excavations in 1973 revealed a number of contemporary tools in addition to the bones of mammoths and hyenas.

The commune also comprises nearby Gamay – a small working village – which was a site of strategic prominence up to the beginning of the 20th century. The old Roman road from St.-Aubin led to a Maison-Forte thus making the village an important crossroads. At the turn of the 20th century, a local priest counted no less than forty-three 'activités commerciales' in the village, including 'a barrel-maker, two cafés, a hotel, a garage, an ironmonger, a cobbler, a grocer and a barber'.

Its illustrious past has gone, but Gamay remains an attractive hamlet, more noted perhaps for the grape-variety to which it gives its name, than for its Maison-Forte. This grape was brought to Burgundy by Seigneur du May in the Middle Ages and widely planted along the Côte until this century, when it was superseded by the Pinot Noir and its produce declared ignoble.

The vignoble of St.-Aubin is extensive – some 80.15.81 ha of Villages and no less than 156.46.09 ha of red and white Premiers Crus. The reds of the village are entitled to be marketed either as 'St.-Aubin, Côte de Beaune' or as Côte de Beaune-Villages; however, much of the commune's output is also sold as Bourgogne Rouge and Blanc. This will no doubt change as people come to appreciate

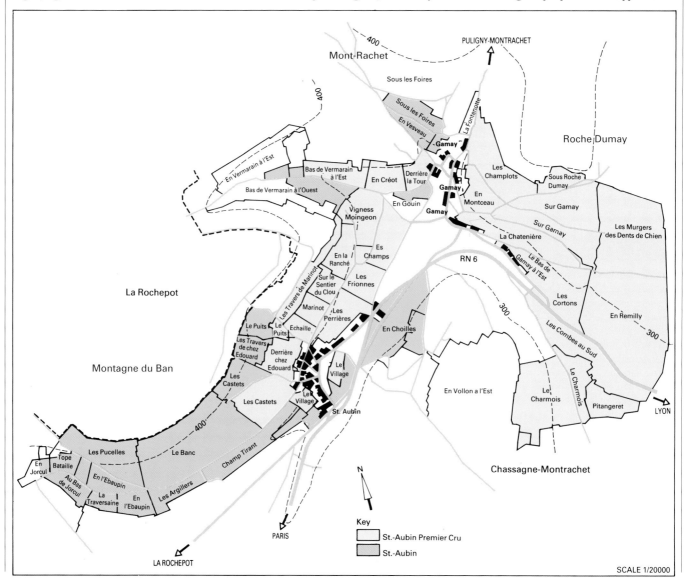

The compact village beneath the bare outcrop of Le Rochepot

the quality of St.-Aubin and as the different Premiers Crus become individually recognised.

There are two separate vineyard sites: one, the Montagne du Ban, is situated on an east-west axis immediately behind the village, with south, south-east and south-west expositions. Here are to be found some of the better Premier Cru vineyards: Les Castets, Les Frionnes and Sur le Sentier du Clou, planted on soils which are mainly limestone marls.

The second swathe of vineyards, all Premiers Crus, lie on the Roche du May, above Gamay, at an altitude of between 240 and 300m, and extends across the RN6 to the Chassagne border. Expositions, although mainly south-westerly, embrace all points of the compass. Here the soils are more varied, with brown limestones admixed with clay on the lower slopes, and more obvious limestones on the higher sites, especially on those immediately backing on to the Mont-Rachet. Here are the finest of the white Premiers Crus, namely Les Murgers des Dents de Chien and La Chatenière on the Puligny side and Le Charmois on the Chassagne slope.

It is worth finding your way up on to the top of the Mont-Rachet – if you can discover the right track – from where a short walk through a hundred metres of snake-infested scrub (it's safe in winter) brings you out just above the Puligny Grand Cru Chevalier-Montrachet. This is the nexus of three communes – St.-Aubin, Chassagne and Puligny and a perfect vantage point over the entire sweep of Puligny and its vines.

The band of limestone rock continues on both sides of the hill – indeed, the continuation of the St.-Aubin Premier Cru Dents de Chien – having lost Les Murgers along the way – reappears as a Chassagne Village appellation. The two St.-Aubin vineyards at the top of the hill are exposed to the drying influence of winds and are generally cooler than those lower down, protected by the hill. This means that they ripen later and thus, in marginal years, are less successful.

The wines themselves are well worth investigation. The reds, especially from the better Premiers Crus are generally robust and earthy in character, developing attractively over 5-10 years in a good vintage. Growers who do not destalk, tend to make wines which are over-tannic and thereby out of balance.

The white wines reach higher peaks than the reds. They have the ability to last and a distinctive *goût de terroir* – definitely an acquired taste – which threads through their maturation. A 15-year-old white St.-Aubin will probably smell of lime-blossom and nuts and have a nutty, earthy flavour which goes well with good fish and white meat dishes. It is worth sticking to the good vintages since the situation of the vineyards means later ripening than Chassagne or Puligny, and consequently wines which in naturally unripe vintages are green and lacking in finesse or fat.

The commune of St.-Aubin is fortunate in having a band of hard-working, skilful, growers whose efforts, until relatively recently, have passed lamentably unrewarded. Now, with prices of more exalted white Burgundy beyond most people's reach, merchants are beating a path to their doors for wines which, while never great, are generally sound, with abundant character and a bearable price-tag.

The best sources in St.-Aubin itself are: Gérard Thomas, Hubert Lamy and Henri Prudhon. Outside the village growers and négociants making good St.-Aubins are Jadot, Chartron et Trebuchet, Olivier Leflaive, Jean-Marc Morey, Bernard Morey and Marc Colin.

With this deservedly increased recognition, more wine is being sold under the Village label, and individual Premier Cru *climats* are beginning to establish their own identities. Provided prices remain sensible, this welcome trend is set to continue.

Domaine Hubert Lamy

ST.-AUBIN

Hubert Lamy is a large, open, deliberate man, who, with a handful of other quality-conscious winegrowers, is helping to establish the reputation of St.-Aubin as a source of sound, attractively priced Burgundy.

There have been Lamys toiling away in the village since 1640. Indeed, the last generation toiled indoors as well as outdoors, producing seven children among whom the vineyards were divided when Hubert took over from his father – who still lives in the village – in 1973. His brother, René, went off to live in Chassagne, whilst Hubert bought out several of his sisters and stayed on to establish his own Domaine – now 7.96 ha of red and 8.54 ha of white, spread over St.-Aubin, Chassagne, Puligny, Santenay and Cheilly-Les-Maranges.

Hubert and his son Olivier make the wines, whilst Hubert's wife looks after the commercial side of the Domaine. 'Mon trésorier,' as Hubert delightfully refers to her, not only deals with sales but also ensures that her husband does not overspend on some shiny, up-to-the-minute piece of equipment which might take his fancy. The treasury has been recently unlocked to the extent of an impressive new cellar near the main road, and smartly shut up again so, for the present, severe economy is in force.

There is no doubt that Hubert's winemaking skills and his vivacious wife's budgeting have combined to create a solid success. Their wines are reasonably priced and the quality represents some of the best to be found in the village.

Hubert clearly relishes being out among his scattered vineyards. This is where quality begins. Minimum fertilisers, plenty of *répiquage*, carefully chosen rootstock, short *cordon* training for the Pinot Fin, are aided by 'precise soil analyses – the clay content of a vineyard can differ within a few metres.'

Olivier's arrival has heralded some important changes in red Lamy vinifications. In particular, bunches are now 100% destalked rather than partially. This change was not seen as permanent, but the quality of the resulting wines caused Hubert to reflect seriously on the wisdom of retaining any significant proportion of stems. Also, *cuvaison* has been lengthened from 8–10 days, as Hubert wisely decided that a further 4 days produced much greater extraction and pre-fermentive maceration increased. This reinforces the argument for fewer stems. Selected yeasts are used – heaven knows why; there is

nothing wrong, and everything right, with the natural population.

The wines are given more or less *press-wine*, depending on its quality, and then kept in cask for about 15 months, fined with either albumen, or gelatine in the case of aggressive tannins, and plate-filtered before bottling. Until recently, only the Santenay and St.-Aubin Les Castets saw any new oak – 'We must go slowly on these expensive casks,' Hubert announces, adding, with a laughing smile at his wife, 'I must first persuade my Treasurer to give me the money!' 'Yes,' adds Mme Lamy, 'if he has a new destalker and all the other new material, he can't expect too many casks as well,' figuratively turning a large key on an invisible cash-box. Now there is 30% new wood, across the range, mainly Nevers, Allier and Vosges, from three different barrel-makers.

There is no doubt that the wines are better for these changes. Earlier vintages seem to have suffered from an excess of astringency and a marked leatheriness. A 24-hour 'maceration à chaud' (40°C) for the Chassagne Village resulted in a softer, warmer wine, with more harmonious tannins. This and the St.-Aubin Premier Cru Les Castets are the best of the reds.

The whites start their fermentation in bulk, so that the temperature can be controlled at 20°C. When the density of the *must* reaches about 1020, two-thirds of the St.-Aubin and Frionnes are transferred to cask to continue their fermentation which, with regular *batonnage*, can last up to two months. The *régionales* remain in cuve.

The St.-Aubins and Pulignys see 25-30% of well-charred, new wood, the rest being raised in older oak. 'I would like to use more new wood, but casks are expensive – the client must pay for it in the end; when I see them making excellent white wine in Chablis, without any wood, I ask myself whether I am doing the right thing.'

If the quality of the reds is still evolving, the whites have already established a level of excellence. Four different St.-Aubin Premiers Crus form the heart of the production; the wines tend to start with a touch of austerity, but show every sign of being built to last. The Frionnes and En Remilly are particularly good – fullish, sappy wines with plenty of depth and interest. The En Remilly comes from young Chardonnay vines, planted on crushed-up rocks, on top of the Mont-Rachet.

Outside the commune, Hubert and Olivier make a Village Puligny, Les Tremblots, and one solitary cask of Grand Cru Criots-Bâtard-Montrachet – both excellent. The Criots is a firm, well-constituted wine, with plenty of depth and concentration, despite the small volume (what on earth does he top up his cask with?).

The delightful Lamys are becoming, deservedly, better known as a fine source of attractive, quality wines at more than reasonable prices.

VINEYARD HOLDINGS

Commune	Level	Lieu-dit/Climat	Area	Vine Age	Status
Chassagne	GC	Criots-Bâtard-Montrachet	0.05	21	F
Chassagne	PC	Les Macherelles (W)	0.16	9	F
Chassagne	V	La Goujonne (R)	1.90	45	F/P
Puligny	V	Les Tremblots	0.89	21/60	P
St.-Aubin	PC	Les Frionnes (W)	2.41	1/20/60	P
St.-Aubin	PC	En Remilly (W)	0.87	8	F
St.-Aubin	PC	Les Cortons (W)	0.57	7	P/F
St.-Aubin	PC	Clos de la Chatenière (W)	1.25	36	P
St.-Aubin	PC	Les Murgers des Dents des Chiens	0.20	11	F
St.-Aubin	PC	Les Castets (R)	2.75	25/35//50	F/P
St.-Aubin	V	La Princée (W)	0.99	10/17	P
St.-Aubin	V	Le Paradis (R)	0.93	25	P
Santenay	V	Les Hâtes (R)	0.60	51	P
St.-Aubin	R	(Bourgogne Aligoté)	1.15	4/15	P
Cheilly	R	(Côte de Beaune Villages)	0.12	36	P
Cheilly	R	(Bourgogne Hautes Côtes de Beaune)	0.76	20/40	P
St.-Aubin	R	(Bourgogne Rouge and PTG)	0.90	20/50	P
Total :			**16.50 ha**		

238

Domaine Gérard Thomas

ST.-AUBIN

Gérard Thomas is one of the best sources of St.-Aubin. From nearly 10 ha of vines, all but two of which are in the commune, the bluff, weather-beaten Gérard produces a range of ten carefully made wines which are invariably of good to very good quality and particularly good value for money.

The Domaine was created after the last war by his father who rented and bought vines. On his retirement in 1982, Gérard took over and started to rationalise what was a highly fragmented estate. In 1986 he added the Premier Cru Les Murgers des Dents de Chien to the estate and the following year bought a plot of the white Premier Cru, La Chatenière.

Both whites and reds are made more or less traditionally. The whites are kept in cask for about one year, and bottled after fining and two separate filtrations. However, nothing is immutable, so when a *cuvée* of St.-Aubin Premier Cru 1988 failed to complete its *malo*, it was simply kept in cask for an extra year until it was in a fit state for bottling.

Gérard Thomas' St.-Aubins are usually ripe, quite plump wines, with good, stylish flavours. His habit of jumping from vineyard to vineyard during harvesting to pick at optimum ripeness seems to pay off with a good concentration of fruit in most of the wines.

The amount of new wood used depends as much on cash-flow as on anything else. In 1989 he managed 10–15%, but in 1988 had to be content with renewing a few cask staves to give a sort of partial new oak. With his spreading renown, things are rather better now.

The cream of the white St.-Aubins are the Premiers Crus Les Murgers des Dents de Chien, just above the satellite hamlet of Gamay, and La Chatenière, below it. Les Murgers, which is also behind the Mont-Rachet, is an exposed vineyard with poor soil giving on to hard bedrock. The wine is characterised by aromas of dried fruit and lime-blossom and with plenty of fat and finesse. Both are mouthfilling and need keeping for several years to reach their prime.

Gérard sells much of his output to private clients and to restaurants, so he deliberately aims at wines which combine fruit and charm for early drinking and the structure to develop in the medium term. This is a difficult fence to straddle, but he does it with considerable aplomb.

The Meursault Blagny and the Puligny

Premier Cru La Garenne are no less neatly crafted. The Meursault often has a touch of St.-Aubin rusticity underneath its powerful exterior, but is none the worse for that. The 1992 and 1993 Blagnys are both excellent efforts – the former having more obvious suppleness, whilst the latter is tighter and distinctly more masculine in character.

The La Garenne has the elegance one expects from a Puligny Premier Cru – deriving power from the soil's relatively high clay content. The 1992 is a discreet, relatively restrained wine, with good underlying power and Puligny finesse.

Gérard is busy extending his small production of reds; at present, these comprise a Bourgogne Rouge, a St.-Aubin, Côte de Beaune and 1 ha of St.-Aubin Premier Cru Les Frionnes.

These are vinified in cement *cuves*, without pre-fermentive maceration and with about 10 days of *cuvaison*. Wisely, Gérard avoids anything more than a touch of new wood – this also makes financial sense – preferring to *saigner* to concentrate the wine rather than to add artificial structure. Much of what is poor in Auxey-Duresses and St.-Aubin red wine can be attributed to an excess of stalk or wood tannin.

Cask *élévage* has been drastically reduced, from 18–24 months to 10 – a very welcome change. Precisely when they are fined, filtered and bottled, depends on when Gérard has time to spare, space to spare and cash to spare. Having said this, he was shocked to be asked whether or not he used a contract bottler – after all, many estimable growers do. The answer, of course, was an emphatic 'non!'

Gérard's reds tend to be quite sizeable wines – not delicate, fruity mouthfuls for the faint-hearted. The Frionnes is, with Les Castets, arguably the best of the St.-Aubin

Vines in full flower

Premiers Crus. Both give wines which are naturally high in tannin and acidity to begin with but which, if carefully vinified, will last well for up to a decade in the best vintages. The 1993 Frionnes, with two years of cask ageing behind it, but no new wood, is tight-framed, but not aggressive. Deep, red, heavyish clay-limestone soils impart a density and natural strength and a consequently slow evolution. Buyers of Gérard's fine 1993 should keep them at least five years to reveal their real qualities.

If you are looking for modestly-priced Burgundy, the amiable Gérard Thomas is an excellent source. St.-Aubin will never reach the aristocratic heights of its neighbour on the other side of the Mont-Rachet, but will continue to provide interesting wines for those prepared to lower their sights a little.

VINEYARD HOLDINGS

Commune	Level	Lieu-dit/Climat	Area	Vine Age	Status
Blagny	PC	Meursault-Blagny	1.00	25	M
Puligny	PC	La Garenne	0.50	30	P/M
Puligny	V	– (W)	0.50	30	M
St.-Aubin	PC	Murgers Des Dents de Chiens (W)	1.30	20	P/M
St.-Aubin	PC	La Chatenière (W)	0.40	15	P
St.-Aubin	PC	Les Frionnes (W)	0.30	30	P
St.-Aubin	PC	Les Frionnes (R)	0.70	1991	P
St.-Aubin	PC	(Several *climats*) (W)	1.80	25	P/M
St.-Aubin	V	—— (R)	0.30	9	P
St.-Aubin	R	(Côte de Beaune) (R)	1.25	35	P
——	R	(Bourgogne Rouge)	1.25	30	P
Total:			**9.30 ha**		

SANTENAY AND REMIGNY

Santenay's imposing Château of Philippe le Hardi

The wines of Santenay have never figured prominently on the map of Burgundy, enjoying a reputation for reliable robustness rather than for elegance or complexity. Of the 113,000 or so cases produced annually, 111,000 are red, made from 378.18 ha of vineyards covering a large area between Chassagne to the north-east and Cheilly-les-Maranges to the south-west. Of these, 124.29 ha – nearly a third – are Premiers Crus, the majority, and best, of which lie in a single band of hillside above the main road.

Although there are officially 11 Premiers Crus, only 5 are encountered with any regularity: La Comme (22.07 ha), Clos des Tavannes (5.32 ha), Les Gravières (23.40 ha), Maladière (13.58 ha) and Clos Rousseau (23.84 ha). Of these, the first three are at the

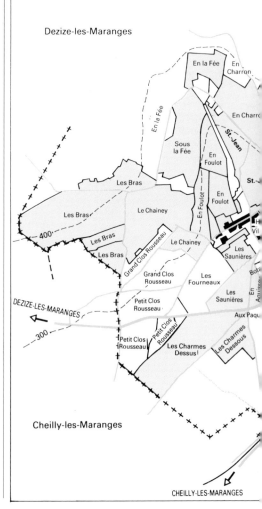

Although not strictly the last wine-producing commune in the Côte d'Or – that honour falls to Cheilly-Les-Maranges – Santenay is generally regarded as its southernmost outpost. For years, buyers have come here in the hope of finding sound quality, reasonably priced red Burgundy to fill the gap between the grander communes and the Rullys, Givrys and Mercureys of the Côte Chalonnaise.

These considerations apart, Santenay is an old and attractive village, more obviously oriented towards its community than to the tourism which infects the atmosphere of much of the Côte. The place is in fact two villages: the more recent and larger part, which sprang up with the advent of the Chagny-Nevers railway line in 1861 and is now home to many of the larger Domaines and to most of the local commerce, is Santenay-le-Bas.

A few kilometres up the hill is Santenay-le-Haut, a much older hamlet with narrow, steep, winding streets and an air of immutable isolation. Nearby are two of Santenay's main tourist attractions – the Casino and the thermal springs.

The former is the town's largest earner, employing some 40 people throughout the summer to cater to a heterogeneous clientele from the 'jeunesse dorée' of the Côte to

crusty old gold-veined Swiss travellers. It operates from a splendid 1914 building with tall, small-paned windows, which looks as though it has been lifted, brick and beam, from Le Touquet or Deauville, fashionable French seaside resorts of the 1920s.

The thermal springs have long been part of Santenay's history. They were almost certainly used by the Romans, who settled on the Mont de Senne, a magnificent vantage point 500m above the valley and, by the early 17th century, were documented for their curative properties. In the late 19th century they were so popular that the single spring was inadequate, and another was sought, and found, by the local pharmacist. This artesian well produces water high in lithium which is especially good for stress-related complaints.

Santenay's heyday as a spa came, according to Henri Cannard, in 1891, when some 10,000 visited to take the waters, which, like that of many spas, boasts broad curative properties, claiming success with everything from constipation to corns. A 100-bed hotel was built and they even tried bottling water to increase sales. Sadly, the hotel survived only one year; it was bought in 1946 by the French railways as a retirement home. A new hotel was opened in 1979, and the cures still contribute to the local economy.

heart of the appellation, in the sector nearest to Chassagne.

Here marly, limestone soils, stony and thus well-drained, give wines of earthy robustness, of which the best need 10 or more years to develop. Whilst Santenays rarely appear as charm-school graduates, with time they take on a certain bawdy elegance which, whilst not quite the real thing, will pass muster for a sort of refinement; the clothes may be expensive but you can still glimpse the tattoos underneath.

La Maladière, a south-east-facing vineyard to the west of the others, has more limestone in its soil which combines with a higher elevation to produce more perfumed but lighter wine. The négociant house, Prosper Maufoux, is the largest owner here, offering a wine which is usually light in colour and rather evanescent in flavour.

The Clos Rousseau, divided into Grand and Petit, sits on deeper, brown limestone soils, richer in clay and iron oxide which, though not best suited to fine wine produc-

tion, can give good richness and genuine depth.

There are two viticultural matters of note about Santenay: firstly, there is a species of Pinot Noir known as the Pinot Fin de Santenay, which growers often refer to as that planted here and in Chassagne, and well adapted to the local soils. Whilst there may have been such a strain in years past, what is now planted are conventional clones, although there remain pockets of *sélection massale* from older Pinot strains.

Secondly, Santenay Pinot Noir vines are trained *en cordon de Royat*, to limit their vigour from naturally productive soils. This has both advantages and disadvantages – the foliage is more spread out, giving better photosynthesis and better ripening, and pruning can be delayed until the spring, since there is no *baguette* to train. However, restarting a *cordon* after frost damage is difficult, and *cordon* training is known to increase the risk of the acariose mite, which eats both fruit and leaves, and of red spider.

Whether or not a bottle of Santenay is likely to be interesting and age-worthy, depends as much on the producer as on the vineyard. Much is light, often stalky and tannic wine, which, whilst perfectly quaffable with well-flavoured stews and roasts, is not worth buying and keeping.

However, there are pockets of excellence, where old vines, small yields and careful winemaking combine to produce wines which have much merit. In addition to the Domaines profiled here, good Santenays are made by Pousse d'Or (Clos des Tavannes), Louis and René Lequin (each now with his own Domaine) and Drouhin.

Santenay Blanc is little seen. However, from good producers (e.g. the Lequins, who make their whites from Pinot Blanc rather than Chardonnay), it can be delicious drinking for its first few years.

Santenay deserved its mild renaissance. Much is worth drinking and, from one or two growers, some seriously fine wine.

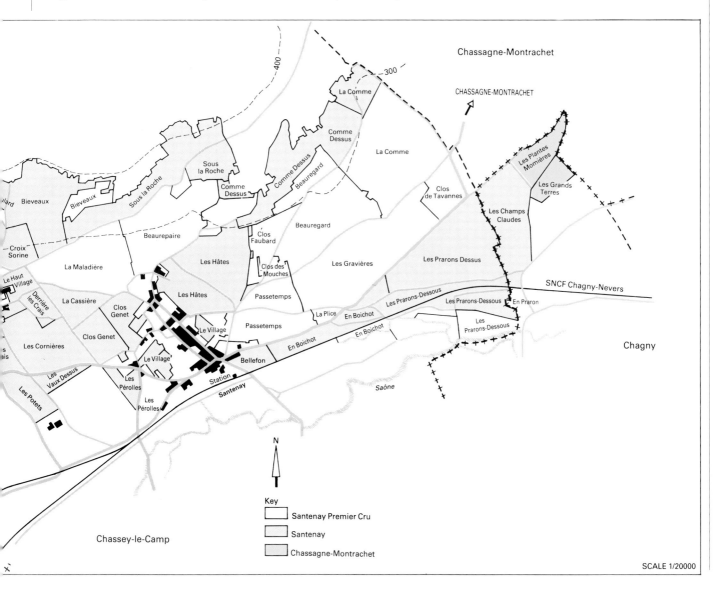

Domaine Adrien Belland

SANTENAY AND REMIGNY

The Côte d'Or is such a fragmented mosaic of smallholdings, that even now, one should not perhaps be surprised to find a long-established Domaine making wine of exceptional quality, apparently still largely unrecognised. Yet it still seems odd – so much extolled are the virtues of the top estates – that there remain discoveries to be made.

Adrien Belland may not see himself in the light of a discovery – after all his family have been vignerons at Santenay for several generations and he has been making wine on his own account for over 40 years – for 15 of them with his son, Jean-Claude. As long as his wine sells well, what do the plaudits of the critics or the glare of international publicity matter – he would probably regard them as more of a nuisance than anything else.

Yet Adrien Belland, lowering his substantial frame into one of his cramped office chairs, does concern himself with what others think of his wines. A large book, propped up behind the wash-basin which doubles as a spitoon, is soon lifted down to show off the numerous medals which the wines have won over the years at fairs in Mâcon and Paris – acclamation in gold, silver and bronze, for Santenays, Cortons and Chambertins.

The medals are well-deserved by this distinguished winemaker. His old parents – both still alive – produced four children, all of whom took their share of vineyards when the division came. Adrien started with 3 ha and added to them, principally by marriage to a girl from nearby Autun who, fortuitously, was of the Latour family. With her came prime parcels of Grand Cru Cortons, Perrières and Clos de la Vigne au Saint, Chambertin, plus some Aloxe-Corton Village. In 1975 he purchased a further 55 ares of Corton Grèves.

Many dismiss the wines of Santenay as being light, without interest and definitely not for keeping. Tasting with Adrien Belland will change their minds; he builds his wines on the architectural principle, from solid timber and is not someone who would ever contemplate, for the slightest instant, the use of plywood.

Visiting the Domaine, situated in one corner of Santenay's torpid little main square, is something of a trip into history. Behind the rather neat façade, leading into a small courtyard, lie the cellars. Here, from the litter of bric-a-brac which bestrews the floor, one might get the impression that winemaking vies as principal activity with gardening,

restoring pre-war heaters and cycle repairs. This would be a mistake.

The first wine offered is a Santenay Village, from a large enamelled cuve in the ground-floor cuverie, with '12' proclaimed on it. The wine is extraordinary: impenetrable and virtually black, with masses of fruit and layers of ripe tannins. A clearly startled look elicits from Adrien: 'It's all in the vines – even the power,' which he regards as enough of an explanation. Comment at the end, the remains of the wine is expectorated into an ancient wheelbarrow which happens to be nearby, full of old grafts. Adrien plants them out in the garden which slopes away to the railway line at the back of the house. Those that don't take are brought in and abandoned in the *cuverie* – emergency supplies of firewood presumably.

Flicking at an exposed bundle of bare wires on the wall of one of the many small cask-lined underground galleries with a wooden stick, Adrien crackles the lights into action and starts drawing off samples from the various casks. If the Santenay is black, what, the visitor might be forgiven for silently wondering, is the Chambertin like?

Next, however, comes the Corton Grèves – equally impenetrable black/purple. Tasted blind, one might easily guess at a young Syrah – although it seems to have a ripe warmth which perhaps would make one hesitate. There is yet more complexity and extraordinary depth and class underneath its mask of tannins.

The cellars are more than two centuries old; they are certainly very bleak on a glacial January afternoon, although Adrien is content to wander round in an open-necked shirt. 'I never touch my wines, neither here nor there,' he explains, referring to his policy of long vinification and waving his stick at a bank of barrels. No pre-fermentive maceration, just a *pied de cuve* to get the yeasts working and 12 days or so of *cuvaison* at a maximum of 34°C.

Adrien attaches great importance to *pigéage*. He tried fermenting with a submerged cap – the principal alternative – but found that it gave less character and less colour to his wines.

However, there is no pumping-over. 'The yeasts work perfectly well without oxygen,' Adrian explains, rummaging fruitlessly round in search of the Domaine's instrument of *pigéage*, of which he is particularly proud.

The Domaine's unobtrusive entrance. Which way to the Casino?

This device, when it finally turns up, propped up behind a vat, against a table full of tools, turns out to be an elaborate sort of rubber lavatory plunger, with the inverted conical end section perforated with small holes. These are covered with flaps, so that they open up on the way down through the cap, to break it up, and close on the way up to suck up the wine – more effective than foot-treading, and eliminating the need for *remontage*.

Another small vault houses the Chambertin which comes from vines at the Morey-St.-Denis end of the vineyard. It is *élévé* in 50% new Allier oak but, like all the other wines, is kept in tank until after the *malo* before being transferred to cask – in March. Surprisingly, it has a shade less colour than the Corton, although this does not herald any relaxation in the structure. The wine has an opulent griotte cherry nose, masses of ripe, densely-packed fruit and extraordinary complexity. The new oak is beautifully integrated and barely noticeable.

The wines generally spend a year in cask before being racked back into *cuves* where they are fined, filtered and bottled between March and September of the second year – a total cycle of 18–24 months.

This is an uncompromising tradition for which his customers ought to be thoroughly grateful. Although he sells a little Santenay in cask *en négoce*, also a few *pièces* of red Corton and Chambertin to Louis Jadot, the rest is bottled at the Domaine, 60% going to export, the rest within France.

The 1989 Corton Grèves and 1989 Chambertin are next on the list. Despite being at ambient cellar temperature (7°C) both taste remarkably fine. The Corton has the characteristic depth of colour, and an attractive aroma of *fruits sauvages* mixed with liquorice. Quite a wild wine on the palate – big, a touch rustic in the best sense, yet long and complex. The Chambertin is dense, although less so than the 1990; the temperature has muted its nose, but on the palate it is a big, spicy wine, strongly liquorice, quite supple and 'flatteur'; a wine of beautiful balance which, but for a touch of hollowness, would be *Grand Vin*. Perhaps at 15°C . . . who knows?

Two vintages of Santenay Les Gravières are produced to show how the wines evolve in bottle. The 1985 is of deepish mid-Victoria-plum hue with a rich, almost burnt tarry nose – liquorice and viscera. Although a touch rustic, the wine is deep and tarry in flavour, a big wine with plenty of concentration and still youthful. Les Gravières is generally less tannic and structured than La Comme – probably the best of the Santenay Premiers Crus.

The 1971 Gravières is still in its prime – moderately deep in colour, with no exaggerated signs of age, a gorgeous open spicy

Adrien Belland topping up his casks

nose and a deliciously delicate, yet positive, Pinot flavour; again hints of spice, coffee and liquorice. A very fine wine which will still last for years.

As to the secrets of making his wines, Adrien has nothing particular to suggest. 'We make vins de garde,' he offers, stating the glaringly obvious. No differences in vinification or *élévage* distinguish a Village Santenay from Grand Cru Chambertin – except that the latter gets some new oak, whereas the former is raised in an older cask. Adrien believes that destemmed grapes from old vines impart enough natural structure and

character, especially with his long vinification, without the need to add more, artificially, with new barrels.

Recent years have seen changes. The office is tidier now – the desk raised on what appear to be four upturned glass ashtrays – as Adrien prepares to hand over entirely to Jean-Claude. There is now a 'new', 200-year-old cask cellar at the top of the village, above Jean-Claude's equally 'new' house. As he has worked with Adrien for so long, there is unlikely to be any seismic change when he finally assumes the reins.

VINEYARD HOLDINGS

Commune	Level	Lieu-dit/Climat	Area	Vine Age	Status
Gevrey	GC	Chambertin	0.41	30	P
Aloxe	GC	Corton, Clos de la Vigne Au Saint	0.49	20	P
Aloxe	GC	Corton-Perrières	0.69	40	P
Aloxe	GC	Corton-Grèves	0.55	25	P
Aloxe	V	Les Boutières	0.58	35	P
Aloxe	GC	Charlemagne	0.36	30	P
Santenay	PC	Clos des Gravières	1.21	35	P
Santenay	PC	La Comme	0.85	22	P
Santenay	V	Clos Genet	1.56	28	P
Santenay	V	Les Hâtes + L6 Charmes-Dessus	2.12	30	P
Chassagne	PC	Morgeot (R)	0.48	30	P
Puligny	V	La Rue Aux Vaches (W)	0.45	35	P
————	R	(Côte de Beaune-Villages)	0.99	35	P
————	R	(Bourgogne Rouge)	0.58	30	P
Total:			**11.32 ha**		

Domaine Vincent Girardin

SANTENAY

In 1982, Vincent Girardin took over his quarter share of his parents' vineyards – 3 ha. Now, from his substantial house and greatly expanded cellars in the angle at the Chassagne exit of Santenay's main square, he makes the wine from thirteen. This mix of owned and rented land, stretching from Beaune to Maranges has been carefully assembled to encompass a fine range of Santenays (including four white Premiers Crus), a couple of Beaunes, a Village Pommard from 60-year-old vines, plus some Meursault and Savigny.

Since his first vintage in 1982, Vincent has proved himself a consistently fine winemaker and built up a solid reputation for quality. In the early 1990s a slim, red-headed Swiss teacher from Fribourg came to taste in the cellars and fell in love with more than the wine. Véronique and Vincent married in 1994, since when a touch of femininity has adorned the house and computerisation arrived in the Domaine's affairs. 'I spend as much time as I can with my wife,' Vincent confesses.

There is nothing exceptional or extraordinary about the care of the vineyards or the winemaking, except perhaps for Vincent's insistence on keeping as much lees as possible for maturing his reds, provided they are clean and not tainted by rot. He sees Côtes de Beaune *Grand Vin* as exuding pure Pinot fruit above all and tries to avoid the sins of tannins which are too dry and aggressive. In pursuit of these goals, the reds are entirely destemmed, vinified in stainless steel and matured for 14–16 months in a maximum of one-third new wood. His annual 160 new cask requirement is supplied by two different barrelmakers, for the rest, second- and third-year casks are used. There has been neither fining nor filtration since 1990.

The white grapes are picked into closed cases and transported as quickly as possible to the cellar, where the juice is expressed and then settled out for 48 hours. Vincent is vehemently against *tables de triage*, preferring to eliminate poor fruit in the vineyard: 'I'm out there for all nine days of the harvest, sorting.' The whites all undergo their malolactic fermentations in cask – up to 40% of which are new. Plenty of *batonnage* and a single August racking are followed by *assemblage* and fish fining before bottling with Kieselguhr and membrane filtration; a deliberately softish treatment to avoid destroying fragile aromatic purity.

Véronique and Vincent Girardin

Both reds and whites are top-class, exemplifying well Vincent's concern with fruit, aromas and balance. The Chassagne Premier Cru Morgeot from mainly 50-year-old vines is the pick of the whites, which includes a remarkably rich and fine Bourgogne Blanc from Santenay vines. The white Santenay Premiers Crus are quite firm, yet rich and honeyed – well worth looking out for, rare and unusual. The range also offers an equally enticing red Bourgogne, from vines at nearby Maranges, a fine clutch of Santenays plus a trio of Pommards and Maranges, and a Beaune Vignes Franches.

The reds at all levels have an abundance

Opposite: Steam-cleaning casks at Romanée-Conti

of soft silky fruit – especially in vintages where the fruit has good natural ripeness. In such years, Vincent's Santenays are some of the best to be found, especially the Maladières and the Domaine's 1.38 ha *Monopole*, Clos de la Confrérie. All come from vines of a respectable age – not little wines to be drunk young, or worse, chilled, but serious Burgundies with a great deal of appeal and good medium-term ageing potential.

Vincent's success is reflected in his representation in some of France's finest restaurants, an achievement of which he is justifiably proud. The fact that they are not overbalanced by tannins makes the reds approachable relatively early, an advantage for establishments without the resources to mature wines themselves.

One quarter of the 100,000 annual bottled production is white, three-quarters red, whilst a volume equivalent to about 50,000 bottles is sold to the négoce. Over 80% is exported, 15% goes to individual clients and the remaining 5% to the great restaurants. As long as too many children don't appear to distract him, Vincent Girardin is certain to consolidate his already fine reputation in the years to come.

VINEYARD HOLDINGS

Commune	Level	Lieu-dit/Climat	Area	Vine Age	Status
Beaune	PC	Clos de Vignes Franches	0.48	10	F
Beaune	V	Les Bons Feuves	0.50	50	F
Pommard	PC	Les Chanlins	0.20	45	P
Pommard	V	Clos de Lambots	0.90	60+	P/F
Pommard	V	Les Vignots	0.55	18	F
Savigny	V	Les Gollardes (R)	0.20	25	P
Savigny	V	Les Vermots Dessus (W)	1.50	20	P/F
Meursault	V	Les Narvaux (W)	0.60	25	P/M
Chassagne	PC	Morgeot (W)	0.40	(2) and 50	P
Santenay	R	(Bourgogne Blanc)	0.50	15	P
Santenay	PC	Clos du Beauregard (W)	0.90	2 and 9	P
Santenay	PC	Le Beaurepaire (W)	0.70	20	P/F
Santenay	V	Le St.-Jean (W)	0.45	15	P
Santenay	V	Clos de la Confrérie (W)	0.18	10	P
Santenay	V	Clos de la Confrérie (R)	1.20	25	P
Santenay	PC	Les Gravières (R)	0.50	20	P
Santenay	PC	La Maladière (R)	1.00	30	P
Maranges	PC	Clos de Loyères	1.30	70+	F
Maranges	PC	Clos Roussot	0.50	12	F
Maranges	V	(Various *climats*)	1.00	35	F/P
Total:			**12.38 ha**		

APPELLATION AND QUALITY CONTROL

The Côte d'Or's 8,000 ha of vines are divided into no fewer than 116 different appellations. With so many in such a relatively small wine region, it is worth clarifying what is meant by an appellation and discussing its significance for the wine drinker.

The first thing to be made clear is that, although colloquially referring both to an area of vines and to the name of the wine produced there, appellations are primarily granted to land. Only in a secondary sense do they attach to wine which must pass certain tasting and other tests before becoming formally entitled to an appellation.

The French system of Appellation Contrôlée (AC) did not spring ready-made from the mind of some enlightened law givers, but evolved over nearly four decades before being progressively codified from the 1920s onwards. Its aim was to provide a legal framework for delimiting and controlling areas of wine production and to set up a structure of local, regional and national committees, first to create the appellations, then to police them.

In the Côte d'Or, appellations are precisely mapped plots ranging in area from vast acreages of Bourgogne Rouge and Blanc to the 0.85 ha of La Romanée. The large number of individual appellations reflects the fact that over the centuries certain vineyards throughout the Côte have been found regularly to produce better wine than others. So, when the AC system was set up, each designated vineyard site was graded on its quality potential into one of four categories – in ascending order:

1. Regional: (e.g. Bourgogne Rouge, Passe-Tout-Grains, Côte de Beaune Villages).
2. Village: (e.g. Pommard, Nuits-St.-Georges, Beaune); obviously Pommard can only be produced from vines in Pommard, and so on.
3. Premier Cru: specific vineyards considered to be capable of consistently producing wine above the level of Village quality; on the label these are designated as 'Village + Premier Cru', (with the option of adding a specific vineyard name if the wine comes solely from that *climat*, e.g. Volnay, Clos des Ducs).
4. Grand Cru: crowning the pyramid are the Grands Crus – 32 individual vineyards of particular excellence, scattered throughout the Côte, each with its own AC (e.g. Chambertin, Montrachet, Corton-Charlemagne). Grands Crus, for which the rules specify lower yields and higher minimum natural alcohol, have the distinction of only using the vineyard name on the label, without the usual accompaniment of the village to which they belong. So, for example, wine from the Grand Cru Chambertin – a single plot of land in the village of Gevrey-Chambertin – would simply be labelled Chambertin, whereas wine from the Gevrey-Chambertin Premier Cru vineyard Les Cazetiers would be labelled Gevrey-Chambertin, Les Cazetiers.

For the buyer, the significance of the AC system is that, other things being equal – vintage, grower, etc. – the higher the vineyard's classification the better, in theory, the wine. Thus a Pommard – Premier Cru Les Epenots – from this single vineyard in the commune of Pommard should be a finer, more complex and better wine than a Village Pommard which should outclass a Bourgogne Rouge made from grapes grown within the boundaries of Pommard.

Unfortunately, things are rarely equal and this neat hierarchy is all but vitiated by the growers the system seeks to regulate, since they themselves differ widely in competence. A Village wine from a top grower will, more often than not, outclass a Premier Cru from a less gifted hand. The system is also devalued by the failure of the authorities to enforce the regulations available to them.

AC classifications are not immutable and changes do occur. Processing applications for new appellations or for upgrading vineyards is the job of the Institut National des Appellations d'Origine (INAO). From their office in Dijon, a staff of four administers the affairs of the entire Côte d'Or. In conjunction with local committees, they decide the earliest permitted date of harvest for each commune.

Although the INAO's principal mission is not control, but delimitation, its inspectors have considerable powers. In addition, two other government services keep a constant eye on the Côte's vignerons: the Direction Générale des Impôts fields three inspectors to ensure that wine taxes are paid, and thus have an interest in harvest declarations and sales.

However, it is to the Direction Générale de la Concurrence, Consommation et Répression des Fraudes' trio of inspectors that the task of policing the appellation regulations principally falls. These are wide-ranging, covering viticultural practices, harvesting, permitted grape varieties, plant density, pruning, etc., and laying down rules for vinification: *chaptalisation,* acidification, blending, sulphur, etc.

According to a senior official of the Répression des Fraudes, apart from overseeing that the *ban de vendange* is respected and permitted yields are not exceeded, the most important controls are those undertaken in vignerons' cellars. Spot checks and inspections are used to ensure that vinification practices are observed and that stocks tally with harvest declarations or paperwork for any wine bought in.

The main aim of all this grading and control is to preserve the authenticity, typicity and quality of AC wines. Before an AC is granted, certain qualifying conditions must be met – including a minimum level of natural alcohol and a maximum yield per hectare of vines. Thereafter, growers are required to present each wine for which an AC is sought – *agrément* – for analysis and tasting. If a wine fails, then it may be submitted twice more. Inspectors also have the powers to visit Domaines unannounced and to take random samples.

A hopeless lack of manpower makes theory and reality widely divergent. The 'Fraudes squad' is up against unbeatable odds, with some 4,400 annual declarations of harvest in the Côte – each comprising several wines – and only three unqualified, part-time inspectors to police them.

In recent years the operation of the appellation controls have been trenchantly criticised, both inside and outside the region, by customers dissatisfied with the standard of many AC Burgundies regularly appearing on the export market. In particular, fire has been directed towards the practice of over-*chaptalisation*, either to increase volume or to cover up faults, and to the apparent tolerance of excessive yields, especially in Premier and Grand Cru vineyards.

Control of yields is no better. The system of base yields, which sets a maximum for each AC, has a built-in mechanism for authorising increases whenever it is deemed fit. This plafond limite de classement (PLC) – typically providing for an extra 20% on base yields – was intended to be invoked in exceptionally abundant vintages. In recent years growers have been demanding, and getting, the PLC in vintages where the case for it has been, at best, marginal.

There is also a strong case for much greater vigilance in the vineyards to scrutinise yields of individual plots. A yield of 50 hl/ha may be acceptable in a well-maintained vineyard, with every vine producing, but not if one third of the vines are missing and the other two thirds are in a degenerate state. Anyone with their eyes open can see the problem in vineyards up and down the Côte.

In an authoritative exposition of the AC legislation, Anthony Hanson (1982), in a chapter subtitled 'The Buyer Deceived', pointed out that, although the laws have been tightened in recent years, loopholes give any grower with a gram of imagination the ability to drive a coach and horses through them, with apparent impunity. He concluded that, 'the good old, bad old days when any rosé can call itself Clos de Vougeot, Chambertin or Corton, so long as it comes from the right soil and vines and fulfils a few conditions, are still with us.'

The vigneron still has considerable scope for cheating. He can overproduce, declare what is authorised and then bottle the surplus for cash sale. The 'second cellar', run on a strictly cash basis, is endemic in the Côte. Alternatively, any production over the legal limit can be declared as a surplus for a lesser AC. Since declarations of harvest need not be presented until 25 November there is plenty of time for the unscrupulous vigneron to arrange his casks, knowing full well that the inspectors have insufficient time to taste everything. If this sleight of hand gives him an extra barrel of Grand Cru, his trouble is well recompensed.

According to the rules, any wine produced over the maximum limit must be sent for distillation into industrial alcohol – it cannot be bottled or sold as wine. In other words, part of a single vat of wine is given the AC and part refused. This is absurd. If the wine is of AC quality, it should all be released for sale; if not, then the whole lot should be declassified or sent for distillation. In any case, there seems little to prevent a pragmatically-minded vigneron with a surplus of Grand Cru from sending the same quantity of Village or Regional wine to the distillery and keeping the better wine for himself.

Fortunately, there is evidence of change. Pressure from a variety of sources has led to a scheme whereby a vigneron presenting for *agrément* a wine which is judged to be of borderline quality will be given the benefit of the doubt for one year, on condition that his cellar practices are monitored by an independent oenologist. However, since he has the right to appoint the oenologist, cynics might consider that there is plenty of scope for collusion. Nonetheless this is a welcome development.

What is the significance of all this for the consumer, perhaps faced with a row of Burgundies on a shop shelf thousands of miles away from the Côte d'Or? Buyers, who cannot always taste first, look to an appellation as a guarantee both of authenticity and of quality. For the first, one expects the contents of the bottle to correspond to what is printed on the label, and this is generally the case. For the second, those relying on an appellation for a certain level of quality will often be disappointed – a dilute poorly vinified, Chambertin is, unfortunately, still a Chambertin.

One widespread practice, which compromised the quality of much post-war Burgundy, has thankfully largely disappeared; *coupage* – the blending of a proportion, usually small, of genuine Burgundy with something cheaper, flourished in the 1950s and 1960s. As André Simon commented: 'Blending is to some extent like kissing – it may by quite innocent, but it may lead one away from the narrow path of duty and propriety.' Many Burgundians were led away!

The principal difficulty faced by the authorities is that growers, particularly those regularly producing at or near the maximum yields, form a powerful pressure group with a vested interest in the status quo. At present, for example, tastings for the *agrément* are conducted between 15 November and 15 April following the harvest – i.e.

when the wine is a few months old. As anyone with even a nodding acquaintance with winemaking knows, much can happen to change a wine in the year or more between then and bottling, even assuming that the grower is honest and careful.

Furthermore, only carefully selected samples of each wine are tasted. This allows a grower with several casks of one wine to submit a single sample to gain the AC for the entire quantity, leaving the door open for all sorts of malpractice. For example, in 1983, a year notable for rot in the Pinot Noir, many buyers discovered that wine they received in bottle bore scant resemblance to what they remembered tasting in cask. Wily growers, knowing that buyers could not taste every cask of each wine, had presented the best casks for tasting and added the contents of the rotten casks just before bottling. The hapless clients had little recourse, except perhaps the sanction of non-payment, whilst the AC officials seemed reluctant to intervene.

Moreover, the official tasting-panels are barely independent of the producers and their interests. There is still no representation of export markets which, as Hanson points out, form the principal output for many of the greatest AC names. The incidence of wines failing their tasting test on grounds of quality is negligible – standards are obviously set so low that all but vinegar passes. Such nonsense strengthens an already irrefutable case for more vigorous use of the existing powers enabling substandard wine to be declassified to a lower appellation. Making clear to growers that poor wine would be downgraded would be a powerful spur to improving overall quality.

One can only conclude that there is still no real will to control either yields or quality. The requisite laws and powers exist, but are ineffectually policed with the inevitable result that substantial volumes of indifferent wine, much with the cachet of exalted appellations, continue to pour on to a gullible export market. This tarnishes the reputation of the region and its appellations, and compromises the efforts of the many conscientious Domaines who strive tirelessly for quality. An appellation system is only as good as its enforcement.

In the end, the customer's only real safeguard is a sound knowledge of what constitutes good and bad Burgundy. If he dislikes what he is being offered, he should vote with his feet and buy elsewhere.

Appellations in the Côte d'Or

	Côte de Nuits	Côte de Beaune	Total
Grands Crus	25	8	33
Commune & Premier Cru	7	18	25
Communes	8	20	28
Sous Communales	1	15	16
Volnay Santenots	–	1	1
Régionales	14		
Totals	**41**	**14**	**62**	**117**

Notes: 1. The Côte d'Or comprises c. 8000 ha. of vineyards (=20,000 acres) spread over 45–55 kms. (28–35 miles) between Dijon and Sampigny.
2. Sous communales appellations are: 14 'Village plus Côte de Beaune', Côte de Nuits-Villages and Côte de Beaune-Villages.

Maximum yields and minimum alcohol levels

	Red Wines		White Wines	
Appellation	R de B	Alc.	R de B	Alc.
Communal/ Village	40	10.5	45	11.0
Premier Cru	40	11.0	45	11.5
Grand Cru	35	11.5	40	12.0

Notes: 1. R de B refers to the *Rendement de base,* the normally permitted maximum yield, expressed in hl/ha
2. Alc. refers to the minimum alcohol requirement and is expressed in degrees.
3. The above figures are those normally set for most appellations of the Côte d'Or.

CLIMATE AND MICROCLIMATES OF THE CÔTE D'OR

An old vigneron's saw proclaims that 'mieux vaut saison que laboraison', which loosely translated means that, when it comes to wine quality, weather usually has the final word. Whilst modern technology may have muted the effects, its general purport remains valid: that, between bud-burst in spring and harvest in autumn, weather contributes significantly to the character of a wine.

The Côte d'Or lies on the 47th parallel, near the northerly limit for regular viticulture, in a zone of continental, temperate climate. Here, away from maritime influences, the vines enjoy relatively short, warm summers and long, cool winters. In most years, this pattern promotes an even vegetative cycle, but irregularities at either end of the season give the weather an important and frequently decisive influence.

Paradoxically, the vine produces its best wines in marginal climates rather than its preferred habitat – the Mediterranean or the tropics. Thus, in more northerly vineyards of Burgundy, Bordeaux, Champagne and Germany, a long, slow ripening contributes to lower alcohol and greater aromatic finesse. Further south, regular hot summers give higher alcohol and greater uniformity, vintage variations having less importance.

The vine has specific minimum needs to fully ripen grapes; broadly these are: 1,400 hours of sunshine during the growing season, 685 mm of rainfall, a temperature of 15°C during flowering, an average summer temperature of 22°C, a winter average of 3°C and an annual average of 10°C (although the ideal is nearer to 15°C). In the Côte d'Or these minimum conditions are generally met; average rainfall exceeds 700 mm and sunshine averages 2,000 hours, providing some compensation for a lower than optimum average summer temperature of 19–20°C. In May the temperature can rise rapidly, helping the vine's buds to swell; in June an average of 16–18°C usually ensures trouble-free flowering, provided there is no rain to damage the fragile flowers and disrupt pollination.

These three critical parameters – sunshine, rainfall and temperature – work together; but how they are distributed throughout the growing season is just as important for quality as their totals or averages. Rainfall, in particular, is more beneficial in small regular doses than as a few memorable downpours. Similarly, an even, hot summer is better than a few weeks of searing heat followed by prolonged cool weather. Viticulteurs have to remember that two analytically equally ripe grapes may disguise completely different patterns of development.

The vine's various needs can be considered separately:

Light: the vine needs daylight for its most important process – photosynthesis, converting carbon dioxide and water to sugar and oxygen. Although sunshine is the most important provider of infra-red and ultra-violet light for this purpose, the process can continue in total cloud cover given reasonable warmth.

How much sunlight a vine receives depends on its gradient and exposure. In the Côte, south and south-east sloping sites are favoured, vines usually being planted down the fall line. But sunshine hours vary greatly from one vineyard to another; Pinot Noir grapes in Corton vineyards in west-facing Pernand-Vergelesses invariably ripen much later than those planted in south-facing Aloxe-Corton.

Pruning and trimming the foliage also affect the amount of direct sunlight that reaches the bunches later in the year. The current fashion is for higher summer-pruning, leaving a much taller canopy of leaves, which has been found to increase sugar levels by up to 2 degrees of potential alcohol. This has sometimes resulted in over-shading the ripening bunches, affecting skin ripening from direct contact with sunlight. Regular sunshine is also essential – the even distribution of sunshine hours being just as important as the total.

Heat: sunshine is also related to temperature – providing heat as well as light. Direct heat from the sun is, however, only one source of warmth: heat can be reflected off the soil or can arrive as convected heat from a warm air-flow – e.g. from low to higher ground.

While heat and light are known to be important in viti-culture, the optimum balance between them is less certain: can more light compensate for less heat or more daylight for less sunlight? Longer days in northern Europe make this of more than academic interest; what is known is that overall temperature is proportional to the sugar content of grapes and inversely proportional to acidity levels.

While extreme heat, which can cook the grapes, is relatively rare, extreme cold is less so. The Côte has on average some 60–70 days of recorded frost annually, which in memorable years such as 1956 and 1985 reached –27°C. Although the vine is a hardy plant and can tolerate short spells at around –25°C, prolonged exposure kills even the dormant vine.

Spring frosts are a particular risk in these northerly latitudes. Cautious growers make allowance for frost damage when pruning, but this is no help when several nights of late frost start scorching early buds. In the last fortnight of April 1991, for example, widespread damage – up to 100% in some lower-lying vineyards – was caused by several nights of severe frost. This presents little risk to the vine's long-term life, but reduces that year's potential crop size. Further north, Chablis growers have long used a variety of frost-protection measures from smudgy oil-stoves to sprays which coat the young buds with a protective layer of ice – this works because the latent heat of freezing acts as insulation. Vignerons of the Côte have yet to take such steps.

Water: water is needed both to keep the vine's vital functions going and for photosynthesis. It is absorbed directly through the leaves – although in very small quantities – and by osmosis through the roots, reaching the plant in a variety of forms: snow, hail, fog, rain, humidity and from spraying. In dry years the vine survives because its deep roots are able to pick up moisture from the bedrock, and it is the *trace elements* and minerals leached out from soil and rocks which supply most of its essential nutrients.

The importance of using rootstocks which rapidly establish a sound deep rooting-system, and cutting proliferous surface lateral roots to encourage this is appreciated by most better Domaines. In years such as 1976, 1988 and 1990, when drought, consequent on prolonged intense heat, put photosynthesis at risk, older vines with well-established roots were much less affected than younger plants. Although much of the Côte is on solid, seemingly impenetrable rock, the vine manages to insinuate its roots to depths of 10 metres or more; such is its survival instinct!

As with light and heat, the distribution of rainfall, particularly just before the vintage, is as important as the annual total. In dry years, enough rain to balance the volume of juice to skins and ensure a viable concentration has often meant the difference between a good and a great vintage. On the other hand, rain at flowering will cause *coulure,* when the flowers fail to set, and will disrupt pollination. Equally, excessive rain at harvest may swell the grapes and over-dilute the juice, or in severe cases cause the berries to burst and thus rot. Rain at almost any time may wash off protective sprays, making life difficult for the harassed vigneron.

In an area as diverse as the Côte, it is impossible to specify an optimum precipitation; so much depends on the soil drainage – one plot of gravel wilI effortlessly absorb several times what would waterlog a patch of clay. So not all vignerons view approaching rainclouds as a blessing.

Light, heat and water are thus the main climatic variables – how these are distributed in any given year constitutes that season's weather. As far as wine quality goes, it is not just the absolute levels of each but how they interact which matters.

Specifically, the ratio of damp to warmth seems critical in determining balance and harmony in a wine. In wet, cool years, wines are dilute and unripe and not much will save them. However, in wet but warm years, when the grapes may be ripe though dilute, wines often have considerable bouquet and finesse. A determined *saignée* will often restore the equilibrium (1982 was an excellent example). Conversely, years of excessive heat and low rainfall produce harsh, tannic, sometimes jammy wines, needing long bottle-age: there is nothing the vigneron can do to put things back in balance; 1976 is a fine example of this sort of vintage. Best of all is normal dampness with great warmth – which usually betokens a great vintage.

So often in such a marginal climate as Burgundy's, freak weather will cause scattered damage somewhere or other. Hail is the most frequent culprit, arriving with little advance notice at any time between April and August. The storms tend to be highly localised – often just a few hundred metres across – cutting savagely through anything in their path. Sheltered sites are far less hail-prone than more exposed vineyards on open plains or hillsides.

Hail is devastating: it can destroy flowers, scar leaves or split the grapes, provoking rot. In the worst cases it splits the wood, killing the plant. There are rockets which seed hail clouds with potassium iodide to disperse them, but these are expensive and of limited efficacy. In the face of a hail-storm the vigneron is virtually helpless.

High wind is less of a risk. Winds prevail from several directions – the best known and coldest being the northerly Bise. However, deleterious effects are usually confined to drying out the vegetation and cooling higher exposed sites, retarding maturity.

Against this array of potential destruction, the grower has only limited protection. Over the centuries fragmentation of the vineyards, which forces vignerons to have holdings scattered throughout one or several communes, has proved their best defence.

In addition, the variety of microclimates up and down the Côte plays an important part in the quality of what is produced. Essential to understanding the Côte d'Or is the realisation that, as well as being a complex geological mosaic, it is also a vast patchwork of microclimates. Growers who know their vineyards will talk of peculiarities and susceptibilities of each little plot as though they were a collection of eccentric humans: some are late developers, some capricious, some early ripeners, some frost-prone, some prone to dampness at the bottom, whilst others suffer unduly from wind.

Microclimates occur above, below and on the soil. The microclimate of the bunches may differ from that of the soil or roots – how the leaves are trellised or summer-pruned will alter one, whereas clay or gravel subsoil will affect the other. Both will be influenced by whether the soil is hoed or simply treated with herbicide and com-

Combes play an important part in the Côte's weather. Here the limestone outcrops of the Combe d'Orveaux form a striking backdrop to the vineyards of Chambolle-Musigny

pacted by heavy machinery as it passes between the rows.

The major factors determining microclimate are aspect, altitude, shelter, drainage and gradient. These, to a greater or lesser extent, modify the vine's environment. Elevation is also important: higher ground will have lower average temperatures than lower – adjusted by a lapse rate of 3 centigrade degrees per 300 vertical metres of displacement.

In the Côte, all these variables play a part. Although the vineyards are mostly exposed south or south-east, a multitude of smaller variations must be considered. Many of the best vineyards are on slopes of different gradients, some exposed, others sheltered by woods or hills. An almost infinite variety of soil types ensures a varied distribution of drainage, from hollow gravel to thick clays.

One of the most significant geographical features of the Côte is the series of recurrent 'combes' which bisect it laterally, generally on an east-west axis. These act as conduits for rain, and for small rivers, as well as forming efficient wind-tunnels which accelerate the air-flow, catching exposed vineyards in their path. Some are wider than others; all play an important part in the microclimate of nearby communes.

Equally significant is the microclimate round and within each bunch of grapes. Bunches near the top or edges of the foliage will mature at a different rate from those more densely shaded towards the centre, and those closer to the soil will enjoy a different heat regime from those farther away.

As growers well know, it is a profound mistake to regard a bunch of grapes as a homogeneous, evenly-ripe entity. The Pinot Noir in particular often produces very tightly-packed bunches which impedes free air-circulation, reducing cooling in hot weather and encouraging the spread of rot in damp conditions. Also it is not unusual for the outside of a bunch to be fully ripe while berries on the inside are still underdeveloped and high in acidity. Careful picking and sorting is thus essential.

A harvested grape represents the sum of a particular growing season. Successive vintages may yield grapes of equal ripeness from the same vineyard but the final wines may differ strongly. Analytical ripeness is therefore only the broadest indication of the likely result of vinification. Against extremes of weather, there is little the grower can do; however his management of soil and foliage, in particular, can significantly influence the quality of the fruit he harvests.

THE ENIGMA OF SOIL

Together with climate and grape variety, soil is among the most important determinants of wine quality. In Burgundy, unlike anywhere else in Europe except perhaps for Alsace and Germany, the classification of vineyard land depends as much on soil as on anything else. Nowhere is this more important than in the Côte d'Or. Looking at a map of the vineyards, it is apparent, though often barely credible, that no more than a few metres may separate a Grand Cru and a humble Village vineyard. These seemingly arbitrary divisions reflect the fact that centuries have convinced winemakers and tasters that there are systematic differences in wine quality between grapes from one plot and those from another. It is on such detailed differences that the AC classifications are based.

Noting differences does not mean that you can necessarily explain them. After all, a vineyard is more than just its soil; it is also *terroir*, a much discussed concept which comprises topsoil, subsoil, slope, exposure and microclimate, each of which contributes to a wine and thus might possibly account for any observed differences in quality. Furthermore, interactions between these various factors probably mean that the totality is more than simply the sum of its constituent parts and that it is meaningless to discuss the influence of one aspect of *terroir* without considering the others.

Nonetheless, experience in Burgundy suggests that, even when other factors have been eliminated, differences remain, for which soil is the most plausible explanation. Specifying the mechanisms involved has fascinated geologists, vignerons and tasters for decades.

Soil is a diffuse concept. In common speech it signifies whatever you put your spade or hoe into, but to the geologist it refers only to the top layer of a vertical profile of the vineyard, those beneath being the underlying superficial sediment and the substratum of solid rock. The way the earth has evolved makes it shaky to conclude that all the layers are of the same composition; on the contrary, each has its own particular properties. What is clear is that soils perform two quite distinct functions for the vine: their physical properties affect its water regime and heat-retentive environment, whilst chemical properties influence its nourishment and growth.

For fine wine the optimum physical properties of soils are those related mainly to their drainage. The balance is delicate: vines die rapidly in places where their roots are waterlogged, but equally need a reservoir of accessible water into which deep roots can tap in years of drought. However, surface damp and consequent high humidity in soils, such as those on plains near the RN74 which are notably high in clay, are undesirable, since they create frost-pockets which can lead to damage. Most of the vines lost in the Côte in the great frosts of 1985 were on this flatter, frost-prone land which, fortunately, is zoned mainly for Regional and Village AC.

As a general rule in the Côte d'Or, the favoured vineyard sites are those on well-drained hillsides, where excess water and cold air can spill off and where exposure to heat and light are maximised. However, the soil at the top of these slopes is generally too thin – giving finesse and subtlety to wines, but without much structure; whilst that at the base is the opposite – too rich and deep, excellent for structure but producing little by way of finesse. Hence the finest vineyards tend to lie in the heart of the hill, where the soils produce an optimal balance of structure and elegance.

In addition to good drainage, the heat-retentive properties of the surface soils play a small, but useful, role. By storing up heat, which is radiated back into the surrounding air, stony soils can, for example, make a difference to the vulnerability of buds to a snap late spring frost, or even raise sugar levels and tip the balance towards success in a marginal vintage.

Among the physical properties of soil, the size and cohesion of topsoil particles are of particular importance. Many Premier and Grand Cru *climats* along the Côte are on slopes as steep as 20 degrees, where rainstorms can easily dislodge large amounts of loose earth, which the unfortunate grower is then obliged to take back up again. This instant soil erosion is particularly destructive, since the finer particles, which are invariably the most easily washed away, are those considered to be among the most important for quality. Fortunately, a high proportion of stones and pebbles in many vineyards helps with soil retention.

Soil erosion is not confined to the steep slopes; even in vineyards such as Le Montrachet or the lower part of Romanée-Conti, on slopes of 5° and 3°40' respectively, rain can remove topsoil to an extent which necessitates replacement. Whatever the soil, if enough continuous rain fails to saturate the topmost few centimetres of the topsoil, it will erode.

To combat this, some growers are experimenting with grasses, sown between vine rows, to act as soil retainers. These are effective, but tend to compete with the vine for water – which is undesirable, especially in hot dry years such as 1976 or 1988 when water is at a premium. Grasses also change the reflectivity of the soil and are notoriously prodigious potassium consumers, so such regimes can also affect the vine's nutrient balance.

Soil is, however, more than just an inert, more or less cohesive, growing medium for the vine; it is also the means by which it obtains much of its nourishment. The overriding need is for water – there is no chemical reaction of the vine which is independent of it – and, apart from minute quantities picked up directly from the leaves during rain or spraying, the vine relies principally on its roots tapping into reservoirs in the subsoil and rock for its supplies.

This ability of roots to delve down and extract water from the subsoils has a further benefit. Since many substances necessary for plant growth are water-soluble, they may be leached out of the soil by water and transferred to the vine by osmosis. Although the precise mechanisms by which plants extract nourishment from soils are imperfectly understood, it seems likely that more is gained from direct contact between root and soil than from waterborne transfer. In a region such as the Côte d'Or, making great wine is more complex than simply planting a vine in sites which are neither waterlogged nor frost-pockets. Widely different soil-types support a large variety of vine-types, so it is a matter of finding which are best adapted to any given soil. Pinot Noir and Chardonnay may perform magnificently in the limestone soils of the Côte d'Or and Champagne, but would be a poor choice for the gravels of the Médoc.

In addition to the appropriate fundamental soil-type, certain *base elements* – principally nitrogen, potassium and phosphorus – are essential to support proper plant growth. Other useful *trace elements,* mostly minerals, may also be present in greater or lesser quantities. It is known that the vine can use either sort of element to meet its needs. What is not known is whether, or how, a particular substance will intervene to affect wine quality. The best the vigneron can do is to commission regular deep soil analyses and use these to fine-tune his soils by sensible use of fertilisers. Once a reasonable balance has been established, fertilisers are largely unnecessary.

Keeping soils properly balanced is skilled work, serious mistakes often having long-term and costly consequences. Vignerons on the Côte well remember the 1960s and 1970s when cash-rich growers were persuaded by eloquent fertiliser salesmen to overindulge their vineyards in potassium. The results, which are still being felt some 30 years later, were disastrously low wine acidity levels and thus wines which disintegrated prematurely. Unfortunately it is known that potassium never fully degrades; a classic study in the UK (Warren & Johnston, 1962) showed that even after 56 years, an application of potassium fertiliser was still having a marked effect. It seems that potassium taken up by the vine will be held until loss through the grapes and thorough pruning gradually removes it.

Although soil undeniably contributes to the taste of a wine, the mechanisms are poorly understood. What is clear is that there is no simple correlation between soil-type and taste; for example, a high iron content does not bring a taste of iron, nor a chalky soil a taste of chalk. The influences appear to be infinitely more subtle.

What, therefore, can be said about the quality of soil which is most likely to produce fine wine? There is a common belief that 'vines, like poets, produce their best when they must struggle for survival . . . in the anaemic soil that is typical of the best growths' (Lichine, 1982). Vignerons also believe this; how often does one hear them declare that 'the vine must be made to suffer'? – and 'vine stress' is common New World currency.

However, the relationship between viticulture and poor soil is far from universal. Whilst the meagre, nitrogen-less soils of the Médoc would support little else, except perhaps forest, much of the Côte d'Or is perfectly adaptable to other cultures. Until just after the last war, blackcurrants were harvested commercially in Puligny from what is now vineyard land.

What is probably true is that, historically, vines being long-lived plants requiring minimum maintenance were planted on soils that were of little use for much else, or too hard to work. Also, because the vine needs a long, warm ripening season, the farther north one goes, the more likely it is that vineyards are to be found on hillsides to catch as much sunlight as possible. This, together with naturally greater erosion on slopes, means that soils tend to be poorer than those on plains, where alluvial deposits and river silts have collected. Hence, perhaps, the enduring myth of poor soils.

The real importance of a relatively nutrient-deficient topsoil is to encourage the vine to establish a deep root system, to extract nourishment from the subsoils and to insure against drought.

Professor Hancock, the eminent British geologist, in a personal communication, points out that 'modern vines based on American rootstock obtain most of their nourishment from relatively shallow roots, often not more than 0.4 m deep . . . However, within many regions of fine wine production, the natural soil layer is very thin, only of the order of 0.2 m; on the other hand, many of the regions that produce largish quantities of mediocre wine have thicker soils.'

Thus, he concludes, the common belief in the importance of poor soil 'has an element of truth, but is a somewhat misleading simplification. It is more a matter of the balance that is suitable for the vines.'

Geologists have long known that the entire Côte sits on a bedrock of limestone, formed around 150–170 million years ago during the Jurassic period. At that time there was a warm shallow sea lapping against the ancient rocks of the Massif Central, a short distance to the west. Limestones, sometimes alternating with various amounts of clay, accumulated slowly in this sea. Since the Jurassic period, sea levels have oscillated many times, but with the lower sea levels of today the Jurassic limestones and clays are exposed at the surface. In many places the strata have collapsed downwards towards the valley, along fractures parallel to the hillside.

During the last glaciation, the remnants of which can still be seen around the Poles, the Côtes were subjected to deep freezing every winter. During each summer thaw, the surface sediments slid down the hillsides over the frozen rocks beneath, even on slopes of only a few degrees. Many of the famous vineyards are located on these slide-deposits, although some, such as Chevalier-Montrachet, are underlain by solid limestone. In addition, over the millennia water has permeated the underlying rocks, removing soluble limestone, leaving the insoluble sand-like and clay impurities, the proportions of which in the topsoil have thus progressively increased.

Against this geological background, the soils on the Côte d'Or have been intensively studied, partly to understand better which vines are best adapted to which soils, and partly to see if there is any discernible correlation between wine quality and soil-type. Limestone appears particularly favourable to the production of *vins de garde* whereas, for example, granitic soils tend to produce more rapidly maturing wines. Differences between Riesling sites in Alsace provide striking demonstrations of this.

In a classic study, published in 1957, Mme Rolande Gadille analysed extensive soil samples from all over the Côte, but, although many interesting relationships emerged, she found no obvious correlation between soil-type and wine quality.

A later study by a group of eminent French geologists (Meriaux et al., 1981) attempted to relate various physical characteristics of the villages of the Côte – slope, stoniness, clay and total limestone content – to quality levels. They found that the better vineyards – i.e. Premiers and Grands Crus – tended to be on slopes of more than 3%, with average stoniness of 5–40% and a clay content which is finer than that of Regional AC or Bourgogne land. Higher limestone contents were also noted in the better sites.

To date, available studies have yielded little information for anyone hoping to list the soil ingredients – either necessary or sufficient – for a Côte d'Or Grand Cru. However, it still seems highly probable that soil is an important determinant of the typicity of the communes and *climats* up and down the Côte, since, removing variables which blur the picture – grower, microclimate, etc. – there remain significant and systematic differences between wines produced in adjacent vineyards and in different communes.

Soil is only part of a complex equation on the Côte. While geologists and other experts are cautious in their conclusions, others generalise and misrepresent its properties and classification in an attempt to unravel the fascinating enigmas of the region. So far, it would seem that it is the physical properties of vineyard soils and rocks which play a greater part in influencing wine quality than any obvious differences in chemical composition.

For anyone tempted to oversimplify the difficulty of disentangling the role of soil from other influences, a neat experiment by Professor Ravasse at Montpellier might just dissuade them: he concreted over half a plot of vines and compared its wine with that produced from the other half. Over 27 years, he found no significant differences in productivity or richness of sugar. However, the concreted vines tended to wilt rather more when it became very hot!

In the words of the eminent French geologist, Professor Noël Leneuf, 'There must always be an element of mystery,' this is what drives curiosity. At the same time, one cannot help but agree with Professor Hancock that whilst 'geology is only a matter of theoretical interest to the drinker, it is of vital importance to the grower.'

PINOT NOIR

The Pinot Noir is the most capricious of all grape varieties – invariably demanding from the grower, winemaker and drinker the utmost forbearance and respect. It is highly sensitive to climate, soil, pruning and training, and especially to how it is handled and vinified. At its best it produces wines which are sensuous, magnificently perfumed and seductively fleshy, at its worst, meagre, angular offerings with charmless, raw, stalky flavours and enough acidity to run a car battery.

One might ask why people persevere with such a mischievous, moody grape; after all, there are plenty of alternatives. On the Côte d'Or growers sometimes express frustration at its unpredictability, but cling like gamblers to the fascination it provides in the face of an attainable, but irritatingly elusive, jackpot.

They have certainly had plenty of experience. Pinot Noir's long history on the Côte began with its debut as a named variety – Pinot Noirien – around 1375, although plantings of a similar vinifera variety were documented as far back as the first century AD. Philippe the Bold, Duc de Bourgogne, saw the need to plant better varieties for the soils in his vineyards to give of their best and, persuaded of its value, issued an edict in 1395 in favour of the Pinot Noir, banning the more prolific and less noble Gamay.

Custom and law have since enshrined the pre-eminence of Pinot Noir as the Côte's noble red grape. However, it is wrong to think of it as a single variety. Not only has it been heavily cloned since the late 1950s, it has also spawned a healthy population of spontaneous genetic mutations. Henri Gouges, for example, started his Nuits-St.-Georges Blanc in the 1930s when he found vines in his Perrière vineyard with both red and white grapes sprouting from the same plant.

Most of the Pinot vines planted on the Côte, whether clones or individual *sélection massale,* have the Pinot Fin as parent. This strain – also known as the Pinot Tordu because of its misshapen trunk – is considered the only Pinot variety suitable for producing the finest Burgundies. But there is another, less fine, strain – Pinot Droit. So named because it grows straight upwards, it is more prolific than the Pinot Fin and much easier to work with. Many growers, seduced by the prospect of less labour and more wine, saw the Pinot Droit as a ready means of increasing their incomes. Plantings mushroomed in the 1960s and 1970s, until the disparity in quality became apparent. Any remaining are gradually being replaced with Pinot Fin, especially in the better sites, as the vines expire.

Physically the Pinot Noir is characterised by small, tight bunches and a small, mid-green leaf. The compact, pine-cone shape of the clusters is thought to be the origin of the name Pinot (it means 'pine' in French). Compared with the Cabernet Sauvignon, for example, the Pinot bunches are some 40–50% smaller and the leaves some 4% smaller in overall dimension. In warm, humid conditions this compactness provides an ideal microclimate for rot to develop and spread, so clones with looser clusters tend to be favoured. Research is currently in progress to develop clones with smaller berries and a looser cluster.

The grape also has a fragile skin, difficult to ripen fully, which is partly responsible for the Pinot's reputation for giving a relatively light-coloured wine. More seriously for the grower, a thin skin provides easy access for the grape-worm, a perennial nuisance in most Côte d'Or vineyards. This insect punctures the grape, leaving a wound which then rapidly becomes rotten; if the rot spreads, it severely affects the quality of the wine.

The Pinot's susceptibility to both mildew and grey rot accounts for at least some of its awkwardness. It is also highly vulnerable to the fan-leaf virus *(court-noué)* which, in the years of neglect both during and immediately following the last war, ran riot through many of the best vineyards. Transmitted by a root-sucking worm, and by grafting, it appears to be encouraged by overtired soil and enfeebled vines. Its effects are clearly visible: the leaves turn yellow and fall off and their veins spread out into a fan-shape. Degeneration and finally the death of the vine are inexorable consequences, without the possibility of a cure. Where vines are infected, the only realistic solution is to grub up, disinfect the soil and replant with virus-free grafts.

The Pinot Noir is a notoriously early budder, making it particularly susceptible to spring frosts. For this reason many growers prune their vines generously to ensure that at least some buds come to fruition. It needs a long, reasonably even growing season to ripen fully, and abhors extremes of heat. Those with plantings in the hotter regions of California and elsewhere have found that no amount of cool fermentation will restore finesse and delicacy, once the grapes have been ripened to their jammy maximum.

There has been much study of how best to train and prune Pinot Noir in the Côte. In Santenay and Chassagne, in particular, it is trained *en cordon de Royat,* experience suggesting that in their rich soils the grape performs better with extended vegetation and a less productive bud distribution. Although no-one can satisfactorily explain why, the strain planted here is also different from elsewhere on the Côte. The 'plante fin de Santenay' seems well adapted to its environment, and growers know how to coax the best from it.

The Pinot's capriciousness extends to its taste. Although adaptable to a variety of methods of vinification, it exhibits a much greater diversity of style than either the Cabernet Sauvignon or the Syrah. Whilst these manage to retain their fingerprints almost wherever they are grown, the chameleon Pinot puts on a different expression for each origin. Tasters faced with a line of Pinots from around the world might be hard put to it to identify the common denominator, so complete are its disguises.

In Burgundy, Pinot Noir responds well to a marginal climate and well-drained, meagre soils predominantly high in limestone. It performs best when vines are old and yields low. However it is truculent and fussy about where it shines. Because of its relative fragility (Pinot skins are in fact more robust than is generally believed), it needs to be fully ripe before it will vinify into a balanced wine.

Wines made from low yields of ripe Pinot will support a good larding of new oak, and can age magnificently. Tantalising glimpses of the majesty of which Pinot Noir is capable are enough to keep growers everywhere, not just on the Côte, struggling to emulate. The greatest of Burgundies will continue to inspire those for whom, whether openly admitted or not, that ravishing silky opulence and extraordinary complexity remain an enduring goal.

The quest for a Pinot Noir wine which comes near to matching a Côte d'Or Grand Cru has become like a Holy Grail, especially for many New World winemakers. To date, Parsifal has yet to appear.

252

CHARDONNAY

In contrast to the Pinot Noir, the Chardonnay is a model of obedience and good behaviour. Not only is it versatile, resilient and content to grow in a variety of soils and climates, it is adaptable to almost any vinification to which it is subjected. At best opulent, rich and concentrated, with remarkable longevity, Chardonnay represents for many the epitome of what dry white wine should be. Wherever planted, it seems to wear its heart on its sleeve and to present an attractive personality, whatever the adversities. For producer or consumer, Chardonnay is exuberantly user-friendly.

The history of Chardonnay is less well documented than that of the Pinot Noir; there is an obscure little village in the Mâconnais called Chardonnay, which may have something to do with its origins, but whether it has, or indeed whether the grape predated the village or vice versa, remains a mystery. When it first arrived in the Côte is also uncertain. Although the nobility of some of the great Grand Cru sites, such as Montrachet and Corton, was recognised as long ago as the eighth century, their plantings were then a mixture of indigenous varieties rather than a single *cépage*. Aligoté was widely planted until the end of the 19th century.

If the origins of Chardonnay are blurred, so is its ancestry. Constant references to 'Pinot Chardonnay' reflected the widespread belief that it was a white mutant of the Pinot Noir. This has been disproved, but growers still talk of it and believe there is a link.

In the vineyard the vine flourishes without giving the vigneron undue trouble. It buds early, which renders it susceptible to spring frosts, but can support prolonged winter cold without suffering. Together with their colleagues in Chablis, the growers of the Côte remember the winter of 1956, when the thermometer plunged to −27°C and stayed there long enough to destroy a high percentage of the Côte's vines, both Pinot Noir and Chardonnay.

Provided it can enjoy a long, even growing season, with reasonable warmth, the Chardonnay will ripen well. It has a knack of attaining high sugar levels in conditions which would leave other varieties wanting and therefore needs less *chaptalisation,* although it can become flabby if it is harvested too late, or with low acidity.

Left to its own devices the Chardonnay will proliferate foliage in every direction. Whilst this may look healthy, it dissipates the vine's energies into leaves rather than bunches. This natural vigour makes it imperative for the vigneron to prune short and to remove excess buds and shoots early on in the summer if he wants to harvest a crop of balanced, concentrated grapes. The Chardonnay vine is also very susceptible to *oïdium* and to *court-noué*.

On the Côte, ripening depends very much on the individual site – the cooler westerly expositions of Pernand and Savigny, for example, or the higher, more exposed slopes of St.-Aubin or Chassagne, needing an extra week or more to bring grapes to maturity than south or south-east facing *climats* of Puligny or Meursault.

The Chardonnay is not at all fussy about soils – doing well, if not spectacularly, on the high pH, acid-neutral soils of the Mâconnais and performing to perfection, if differently, on the Kimmeridgian clays of Chablis. However, the better adaptability of the soils to Pinot Noir means there are no significant plantings of Chardonnay in the Côte de Nuits. The few plots that do exist – Musigny and Morey in particular – suggest that it would probably perform respectably if given the chance.

A ripe bunch of Chardonnay grapes. Mottled skin discolours the wine if the juice is left in contact with it for too long

In the Côte de Beaune the best sites, including the Grands Crus, are those with well-drained, predominantly limestone soils; however, attempts to correlate soil-type and quality have so far produced nothing more than a plethora of inconclusive statistics. Montrachet has obviously no intention of divulging its secret.

One of the great virtues of Chardonnay is its ability to produce fine wine at yields at which the Pinot Noir would taste positively watery. Top growers who would put an upper bound of 35 hl/ha or so on Pinot Noir will show no sign of undue discomfort if their Chardonnay brings in half as much again. This may have more to do with not needing to balance solids to liquids in white vinification than to any special characteristic of Chardonnay.

In the cellar, the Chardonnay is equally malleable. It will deliver fine quality whether fermented cool or warm, whether vinified in new oak, old oak or stainless steel, and will be happy bottled early or after a year or more in cask. It supports *élévage* in virtually any type of new oak barrels, rarely becoming unduly tannic or *boisé*.

However, its tendency to develop high sugar levels, particularly during the final stages of ripening, usually occurs at the expense of acidity. So in exceptionally hot vintages, such as 1983, it can become clumsy and alcoholic, unless steps are taken to retain natural acidity. Growers who are tempted to delay picking can find themselves with very rich, soft, super-ripe wines which appear over-blown and deficient in grip; in short, too much fat and no stays!

The greatest of the Chardonnay's attributes is its ability to age. Whilst a young Grand Cru may be pleasant to drink, it is with years in bottle that it really begins to express its origins and to show its breeding. The balance between youth and age is, however, finer with white wine than with red – the absence of significant tannin bringing even the slightest hint of over-oxidation into sharp relief.

Although growers throughout the viticultural world have scaled notably greater heights with Chardonnay than with Pinot Noir, their untiring efforts to match the restrained depth and power of the Côte's white Grands Crus continue to meet with limited success. There is a dimension of understated elegance and class in a fine Corton, Meursault or Puligny, which seems to defy mimicry.

CHOOSING WHAT TO PLANT

However sophisticated one's vinification techniques, quality ultimately depends on the raw material – the grapes. These, in turn, are determined by the location of the vineyard, the climate and, above all the type and quality of the plant.

A European vine plant consists of two distinct halves grafted together: a scion, the top section which determines the grape variety, and a rootstock, the lower section, which establishes the rooting-system and contributes to the adaptability of the plant to its soil and to its general growth characteristics. Both halves are important as is the vigneron deciding what to plant.

Half a century ago he had little choice; he could either buy plants ready grafted or *phylloxera*-resistant rootstock, make a selection of scion from his own vines *(sélection massale)* and cobble together his own grafts. Though most conscientious vignerons preferred their own grafts, the results were haphazard; if these survived the first year or so, they could not be relied upon either to be disease-free or to produce regularly.

It was not until the late l960s that the science of plant selection and breeding turned its attention to the vine: by 1969 it was able to offer growers a choice of individually selected and bred clones of Pinot Noir and Chardonnay, together with a range of rootstocks to suit a variety of soil types. Gradually, as the results of these early clones were studied and the industry developed, growers were persuaded to abandon home-made selections in favour of the commercially produced alternatives. But the Burgundian vigneron is not to be rushed; a few still distrust the quality of standard clones and continue to produce their own plant material.

Clones: A clone is 'a group of individuals produced by means of vegetative propagation of a single organism' (Becker, 1982). In fact, both the Pinot Noir and the Chardonnay one sees in the vineyards are not one genotype but a population – thousands of clones and mutations – from which some few hundred have been studied intensely to produce the handful currently marketed.

To establish an individual variety it is necessary to start from a single pip, bud or eye from the vine; however, efforts are now being made to propagate direct from genetic material, to refine the selection further. Developing a clone takes 12–15 years, since at each stage the propagated plants have to be observed and further culled before they can be multiplied in commercial quantities.

The original impetus for cloning was the widespread virus degeneration, especially of Chardonnay, which ravaged the Côte in the 1950s. Once virus-free strains had been developed, the emphasis changed to selecting for varietal purity and for quality.

The aim of cloning is not to change the spectrum of a grape variety but to refine the strain so that there is less variability. This means maximising both the strain's state of health and its varietal purity. In developing a clone, selection is made both for positive attributes – higher sugar levels and better sugar/acid balance, stability of performance, resistance to frost, pigment quality, date of budding and ripening, berry size, leaf and wood development, etc. – and for absence of negative qualities – disease and viral infection.

In Europe, emphasis is placed on obtaining disease-resistant stock, whereas in the USA it tends to be on developing disease-free stock – these are not the same. Disease-free stock has been found to produce better yields and sugar levels which in the end result in better wines.

At each stage of clone selection – there are usually three 3-5-year stages in all – as well as consideration of observable qualities of the kind outlined above, account is taken of such matters as soil and exposure requirements and how the vine will be pruned and trained. In addition, grapes from each population of clones are micro-vinified to determine what qualities each imparts to a finished wine, and some 5 years' tasting establishes consistency of quality and ascertains how the wine stands up to bottle-ageing.

The final stage in clonal development is to ensure that each individual plant is virus-free. Originally the entire vine would be heat-treated to achieve this, but modern techniques rely on irradiation of just the shoots. However, freedom from viruses is no guarantee that once in the hurly-burly of the vineyard, a vine will develop none. So once planted out in the real world, clones are closely observed and periodically overhauled and reselected. The grower can remain blissfully ignorant of all this – 'You don't have to know how the tractor works to drive it,' remarked one. However, most on the Côte take a keen interest in clones and their habits, and the matter of *sélection clonale* versus *sélection massale* is much discussed in café society.

When it comes to choosing what to plant, the careful grower must take several factors into account. Some varieties of Pinot Noir yield markedly more than others – for example, the infamous Pinot Droit strain has several permitted clones which are responsible for much of the overproduction in Burgundy; although eschewed by most top-quality growers, it is still quite widely planted.

Furthermore, it is generally believed best to plant several different clones of one variety in each vineyard rather than just one. This encompasses two important ideas: firstly, that a single clone will yield a rather standard wine, whereas three or four mixed together will produce greater complexity, and secondly, that if you rely on a single clone and it happens to develop a fault or a disease, then you have lost your production in that vineyard until you replant – an unacceptable risk.

The second idea is perhaps sound sense. The first, however, is false – according to Professor Raymond Bernard, who was one of the developers of clones in Burgundy in the late 1950s. His experiments have shown that a single clone will often produce the best wine. In his view, clones are often blamed for poor quality, when the true culprit is excessive yield. Growers are also perhaps operating in the mistaken belief that the best quartet is a combination of the best four soloists. Whatever his planting policy, a grower must realise that each clone has its own characteristics: some give higher sugar/alcohol levels whilst others ripen earlier or give more even ripeness, and so on.

The Burgundian vigneron is a distinctly cautious species. Although many are devout partisans of clones, others, whilst grudging converts, continue to regard them as a mixed blessing. Some, perhaps persuaded by neighbours, are just beginning to try a few clones to see what happens, whilst a few Domaines remain steadfast in their refusal to countenance clones under any circumstances. However, after 25 years' experience, there is much for which growers along the Côte may thank Raymond Bernard.

Degenerative viruses – especially *court-noué,* which severely

Fresh grafts, ready for planting

attacked the Chardonnay plants of Puligny and Chassagne after the Second World War – are under control and, in consequence, a vigneron can now be sure that some 90–95% of his vines will produce every year, whereas before the proportion was no greater than 60–75%, a factor which partly accounts for today's higher yields.

Whilst new clones appear and established ones are taken in for routine maintenance, much is being done to improve what there is, particularly in the area of virus susceptibility. Experiments in Colmar, Alsace, with vines which are given a low dose of virus and then planted out in a plot affected by that same virus, seem to indicate that it may be possible to effectively 'vaccinate' plants against specific infections. But the emergence of new strains of virus make this more complex than it might at first appear.

Out in the field, some 80% of vignerons are now using Chardonnay clones, whereas only 50% have accepted clones of Pinot Noir. Among the experts there is concern that the variety of commercially available clones in both varieties has become too great. There is a compelling argument for adding to the INAO's controls a list of approved clones for planting on AC land, especially in the Premier and Grand Cru *climats* where the temptation to go for high yields most needs to be restrained.

Rootstocks: Before the epidemic of *phylloxera* which progressively destroyed some 75% of viticultural France from about 1863 to 1900, and much of the rest of Europe's vineyards later, vines were planted on their own roots. However, after considerable misery and fruitless experiment, it was discovered that the only effective protection against attacks from this louse was to plant vines on to *phylloxera*-resistant American roots. Thus was the rootstock born.

Today, except for some New World plantings and a handful of surviving pre-*phylloxera* vineyards in Champagne, the Douro valley and elsewhere, vines are customarily planted on to selected resistant rootstock. However, choosing a suitable rootstock is almost as complicated as choosing the scion on to which it is to be grafted. As Kunkee and Goswell noted in 1976, 'selection of . . . rootstock for use in control of nematodes and *phylloxera* is far more complicated than merely assessing resistance and making the graft.'

The most commonly used rootstocks, developed by much the same techniques as clones from crossings derived from two of three American parents (vitis rupestris, vitis riparia or vitis berlandieri), have their own strengths and characteristics. From these, further crossings of European vines with American rootstocks are made to produce the ideal roots for various combinations of soil, climate,

graft, etc. The result is a wide variety of acceptable resistant roots from which, theoretically, the vigneron can choose.

However, years of experiment and observation have narrowed the choice down to a handful of practicable affinities. It would be a foolish grower who ignored decades of distilled collective wisdom and planted his vines on something wildly heterodox.

The principal considerations in choosing suitable roots, for the Côte d'Or or for anywhere else, are the vigour of the root, the soil into which it is to be planted and adaptability to the scion and the microclimate. It is important to realise that the rootstock is not inert, but interacts with the scion during their life together and, as with any marriage, success is due as much to compatibility, however ill-suited they may sometimes appear, as to income – i.e. yield.

In particular, the vigour of the roots must balance that of the scion: too much and the flowers may abort or unwanted foliage abound – the headless chicken phenomenon; too little and the grapes will not mature properly. The S04 rootstock, of which there are still significant plantings in all parts of the Côte d'Or, produces high vigour to start with and then seems to degenerate, probably because of low resistance to active lime in the soil; however, some growers have older plots of vines on S04 which are still producing superbly.

Soil affinity is also critical – some roots have a high tolerance of calcium, excess salinity, acidity, etc. whilst others are less successful in richer soils with a high clay content. This is especially important in the Côte d'Or where soils can vary significantly within the space of a few metres. For example, the latest strain of 161/49, which is now replacing the S04 on sloping sites, is particularly well adapted to soils with a high active lime content whereas other, less adaptive roots result in the development of *chlorosis*.

Not all roots are suitable partners for all scions. This is not a matter of gross incompatibility, rather of fine tuning. For example, an inappropriate rootstock could lead to uneven development of sap, too early a flowering or too late a ripening, all of which matter in Burgundy's marginal, continental climate.

The conscientious grower will also take account of the microclimate of the individual site which is to be planted. Is it excessively humid, a frost-pocket, or perhaps particularly wet or windy? If it is low-lying, as is much of the Côte, and thus near to the water-table – as at Puligny-Montrachet or in the lower parts of the Clos de Vougeot –then a shallower-rooting stock is preferable.

Along the Côte d'Or a handful of clones and roots are currently in widespread use. Of the Pinot Noir clones, 113, 114 and 115 – all developed from a mother vine in Morey-St.-Denis and first marketed in 1971 – are popular, as are 667 and 777 which became available in 1980. For Chardonnay, B75, B76, B77, B95 and B96 are common, as is the B548 propagated from a *vigne mère* at La Vineuse in the Saône-et-Loire and first marketed in 1978.

The most widely planted rootstocks in the Côte are the 161/49, which performs best on well-drained sloping terrain, the 3309, a *chlorosis*-prone rootstock which prefers soils with less active lime and is used in semi-sloping vineyards where the soil is richer, and the S04 which is still used by some growers who seem able to make it work. There is also a renaissance of Riparia, which is particularly adapted to deeper soils and is effective in limiting vine vigour.

The distillation of all this is that there are a great number of factors to be considered before planting a vineyard. Fortunately for the vigneron there is much free expert help at hand, so he does not have to cudgel his brains to disentangle the intricacies. Provided he remembers that you cannot make an inappropriate grape-variety succeed by the expedient of grafting it on to an 'appropriate' root-stock, he is unlikely to make any earth-shattering mistakes.

MAINTAINING THE VINE

The vigneron who has chosen and planted his vines with care must then coax them into producing the best possible fruit. In deciding how to achieve this, he must project his thoughts beyond the short-term, extrapolating the effects of each treatment or practice beyond one growing season, over the life-expectancy of the vine. There are two undisputed keys to producing quality wine: healthy vines and low yields. These are not alternatives: it is no use having exuberantly healthy plants overproducing, or tiny yields from diseased vines.

How a plant performs depends as much as anything upon the soil it grows in. Neither in chemical nor in physical structure is the soil beyond the vigneron's sphere of influence. Chemically, repeated use of strong, toxic sprays will destroy the fragile balance of yeasts and bacteria which constitute the soil's micro-flora, and can alter soil pH. Physically, modern heavy machinery will gradually break up and compact the topsoil, altering its drainage properties.

Many of the Côte's finest vineyards, for example the hill of Corton and the top sectors of Vosne-Romanée, are on steep slopes. Not only does this make mechanical working difficult, it also increases the likelihood of soil erosion, when heavy rain washes down valuable topsoil which the wretched vigneron then has to take back up again. To combat this, he may allow natural grasses to grow or consider planting special grasses to help retain the soils. This *enherbement* is still experimental; whilst it appears to be an excellent preventive the grass tends to retain moisture which both increases frost-risk and also takes valuable water from the vines in dry summers.

Under normal circumstances vignerons have to decide whether to hoe their vineyards or to use chemical herbicides to eradicate grass and weeds. The former aerates the soil but also makes it sticky, restricting access to the vineyards after rain. Furthermore, the mechanical hoes used may physically damage the vine trunks, which can lead to Esca – a sort of vine apoplexy which kills the plant. The alternative is to use herbicides, but these contaminate the soil. There is significantly less erosion when the soil is hoed since water penetrates more easily and binds the topsoil. Twenty-five years ago, only 10% of the Côte's vineyards were treated with herbicides – hence less erosion; nowadays the proportion is estimated at 85%.

The growth and health of the vine, as well as the structure of the soil, are also affected by fertilisation. In the 1960s and 1970s fertiliser salesmen and prosperous vignerons combined to saturate much of the Côte with potassium-rich fertiliser. Thirty years later, the soils are finally shaking off this imbalance, which led to wines with high pHs and low acidities. Vignerons are more enlightened, and the best only use the minimum of organic humus, manure, or nothing at all.

Even the minimum may be a mistake, since some 80% of commercial organic fertilisers have no nutritive value beyond adding unwanted nitrogen to the soil. Nonetheless, a well fermented humus may help prevent soil erosion and can act as a small water reservoir, which is especially valuable on hillsides. Some vignerons mulch vine prunings back into the soils, for much the same reasons, but this merely recycles the potassium they contain.

Vignerons are now realising the need to take much greater care with their soil management. Neither excess plant vigour nor destabilised micro-flora contribute anything positive to wine quality.

Left to itself, the vine is a rambling plant and a notoriously irregular producer – a few bunches one year and perhaps a glut the next. To reduce its proliferousness and to ensure that foliage and bunches receive maximum insolation, it must be trained and pruned. Vines are also individuals – some are more vigorous than others, some mature their fruit better, etc. – so, within the rules of each appellation the vigneron must adapt his work to his vines.

There is no doubt that the severity of each winter's pruning, how many eyes per vine the grower leaves, is fundamental in determining the potential quality of the wine he makes. In the Côte d'Or the law sets a limit of 80,000 buds per ha – i.e. 8 buds per vine, assuming the usual vine-density of 10,000 per ha. This corresponds to a yield of some 40-45 hl/ha – too much, at least for Pinot Noir in Grand Cru sites. Growers for whom quality really matters, prune more strictly; this entails a risk, if there is frost or hail.

Once the vine has started to grow, the vigneron must remove any double shoots or excess buds from each vine. This task, *évasivage/dédoublage,* normally undertaken in early spring, is an essential operation in limiting yields; how many passes a grower makes through his vines is an indicator of quality; some are noticeably more conscientious than others. Research at Dijon indicates that if more than 6 buds remain on a vine, then only quality drops, whereas below 6 there is a progressive diminution in quantity.

Throughout the summer, excess foliage is removed to avoid humid microclimates for the bunches and to ensure that they get as much sun as possible. Nowadays, the tendency is to train and summer-prune the vines higher because this increases maturity and sugar levels. There is much research into the precise shape and height of *palissage* which is proving valuable in Burgundy's climate. However, too high a trellis risks creating patches of shade, preventing sunlight from reaching bunches at the centre.

In some years, despite his best efforts at pruning and thinning, the grower may still have too many bunches and decide to remove some. The theory is simple: the more bunches per vine, the less it can ripen them; reducing the charge will restore the balance.

However, there is heated disagreement as to whether this green-pruning works. Some growers believe it is nothing more than gimmickry since, when the time arrives, most of the potential has passed from the vine into the bunches – which are then cut off; in any case, the antagonists argue, the vines just compensate, so you are effectively back where you started. Others claim that the process works well, provided you do it at the right moment – at *veraison,* when the grapes are turning from green to black.

Green-pruning is very fashionable at the moment: local newspapers are full of photographs of people bent double, hard at work removing bunches from famous vineyards. Those who disagree scathingly counter that if you need to remove bunches then you had too many buds to start with – a self-inflicted excess. This controversy splits even top Domaines, and seems set to last.

Whatever he decides to do about excess bunches, the vigneron will probably be more preoccupied with keeping his vines free of the multifarious infestations which threaten from bud-burst to harvest. The problems are not simple – viruses may remain undetectable until it is too late to save the vine; pests rarely announce their arrival; an overnight storm can cause an outbreak of rot; the berries may swell and burst or the man next door may forget to spray, leaving your

One cure for soil erosion is to plant soil-retentive grass between the rows – as here in Domaine Gouge's Les Vaucrains vines in Nuits

vines vulnerable; the catalogue is endless.

A grower must determine a treatment policy and plan the skeleton of his annual regime in advance. He must decide whether to use only surface, contact products, which are the least harmful but which wash off at the merest drop of rain, or to opt for products which penetrate the vine or for systemics which remain active for much longer. He can either opt for the security of preventive treatments which may turn out to be unnecessary, or wait for the signs of infestation and then treat curatively with one of the excellent new products which, at least for *oïdium* and mildew, work recursively. Each system has its benefits and disadvantages.

In formulating his policy, the vigneron should take account of the longer-term effects of what he does. Problems of resistance and toxicity have caused a major reassessment, with many growers backing off from the ever-stronger synthetic products, which select out all but the most virulent forms of a disease, and turning towards a more natural, organic regime. Beyond promoting the immediate health of the vines, products may also leave residues which can significantly affect the course of fermentation.

Understandably, most growers are by nature cautious – preferring an extra treatment or two to the risk of disease – and having prospered, can afford to be so. However, many blatantly overtreat, which encourages rot and is beneficial neither for their wine nor, in the long term, for the vines. Others are making strenuous efforts to reduce treatments – in particular for rot. Problems with an effective, widely used anti-rot product containing the procymidone molecule, have forced a rethink, since there is as yet no viable alternative.

At present, the annual invasion of pests can only be contained with insecticides. These breed their own resistance problems, so products with greater specificity are being researched in order that ecologically beneficent fauna are not indiscriminately destroyed along with the unwanted spiders and larvae. Fortunately, favourable weather over the last few years has allowed growers who treated curatively to reduce insect sprays, saving time and money.

Most growers subscribe to the Service de Protection des Végétaux – an organisation which disseminates specific advice on risks and treatments throughout the Côte, by means of regular bulletins. Its aim is to persuade viticulteurs to limit treatments and to point them in the direction of ecologically friendly products. So once a Domaine has its broad treatment strategy in place, much of the detailed decision-making is taken out of its hands.

Despite all the up-to-the-minute offerings from the chemical companies, many growers are returning to the traditional copper- and sulphur-based treatments for mildew and *oïdium*. Copper is a useful substance but needs careful usage: it tends to provoke *coulure* at flowering, slows down vegetation and tends to accumulate slow-degrading toxic residues in the soil. However, if used towards the

end of the season, it hardens the somewhat naturally fragile Pinot Noir skins, keeping the dreaded grape-worm at bay. It is thus, indirectly, a valuable aid in rot control, since the wounds made by this worm rapidly turn rotten. However, copper and sulphur are both contact products which are readily washed off.

There is one disease which is causing justifiable concern along the Côte – *eutypiose*. This is particularly insidious since, after brief but visible early symptoms, it can take 7 years to reappear in an infected vine, by which time it is too late. *Eutypiose* is spread by air-borne spores, especially in damp windy conditions, and enters through pruning cuts and other wounds. It is virtually untreatable, although sealing cuts immediately after pruning seems to help.

Many older growers refuse to take *eutypiose* seriously, ascribing it either to prolonged sunshine or to the inventiveness of chemical companies, short of business. Sadly, it is all too real. Studies in 1990 indicated that 83% of Pinot Noir and 90% of Chardonnay vineyards throughout the Côte were affected. The highest level with Pinot was 23.2% and with Chardonnay 25.9%, and the incidence is increasing. The only solution is to grub up affected vines and burn them immediately, and it is encouraging that communes have taken the role of policeman into their own hands to ensure compliance.

With all the difficulties and problems of maintaining the vine, it is good to note some promising new developments. There is much research afoot into alternative ways of dealing with insects, especially the grape-worm. Mimetic, growth-regulator sprays, which disrupt the musk odours which are essential to mating and so destabilise insects' reproductive cycles, are currently on trial in several vineyards, with apparent success. These are of much lower toxicity than conventional insecticides. The use of glue pads to trap grape-worm moths is also proving useful in determining the precise moment to treat larvae, thus minimising the strength and number of treatments needed. There is also hope of increasing the level of benign predators on a variety of species – including red and yellow spiders, which pump sap from the vine; this would remove the need for most treatments without destroying the eco-balance. Some growers are now using chemicals to encourage flowers and abort as a means of yield control – a high-risk strategy.

On a more general level, there is much interest in the system of vine maintenence known as 'biodynamie'. This is based on the 19th-century work of Rudolf Steiner elaborated by Claude Bourguignon and others in recent times and consists of using very low doses of product, applied at specific times – a sort of viticultural homoeopathy. A few Domaines, including Leflaive and Leroy, have now dipped their feet into this rather revolutionary water, and many others seem eager to go paddling.

On the hardware front, mechanical harvesters have been spotted in Meursault and Gevrey, and elsewhere on the Côte. These are of doubtful benefit – research suggests that up to 3 years old, machine and manually harvested wines do not differ, whereas thereafter the machine wines start to age more rapidly. Also, there are serious concerns about the long-term effects, on their root-systems and general health, of shaking the vines to dislodge the grapes.

There is undisputed consensus that the most significant improvements in quality will derive from better viticulture than from changes in the cellar. However, although most of the Côte's 4,000+ vignerons are more confident growers than winemakers, there is still far to go, especially in persuading them to reduce yields further and to limit the number of products and the frequency of individual treatments. Many viticulteurs still cling to the belief that a lush, abundantly green vineyard with neatly trimmed foliage is invariably preferable to one less manicured. Perhaps they are just gardeners at heart.

THE IMPORTANCE AND USE OF WOOD

For more than 2,000 years, the wooden cask was the only serviceable medium for bulk liquid storage. Herodotus records the use of palm wood casks for transporting wine to Babylon, and artefacts and documents provide further evidence of barrels in widespread use in winemaking. With no sensible alternative, the barrel became part of the tradition of winemaking in much of Europe.

However, the 228-litre casks one sees in any worthwhile Burgundian cellar represent not only the legacy of history but also recent advances in the understanding of how a wine develops. Only since the late 1970s has serious attention been devoted to understanding the effects of wood on wine, but these few years of research suggest that the subject is much more complex than generally supposed.

The principle of storing young wine in cask is based on the value of a gradual contact with oxygen – slow oxygenation, rather than rapid oxidation – which does not occur with an inert storage medium such as stainless steel. In this respect, wood has two important sets of properties: those related directly to the nature of the cask itself, and those related to the oxygen chemistry of wine.

It is now well known that the make-up of a cask – shape, size, ratio of wood surface to wine volume and method of cooperage – contributes to a wine's development. Equally important is the type of wood used, the age of the tree from which the staves are hewn and how they are treated before the cask is made up.

Historically, the predominance of oak and chestnut merely reflected availability. Nowadays, choices are more sophisticated, with extensive research devoted to codifying differences attributable to the provenance of the wood and to the way it is treated.

The current feeling is that the importance of wood provenance has been overstressed – tastings revealing diminishing differences between wood from different forests as a wine ages. Growers realise that what matters is the fineness of the grain and how the wood is treated. Moreover, soils and climates differ from forest to forest, resulting in significant differences – especially in the tightness of the grain and its porosity; so mere provenance, by itself, can mislead.

Tastings also indicate that the tighter the grain the better the wine. Tight-grained wood from Nevers will impart a finer, more subtle flavour to a Chardonnay than more loose-grained Limousin. Heart wood will give a different taste from wood from the outside of the trunk which contains more sap. In general the wider the pores the greater the extraction of oak compounds into the wine, thus the greater their contribution to its aromatic and flavour development. Also, wood from a younger tree will not have the same physical and chemical characteristics as that from an older one.

The matter is further complicated by the fact that, as with grape varieties, each species of tree has multiple clones, some producing better wood than others. It has even been suggested that a system of Appellation Contrôllée be introduced to control the provenance and quality of any wood sold for wine casks; this initiative is being supported by research to develop a system of 'finger-printing' oak from different forests. Experts distinguish summer from spring wood, since a tree-trunk only grows during the summer, emphasising that the proportions of each matter as much as precise provenance. Tannins are localised in summer wood, so the fact that Tronçais oak contains less of this than Limousin is essential to deciding which to use.

The amount of sap (undesirable) in the wood depends on when the tree is felled. Wood cut when the sap is rising perforce contains more. So autumn and winter are the best times to fell, when it is descending.

Whatever the wood, how it is dried and prepared can determine its contribution to a wine. Many growers, realising this, are now buying their own wood and arranging for it to be dried naturally rather than in kilns, since this removes the harsher tannins more effectively and ensures complete dryness, reducing the risk of *volatile acidity* in the final wine. It is generally considered that one year's exposure to the open air is necessary for each centimetre thickness of the plank; so, on average two-three years outside is desirable.

Before a cask is assembled, the individual staves must be heated to bend them into shape. Whether they are lightly, moderately or heavily toasted modifies polyphenol compounds and thereby affects the intensity of oak flavours imparted to the wine. In general, a light toast produces more complexity and heavy toast more roundness. Classic trials by Robert Mondavi in the Napa Valley, putting the same base wine into differently coopered barrels, demonstrated not only this effect but also that hand-splitting staves versus sawing, the specific means of heating, toasting versus charring and the thickness of the staves all produced marked variations in wine character.

The age of the wood must also be considered. New oak tends to impart more vinosity to a wine; older wood will give a riper spectrum of flavours. Tastings of the same wine aged in different casks strikingly demonstrate the effect of each of these factors.

Finally, to these complexities one must add the cooper; each works in his own individual fashion, so even given identical ingredients one would hardly expect identical results.

Most winemakers remain blissfully unaware of these intricacies. They tend to deal with one cooper and, whilst the more sophisticated might specify the provenance of their wood or try out casks from several forests, the only constant factor affecting their calculations is how many to buy each year.

Too much new wood, too high a proportion or too long in cask, can ruin a wine. A careful vigneron will judge these factors on tasting alone: a naturally more structured vintage or a Grand Cru will integrate more new wood than wines of lesser pedigree.

If matching the wood to the characteristics of the wine taxes the comprehension, it is no less complex to grasp what goes on inside the barrel once it is full. The cask itself and the air both contribute significantly to a wine's development.

It was long believed that oxygen enters a cask by transpiration across the staves. This is now known to be false: Peterson (1976) convincingly demonstrated that in a full, tightly-bunged barrel, on its side, there progressively develops a vacuum. If the wine does take up oxygen during its stay in cask, it does not do so through the staves.

What are the alternatives? Oxygen can enter either by absorption from that already dissolved in the pores of the wood or in the wine, or else – perhaps more plausible in an imperfect world – via either the interstices between the staves which are a less than perfect seal, or through a non-airtight bung. Up-to-date cellars may have replaced the old wooden bungs (which tended to warp) secured by rags harbouring zoos-full of microbes, with rubber and glass bungs which improve both hygiene and security, but even these are probably not 100% airtight. In reality, however, far more oxygen finds its way in through routine cellar operations – racking, fining, moving casks, and when the barrel is unbunged to extract a tasting sample – than through any other means.

Whatever its method of ingress, oxygen affects the way a wine develops. Until it is bottled, when it enters a 'reduced' state in which oxygen is virtually absent, wine is prey to the many chemical transformations which take place in the presence of even minute amounts of oxygen. At the limit, a wine completely open to the air will turn into vinegar. However, controlled access to lesser amounts of oxygen over a period of months before bottling is generally beneficial, especially for wines intended for keeping.

The role of oxygen is many-stranded: it oxidises tartaric acids, polyphenols and alcohol – all compounds naturally occurring in wine – softens the taste of tannins and stabilises colour pigments. The net effects of all this biochemical activity are a decrease in fixed acids and tannins, the precipitation out of colouring matter and the oxidation of tannins, in both red and white wine, to a brown tint.

The contribution of the cask-wood itself is no less important. Wood adds structure – elements of backbone and firmness. Tannins and other 'phenolic' substances pass from wood to wine in amounts affected by the nature of the cask and the length of time the wine spends in it. However, the effects on tannin structure are generally less pronounced than those on other aroma and flavour compounds. To complicate matters further, the tannins imparted from a new cask are different in character – particularly taste – from those deriving from the grape-skin (their traditional source) and again from those from pips and stalks. Although oak tannins tend to be harder in flavour than skin tannins, they are ideal for wines such as Côte d'Or Chardonnays which benefit from added richness and structure without a harsh, unharmonious backbone.

In each vintage, the grower has to make several key decisions for each *cuvée*: how much new wood, what type and how long should the wine stay in contact with it? If he knows his job, he will seek to add what is attractive without allowing the wood to dominate or destroy the characteristics of grape and *terroir* which make, for example, a Puligny different from a Meursault.

Few top-class Domaines stick unswervingly to a fixed percentage of new oak each year. They have to bear in mind that injudicious use of oak can leave a wine out of balance – the subtle equilibrium between tannin, oak and fruit is easily upset and, once destroyed, may never entirely recover. Too much new wood or too long in cask will often desiccate a wine – it loses fruit and flesh which it never regains. The balance between enhancement and loss is therefore remarkably fine. These judgements can only be made satisfactorily on tasting.

However skilled a grower may be at judging when to bottle his wine, in reality it is often his family finances which determine how many new casks he can afford each year. A new barrel will cost 2,500 francs and he needs 50. They will add 15 francs to the price of every bottle he sells – the market is tight, will he still sell the wine? Perhaps the third-year barrels might just do for a fourth.

He will also be acutely conscious of the 10 per cent loss from evaporation and cellar operations involved in keeping wine in his expensive new casks – and of the costly labour involved in weekly topping-up. He may not, however, realise that there is greater evaporation from an older cask or that the wine in it matures more quickly. Stainless-steel vats must often seem an appealing way out; hardly surprising, therefore, that many take the soft option and put less wine into cask and replace them less often.

The proportion of new oak a grower uses will vary from year to year. The unwritten rule is that the potentially finer the wine the more new oak it can support. A Grand Cru will typically be matured in up to 100% of new wood and a Premier Cru up to 40–60%. However,

these guidelines must be tempered with others: leaner vintages tolerate less new wood than riper ones, and some communes – for example, Volnay and Chambolle-Musigny – produce more delicate wines which are easily overbalanced by too much new oak. It must also be remembered that the contents of second-year and older casks of the same wine will eventually be amalgamated with that of any new barrels to make up the final *cuvée*.

Although it is generally considered uneconomic to put anything less than Premier Cru into new wood some growers put their Bourgogne Rouge and Bourgogne Blanc into a proportion of new oak, often with fine results – and prices to match.

The effect of wood diminishes with each year a cask is used. After about 5 years it has given what it usefully can and will either be resold to someone less scrupulous or sawn up for the geranium tub. The noticeable taste impact of new wood, so evident during the first few years, also diminishes as a wine ages in bottle – the scaffolding somehow integrates with the building. The vanilla and toast aromas and the extra tannins become part of the developing wine.

For white wines, many vignerons now appreciate that the sooner the juice is put into the casks the better, especially if these are new. Not only do white wines fermented in cask have more regular and rapid *malos,* but they also taste rounder and more harmonious than those fermented in bulk and then transferred to new wood.

Wood is thus an important, but highly complex, part of fine wine production. No grower of quality can remain ignorant of its potential or of its pitfalls. Conversely, one can learn more about a grower's attitude to quality from his views on wood and how he uses it, than from any map on the wall vibrantly inked in to demonstrate his exalted land holdings.

A cooper at Maison Louis Latour heating oak staves to bend them into shape

MAKING RED WINE

One of the Côte d'Or's more confusing features is the wide diversity of style and quality. How is it that one vigneron crafts sublime wine whilst his neighbour only manages something uninspiring and pedestrian? For example, only a handful of Clos Vougeot's 82 owners produces top-quality. Too much indifferent Burgundy leaves growers cellars for there to be any doubt that much is going awry. Whilst poor quality can often be traced back to ignorance or lack of cash for proper equipment, in many instances it is the direct result of laziness or incompentence. Any grower with healthy, ripe grapes, has all the raw material necessary for making fine wine; so what is going wrong?

To understand why this happens, it is necessary to get to grips with the broad principles of vinification, which strike more or less common ground. Being aware of the processes involved in transforming grapes into wine increases the ability to relate quality to wine-making techniques and thus to pinpoint problems.

Top-class growers stress the importance of ripe healthy fruit and are prepared to wait for optimum maturity, balanced natural sugar and acidity, and as favourable a ratio of juice to solids as the weather will allow. This entails spending time and money removing rotten, damaged or unripe fruit before it gets into the vats, and using only small harvesting containers to avoid prematurely crushing the grapes. Expenditure on harvest has increased at many top Domaines, most of whom have bought special sorting-tables to facilitate the process. If growers fail here, they load the dice against themselves, even before they have started making their wine.

In the *cuverie*, the first important decision is whether or not to separate the berries from their stems – destalking. Stems, which are nothing more than ripe or unripe wood, absorb colour and contribute little but astringent tannins, which are less noble than those extracted from the skins, so most prefer to remove them. However, this early injection of tannin helps fix unstable, but valuable, colour compounds – anthocyanins.

A few doggedly "old-fashioned" growers still refuse to destem, whatever the vintage, and their wines invariably have an irremediable raw, unpleasantly herbaceous streak which destroys their balance. Most now accept that stalks bring little benefit and generally remove the majority, leaving perhaps 20-30% in particularly ripe years to add structure and to facilitate the drainage of juice through the cap of skins and pips which forms on top of each vat. In many Domaines this has resulted in a significant improvement in quality, especially in unripe vintages. Some refer to 'old' and 'new' styles of Burgundy; what matters is that tailoring the level of stalks to the vintage makes for a better, more durable, balance. The ability of 'old style' wine to last a century means nothing if all that's left is harsh tannin.

Ripe Pinot Noir grapes contain all the necessary potential for lasting colour, aroma and flavour, mostly located in pigment compounds in, and just under, the skin, with very few in the pulp. Only to the extent that the vigneron manages to both extract and retain these will his wine succeed.

Extraction occurs before, during and after fermentation and depends on both time and temperature – the longer you macerate the skins with the juice, the more you leach out, especially colour. However, what is extracted before fermentation differs from that extracted during and afterwards. The current trend is for a few days pre-fermentive maceration to increase extraction, achieved either by cooling the pulp or by adding sulphur dioxide (SO_2) to temporarily anaesthetise the yeasts. Others dislike the practice and consider inhibiting fermentation thoroughly unnatural. While neither view is wrong, it is beyond dispute that a few days of pre-fermentive maceration gives more deeply coloured and intensely aromatic juice.

The heart of winemaking, fermentation, is a complex of processes, at present imperfectly understood, in which yeasts transform grape-sugar into alcohol. It is known to be affected by temperature, size and shape of vat and by whether natural or 'cultured' yeasts are used. Once fermentation is under way, the temperature rises and a cap of solids floats to the surface on released carbon-dioxide gas. Both need careful management.

The vigneron has a choice: if he ferments at a high temperature – anything over a maximum of 35°C is regarded as risky – he increases the extraction of aroma and flavour compounds from the grapes, but the yeasts may stop working, allowing bacteria naturally present in the juice to degrade any remaining sugar into acetic acid – i.e. vinegar. In high concentrations this *volatile acidity* has an unpleasantly pungent smell and a sharp, sour taste. If, however, he chooses to ferment at too low a temperature, the wine will lack depth and substance.

He also must decide how often to break up the cap on top of the juice to keep it moist (*pigeage*). In Burgundy this is done either at least once or twice daily, by jumping into the vat and using your feet or by some automated piston device. Greater frequency increases extraction from the skins, but this can be overdone. Lazy vignerons tend to *piger* infrequently with predictable results.

Many growers, attracted by the security of regular, controllable, fermentations, now use cultured Burgundy yeasts in place of the natural yeast population – the bloom on the grapes. Others contend that each commune and *climat* has its specific yeast population, and that only these are capable of real typicity and complexity. Cultured yeasts, they argue, often vociferously, blur these differences and standardise wines.

Although cultured yeasts are being constantly refined to reflect the Cote's original yeast populations, and sophisticated techniques have been developed for the genetic identification of individual yeasts, there is scant research support for the hypothesis of commune or vineyard-specific micro-flora, or for the suggestion that, even if these existed, they would play a significant role in wine typicity. Security apart, one might justifiably question the need for cultured yeasts when the indigenous ones work perfectly well.

The process of turning red grapes into wine – *cuvaison* – extends from the moment the grapes are vatted to the moment the new wine is run off so that the pulp can be pressed. Each stage has its part to play, extracting different substances from the grapes and transforming others. Prefermentive maceration maximises the extraction of highly water-soluble colour pigments, whereas aromatic compounds are mostly extracted during fermentation, during the conversion of grape-sugars to alcohol.

Tannins, so important to a red wine's longevity, are most soluble in alcohol, and are thus maximally extracted during and after fermentation. As they are leached into the new wine, they also act to 'fix' unstable colour compounds extracted by water into the pulp before fermentation started.

Preferred length of *cuvaison* varies widely – from 7-10 days to 3 weeks or longer. A vigneron with too few vats will be forced to shorten it; if the skins are fragile and not entirely ripe, he may lengthen it to extract more substance and colour. Whilst there are no formulae, it is doubtful whether a wine of serious depth and staying power can be made with a *cuvaison* of less than about 10–12 days.

When grapes lack sufficient sugar to produce the legal minimum alcohol necessary for a balance in the finished wine, a vigneron is permitted to make up the deficiency with sucrose, during fermentation – up to a maximum increase of 2 degrees of alcohol. How this *chaptalisation* is done can affect the quality of the resulting wine. Recent changes to the rules allow sugar to be added in several small doses, which most conscientious growers prefer, since this has the desirable consequences of minimising the heat generated and prolonging fermentation. Many also prefer to add any sugar needed towards the end of fermentation, to further lengthen it. Unfortunately, some Domaines regularly over-*chaptalise* their wines, adding to alcohol and thus smoothness, at the expense of freshness and typicity.

Faced with a natural imbalance between juice and solids in their grapes, the more conscientious will bleed off (=*saigner*) some juice from each vat to restore equilibrium. Any *saignée* should take place immediately after vatting, since delay will only increase the amount of precious aroma and colour compounds removed with the unwanted pulp-juice. For some, the sacrifice is too much – since the juice *saigneed* represents saleable wine and is useless for anything but 'vin ordinaire' or sparkling wine. A grower's willingness to *saigner* is a good indicator of his attitude to quality, but the procedure is not a substitute for failing to prune short, or otherwise over-cropping.

With a vat full of new wine, the next step is to decand the "free-run wine" and then press the pulp which remains. Too harsh a squeezing will express more wine, but this will be higher in tannins and lower in quality than the *vin de goutte*. Growers will often claim to blend in only wine from the first, gentle pressing, but their wines often give them away. Asking what proportion of the total press-wine represents is often very revealing – 25% indicates too severe a pressing, while 5-10% is a more acceptable average.

Once the press- and free-run wine have been assembled and allowed to settle, the new wine is run into 228 litre casks for its *élevage* – literally 'pupillage', or 'upbringing'. It is during these 9–24 months that the vigneron has most scope for destruction. He may use too much, or too little, new wood; he mayleave the wine too long in cask, so it loses freshness and shrivels up; or, he may fail to top up his casks regularly, so oxygen gets in and starts the inexorable process towards vinegar.

Shortly after alcoholic fermentation, the new wine will undergo a second, natural, *malolactic* fermentation. This is the transformation of harsh malic (apple) acid into softer tasting lactic (milk) acid and is mediated not by yeasts, but by bacterial.

During its *élevage* the wine will be periodically racked, to get it off its lees, which after a time impart an unpleasant and individual taste. How often, when, and how a wine is racked are of vital importance to its development. In general, red wines are usually racked twice – in the spring after their *malo*, and again about three months before bottling. The important matter is that the precise timing of each racking should not depend on some predetermined formula, or the need for casks, but on the wine's development, a factor in the assessment of which tasting is essential.

The first racking is so timed because, during the *malo* the wine is relatively unprotected from oxygen – there is no CO_2 around and the vigneron mustn't add more SO_2, since this would knock-out the very bacteria which break down the malic acid.

Recent years have seen a marked tendency towards longer, slower *malos*, even in some cases *batonnage*, traditionally restricted to white wines, and to leaving the wine on its lees for a month or so after *malo*. All this enriches and adds aroma and flavour complexity.

A grower is most likely to wreck his wine in preparing it for bottling. Two traditional operations – fining and filtration – enable him to ensure that it is free of gross deposits and generally bright and stable. Fining adds a substance which has no taste impact, to remove finely suspended particles, often invisible, which would not normally settle by themselves. It may, incidentally, smooth out rough tannic edges. Filtration, through a more or less porous medium, removes deposits from the larger visible particles down to the smallest of micromolecules.

However, these processes often destroy aromatic persistence and finesse, and can take guts and substance from a wine, so many growers strive to avoid them. Others, anxious for the security of knowing they will not be awoken in the middle of the night by an incensed customer complaining that his expensive Chambertin has become cloudy and started to fizz, fine and filter to excess. In general, careful wine-making should render all but the lightest intervention unnecessary. Recent years have seen a 'cult' of 'unfiltered' wine. While it is generally, though not always, better not to filter, most sensible growers will do so if they consider it necessary. There is nothing magic about *vin non filtre*.

Having reached this far, the grower still has to get his wine into bottles – a process fraught with danger. First, he must time it right, for which constant tasting is the only sensible test; a week or two either way can make a massive difference. Then he must cope with the operation of bottling itself. Many growers, particularly those reluctant to finance sophisticated equipment which they will only use for a week or two each year, entrust bottling to a specialist contractor. Unfortunately, most of these enterprises are remunerated on a piece-work basis, so it is in their interest to take as little time as possible – far from beneficial to the wine. The sensible compromise is shared equipment – which is beginning to happen.

More refined and widely available technical know-how, and better all-round skills have significantly improved standards – in terms both of consistency and of overall quality levels. In addition, peer pressures have played their part in jolting under-achievers to change their ways.

One can learn much from looking round a cellar; it often reveals what is going wrong. Apart from any technical incompetence, vignerons make silly mistakes in the cellar – for example, repeatedly using the same cask tastings – so that it is being constantly unbunged, letting in the air; or, failing to replace the piece of jute separating a wooden bung from the cask-hole, encouraging spoilage bacteria.

At the top level, there is much talk of tannin and discussion of how it might be refined. Markets used to soft, full, oaky, New World reds, have little appetite for harsh tannin, whatever else may accompany it, and growers have long realised that the quality of tannins, as well as their quantity, is an important element in a wine's balance and appeal.

Despite all the advances, there is still much poor quality. One eminent Burgundian notes that, whereas some 80% of wines taste good before *malo*, only 40% do so after, and a paltry 20% are still fine in bottle. Although much potentially fine wine is destroyed by poor fruit quality, much is also due to lack of technical skill. Most vignerons are superb grape-growers, but sadly, all too many are less than competent wine-makers.

MAKING WHITE WINE

Talking to growers, there is no doubt that most find making white wine considerably more straightforward than making red. It is indeed exceptional to find one who makes equally fine red and white wine – you are, apparently, either a 'patissier' or a 'saucier' but rarely both.

The most important differences between red and white wine are colour and tannin. White grapes are never truly white, but various shades of mottled yellow and green – which easily discolour wine. So, while red grapes are allowed to macerate with their juice to extract as much 'matière' as possible from the skins before the grapes are pressed, white grapes are pressed immediately, and the juice removed before it can pick up colour from the skins.

Because of this minimal skin contact, white wine contains negligible tannin – an ingredient which adds so importantly to the structure and longevity of a red wine. To compensate for this, and to provide a fine white wine with the ability to age, the vigneron must ensure that enough acidity is retained to balance the fruit and alcohol. In short, tannin and colour are undesirable and acidity essential.

Because of its lack of tannin and anti-oxidant enzymes, white juice is more prone to oxidation than red juice. As a cut apple discolours rapidly unless protected by acidity (lemon juice for example), so white grape-juice will irreversibly brown if exposed to the air. This exacts from the vigneron a high standard of care and hygiene if the wine is to arrive at bottling light-coloured and bright.

This means scrupulous cleaning of everything from cask bungs to the cellar floor and any cellar equipment used. Careful use of SO_2 as a disinfectant throughout the life of the young wine also helps the vigneron to this end. However, most of the best growers prefer to concentrate on cellar hygiene in order to reduce SO_2 levels to the barest minimum, since beyond a certain concentration this adds an unpleasant, flat dimension to both smell and taste. A few vignerons manage to make excellent wine without using any SO_2; however, like cycling with no hands, there is an increased risk of accidents.

Harvest can make or break quality. Sugar and acidity must be balanced for success later, and whilst *pourriture humide*, the *noble rot* of the great sweet whites, is of less concern than with reds, grey rot is damaging and must be eliminated before pressing.

The main difficulty at this stage is to ensure that the grapes remain intact. Split berries, unprotected by SO_2, rapidly oxidise and discolour in the absence of tannins to buffer the oxidase enzymes which work so fast once juice is liberated. Thus undamaged, ripe and healthy grapes are what the vigneron needs as his raw material. There used to be a vogue, particularly among New World estates, for adding sulphur to bunches of grapes as soon as they had been cut; however, research revealed that this provided wine made from them with less long-term protection from oxidation than simply leaving them unsulphured until after pressing.

Once at the *cuverie*, the grapes are pressed as soon as possible to extract the juice and remove it from the skins and pips. Research in America and Australia has found that if the berries are simply crushed, just to break the skins, and then macerated at relatively cool temperatures for several hours, whilst undesirable tannins do not leach out, much more by way of aroma and flavour is extracted, since these compounds are located just beneath the skins and are not extracted by pressing.

Some growers in Puligny, Meursault, Aloxe-Corton and Chassagne are now using this *macération pelliculaire* to give their wines greater depth of extract.

Until quite recently, white grapes were pressed in the same type of presses as red grapes – generally devices with a screw-thread which either brought together two horizontal metal plates, or else descended one plate vertically to press the grapes. Modern presses operate on the principle of an expandable bladder which slowly inflates outwards, crushing the grapes against the wall of a cylindrical drum. These allow gentle, controlled pressure, which liberates the juice without extracting undesirable tannins from the skins or, worse still, from the pips which contain particularly harsh tannins.

Once extracted, the juice is allowed to settle to remove any gross lees before being fermented, in either stainless-steel or glass-lined tanks – or for smaller quantities and better wines, in oak casks. Fermentation in cask is possible with white wine and not with red because there is no cap of skins to be broken up. Moreover, in small volume, the temperature does not rise as high as it would with the same juice in large volume. However, once in cask, the grower has little control over fermentation temperature, beyond cooling the cellar which is both slow and ineffective.

The maximum temperature to which fermentation is allowed to rise decisively affects the character of the wine. Cool fermentation, around 15°C, currently highly fashionable in bulk wine production, gives clean, neutral wines, often with little varietal character. Fermenting Chardonnay at such low temperatures tends to give exotic fruit aromas and flavours which, while pleasant, produce wines which lack individuality. This standardisation also expunges the typicity of each appellation, which is so much part of the interest and finesse of great white Burgundy. Fermentation for Chardonnay seems to work best at 17-25°C – above this level, the wines rapidly

Ancient and modern: the bucket is no less essential than the high-tech Vaslin press

become flabby and heavy, and lose freshness.

Growers may ferment wholly in cask or part of each lot in cask, and part in stainless steel to preserve freshness and acidity and then amalgamate the two parts. If new oak is used, then it is better to ferment the wine in the new cask rather than elsewhere and put it into new oak later – the results are more harmonious and both alcoholic and *malolactic* fermentation more regular.

As with red wines, cultured yeasts may be used to replace the indigenous ones and some vignerons are unshakably convinced that the results are better. However, most see no reason to meddle with nature and happily stick to what it supplies. Even though the available selection of cultured yeasts is becoming progressively more refined, there is scant evidence to indicate that they are any better or worse than those harvested with the grape.

Once the new wine is made it has to be nurtured until the time comes for bottling. An important part of this work is ensuring that the wine benefits as much as possible from contact with its lees. The lees nourish the wine, bringing it fatness and aromatic complexity, so the longer the lees-contact the better. However, unhealthy lees or excessive contact can result in an unpleasant *goût de lie*, so constant tasting and vigilance are needed.

Periodically, in order to keep the lees evenly distributed throughout the cask, a stainless-steel instrument rather like a scythe with holes in one end, or a length of chain, are put into the wine and rotated with more or less vigour. The frequency of this *batonnage* varies from grower to grower, but once or twice a week up to the *malo* is normal. One grower's own peculiar system: he simply takes a rubber mallet and taps each cask as he passes; this sends a shockwave through the liquid and keeps the lees in suspension.

Lees are also important in retaining the fresh colour of a white wine. They absorb colour – keeping the wine 'white' rather than yellow; it is this property which makes lees undesirable to any great extent in red wine *élevage* and is why red wines are not *batonnés*.

As well as extracting maximum fat from the lees, the vigneron has to take pains to ensure that the balance of acidity is not upset. In very ripe vintages, when natural acidities are low, he may pick some grapes early to ensure part of each *cuvée* has higher acidity; alternatively, he may – with red grapes as well as with white – deliberately harvest a proportion of the second generation of bunches from the vines; these *verjus* are less mature and thus higher in acidity. Alternatively, he can act to suppress the *malolactic* fermentation, thereby retaining some of the crisper malic acid which would otherwise have been converted into softer lactic acid.

If all else fails, the wine can be acidified. This is a strictly controlled operation which involves either adding tartaric acid to the fermenting *must* or adjusting the finished wine with citric acid just before bottling. Neither alternative is particularly satisfactory, for a variety of reasons, but principally because added acid is never entirely harmonious and seems to sit apart rather than integrating with the flavours of the wine.

The lack of tannin makes white wine more fragile than red and more easily upset by too much handling. Top-class Domaines, such as Leflaive, Sauzet or Lafon, stress the importance of both maximum hygiene and minimum interference. The less a wine is moved – racked, oxygenated or pumped – the better, especially for aromatic complexity and freshness. This also reduces the amount of SO_2 needed to keep the wine stable after bottling.

Two of the vigneron's most difficult decisions are how to prepare the wine for bottling and when to bottle. Clarity and stability are essential if bottles are not to find their way back 6 months later from a dissatisfied client several thousand miles away. Much the same considerations apply to white wine as to red. In deciding his policy,

An impressive battery of stainless-steel vats for their Corton-Charlemagne at Domaine Bonneau de Martray

the vigneron has to balance the advantages of fining and filtration with the sure knowledge that too much treatment may irreversibly destroy a wine's delicate equilibrium.

While red wines are fined by adding protein – e.g. egg-white or special milk products – white wines are fined to remove fine protein molecules which can make them hazy, and to correct premature yellowing and render them bright. Filtration comes in varying degrees of harshness, from a light polish to remove anything from old boots to dead wasps to a sterile filtration which removes the smallest of the micro-molecules which are potential long-term troublemakers. As with red wine, a careful fining can refine a wine's aroma by removing larger tannin molecules (white wine does contain some natural tannin). Overfining or too harsh a filtration may reassure the grower, but removes guts and finesse from the wine.

The decision about when to bottle is critical. A wine may be delicious in cask, with plenty of freshness and fruit, and yet be ruined if left to dry out for too long before bottling. Frequent tasting is essential to monitor wines, since they can change from week to week.

In the Côte d'Or white wines are generally bottled any time from a few months after harvest, for a fresh, sappy Aligoté, to a couple of years later, for a powerful Grand Cru.

Although the absence of the need to extract colour and tannin makes white-winemaking rather more straightforward than red, mistakes are often made. The most common fault is excessive use of SO_2 to protect a wine against discolouring or re-fermenting in bottle. Since SO_2 levels are usually adjusted at bottling, an apparent excess may be detected if the wine is tasted within a few months. However, with time, much of this added SO_2 will be absorbed by the wine and so will become less noticeable. A serious over-sulphuring, however, is a fault which will result in a flat, irreversible dullness in the wine.

Why do some winemakers systematically make a better job of the tricky business of turning grapes into wine than others? Whilst there is no straightforward answer, it is clear that much of the abundant poor quality, in both red and white wines, is the result of flaws in vinification or in *élevage* which are easily corrected. Furthermore, a great deal of indifferent, but correct, wine comes from Domaines which regularly overcrop their vines. There is absolutely no doubt that in many cases, the difference between good and great wine can be attributed to excessive yields.

While all this may be true, there remains the indisputable fact that some vignerons have a gift for winemaking which transcends the mere application of scientific principle. These talented few can ennoble an Aligoté or extract Grand Cru complexity from a humble Village vineyard. This is the difference between skill and genius; the Côte d'Or has enough of these stars to illuminate its firmament.

GUY ACCAD

The Lebanese oenologist and agronomist Guy Accad is one of Burgundy's most controversial – and criticised – figures. He set up a winemaking consultancy in the Côte in 1975 and at his peak, advised some 40 Domaines. Though many have now dispensed with his services, his influence – and the controversy his approach generated – remain.

The arguments revolve round whether or not his method is 'traditional', whether his wines reflect the diversity and typicity of their appellations, and whether they have the capacity to age. Much of the public debate was conducted by critics who did little more than taste some of his clients' wines; none took the trouble to meet him and examine his philosophy at first hand.

What follows is the result of several hours spent with Accad and many more talking to and tasting with his most prestigious clients.

Accad's inspiration derives from old Burgundies which seemed to scale far greater heights than those produced today – 'If Burgundy was born 50 years ago, it wouldn't have the reputation it does now.' His argument is not that growers make bad wine, but that most fail to extract the maximum potential from their land.

His approach starts in the vineyards: 'good terrain, healthy vines and ripe grapes' are pre-requisites of *Grand Vin*, and this means the best possible soil-equilibrium. Soil imbalance affects wine quality.

Super-ripe, but not over-ripe, fruit is also a cornerstone of his strategy. He has three lines of attack: higher vine density, reduced yields and late harvesting. Many people forget, he argues, that in the last century vines were planted untrained, at a density of some 25,000 per ha. From these came wines of great depth and quality.

As plant density increases, the ability of the sun to fully ripen grapes, especially in cooler climates, diminishes, whilst at low plant densities, the quantity of fruit on each plant increases, to the detriment of quality. It is therefore necessary to adapt density to the climate. In general, his rules are that the hotter the climate, the lower the optimal density of planting; conversely, the cooler it is, the higher the density. He therefore advises his Côte d'Or clients to increase their plant-density to 12,500 per ha. The more grapes per vine, the less ripe they will be. So decrease the charge per plant.

Ripe fruit contains more, and more complex, aromas than unripe fruit (think of a ripe/unripe apple) and the ripe tannins which accompany it taste rounder and softer. Late harvesting also intensifies colour and minimises the need for *chaptalisation*.

The real controversy starts in the *cuverie*. He complains that too much wine – good and bad – is being made to a 'recipe' and criticises those who use the vintage as an excuse for poor quality. Grapes from two analytically beautifully-ripe vintages can differ significantly in quality. This means elaborating the crude analysis for sugars and acids, to encompass skin thickness and tannin and pigment properties. Then you can make an intelligent decision about how best to vinify.

For Accad, vinification comports a series of choices; you must know what questions to ask and the options opened up by possible answers. For him *Grand Vin* means at least (though not at most) *vin de garde*. In Burgundy, the notion of Grand Cru is inextricably linked to the ageing potential of its wines. To the suggestion that a still deeply-coloured, sound, 1909 Nuits St.-Georges was probably 'cut' with something inferior, he riposte: 'Cut with what – what could live for 80 years except for a Grand Cru?'

It is thus necessary to develop a vinification which both rejects undesirable elements from grapes, whilst extracting and retaining desirable ones (pigment, for example, is notoriously unstable).

His *grandes lignes* are simple: partial destalking (50–75%), sulphuring at 2–3 litres per tonne (2–3 times the usual dose), then cooling to 8–15^{0}C for 5–10 days maceration. Thereafter, fermentation starts slowly and continues, at a maximum temperature of 30^{0}C, until all the sugar is consumed, when the *vin de goutte* is run off without any further maceration. The press-wine is added and the new wine then put into cask foir a classical *élévage*.

Accad relies strongly on colour as an indicator of a wine's development and on his belief that the best colour and aroma compounds are extracted early, in the absence of alcohol. These actuate his use of both SO_2 and cooling to achieve a long maceration.

The high sulphur levels, often considered the hallmark of Accad's vinification, are to augment colour and tannin extraction, rather than to delay fermentation, since wine yeasts will normally work at the concentrations he employs. However, once the initial dose has been added, there is no further SO_2 adjustment.

Such sulphur levels are said to give wines a flat, cardboardy taste. Accad counters that if one sums all the small doses of conventional winemaking, his are barely higher and that wines so vinified do not, in fact, taste of sulphites.

The rate of change of temperature also plays a part – a slow fermentation will produce different results from a faster fermentation at the same temperature. So timing of *chaptalisation* is also critical.

Efforts are also made to avoid the otherwise common practice of maceration at the end of fermentation – since the alcohol then present produces a highly unselective extraction leaching out undesirable compounds, in particular enzymes which contribute to the irreversible degradation of red wine.

Guy Accad's philosophy is both direct, almost platitudinous: at each stage, the winemaker must ask himself: 'Is it necessary to do X?', or 'Is it a good moment to do X?' or again, 'Why do X at all?'. 'Tradition' should not be an acceptable excuse for incompetence.

His clients produce consistently impressive wines – richly coloured, exuberantly aromatic and distinctively individual. Tasting 1987s, 1988s, 1989s and 1990s from Senard, Grivot, Labet and Confuron leaves no doubt of clear differences between *climats* and vintages. Growers' styles make comparisons problematic. With more 'Accad' wines, perhaps typicity itself will change .

Ageability asks two separate questions: will these wines last and will they turn into 'typical Burgundy'? Their massive initial structures leave one in no doubt that they are as durable, if not more, than most conventional Burgundies from similar vineyards and those now reaching maturity have as much 'typicity' as any others.

Accad's ideas are cohesive. People will doubtless continue to debate whether heavy doses of sulphur and cool pre-fermentive maceration is genuine innovation or merely a modernisation of traditional practice. The argument is sterile and the conclusion immaterial.

Most of the wines produced under Accad's aegis are undubitably fine, so few who eventually drink them are likely to complain. Should some evolve lacking a certain Burgundian classicism, would it be heresy to suggest that perhaps it wouldn't really matter?

HENRI JAYER

In contrast to cash-rich Bordeaux, Burgundy's fragmentation has limited growers' means and thus the scope for the emergence of gurus. Here, perceptions seem to be introspective, conditioned more by family tradition than by international comparisons.

If any single person has influenced the skill and morale of younger growers it is Henri Jayer. Over four decades, this modest, kindly man has counselled and befriended many of those now considered Burgundy's first-division wine-makers.

Meeting him, in his unostentatious modern house on the edge of Vosne, one is aware of quiet wisdom and self-effacing modesty. He does not, as many have noted, suffer fools; maybe, but his over-riding concern is with the reputation of the region he has worked in for 60 years and with its new generation.

Henri Jayer's reputation is founded on a succession of superlative wines from his small, Vosne-based Domaine. After the 1995 vintage, he handed over his vines to his nephew Emmanuel Rouget (qv), whom he trained. Now officially retired and thus freed from daily labour, he spends his time helping him and advising Jean-Nicolas Méo, to whose Domaine he has long been consultant, and remains much in demand from vignerons of all ages needing advice.

He has thought deeply about what really determines the quality of a wine. In his view, *terroir* is paramount – a Gevrey can never be as fine as a Vosne because their atmospheres and soils differ. Moreover, one vigneron's personal perspective differs from his neighbour's and inevitably influences how he sets about winemaking.

Jayer's own scheme is robustly straightforward and remarkably uncomplicated. 'Wine,' he reminds, 'is for pleasure, so one seeks as perfect an equilibrium as possible.' His personal philosophy rests on two principles: first, that 'wine must not be brought up in cotton-wool – let nature go', and second, that one cannot artificially replace constituents lacking at the start and expect success. Tinkering to compensate for inadequate fruit is no path to quality. He also avers that mystery is part of wine's fascination.

Henri Jayer stresses the importance of expending maximum effort to produce top-class raw material. Most of his own vines were over 50 years old and he harvested 'neither late nor early', to achieve optimal quality, which he cryptically defines as '90% of potential maximum'. If you wait longer, gains are likely to be counterbalanced by losses.

Ideal fruit is broadly quantified as two thirds liquid to one third solids. This entails removing grape-stalks which bring nothing to a wine, except astringency. Jayer defends the value of a period of pre-fermentive maceration: 'the wines with the most bouquet and the finest robe have 5-7 days' soaking – this releases extraordinary aromas and colours'. In this, he agrees with Guy Accad; however, whilst Accad delays fermentation by chemical means – a heavy dose of SO_2 – Jayer achieves the same result by cooling his pulp to 15°C – a mechanical operation. As the pulp warms, the natural yeasts start working, helped by one or two daily *remontages*. Once fermentation is under way and any necessary *chaptalisation* has been made, *pigéage* takes over from *remontage*.

Great weight is placed on using only indigenous yeasts: 'everything is in the yeast,' says Jayer, recalling with a groan a Californian 'Pinot Noir' which tasted just like Cabernet Sauvignon. 'They had yeasted it with 80% Cabernet and 10% Pinot yeasts,' he explained; restraining himself from adding: 'what do they expect?'

His dislike of tinkering extends to the *saignée de cuve*, which he regards as a palliative for those whose juice is too dilute because their debudding was inadequate. 'No one is prepared to take risks these days – they all want assurance.'

Jayer prefers cement *cuves* arguing that these give less risk of atypical flavours and help keep temperatures down below 34°C. His *cuvaison* lasted 15-20 days – until the cap of solids started to fall, indicating the end of fermentation. After adding the press-wine, the new wine was transferred to 100% new oak for about 18 months. Jayer believes that a correctly balanced wine can support such a regime, even in less naturally ripe vintages: 'it is a question of concentration,' he affirms.

Malolactic fermentation proceeded at its own pace as Jayer dislikes heating to provoke the lactic bacteria into action: 'it's no use being in a hurry'. If low pH (i.e. high acidity) wines take longer to ferment than those with a high pH, so be it; don't interfere. Each *cuvée* is an individual and should be allowed to evolve in its own way. After two rackings, the wines were bottled off their fining, directly from cask at the prodigious rate of 5 casks per day.

The results of Henri Jayer's skill need little description here. Anyone fortunate enough to have tasted his wines from the yardstick Bourgogne Rouge, through a deep, silky Vosne Beaumonts and the magnificent Vosne Cros Parantoux to a magisterial (though not invariably finer) Echézeaux, will have experienced the wonders this man is capable of extracting from bunches of grapes.

If Jayer endows the winemaking process which such thoughtful simplicity, where do so many go wrong? In his view, Burgundy's 'wound' is that whilst 80% of its wines are good, if tasted before *malo*, considerably fewer are after, only 20% are worth considering in bottle – a bleeding to neutrality or worse.

Specifically, Jayer believes that excess sulphur and too many manipulations have impoverished quality. Also, vignerons fail to top up casks regularly and to taste the wine each time they do so. Cellar hygiene is often skimped – especially with older casks.

Then again, fine wine is easily ruined by over-fining or severe filtration. Indeed, Jayer sees no need to filter, giving his Burgundies just the purest of finings. Harsh manipulations may produce bright, sterile wines, and thus peace of mind, but this is achieved at the expense of balance and quality.

For Jayer, the customer is the key to influencing standards in Burgundy. 'It is up to the client not to buy bad wine, he has more power than he realises.' He advises a distrust of the 'cellar ambience'; this, animated by a persuasive vigneron, is no place to make a dispassionate buying decision.

Of his own achievements he is dismissively modest: 'Perhaps I have helped some younger vignerons not to make mistakes.' As for the future, he is optimistic: 'The young have both the finance and the technical means to make fine wine. They don't work in the same way as the older vignerons – by 'pif', by instinct . They have more curiosity; get out more and taste more, so can see if they are incompetent. Vignerons were individuals before, they are more communicative now; the better ones are models for the rest – there are no secrets.'

If anyone is in a position to make such judgements it is Henri Jayer. Burgundy and its present generation owe much to his wisdom and generosity of spirit.

FROM GROWER TO CONSUMER – HOW BURGUNDY IS SOLD

Although only some 50 kms long and between 500 and 2,000 m wide, the Côte d'Or is in fact a highly fragmented patchwork of individual vineyards divided among upwards of 2000 growers, each owning an average of 5 ha of vines, spread over several appellations.

A typical grower might have in his cellar some ten different wines – a Bourgogne Aligoté, some Bourgogne Rouge or Blanc, perhaps two or three Village wines, several Premier Crus and one or two Grand Crus if he is lucky. How does all this wine find its way on to the market ?

While the wine is still unbottled the grower has two choices: either to sell it in bulk or to mature it and sell it in bottle. If the former, his customers are likely to be the negociant houses who in the main own no vineyards, but rely on a network of small growers to supply their needs. It is estimated that some 60-70% of all Burgundy currently passes through the hands of the negoce, although the proportion will be significantly less in the Côte d'Or because many Domaines now bottle and sell directly.

If the grower chooses to keep the wine and bottle it, he can label the bottles and sell them at his cellar door to private customers or, at less exalted prices wholesale; or he can leave them unlabelled for sale to negociants who find themselves short of stock.

In practice, there are three stages at which a grower can sell his wine to the negoce – 'sur le marché' as it is called: i) as grapes, juice or very new wine, ii) in cask, or iii) in bottle. Many negociants have annual contracts with a large number of growers offering different appellations throughout the Côte – by this means they make up a list to offer their customers.

These arrangements, which may or may not oblige the negociant to take the crop, are often unwritten gentleman's agreements which have been in place for decades. The good negociant knows his vignerons personally and will give them advice and technical help to ensure that they produce the quality that meets his needs.

The better houses will only buy in grapes or unfermented juice and vinify the wine themselves; this gives them complete control and the freedom to make the wine in their preferred style. The less careful tend to buy finished wine in bulk, which they mature and then bottle in their cellars. The least quality-conscious houses buy unlabelled bottles, 'sur pile', and simply stick on their own labels.

Most of the finest Burgundy is bottled, and sold in bottle, by the Domaine which made it. This has been an accelerating trend, even for smaller Domaines from less prestigious appellations. In the early 1900s, virtually all Burgundy found its way through the negociant system. This remained so until relatively recently: in 1970 only some 5% of all Burgundy produced was sold in bottle by the Domaine which produced it; now, in the Côte d'Or, that percentage is probably nearer to 50.

For a variety of reasons, it sometimes happens that a top Domaine has wine which it would prefer to dispose of in bulk. For example, it may have cash-flow problems – great vignerons are rarely talented financiers; or again, in years when the crop is dilute or when, perhaps, a few casks turn out sub-standard, a Domaine may choose, rather than compromise its reputation by selling under its own label, to sell 'sur le marché'.

Although there is nothing in law to prevent a grower and his customer dealing directly with each other, for a multitude of reasons most prefer to use the services of a 'courtier en vins' as a go-between.

Courtiers have been an established part of the marketplace for several centuries. They thrived in the Middle Ages, when communications and travel were difficult, going about among growers and merchants making a market in whatever was for sale. Courtiers were known to have existed in Beaune in 1375 and, despite modern communications, have remained an indispensible part of the trading structure.

There are presently some 60 courtiers in the Côte d'Or. These are independent operators, often just one man and a secretary, without any formal qualifications, holding no stocks, who may be approached by either a prospective purchaser or vendor – to sell the surplus of one or to fill the cellar of the other. The courtier is expected to know the market and either to find clients or source whatever is required. Each Domaine generally works with a small number of courtiers it trusts and, conversely, a conscientious courtier will specialise in a limited number of appellations. Since there tend to be periods of intense activity, a single courtier could never manage to cover more than a handful of communes.

Apart from relying on the courtier for his contacts, a purchaser will expect him to oversee each transaction. Curiously, whilst elsewhere in wine-producing France the courtier invariably works on commission from the buyer, for the large number of small lots he will generally transact in Burgundy, custom decrees that both purchaser and seller pay him commission – the usual rate being 2% from the one and 3% from the other.

For this he is expected to deliver tasting samples and to ensure that the wine eventually delivered matches that ordered. Although he sends the client the bill for his purchase and is responsible for any faults the wine may have, the contract is between grower and purchaser; if the grower thinks that the customer is a debt risk, he can refuse to deal.

Although many negociants value the personal contact involved in dealing direct with growers, others prefer the anonymity which courtiers provide. Time-wasting travelling and social pleasantries are dispensed with, and hundreds of samples can be tasted without leaving their own tasting-rooms, and rejected without embarrassment.

Another species of middle-man, with whom the courtier is frequently confused, is the 'representant'. This entity – often a company – arranges with Domaines or growers to sell their wines, usually in bottle, on a regular basis. Unlike a courtier, the 'representant' will generally produce a catalogue of the wines he has to offer and the larger firms will also have some kind of marketing and distribution organisation. He may also choose to add a profit margin, over and above the normal commission, to cover increased overheads.

Nowadays, the finest Burgundy Domaines frequently find themselves with more customers than stock, and are able to dictate precisely to whom they sell, channelling their wines to those most likely to nurture and appreciate them. Some prefer to concentrate on 'La grande restauration', often measuring their prowess by the number of three-star Michelin establishments featuring their wines.

Many growers take their eating as seriously as their drinking, and enjoy the reciprocity involved in supplying such as Lameloise, Troisgros, Chapel or Taillevent. Dine, on a Friday or Saturday evening, at one of the more exalted local troughs and you are almost bound to find an uncomfortably overdressed, or nonchalantly under-dressed, wine-grower and his family working their way through the Menu de Dégustation with evident delight, fussed over by the proprietor, ever hopeful of increasing his meagre allocation.

Others concentrate on exports and deal only reluctantly with private customers or restaurants. They point to the twin benefits of larger individual orders and less time taken out of over-charged days for social politesse and tasting. Some Domaines – in Chassagne and Pommard, for example – have tried to solve the problem of constant visitors by setting up shops offering a number of growers' wines for sale. This saves the customer the trouble of finding and visiting several growers, and the growers the trouble of receiving him – particularly awkward when language barriers reduce communication between the parties to hand-signals and an assortment of inadequate facial contortions. However, such shops undeniably take much of the pleasure out of the buying and discovering process.

Notwithstanding, there has been a steady trend towards direct selling along the Côte. From Easter to late Autumn swarms of wine-loving tourists descend on Burgundy to replenish their cellars and to visit their favourite growers. International media attention has turned some of these hard-working sons of the earth into minor celebrities. In many cases, although most wouldn't admit it, their egos enjoy such frequent ritual massaging and they start to develop modest eccentricities to embellish their act, leaning on a barrel or wandering from cask to cask, pipette in hand as they expatiate on this technicality or on that vintage.

Some are genuinely bemused by all the attention they receive and find it difficult to understand what the fuss is about. Whatever their technique for dealing with the tide of endless personal callers, most growers welcome the cash and exposure that they bring, and there is no doubt that the trend is set to continue. If the astute grower can lever a price advantage out of the process, so much the better.

Many vignerons deliberately sell a high proportion of their production outside France and enjoy taking their families off on exotic wanderings to see where their wine ends up. Over the decades, such arrangements have sown the seeds of many long-established friend-ships between grower and importer. Others, disliking travel and the anonymity of foreign markets, prefer to sell to French and European customers, with whom they perhaps feel they have more in common. However they eventually distribute their wares, most vignerons take pleasure in the thought that their bottles are finding their way on to tables where they will receive informed and comprehending appreciation.

In the end, whether a buyer gets anything at all, and indeed how much he pays, may depend on nothing more sophisticated than the whim of the grower. If he doesn't like you, however big your budget or impeccable your credentials, you plead in vain. Equally, there is always a case or two to be squeezed out of precious stocks for the favoured few. How many buyers have made to leave, after an hour or so tasting, downcast to find their hesitant request for wine met by an expressive shrug accompanied by the ritual lamentation: 'je n'ai plus rien; c'est tout vendu' only to have their spirits uplifted moments later with the vestige of a smile accompanied by 'but, I will go and see if, perhaps, I could find you a few bottles'.

One way of selling your wine – direct to the consumer

BUYING AND ENJOYING BURGUNDY

In the 1995 vintage, over 4,400 individual growers declared a harvest in the Côte d'Or. Assuming each grower bottles 6 wines, one arrives at a total of 26,400 Domaine-bottled wines finding their way onto the market. Among these will be more than 60 different Clos de Vougeots, as many Echézeaux, at least 15 Montrachets, a plethora of Pulignys and a positively tidal wave of Nuits St.-Georges. How can a prospective buyer hope to find his way through the maze?

Burgundy is a minefield – a buyer's nightmare, where quality often bears little relation to price and where vested interest and ineffectual controls give unscrupulous growers year-round open-season on the ignorant or gullible.

Unfortunately, even if you know which Domaines to buy from, available quantities of the best wines are pitifully small and demand regularly far outstrips supply. What is available, especially in top-flight vintages, is eagerly sought after and rapidly snapped up. This leaves legions of unsatisfied trade buyers wandering round the Côte looking for reliable sources of supply, whilst private individuals find themselves paying their local merchants hefty mark-ups for the golden Domaines – that is, assuming they manage to get an allocation.

Whilst supply cannot be increased and there are few bargains, certainly at Premier and Grand levels, it is possible to buy fine Burgundy provided you are prepared to take a little trouble and are not mesmerised by labels.

Recent vintages have seen good crops of excellent wine and recession has left growers with comparatively full cellars, but this modest glut is unlikely to last for long. It only needs a vintage or two of moderate quality to put growers back in the driving seat.

Anyone contemplating building up a cellar of Burgundy, whether trader or private buyer, must ask: where to buy, what to buy, how to buy and when to buy? Fortunately in Burgundy, unlike Bordeaux, larger and smaller customers usually compete on equal terms since growers have small stocks and tend to enjoy the personal contact which the Bordelais often seem happy to avoid. Prices are non-negotiable and quantity discounts virtually unheard of – for all but the more plentiful régionales. So what is the best strategy ?

Where to buy? If quality matters, then there is no alternative to the type of grower profiled here, or else to one of the handful of reputable negociants. Covering Burgundy by the grower route is both time-consuming and costly in shipping and administration if you buy direct, or in locating importers and retailers if you buy locally; the negociants, on the other hand, offer a full range of wines although rarely of uniformly top-quality – in short, a one-stop shop.

In most countries without import restrictions, it is possible to find merchants who specialise in Domaine-bottled Burgundy. For those wanting mixed cases and advice, these can represent excellent sources of supply. However, the range may be restricted and availability limited, making it necessary to deal with more than one merchant. Most conscientious retailers will offer periodic tastings, often of single vintages or Domaines, which are a useful means of education and of deciding what to buy. It is important to beware of persuasive prose and to make up one's own mind as far as possible free from a merchant's influence.

For older wines, auction houses are often worthwhile hunting-grounds, but it is important to be sure that wine-levels are acceptable

and that storage has been appropriate. For some as yet unexplained reason, Pinot Noir seems to support a much greater ullage in bottle (loss of wine) than Cabernet Sauvignon. Bottles with up to 5 cms air between cork and meniscus can be excellent, provided the colour is sound and the wine clear. Chardonnay, however, is more susceptible to level and older wines should be examined carefully for browning – a sure sign of oxidation.

What to buy? There is no alchemy by which age will transform poor wine into something fine, so laying down indifferent Burgundy, even of a great vintage, is a waste of money, cellar space and time. There is much to be said for trying to build up sufficient supplies of decent young wine to enable bottles to be kept until they are mature – after all that is what most growers make them for.

It will be clear from reading the grower and commune profiles that, whilst the top wines are in short supply and beyond the pockets of most people, there is plenty of interesting Burgundy to be found below the stratosphere. Less popular communes – Monthelie, St. Aubin, Fixin, Marsannay, Auxey-Duresses, St.-Romain, etc. – are well worth mining for good sensibly-priced wine.

At the everyday level, many of the top growers make sensibly priced *régionales* – Bourgogne Rouge and Blanc, Côte de Nuits or Beaune Villages – which receive the same skill and care as their Grands Crus. These are not cheap, but there is, unquestionably, greater pleasure to be had from such wine than from incompetently made, and certainly more expensive, Village or Premier Cru. If in doubt, try a comparative tasting – one sip should convince you.

Once you have found a clutch of growers whose style you like, then there is plenty to be said in favour of sticking with them from vintage to vintage. Certainly, no Domaine is without its failures and none is immune from the caprice of weather or fate. However, providing you steer clear of really appalling vintages (of which there are very few nowadays), the grower's name on the label is a better guarantee of pleasure than either vintage or vineyard from elsewhere.

The second-rank vintages often offer some of the best bargains – merchants often by-pass them because they are anxious to avoid being landed with unsaleable stock, and the grower prices them attractively for similar reasons. The modern reality is that the best vignerons will make a respectable job of nine out of ten vintages, so the chance of encountering a really disappointing wine from a Great Domaine is slender.

Unfashionable vintages, such as 1991, 1987, 1986 and 1982, in fact produced some concentrated and delicious wines which, whilst not in the top class, are well worth buying and laying down. In any case, all but the most bone-headed would prefer to be pleasantly surprised by a wine of which they had low expectations, than to be disappointed by the unfulfilled promise of an expensive label from a great vintage.

We live in an age of gurus. There is no shortage of 'experts' willing to rush into print on a vintage, barely before the vats have ceased to ferment. The growers refuse to judge in this way, but these people seem to know better. Some are qualified and experienced tasters, but most, unfortunately, are not. Unlike merchants, these pundits are rarely answerable for their mistakes. If you find someone whose opinions you trust, then follow them; but, in general, there is no substitute for forming your own, independent, judgement.

How to buy? If you are an importer or wholesale buyer, then you can either buy direct from the Domaine, or through a broker. The chapter on 'How Burgundy is traded' (p. 266) explains how the system operates. For a private buyer, there is no substitute for a friendly merchant, if you can find one whose judgement you trust. Whilst those near enough to visit Burgundy can enjoy the experience of visiting Domaines and tasting first-hand, they should be aware that many of the best growers are reluctant to receive individual visitors – at least without a personal introduction – and that even if they manage to breach the front-door, they may well come away empty-handed.

Although being turned politely refused may often seem like a personal affront, especially if you have come half way across the globe to worship, this reflects neither cussedness nor arrogance. The scale on which wine is produced in the Côte means that many Domaines are family operations, run by husband and wife with the help, perhaps, of a couple of workers. Visitors consume a great deal of time, which they can ill afford, let alone the cost of opening expensive bottles for tasting. If, in addition, a Domaine can sell its entire produce several times over with a few telephone calls, there is little incentive to receive visitors, however much the owners enjoy customer contact. If you feel that there is any risk of rebuttal, come armed with an introduction and an appointment.

This said, for many of Burgundy's better Domaines, receiving visitors is part of their way of life and there are few who do not respond warmly to genuinely interested wine-lovers, provided that they are given reasonable notice. Direct sales have grown substantially in recent years, especially to regular Swiss and German clientele who invade the Côte from Easter to All Saints, re-stocking at advantageous prices and having fun into the bargain.

When to buy? Time was when merchants, unhurried by inflation or demand, would make two or three visits to their selected Domaines, tasting in cask and in bottle, before placing their valued orders. Now, if you are lucky, you receive a fax stating your allocation which must be confirmed within weeks, if not days, long before the wine has come anywhere near to seeing a bottle. The price is usually non-negotiable and the offer often carries the unwritten rider that if you don't like it, there is a queue of supplicants who will take your place in the queue (and pay up there and then, if necessary). Also, importers who try to skip a disappointing year, soon find that they have forfeited their allocation when the next five-star vintage comes along.

This pressure has passed through to the consumer – if you don't buy 'en primeur', the story goes, then you risk having to pay more, or worse, getting none of your favourite Domaine's wonders at all.

A succession of over-hyped, over-priced vintages in the Côte, have left many buyers disillusioned and overstocked. Following the almost universal media mis-judgement of the 1983s, many trade importers have become wary of confirming orders before they have had the chance to taste the wines in bottle. The realisation that a wine which is a well-proportioned, elegant and irresistable maiden in cask, can rapidly turn into a gnarled, shrivelled and thoroughly resistable old witch in bottle, has caused people to rely less on advance press ratings and more on their own convictions – a welcome trend.

Buying 'en primeur' can only be justified when the quality is so high and the market so short of stock that the chance, once missed, is unlikely to recur. These circumstances being rare – once or twice in a decade possibly – dispassionate caution should override instant gratification.

What of the future? Whilst there may be temporary hiccups in supply and demand which work to the buyers' or sellers' advantage, the long-term trend is clear as tiny quantities of superb wine from a coterie of top Domaines are chased by an ever-increasing international market. In such circumstances, and with no sign of any real threat, to Pinot Noir at least, from outside Burgundy, prices must rise. The best wine-makers are becoming cult figures, and their wines demanded by those with the means to pay for them.

For the careful buyer, things are not entirely gloomy. There may be no escape from the price-spiral for the finest Burgundies, but there is much of quality and interest a little further down the pyramid. In addition to the starred growers one knows about, there are many lesser luminaries whose mentality is gradually changing from a policy of quantity to one of quality. Younger, more skilled wine-makers are returning to the Côte, attracted by better prospects and viable returns, to take over from the old guard as they retire, and with them the prospects for finer wines from what are now mediocre Domaines.

Cellaring and drinking burgundy: Enough has been written about how to treat wine – even-temperatured storage, laying bottles down, decanting an older wine off any sediment and so on to make reiteration unnecessary. However, there are some points peculiar to the wines of Burgundy which are worth highlighting.

1. Fine white Burgundy, though lacking in tannin, needs keeping as much as red. The best of Puligny, Corton and Meursault, whilst often delicious young, will give so much more if kept for a few years; how long, of course, depends on the style of wine and the vintage. In general, Grands Crus will benefit from longer in bottle than Premiers Crus, which in turn mature later than straight Village wines.

2. For all Burgundies, but white wines in particular, the warmer their storage the faster their maturation.

3. Much of the quality of fine white Burgundy is lost if it is over-chilled. This loss is often irreversible – what has been chilled out does not re-emerge when the wine warms up. Putting a precious Puligny in the freezer may chill it quickly – even this isn't certain – but will do it little good. Half an hour in an ice-bucket is better for the wine and just as effective.

4. In general, red wine is far more robust than the neurotic anxieties of some collectors and commentators would have us believe. It can withstand a fair amount of moderately rough treatment without too much complaint. Whilst perfect cellarage and service are the ideal, they are rarely the reality. Those with imperfect cellarage, too warm a dining-room or no decanters should take heart. Far too often inherently poor quality is attributed to defective handling.

5. Decanting: much pointless hot-air has been expended on this subject. What should be remembered, above all, is that wine contains many highly volatile substances which contribute to its complexity and which may be irretrievably lost if a bottle is opened too long before drinking. In addition, decanting aerates the wine, provoking further changes from this contact with oxygen. Older wine with a granular sediment may be served straight from the bottle, to avoid unnecessary aeration, provided it is stood upright for a few hours to settle the deposit.

6. Too often red wine is damaged by being left in an over-heated room before being served. The Pinot Noir is capable of magnificently complex and abundantly subtle perfumes which are easily destroyed by heat which rapidly releases the more evanescent into the surrounding atmosphere. The French term 'chambré', used to describe the room temperature at which red wines are best drunk, suggests a temperature of around 18-200C, rather than the near tropical paradise of many centrally-heated dining-rooms.

TASTING BURGUNDY

However much one reads about a wine region, there is no substitute for tasting. And that, far from being the recherché art that many would have us believe, is a skill that can be acquired by anyone with reasonably normal sensory acuity and the self-discipline to practise intelligently. What matters, above all, is the willingness to exclude prejudice and to taste honestly.

Much has been written by way of introduction to the mechanics of tasting – Broadbent (1970), Spurrier & Dovaz (1983) and Peynaud (1987) all provide useful background material and advice. This short essay is not designed to supplant these excellent sources, but to indicate what one should be looking for in a wine, and especially in Côte d'Or Pinot Noir and Chardonnay.

It is worth restating the oft-forgotten fact that physiologists recognise only four 'true' tastes: acidity, sweetness, bitterness and saltiness, of which all, but the last, are important in wine. Beyond these, there are 'taste sensations' – temperature, viscosity, volume, texture, astringency, etc. – which also form part of a wine's overall taste profile. Together with a vast array of aromas, these provide the raw material which the taster has to analyse, describe and assess.

Tasting is complicated by the fact that aromas and flavours do not exist in isolation, but interact, either re-inforcing or masking each other. For example, sweetness disguises acidity and is enhanced by alcohol, whilst tannin can hide fruit, and bitterness almost anything. These interactions can be powerfully distorting, especially in young wines, whose constituents need time to integrate and for their true qualities to emerge. This is why early judgements of a wine or vintage are so often misleading.

In a well-made wine, no single characteristic should dominate – fruit must balance acidity, acidity must balance alcohol, and in red wine, all must balance tannins. This does not mean that the components of taste and aroma cancel each other out, rather that they constitute an active harmony – the dynamic equilibrium of the gymnast, rather than the passive balance of the sleeper.

What constitutes good balance remains subjective, but one soon develops a sixth sense for wines which are out of kilter. For those inexperienced in tasting, young wines often seem jagged and unharmonious – all in pieces. Only with practice does one learn to recognise an imbalance which is unlikely to be corrected by age.

In addition reliable guides to a wine's quality are its length (how far back on the palate the taste goes), its persistence (how long the flavours linger after swallowing or spitting), and its complexity (each sniff or mouthful giving something different). However renowned or expensive a wine, if these qualities are lacking, then it is not truly great.

Tasting blind is a most exacting skill and the only true test of a wine's intrinsic worth. For anyone learning to taste, it is an invaluable tool for sharpening the palate and for developing an unprejudiced sense of quality. Every effort should be made to taste blind as often as possible.

Making a definitive quality assessment provides the taster with the severest test – his ability to exclude the potent influences of reputation, politeness, occasion, or just the opinions of those around him. It is here that self-deceit creeps in, often bolstered by the fear of being a lone dissenter. All too often is it forgotten that the quality of a wine is determined by what is in the glass, not the label on the bottle.

Whatever the circumstances, one should try to develop a systematic routine of looking at, smelling, then finally tasting, a wine, in order to determine the strengths and weaknesses of its component parts as a preliminary to deciding its quality level, how well it will age, or has developed, whether or not to buy it, and how it compares with whatever else is being tasted. Tasting and comparing within and between grape varieties and regions is invaluable.

In all this ritual, one should never forget that, whatever its individual qualities, wine is invariably more than the sum of its constituents. Neither should one lose sight of the fact that wine is intended for drinking, and not as the raw material for analytical gymnastics. In general, a wine should be pleasurable, and appetizing, to eye, nose and palate; it should have balance between its constituents – acids, alcohols and tannins, etc; and above all, it should have a good measure of ripe fruit. Any excess or deficiency compromises quality and risks upsetting a smooth evolution.

Of all the sensory qualities, aroma is especially valuable, since it most powerfully reflects the typicity deriving from terroir and grape-variety; its type and intensity are key features of wine assessment. Grapes contain two different substances – directly smelling odour molecules and those which are only 'precursors' of aromas. While the former are dominant in aromatic varieties such as Muscat, which, as grapes, taste much as they smell, the latter are some 20 times more concentrated in non-aromatic varieties, such as Chardonnay. However, being tied to sugar molecules, these are non-aromatic in their pre-fermentive state and rely upon fermentation to detach and transform them into fully aromatic compounds. During this phase, aromatic concentration rises by a factor of 5-6 as the typicity of the grape begins to emerge.

The temperature at which grapes are fermented is thus a major determinant of a wine's aromatic qualities. Whilst Pinot Noir seems capable of fermenting at relatively high temperatures – up to 35°C – without undue aromatic distortion, Chardonnay is more sensitive. Above an ideal band of 17-25°C, aromatic intensity increases sharply, but to the detriment of finesse and freshness; below, fermentation produces somewhat colourless, neutral wine, with little varietal characteristics. The importance of temperature also applies to tasting, and is not peculiar to wine; many flowers smell different in different conditions – time of day, dry or humid atmosphere, hot or cold temperature. This is nothing more than subtle modification in volatile, organic compounds, common to many forms of plant life which easily alters their aromatic profile.

Tasting young wine, especially in cask, is generally more difficult, and less gratifying, than tasting something mature. It is also more challenging, since young wines tend to present themselves as an awkward amalgam of unharmonious constituents – rather like a pile of bricks, from which one is invited to imagine the finished building.

In cask, wine changes rapidly from week to week, particularly when it is moved, racked, fined or filtered, and dramatically when it is bottled – a shock from which it may take months, or even years, to recover. Different casks of the same wine may taste very different – new wood from old, racked from unracked – so cask samples can only ever be an approximation of the finished product.

It should be added that , atmospheric as they often are, cellars are physically inconvenient places for tasting, since artificial light and cold distort a wine's qualities. Henri Jayer's uncompromising advice is to taste in the cellar by all means, then take your euphoria back home and retaste in controlled conditions; mistrust the grower's theatrical blandishments, his exotic prose and his carefully rehearsed asides about dwindling stocks and having sold the last few cases, only yesterday, to this or that illustrious client.

To the eye, Pinot Noir rarely gives the dense, impenetrable appearance one often finds in young Cabernet Sauvignon or Syrah, although some growers with very old vines, practising long *cuvaison*, may produce extraordinarily dark wines. However, lightness must not be confused with lack of substance – a wine may appear almost rosé, but be packed with concentrated, ripe fruit. Young Burgundy can vary in hue from ruby red to black-cherry, and from light to dark in saturation; the spectrum is wide.

Hue and depth are valuable indicators of a wine's age and likely development. Young Pinot often comes with a purple colour component, derived from anthocyanin pigments which are later transformed into a more stable deep red. In addition, the finest red Burgundies are often accompanied by a limpidity, a softness of texture, which is particularly distinctive and attractive to the eye.

Whatever the hue, it should form a continuous 'robe', from the centre to the edge of a tilted tasting-glass. A watery meniscus or a degradation of colour is not an encouraging sign. Prematurely brown or brick-edged reds, or dull, ochre-tinted whites are often the result of over-exposure to oxygen or too long in wood and are unlikely to age satisfactorily. Whilst white wines may be hazy or turbid during *elevage*, in bottle they should be bright and clear, pale straw or green or yellow-gold.

On the nose, young wines may present themselves in a variety of ways. Chardonnays can be flowery or not and Pinots can smell of *petits fruits rouges*, of *fruits noirs* – or sometimes, of nothing at all. During *elevage* the aromatic intensity may change from exuberantly fruity to dumb and unforthcoming. This is normal and explains why, in assessing young wines, one relies less on aroma and more on basic taste components.

A wine which has spent time in new oak will generally have a marked toasty or vanilla component to its aroma. This often dominates for a year or two, making it essential to look underneath to ensure that there is enough fruit there to keep the wine alive. The ability to ignore attensive wood or tannin is an essential skill in tasting young wine, only developed with practice.

On the palate, the absence of significant tannins and 'green', stalky, flavours makes young Chardonnay infinitely more approachable than young Pinot. To compensate, and ensure a sound development in bottle, wines must have enough acidity. Lack of acidity is a common fault in Chardonnays, especially in very ripe Burgundy vintages, such as 1983,1989 and 1992.

Fine Côte d'Or Pinot Noir spans a wide spectrum of flavours – often characterised by a strong element of soft berries – pure, ripe, crushed fruit, mouthfilling and succulent. The wines of the Côte de Beaune, whilst similar to those of the Côte de Nuits, tend to have less obvious muscle and density and are not quite so long-lived.

In general, all that can be usefully extracted from a very young wine is a rough idea of its underlying structure and depth – acids and tannins being less susceptible to short-term change than aromas and other flavours. This give a good guide to its overall quality and ageing potential. It is also essential at this stage to identify any glaring deficiencies or faults – such as dilution, a lack of fruit, or an

A tasting in progress in London

irremediable taste of rot and to be aware that wines change during *élevage*.

Although some wines are attractive, even drinkable, from cask, it is with age that great Burgundy comes into its own. Once in bottle, deprived of the opportunity for freely combining with oxygen, a fine wine undergoes a much slower, more subtle transformation. Reactions between its various chemical constituents – principally alcohols, acids and tannins – gradually change its colour composition, lightening reds and deepening whites, and produce trace quantities of a variety of volatile, highly aromatic compounds, in particular esters, which contribute significantly to aroma and flavour.

With time, a wine's protection from oxygen lessens and it starts to change. The Pinot Noir, not darkly coloured by nature, loses redness and develops a brownish tinge, whilst the Chardonnay loses its youthful green glint and deepens towards yellow or gold. These changes are accompanied by a shift from the primary, fruit and floral-based smells to more subtle and complex dried fruit and broadly vegetal aromas in the Pinot, often with strong hints of violets and mushrooms, and to those of honey, lime-blossom and nuts in Chardonnay. Wines open out, both in aroma and flavour, and their individual elements integrate. A mature Pinot or Chardonnay should be pure, uncluttered by new wood, and richly fragrant. The time span of a wine's evolution will depend on its individual character; those with more structure – tannins and acids in particular – will be slower to reach maturity and will remain at their peaks for longer than those with weaker frames.

As the years pass, aromas become more elegant, with notes of animal, visceral and musk in reds and the more oxidative smells of nuts and butter in whites. Pinot Noir can also develop hints of leather, fur, and especially sous-bois (undergrowth, leaves, etc.) and sometimes well-hung game. However, these tertiary aromas do not develop entirely at the expense of fruit – Pinot Noir often reverts to its more youthful fruity aromas – strawberries, raspberries, etc. The finest of old Pinots have great richness and opulence – fruit which is almost sweet but exotically ripe, with a silky, velvet texture and a complexity and balance which inspire admiration. A great Burgundy should have power and subtlety, depth and delicacy, and above all something intriguing which makes each sip a revelation.

The great white Burgundies are no less enthralling. After 5-10 years they begin to reveal a richness and elegance, allied to a powerful backbone. The best are invariably understated, complex and intense, but never overblown – inviting the drinker to exercise his imagination and read between the lines, rather than having every detail set uncompromisingly forth.

Tasters should always be on the alert for faults. Whilst nowadays one rarely encounters Burgundy which is defective to the point of being undrinkable, there are many subtle faults which point to laziness or to poor wine-making which can scar a wine permanently. A frequent problem in the Côte's marginal climate is a lack of ripe fruit, resulting in thin, hollow wines. At the opposite extreme, in intensely hot vintages (eg. 1976 and 1983) too much, over-ripe fruit can overpower a wine, with unpleasant cooked, jammy flavours – a failing more often encountered in New World Pinot Noir.

Other common faults relate to the use of wood. Excessive new wood will mask the fruit in a wine and destroy its finesse and typicity. Equally, too long an *élevage*, in either new or old oak, dries out a wine – it just loses its freshness and flesh, leaving behind a meagre, more or less tannic and acidic skeleton.

Excessive chaptalisation, either to increase volume or to mask other faults, is responsible for much dreadful Burgundy. Whilst the resulting extra alcohol and glycerol may give wines greater smoothness and thus some initial appeal, to the experienced taster they destroy purity and finesse.

Rot, with its distinctive, musty stamp, is often found in Burgundy. Though marginally more tolerable in Chardonnay, it usually indicates a deliberate disregard for quality and carelessness in sorting grapes. In 1983, many growers failed to eliminate rot and their wines are indelibly tainted.

In the cellar, over-use of sulphur (SO_2) – in measured doses an invaluable aid to ensuring stability – is usually a sign of sloppy wine-making. Excessive sulphur blunts freshness, particularly in white wine, giving an unpleasant, pungent aroma and a flat, cardboardy taste. It is normal for a newly-bottled wine to smell strongly of SO_2, but this should dissipate with time. With experience one develops a sense for excess.

Mature wines can show various other faults: bottles can be corked (an unfortunate, relatively rare occurrence), or oxidised, making whites flat and sherryish and reds unpleasantly stale. Wine can be volatile with a distinct whiff of vinegar which, in small quantities, may enhance it but is unpleasant in concentration; or they may be maderised – usually the result of over-heated storage.

Superimposed on the general personalities of Pinot Noir and Chardonnay are the individual taste characteristics of the various vineyards and communes along the Côte. These, combined with the immense diversity of individual wine-making styles, make the notion of a 'typical' Gevrey, Chambolle, Corton, Volnay or anything else difficult to sustain. Although by tasting the wines of reliable growers, one does come to identify broad stylistic differences between communes, for anyone learning to taste Burgundy, it is more profitable to concentrate on the spectrum of flavours and aromas that characterise fine Pinot Noir and Chardonnay than on what to expect from Pommard or Chassagne-Montrachet.

The grading system of the Côte's appellations leads one to expect, above all, a gradation of complexity, finesse and power as one ascends the ladder. What therefore, in broad terms, differentiates Grand Cru from well-made Bourgogne ordinaire?

Analytically, not much. The main differences lie in dimensions which are not susceptible to quantifiable molecular analysis. The grander the appellation the more its wine should have subtlety and nuance, length and persistence, depth and interest, power and complexity, and so on. To the senses, it is aromatic complexity and depth of flavour which are the most reliable markers of quality. The latter is doubly important, since it contains a strong aroma component.

If a true Grand Cru should be an amalgam of finely-judged balances, for the unofficial accolade accorded to only the greatest wines – Grand Vin – a wine must have something extra.

What one is particularly looking for is class – something exciting, yet undefinable, something which cannot be reduced to specifics. Recognising class is, arguably, the one element of tasting which cannot be taught – you either have the feel for it or not. What is certain is that, if you have to search too hard, it probably isn't there. Even young wines, difficult and gawky as they may be, will show class, paradoxically, through all their youthful rough edges. Class gives a wine an indelible stamp – a birthmark which it carries for life. Wines often come near to having class, but most fail through trying too hard – just too much of everything, too ostentatious and revealing; the body-builder's 'show-it-all' rather than the dancer's relaxed, elegant poise.

Words, by themselves, can never do justice to the nuances of great wine. This is how it should be – especially in the Côte d'Or, where such rich diversity makes the task of true appreciation so challenging. Great Burgundy is rare and expensive, but the effort to understand it is more than recompensed by what, after all, is the ultimate purpose of drinking. . . the pleasure it provides.

VINTAGES 1971–1995

These notes represent a general indication of the climate, character and evolution of 25 vintages in the Côte d'Or.

In reading them, it must be remembered that the vintage is only one tile in the total mosaic, especially in Burgundy where the grower, vineyard and micro-climate are all of equal, and sometimes greater, importance. Also, given small yields, thorough *triage* and careful wine-making, a skilled vigneron will often surpass the overall quality of the vintage, especially in more difficult years.

Neither should differences between individual communes and vineyard sites be ignored; drainage, vine exposition and micro-climate all distort the general vintage pattern, for good or ill, and when you add fertilisation, vine age, pruning and the impact of an early or late harvest, the picture becomes much more complex than ratings or vintage charts lead one to suppose. This is why the integrity of the grower matters so much.

The localised weather patterns of the Côte also frustrate global assessments. A severe hailstorm or snap-frost, in an otherwise good vintage, may mean that the vines of one commune, or even one narrow strip of vineyards, are damaged beyond the redemption of even the most skilled of vignerons.

If a grower cannot buck the weather, neither can the finest of growing seasons compensate for incompetent vinification. So, a vintage assessment is therefore never more than a large canvas, whose confident, broad brush-strokes hide a wealth of variation between communes, within communes, and between individual Domaines.

In these days of easy travel and instant communication, international perception of each vintage is fixed almost before fermentations are over – often earlier. Each November, there is a mad scramble among journalists, especially those from the USA, to be first to report on the new wines. Their assessments fix an impression of the vintage in the public's mind, which – however wrong it subsequently turns out to be (monumentally, in 1983, and badly enough in 1985 and 1991) – is virtually indelible. Whilst perhaps helpful to merchants unable to visit all their sources every year and needing to decide, as early as possible, whether the vintage is one to buy or to avoid, these absurdly premature assessments should be treated with considerable caution.

This way of working also creates unhealthy pressure on the market, especially on the best Domaines who now demand early reservations if you are to stand any chance of getting a decent allocation of stock. The days of tasting each vintage twice or more in cask and then after a year in bottle before making a buying decision, are, in all but the leanest vintages, over.

The public pronouncements emanate from journalists and commentators, not the growers. Some are authoritative and reliable, many are not. There is usually nothing tentative about these judgements – the vintage is either black or white – and those who make them wield disproportionate power over markets which are content to be led by the nose and lack either the opportunity or the spine to judge for themselves.

None of this is good news for the consumer who has to buy, often at high prices, sight unseen. Producers would do themselves and the public a signal service if they collectively refused tastings of new wines to all but the trade, bona fide, and then only when they had finished their *malos* and were in a reasonably fit state to be evaluated.

The assessments which follow reflect one taster's palate and experience. In reading them it should be remembered that after a very short time, the storage conditions of a bottle of wine, of any provenance, will play a major part in determining what it tastes like. Even the freshest of vintages, of either colour, which sit, unsold, in restaurant refrigerators or sunny shop-windows for long periods will not be improved by that experience, whereas well-cellared wines from a distant decade, may still be lively and interesting.

With age, bottles progressively develop ullage – that is wine is lost and the space between cork and liquid increases. Why some wines ullage more than others is a mystery, but cork quality and storage undoubtedly contribute. Whilst Chardonnay suffers unduly if the level in the bottle has dropped by more than 1-2 cms (clarity and colour are the best indicators with white wines), Pinot Noir is less susceptible. Provided the other signs are good – bright, sound, translucent colour, etc. – ullages of several centimetres are perfectly tolerable.

There is an idea abroad that Burgundy will not live for very long. This is a myth. As Michael Broadbent (1980) succinctly put it: 'well constituted (red) Burgundy will last as long as a good Bordeaux. Lightness of colour and style can be misleading: the key is the intrinsic quality and balance of the component parts'.

Burgundy's fragmentation and diversity make vintage generalisations highly insecure. The (theoretically) finest years can disappoint and the abjectly dismal delight; there are always surprises. This is a region where it is better to rely on the reputation of a grower than on that of vintage or appellation.

1971 From its youth this was a gilded vintage – rather like the 1971 St. Emilions and Pomerols, the 1971 Burgundies, both white and red, started with their hearts on their sleeves. *Coulure* at flowering, which sheds flowers and thus reduces the crop, followed by a long hot summer punctuated by some August hail, resulted in a fine concentration of juice and well ripened skins. The Côte de Beaune, which suffered most from the hail, produced a small crop of superlative whites and some immensely seductive reds. The whites still continue to give pleasure – an Hospices Meursault, Cuvée Grivault, was firm, rich and deep in 1989 – on its way to a delightfully nutty old age, and a Chassagne Morgeot, from Ramonet-Prudhon, sampled in 1990 was magisterially powerful and complex, a fine wine, not just a necrophiliac curiosity.

The reds, providing they have been well cellared, are still remarkable drinking. A warm, opulent and complex Volnay Taillepieds from de Montille, quite wondrous Beaune Marconnets, Bressandes and Grèves from Albert Morot (an experienced taster thought that the Bressandes was La Tâche, so rich and complex was it), a ripe, youthful, Santenay La Gravière tasted in 1991 with Adrien Belland, some fine English bottlings, and a well-nigh impeccable La Tâche from DRC – the litany is endless.

This is a vintage which has evolved well – more attractively, in general, than their Libournais counterparts. Both reds and whites are now 'à point' and should not be kept much longer if you want to catch them before they lose their eminently seductive charm.

1972 This was a vintage which was virtually unsaleable, at least in the UK. It was initially misjudged – partly, no doubt, because of the weak-kneed 1972 Bordeaux and also because of the huge crop size. The weather conditions demonstrated again the marginality of the Côte d'Or climate – a cold, damp spring, late flowering, followed by a cool, dry summer and then, a magnificent September which brought the grapes to relatively healthy maturity and thereby saved the vintage. The white wines never really caught the imagination, although Michael Broadbent reports some to be 'very stylish'.

The reds, however, many of which started out with so much acidity that they were abandoned by their growers as untasteable, have, with perverse torpor, thrown off their acidity and quietly evolved into wines of some distinction. Many, tasted with growers during late 1990 and early 1991, are thoroughly worthy bottles for current drinking – a few have real finesse and depth. Most have an attractive old pinot gaminess, without the opulence and depth of the 1971s. There are probably more surprises than disappointments with the 1972s. However, they are wines for drinking over the next few years and will not repay much further keeping.

1973 Initially a warm, very dry summer, preceded by a good, even flowering promised a fine vintage. However intermittent heavy rain from July through to the harvest in late September and most of October washed out this hope. Limited experience of the reds justifies their reputation as 'light, pallid and undistinguished' (Broadbent, 1980).

The whites are altogether different – generally firm, structured wines with considerable aromatic development, which have aged well. This is largely attributable to the earlier harvesting of the Chardonnay, thereby avoiding the deleterious effects of autumn rain. A Corton-Charlemagne from Tollot-Beaut, tasted in 1990, was in fine condition with a splendidly deep colour, a nose of grilled almonds and lime-blossom and a tight, masculine flavour of length and distinction.

Well-cellared bottles of 1973 white, of respectable provenance, should still be sound and even interesting.

1974 In general 1974 is abysmal, for both reds and whites. A moderately good summer was ruined by an atypically cold, wet harvest. The wines were dilute and lacking in both stuffing and balance. From time to time the odd bottle of 1974 red surfaces and surprises – a St. Romain tasted in 1989 was still alive, though hopelessly overendowed with acidity and underendowed with fruit – but the whites seem to have disappeared into oblivion. One occasionally sees wines from this vintage on French restaurant lists, at escurient prices – perhaps they know something we don't?

1975 If anything, the wines were even worse than 1974. A good, warm spring and early summer gave way to miserable weather, which persisted, apart from a spell of dry, sunny weather at the end of August, until the harvest at the end of

September. Humidity provoked widespread rot, and hail in July and August – especially in the Côte de Nuits (Vosne was particularly affected) – simply made matters worse. The result was a dismal array of wines – many irremediably rot- and hail-tainted, otherwise dilute and fruitless.

Many Domaines who ought to have known better put out wines under their own labels – it did nothing for their reputations, but after 1973 and 1974 the decision was probably actuated by more than a touch of economic necessity.

The much-publicised report of a tasting of 1975 wines from the Domaine de la Romanée-Conti in London in April 1980 in which it was generally concluded that, even judged as restaurant carafe wines, they all left much to be desired and should never have been sold under the Domaine's label, brought a swift and scathing rebuke from Mme Bize-Leroy. Her asseveration was that the wines need time to evolve, and, as she staunchly maintains, much longer in lesser vintages. However, they are still dismal – how long does one have to persevere before the Domaine admits its mistake?

Oddly enough there are one or two white wines of fine quality. A Meursault Monatine, from Domaine Rougeot, is still drinking beautifully – rich, ripe and round – nothing thin or second rate about it. It was Marc Rougeot's first vintage and when his father tasted the wine he swiftly pronounced on the incompetence of his son, bottled the wine and put it aside. Years later it started to blossom and has continued to do so. No doubt Rougeot, père, apologised profusely !

1976 The long, hot summer, when cities sweltered, roads melted and the air hung leaden and breathless. Vines, as well as humans suffered from drought and heat, and had to dig deep to pick up moisture and nourishment. Despite a very early *veraison* and an atypical early September harvest, the Pinots were deeply coloured and high in tannins and extract. Such concentration of musts made for difficult vinifications – thick skins required a long, slow *cuvaison*, yet growers were aware of the dangers of extracting too much tannin.

Those who rushed to snap judgements before the vats were barely empty, proclaimed another 1947 or 1959. Unfortunately as the wines began to develop in bottle it became apparent that many had a serious excess of tannin and would take some considerable time to 'come round'. Growers still tell you to have patience and wait – even so, there is no certainty that you will end up with something more than middle or upper-middle class.

Many of the reds are still closed up, big, burly tarry specimens which lack balance

and breeding. Some of the whites are still attractive – a Chassagne Les Ruchottes from Ramonet-Prudhon was full and nutty, in an old-fashioned sort of way in 1990 – but their low acidities have presaged a premature decline. The best advice to those with bottles of either colour is 'try one and see'.

1977 In general, an indifferent vintage. The summer started very wet, but the rot which threatened never appeared; catastrophe was averted by a warm, sunny September. However, the grapes failed to reach reasonable sugar levels and much *chaptalisation* was needed to achieve any sort of balance. Most wines are dilute and gutless with too much acidity – at best light and lean. Even the rather better structured whites must be falling apart by now.

1978 This is an 'annus mirabilis' both for the weather and for the wines. Cold and rainy weather prolonged the flowering and brought with it both *coulure* and *millerandage*, which reduced potential crop size. It continued wet and cold up to the last ten days in August. The vines, weeks behind normal maturity, needed a spell of dry hot weather for any prospect of a decent vintage. Then the weather changed and there followed two months of just what was needed. The vegetation caught up until, in mid-October, still in hot sunshine, the harvest started.

It is no exaggeration to say that these last weeks of warmth and dryness made the vintage. Clive Coates records a supplier in the Côte Chalonnaise telling him that his vines added an extra 2 degrees potential alcohol (i.e. sugar) in the last fortnight before picking – it was the same up and down the Côte.

From the start, the fine quality of the wines was apparent – attractive positive aromas, quite fleshy, pliable fruit and sound, moderately firm, structures. An initial elegance and softness made for rich, mouthfilling wines, with none of the hard, tarry tannins which marked the young 1976s.

The Chardonnay was more prolific than the Pinot Noir but not, fortunately, to the detriment of the wines – the grape can support higher yields than the Pinot without commensurate loss of quality. However, there is a certain unattractive quality about many of the Côte d'Or 1978 whites which makes it a much less fine vintage than for the reds. Although there are undoubtedly some fine wines – Leflaive, Ramonet, Ampeau and Lafon stand out – some, even from good stables, lack finesse and have a thick-skinned, overblown character. Some also, including many of Sauzet's Pulignys, had an unattractive vein of 'limey' acidity which left them with a distinctly dirty finish. This is not to put people off trying 1978 whites, but to temper the anticipation with a note of caution.

The reds, however, have no such problems and have blossomed into wines of great richness and distinction which will continue to give much pleasure. Unlike 1976 or 1969, where one has to pick and choose, the 1978s from conscientious growers, are uniformly delicious, from the humblest Bourgogne to the most exalted Musigny. Whilst the *régionales* should have been drunk by now, the village wines are drinking well, although some from the Côte de Beaune are starting to fade.

In contrast, most of the Premiers and Grands Crus have plenty of vigour and life left in them and will continue to develop over the next few years. At the luxury end of the scale, there are some truly magnificent wines from many of the Great Domaines which are as good a lesson in what fine Burgundy is all about as one is ever likely to get. Some will happily see in the new century, especially in Magnums or larger formats but they do not, by and large, have the structure to last well for another generation. How long you keep them depends somewhat on how you like your Burgundy – with the softer, tender flesh of youth, or leaner and thoroughly well hung.

1979

This was a year of plenty – a huge 'sortie' of bunches and an almost perfect flowering presaged a large crop and although the summer was not particularly hot, neither was it particularly wet. Apart from damage from some severe, but thankfully localised, hail-storms which wreaked havoc around Nuits and Vosne – the bunches remained intact and came slowly to what, if not perfect ripeness, was an acceptable level of maturity. (There are two aspects of ripeness which are often confounded: firstly, ripeness of the invdividual components of the bunches – skins, wood and pulp, etc.; and secondly, the ratio of solids to liquid in the berries. Analytical ripeness – acids, sugars, etc. – does not address this second aspect. Both matter for quality.)

This is a vintage in which individual growers' yields were a major factor in determining quality – too high and the wines were hopelessly dilute; moderate, and there was the chance of an acceptable balance. Sadly, many of the red wines, especially from the Côte de Nuits and often from impeccable Domaines, have turned out dilute, deficient in both stuffing and tannins.

However, there are some attractive wines about throughout the Côte; Pommard, Volnay and Beaune seem to have been more successful than most communes, but this was a year when try as they might some growers just failed to produce anything more than short-lived, unbalanced wines.

The whites are another story. Here again is demonstrated the ability of Chardonnay to succeed at relatively high yields. Although lacking the structure and concentration of the white 1978s, the 1979s are noticeably finer, with an elegance of flavour and aroma which the former lack. Both Leflaive and Sauzet produced much more stylish and suave wines in '79 than in '78, which are about at their peak. The '79s continue to give immense pleasure to those still fortunate enough to have them.

1980

Qualitatively, 1980 mirrors 1979 – with the red wines generally eclipsing the whites.

A cold, thoroughly inclement spring caused the latest harvest of the decade – most growers waiting until the middle of October to pick. Fortunately August and September had been hot and dry, so although the crop was small, it was healthy.

The vintage was generally written off by those who comment in advance on such things. Matters were not helped by Louis Latour, head of the Maison Louis Latour, who gave it out that he had not bought a bottle of 1980. Whilst it is true that most of the white wines were flabby and charmless, the reds turned out to be delightful and in some cases, superb wines. They are characterised by elegance rather than ample roundness – Gainsborough rather than Rubens. There are some yardstick wines from Dujac and Rousseau – deceptively pale in colour but lacking nothing in power and concentration. Most now need drinking.

1981

Louis Latour's vintage report well encapsulated the background: 'The 1981 vintage ranks among the smallest of the century, especially for red wines. . . From the outset, meagre quantities of fruit were to be seen on the vines, but successive climatic accidents further reduced the projected size of the vintage.' Specifically, although the vegetative cycle started off well, despite some spring frost, it was not until September that there was any really warm and settled weather. This continued into October, but then storms and hail struck – in particular the northern section of the Côte de Nuits. This physically damaged the grapes and diluted the juice. The result was less than half the normal crop.

The whites fared markedly better than the reds. There are some excellent, if rather skinny, offerings from Leflaive, some attractive wines from Ramonet and Sauzet – a fleshy and beautifully balanced Champ Canet, in particular. These should be drunk sooner rather than later.

The reds are generally indifferent. The exigencies of removing all traces of rot and the need for heavy *chaptalisation* put growers to the test. Most failed. Within the dismal totality there is the odd bright spot – from the obvious perfectionists. A Village Gevrey, from Joseph Roty, was dark in colour, with an imprecise, unctuous sort of nose and a soft pulpy flavour which developed well enough in the glass – perfectly drinkable and respectable, but only grudgingly interesting. However, with his customary care, François Faiveley managed to transcend the general mediocrity with a fine, rich and mouthfilling Echézeaux and elsewhere, Jacques Seysses, Charles Rousseau and Romanée-Conti produced complex and worthy wines. However, in the ensemble, 1981 is not a vintage to be taken too seriously.

1982

This was a year in which, as far as the weather went, nothing negative happened. A warm, sunny spring and early summer produced a full flowering, without significant *coulure* or *millerandage*, and succeeding months did nothing to disturb this embryo bumper crop. Rain in August added to the volume which continued to ripen until the middle of September, when the harvest began.

Growers faced two principal problems: first the sheer volume presented, for many, acute problems of storage. There was simply not enough vat-space in the cellars to house the fermenting juice. Anything that could hold grapes was pressed into service – one grower even confessed to be fermenting some in a bath-tub. Unfortunately, many growers shortened their vinifications to empty vats for the next batch, with consequent loss of depth, colour and extract. The problem of excessive *rendements* is generally self-inflicted. Any grower who is serious about keeping yields within levels compatible with top-quality is perfectly capable of doing so.

The second, and more damaging problem, was the high temperatures at which much of the harvest reached the cuveries. Growers with the means of cooling their *musts* avoided spoilage; those without, who worked on the 'we'll manage somehow' principle, were faced with soaring temperatures, stuck fermentations no doubt – though it is a matter of pride never to admit to it – and high levels of volatile acidity. As a result of this experience, many shiny new heat exchangers are now to be seen lurking in the corners of cellars or waiting above the *cuves*.

The wines have nothing of the qualities of 1982 in Bordeaux. In general the best are well-constituted, with plenty of succulent soft fruit and good depth, though sometimes deficient in acidity. The worst are dilute, over-chaptalised and charmless – pap everywhere and no corsets.

The whites are also a mixed bunch. The top Domaines by and large, produced fine wines – not for long ageing, but with good ripe fruit and an easy charm. Bottles from Leflaive – especially the Premier and Grand Crus – Lafon, Coche-Dury and Ramonet have all been interesting and enjoyable.

In short, if you are lucky enough and stumble upon a sound 1982, it may still be attractive. Most, by now, will have faded past their (mediocre) best.

1983
This is a thoroughly inconsistent and enigmatic vintage, especially for the red wines. The key to understanding it lies in the weather during the growing season. Spring was late in arriving, cold and wet, delaying the rise of the sap in the vines and thus the start of the vegetative cycle. May saw a distinct improvement and flowering took place in excellent conditions. From then until the end of August, the weather was largely hot and dry. However, in July, severe hail-storms struck the area bounded by Chambolle-Musigny to the north and Vosne-Romanée to the south, including Echézeaux and Vougeot in between. Then, in the early days of September the rains came – nearly three weeks of relentless torrent which, despite some protection from heat-thickened skins, caused widespread rot throughout the Côte. The *fin de saison* saw a period of extreme heat, which concentrated the grapes to the point of *surmaturité*. The harvest, which started on the 25th of September, passed off in fine conditions.

There are several factors in this pattern to note: firstly, rot. Unless rotten grapes are excised, they will irreversibly taint wines made from them. This affects whites less than reds, since these are vinified without their skins. Once in situ, rot spreads and is difficult to treat. An element of protection is provided by the physical thickness of grape skins, hardened by the use of copper-based vine treatments and by intense heat, as in 1983.

Secondly, hail: this splits berries and taints wines. Low concentrations of rot and hail can be masked by blending with sound wine, but this is not particulary satisfactory; the taint may sometimes disappear with aeration. The impact of hail on taste depends on when it occurs – before *veraison*, when berries change from green to black, is less damaging than after, when the skins are more vulnerable.

Thirdly, *surmaturité*: when grapes are subjected to prolonged heat they become more concentrated and raisiny. The volume of juice is reduced, the skins thicken and the sugar, acids and extracts in the grape are all increased at the expense of their water content. This can make for difficult fermentations, and for a cooked, figgy flavour which, in moderation, can be attractive.

All these factors contributed in one way or another to the diversity of the 1983s. In cask

the wines generally tasted excellent – good concentrated, ripe, if not over-ripe, fruit with plenty of depth and extract; in short, a great vintage in the making. However, between cask and bottle something appeared to go wrong. The wines lost their flesh, hardened, and became tough and often astringent. Many curiously developed a taste of rot – probably because prospective buyers were only given samples from 'clean' casks, the tainted wine being blended in later. This, especially from fine Domaines, was nothing less than dishonesty and is unforgiveable.

However, whilst as Clive Coates has summarised them, the 1983s continue to 'excite, disappoint, amaze, infuriate and mislead', the prognosis is not entirely gloomy. Although there is no future for wines which are badly rotten or hailed, those that are simply hard have a reasonable chance of softening, provided there is a balance of fruit and acidity to weigh against the tannins.

Even among the better Domaines there is a wide diversity of quality. Some cut short their *cuvaisons*, for fear of extracting off-flavours and too much tannin; others did the opposite, aiming to extract more richness. Fining, especially with gelatine, was often over-done by growers desperate to reduce tannins – the wines were thereby badly eviscerated and now lack balance – and clumsy filtrations frequently made things worse.

Nonetheless, there are some remarkable wines from this heterogeneous vintage. Very fine Romanée-Contis, some splendid Ponsots, and attractive harmonious Jadots, Grivots and Jean Gros. There are, equally, many growers whose wines remain hard, dry and unyielding; their future is uncertain. The only course for those with 1983s is to hang on, and hope.

The white wines are less heterodox. Over-ripeness in Chardonnay produces wines of abnormally high alcohols, but does not impact on the taste in the same way as it does with Pinot. The 1983s tended to excess alcohol and some are rather lumpen and clumsy. However, there are some superlative wines – especially from the likes of Sauzet, Leflaive, Ramonet, Lafon, Drouhin and Jadot. The Leflaive and Sauzet Grands Crus are inspirational, and will keep superbly.

1984
Sandwiched between a heterogeneous 1983 and a uniformly ripe and plush 1985, 1984 is something of a vinous dwarf. The summer was unremittingly cold, with some sunshine but no great warmth to ripen the grapes. It rained for much of September although cool temperatures kept rot at bay. When the harvest finally came, those who picked last benefitted, whilst the rest did their best with a large volume of unevenly ripe bunches.

In the cellars, growers accustomed to

bleeding the vats to increase the ratio of solids to liquid made a better fist of things than those who simply blundered on in whatever way they were used to.

In such conditions, generalisations are worthless. However, what can be safely said is that as always, the reputable, conscientious growers made good, acceptable wines. Now the best *cuvées* are showing medium weight, elegant, flavoury ripeness and good balance, almost as if they were developing structure as they went along. Judicious use of new oak has, in some cases, added gentle stuffing to wines which by themselves would have been ineffably meagre. In this, as in other vintages, individual vineyard sites, with their particular micro-climates, played an important role in the relative maturity of the grapes – so the Cru is important as well as the integrity of the grower. Buying Burgundy is no easy business.

1985
Whatever the quality of the wines, the growers will remember 1985 for the savage frosts which hit the Côte d'Or during January and February, destroying a significant area of vines outright, and leaving many others weakened and degenerating. In Gevrey-Chambertin alone, possibly the worst-hit sector of the Côte, the estimates of vines lost – mainly in the flatter village and Bourgogne Rouge vineyards near to the RN74 – vary from 100 to 150 hectares. This is a serious level of damage which had 'knock-on' effects for several years.

However, the growing season passed off uneventfully, with a dry, if not particularly warm summer, followed by a fine and exceptionally hot September and October: 'not a cloud in the sky, 25 to 30 degrees centigrade during the day, constant sunshine and soft nights more remindful of the Riviera than Burgundy' (L. Latour, vintage report).

The harvest, which started during the last week in September, produced a normal volume of full, ripe, healthy grapes. Vinification turned these into seductive, deep, rich wines, of great finesse and silkiness. As with the 1978s, these were accessible from their earliest months, and have lost none of the open, ripe fruit which has characterised them throughout. However, most have low acidities, which taken with their round, softish tannins, must put a question mark over their long-term future. Perhaps, like 1947 and 1959 they will conspire to defy the rules and last for half a century!

The white wines have a similar feel – plenty of ripe, soft fruit, rather fat and creamy; lovely drinking up to the mid- to late-'90s, but not for keeping much beyond then. There was a significant risk of overheating fermentations from a hot harvest, but most sensible growers had learned the lessons of earlier difficult vintages and invested in cooling equipment. The most common deficiency – it would be misleading to term it a fault – is low acidity. However, growers with older vines and thus smaller yields seem to have made wines with a good enough firm belt for a lack of braces to be of little consequence.

1986 This, and 1987, are vintages when the skills of the grower were, as the French, say 'primordial'. Firstly, he had to choose whether to pick early – the harvest started in the third week of September – or to risk waiting. An uneven growing season had been further disrupted by cold and wet weather from the middle of August onwards; however, in September, which was exceptionally wet, humidity had led to the spread of rot, which persuaded many growers to harvest as soon as possible. These early pickers found themselves with volumes of dilute, characterless wine. However, those who were prepared to take the risk and wait were, as is so often the case in Burgundy, well rewarded. A spell of dry, breezy weather, which both dried off the grapes and added a little concentration, enabled many to harvest, from the beginning of October, fruit which was both riper and more concentrated than that garnered by their more cautious colleagues.

Secondly, having picked his grapes, the grower had to take considerable pains to ensure that nothing rotten found its way into the vats. The best Domaines spent heavily on personnel sorting through bunches and removing rotten berries. Those who were slipshod produced wines which taste of rot.

In dilute years such as this and 1982, if the *cuves* are left to ferment by themselves, the wines will end up with weak frames – too much juice and not enough ripe solids to balance them. Many growers, faced with this prospect, will draw off a percentage of the juice from each vat – *saignée de cuve*. This process, performed as soon as possible to avoid removing extract as well as juice, depends on guesswork rather than science – one can *saigner* 10% or 60% – you just have to have a feel for what will work. Although it is no real substitute for proper ripeness, a careful *saignée* can help restore a wine's equilibrium. Some growers, however, such as Charles Rousseau in Gevrey, believe that this is in effect a defeat – an admission that you have not pruned short enough, or removed enough buds and shoots during the spring.

As a result, 1986 reds are a mixture of good – a few very good – and dilute mediocrity. Where the vigneron has taken care, the wines are quite soft, well-perfumed, with reasonable fruit. However, many could not avoid a layer of rather unattractive dry tannins which are unlikely to round out.

A few growers made very fine wines in 1986 – those of François Faiveley, Charles Rousseau and Daniel Chopin-Groffier coming directly to mind. Christophe Roumier, in Chambolle-Musigny, also made fine 1986s. The best still have life in them, but most reds are rapidly losing cohesion, if they ever had it in the first place.

The whites are considerably more reliable than the reds. The Indian summer which followed the September downpours transformed sugar levels at, according to one report 'the rate of nearly half a degree per day', resulting in excellent harvest sugar counts for those who waited. Some grapes even had a touch of *noble rot*, adding a dimension of fatness and complexity.

Those buying 1986 whites to lay down had a wealth of choice. The best Domaines produced delicious wines of finesse and elegance, perhaps reminiscent of the 1979s in concentration and style. These wines have developed attractively and most are now fully mature. The 1986 whites generally outclass the 1985s – although these are very different in style.

All in all 1986 was a satisfactory vintage with some good wines to enjoy whilst waiting for the 1985s, 1988s, 1989s and 1990s to mature. As always, there are considerable variations in quality between Domaines.

1987 As with 1983, this vintage was rescued from oblivion by an exceptionally hot September. A dismal spring, relieved only by about three weeks of warm, fine weather in March, was followed by an equally dismal summer; the flowering was both late and uneven, with a high incidence of *millerandage* – these are embryonic bunches which never fully develop but remain small; if they ripen, they are highly concentrated and can contribute much to a wine. Equally, their very presence reduces the overall volume of the harvest, so they are of double benefit.

'August makes the grape, September makes the wine' is a Burgundian saw. This was certainly true in 1987.

The red harvest was some 20% down on 1986, the white harvest nearly 25% less. Fortunately, September was largely dry as well as hot, so rot was minimal and the health of the grape generally good. This meant that in Domaines where trouble is taken at every stage of the vegetative cycle to keep yields down, concentrations were good and quality consequently high.

Many of the wine writers, as usual, leapt in to judge the vintage and, largely influenced by tales of rain during the late September/early October harvest, dismissed it as one of low quality and little consequence. They were wrong.

Although most of the reds began life with a shell of hard tannins from which they are just emerging, they were deeply coloured, with good fruit and extract – helped by the *millerandage* – and had good acidities. Tasting a broad range from both parts of the Côte, during 1991 and 1996, confirmed the initial impression of a vintage with all the elements of quality, but needing time to settle down and integrate. Given their high acidities and tannins, it is not difficult to see how people might be led to conclude that these wines are out of balance. However, one has to look beneath the wrapping to find good, firm, concentrated fruit. Some growers compare the style and likely evolution to that of 1972 – if so, then there will be some marvellous bottles about in the first decade of the new century.

Among the whites, there are some delicious wines – not immensely charged with fruit, but fine and delicate in style. Most are characterised by a nerve of acidity which in some instances is green and malic. However, time has wrought a better harmony. The top estates, as one might expect, pulled all the rabbits out of their respective hats and produced fine quality – Leflaive, Ramonet, Sauzet and Lafon in particular.

1988 In 1988 the vegetative cycle was almost a model of regularity: a warm, dry mid-June saw the flowering pass in ideal conditions. Thereafter, cool, rainy weather gave way to a warm, often hot, summer with lower than normal rainfall which marginally retarded the full maturation of the grapes. A fine September – the month which can make or break a vintage – brought a little rain, but barely enough to produce optimal maturity.

Some growers leapt into their vineyards and started picking in the Côte de Beaune during the third week of September. The results of their haste were grapes which needed heavy *chaptalisation* to generate enough alcohol for balance.

Those who took the risk and waited until the end of the month made much richer, more naturally harmonious wines.

This fine growing season produced a large harvest – the reds some 11% more than in 1987 but 12% less than 1986, the whites some 26% more than 1987 but only 2% less than 1986. These figures, however, conceal considerable variation between communes up and down the Côte .

Vinifications were fortunately not complicated by excessive heat during the harvest. However, the volume of the crop meant that a *saignée* was obligatory, for all but the few who summer-pruned or who had particularly old vines. The red wines are generally deeper and more consistent than their 1987 counterparts in the twin senses that, not only is there overall a higher level of quality in a given grower's cellar, there is also a uniformly fine average along the Côte, from Marsanny to Santenay. Although these wines presently lack the obvious 'ampleur' and fleshy charm of the 1989s, there is a general consensus among growers that they will outlast them.

In style, the 1988s started off dominated by a layer of rather austere, though perfectly ripe, tannins. These are beginning to integrate, but the best need several years more for the splendid fruit underneath to really show itself. They are a complete contrast to the 1985s, which have opulent, soft, ripe fruit in abundance. The 1988s have the fruit, but of a more reserved kind. With so many Domaines making excellent wines it would be invidious to select any for particular mention. On the contrary, there should be serious doubt about the capabilities of any grower who failed to produce fine 1988s.

As for the whites, the large harvest also presented problems. Unfortunately, since the skins do not influence their vinification, *saignée* is not an option for white vinification, so growers who over-cropped ended up with dilute wines. Overall, tastings suggest that, whilst this is undeniably a fine, healthy, vintage, it does not quite come up to the quality of either 1985 or 1986. Many wines were still skinny and lacked a real depth and concentration that no amount of maturation will rectify. However, for the medium term they will provide delicious drinking – with attractive aromas beginning to evolve and quite reasonable acidity to give them balance and life.

Among the ensemble, there are some notably classy offerings – as usual Leflaive, Lafon, Bonneau du Martray, Coche-Dury, Jadot, Sauzet and Ramonet are perched at the top of the tree, with Pierre Morey, Yves Boyer, Guy Roulot, Jean-Noel Gagnard, Michel Colin and Bernard Morey hanging on to the branch below.

1989
Throughout most of the Côte 1989 was a year of near-perfection for the vine. The vegetative cycle started off some two weeks ahead of schedule, and remained so up to the harvest. March was warm and sunny, with average temperatures well above the monthly 5°C. average. However the late spring had some surprises: April, though not especially cold, brought nearly 115 millimetres of rain; a sharp frost at the beginning of May wreaked significant damage in low-lying frost pockets in general, and on the southern, Puligny side of Meursault in particular and finally, going out with a veritable kick, a hailstorm on the 25th. May caused widespread damage, especially to the Corton hill and in nearby Pernand-Vergelesses, reducing the potential crop by half.

The flowering lasted for nearly 15 days – which meant that, within the same parcel of vines, there were to be several different degrees of maturity. Fine weather returned in July and remained until after the harvest, which started relatively early, at the end of the second week in September. However, without much rain, some vines, particularly the younger ones on well-drained sites, suffered badly, not having sufficiently deep root-systems to find water elsewhere. Although the grapes were ripe, many vignerons were disappointed that when they looked at the sugar levels at harvest, they had not reached the important 13.5 degrees potential alcohol – the level at which, as Monsieur Duvaud-Blochet, a famous 19th century Burgundian wine-grower theorised, natural alchemy transforms a good year into a great one.

The drought, hail and frost, together with some *coulure* and *millerandage*, reduced the white crop by some 14% on its 1988 level, whilst the red harvest was insignificantly higher than in 1988 . Yields in the Côte de Nuits were marginally higher, on average, than those in the Côte de Beaune, accounted for by a late September rainfall, just before the harvest. Such differences in weather patterns between the two parts of the Côte d'Or, also explains a small difference in average ripeness – Nuits having marginally less natural sugar than Beaune.

Important differences in ripeness may occur even in a more circumscribed area; for example in 1989, Le Montrachet reached a natural average ripeness of 12.3 degrees, whereas nearby Bâtard-Montrachet and Criots-Bâtard-Montrachet were harvested at just over 13 degrees.

In cask, both reds and whites shared one over-riding characteristic – heaps of fat, ripe fruit; they are mostly opulent, big, soft fleshy wines with enormous charm and elegance; even the reds were almost drinkable straight from the barrel. This exuberant fruit, coupled with low acidity levels, tempted many seasoned growers into comparisons with the 1947s and 1959s. The 1989s are destined to make gorgeously attractive drinking for the medium term.

If there is an indicator which sorts out the good from the very good Domaines in a vintage like 1989, it is yield. In as much as these lie within growers' power (site and vine age making their own important contribution), there are wide variations. Some tell you that they made fine quality from Pinots yielding 50 hl/ha whilst others talk of excessive yields at 45 hl/ha. Some growers *saignéed* in 1989, although many did not.

There are some exceptional wines in the making: Daniel Chopin-Groffier's massive, deep, Clos Vougeot, a string of thoroughbred beauties from Méo Camuset, a fine 'sortie' from Romanée-Conti plus a galaxy of delights from top growers in each commune. The best, both red and white, will give immense pleasure for a dozen or so years from the mid-nineties.

In fine, 1989 has a distinct touch of the 'barmaid' about it – plenty of obvious charm and up-front flesh, but perhaps marginally short on intellect.

1990
In combining 1989's richness and opulence with 1988's structure and concentration, 1990 has all the elements of an exceptional vintage.

The early part of the 'période vegetative' was not favourable – an almost summery March was followed by a wintry April with some nocturnal frost. June was average in temperature and rainfall, but deficient in sunshine. However, from 5th July an anti-cyclone set in, bringing hot, sunny and dry weather, and remained until after the harvest. Unprecedented drought, which threatened the balanced maturation of the grapes, was relieved only by a few isolated storms. However, on 30th August when even the most phlegmatic vigneron was beginning to look anxious, a storm broke precipitating between 30 and 60 mm of rain on the Côte d'Or in little over 24 hours. This was just enough to keep photosynthesis going and effectively saved the crop, since the fine hot weather continued unabated.

The harvest started in mid-September – some 15 days ahead of normal – and the last grapes were brought in around 10th October. In 1990 the vigneron had no reason to delay his picking – the grapes were more than fully ripe.

Yields were high. In fact, many Domaines, fearing excess, green-pruned, to reduce the crop-size. Even the authorities were carried away, extending the *rendement de base* for white wines by a full 5% throughout the Côte.

Most growers, looking at the last two vintages of the 1980s and 1990, rank their reds, in ascending order of maturity, and preference: 1989, 1988 and 1990. However, whilst there are a few who prefer their 1989s to their 1988s it is difficult to find any who rate either their 1988s or their 1989s more highly than their 1990s.

Now the wines have had the chance to settle down in bottle, it is clear that the early prognostications were well-founded. Despite high yields (whites globally 27.4% up on 1989 and 10.3% on 1988) sugar levels were high too, and acidities on the low side (though generally higher than in 1989). In character, the reds have good concentrations of firm, ripe fruit – some definitely over-ripe – and notably greater finesse than the delicious, if atypical, 1989s. This is also a vintage, of classic, well-balanced whites, which should make fine bottles over the medium term.

The reds are developing beautifully, with great charm, abundant richness and undeniable class. Even the *régionales* have a dimension of nobility only found in exceptional vintages. These, the Villages and some of the Côte de Beaune and Chambolle Premiers Crus are beginning to drink well, but the Côte de Nuits and Grands Crus are still firm and closed in. Although one could derive pleasure from these latter, it would be a pity to try yet, as they have so much more to give.

In short, 1990 is set to deliver its early promise – a magnificent, classic Burgundy vintage.

1991
After several years of mild winters, the 1990/91 Burgundian winter began with a beneficial freezing cold spell and atypical November snow. Despite this, vegetative activity started earlier than normal the following spring. March in the Côte d'Or was mild but wet allowing vegetation to develop apace. Then, cold weather re-established itself, blocking normal vegetative development; there was snow in the Yonne on 19th April, and on the nights of 20-21 and 23-24 April, following unseasonally high temperatures at the beginning of the month, severe frost struck the Côte. This destroyed many of the first buds and also some latent growth – not just in the known frost-pockets, but throughout the vignoble. Meursault, Puligny and Prémeaux were particularly affected.

Flowering extended over about two weeks from mid June, presaging at least an uneven ripeness of what crop remained. Then the vigneron's nightmare – summer hail – struck, twice. On 22 June a hail-storm hit the north of the Côte de Nuits, causing severe damage in the Hautes Côtes and in the Grands Crus between Morey and Gevrey. Two months later, on 22 August, a further storm ravaged Ladoix and the Hautes Côtes also damaging Beaune, Chorey, Aloxe, Savigny, Pernand and Corgoloin.

The summer was not particularly propitious – a cool June followed by a warmer July, which saw a rapid evolution of vegetation throughout the Côte. *Veraison* was largely complete by the end of August. By the beginning of September however, sugar levels had generally caught up, despite a lack of rain. Pests were noticeably less abundant than normal, reducing the need for repeated treatments – either preventive or curative.

The *ban de vendange* was generally proclaimed for 25/26 September and, as usual, many rushed in to pick, especially where sugar levels were high. Those who waited were rewarded with several days of unstable weather and a downpour over the weekend of 28-30 September. The sun then came out, enabling sugar levels to increase and grapes to be harvested dry. However, by this time, rot had spread through much of the Côte and a severe *trie* was necessary to remove this and small, dessicated, hail-damaged grapes. In most communes, bunches were of uneven ripeness, so only those who took extra care

in sorting succeeded in making wines of good balance and concentration.

In parts of the Côte de Beaune, the weather pattern was curious and atypical: in Chassagne-Montrachet, for example, frost damage occurred on the hillsides but not on the plains – in Puligny it tended to be the reverse. Notwithstanding, healthy Grands Crus were being harvested on 1st October at 13.8 degrees natural sugar.

Despite the rot and hail, conscientious growers made strenuous efforts to eliminate any damaged fruit and there is no evidence of taint in any of a considerable number of wines from this vintage tasted in 1995. Indeed, the overall quality is good to very good, with some genuinely fine wines to be found, both red and white.

Global yields were well down on the high levels of 1990 – nearly 13% less for both reds and whites. This conceals a wide variation: red Grands Crus suffered worst, 23% down on 1990, whilst the white Grands Crus were 5.5% lower, the Village and Premiers Crus taking a 13% hit. The top estates produced considerably less than the averages, so quantities of the best wines are small.

After the relative glut of 1988/89/90, and a largely unfavourable press, prices fell sharply. Growers were stuck with stock – and many still had 1991s to sell in 1995. For the buyer prepared to swim against the tide there are some excellent wines to be had, at keen prices, but careful selection is essential. In reds, the further one descends the scale the greater the variability. The top Premiers and Grands Crus – especially in the Côtes de Nuits and Corton, are the best bet – wines to keep for several years. Many Village wines throughout the Côte lack *ampleur* and balance. The best strategy: stick to top Domaines and avoid lesser communes.

Among the whites, the picture is no easier. Whilst there are some excellent Chassagnes, both Meursaults and, curiously, Pulignys are more variable. Many simply lack flesh and balance, although if you pick and choose there are some very attractive wines to be found.

The 1991 Burgundy vintage was damned – prematurely, as usual – by many, apparently reputable, journalists, who tasted too early and didn't, by and large, visit individual growers. This way of working is nonsensical and causes – as it did with the 1991s – a great deal of damage to growers who can ill afford it. Those with the influence which judging brings, should accept the attendant duties and behave more responsibly.

1992
This is a vintage which, as so often in the Côte, privileged those prepared to reduce yields. Global figures show a large crop, 3.5% down on 1990 for reds and 6.1% for whites. Whilst the

quality of the whites is relatively uniform, the reds are distinctly uneven.

An exceptionally mild winter and spring led to an early start to the vegetation. Budburst occurred around 25 April, then a warm May leading to an uneventful flowering, with a touch of *coulure* and *millerandange* in certain places. A wet and humid June followed. All this presaged a large harvest, and led many growers to green-prune at the end of July. August was hot enough to slow down vegetation which, by then, was some 15 days in advance of normal. Rain at the end of August started things going again, but brought unwelcome patches of botrytis to the Chardonnays. Then came a hot, dry sunny spell which stopped the rot in its tracks and increased sugar levels dramatically. This was not to last and the weather deteriorated, with a couple of days of heavy rain (22nd-23rd). The Côte de Beaune Chardonnays, picked from 14 September on, were well ripened; the Pinot Noirs, however, harvested towards the middle-end of the month, whilst in the main ripe, did not have the depth and concentration for greatness.

The whites have, understandably, received a great deal of critical praise. The wines are delicious, accessible, with great depth of flavour and fair acidities; fat, rich and generous with bags of up-front charm. Thought not long-stayers, the best have the structure to evolve well until the early years of the 21st century. This is a vintage where the second-rank villages – St. Aubin, Auxey-Duresses, Monthélie, Savigny, Pernand, etc. – produced lovely, open, enjoyable wines and are well worth mining. However, the 1990s and some of the 1993s, with firmer structures and better balance, will undoubtedly outdistance the 1992s which are decidedly short on brains.

The reds are a mixed bunch. Very little of really exciting quality, but much that is sound and attractive, though relatively forward. This was a vintage in which low yields were 'primordiale'; debudding, green pruning and a rigorous *triage* were essential. Many vignerons also bled their *cuves* to further concentrate the wines. Those who went up to, or beyond, the permitted *rendement de base* made indifferent wine. So simply selecting your grower and asking for his yields would be a valid buying strategy in 1992.

In general the best wines are well-constituted, though not massively deep, and elegant in a strawberryish, raspberryish mode with enough matter underneath to support a few years ageing. Pretty wines, ideal for the medium term whilst awaiting the entrance of the grander 1988s, 1989s, 1990s and 1991s.

1993
This is one of those vintages whose wines may, for the reds at least, arrive at a very different destination

from that towards which they appeared to set out. The scene was set by the weather which, through the summer, was warm but sporadically wet – alternating hot and humid days – which encouraged both *oidium* and mildew. The summer saw several hail storms, most notably on 16 and 27 May in and around Morey St.-Denis and on 20 June which damaged a swathe straddling Meursault and Puligny. From mid-July until mid-September, hot, sunny days returned, punctuated only by a storm on 10 September bringing useful rain. Cooler weather returned, interspersed by both dry and sunny, and damp and cloudy days. The harvest started in the Côte on 15 September and was marred by intermittent rain throughout. Those who were able to be flexible and rapid in their harvesting fared best.

Some refused to treat chemically against *oidium* and mildew and saw their crops destroyed (for what gain is not apparent). For the rest (who had to treat it much more frequently than normal), the cool weather helped block the spread of *botrytis* and preserve colour pigments in the Pinot skins.

The fruit arriving at cuveries did not fill growers with optimism; acidities were high and tannins seemed hard. Indeed, many report themselves as thinking: 'what on earth are we going to do with this?'. It was not until much later – after *malo* for most – that the intrinsic quality of the contents of their casks started to become apparent. The main transformation affected both tannins, which softened considerably, and aromas, which developed and intensified. One of the characteristics of 1993 reds, across the Côte, is their interesting aromatic potential. It was as if these long, slow, malolactic fermentations with the wines on healthy lees, not the alcoholic fermentation, had unlocked dormant complexities. Tasting the wines, mostly in cask, from April-September 1995, made it clear how exciting is this dimension of the vintage.

What struck many growers was that although the skins were, by and large, well ripened (certainly the all-important pigments detached themselves easily enough in the vats), Pinot sugar levels were far from high. A curious conundrum – ripeness on the outside but not within the grapes.

As a result, the reds are well-coloured, not perhaps as deep as the 1990s, but fine and limpid. Acidities are high, in a few instances, very high, but in general compatible with a slow evolution. In any case, after 1972 which started out with mouth-puckering acidity and was deemed by many a write-off, high acidity should not be a cause for alarm. Tannins are firm, with some wines having hard edges but, by and large, round enough to integrate with rather than dominate, the acids and fruit. So expect a longish period in bottle

before they reach their apogee. Whether 1993 deserves all the hype bestowed on it remains to be seen. Many *cuvées* are clearly excellent, some even Grand Vin, but this vintage's general evolution is less easy to predict than that of 1990, with which it will inevitably be compared.

Growers are divided in their preferences between 1993 and 1990. At present, many wines appear to lack the plumpness and *fond de matière* of 1990, but *élevage* and a year or two in bottle could change all that.

The white wines needed fairly heavy *chaptalisation* – the crop was large (though some 4% lower than 1990 and broadly similar in volume to 1992) – but in the main healthy. Vinification needed care and thought to deal with fruit which was not packed full of matter. High acidities entrained very long *malos* which bubbled on through the summer. Many growers increased the frequency of *batonnage* to add richness to their wines (fine, provided the lees were healthy) and reined back on new wood so as not to stifle them with oak.

At the top level the whites are elegant, firm, classically structured wines, gripped tightly at present by acidity (tartaric) which they will take time to shed. Many are clearly going to be very attractive – long, midweight, with enough power and style. Don't expect the flesh and *rondeur* of the 1992s, but buy these as mid/long term prospects. Although still young, the best 1993s could well outclass the 1992s, given time. They will certainly outlast them.

1994

A warm spring led, for the seventh consecutive year, to an early start to the growing season. Late May, early June, saw a short, even flowering and a very hot, dry July and August followed. A memorable hail-storm, on 20 June, cut through parts of Puligny, Blagny and Meursault, most notably in Puligny's Premiers and Grands Crus, including Montrachet and Chevalier. Here the Chardonnay harvest was reduced and, in places, touched with botrytis.

Rain throughout the Côte at the start of September kept the vegetation, and thus sugar production, going, although punctuated by dry sunny periods which limited the spread of rot. As in 1993 and 1995, the heat-thickened Pinot skins resisted well and the harvest was by and large healthy. As always, those who took care to weed out rotten, damaged fruit to keep yields low achieved excellent results.

Tasting during the spring and summer of 1995 showed a great variation in quality, both between growers in the same commune or appellation, and also between different *cuvées* in individual cellars. This is especially so of the reds, where many wines, though well-

coloured, lack flesh and balance, having a hard, unattractive tannic edge without enough concentration underneath. Elsewhere, one finds more harmonious wines which are destined to become, if not great, then attractive and 'pretty' over the medium term.

The whites present a more interesting prospect. Those who harvested early, before the rot really spread beyond reasonable redemption, produced very attractive, if febrile, wines, many with an enriching overlay of botrytis; sugar levels were nowhere near those of 1992, and in many instances the wines don't have the inherent constitution to make it sensible to cellar them beyond a few years. Those who picked late fared well, provided they had used anti-rot sprays (which many don't for Chardonnay). In short, this is a vintage where there are good things to be found, but you have to do your homework.

1995

April was miserably cold and wet, as was most of May and early June. Flowering throughout the Côte was retarded and uneven, which presaged a late and difficult harvest. In the event, when warm weather finally arrived, with a very hot and dry July, things caught up to a certain extent. By early September grapes were showing signs of reasonable analytical maturity (sugars, acids, etc.) but there were fears that tannins were unripe and would be hard. In the Côte de Nuits, growers harvested around the final week of September and many were still picking into the first week of October. In general, sugar levels were satisfactory at all levels and tannins ripe. However, intermittent rain in September meant that those unequipped or unprepared to *trie* seriously risked having tainted wines. Yields were low in the reds, and extremely low in the whites, especially in Premiers and Grands Crus.

Early indications suggest good and very good quality for both reds and whites across the Côte.

GLOSSARY

Agrément: the official approval of a wine for its respective appellation. This is based on an analysis and tasting test, carried out between November and April immediately following the harvest.

Assemblage: the process of amalgamating the contents of various vats or casks to unify the wine and to make a single *cuvée* for bottling. This can take place at any time after vinification, but usually occurs at racking or just before bottling. This is also the moment when the conscientious grower will weed out any sub-standard casks.

Baguette: the principal fruiting cane(s) which remain after pruning.

Ban de vendange: the official proclamation of the start of harvest decided by the local *INAO* committee. Growers who pick before this date are liable to certain vinification restrictions.

Base elements: nitrogen, potassium and phosphorus. These are the essential active soil-ingredients to support plant life. They are not the same as *trace elements.*

Batonnage: the traditional practice of stirring white wines to ensure even distribution of the lees through the liquid. Its frequency and extent vary from Domaine to Domaine.

Botrytis: a fungus which attacks grapes and rots them. It appears in both dry and damp forms and is never desirable in red grapes. In white grapes a touch of damp rot may add quality to a dry wine. The taste of rot, in either form, is ineradicable.

Buttage: traditional practice of ploughing up soil around roots of vines to protect them from winter frosts. Now largely discontinued.

Carbonic maceration: a system of fermentation in which whole, uncrushed grapes are fermented in the absence of air. Colour is extracted without tannin, so the wine is supple and drinkable early. Much Beaujolais and bulk table wine is made in this way.

Cépage: grape variety.

Chapeau: the cap of solids – skins, pips and stalks – which forms at the top of a vat of fermenting red juice, held up by escaping CO_2 gas. If not kept moist, this cap rapidly dries out and sours the entire vat. *Pigéage* both performs this function and also ensures maximum contact between liquid and solids, thereby maximum extraction.

Chapeau immergé: the practice of keeping the cap of skins and pips moist, in a vat of red *must,* by submerging it permanently underneath a ceiling of wooden planks. Although this eliminates the need for *pigéage,* many growers do not favour it because the cap remains intact. They consider that periodic breaking up of the cap is essential to proper extraction of colour, tannins, aromas, etc.

Chaptalisation: the addition of sugar to fermenting *must* to correct a natural deficiency and thus bring the final alcohol level up to the legal minimum. Introduced by Chaptal in 1801, the process is not designed to increase sweetness. The method and amount of *chaptalisation* are subject to legal control.

Charpente: literally 'carpentry'; tasting-term, used to signify structure. Up to a point, the more *charpente* a wine has the better.

Chlorosis: vine disease caused principally by excess calcium in the soil in which leaves turn yellow and stop photosynthesis through lack of chlorophyll. Inappropriate rootstock is a principal cause.

Climat: vineyard site. In the Côte d'Or, *climats* usually have names – Les Cras, Sous la Velle, etc. The term is interchangeable with *lieu-dit,* designed to classify wine before bottling.

Col: a *col* is a fining, designed to clarify wine before bottling. A wine remains *sur col* for several weeks or even months, during which period its taste qualities may be distorted.

Cordon de Royat: a system of training vines by laying the main vine stem horizontally along a wire, off which several vertical fruiting canes are taken. This is widely used in Chassagne and Santenay to limit yields and is becoming increasingly popular among top Domaines elsewhere in the Côte.

Corsé: a term of approbation used by tasters which has no precise translation, but generally refers to a wine which is well-constituted and robust. It does not mean coarse.

Coulure: the failure of flowers to set on a vine; often caused by adverse weather conditions which make them drop. Fewer flowers mean fewer bunches and thus a reduced yield.

Coupage: the practice of cutting (blending) one, usually more expensive, wine with something inferior. In the Côte this was common until the 1970s; the cutting wine was usually from the southern Rhône or Algeria.

Coup de feu: the moment of most intense heat during fermentation.

Courson: a short pruning spur, often providing the fruiting wood for the following year.

Court-noué: a virus disease, endemic in Burgundy, especially in white vines. Known as the 'fan-leaf', this malady attacks the vine's leaves, reducing their photosynthetic ability. Grubbing up and replanting is the only solution.

Crochet: method of training the vine, a modified *gobelet,* with fruiting canes pruned short to one or two buds on each. Principally used for very young vines, to limit vigour, or for very old ones which have grown too tall to bend a cane onto the wire without breaking it.

Cryptogams: a family of vine maladies which includes *botrytis, oïdium* and mildew. These are normally treated with specific sprays.

Cuvaison: the process of vatting. The time during which grapes are transformed into wine, starting when the grapes are put into vats to ferment and ending when the new wine is run off to cask. This only applies to red grapes.

Cuve: the vessel in which fermentation takes place. This can be made of wood, stainless-steel, glass-lined epoxy, etc.

Cuve auto-pigéante: simply a stainless-steel *cuve* which contains apparatus for automatic *pigéage.* These take several forms – from rotating *cuves* to static ones with rotating paddles. Some growers think that they improve quality; others regard them with deep distrust.

Cuvée: an ambiguous term, referring either to an individual vat – as in 'from several *cuvées* of Meursault he selected one' – or to the bottled wine – as in 'he has a *cuvée* of Gevrey and one of Chambolle'. So a grower might blend several *cuvées* of Meursault to form a single *cuvée* which he then bottles.

Débourbage: the process of settling to allow the heavier, less desirable lees (*les bourbes*), to precipitate out.

Décuvage: decanting a wine from vat after fermentation. This really only applies to red vinification, where the new wine is run off the residue of solids, which are then pressed to yield the *vin de presse.* The precise moment of *décuvage* involves a delicate decision – which can markedly affect wine quality.

Dedoubler: the removal, during the spring, of any double shoots or buds. This reduces potential yields and spreads out the foliage.

Ébrossage: another word for *ébourgonnage, échtonnage, dédoublage* or *évasivage.*

Écoulage: running off juice from a vat or press.

Égalisage: the process of unifying several casks of wine from the same vineyard or appellation, to eliminate any differences in taste between them. This usually takes place at racking or at *relève de col* just before bottling.

Égrappage: destalking; separating grape berries from stems either by hand or machine.

Élevage: literally means upbringing. The skilled process involved in caring for a wine between vinification and bottling. Racking, fining, filtration, etc. are all part of a wine's *élevage.* The wine-maker and *éleveur* may be different people – e.g. where wine is sold young in cask; hence 'négociant-éleveur'.

En foule: the system of vineyard planting common up to the end of the nineteenth century, whereby vines were densely planted en masse and simply allowed to ramble – their natural propensity.

En friche: unplanted vineyard land, often scrub.

Enherbement: the practice of deliberately sowing grass between vine rows to retain top-soil and prevent erosion.

Eutypiose: an insidious vine infection, probably spread by mushroom-like spores especially in damp, windy conditions Pruning wounds are the most susceptible means of entry. Although most noticeable early on in its development cycle, it retreats, giving the impression that the vine has healed. Thereafter, it can take up to 7 years before any further symptoms appear, by which time it is too late. Some parts of the Côte d'Or are more affected than others. Too many vignerons are failing to take *eutypiose* seriously.

Évasivage: the removal of excess buds from the vine; usually carried out between bud-burst and flowering. An important operation which is essential in restricting growth and reducing yields.

Fermage: a system of vineyard tenancy whereby the tenant farms the land and enjoys the totality of the crop in return for an annual rental, fixed at the cash equivalent of an agreed number of pièces of that vineyard's wine. Even if there is no harvest, the rental is payable. See *Métayage.*

Figué: literally, figgy. Over-ripe Pinot Noir can taste and smell figgy, especially when the skins have been cooked by prolonged hot sunshine in dry weather. Up to a point this can enhance a wine.

Foudre: a large, wooden, fermenting vat.

Framboisé: literally, raspberried; an aroma often found in young Pinot Noir.

Fruits noirs: literally 'black fruits' – a tasting term referring principally to blackberries, blackcurrants, bilberries and plums.

Fruits rouges: literally 'red fruits' – a tasting term referring to strawberries, raspberries, loganberries, redcurrants, cherries, etc.

Fruits sauvages: literally 'wild fruits' – a carpet-bag tasting term which tends to refer more to the style of fruit than to the particular variety; it connotes hedgerow smells of freshly picked berries.

Gobelet: system of training a vine with several upright shoots from the main stem – resembling a goblet. Used widely for young and old vines in the Côte, the *gobelet* is particularly associated in France with the Beaujolais, the southern Rhône and Provence.

Goût de lie: a sort of yeasty, cardboardy taste which derives from too much contact between wine and lees and can render a wine flat and disagreeable. A pronounced *goût de lie* is a signal that racking is due – or overdue!

Goût de silex: a particular earthy taste, found especially in white wines from Pernand-Vergelesses and Savigny-lès-Beaune.

Goût de terroir: a tasting term meaning 'earthy taste'. It is often found in Burgundies from lesser communes – e.g. St.-Aubin, Auxey-Duresses – or from vineyards where the soil gives a distinct flavour of its own – e.g. the taste of silex in some Pernand and Savigny whites.

Guyot: system of training invented by Dr Guyot in the mid-eighteenth century, consisting of either a single or double fruiting cane trained laterally off the main vine stem.

INAO: Institut National des Appellations d'Origine. The French governmental organisation which delimits and controls appellations including those for pottery and chickens as well as for wine.

Lieu-dit: this means a specific vineyard site;

the term is, to all intents and purposes, interchangeable with *climat.*

Macération: the practice of letting grape-juice or new wine mix with its solids – skins, pips, etc. – before, during or after fermentation. *Macération pelliculaire* refers particularly to a pre-fermentive maceration of white juice.

Mâche: a frequently used tasting term; difficult to translate – but has the sense of chewy-gutsiness.

Malade de mise: bottling-sickness. A term referring to the phenomenon where, for a period immediately following bottling, a wine may not taste true to form. Bottling frequently shocks a wine into itself, a state from which it may take up to several years to recover.

Malolactic/Malo: a bacterially-mediated fermentation which turns harsh malic (apple) acid, naturally present in wine, into softer-tasting lactic (milk) acid. It follows alcoholic fermentation.

Marc: (i) the cake of solids left after pressing; (ii) a form of brandy made by distilling this cake.

Métayage: an alternative system of land rental to *fermage* in which rent is paid, not in cash, but in an agreed proportion of grapes or wine usually one-third, a half or two-thirds. The share-cropper or *métayer* is normally responsible for all the running expenses of the vineyard, except for new plants, posts and wires. The landlord sometimes pays an agreed proportion of fertilisers, sprays, etc.

Millerandage: a phenomenon of flowering, when embryo bunches form but fail to develop further. These *millerands* reduce yields but also contain tiny amounts of very rich concentrated juice, which can add significantly to wine concentration.

Monopole: a vineyard in single ownership.

Must: the grape juice before it has finished fermenting and thus become wine.

Noble rot (Pourriture noble): whilst a wholly desirable condition in grapes destined for sweet white wine, a small amount can enhance a dry white wine with its quality of richness both on the nose and on the palate. This is largely derived from botrycine – a by-product of *botrytis.*

Oïdium: powdery mildew; a rapidly spread fungus disease of American origin which attacks new leaves and shoots, and splits and rots the grapes. First observed at the Royal Botanical Gardens, Kew, London, in 1845, *oïdium* ravaged viticultural France in the 1850s. It is effectively treated with sulphur.

Palissage: the training of vine-shoots and foliage onto the upper two strands of wire during summer. At the same time, the middle pair of wires are clipped together.

Pénétrant: a class of treatment products which act by penetrating the vine's capillary system. These contrast with contact products – which don't penetrate the system but wash off easily and systemics which penetrate more deeply. Each has advantages and disadvantages.

Phylloxera: an aphid, 0.5-l mm. long, with a complex life cycle, which feeds on vine-roots, eventually killing the plant. It multiplies vigorously and is permanently resident in the soils of

most European vineyards, which it devastated at the end of the nineteenth century. There is no cure, but planting onto resistant rootstock renders the insect harmless. A few French and other vineyards remain on their original, pre-*phylloxera,* roots.

Pièce: the standard Burgundy barrel, containing 228 litres. The standard Bordeaux 'barrique' contains 225 litres.

Pied de cuve: a starter-culture comprising of artificial yeasts and wine, or which is used to inoculate vats, to induce fermentation.

Pigéage: the practice of breaking up the cap of solids which forms on top of a vat of fermenting red grapes to prevent it drying out. Although traditionally done by human feet, many Domaines use mechanical pistons or hand-wielded plungers to do this task. *Pigéage* also mixes up solids and liquid, thus improving extraction.

PLC (Plafond Limite de Classement): this is the ceiling yield for any given appellation, expressed in hl/ha, and represents a percentage increase – normally 20% – on the *rendement de base.* It is supposedly only authorised in prolific years.

Pourriture: rot, which can come in one of two forms – 'sec' or 'humide'. Neither is desirable, but 'humide' is less disagreeable on the palate than dry rot. *Noble rot (botrytis)* is important in the production of high-quality sweet white wines, but not in Burgundy.

Prélèvement: the practice of taking random samples of grapes from a vineyard to determine maturity/ripeness and thus the right moment to harvest.

Reduit: literally 'reduced' – the opposite of oxygenated. A tasting term for a more or less disagreeable smell brought about by storage in a reduced state – i.e. in the absence of air. The smell is not permanent and is easily eliminated by aeration. When a wine in cask becomes noticeably reduced it should be racked.

Régisseur: the manager or cellar-master of an estate.

Régionales: wines from regional appellations – e.g. Bourgogne Aligoté, Passe-Tout-Grains, Côte de Beaune-Villages, Bourgogne Blanc, etc. These come from land in each commune which is deemed unsuitable for a higher appellation.

Relève de col: racking the wine clear of its fining.

Remontage: pumping-over juice from the bottom to the top of a vat during red wine fermentation. This aerates the yeasts and gets them working. It also equalises the temperature in the vat and helps keep the cap moist.

Rendement: yield, normally expressed in hl/ha.

Rendement de base: the base yield. This is the maximum yield set for each appellation, for a normal vintage. It is expressed in hl/ha – i.e. x 100 litres for each hectare. In prolific vintages, it may be augmented by the *PLC.*

Repiquage: the practice of replacing individually vines which die or get too old, rather than grubbing up an entire parcel. Preferred by many top growers as it helps maintain a high average vine age.

Rondeur: Roundness. A taste-sensation rather than a literal description.

Saigner/Saignée/Saignée de cuve: the practice of bleeding off juice from a vat of red grapes, especially in dilute vintages to concentrate what remains. The later you leave it, the more extract you remove. Many growers maintain that the need to *saigner* indicates over-production in the vineyard.

Sélection clonale: refers (i) to the use of selected clones by the vigneron as opposed to *sélection massale* and (ii) to the highly skilled process of developing clones for commercial propagation.

Sélection massale: traditional process of selecting suitable plant material, by taking wood or shoots from the best and healthiest vines direct from the vineyard. The precursor of clones, and still used by some vignerons.

SO₂: sulphur dioxide. This is widely used in wine-making as an all-purpose disinfectant, since it kills destructive microbes and prevents oxidation. In excessive doses it has a pungent smell and gives wine a flat, cardboardy taste. It should not be confused with bad eggs – that is H_2S, hydrogen sulphide.

Sous-bois: an often used term signifying undergrowth or damp vegetation – an attractive mushroomy smell which is frequently encountered in older Côte d'Or wines.

Sur col: literally 'on fining'. A wine which is in the process of being fined is referred to as *sur col*. In this state, which may last for several months, wines may not taste true to form.

Surmaturité: over-ripeness. Grapes left on the vine in hot dry weather concentrate and shrivel. This gives added depth of flavour but beyond a certain point can bring a tarry, cooked taste to a wine. Over-ripened grapes often have an element of *botrytis* which in white wine frequently results in a special aromatic richness.

Sur pressoir: from the press. Used to refer to wine sold as juice or in an unfinished state.

Tâcheron: literally, a worker who is paid by task – a piece-worker; however, in current parlance, someone who tends vines for someone else – quite common in the Côte.

Taille: pruning.

Tendre: a tasting term – supple, tender.

Terre rouge: this is red earth, soil often found in the Côte which has been tinted by oxidised iron deposits.

Terre à rouge: soil more suitable for the production of red wine.

Terroir: an elusive but important concept, encapsulating the general physical environment of a vineyard. It includes micro-climate, soil, slope, exposure, drainage, etc.

Trace elements: inorganic compounds found in usually minute quantities in soil for example: beryllium, iron, cobalt, manganese, magnesium, chromium. They contribute in different ways to grape-maturity, fertilisation, photosynthesis and sugar accumulation. However, the precise causal relationships are imperfectly understood.

Triage/Trie: the practice of sorting through the crop to pick only ripe, healthy grapes. A *trie* can be done on the vine, or by hand at the cuverie. It is especially necessary in years of rot or hail damage.

Vendange verte: literally 'green harvest' – cutting a proportion of bunches before the proper harvest to reduce the load on each vine. This is a controversial practice, since many believe that the vine simply compensates with larger, more dilute berries.

Veraison: the moment at which the berries of red grape varieties turn from green to black on the vine (usually in August on the Côte).

Ver de la grappe: grape-worm. Insect which punctures the skin of the grape leaving a wound which rapidly turns rotten. There are two generations during each vine-growing cycle, the first harmless, the second not. For no known reason some communes are regularly more infected than others.

Verjus: the second crop of grapes; small and usually unripe, these are mostly found at the top of the vine. They must be removed well before harvest since they both sap vital energy from the vine and also add unripe acidity and greenness to wines if they get into the vats. An important quality factor in Burgundy, since pickers often cannot distinguish *verjus* from the main crop.

Vigne mère: mother vine – the vineyard or set of vines from which clones or *sélection massale* are propagated.

Vin de garde: wine for keeping, as opposed to wine designed for early drinking.

Vin de presse/Vin de goutte: the press-wine is that extracted by pressing the pulp from a red wine vat after the free-run wine *(vin de goutte)* has been decanted. It is usually harsher and more tannic, depending on the pressure used to extract it.

Volatile acidity: acetic acid, vinegar. This comes generally from careless vinification or sloppy hygiene. In tiny quantities it can enhance a wine, but in large doses becomes offensive to both nose and palate.

MEASURES AND CONVERSIONS

Measures of area
1 hectare =2.471 acres = 10,000 sq. metres = 100 ares = 24 ouvrées
1 are = 100 sq. metres (100 ares = 1 hectare)
1 ouvrée = 4.285 ares = 0.417 hectares
1 journal = 8 ouvrées = ⅓ hectare (3 journeaux = 1 hectare)

Measures of capacity
0.75 litres = 1 standard bottle
1.5 litres = 1 magnum = 2 bottles
3.0 litres = 1 double magnum = 1 jeraboam
9 litres = 12 bottles = 1 case

1 queue = 2 tonneaux = 456 litres = 608 bottles
1 tonneau = 1 pièce = 228 litres = 304 bottles (the standard Burgundy cask size)
1 feuillette = ½ tonneau = 114 litres = 152 bottles
1 quarteau = ¼ tonneau = 57 litres = 76 bottles

Vat capacity is usually measured in hectolitres:
1 hectolitre = 100 litres = 133.3 bottles = 11.1 cases

Measures of yield
Yields are usually expressed in hectolitres per hectare (hl./ha.)

1 hl./ha. = 100 litres / ha.
1 hl./ha. = 133.3 bottles / ha. = 11.1 cases / hectare
1 hl./ha. - 53.9 bottles / acre - 4.5 cases / acre
40 hl./ha. = 4000 litres / hectare = 444 cases / hectare
40 hl./ha. = 2158 bottles / acre = 180 cases / acre
40 hl./ha. is equivalent to about half a bottle of wine per vine

Measures of production
130 kilograms of grapes produce approximately 1 hectolitre of wine. A plant density of 11,000 vines per hectare and 8 bunches per vine is approximately equivalent to a yield of 55 hl./ha. This is also equivalent to 1 pièce (cask) per ouvrée = 24 pièces per hectare. This amounts to some 650 grams of grapes, or half a litre of wine per vine.

Index

Each commune or village featured in this book is referred to in **bold** type. Vineyards indexed under each commune refer to places where they are mentioned in the text and not to maps or domaine holdings, to which readers are also referred. There are often different – equally correct – spellings of vineyard names. The most common are used here.

Acknowledgements

The lengthy preparation of this book has been greatly assisted by many, both in the UK and in France. I am particularly grateful to all the Domaines, whether included here or not, who generously opened their doors, cuveries, cellars and tasting-rooms, gave so much of their time and so freely shared their ideas. Their spontaneous welcome and encouragement will long be remembered.
The following people also gave generously of their time and expertise: Professeur Raymond Bernard of ONIVINS, Dijon; Professeur Michel Feuillat of the Laboratoire d'Oenologie, Université de Bourgogne, Dijon; M. Remi Gonin of the Répression des Fraudes, Dijon; Professor Jake Hancock, Dept. of Geology, Imperial College,

University of London; Professeur Noël Leneuf, Director of Université, Dijon Research Centre, Marsannay; M. René Naudin of the Institut Technique de la Vigne et du Vin, Beaune; M. Riffiod of the Protection des Végétaux, Beaune; Mssrs. Jean-Luc Servan and Philippe Trollat of the BIVB, Beaune; Dr. Jean Siegrist, of the Institut National de la Recherche Agronome, Dijon and M. Jules Tourmeau of the InAO, Dijon.
Personal introductions to many growers were obtained through the kindess of merchants and specialist Uk importers – in particular: Nick Clarke MW of O.W. Loeb & Co. Ltd.; Simon Cock of Heyman Brothers Ltd.; Claude Giret of Berkmann's Ltd.; Becky and Russell Hone of Le Serbet, Bouilland, Côte d'Or; Robert Rolls of Market Vintners Ltd. and Simon Taylor-Gill of Domaine Direct Ltd.

Sara-Jane Vere Nicoll at Kyle Cathie Ltd. efficiently copied, collated and despatched mountains of letters to Domaines.
Also, this book would not be the same without the photographs of Janet Price and Geraldine Norman. Both made several trips to Burgundy and spent hours persuading surprised vignerons not to pose in their best suits and encouraging them to relax. The results often say more than my words.
Finally, my special thanks to Dr. Christopher Davenport-Jones, a knowledgeable wine-enthusiast and kind friend, who introduced me to Kyle Cathie, to Kyle herself for her enthusiasm and support, and to my wife, Geraldine, who read and re-read the manuscript, correcting everything from errors of grammar to stylistic infelicities. Without them, this book would never have been.